LUST FOR LIBERTY

Samuel K. Cohn, Jr.

Lust for Liberty

The Politics of Social Revolt in Medieval Europe, 1200–1425

ITALY, FRANCE, AND FLANDERS

HARVARD UNIVERSITY PRESS

Cambridge, Massachusetts, and London, England   2006

Library of Congress Cataloging-in-Publication Data

Cohn, Samuel Kline.
   Lust for liberty : the politics of social revolt in medieval Europe, 1200–1425 : Italy, France, and Flanders / Samuel K. Cohn, Jr.
      p. cm.
   Includes bibliographical references and index.
   ISBN 0-674-02162-2 (alk. paper)
   1. Revolutions—Europe—History. 2. Social change—Europe—History.
3. Civilization, Medieval. I. Title.

HN373C73 2006
303.6'40940902—dc22   2005056388

To the memory of Rodney Hilton

Contents

Acknowledgments

This book arose from my work of translation and commentary, *Popular Protest in Late Medieval Europe,* in the Manchester Medieval Sources Series. Although that volume presented over two hundred documents covering about a hundred revolts, it focused on the major ones of late medieval continental Europe. While finishing that volume, I found many more, lesser-known revolts worthy of description. The assemblage of these revolts (and still others found later) amounted to more than the individual parts. It is this collective story and its trends, along with the great variety of individual tales of human suffering and aspiration, that I now wish to convey.

As I did for the source book, I thank Graeme Small again for stuffing my pigeonhole with references to French and Netherlandish sources and for reading through an early version of the manuscript, spotting errors, and making insightful suggestions. Several others read the manuscript at various stages: Thomas Munck, from an early modern perspective; Steven Rigby, with a rare theoretical sophistication and from the angle of English history; Rudy Binion, always with his red pen out for infelicities in language and fuzzy logic; Ernesto Screpanti, with an eye on the Ciompi and Italian material; Peter Arnade, with his expertise in the Low Countries; and the anonymous readers at Harvard University Press. Still others read parts—Matthew and Debra Strickland, Genevieve Warwick, and John Padgett—and their comments forced me to rethink and rewrite arguments.

I presented portions of this book as conference papers and as a pilot study for a workshop on work and organization in the political science department, University of Chicago. Later versions were given at the Social Science History conference at St. Louis, for "Rodney Hilton's Middle Ages" at Birmingham (U.K.), at a graduate seminar at the University of Texas (Austin), for the medieval seminar at St. Andrews, and at the Historical Association, Durham Branch. I gave earlier versions of "Flags and Words" at a conference in honor of Richard Trexler and at a conference on ritual in Arezzo. I benefited from these occasions. In particular, I thank John Padgett, Chris Wickham, Chris Dyer, Peter Arnade, Natalie Davis, John Najemy, Richard Trexler, Fabrizio Ricciardelli, Franco Franceschi, Neil Kamil, Frances Andrews, M. Michele Mulchahey, and Neil Evans for their invitations, criticisms, and encouragement. Finally, I am indebted to Kathleen McDermott for shepherding the volume through the press and to Joan Kocsis for her critical reading and copy editing. The errors and infelicities that remain are of course my own. I dedicate the book to Rodney Hilton, friend and source of great inspiration.

Note: The book contains translations from chronicles and archives in medieval French, Italian, and Latin. Occasionally, I have supplied key words from the originals and have left them in their old spellings, such as *pluseurs* for *plusieurs, picoli* for *piccoli,* and *Saint-Denys* for *Saint-Denis.*

LUST FOR LIBERTY

CHAPTER 1

Introduction

In the 1960s, works by Barrington Moore, Jr., Eric Hobsbawm, George Rudé, E. P. Thompson,[1] and others, coupled with the student movements of that decade, stimulated a new vogue for the study of comparative revolts in early modern, modern, and contemporary Europe and elsewhere. Curiously, the trend did not extend to medieval Europe, despite its periodic large-scale revolts beginning in the thirteenth century and especially in the wake of the Black Death. Individual revolts—the Jacquerie (1358), the Florentine Ciompi (1378), the English Uprising of 1381, the Hussite rebellions of the first half of the fifteenth century, and the *remensas* in Spain[2]—continue to receive detailed archival research and interpretation. But medievalists have been reluctant to venture beyond local settings and compare these movements across time or especially across linguistic and (later) national boundaries. Furthermore, few attempts have been made to study revolts other than this handful of famous late medieval ones, all of which were repressed. Thus the literature has tended to stress that preindustrial revolts were rare and invariably smashed.

Not only have revolts well known to nineteenth- and twentieth-century historians, such as the *Harelle* of Rouen and the Hammer men of Paris, failed to draw new research since Léon Mirot's study of a hundred years ago,[3] but also little attention has been paid to a plethora of other revolts now largely unknown to scholars. Examples include "the people without underpants" who brought down the government of Bologna in 1289; a successful tax revolt of weavers, fullers, and other artisans in Tournai in 1307; a revolt claimed to have involved 40,000 serfs (certainly exaggerated) from over twenty-two named villages around 1338, who refused their dues to the dean and canons of Notre-Dame of Laon, resulting in nine men being executed and "many" women branded on their cheeks;[4] a "Jacquerie" that slaughtered noblemen, ladies, and their servants in the region of Toulouse in 1364 and went unpunished despite the crown's efforts;[5] a riot in Viterbo in 1367, sparked by the washing of the cardinal's "pretty little dog [*cagnolino*]" in a communal drinking fountain, which ended in a bloodbath of foreign dignitaries;[6] the wave of antipapal revolts in 1375 and 1376 that swept from Milan to Naples, replacing signorial regimes with guild-based popular governments;[7] the Roman crowds' riot that pressured the College of Cardinals into electing an Italian pope in April 1378; a vineyard laborer who gave political speeches over a five- or six-year stretch, criticizing the town council's works and administration and rousing his fellow workers and artisans *(petit peuple)* in Châlons-en-Champagne to attempt the overthrow of government and embark on reforms in the second decade of the fifteenth century.[8]

These are but a few of well over a thousand examples of collective protest, social movements, and revolts that I have collected mainly from published chronicles and a scattering of archival records in Italy, France, and Flanders, including Liège and its region. Some, such as the revolt over the cardinal's pretty little dog and the Roman crowd's pressure on the College of Cardinals in 1378, received more extensive coverage from contemporaries across Europe than the now more famous "big three" of the later fourteenth century: the Ciompi, the Jacquerie, and the English Uprising of 1381. Only a couple of contemporaries who resided outside the national boundaries of these revolts reported either the Jacquerie or the English Uprising of 1381: the Florentine Matteo Villani[9] and an anonymous monk at St. Mary's Abbey, York,[10] who wrote in Anglo-Norman, recorded the Jacquerie; Michel Pintoin (known as the religieux de Saint-Denys) and Jean Froissart reported the English revolt.[11] The Florentine Ciompi received even less international attention: I know of no contemporary comment on it north of the Alps. Even within Italy beyond the borders of Tuscany it received scant notice—a brief account from a chronicler of neighboring Bologna and another from Gubbio.[12] By contrast, at least fourteen chroniclers outside Rome described the riots of the Roman people, who in May of that same year (1378) pressured the College of Cardinals to elect an Italian pope. Four of these contemporaries wrote from the other side of the Alps.[13] Similarly, the riot over the cardinal's pretty little dog received interregional and international attention as far afield as the king's official chronicler at Saint-Denis as well as from a local town chronicler of Montpellier.[14]

Historiography and Notions of Popular Movements

The only book-length attempts to analyze revolts and popular movements comparatively and beyond single national contexts have been Michel Mollat and Philippe Wolff's *Ongles bleus* and Rodney Hilton's *Bond Men Made Free*, both published over thirty years ago.[15] Moreover, Hilton's work was confined to rural movements and, as his subtitle suggests, his comparative context was the prelude to studying a single revolt: the English Uprising of 1381. Thus only one work has attempted an investigation of the broad sweep of late medieval rebellions, *Ongles bleus*. Based on prodigious research, its authors began with analytical questions: Were the "revolutionary waves" more or less sponta-neous? Can they be explained by a revolutionary contagion, or were they iso-lated events to be examined within their own national or regional settings? Does comparison of these movements reveal general characteristics or distinc-tive traits? What difference did the Black Death make to a supposed increase in revolts, especially a generation after the Black Death, when (according to Mollat and Wolff) a remarkable cluster of revolts sprang up across Europe in the years 1378 to 1382? Although they amassed a valuable array of social revolts, they left these important questions mostly unanswered.[16]

In the analysis that does structure *Ongles bleus*, Mollat and Wolff hunted for similarities rather than differences in popular protest across Western Europe. The only major distinctions they drew pointed to differences over time. Here, as with their title, they borrowed from the great historian of the Low Coun-tries, Henri Pirenne.[17] They called the revolts of the late thirteenth and early fourteenth centuries "revolutions of the crafts" and claimed that those after the Black Death erupted from misery. While solid craftsmen had planned revolts earlier, those after the plague comprised either poor peasants or the urban poor, that is, nascent proletarians.[18] Such a conclusion will be ques-tioned later in this work; for now, however, I wish to signal that regional dif-ferences are worthy of investigation for understanding the history of late medieval revolts, even if the explanations for them may remain elusive.

Historians have attempted to construct hierarchies of popular rebellion, drawing distinctions between "rebellion," "revolt," and "riot." For instance, Guy Fourquin has maintained that "rebellion," or the complete overthrow of a society's foundations, was impossible in the Middle Ages and had to await the French Revolution. Such distinctions come from modern sociology or modern historians' own definitions with little regard for what the sources say.[19] I know of no medieval theoretician—such as a John of Salisbury or a Marsilius of Padua—who elaborated any model or hierarchy of violence or rebellion.[20]

While it is not a mistake for historians today to draw models of revolt or violence,[21] it is important to recognize how contemporaries used certain key words for revolt. Statutes, criminal records, town council proceedings, and chronicles often restricted the use of the word "rebellion" for aristocratic challenges to the dominant power, be it a king, count, or city-state, or the "rebellion" of a subject village or city, especially in Italy, but not because these actions were any more dangerous, important, or despicable than those from other orders or classes of society; the actions of lower orders or classes were often seen as serious threats to social peace and political order, and their advocates were often accused of treason *(lèse majesté)*. If the dominant power prevailed, the conflict arising from the lower orders could be settled with negotiated leniency or brutal and disproportionate repression. Contemporary authors did not use precise terms to distinguish a skirmish from a disturbance, a riot from a revolt, or a revolt from rebellion. For popular rebellion, the phrase was generally "to rise up." In France and Flanders insurgents most often "moved" and thus were guilty of creating *commociones.* In Italy they made noise; thus their revolts or riots were *rumori.* In Flanders, France (Langue d'oïl and Languedoc), and Italy, nearly all the records, judicial and narrative, accused these "movements" or "noises" of hatching "conspiracies," "plots," "plans," illicit assemblies, and disturbances against the "peace and tranquility of the state" or "status quo."

More important than such distinctions is another, which neither Mollat, Wolff, Fourquin, Hilton, nor any other historian to my knowledge has yet to draw with clarity: what constituted a popular revolt, riot, or movement and how are such events to be selected from the sources? First, did these acts have to involve violence? By my definition they did not. Popular movements could, for instance, include peace movements, which might not resort to violence: witness the remarkable protest of small children in 1347, who marched through the streets of Naples to the royal palace of the Angevin Queen Joanna I (1343–1382), crying "Pace, pace," and waving banners of the two Sicilies to end Naples' war with Sicily.[22] They could include organized political pressure and petitioning, as with serfs on the estates of canons of Notre-Dame at Orly, Châtenay, and other nearby villages. The canons imprisoned the men of the villages in their charter house for failure to pay their rents and left them to die without providing any sustenance. In response, their wives filed a for-

mal complaint in 1251 before Queen Blanche, St. Louis's mother, but as far
as the sources reveal they did not engage in violence, even though they eventually prevailed over their clerical lords, who claimed to have legal powers
of life and death over them.[23]

Tax revolts, usually one of the most violent forms of revolt, could also succeed without violence. For instance, in contrast to the French crown's attempt
to raise taxes in Flanders, which led to rebellion between 1297 and 1304—one
of the bloodiest and most widespread of the later Middle Ages—Philip the
Fair's attempts to raise taxes to wage war against Flanders in 1314 were met
with general grumbling and discontent throughout his realm. A year later his
son, Louis X le Hutin, was forced to withdraw the fiscal demands, not because
of rioting in the streets but because of actions in local assemblies.[24]

Student movements also won concessions without resorting to violence.
To be sure, students in the Middle Ages were hardly peace-loving, docile types,
in fact probably less so than in modern times. Decked out in full military garb
and armed with the latest weaponry, their gang wars often terrorized locals.[25]
But their most effective actions were peaceful ones: organized refusal to attend
classes and threats of mass migration to form new universities with poten-
tially disastrous effects for the local economies they left behind. Often town-
gown conflicts or a perceived gross miscarriage of justice prompted students
to take such collective action. In 1230 a disturbance between the university
and citizens *(bourgeois)* of Paris caused students to leave the city until the
citizens invited them back on favorable terms.[26] The podestà of Bologna
beheaded a Catalan student in 1321 for having slept with the niece of the
famous canon lawyer and professor Lord Giovanni d'Andrea.[27] The foreign
students organized a strike and threatened to leave Bologna if the podestà was
not brought to justice. In response, the podestà arrested four student ringleaders and decapitated them, provoking all the masters, doctors, and students to leave for Imola. Further, the dons sent notices to cities throughout
Tuscany to establish new universities. A year later, feeling the commercial
pinch and loss of prestige, Bologna offered economic enticements and persuaded some students and their professors to return.[28] Finally, revolts against
the violence of aristocrats, even one of the most famous ones of the Middle
Ages—Cola di Rienzo's establishment of popular government and the expul-
sion of the barons from Rome—at least initially were bloodless revolutions.[29]

In addition, I have included in my samples popular movements that gathered great crowds but on first impression may not have appeared as obvious
forms of protest, such as the Alleluia movement of 1233. According to the

chronicler Salimbene of Parma, this religious movement spread throughout Italy, bringing together noblemen and commoners, burghers and peasants, adolescents and virgins, the old and the young, singing songs in praise of the Lord. But this was not solely a religious procession or movement; rather, it reached simple peasants and artisans and demanded political peace and an end to magnate violence.[30] Other religious peace movements could be more overtly political, such as the flagellants who organized demonstrations at San Miniato in June 1311 and processed through the territories of Lucca and Pisa. Stripped to the waist, they "clamored in loud voices for mercy, peace, and penitence,"[31] went on to draft new town statutes, successfully pressured the podestà of San Miniato to call a cease-fire among the region's warring factions, and renounced all sentences of banishment.

The vast majority of these revolts, however, were violent, and brought armed men into city squares or fields even if sometimes equipped only with sticks, stones, and mud. Even peace movements could become violent and achieved political reform through fear and terror, as when the *popolo*[32] of Osimo, a hill town in the district of Ancona, rioted against their governors in May 1322 and demanded peace with the Church. From fear of what had just happened to Count Federico da Montefeltro in Urbino,[33] the city council fled and the "commune and *popolo* of Osimo surrendered the town to the Papacy."[34]

To be considered "popular protest," should these movements include a critical mass of participants? Chroniclers rarely specified the numbers involved; usually their descriptions were qualitative—a great rebellion or riot (*grant commocion, un gran romore, grande tumulto, maximus tumultus, maximus rumor*), many rebellions (*pluseurs rébellions*), many commoners (*plusieurs communes gens*), a great multitude (*grant multitude, seditio maxima in populo, populus multo numero*). Chroniclers certainly could exaggerate the insurgents' numbers, as when the *Anonimalle chronicle* claimed that the Jacquerie of northern France put 190,000 into the field of battle,[35] or when Jean Froissart estimated the Roman crowd that pressured the College of Cardinals to elect an Italian pope in 1378 at 30,000, even though the adult population of Rome at that time was probably well below that figure.[36] On the other hand, chroniclers and town or royal clerks and notaries, who drafted letters of remissions or criminal inquests, do not seem to have been invariably prone to gross overstatement (despite historians' general notions about the use of numbers in the Middle Ages).[37] Several, for instance, put the Jacques forces at only between six and seven thousand even when gloating over the numbers slaughtered,[38] despite the number of villages involved, the high density of settlement, and the vast territory covered by the Jacquerie, as can be seen from around sixty letters of remission that have been published.[39]

Moreover, chroniclers and clerks occasionally gave numbers to what they called "a great multitude of commoners and tumultuous men." A remission pardoning an apothecary, who was singled out in a sedition against the king's councilor in the southern French town of Béziers in 1363, counted "about sixty or so" in the uprising.[40] In 1412 the governors of Verona uncovered a conspiracy to overthrow the government and free it from Venetian control. "About seventy to eighty men of the lowest condition" were caught waving a flag and chanting "Long live the emperor and the Scala [the ruling family of Padua]." They were seized and most were drowned in the river Adige.[41] Chroniclers and registers report other reasonable estimates of the numbers of insurgents, ranging from a handful of co-conspirators to several thousand, such as the peasants who stormed the city walls of Parma in 1385, the wool workers in the Ciompi revolt who broke into the Palazzo Signoria on 20 July 1378, or the throng in Paris who in March 1382 broke into the Châtelet, stole the hammers, and rioted against Charles VI's taxes on commodities (subsidies). The Flemish revolts of 1297–1304 and 1323–1328 mobilized far greater numbers of peasants and artisans across regions and cities and were the largest and most widespread rebellions of the Middle Ages.[42]

For this study I have tried to weed out the actions that appeared to be taken by isolated individuals or families against bosses, landlords, or government officials—what James C. Scott has called "everyday forms of resistance"[43]— from incidents of collective action that went beyond the family cell. Indeed, chroniclers rarely reported individual acts of sedition. When they did, the incidents were either remarkably atrocious or colorful, or perhaps indicative of a more general resentment underlying an individual's actions. Such resentment may explain a Sienese chronicler's recording of a seditious assault in 1346. One night Vivuccio, the illegitimate son of a parish priest of the village of Corzano, dumped "a bucket of piss and other filth" on the head of a certain Bindo Tenghi, a merchant in the street of the cobblers (*calzolaria*). When caught, Vivuccio confessed that he had been in cahoots (*l'avea fatto a stanza*) with a Giovanni di Nadino Belanti. Sometime earlier, both had been fined a thousand gold florins in the merchants' court, where Bindo had sat on the bench.[44] Although rare in late medieval chronicles, such individual acts of revenge, hatred, and disrespect of those in authority are sprinkled liberally through the judicial acts (when they survive) and the royal letters of remission issued by the king of France and his lieutenants. Often these were crimes committed as part of larger social conflicts, as can be seen in numerous remissions granted to peasant insurgents of the Jacquerie of 1358, Tuchin bandits from 1364 into the 1390s, artisan supporters of the *Harelle* of Rouen in 1382, and the *Maillotins* of Paris of the same year. However, it is difficult to be certain whether such acts were isolated or part of larger collective protests. For instance, in 1376, Pierre, "a poor farm laborer [*pouvre laboureur*]" of Sainte Gemme in the diocese of Luçon (Poitou), received a royal letter pardoning him of the murder of a fellow villager, Jehan Paquerea. This Jehan had threatened to put in his cooking pot the collector of the royal hearth tax *(fouage)* who had come to collect the remainder of the tax Jehan owed. Jehan had also insulted the tax collector's wife, saying that "she lied worse than any crooked rotten hag." The tax collector was Pierre's brother.[45] Was the scrape simply a personal vendetta between an isolated disgruntled taxpayer and a collector doing his job, or did it reflect deeper village resentment over royal taxes (with many other unreported assaults) at the very moment when Charles V, in fact, had sharply escalated the hearth tax in various regions of France? From this single surviving letter it is impossible to say, so I have not included it (along with similar cases at other times and places) in my samples of popular protest. As important as such individual acts of protest and insult to agents of the crown may be for understanding conflict and opposition to dominant powers, this study will define popular protest as collective action (violent or nonviolent) against those of higher social status, whether they were wool bosses, landlords, or representatives of the state.[46]

Even more difficult is distinguishing what constituted a popular revolt as opposed to revolts of higher classes or orders; where should the line be drawn? Although most of the revolts, acts of resistance, and protests in this book concern peasants, workers, and artisans, they are not the only ones that I have included as "popular." Age too could demarcate the popular from the power elite, as with the children's peace march in Naples in 1347 (the children's social status is not indicated). Students likewise may have included marginal and unfortunate foreigners, such as the Catalan whose love of a "donzella" from a prestigious Bolognese family cost him his head, but they may also have included other students from well-off families, who acted in solidarity with other marginals against the city elites, judges, podestà, and ennobled professors and who later in life may have filled the ranks of these elites.

The line delimiting the popular can never be simple or absolute: rebels often crossed social barriers, as historians of the Jacquerie and the English Peasants'

Revolt of 1381 have recently emphasized. "Popular" needs to be seen as dependent on the particular dynamics of a conflict, who was opposing whom. For instance, I have included revolts led, organized, and staffed by city councils and the bourgeoisie against representatives of the crown, such as the revolt of Carcassonne in 1364, when counselors organized their citizens to lay siege to the royal castle of Trèbes, about five kilometers beyond their city walls.[47] At other moments the same "bourgeois" insurgents could become instead the city elite, oppressing those further down the social hierarchy, whether artisans, disenfranchised workers, or peasants.[48]

Although I have ruled out rebellions by the aristocracy even against superior lords or the crown, it is often difficult to know exactly who comprised insurrectionary crowds. For example, who were the "inhabitants of Turin" (the capital of Savoy), who in 1255, "with the support and advice from those of the city of Asti," imprisoned their lord, Thomas, the count of Savoy?[49] Who were "the people" of Valenciennes *(gens castri quod Valencianis dicitur)*, who in 1291 forced their lord, John, the count of Hainault (Jean d'Avesnes), out of town because "he had oppressed them beyond all measure"?[50] Occasionally, further descriptions of the riot or its context and its repression give clues as to who these "inhabitants" or "people" were. One example was a tax revolt in Rouen in 1292, when the commoners *(minor populus)* rose up against the magistrates of the exchequer and the king's officers "because of the evil way they had been squeezed for taxes beyond any measure"; they waged war against the officers in the city's castle, destroyed the house where the taxes were collected, and threw the money into the city's squares. In comparison with Carcassonne in 1364, or possibly Turin in 1255 and Valenciennes in 1291, this revolt at Rouen cut at a lower class level. Here the insurgents did not constitute a united, citywide front against the crown. Instead, the elites of the city allied with the crown; the mayor and bourgeois stepped in, "put an end" to the rebellion, "hanged very many of the insurgents, and imprisoned many others in various royal prisons."[51]

It is often difficult to know in different contexts, with different authors and over time, what key words such as *peuple, plebes, communes, popolo, menu peuple,* and *popolo minuto* meant with any precise sense of occupations or levels of wealth.[52] Chroniclers could be even vaguer, referring (as we have seen) to uprisings of "inhabitants" or "those of" a particular village, city, or region. Even at the hands of the same author a term such as *popolo* could shift meanings from the masses to the government of a city. In Italian city-states, the *popolo* rose and organized neighborhood cadres to oppose their oppression by knights—*milites* or magnates. While chroniclers especially before 1300 rarely specified the occupations of those who comprised the *peuple* or *popolo*, often the weapons that such groups could command sharply differentiated them from their knightly superiors. For instance, a fistfight between a nobleman and a commoner sparked a major riot *(seditio magna)* in February 1090 in the northern town of Piacenza. The fight between those without horses *(pedites)* and noblemen *(milites)* broke out in a vacant lot by the Church of Santa Maria; the two social groups then gathered in two different neighborhoods of the city before engaging in a battle that lasted two days. The weapons of the *populares* were stone-age: they hurled rocks and mud at the nobles and "gravely wounded them with knobbed sticks." Even with such weaponry the commoners prevailed. By the second day the entire city had joined the fray, chasing the *milites* from town. The *pedites* then followed the noblemen to their ancestral village of Saint George and burned it down. Their purported chant gives their social status further clarity: "It is better to die in battle than to live in desolation and perish of hunger," and the chronicler added that a shortage of foodstuffs *(carere victualiis)* had precipitated the revolt.[53] As against the usual notion of preindustrial revolts, this is one of the very few of over a thousand in my sample where the sources specified famine or food shortage as the cause of a revolt. Even here that shortage was secondary—a matter of background—to the primary cause, which was political: the *pedites* "hounded out" the *milites* because of political oppression. These commoners successfully took over the reins of city government.

By the late thirteenth century, however, if not earlier, the character of the struggle between the *popolo* and magnates in such towns as Bologna, Florence, and Perugia had changed, especially after the *popolo* gained the upper hand, promulgating laws that outlawed nobles, leveling their towers, imposing special taxes on them, and penalizing them more harshly than commoners for the same crimes. Historians following in the footsteps of Nicola Ottokar,[54] such as Emilio Cristiani[55] and Jacques Heers,[56] have argued that the conflicts between *popolo* and magnates of the late thirteenth and fourteenth centuries were not matters of class or social conflict at all; rather, the two groups had intermarried, becoming indistinguishable in wealth and economic activity. More recently, historians investigating the lifestyle, dependence on violence, and ideology of these groups have returned to a position closer to Gaetano Salvemini's,[57] seeing these groups as more sharply divided social classes.[58]

Thus I have included many of the *popolo*'s assaults on the nobility in my database of popular protest. I have, however, excluded their defensive "revolts" against the nobility once they had risen to power in city-states.[59] In certain circumstances, as in Milan in February 1311 when the ex–ruling party of the Visconti led an uprising against the emperor, Henry VII, it is difficult to know whether the assault comprised any popular element at all, no matter how liberally the boundaries of "popular" are interpreted. True, the chronicler reports that the citizens of Milan had been "greatly burdened" by the emperor's new tax intended to raise 100,000 gold florins, and "since they had not been taxed for a long time, they complained forcefully." It was left, however, to members of Milan's old feudal elite, Lords Guidetto della Torre and Maffeo Visconti, to bring the matter openly before the emperor and to conspire "with their friends" to chase the emperor and his men out of Milan. The conspiracy failed because Lord Maffeo betrayed his co-conspirator and informed the emperor, whose troops then destroyed all the palaces of the della Torre clan.[60] Almost a century later, following the death of Milan's duchess (the widow of Giangaleazzo Visconti, Count of Virtù), the *popolo* of Milan wanted to control Milan's fortifications, but they turned to a member of the Visconti family, Lord Francesco, to lead the revolt against the German soldiers of Francesco Barbavara.[61] To what extent the *popolo* were engaged in this revolt and who exactly comprised their ranks is again difficult to gauge from the account of the usually exacting and meticulous Florentine chronicler, the pseudo-Minerbetti, who in recording many other revolts of the late fourteenth and early fifteenth centuries was attentive to matters of social class. A later Milanese historian of the early sixteenth century, Bernardino Corio, gives further clues about an insurrection against Barbavara on San Giovanni day of the previous summer, when several noble families rounded up their henchmen to assassinate him. The plot failed, but under the leadership of Antonio Porro, a wealthy Milanese patrician, the *popolo* took arms, and a crowd of 15,000 *plebei* (according to Corio) terrorized Barbavara, locked him in his castle, and killed a number of his supporters, including the abbot of Sant' Ambrogio. Yet this *popolo* sounds different from the antimagnate forces of late medieval Tuscan history. Instead of chants of "Long live the people," "Death to the nobles," or "Long live the guilds," their cry was "Long live the duke."[62] Clearly, over time and space, revolts of "the people" in northern and central Italy varied radically in character. Some I have judged as "popular"; others I have not. It is a gray area that depends as much on which chronicler's report is read and believed as it does on any definition of what constitutes "popular" or "a revolt," no matter how theoretically sound.

Similarly, peasant revolts are not so easy to delineate as it might seem. For instance, peasants were often the main actors in the revolts of villages or even small towns against the domination by larger city-states. Such rebellions were particularly frequent in the hills and valleys of Voltri, Polcevera, and Bisagno surrounding Genoa during the last quarter of the fourteenth and the early fifteenth centuries. They rose up against Genoese taxation, killed their rural governors (podestà), and even invaded the city, occasionally joining artisans against Genoese patrician rule. Sometimes chroniclers referred to these insurgents as *rustici*, sometimes as the *popolo,* and sometimes as Guelfs or Ghibellines, but given the absence of towns of any size in these valleys, they were in any economic sense mountain peasants or those who mixed farming with fishing and other simple maritime activities and should be analyzed as such. Yet I know of no historian to consider these revolts as peasant movements.

It is also difficult to distinguish military operations in which nobles or merchant patricians employed or organized peasants to serve as the shock troops for pursuing aristocratic factional warfare or for suppressing urban revolt, as opposed to peasants joining with nobles or merchants in pursuit of their own interests. The former I have not considered as popular rebellions, while the latter I have. Oligarchs of Florence organized peasants from their estates and the rural militia to invade the city and oppose workers and artisans in the early stages of the Ciompi revolt of 1378,[63] but no evidence suggests that these peasants had political initiatives of their own. On the other hand, I have classified as a peasant revolt an invasion of peasants into the city of Parma on 26 March 1308, even though these *rustici* came there under the command of Rolandino Scorza in a battle between the forces of the emperor and those of the bishop of Parma. I have done so because once in the city the peasants pursued their own goals, turning what was originally an internecine conflict among elites into a tax revolt by peasants. They broke into the communal palaces and offices of the podestà, the Captain of the People, and the gabelles (i.e., indirect taxes) and judges of communal taxation, broke apart archival cabinets, and ripped to shreds judicial ledgers and lists of taxes and fines. Throwing the documents from the palace windows, they "created great clouds of torn charters that entirely covered the square below. And in this way, these peasants cancelled their fines and released themselves from what they owed."[64] Forty-eight years later the same happened in Novara. Peasants from the neighboring villages of Trecate and Galliate supported the troops of the marchese of Monteferrato to invade the city, but once inside "the rustics raided the town hall and ripped, burnt, and dumped down a well the city's notarial records, from its most ancient charters to recent judicial condemnations [against these peasants], thus freeing themselves of fines and taxes."[65]

Often it is easy to distinguish internecine struggle among elites (struggles within and between city-states) from incidents of popular revolt. Thus those struggles within Italian city-states that chroniclers labeled as Guelf-Ghibelline conflicts can for the most part be dismissed. However, at certain times and places, particularly in smaller cities, these struggles were not exclusively battles among aristocratic or merchant elites vying for political control of city-states as in Florence or Milan; instead these "parties" occasionally saw different social classes struggling for political inclusion. For instance, at Todi the people *(lo populo)* were called Guelfs and the elites *(li boni homini* or *gintil-homini)*, Ghibellines.[66] As we have seen, the rural populations that periodically invaded Genoa, opposing magnate rule and supporting the cause of the *popolo*, were also called or called themselves Ghibellines.

The Sources

As the examples above suggest, the primary material for this book comes largely from late medieval chroniclers. In attempting syntheses across regions, historians often turn to their own primary research for a particular locality but rely on the work of other historians for areas beyond their expertise. My method has been different. I have combed through the major collections of narrative sources, mainly chronicles, for the various regions of this book's investigation: the *Rerum Italicarum Scriptores,* edited and directed by the eighteenth-century erudite Ludovico Muratori; the revised and expanded *Rerum Italicarum Scriptores* of the Istituto Storico Italiano per il Medio Evo, initiated by Giosué Carducci and Vittorio Fiorini in 1900; the *Rerum Gallicarum et Francicarum Scriptores* or *Recueil des Historiens des Gaules et de la France,* begun by Léopold Deslisle in 1869; the *Société d'histoire de France,* founded by François P. G. Guizot in 1833; the *Monumenta Germaniae Historica, Scriptores,* directed originally by G. H. Pertz (for chronicles and annals pertaining to Flanders, France, and Italy); the *Corpus Chronicorum Flandriae,* directed by J.-J. de Smet from 1837; and the *Chroniques liégeoises,* directed by Sylvian Balau et Émile Fairon of the Académie royale de Belgique, commission royale d'histoire, from 1931. In addition, I consulted series holding fewer medieval chronicles, such as in the *Fonti per la storia d'Italia* of the Istituto Storico Italiano per il Medio Evo; *Documenti di storia italiana;* the late-eighteenth-century *Delizie degli eruditi toscani,* directed by friar Ildefonso di San Luigi; the *Sociétés des anciens textes français; Collection de documents inédits sur l'histoire de France; Collection de textes pour servir à l'étude et à l'enseignement de l'histoire de France;* and many other minor or local collections as well as new editions of chronicles not included in multivolume collections, such as *Journal d'un bourgeois de Paris de 1405 à 1449*[67] and *Chronicon Regiense: La Cronaca di Pietro della Gazzata nella tradizione del codice Crispi.*[68]

I searched through these sources for contemporary narrative reports of social movements circa 1200–1425.[69] If a chronicle that began earlier continued into these years, I would also search it for examples of popular movements and disturbances back to the eleventh century. I collected, however, only a handful of examples predating 1200; the statistical trends of this book begin in 1200. My original question for this book—what was the impact of the Black Death on popular revolt?—guided the choice of dates, a time span long enough to reveal differences before and after 1348.

I scanned numerous chronicles, annals, journals, and diaries; found 298 with at least one revolt;[70] and collected from them over 1,600 descriptions of popular movements, which amount to 1,112 separate incidents. Most are reported only once. At the other extreme, the Sicilian Vespers, a revolt that began against the arrogance and sexual misconduct of French soldiers at a festival outside Palermo on Easter Monday 1282, appears in thirty-four chronicles in this sample, having gained the attention of writers as far away as Liège.[71] To these chronicles, I have added judicial cases from archives in Florence, Lucca, Siena, and Bologna, along with a hundred cases discovered among the thousands of documents conserved in the Trésor des chartes in the Archives nationales of Paris or published for the regions of Poitou and Languedoc.

Chronicles

Chronicles have come under attack from historians: these sources, some have argued, are biased, inaccurate, and contradictory and are best studied for questions of mentality rather than for the "facts" they purport to relate.[72] Certainly, the narrative sources selected for this study can provide grist for these mills. First, chroniclers often misdated events, especially minor revolts, even when they lived in the regions and at the time of the events. Usually, the mistake was a matter of months or a single year as with the Bolognese chroniclers who dated an artisan uprising of 1393 in Florence to 1394.[73] But on occasion chroniclers could be wider of the mark, as when a Parisian chronicler misdated

Fra Dolcino's heretical community and its suppression to 1312 instead of 1304–1307.[74] Not to be outdone, a late-Trecento chronicler of Gubbio seemed to get most of his dates wrong by seven to nine years, switching to 1360 the 1367 uprising in Viterbo against cardinals and courtiers, the Perugian uprising of 1369 against the church, and even Messer Brascia's overthrow of Gubbio itself in 1367.[75]

More striking is the panoply of opinions and prejudices that can be seen for events such as the Jacquerie of 1358, for which large numbers of chronicles and other archival documents survive. This revolt, perhaps France's best known before the French Revolution, sparked deep-seated passions. While the Carmelite friar Jean de Venette[76] saw reasons for the peasants' discontent and charged the nobility with betrayal, the aristocratic canon of Laon, Jean le Bel, reported the peasants' actions as "uncontrolled, diabolical madness," the consequence of a "senseless beastly rage." Le Bel considered the Jacques to have been "leaderless people" but marveled at how these revolts could have spread over so vast a terrain, all flaring at the same time. To his mind peasants were incapable of acting on their own; hence outsiders from higher social classes—such as Charles the Bad, the king of Navarre; Robert Le Coq, the bishop of Laon; or Étienne Marcel, the provost of the Parisian merchants—must have secretly set the revolts in motion, even if the first of these nominees massacred the peasants only two weeks later.[77] By contrast, other chroniclers described the Jacques' principal captain, Guillaume Cale, some even favorably,[78] and letters of remission list a myriad of local leaders from the ranks of the villagers themselves.[79]

Far less famous revolts with fewer sources can show similar diversity in reporting. For instance, two doges and a later patrician of Venice, Marino Sanuto the elder, briefly described a popular revolt in Venice in 1266 against an increase in the gabelle on milled grain *(la macina)*.[80] According to the doges, the rock-throwing crowd that gathered in front of the Palazzo Ducale were easily dispersed, with "the principal authors of the wickedness" hanged. Sanuto's account, based on earlier chronicles now partially lost, such as that of the merchant Ser Pietro Dolfino Barone,[81] tells a different story: rather than being motivated by simple "wickedness," the people were "impatient with such unaccustomed abuse"; and the doge, far from being in complete control of a frivolous uprising, had "to choose judicious words" to stop the crowd from raiding the country and destroying property. Further, mediation by the heads of the neighborhoods *(contrade)* was needed to quell the riot *(tumulto)*; and, most important, against the doges' claims, the revolt proved more than a flash in the pan. Although several leaders were hanged at the columns near the church of San Marco, the insurgents won their cause: the doge was forced to back down and revoke the increase in the gabelle.

Although most of the revolts are found in chronicle descriptions alone, others can be traced in archival documents: criminal inquests or sentences; governmental decrees *(provvisioni);* and, in France, letters of remission. For a popular insurrection in Lucca against the ruling Guinigi oligarchy, for instance, the assessments of the chronicler Giovanni Sercambi, a spice merchant loyal to the Guinigi, and who supplied them with stationery and medicines, can be juxtaposed with the more clinical reportage of judicial records. Sercambi portrayed this revolt—the only popular one that historians have thus far noted in late medieval Lucca[82]—as a frivolous affair, turning on nothing more than a change in the name of the city's government from "Commune" to "People." By his account, the revolt (which he misdates one year early, to February 1372) was a factional conflict among citizens, Guelfs versus Ghibellines, with little hint that different classes or those excluded from government were its protagonists. Only Sercambi's listing of the rabble-rousers beheaded or fined—Nicolao di Lippo, a needle worker; Pieretto, a weaver; Stefano, called Trombante (loudmouth) from Quarto; and others without family names—suggest any possible class difference between the leaders of the protest and the oligarchic merchant elite, the ruling Guinigi family.[83]

The judicial records tell a different story, though not without the judges' and notaries' own prejudices.[84] Faced with grievous crimes and especially revolts, the courts showed little sympathy for or attention to insurgents' motives. Rebels' acts by definition "were instigated by the spirit of the devil."[85] According to the judicial formula, rebels did not "have God in their sight"; their guidance instead came from "the enemy of humankind." Nonetheless, the court's inquest shows that this revolt was one of artisans, mostly in the cloth industry, who rallied their fellow workers and other artisans against Lucca's most powerful family and its oligarchic rulers. In addition to the needle worker Nicolao di Lippo, Stefano the "loudmouth," and the weaver Pieretto, the inquest lists another leader who organized secret meetings—Lorenzo, a master cobbler.

> Not from evil or suspicious testimony but by trustworthy, loyal, and honorable persons, it has often been brought to our attention that this Nuccino together with Master Lorenzo, a cobbler, and Bindinello di Tadicione . . . often held discussions and made plans with this Master

Lorenzo, Bindinello, and certain other citizens of the city of Lucca, which disturbed the peace and tranquility of this city of Lucca. To execute the promises, plans, and orders given on Thursday, 25 July, this Nuccino, together with Master Lorenzo, Bindinello, and others of their accomplices and associates, were supposed to meet in the church of Saint George and from there lead all their friends, who were armed, to come together at the Palace of the Lord Elders of the city of Lucca, where they were to expel these lord elders, the imperial vicars,[86] and to chose and summon other new ones to take their place. After accomplishing this, they were to make their way to the houses of those of the Guinigi family,[87] the Bucciolli family, Lord Simone of Barga, Orlandino di Volpello, and many other citizens of the city of Lucca, to set them on fire, rob them, and kill any who might resist, thus subverting the present state, peace, and tranquility of the city of Lucca.

The plot failed, but the conspirators held another meeting and attacked the palace of the Guinigi family. Forewarned, their kinsmen and friends mounted an armed guard and rebuffed the artisans' assault. In a separate trial, Pieretto was convicted of charging "with his knife unsheathed under his cloak" into a council meeting of the ruling elders of Lucca. Once discovered, he fled, sparking a major riot throughout Lucca with shouts of "Long live the People." Further, in the square of San Michele in Foro, where "the majority of the people of Lucca" were assembled, Nicolao the needle worker harangued the crowd, "shouting loudly, many, many times: 'Do not leave us, you must lead the citizens of Lucca.' " In yet another trial, another weaver was convicted as a co-conspirator. Perhaps these rebels' chant, "Long live the People," was Sercambi's cue for belittling the conflict as of no greater significance than a government's name. But as the judicial proceedings show, behind the name *popolo* meant toppling the regime of a narrow oligarchy of merchant patricians and replacing it with a new, much wider representative government that would include, as the inquest put it, "the majority of the people of Lucca." As the revolt's popular leadership suggests, this majority included those at the bottom of Lucca's social ladder—weavers and needle workers.[88]

In previous studies I have added to the critical chorus against relying on the chronicles as sources for political and social history, especially when used in isolation from other sources. During Florence's dramatic struggle against Milan, which reached its boiling point in the summer of 1402, peasant communities across the northern and western mountainous perimeter of the

Florentine state revolted against Florentine taxes that targeted mountain peasants at much higher rates than those lower down the slopes, closer to the city, where Florentine patricians held their lands. In collaboration with enemy generals and old feudal families (the Ubaldini, Uberti, and Pazzi), mountain peasants assailed Florence's frontier citadels and established their own mountaintop bastions, where they intercepted Florentine messengers, raided the countryside, and threatened the security of the Florentine state. Florence failed to suppress these mountain rebels with its military might and eventually had to negotiate with them. In these negotiations, summarized in Florence's rich archival sources, principally its *Provvisioni*, Florence ended by granting remarkable privileges and even lifetime tax exemptions to these rebels, who a year before had been condemned to death as traitors.[89] Against this history sketched from archival documents, the merchant chronicler Gregorio Dati (whom modern scholars such as Hans Baron and Antonio Lanza[90] have praised as having brought to the Renaissance a new historical perspicuity) portrayed these mountain peasants on the Florentine periphery as the stalwarts of Florentine liberty, virtuously defending the republic against the threat of Milanese tyranny. According to Dati, each villager was "worth two foreign soldiers in these hard and bitter places."[91] No mention was made of the high taxes they were forced to shoulder or their consequential successful rebellion. Chroniclers, like historians and statesmen in more modern times, can falsify and rewrite history to justify their ideologies and self-importance. Worse yet, they can cover up history by refraining from reporting incidents that contradicted their notions of republican liberty or supposedly enlightened and benevolent rule. How many revolts remain hidden from history, even sizable ones, such as those that raged over the mountaintops of Florence between 1400 and 1403, involving thousands of peasants in well over 200 villages?

Did the authorship of these chronicles differ significantly between Italy and the lands north of the Alps? If so, would the differences seriously affect a comparative study of revolts? First, over one-third of the authors remain unknown, but for some of these it is often possible to surmise whether they were members of the clergy or laity, aristocrats, patricians, or merchants. Several series of anonymous chronicles represent collective monastic enterprises. Italy shows a greater predominance of merchant and notarial chroniclers, and Florence and Siena are the only places in my samples where artisans (only two) and even a worker left a chronicle. By contrast, clerics dominated chronicle writing in the north, followed by aristocrats. It might therefore be expected that revolts with religious leaders or those that revolved around religious ideology would be reported in greater numbers in the north, but this was not the case. To anticipate a conclusion drawn toward the end of this book, revolts with religious overtones and religious movements both north and south of the Alps peppered popular rebellion from the twelfth century to 1349; afterward (at least to the end of this analysis, when new religious movements branded as Hussites were on the horizon in France and Flanders), revolts with religious leaders or religious ideals disappeared almost completely, in fact more so in the Low Countries and France than in Italy.

Despite questions about chronicles, they may not be "the least reliable" of sources, as Guy Fourquin and others now charge.[92] On occasion, they give a more rounded sense of an insurrection than that supplied by an isolated judicial record. As we have seen, such records rarely alluded to insurgents' motivations or the causes of revolt. Between 11 and 16 April 1376, the Bolognese court of the podestà, for instance, sentenced twenty-three mountain men from Apennine villages separating the territories of Florence and Bologna, who had invaded Bologna. The men had burst through a sluice gate in the city walls, rushed to the cardinal legate's palace, dragged him into the piazza, stolen his horse, and ripped the rings off his fingers, thereby gravely humiliating the pope's representative and temporal authority in Bologna. Other than acting "under the influence of the devil, from contempt of the sanctity of the Holy Roman Church, with reckless abandon and a sacrilegious mind," the judicial records give no sense why these mountain peasants had journeyed so far to Bologna to humiliate the legate. Further, only in a brief aside do these records suggest that others may have been allied with or had commanded the mountaineers: "In committing this crime, each and every one of the indicted received help, advice, and favors."[93]

The chronicles of Bologna[94] and elsewhere[95] give context to the mountain men's actions left inexplicable in the judicial ledgers. According to *Cronaca B* and the *Cronica Bolognetti,* "several magnates of Bologna organized a large gathering of men from the city with many nobles from the *contado* [surrounding countryside] of Bologna" to overturn church rule and return authority to the people of Bologna. The Count of Bruscoli (a mountain village high in the Apennines) was a prime mover of the revolt, and he (not a peasant) was in fact the one who ripped the rings from the cardinal legate's fingers. For the Bolognese *Cronaca gestorum* of Friar Jerome Burselli and chroniclers outside

Bologna, it was a revolt to restore an elected government of the people. (At this point in Bolognese history its government was led by patrician families such as the Bentivoglio, the Counts of Castiglione dei Pepoli, and others "of Bologna's most important citizens [*principalioribus civibus*].") Further, the chronicles report that a mass armed demonstration of the *popolo* with their neighborhood flags raised and cries of "Death to the Church" and "Long live the People" followed the mountain men's invasion. As a consequence of the revolt, not only was the cardinal legate spirited from town and his palace returned to the Bolognese; in addition, the uprising was nearly bloodless and returned rule to an elected council of elders representing the four quarters of the city, the banners were returned to the neighborhood districts, and an elected Standard-bearer *(Gonfaloniere)* of Justice was made the highest officer of the city and given the banner bearing the symbol of the people.[96] Chronicler "A" further comments that the newly elected leaders and representatives of the people were "an enlightened bunch," comprising magnates and those from the middling ranks *(mezani).* Unfortunately, none of the chroniclers attempts to explain the motivation of the mountain rustics or why they were later sentenced by the new popular government. Were they simply following the orders of their feudal lords as *Cronaca A* implies? If so, why did some willingly risk their necks while others, such as the villagers of Panico, refused to join in? Did the excessive taxation of the papacy, which sparked revolts from Milan to Puglia, impinge with particular severity on these mountain people?[97] Whatever the answers, these chronicles show that despite prejudice and selective attention to certain aspects of the revolt, a reasonable story can be told, often with a greater understanding of the motivation for various social ranks in the rebellion than can be derived from the dry and formulaic judicial records.

The Archives

Apart from chroniclers, with their mistakes, prejudices, and selectivity, what other sources are left to the historian who wishes to investigate the plethora of late medieval revolts across large areas of Western Europe? The archival sources most commonly consulted for popular movements in the late Middle Ages and early modern periods—judicial records—survive in only small numbers before 1400 and are concentrated in a handful of northern Italian city-states, such as Florence and Bologna. Even for a city whose archival resources are as rich as those of Siena, surviving judicial records are patchy before the sixteenth century. North of the Alps such records are even harder to come by: for the largest city in Western Europe—Paris—they begin only in the fifteenth century. Surviving records of town councils and daily decrees are also rare before the fifteenth century, especially north of the Alps.[98]

France, however, is blessed with another source, which has yet to be tapped for the study of late medieval insurrection except for the Jacquerie,[99] the Tuchins around Saint-Flour,[100] and to a lesser extent, the *Harelle* of Rouen and the *Maillotins* of Paris in 1382.[101] The registers of the Trésor des chartes, housed in the Archives nationales (JJ 35 to JJ 266), contain letters and decrees emanating from the king and registered in the royal chancellery. With few lacunae they extend from the reign of Philip the Fair (1302) to Charles IX (1568) and contain 95,000 documents.[102] Of these royal acts and letters, most cases of popular rebellion are found in letters of remission granted to individuals. On rare occasions, these letters were also granted to cities or even entire regions of France: such was the pardon of Charles VI's lieutenant in Languedoc, John, Duke of Berry, who in the 1380s granted a pardon to all inhabitants within the seneschals of Toulouse, Carcassonne, and Beaucaire because of insurrections in return for a fine of 800,000 gold francs.[103] Unfortunately, grants of letters of remission to individuals or communities were not constant over time. Instead, only by the 1340s did kings begin to realize their value for raising revenue, and the letters were relatively rare before Philip VI's reign (1328–1350). Afterward, their numbers mounted steeply. For the years 1345–1349, they constituted about one-third of the acts in the Trésor des chartes; by the end of the century their proportion had risen to four-fifths.[104] Thus it would be problematic to study the impact of the Black Death on popular insurrection from these sources alone. In addition, the records after the Black Death, except for certain regions such as Languedoc, Gascony, and Berry, have yet to be inventoried analytically,[105] and no comparable records exist for Italy. Nonetheless, a sample of these letters has been employed in this study. They are particularly useful for the south of France (Languedoc), where curiously the chronicle tradition was much weaker than in the north of France or in Italy.

Finally, an analysis of popular revolt based on unpublished archival sources, even given their fragmentary nature and limited survival across late medieval Europe, would require a multinational collective endeavor. For Flanders alone the retrieval and publishing of such documents relating only to the wool industry relied on a team of scholars whose efforts stretched across much of the twentieth century.[106]

The Samples and Their Selection

The examples of popular protest across Italy, France, Flanders, and the Liégeois collected for this study are only a sample and not a random one. They reflect the predominance of chronicle writing in various regions combined with later scholarly efforts in the eighteenth and nineteenth centuries to preserve and edit them. Thus it comes as little surprise that the cities with the strongest chronicle traditions are often those with the greatest number of revolts. Chroniclers from Paris and the royal abbey of Saint-Denis on its outskirts supply the largest number of descriptions of social movements in my collection and over half of those found for the realm of France: 208. Paris, accordingly, emerges as the most rebellious French city. Strikingly few cases of popular insurrection appear in some regions, such as Gascony, controlled by the English during the period of my analysis, and Poitou, a frontier zone caught in the crossfire of English and French allegiances, where great social turmoil and revolt might be expected. For Poitou, however, Paul Guérin's editions of all the surviving documents in the Trésor des chartes found for this region can serve as a control. These archival sources show indeed that the region was rife with violence, war, broken truces, and roaming bands of marauders. However, examples of tax revolts or other forms of popular resistance, as the chronicles reflect, appear remarkably few, especially compared with those areas of France that the chronicles portray as the hotbeds of social revolt—Flanders, Rouen, and Paris.[107] The same can be said for the Bordelais during the fourteenth and early fifteenth centuries. Despite Robert Boutruche's exhaustive research in archival documents, little evidence of any popular movements either in cities or the countryside surfaces for the later Middle Ages in this war-ridden, over-taxed region.[108]

Nonetheless, some areas are poorly represented by chronicles, which certainly understate the rebellious behavior in those areas. For instance, Sicily and large parts of southern Italy are poorly served by surviving chronicles. Except for waves of highway robbers *(maladrini)* terrorizing the countryside within the kingdom of Naples,[109] little is heard from chronicles of local uprisings in the towns and villages of Campania, Calabria, and Puglia, and only slightly more for the Abruzzi.[110] By contrast, Romolo Caggese's study of the registers of the Angevin chancellery (destroyed by the German army in 1943) portrays these districts as being as rife with rioting during the late thirteenth and fourteenth centuries as Tuscany was, especially during the reign of Robert of Anjou (1309–1343), when myriad insurrections arose against tax officials and noblemen in cities, towns, and the countryside.[111] Similarly, not a single revolt appears in my sources from the south-central county of Forez, which also is poorly served by contemporary chronicles. Yet from the archival research of Étienne Fournial, we now know that this region also had its share of popular insurrection, with major tax revolts at Montbrison in 1308 and Saint-Galmier in 1310, a wave of fiscal revolts in 1358, and revolutionary brigands from 1422 to 1431, who, according to their captain, were "intent on killing all the nobility, then the priests, and after them, all the bourgeois."[112]

On the other hand, chronicles such as those compiled by the monks of Saint-Denis or the merchant bankers of Florence were often concerned with more than their own backyards. They strove to be "universal" in coverage and relied on wide networks of religious, diplomatic, and commercial correspondence supplied by traveling clerics, merchants, and ambassadors to extend their histories over vast areas of Europe. These often provide our best narrative accounts for distant places such as the south of France during the period of the Tuchins or for revolts in southern Italy such as the port of Gaeta in 1353.

Despite their problems, chronicles provide the best means for viewing popular movements across Europe. Although written almost exclusively by observers in social classes above the status of rebelling artisans, workers, and peasants, these sources might well be expected to support conclusions drawn by current historians on the leadership, organization, ideology, and success of popular protests in the later Middle Ages. Historians generally agree that these protests erupted spontaneously among "leaderless men," their leaders came from outside the rebels' ranks, their organization was at best primitive, their ideology harkened back to a mythical golden age, they naively strove to restore lost rights, and to achieve their ends they appealed to their "natural" leaders—king, emperor, or pope. Further, these elite chroniclers might be expected to demonstrate that popular breaches of the rightful order of things happened infrequently, inevitably failed, and were brutally repressed in order to teach lessons that heightened the self-confidence of ruling elites, preserved the status quo, and instilled a sense of the righteousness of oligarchic or royal rule for posterity. Thereby, their reporting would confirm recent historians' conclusions: social revolts were "a will-o'-the wisp, all glow and no substance,"[113] that real struggles for power "unfold exclusively within the very restricted world of the patriciate."[114] However, despite the vested interests of the vast majority of these chroniclers, this study shows that their descriptions considered collectively paint a different picture. First, they were not loath to report the uprisings of commoners and did not judge them "devoid of interest or so foul that reporting them would soil the parchment."[115] More important, despite the chroniclers' prejudices, their descriptions provide rich documentation that casts into question current notions about the leadership, causes, ideology, role of women in, and success of popular revolt, not only for medieval Europe but for the preindustrial past more globally.[116]

CHAPTER **2**

Peasant Revolts

Historians have rallied behind or brushed aside Marc Bloch's dictum: "peasant revolts were as natural to traditional Europe as strikes are today."[1] Current thinking on peasant revolts over the last decade or more, however, would deny Bloch's claims. More than forty years ago, Jacques Le Goff claimed that "the habitual form of peasant struggle" was instead individual "passive resistance": "the silent guerrilla warfare of looting on the lord's lands, poaching in his forests, burning crops, refusing to pay dues . . . leading sometimes to flight and desertion."[2] More recently, the political scientist James C. Scott has expounded further on this position for preindustrial societies writ large.

> What is missing from this perspective, I believe, is the simple fact that most subordinate classes throughout most of history have rarely been afforded the luxury of open, organized, political activity. Or, better stated, such activity was dangerous, if not suicidal; even when the option did exist, it is not clear that the same objectives might not also be pursued by other stratagems. Most subordinate classes are, after all, far less interested in changing the larger structures of the state and the law than in what Hobsbawm has appropriately called "working the system . . . to their minimum disadvantage." Formal, organized political activity, even if clandestine and revolutionary, is typically the preserve of the middle class and the intelligentsia.[3]

In several places Scott stresses the difference between open rebellion, on the one hand, and noncollective and noncombatant means of resistance on the other, concluding that "the emphasis on peasant rebellion [is] misplaced." What matters more is

> to understand what we might call *everyday* forms of peasant resistance—
> the prosaic but constant struggle between the peasantry and those who
> seek to extract labor, food, taxes, rents and interest from them . . . foot-
> dragging, dissimulation, desertion, false compliance, pilfering, feigned
> ignorance, slander, arson, sabotage, and so on . . . These Brechtian forms
> of class struggle . . . often represent a form of individual self-help . . .
> avoid[ing] any direct symbolic confrontation with authority . . . Every-
> day forms of resistance make no headlines. Just as millions of anthozoan
> polyps create, willy-nilly, a coral reef, so do thousands upon thousands
> of individual acts of insubordination and evasion create a political or
> economic barrier reef of their own. There is rarely any dramatic con-
> frontation, any moment that is particularly newsworthy . . . The nature
> of the acts themselves and the self-interested muteness of the antago-
> nists thus conspire to create a kind of complicitous silence that all but
> expunges everyday forms of resistance from the historical record . . .
> History and social science, because they are written by an intelligentsia
> using written records that are also created largely by literate officials, is
> simply not well-equipped to uncover the silent and anonymous forms
> of class struggle that typify the peasant . . . By contrast, peasant insur-
> rections seem like visceral reactions of blind fury.[4]

With such a schema, is not the study of subaltern classes and class conflict in past times a useless exercise? By Scott's reckoning, their struggles appear simply as a continuum of mounting everyday tasks without significant breaks, progress, or reversals. Furthermore, because these acts lie beneath the surface of privileged written records and make no headlines (according to Scott), the historian has little chance to study class conflict in preindustrial societies.[5]

This chapter does not vindicate Bloch's position against Scott's; rather, it questions both positions. In general, my survey of the chronicle literature, letters of remission, and criminal acts suggests that open confrontation by peasants, workers, and artisans was far more common than recent historians have assumed or than social scientists would believe possible of the prein-dustrial past. On the other hand, although strikes can be found in both the city and countryside in documents from the late Middle Ages, the general char-acter of late medieval revolts did not run parallel to the industrial strike, which mounted in importance with the industrial revolution through the twentieth century. Instead, late medieval class conflict perhaps has a greater parallel with struggles in "postindustrial societies" since the mid-twentieth century, where the state, more often than capitalist bosses or landlords, has become the principal butt of protest. Here, once again the focus on the three or four most prominently studied revolts of late medieval Europe—the Jacquerie, the Ciompi, the English Peasants' Revolt of 1381, and the Hussite rebellions— can be misleading. In all these revolts, peasants, artisans, or workers confronted their landlords or employers, even if economic exploitation may not have been the sole, or even the main, spark for class conflict.[6]

Economic Revolts of Peasants

As even those who use the terms warn, distinctions between social and economic or between political and economic revolts are ultimately heuristic, especially for preindustrial societies. Not only did one sphere overlap the other, they were intricately coupled.[7] For instance, all states, even the most primitive ones, are intimately involved in the redistribution of resources. In Karl Polanyi's words "redistribution also tends to enmesh the economic system proper in social relationships."[8] Certainly, any successful struggle by any group for political inclusion would have direct economic ramifications. Nevertheless, a difference can be drawn between conflicts that occurred at the point of production and over the means of production, even though such challenges would also affect social status and freedom. On the other hand, was the tax revolt an economic or political revolt? Of course it was both, but it cannot be construed to have been the medieval equivalent of the industrial strike; the tax revolt reflected discontent with the state, not with employers. Even if landlords or wool bosses may have been a central part of the ruling elites of those states, their interests were not always the same as the states; bosses and governors could even oppose one another. Splits in the ruling class often accompanied revolts from the subaltern classes, with employers and the state competing for the same pool of labor surplus.[9]

Of 1,112 revolts and social movements in my samples, only ten were ones in which peasants confronted their landlords directly, and even with these, questions of economic exploitation did not necessarily lie at the heart of the conflict. Perhaps as surprising given recent literature on the rarity of peasant revolts in Italy in comparison with lands north of the Alps, only four came from France: the Jacquerie of 1358; the revolt of the villagers of Orly and Châtenay, who refused to pay an increase of the *taille* to the canons in 1251;

an uprising of the villages subject to the dean and chapter of the church of Notre-Dame de Laon in 1338;[10] and "the Jacquerie" of 1364, when the inhabitants of the market towns of Gimont and Simorre in the district of Toulouse "like mad men battled" against their lord, Pierre Raimond of Rabastens.[11] But like the Jacquerie of 1358, which in miniature the 1364 uprising resembled, no evidence links this violent protest to economic oppression or demands about rights in common, feudal rents, and the like.

Of peasant revolts against local landlords in Italy, one broke out in the mountainous valleys outside Genoa, another in the hinterland of L'Aquila, and the other three in mountainous zones of Florence, where feudal families still survived: the Pazzi in the Valdichiana, the Ubertini in Valdambra, and the Guidi and Tarlati in the Casentino. But none of these were simple, straightforward revolts against feudal dues: in each case resistance to a city-state's attempts to incorporate peripheral mountainous zones into its ambit appears at the heart of the conflict. First, in 1233, the peasants *(rustici)* of the valleys of Onéglia and Arroscia conspired against their lords; the bishop of Albenga[12] and the marquises of Cravesana—Taliaferrus; and Lady Mabilia, widow of Otto from Cravesana. The peasants were "disobedient" to both secular and ecclesiastical lords. The chronicler does not elaborate on this disobedience— was it a rent strike or some form of disrespect not directly tied to the landlords' expropriation of the peasants' surplus? At any rate, the conflict soon spilled beyond the confines of a landlord-peasant dispute. The lords traveled to Genoa and persuaded their city "friends," the podestà, and lords from neighboring valleys to support them in their war against the peasants. They formed two armies and attacked on two fronts. The peasants repulsed both assaults, "converting them into flight." Further, "with mindless fury," the peasants took a walled town in the diocese of Albenga from the bishop and another that belonged to the commune of Genoa. "They destroyed these villages and looted other places, wickedly killing some of the best citizens of Genoa, Ventimiglia, and Savona: they did not refrain from their evil doings, day and night, until the regime of this podestà had come to an end." In his place the peasants chose one of their own, Bergondio Pugno.[13]

The chronicler in verse Buccio di Ranallo provides even less information for a peasant uprising in the *contado* of L'Aquila around 1267. We are told only that the peasants with great arrogance destroyed all the castles around the city of L'Aquila, but we are not informed why or even whether these castles belonged specifically to the lords who ruled over these peasants.[14] In the three Florentine peasant revolts against local lords reported in chronicles, Florentine politics of territorial aggrandizement peers behind the scenes, even if economic and social exploitation may have been underlying causes. In March 1349 the subjects *(i fedeli)* of Count Galeotto of the feudal Guidi clan, "who had always been Ghibellines and enemies of Florence," revolted against him because of "his cruelty and his dissolute life, and because he had treated them badly for a long time." His men took his castle of San Niccolò, all its lands, holdings, tools, treasures, and noble furnishings, and turned them over to the Commune of Florence but with certain conditions. These conditions reveal underlying initiatives of the Florentine state: the peasants were to be made *"popolani e contadini"* of Florence, registered on the communal tax rolls with certain temporary immunities (as in most agreements of subordination in Florentine history). But control over their castle was put into Florentine hands and their village of San Niccolò was absorbed into the Florentine *contado*.[15]

Matteo Villani describes another revolt against feudal control, this time against the Tarlati lords on the mountainous frontiers of Florence bordering Arezzo. Again, the revolt appears to have been as much a struggle for political independence as a protest against economic burdens. In fact, Villani's metaphor for their condition suggests that in material terms life under the Tarlati may not have been so onerous: "birds sweetly nourished in their cage rejoice at seeing the open wood and, if they can, flee from their imprisonment to return to the forest. Also men who have long endured servitude under the yoke of a tyrant yearn for the moment when they can recover their liberty." Villani argues that the "subjects" of the Tarlati did just this on 13 February 1360, when they revolted against their lords and handed their village, la Serra, over to the Commune of Florence.[16]

Finally, the Minerbetti chronicler is more explicit about Florentine responsibility in prompting a peasant rebellion against feudal lords in 1404. Realpolitik and military imperatives, rather than economic exploitation, impelled these subjects to betray their lords and accept Florentine rule:

Florentine soldiers then in the Valdambra made war against all the castles that Andreino degli Ubertini held in these districts. As a result, the men of these castles, who were Andreino's subjects [*fedeli*], saw that everything would be destroyed, that no one would come to their aid, and that they could not defend themselves. For the better part of valor, they took the side of the Florentines and secretly negotiated with Florence's War Committee [*Dieci della Balia*]. Then on 8 April, they all rebelled against their lord and gave themselves over to the Florentines. They received the Florentine troops into their homes and cut good and favorable deals for themselves [*ebbono buoni e larghi patti per loro*].[17]

The Florentine *provvisioni*, or day-by-day record of decisions passed by Florence's legislative councils, bears out Minerbetti's claims: numerous parishes in the Valdambra and Chianti won tax exemptions and had their debts wiped off the books.[18] Thus, even this miniscule group of Italian peasant revolts in which peasants opposed feudal lords shows little sign of laborers directing their anger explicitly against feudal dues, rents, or other economic conditions.

The historian might argue that Florentine merchant chroniclers or the monks of Saint-Denis entrusted with preserving the history of kings would not consider peasant struggles against lords as "headline news," even when these struggles were collective actions and involved casts of thousands. They would only appear in cases like that of the Queen Mother's freeing the peasants at Orly and Châtenay, thereby illustrating her virtue and hence that of royal power. Several cases found in other sources lend credence to such suspicions. In January 1348, landlords in the *contado* of Florence submitted a petition to the government protesting the actions of their rural tenants and their rural communes. They alleged that "certain communities, baptismal districts [*plebatus*], and parishes [*populi*] in the *contado* and district of Florence" coerced their fellow villagers to boycott their landlords' grain mills and to go on strike. They refused to cultivate their landlords' fields or "to do business with these landowners." Thus they left the landowners' goods and produce to rot. According to the petition, these communities had imposed taxes and other burdens on the landowners' rustics (*colonos*) and tenants, and had collected their own gabelles on the landowners' produce and profits. Moreover, they had enacted "iniquitous decrees and statutes" against the landowners and "conspired, plotted, and performed many other unjust acts against them by various devious means and machinations in violation of the statutes and decrees of the commune of Florence." The government approved the petition and levied the colossal fine of 500 pounds on each parish or commune, as well as 200 to 300 pounds to any who had committed these deeds.[19] Although this archival record does not list the parishes involved, it declares that they stretched throughout both the *contado* and district[20] of Florence. Yet, as far as I am aware, no chronicler mentions this collective action, not even the meticulous Giovanni Villani.

A second case north of the Alps appears even more remarkable in escaping chroniclers' notice given its geographic and demographic scale. It did engage the king's attention, however, and led to the drafting of at least three royal letters over seven-and-a-half years, two of which survive in the Trésor des chartes. In the first, King Philip VI's position was exactly the opposite of that taken by Queen Mother Blanche eighty-seven years before, when serfs refused to pay new rents imposed by their ecclesiastical landlords. In May 1338 Philip approved a death sentence "against many men and the branding of the cheeks of many women from the villages of Brissy, Remies, and other localities subject to the dean and chapter of the church of Notre-Dame de Laon." They had revolted against their ecclesiastical lords and fought against the king's soldiers, who had rushed in to suppress the revolt. A third royal letter of December 1344 lists twenty-two villages (and says there were more) that formed an alliance to refuse payment of the church's *tailles* and other dues *(redevances)*. Further, the king granted letters of remission to all the officers who "might not have been able to observe the letter of the law in carrying out the executions, for they had needed to act quickly, without time-consuming investigations, in order to avoid further rioting [*la comocion*] by these people." By the time this letter was written, the village insurgents (according to the royal letters) numbered well over 40,000. This third letter refers to a second one dated 22 July 1339, which no longer survives,[21] specifying that nine serfs were executed and many of their women folk branded and that these peasants were to remain the chapter's serfs and pay *chevage, formariage,* and *mortmain.*[22] Further, perhaps to rub salt into the wounds, the decree allowed the serfs to buy their freedom in exchange for the colossal annual rent of 1,000 Parisian pounds, provided that they also no longer treat the chapter of Laon with contempt.[23]

Such rebellions, however, do not fill the royal letters and acts of the Trésor des chartes. In more than a thousand such acts published for Poitou and in almost ten thousand letters that have thus far been catalogued analytically in various geographic surveys, only one other case even suggests an economic conflict between peasants and lords. It was hardly a revolt at that, showing no signs of the violence evident in the 1251 assault by the canons of Paris against their serfs or that of the serfs against their landlords in 1338. On 2 July 1351, the peasants of the walled village *(bastide)* of Revel petitioned their lord, the prior of Saint-Martin des Champs, to abate the fees owed to the priory. They argued that "depopulation and devastation during these troubled times, the plague of 1348, and payments owed for royal taxes [*subsidia regia et onera*]" had led to mass migration of their villagers, which had severely reduced their tax base. The prior was sympathetic and agreed to a reduction of their payments.[24]

Political Revolts of Peasants

On the other hand, peasant revolts were not so rare in these sources, especially in chronicles, but these uprisings revolved around political—not economic—issues and assailed various levels of the state and not their landlords. Despite chroniclers' preference for the affairs of ruling elites, noble armed conflict, and intrigues involving members of their own social classes, they were not oblivious to peasant uprisings or opposed to passing them down to posterity. Compared with a mere handful of peasant revolts against feudal or urban landlords reported by chroniclers—few of which arose explicitly from disputes over economic exploitation at that—no fewer than fifty-seven peasant revolts can be fished from the chronicles in which economic oppression was not the immediate cause, and landlords—capitalist or feudal—were not the targets. This figure does not include the many other revolts by villages or small market towns, composed mostly of rustics, against a city-state in which the sources do not clarify who the rebels were. For instance, the chronicler Michele da Piazza reported numerous *terrae* (rural districts) revolting against local counts or royal power in the 1350s but did not reveal who led or formed the ranks of these revolts.[25] Furthermore, recent historiography ascribes such uprisings primarily to the more rural economies north of the Alps; in fact, three-fourths of them (42 of 57) erupted in the urban-dominated zones of late medieval central and northern Italy.[26]

To be sure, all peasant revolts were not equal in duration, geographical scope, numbers of combatants, and the terror they inflicted on local communities, heads of state, and the chroniclers who recorded them. The three most important revolts by these standards were three of the most important peasant revolts in Western European history—the revolts in Flanders 1297–1304 and 1323–1328 and the Jacquerie of the Île de France, Picardy, the Beauvaisis, and neighboring villages further afield in May 1358. All three (along with the English Peasants' Revolt) were north of the Alps.

These revolts, especially those in Flanders, certainly were not purely "peasant revolts," in that commoners and to some extent bourgeois from the cities formed alliances with the peasants. In addition, since the twelfth century many in the countryside had the status and rights of urban burghers as "external bourgeois" *(haghepoorters* or *buitenpoorters)*, and in contrast to Italy, many weavers and fullers resided in small towns and villages.[27] The literature on these Flemish revolts is vast, and there is no need to summarize the events or the historiography yet again.[28] Suffice it to say that although the peasants and their allies massacred hundreds of rural landlords and their families, the evidence suggests that politics rather than economic exploitation by landlords, urban or feudal, were at the core of the rebels' discontent. First, it was not landlords but the French king Philip IV, called the Fair (1285–1314), who sparked the Flemish revolts of 1297–1304 with his political aim of bringing Flanders under tighter French control. His aggressive politics circumvented the power and prerogatives of the count of Flanders, Guy de Dampierre, and through the king's chief officer in Flanders, James of Saint-Pol, imposed new and heavy consumption taxes on commoners in the cities and the country-side. The decision of landlords and urban patricians to comply with these orders divided the country into two parties: those sympathetic to France, the *Leliaerts* (the fleur-de-lis), and the proto-nationalist Flemings, or *Clauwaerts*.[29] Philip and his patrician sympathizers brought on the wrath of commoners in the cities and the countryside, first in the Franc of Bruges, then throughout western Flanders. Further, the victims of the massacres that ensued were not principally landlords but the French—first soldiers and royal officers, and then anyone who spoke French.[30]

The second revolt of Flanders, 1323–1328, came closer to being a con-frontation between landlords and peasants. The principal leaders—Clais Zan-nekin, Segher Jonssone, and Jacques Peit—came from the countryside. The social and political alliances of this revolt differed from those twenty years before. The new count, Louis of Nevers (1323–1346), grandson of Guy Dampierre, renounced his grandfather's political resistance to the French crown and in 1323 sought to enforce the financial penalties owed by Flanders to France under the peace of Athis (1305), even though Philip the Fair by 1309 had agreed not to enforce them strictly. Thus the peasantry was suddenly faced again with an enormous indemnity, with ransoms for nobles imprisoned in France, and with the return of many banished pro-French nobles, some of whom had been their lords and enemies during the previous rebellion.[31] But while commoners from the countryside led the revolt, it spread to artisans through the cities of Flanders and, as before, evolved into an anti-French movement to rid Flanders of foreign rule and taxation. Again, their rallying cries turned against the French and did not strike out against matters of the manor, demands over working conditions, rights in common, or rents.

Of these revolts, the Jacquerie presents the richest literature and debate as well as the most obscure motives for a major uprising, despite its numerous chroniclers and the survival of over two hundred letters of remission, thirty-eight of which have been published. Against the claim of David Bessen that the Jacquerie was neither a peasant revolt nor a revolt against the nobility, and of Raymond Cazelles, that it was not even a revolt,[32] the sources—both chronicles and remissions—tell another story.[33] What continues to defy explanation is not that peasants provided the backbone of this rebellion, even if country artisans joined the peasant forces; rather, it is why peasants from the richest areas of France rose up with such vigor and hatred against their lords.[34]

Since the meticulous archival research of Siméon Luce in the latter half of the nineteenth century, historians have shown that the Jacquerie was hardly a spontaneous rebellion of "leaderless" or crazed men, as Jean le Bel and Jean Froissart passionately portray it.[35] Rather, letters of remission reveal prior planning and discussion at the village level, as well as elected village leaders, across the Île de France, Picardy, Beauvaisis, and Champagne. Rarely, however, do these sources give any inkling of the peasants' motives. Few chroniclers cite peasant chants or attribute to them any words that may explain their sudden violence or the reasons for risking their lives and property. Further, the remissions concentrate on excusing individuals, denying their willful participation, or arguing in several cases that they showed restraint against more radical forces either within their villages or from Paris.[36]

The best explanations, nonetheless, come from the chroniclers. Those such as Jean le Bel, Froissart, and the Anonimalle chronicler attributed the peasant rage to brute animal instinct. The chroniclers Jean de Venette, the continuator of Richard Lescot's chronicle from Saint-Denis, and a provincial knight either from Normandy or Flanders (*Chronique normande du XIVᵉ siècle*)[37] saw the peasant rage as arising from nobles' betrayal of and failure to protect their communities. Before describing peasant atrocities against nobles and their ladies, Jean de Venette gives the peasants some justification for their outrage: "seeing the wrongs and oppression inflicted on them on every side . . . the nobles gave them no protection but rather oppressed them as heavily as did the enemy." A speech invented by the continuator of Richard Lescot (although pronounced by a bourgeois) corroborates these reasons for peasant outrage: "We charge against these noble traitors, who have shirked their duties to defend the kingdom, who desire to do nothing but devour the sustenance of the commoners."[38] Finally, *Chronique normande* goes furthest in clarifying the causes of the Jacques' outrage:

> Then the regent was advised to order those of his knights in [the Île de] France and the Beauvaisis who had fortresses to stock their garrisons quickly with plenty of provisions and to blockade Paris from receiving food and merchandise. Those knights with fortresses gathered together to decide how to implement the regent's order; some did not have the means to supply the provisions for their castles. So they were advised to take the provisions from their own men.[39] They followed this counsel and outrageously took the goods from their own men. Thus these peasants [*paisans*] were mortified that the knights who were supposed to protect them had decided to seize their property. For this reason, the peasants rose up with prodigious force and charged against the knights and all the nobles, even their own lords.[40]

While this chronicler alone hints at an underlying economic cause for the Jacquerie, even he mentions no new or increased feudal dues or other exactions as such. Instead, as with the revolts in Flanders earlier in the century, politics, betrayal, and abuse were the sparks of rebellion, not conditions of misery or increased feudal exactions. It was the nobles' political failures that led to the Jacquerie: their failure to protect their villagers from assaults by the English or by the regent of France and their collusion with the enemy in warlike pillaging of peasant property.[41]

Furthermore, these revolts differed from the English Peasants' Revolt of 1381: the Jacques presented no programs to end feudal or manorial extractions or to change capitalist or commercial relations. Nor did they list grievances over lost rights in common, as German peasants in 1524–1525 would later do, as with "a peasant war" in Normandy in 996, or when peasants resisted aristocratic encroachments on their economic independence from the eighth to the tenth century.[42] Nonetheless, the absence of such direct economic grievances should not lead us to follow Guy Fourquin and others who claim that because the peasants lacked such programs, no class struggle is evident, and that the peasants were reactionary, desiring only to turn back the clock to some mythical golden age. The sources do not justify such conclusions. Instead they show peasants engaging in politics, forming assemblies and village alliances, electing their own leaders, and defending their rights by attacking their class superiors who had betrayed them.[43]

Peasant Revolts in France and Flanders

Let us now turn to the bulk of the evidence given for peasant uprisings over the two centuries of this analysis across Italy, France, and Flanders. First, although Flanders produced the largest and longest-enduring peasant revolt in Western Europe of the Middle Ages (that of 1323–1328), the chroniclers report few other Flemish peasant uprisings for the rest of the fourteenth and early fifteenth centuries. Peasants comprised the troops that Jacob van Artevelde sent into the field in the 1330s and those that his son Philippe mobilized from 1379 to 1383, but these wars emanated from the cities and expressed no explicit peasant grievances of either an economic or a political character.[44]

Peasant uprisings were rare in France too. The Jacquerie was the exception. Only six others appear in the chronicles, and none of these was a peasant revolt in the strict sense (whether against landlords or the state). Geographically, certainly the most extensive of the six were the shepherds' and children's crusades of 1250 and 1320. These also received more attention from chroniclers than almost any other revolt or movement. In my samples at least fourteen chroniclers described the earlier movement and another fourteen the later one. One chronicle remarked on the extraordinary similarity between the two, which spread from Picardy to Aquitaine and Languedoc and into German-speaking areas. Even though the rebels were described as "impoverished shepherds [*misera pastorum*]" and "*populares simplices*," they did not single out local lords or the wealthy as the targets of their rage. Instead, Jews and clerics were the targets. If they had any economic or political agenda, the chroniclers did not express them. No new tax singled out these herders or children (who in fact paid no taxes). Unlike tax revolts, as we shall see, these movements leave no evidence of chants against gabelles or other taxes, nor did they attack tax officials, as was the hallmark of other tax revolts.[45]

Three other French peasant revolts or armed movements appear immediately following the Jacquerie and originate in the very villages of the Beauvaisis and the Île de France where peasants had assembled to fight their lords and had been brutally massacred by the troops of the King of Navarre and other noblemen. Given the consensus on the dimensions of that slaughter, it is a wonder that peasants would or could have mobilized any armed resistance only a year later, much less a successful one. The first such rising is the most famous. A male forerunner of Joan-of-Arc peasant heroism and patriotism, it resounded in local folklore down to the nineteenth century,[46] even though more recent historians, including Mollat and Wolff, have not recalled or classified it as a peasant movement or form of resistance. The story has several versions. According to the noble Flemish or Norman chronicler, after the Jacquerie the united troops of the King of Navarre and the English Captain Robert Knowles rampaged through large parts of the Beauvaisis and Picardy, conquering and plundering villages. In 1359 at Longueil-Sainte-Marie, near Compiègne, the peasants took a stand. Under the command of a peasant named Guillaume l'Aloue, they assembled around three hundred peasants from various places in the Beauvaisis *(paisans de Beauvoisin)*, occupied and fortified a farmhouse, and waged war in self-defense against the English cavalry stationed at Creel and other fortresses, who rode out against them. With six hundred soldiers under the command of Jehan Fonicque, the English besieged the farmhouse, climbed over its walls, "and thought only of killing them all, there being no point in taking any of them for ransom." Guillaume rallied the peasants, crying out that "it was better to die defending themselves in hand-to-hand combat against the enemy than to be burnt alive with their women and children in this farmhouse." They ran out, charging the English, and defeated them, killing at least 120, twenty-four of whom were knights. The victorious peasants suffered only two casualties; one was their leader, Guillaume.

Afterward, they elected another captain "from their ranks" named Colart Sade, and their success attracted other peasants in the region to join their stronghold at Longueil-Sainte-Marie.[47] By other versions, especially that of the Carmelite Jean de Venette, a second hero emerged: a young and gigantic peasant, the valet of Guillaume, called the Big Iron Man, *Grandferré*, or in Latin texts, *magnus Ferratus*. Almost single-handedly, he repulsed a second attack by the English cavalry but lost his life in so doing. Despite the legend surrounding this story, the tale gives credence to the disappointment and sense of betrayal that several chroniclers pointed to as the cause of the Jacquerie the year before: the peasants could no longer trust their own lords to protect them, so they took up arms themselves, thus subverting "the three orders" and functions of medieval society, in this case with remarkable success.[48]

The chroniclers tell another story of peasant organization and resistance the following year, this time south of Paris, but without such a happy ending for peasants or heroic lessons for the patriotic. During Easter week, the people of Châtres, now Arpajon *(homines et populus de villa de Chatres)*, near the château of Chanleloup, fortified their church by digging a wide and deep moat

around it, covering its roof with lead, and stocking it with provisions. They
put their women and children in the church and chose a leader to defend
them. Noticing these preparations, the English encamped on a hill above the
church and brought in war machines to hurl boulders against it. Frightened
by the machines, the villagers' captain along with some of the most important
villagers *(aliqui de magis potentibus)* abandoned their poorer comrades in the
church steeple and went off to occupy a better and stronger tower in the
church. Seeing that they had been put in danger, the "people" screamed out
against the captain. Fearing their threats, he and his wealthier companions
set fire to the church where the people were entrapped. Of 1,200, only three
hundred escaped, by jumping from the windows. But the escapees were no
luckier. Once on the ground they faced the English, who butchered them
mercilessly. Only the captain escaped because the English saw that he was a
nobleman.[49] Clearly, unlike the villagers of Longueil-Sainte-Marie, those of
Arpajon had not learned the lessons of the Jacquerie: they trusted the local
nobility and paid the price.

A third story of peasant resistance comes from the same region as Longueil,
at Thouri-en-Beauce, near Compiègne in 1360. Although this incident did not
provide future grist for folkloric mills, the peasants here appear to have followed the examples of Guillaume l'Aloue and the Big Iron Man of a year earlier. Without turning to their local nobles, they too fended off the English.[50]

A further example of peasant initiative, organization, and resistance to foreign oppression comes later, from the civil war between the Burgundians and
the Armagnacs in the early fifteenth century. In 1411 peasants living between
the Seine and the Oise presented petitions to the king and the provost of
Paris complaining that the enemy was threatening their villages worse than
usual. As a result, they received permission to abandon work in the fields and
to form an army to defend themselves. But unlike the Jacques or even the
men of Langueil and Arpajon, they hardly bucked the hierarchy in their
recourse to self-defense. They formed bands and "as a sign of their unity wore
on their shoulders white crosses with the fleur-de-lis in the middle, carried
flags that bore the words, 'Long live the King,' " and declared themselves to be
"the king's most loyal friends." Nonetheless, their military success over the
enemy led to a subtle transformation in hierarchical relations, which proved
less than salubrious for the king or the bourgeois of Paris: "having taken up
the habit of raiding, soon they had learnt a profession that would continue
after the war had ended. They would ambush anyone they met along the

roads, whether friend or stranger, so that no one dared to cross through woods without being well guarded."[51]

After the Jacquerie, the revolts of the Tuchins in southern France might rank as the most important peasant movement of late medieval French history, that is, if we judge that they were peasants. To be sure, these ragtag bands of bandits, who troubled merchants, towns, and royal authorities from the borders of Aragon to Poitou in the west from 1364 until their suppression by the Duke of Berry twenty years later, were a conglomerate of peasants, ex-soldiers, lesser noblemen, and even some townsmen. As far as I know or Boudet reports in his documentary account of the Tuchins,[52] only one chronicler has described them, and he came from distant Saint-Denis, north of Paris.[53] His account stressed their atrocities reminiscent of Jean le Bel's horror stories of the Jacquerie. Added to the roasting of their class enemies on spits[54] and crowning them with "trivets of red-hot iron" were tales of the slow torture of itinerant clerics, by cutting off fingertips, flaying the flesh of entire bodies with shears, and burning victims alive. This single narrative account, as well as the etymology of their name,[55] portrays the Tuchins as predominantly peasants or rural artisans engaged in a social or class struggle as opposed to being merely opportunistic bandits. According to the Saint-Denis chronicler, Michel Pintoin, they were "a multitude of the most impoverished men . . . who abandoned their menial crafts and agriculture and banded together." Further, according to Pintoin, their movement began as a tax revolt against the new impositions of Charles V: "Spurred on by terrible speeches they were moved to submit no longer to shouldering the yoke of the subsidies and instead were inspired to preserve their ancient liberties, to try to throw off this harmful yoke placed on men."[56]

The more prominent and numerous sources for the Tuchins are letters of remission, which raise questions about whether the Tuchins should be labeled as peasant rebels.[57] First, the leaders and even the rank and file appear to have been military men more than rural toilers; many, in fact, came from the lesser nobility.[58] Of course, this view of the movement may result from a bias in the source, especially as regards its rank and file. Those with sufficient political clout and economic resources to petition the king or his lieutenant in Languedoc, John, Duke of Berry, may have included only the leaders, who were military men of the lesser nobility. Moreover, the letters do not cast "these rebels" as clearly engaged in any sort of class struggle. As against Pintoin, none of the remissions for the Auvergne and mountain ranges around Saint-Flour mention taxes as the spark of these men's anger. Instead, most of the remissions portray internecine conflict between locals who seem to be more or less equals, settling old scores.[59] Further, the crimes described in these remissions—cattle raids and other forms of banditry—appear more as opportunistic endeavors for personal profit than class-based outrage. From these letters little distinguishes the Tuchins from other highway robbers or *maladrini,* who inhabited mountainous and frontier zones at various times and places in European history and were composed of a mix of classes: peasants, under- or unemployed soldiers, wayward sons of prominent noble houses, or even entire noble clans such as the Ubaldini, who preyed on merchants crossing the mountain passes between Florence and Bologna during the fourteenth century.[60]

However, south of the Massif Central, in the districts of Toulouse, Carcassonne, and Beaucaire and possibly in the Limousin,[61] the letters of remission cast groups also called Tuchins in a different light from the bandits of the Auvergne above Saint-Flour.[62] We see these more southern groups principally in a general remission granted to all the inhabitants of the cities and countryside of Toulouse, Carcassonne, and Beaucaire in return for the colossal fine of 800,000 gold francs.[63] In this remission of March 1384, immediately after the Duke of Berry's troops had brutally marched through the south, torching villages to suppress the Tuchins, the residents were accused of "forming unions, conspiring, plotting, giving advice, forming cells, revolting, behaving abusively, engaging in acts of arson, murder, capturing, imprisoning, drowning and hanging royal officers, soldiers, and others of our subjects, breaking and mangling their limbs, creating blockades, engaging in war, invading, capturing castles, villages, and our forts at Buzet (Haute-Garonne) and Cornarieu." Further, the Tuchins' crimes included treason, rebelling against royal taxes—the subsidies and other exactions—and committing other forms of disobedience to the king, his lieutenant, and the royal officers of Languedoc over a period of six years. These Tuchins and their sympathizers were a far cry from the gangs and bandits portrayed in the remissions for the Massif Central called by the same name. But were these rebels from farther south peasants?

From the scraps of information given in the remissions there is no reason to believe that peasants more than city dwellers led or filled the ranks of these rebellions.[64] Indeed, a remission granted in 1390 to the lawyer, Master Pierre Boyer of Carcassonne, suggests that this southern wave of revolt may have been more urban than rural. According to the preamble, "in these times, many communes, organizations [*universitez*], and individuals rebelled and were disobedient to the king and his lieutenant the duke of Berry and of Auvergne . . . people called Tuchins reigned in this country and this master Pierre Boyer gave advice to their councils, organizations, and individuals on many occasions to those in towns [*bourc*] as well as in the districts [*la seneschauciée*] of Carcassonne, Toulouse, and Beaucaire on how to arm and resist . . . the troops of the king and the Duke of Berry." In addition, he advised them on how to tax and raise subsidies from the people to pay and maintain their soldiers in their resistance "against these lords" (the king and the Duke of Berry). The remission lists six more accusations against this lawyer, including his advice to town councils and Tuchin soldiers on raising their own subsidies and opposing those of the king, his writing of inflammatory letters to bishops and other counselors of the king, and still other crimes of treason. For the remission of these crimes the lawyer was fined 500 gold francs.[65]

Even if we include "the Tuchinate" as a peasant revolt (and I do not think we should), neither the chronicles nor the letters of remission (either as published in full for Poitou and Languedoc or as summarized in the analytical inventories for other regions) give any hint that peasant revolt was widespread in France during the later Middle Ages. Beyond those mentioned above, perhaps the most important of the collective acts of peasants exposed in the letters of remission was one of February 1347, but one can understand why it did not make chronicle headlines. Jean of Saint-Laurent, a minor royal officer *(sergent)* in the district of Auvergne, who was imprisoned in Riom, was pardoned because of his services rendered to the crown over a long period of time. In self-defense he had killed Jean de La Villate, who with other inhabitants of the manor *(mas)* of La Villate, serfs of the knight Guillaume de Durat, had resisted this officer's seizure of their cattle. The officer Jean had raided their cattle to collect a fine they owed the king. The serfs attacked the officer with scythes and sticks.[66]

Perhaps peasant unrest was on a wider scale during an incident in 1365, when the king and his lieutenant in Languedoc pardoned the councils and inhabitants of the villages of Rappistagno and Insula and several others outside the district of Albi. The peasants had molested royal officers of the region. Unfortunately, the remission leaves vague just what the "vexations" amounted to.[67] Though peasant revolts were not the mainstay of social rebellion, at least in France, the evidence does not support the view that preindustrial peasant revolts were so risky that they almost never happened, and when they did, inevitably failed. Even before turning to the richer evidence from

Italy, the examples above, with their mix of success and failure, do not give credence to such an extreme view.

Peasant Revolts in Italy

A far greater number of peasant movements and rebellions are on record for that land of city-states, where supposedly such incidents did not take place—northern and central Italy. At least forty-nine peasant uprisings are described in the chronicles I surveyed, again without counting revolts of villages or small towns against the rule of dominant cities.[68] Furthermore, revolts of places such as Grosseto, Montalcino, Montepulciano, and even towns as large as Cortona, comprising populations of five hundred or so after the Black Death, would have involved populations with substantial numbers of agricultural laborers, but I did not classify them as peasant revolts.[69] Nor did I consider revolts of colonies such as Corsica, Crete, Zara, or other places along the Dalmatian coast against Genoese or Venetian rule as peasant revolts, even though they certainly engaged rural populations.[70]

Further, peasant revolts in southern Italy or isolated Alpine valleys in the north, distant from urban and commercial centers, do not predominate in chronicles. Instead, the greatest number of them (19) erupted along the coastal hills and valleys adjacent to one of the most advanced and powerful commercial centers of the later Middle Ages, Genoa. In addition, these Italian revolts did not take place in the earliest years of this study, the twelfth and thirteenth centuries, which might reflect a past when feudal values clashed with those of an emerging commercial milieu. Rather, they clustered primarily after the Black Death, with more than three times as many in the years from 1355 to 1419 as in the two hundred years preceding the plague.

For Genoa, the frequency of peasant revolts post-1348 was sharper than elsewhere and may have resulted in part from its peculiar chronicle tradition. From 1081 to 1300, seventeen extant chronicles, known as *Annali genovesi* of Caffaro and his continuators, covered Genoese history with a meticulousness that would be the envy of any city-state.[71] Then a hiatus stretches through the early fourteenth century. Sometime after the Black Death, Giorgio and then Giovanni Stella (brothers) picked up the story, and by 1365 their attention to the details of Genoese history, especially its political and social struggles, begins to match or even excel that of the earlier *Annali*.[72] Nonetheless, peasant revolts are rare in the seventeen chronicles of Genoa's history from the late eleventh to the fourteenth century. The only notable ones were in 1233 and 1234, examined above, when peasants *(rustici)* from the valleys of Onéglia,

Arroscia, and Iura armed themselves against the Genoese state and its regional podestà.[73]

After these, no other peasant uprising appears in the dominion of Genoa until 1383, that is, nearly twenty years after the Stellas had resumed a close, almost daily chronicling of political events and social strife in Genoa, its mainland territories, and its island colonies.[74] The hotbed of insurrection came from the three valleys that surrounded the city—Voltri, Polcevera, and Bisagno. Except possibly for one revolt, these were overwhelmingly political in character. The peasants even called themselves the *popolo* and waged war directly against the doge. On occasion, they invaded the city and with cries of "Vivat il popolo!" attempted to arouse artisans and other commoners to join their forces, expelled the doge, and brought about a government of the people.[75] Several of these were tax revolts, as with the revolt of the three valleys in 1383. After a church service at 9 in the morning on 21 March, the peasants rang their bells, assembled about a thousand armed villagers, and began chanting: "Long live the people, down with the city's taxes" and "Death to the gabelles."[76] In almost all these revolts, peasants confronted the ruling class of Genoa and not their local landlords. Further, their demands failed to mention wages, rents, or feudal dues and obligations.

One exception may have been the revolt of Genoese galley men returning from service under the arms of the king of France in Flanders in 1338, who demanded their wages and interest on the delay. But this was a revolt of the sea, and by the time it had spread to coastal communities, it no longer revolved around the seamen's pay.[77] Another possible exception may have come in November 1399 when the inhabitants of Sigestro, a village on the eastern Riviera, "all Ghibellines," "zealously rose up in an armed rebellion because of their hatred for the Genoese noblemen and ruling families of the Doria and Spinola," who were Guelfs. The revolt "led to acts of arson and destruction at great expense." But there is no indication that these lords were local landlords; instead they ruled Genoa. The chronicler pitched the revolt as a political, not an economic, conflict, one between Guelfs and Ghibellines over the leadership of Genoa, not one between peasants and lords.[78]

The pattern of peasant revolts seen in Genoa is reflected elsewhere in Italy. Politics and political rights, not economics or the social relations of production, were at the heart of these conflicts; rulers, not landlords, were the objects of peasant anger and resentment. Moreover, these revolts focused on towns and did not arise in distant or backward areas of the peninsula, where feudal lords may have held great estates. The earliest of these erupted in Faenza, 1238, when "its farmers [*suos agricolas*]" invaded and captured the city.[79] From the laconic entry of the chronicler, it is not clear who these *agricolae* were—peasants or minor lords from Faenza's *contado*. The same chronicler, however, gives greater attention to a later revolt and invasion from the countryside into Modena. In 1305 "because of the great freeze that winter, the rivers, streams, and hollows froze over, so that men from the countryside could come into the city by foot and horseback and with carts as though crossing over land." Thus along these frozen streams, city dwellers *(burgenses)* and peasants *(villani)* broke though the ranks of the soldiers of the marquis and invaded the city, knocking down the city's battlements from all sides. These peasants *(rustici)* joined unskilled laborers of the city *(imperiti cives)*, broke into the communal palace of Modena, and in a rage ripped apart or carried off judicial registers of civil and criminal cases, notarial books, and other government records, including the tax surveys *(Libros Aestimorum)*.[80]

Two other of these preplague revolts came from the urban regions of Emilia-Romagna. One in Parma in 1308 (mentioned in Chapter 1) and another in Bologna in 1334 involved peasant armies that invaded the cities in the service of lords. As we have seen, the peasant troops who invaded Parma under Rolandino Scorza's command pursued their own interests once in the city, storming public buildings and tearing asunder taxes, records, and judicial documents that had imposed fines on them. For Bologna in 1334, the chronicler does not reveal the peasants' motives, but their leader was a mountain peasant and their ranks were composed solely of mountaineers. On 17 March, the Bolognese had freed the city from church rule, and because of this a man named Mazarelo from the mountain village of Cuzano entered the city "with a big group of mountain men [*con grande montanarelda in alturo del popolo*]," who began robbing the neighborhood of San Donato, but the locals came out and killed many of them.[81]

The only other preplague peasant uprising reported in these chronicles for Italy north of the Regno did not hinge on the politics of a particular city-state or originate in the ambit of a major commercial center. Nonetheless, it was political. In 1247 the men from the mountainous regions of Lunigiana and the Garfagnana, then under the protection of Emperor Frederick II, rebelled against him and captured and locked up his chief officer *(vicarius)* in Castro Gropo San Pietro. The chronicler does not specify who these *homines* of the valleys and mountains were, who led them, or what their motives may have been other than repulsing the rule of the emperor.[82]

On the other hand, L'Aquila was exceptional, with three preplague peasant revolts erupting in its territory. The first sprang up on the northern "extremities" or borders of L'Aquila and the Neapolitan Regno in 1257. The peasants revolted against Conrad's and then Manfred's attempts to build new fortifications that encircled their fields and villages. The peasants rebelled to free themselves from the dominion of this kingdom.[83] A decade later (1266), peasants from roughly the same zones along these northern borders revolted again against Manfred.[84] A year later peasants around L'Aquila destroyed all the castles in its immediate district (dintorni); again, the chronicler leaves no hint of their motivations other than defending their political independence.[85]

The postplague years show greater numbers of peasant uprisings than before the plague, and their motives and plans are clearer, even if chroniclers on occasion called them leaderless and without order. Most were tax revolts. On 16 June 1355, the cardinal legate of Rimini imposed a heavy forced loan (una grande prestanza), which citizens complained of bitterly. But it was the peasants (una grandissima gente de' Contadini alla Terra) who a week later invaded the city with scythes and other tools and, according to a chronicler of Rimini, "shockingly without any leader or order left the next morning with little honor."[86]

In the same year, another peasant revolt flared in Lucca, which, as in Rimini, had crippling taxes as at least one of its triggers. On hearing the news of Emperor Charles IV's entry into Lucca and the ousting of the Gambacorta of Pisa and other leading families, the Lucchesi, then under Pisan dominion, sought to take advantage of the confusion to free themselves "from the heavy yoke and taxes [servaggio]" that the Pisans had imposed on them. But, as in Rimini, it was "their peasants who came to liberate the city." On 22 May, "inspired by their hatred of the Pisans and oppressive taxes," the Lucchese peasants, "even though poorly armed, broke into the city on all sides" and attacked all the guards of the gates. Since the imperial troops did not bother to defend it, the city was "liberated."[87]

At the beginning of July 1360, the peasants from three fortified villages in the Marche—Boschereto, Corinalto, and Montenuovo—rebelled against the papal legate because of arbitrary taxation (le disordinate gravezze). Learning of this ribellione, the legate immediately sent for the soldiers of the knight, Lord Galeotto di Malatesta, who came in support of the church. Corinalto was forced to surrender, its castle burnt, and the village destroyed, but the other two villages were stronger, put up a more "orderly" defense, and held out until the forces of messer Bernabò (Visconti) of Milan arrived and lifted the siege.[88]

On 10 September medical doctors, notaries, tailors, and other artisans conspired to bring down the signoria of the Marchioni of Ferrara and establish a popular regime. Though it was a revolt more of the urban *popolo* than of peasants, the plan was to have great numbers of peasants from the surrounding countryside break down a city gate and serve as the revolt's shock troops. The rallying cry to prick discontent and curry favor again turned to excessive taxation: *"Muora i Dacii e Gabelle."* The plot was discovered and the principal conspirators ridden on donkeys to Ferrara's main square and hanged.[89]

As mentioned in Chapter 1, neither the chroniclers nor the judicial records make clear the motives for an invasion into the city of Bologna on 19 March 1376 by mountain men from the communities of Valdereno, Loiano, Bruscoli, and Tirli, high in the Apennines near the frontier with Florence. In the dark of night they broke through a sluice gate in the city walls, pulled the papal legate of Bologna from his palace, stole his rings and property, and set off a revolt that freed Bologna from Church rule. To judge by the chronicles, these mountaineers appear simply to have been following the commands of their lords, the Counts of Loiano, Bruscoli, and Panico. By the judicial records, however, which appeared nearly a month later (11 April) after a popular government had been restored to Bologna, the condemned mountain men seem to have been pursuing their own purposes even if these ledgers did not specify what they were. Of course, they may have been just hired toughs in the employ of the counts. But excessive papal taxation of the countryside, a complaint voiced about Bologna's cardinal legate from other sources, may have been their grievance. Nonetheless, the chronicles labeled this revolt "tumultus rusticorum."[90]

On 14 August 1385 a much larger force of peasants stormed a disused walled-up city gate of Parma. One chronicler estimated the size of the force at two thousand or more men, another at four thousand.[91] No matter what its precise numbers, the chroniclers this time made its motives and mission clear. After killing the guards of the gate, "the peasants [*rustici*] charged to the town square searching to kill the tax collectors [*daciarios*][92] and to commit even more dreadful crimes." According to a chronicler from Vicenza: "From fear, neither the Captain [of the People], nor the podestà, nor any other citizen of Parma dared to oppose them openly, seeing that the townsmen were grossly outnumbered. But, by chance, a cavalry of three-hundred lances in the service of the Count of Virtù (Giangaleazzo Visconti, Duke of Milan) was on its way from Romagna and came to the citadel of Parma to rest on this feast day. Immediately, they charged the peasants, killing over three hundred of them and forcing the others to flee."[93] According to another source, the peasants planned their invasion and attack on the city tax collectors with artisans within the city walls, and their common battle cry was "Long live the Plebes; down with the taxes."[94]

Taxes were not the only reason peasants revolted in postplague northern Italy. In November 1388 Padua under the signoria of Francesco Novella da Carrara suffered the loss of Castelcaro, the fortified villages *(bastite)* of Santa Maria di Lugo, Bovolenta, and other places: all had gone up in flames. On hearing of these military defeats, "a crowd of peasants [*vilani*] formed a large gathering and began to riot. From fear that the peasants would destroy their houses, citizens joined them, forming a crowd [*sunanza*] in the piazza della Piava, all shouting against the state." They blamed their signore, Francesco, for the defeats, threatened to burn him and his progeny alive, and marched into the Piazza della Signoria to make other "dishonorable" pronouncements. Fearing the threat of further rioting and unable to raise taxes to pay his soldiers, Francesco sold his silver and other furnishings worth (according to the chronicler) around 200,000 gold ducats.[95]

The military misfortunes of Francesco were re-created at the end of November in Treviso: on hearing the news of Francesco's defeat, peasants *(rustici)* who happened to be in the town began sacking it *(inceperant saccomanare)* and marched straight to the main square shouting, "Long live Saint Mark and the Lord Count of Virtù" (the two enemies of the Paduan Carrara, one from Venice, the other from Milan). As in Padua a few days before, the commoners *(popolares)* followed the peasants' lead, chased out the Carrara soldiers and officers *(stipendiarijs)*, and took control of the city from Francesco's chief officer.[96]

Chroniclers often failed to state the reasons for other rural revolts, but where the evidence can be reconstructed from archival sources, the motives often turned on fiscal abuse. Such was the case with the mountain village of Raggiolo in the northern tip of the Casentino (called the Montagna Fiorentina), which straddled Florence's frontier with Arezzo. In March 1391, this mountain commune sought help from its former feudal lord, Giovanni Tedesco da Pietramala, who sent them 150 soldiers. The peasants then rebelled against Florentine rule but eventually capitulated after two months of fighting. Instead of mentioning the causes of these villagers' discontent, the Florentine chroniclers focused on Florence's triumph and the repression that awaited those who had dared resist Florentine military might.[97] From this Florentine view, the revolt arose either from peasant opportunism—seeking one set of lords to replace another—or from the feudal lords using the peasants in their power struggle against Florentine territorial domination. The chroniclers failed to mention, however, an underlying cause that can be inferred from the Florentine tax records: during the last decades of the fourteenth century, Florence had taxed those peasants along its northern and eastern mountain frontiers far more heavily than any others within its territorial state, and thus former feudal lords suddenly appeared as benevolent liberators in comparison with the rapacity of the peasants' new lords, republican oligarchs, despite their rhetoric of liberty.[98]

In 1395, a much larger revolt *(rusticorum sedicio)* erupted, involving thousands of peasants from an entire region within the territory of Ferrara. Its political context was similar to that of the revolt of Raggiolo in that the chronicles suggest peasants were enticed into action by one lord challenging the rule of another. In this case the conflict arose between two members of the same ruling dynasty, the Este, which suddenly opened space for peasants to press for their own demands.[99] As one chronicler told it, the Marchese d'Azzo[100] conspired with noblemen from the city and the mountains of Ferrara and "attracted thousands of peasants to take up arms with promises of great profits."[101] According to another, the rustics *(villani)* were "given a great quantity of grain and other supplies."[102] Unlike the descriptions of the Raggiolo revolt, however, the same Florentine chronicler (Minerbetti) gives these peasants a voice by reporting their chants when they invaded the city of Ferrara—"Long live the house of Este[103] and death to the gabelles and the *dazi.*"[104] As in Raggiolo, here too revolt failed and was brutally repressed. In the final battle alone, "six hundred or more were killed, not counting those who were drowned but may have survived, and two thousand were taken captive."[105] As with the Jacquerie, in postplague Italy the most desperate and impoverished were not the ones to carry out such revolts. Here, the chronicler is explicit: "All these peasants were rich, because there had never been wars here and the land was fat. Thus the booty was great, so much so that no one could put a price on it."[106]

After the death of Giangaleazzo Visconti in 1402, the Milanese empire began to crumble, with one faction seizing the new political opportunities to oust parties that previously favored the Visconti. The chroniclers expressed these conflicts as internecine, factional struggles, Guelfs versus Ghibellines. Yet other issues were brewing, and the lines of conflict were not only horizontal. As the case of Brescia illustrates, such movements could begin in the countryside and could be more complex, as old scores were settled and peasants took their own political and economic initiatives. In this case, the "Guelfs" were principally mountaineers *(i montanari)* "who with the help of others invaded the city and sacked and burnt the houses of the opposite party and those of the duke [of Milan]'s officers." The early sixteenth-century historian Bernardino Corio described the peasants' vengeance—what might be called their Jacquerie: "since they had no regard for sex or age, they sacrificed their victims as though they were lambs. Dragging [city] women by the hair, they raped and then killed them, and from hatred of the party [the previous ruling Ghibellines], they sold their human remains in the meat stalls; such nefarious and incredible cruelty is difficult to embrace in the hearts of the living."[107]

While the vast majority of the peasant uprisings revolved around some of the most commercially developed cities of northern and central Italy, Florence, Ferrara, Milan, Parma, and Bologna, the more feudalized zones of Friuli[108] produced at least two peasant outbreaks in the early fifteenth century, but even these sprung up close to its principal city, Udine. First, in January 1413 war provided an opportunity for peasants around this capital to protest and cut special deals with the Venetian state. The king of Hungary (whose troops then occupied the area) imposed a new tax *(colta)* of 25,000 ducats on the region, but the peasants *(villani)* refused to pay, claiming they did not have the means, and turned to San Marco for support. Further, the peasants of the Trevignano[109] and Mestrino,[110] "because of their good behavior" (meaning their loyalty to Venice) petitioned the Council of One Hundred and were exempted from the salt tax and in its place charged a smaller monthly head tax.

For other zones of the Terraferma, the Venetians were not as generous: instead of lowering the salt tax, they refused to supply certain towns and villages with any more salt. As a consequence peasants in the hills between Asolo and Bassano rebelled. Further, they were incensed by the Hungarian troops encamped at the bastion of Arcignano (between Verona and Vicenza), who refused to pay for their provisions. During the night of 7 February, the peasants *(villani)* jumped the troops, killing six soldiers and 150 horses. As a result, the next day the Hungarians retreated and made their way back to Hungary, but along the way they captured and enslaved young children and peasants and burnt country houses and palaces.[111]

Possibly the largest and most successful of the peasant revolts in late medieval Italy comes from the region where, given the current historiography,[112] we would least expect to see one: Florence. Between 1401 and 1404, waves of revolts ripped across the mountainous frontiers of Pistoia to the hills of the Chianti, engulfing over two hundred villages. Although first condemned in their absence as rebels with gruesome death sentences, these mountain peasants a year later negotiated handsome deals with the Florentine state, winning communal and individual tax exemptions, cancellation or reduction of debts, the right to carry weapons, and even the power to admit foreigners into their villages.[113] Without doubt, the war with Milan and the threat of enemy invasion through the territory of Florence enabled these mountain peasants to receive munitions, to revolt, and to negotiate large concessions from the Florentine state. But the archival records do not portray these peasants simply as pawns of the Milanesi or of their previous feudal lords. Instead, peasants planned military operations such as the seizure of the Florentine frontier town and stronghold of Firenzuola, even giving orders to the Milan's highest commander (Jacopo del Verme)[114] and building hilltop bastions to raid the countryside and torment the Florentine government.[115]

The richness of the Florentine archives, moreover, allows us to reconstruct the context and causes of these revolts left more or less opaque in the narrative sources. A quantitative analysis of tax registers reveals that the areas to revolt were the ones most heavily taxed. By the last years of the fourteenth century, certain communities in Alpi Fiorentine along Florence's troubled mountainous border with Bologna were charged as much as thirty-two times that of rural parishes down the valleys close to Florence's city walls, where Florentine patricians and even artisans held rural estates or strips of land. Had Florence been able to collect in full the taxes they charged, the wealth of these mountain peasants would have been completely dissipated within four years. Before revolting with their arms, these peasants did so with their feet, draining the war-sensitive borders of the Florentine state of its human resources. Although no document labels them as such, these peasant uprisings at the turn of the fifteenth century were tax revolts. At least one chronicler pointed in this direction: "The country was deeply divided because of heavy taxation and because of discord [*novità*] among the citizens, as can in part be understood. The countryside was more exhausted, impoverished, and deeply divided than the city: there was not a peasant [*contadino*] who would not have gone happily to Florence to burn it down."[116]

Detailed archival research for other cities and their rural surroundings might produce comparable surprises. For now, though, the results gleaned from various archival sources for Florence seem to corroborate patterns seen by chroniclers across Italy[117] and especially in Genoa, the region whose chroniclers reported the greatest number of peasant revolts: peasant revolts mounted in number and significance after the Black Death, and they clustered around some of the richest and most commercially advanced centers of Italy, not in the backwater feudal zones of Sicily or Friuli. Though warfare and enemy occupation touched off many of these postplague peasant revolts, the great majority resulted from taxes imposed by ambitious city patricians and expanding territorial states. On the other hand, feudal lords, rather than being the peasants' enemies, were more often their allies.

In conclusion, despite the prejudices and omissions of the chroniclers, the general trends of peasant revolt in late medieval France, Flanders, and Italy as presented by them do not diverge widely from the patterns that emerge from more detailed archival records found in particular places: Poitou, Languedoc, and Florence. Both north and south of the Alps, peasant revolts against landlords, whether feudal or commercial, were rare. So were demands to change and reshape the social relations of work or other conditions of production. Other records, such as manorial rolls and judicial inquests, might provide further detail on another world of protest—the quotidian foot-dragging, petty thievery, and even the rent strikes of the subaltern classes. Such issues surrounding work, however, did not galvanize large-scale peasant uprisings or even minor examples of collective peasant action. Nor do the archival records collected for this study show many challenges to landlords' prerogatives or feudal principles (even by atomized individual acts). Instead, as in the territory of Florence at the beginning of the fifteenth century, peasants allied themselves with their lords to battle against the increasing encroachments of city-states. The one striking exception comes from the archival records of the Trésor des chartes—the mass peasant protest of the late 1330s, which led to more than twenty-two villages uniting and refusing to pay new feudal dues to the dean and chapter of Notre-Dame at Laon.

The rarity of such riots did not result, however, because such acts were perceived as "suicidal," therefore limiting peasant resistance to a hidden world of atomized acts of silent subversion. Instead, the targets of late medieval peasant revolts were even bigger and more dangerous than feudal lords or patrician *rentiers;* they were city-state governments and the crown, which could mobilize militias and armies beyond the local resources of a mere landlord or two. Such peasant revolts were not so infrequent, especially in Italy, where over fifty can be counted from the narrative sources alone and many more from archival sources. Most of these, moreover, clustered in the quarter century around 1400.

Concentration on the English Peasant's Revolt of 1381, the Jacquerie, the Spanish *remensas,* and the Hussite rebellions of the first half of the fifteenth century—all of which arose in part against serfdom with demands to alter relations of production—has deformed our notion of late medieval revolt in general. The English case has been the best studied, and at least one historian,

R. H. Hilton, has placed it in a European context to draw similarities with rather than differences from the continent.[118] But peasant rebellion in England was rare by comparison. Before 1381, despite careful sifting through manorial records, historians have shown few examples of English revolts galvanizing into collective action beyond a manor or two; instead, they appear to have been more a part of James C. Scott's world of atomized acts of pilfering and the like. According to Hilton, "[T]ypical of these offences [from the thirteenth century to the Black Death] are refusal to obey a summons to the ploughing service; absence from the autumn boon-work; refusal to thresh the lord's wheat; non-performance of carrying services."[119] After 1381, historians claim that the Peasants' Revolt set off a "tradition" of rebellion, but they can point only to two or three revolts before the sixteenth century.[120] By contrast, not only were peasant revolts in France, Flanders, and especially Italy considerably more in evidence than in England, they centered on politics, not questions of rights in common or rents (feudal or otherwise). Can the same be said of workers and artisans, that their revolts also revolved around politics and confronted the state more often than employers? Or was that most studied of late medieval urban revolts—the Tumulto dei Ciompi—here more typical, the tip of an iceberg of protoproletarian struggle?

CHAPTER 3

Economic Revolts

Over 90 percent of popular revolts and movements described by chronicles took place in towns and, as best as can be seen from the laconic texts, they involved bourgeois, urban artisans, or workers without guild or citizen status.[1] To be sure, some movements combined the forces of peasants with commoners in cities, as with the Parma tax revolt of 1385 or the waves of insurrection throughout Flanders from 1297 to 1304 and again 1323–1328. But even if these are considered as purely peasant revolts—which they were not—the percentage is much the same. That riots and rebellion in medieval or preindustrial settings were extremely rare, even suicidal, and that the lower orders avoided them at all costs must be questioned, especially when towns are considered. Over a thousand popular movements and revolts can be found from a sample of published chronicles alone and in little more than two centuries. In Paris or Florence, with strong chronicle traditions, their numbers touched around two hundred, and no doubt these figures are the tip of the proverbial iceberg, as the archival sources suggest.

Do urban revolts, though much more frequent, show patterns similar to peasant uprisings? Were their objectives principally political, matters of political inclusion, and conflicts against oppressive regimes and the political abuse of upper classes, or did they spring from conditions of employment, tensions at the workplace that pitched workers against their bosses? As we shall see in Chapter 9, the history of revolt in Western Europe was not all of one piece, especially before the Black Death. Because of the significance of the Florentine Revolt of the Ciompi, historians have stressed that Tuscany was on a par with Flanders as a hotbed of popular insurrection. But more than scholars of popular movements such as Mollat and Wolff, Vanderkindere, Kurth, or Pirenne[2] realized, a comparison of the two regions' insurrectionary activity (their organization, aims, duration, and repertoires of revolt) shows northern France and Flanders a good hundred years ahead of anywhere in Italy.

France and Flanders before the Black Death

In Flanders, abundant evidence of workingmen's associations, assemblies, industrial strikes, and machine-breaking appears in city ordinances, court cases, and chronicles as early as the mid-thirteenth century. In 1245, the city council of Douai legislated against people of any occupation going on strike *(face takehan)* or calling assemblies for such purposes. The rather moderate penalties for such actions—fines and banishment for a year instead of beheading, as in Florence on the eve of the Black Death, when the earliest evidence of an industrial strike in any Italian town appears—suggest that in Flanders and northern France these activities may not have been uncommon.[3] Evidence of strikes in the late thirteenth and fourteenth centuries, moreover, is not limited to major cloth-producing centers such as Douai.[4] In the fourteenth century, the Flemish town of Béthune legislated against any journeymen or apprentices *(varlés)* of cloth producers going on strike.[5] The town council of Saint-Omer passed laws as early as 1250 against workers assembling or forming societies *(compaignie)* in the cloth industry.[6] Evidence for the even smaller town of Clermont-en-Beauvaisis, north of Paris, is still more explicit: "Conspiracy against the common good is when some kind of workers promise or agree or contract that they will not work for as low wages as they used to, but they increase the price on their own authority and agree that they will not work for less, and impose threats and punishments [*peine*] on their fellows who will not join their conspiracy."[7] Industrial conflict also appears in criminal sentences and other injunctions *(mandements)* against cloth works in Flanders after strikes of cloth workers in Douai in 1276 and 1280;[8] the rebellion of the Cockerulle in Ypres and its satellite town, Poperinge, in the same year;[9] and when the fullers, weavers, and beaters in the surrounding district of Saint-Omer broke and burned their tools in 1325 and again in 1383.[10] I know of no such strike activity or workers' organizations in any Italian revolts until the 1340s.[11]

Finally, in contrast to Italy or the south of France, the chroniclers of northern France and Flanders described riots composed of, organized, and led by textile workers and others of the *menu peuple*. To point out several of these: in 1281, the *plebes* of Rouen murdered their mayor.[12] In the same year, the poet, chronicler, and abbot of the Benedictine abbey Saint-Martin in Tournai, Gilles li Muisis, recorded an abortive uprising of weavers in Tournai to overturn the government. In 1307 he described two more such uprisings—a successful tax revolt by "weavers, the poor, the fullers, and others," who chose leaders that came from their own ranks and attacked tax collectors and the city governors, and an unsuccessful one of fullers whose motives the abbot unfortunately left undefined.[13] Guillaume de Nangis chronicles another attempt in Rouen by the lower orders (*minor populus*) to topple the city government, this time in 1292.[14] At least seven chroniclers described the revolt against royal monetary policy that resulted in tripling house rents for the *menu peuple* of Paris in 1306.[15] Several defined these commoners more precisely as "fullers, weavers, tavern keepers, and many other workers [*ouvriers*] in other crafts."[16] Farther east, revolts of the *plebes* in Liège, Huy, and Sint-Truiden against the Episcopal regime overturned governments from the mid-thirteenth century to the Black Death.[17]

By far the most important popular rebellion of the thirteenth and early years of the fourteenth century—the only one to cut across the regional boundaries of a single city and its hinterland and to draw the attention of chroniclers beyond northern France and Flanders[18]—was the movement against the efforts of Philip the Fair to bring Flanders within the ambit of French control. Though the supporters of this revolt ranged across Flemish society from the Count of Flanders to disenfranchised workers, a weaver led the revolt, and fullers, weavers, and other workers organized the first assemblies to protest the new French taxes. Their general strike in Bruges led to armed confrontations that would spread through West Flanders and as far east as Liège. Moreover, although the revolt ultimately failed to oust the French from Flanders or rid the country entirely of the crown's impositions, it did succeed in changing fundamentally the civil status of workers in the cloth trade, allowing weavers and fullers full rights as citizens, to form their own associations, and to be elected to governmental office[19]—a change for which the chroniclers spilled little ink. In effect, the Flemish rebellions of 1297–1304 were the northern equivalent of Florence's Revolt of the Ciompi (1378), although in Flanders it comprised a much larger canvas of cities and towns and had more significant and durable results. While some workers in the Florentine wool industry gained rights of citizenship for forty-seven days from 21 July to 5 September 1378 and others for three-and-a-half years until 19 January 1382, in Flanders weavers and fullers retained these rights (despite spells of suspension) into the early modern period.[20]

The only other urban European revolt to spread fully across regions was again Flemish, that of 1323–1328. As we have seen, it was at least as much a peasant as an urban revolt. The revolt of 1323–1328 sprang in large part from the unfinished business of the earlier Flanders-wide insurrection: the treaty of Athis-sur-Orge (June 1305), its imposition of excessive reparations and fines, and the decision of the new count, Louis of Nevers, to reimpose the penalties after they had largely fallen into abeyance.[21]

Yet, despite evidence of strikes, assemblies, illicit organizations, machine-breaking, and workers setting the maximum hours they would work, few of the revolts in late medieval France and Flanders sprang directly from controversies between workers and their employers, challenged labor relations, or turned explicitly on economic issues beyond taxes, which as we have argued were first and foremost a matter of the state and its politics. Even the two most important rebellions of the preplague period, the Flemish ones of 1297–1304 and 1323–1328, were essentially political: they challenged French overlord-ship and what peasants, workers, artisans, and others perceived as excessive and unjust taxation and an abusive infringement on rights.

Moreover, even the conflicts that brought workers and artisans into town squares over economic issues were not fought against bosses but against the state, whether it was a town council or the crown. Other battles that concerned economic rights were again not those that necessarily pitched workers against bosses: often they were internecine conflicts between crafts or between cities and their smaller satellites. Such were the relations between the weavers and fullers in Ghent, Bruges, Ypres, and other cloth-producing cities after 1302, when these trades began to hold offices in town councils. Further, the craft battle that brought Jacob van Artevelde to control Ghent in 1338 was one between the weavers, on one side, and fullers and other craftsmen, on the other. So was the armed conflict in the main square of Ghent that led to his death and that of "almost five hundred" artisans. The fullers demanded an increase of 4 gros in the price of the cloth that they sold on to the weavers. But the weavers, supported by the drapers, won. Afterward, the small town of Dendermonde rebelled against Ghent, after the Gentenars tried to snuff out competition from their smaller neighbors by prohibiting their manufacture of cloth.[22]

Two years earlier a similar conflict between craftsmen of the same profession had erupted in the region of Ypres. The weavers of Ypres invaded their satellite town of Poperinge and attacked the weavers there for cutting into their trade. The weavers of Ypres prevailed, killing the leader of Poperinge's weavers and several of his associates. With victory the weavers of Ypres forced those of Poperinge into "total submission."[23]

In 1348–1349 the new count of Flanders, Louis de Male, sought to diminish the power of the three major cities of Flanders, especially of Ghent. His method was to support the fullers against the dominant weavers, and satellite towns such as Aalst against the urban centers.[24] Revolts between these crafts spread through Ypres, Courtrai, and Ghent. In Ghent the weavers resisted the count's restrictions on their governance and their dominance over the fullers, but they lost: many were drowned in the Escaut River; others left town.[25] Not until 1360 did the Flemish cities finally challenge successfully the count's authority and regain their lost rights of 1349; as earlier in the century, they did so by presenting a united front of the crafts in the cloth industry against the count.

Italy before the Black Death

In preplague Italy, even for a city with as well developed a cloth industry as Florence, its statutes, rich collections of town-council deliberations, judicial records, and chronicles leave no evidence of strikes, workers' organizations, or insurrections primarily organized, staffed, or led by disenfranchised workers in the cloth industry before 1343. Even revolts organized by artisans with recognized guilds were extremely rare in Italy before the Black Death, despite Italy's rich history of the "popolo" and struggles for political power against the arrogance and brutality of magnates that reach back to the tenth century.[26] Further, the earliest Italian craft revolts did not hinge on economic questions at all; nor did they emerge from Tuscany (generally considered Italy's cradle of popular insurrection) but from Emilia-Romagna. The first in my samples comes from Parma, when the city's butchers helped Lord Ghibertus de Gente seize control over the city in 1252.[27] But the first revolt by artisan groups or specific crafts for their own corporate purposes presented in chronicles dates from 1267, when the guild of cobblers (*societas calçolariorum*) of Bologna set the Palace of the Podestà ablaze. They did so not because of any grievances over work or commerce but because of a perceived miscarriage of justice: the podestà had imprisoned one of their members for killing a man who had committed adultery with his wife. Their ardent protest succeeded: the podestà was expelled from office and a new one elected.[28] In Parma craftsmen again united for political purposes in 1291. To challenge the power of magnates, four crafts (*quatuor misteria*)—the butchers, ironmongers, cobblers, and furriers—

assembled, rioted, and swore oaths to support one another. To topple the magnates, they also allied with the city's notaries and judges.[29] This alliance of the four crafts would prove to be the core of popular governments in Parma until the fifteenth century. In the early fourteenth century, with their guild flags raised and cries of "il popolo, il popolo," they often led raids against magnate families in the city and through the countryside.[30]

In 1295 the guild of the cobblers revolted again in Bologna, again not over wages or working conditions, but over a judicial grievance. Their anger turned on another case of a perceived miscarriage of justice, this time for unspecified acquittals rather than condemnations. The cobblers charged the Palace of the Captain of the People, stole the Captain's horses, and chanted, "Death to the captain and his officers [*sua familla*]." Unlike their colleagues a generation earlier, they did not succeed. The captain fined the guild collectively 2,000 lire and further humiliated them by forcing them to part with their money chests and belongings *(da le pertinentie . . . scrigni e banche)* in the main square of Bologna.[31] In 1306 the butchers of Bologna fared better: supporting a successful coup d'état they chased Napoleone Orsini, the cardinal legate, and the Guelf Party from power and replaced them with a new popular regime centered on the seven guilds of Bologna.[32]

Not until 1317 did any of the Italian chroniclers describe an insurrection of corporate groups representing specific professions or trades for a Tuscan town, and Siena, not Florence, was the hot spot. Six hundred foot soldiers of the craft militias of Siena—the butchers, wool manufacturers, and blacksmiths— returned from battle at Gerfalco in Siena's hinterland, angry over the decision of the cavalry and their captain to retreat without victory. When the war captain and these magnates entered Siena's town square, the Campo, the *popolo* took up arms and threw stones at the captain, who ducked into the communal palace for protection. The people and the trade militias continued their revolt, threatening the Government of the Nine, the regime in power, which had negotiated the military decisions.[33] Like the revolts of artisan groups in Emilia-Romagna, this one turned on politics, not economic issues or disputes at the point of production.

Italy after the Black Death: The Bruco and the Ciompi

After the Black Death, revolts that pitched workers against employers or challenged social relations of production can be counted on the fingers of one hand. The most explicit of these came from Tuscany and not from northern France or Flanders, as was true before the plague. Foremost among them were the revolts of the Company of the Caterpillar in Siena in 1371 (the Bruco) and the Florentine Tumulto dei Ciompi in 1378. The former is an exceptional case within the chronicle literature of revolt: it began over a wage dispute. Sometime after the middle of May:

> workers [*lavorenti*] and carders of the wool guild had words and disputes with their bosses [*li loro maestri*] over pay, whether their wages should be set according to the norms established by the Commune of Siena or those of the guild. They marched on the town hall but were not allowed to enter; so they rioted, made threats, and wished to kill their bosses in the wool guild and others . . . These [insurgents] were the carders of the Company of the Caterpillar [*Compagnia del Bruco*].[34]

By 14 July, however, the battle lines had changed, and the targets were no longer the wool bosses. The Company armed themselves, rioted, and charged the palace of the chief officer of Siena, killing many of his men. The battle cry of the carders now had nothing to do with wages, conditions of work, or their employers. Instead it was about politics: "The [government] of the Twelve and the Nine have betrayed Siena; death to the Twelve, and long live the People."[35]

Seven years later, the economic demands of the Ciompi were more remarkable still; nothing comparable to them has been unearthed anywhere else in Europe for the Middle Ages. First, the wool workers (who comprised as much as one-third of the work force in Florence), along with journeymen and those who were under the control of other guilds, successfully challenged the prevailing social relations of production in Florence by forming three new guilds. These were not, however, guilds in the traditional sense of occupational societies; rather, they consciously cut across trades and skills to form guilds of class, mixing dependent workers across various crafts.[36]

First, the newly formed revolutionary corporate body of the *popolo minuto*, the Emergency Council of Thirty-two, formed three new guilds. The guilds conveyed to previously dependent workers and artisans new economic rights to regulate their own work practices and abolished the wool guild's absolute authority over their behavior, which was oppressively adjudicated by the wool guild's special internal tribunal and its judge, the much-hated *forastiere*. Previously, this court had stripped wool workers of their civil liberties, barring recourse to the city's civil or criminal tribunals on any matter related to cloth production.[37] After the revolt of the Ciompi, wool workers now placed conditions on their employers. To ensure stable levels of employment, the new government legislated that the industry as a whole was to produce at least

2,000 wool cloths *(panni)* a month, "whether they wanted to or not, or suffer great penalties."[38]

However, more than economics or disputes at the point of production were at stake. The formation first of the *popolo minuto* as a constitutionally defined body and soon afterward the three new guilds were political acts by which workers gained political prerogatives. Now previously dependent workers of the wool industry, apprentices, and other disenfranchised tradesmen and workers possessed guild status. By these means the workers became citizens with rights to elect members to Florence's highest councils—the *Tre Maggiori*—and to be elected to them, even becoming Florence's highest-ranking officer, the Standard-Bearer of Justice.[39]

Recent scholars of the Revolt of the Ciompi have ended their analysis of it with the failure of the radical Eight of Santa Maria Novella to push the revolution further at the end of August 1378 and the subsequent disbanding of the third revolutionary guild, that of the Ciompi. Sometimes called the carders, sometimes "the people of God," they were the most unskilled workers of the three guilds. It is almost forgotten that this was the only constitutional change to occur in September after the Eight's defeat: elections for the new priors continued as scheduled, workers in the wool industry continued to serve in the commune's highest offices, and the two other revolutionary guilds, those of the dyers and doublet makers, continued to exercise their rights as before. Certainly, most contemporaries did not see the defeat of the Eight as the end of workers' power in Florence. For some, such as Marchionne di Coppo Stefani, who had served in the government in 1379, the power and arrogance of workers continued to mount during the so-called government of the Arti Minori (Minor Guilds). In December 1380 he saw the power and privilege of the wool bosses continuing their downward spiral, sinking to lower levels of prestige than during the forty-seven days of the "Ciompi regime." Not only did members of the two surviving workers' guilds push for new privileges and reforms, but also apprentices, who had belonged to the third guild, appear not to have fared so badly since their guild's demise, at least by Stefani's account.

> This guild of the dyers became so audacious that they lost sight of who they were in relation to others in the city and in terms of their own worth. They had been ruled and had been under the thumbs [*retti e sottoposti*] of the wool bosses [*lanaiuoli*], obliged to accept their laws and be ruled by their statutes; now they acted with such arrogance: while all the other guilds were required to take on only a certain amount of work

and no more, or face a penalty of a certain number of pounds, these people made laws that gave workers the right to accept any amount of work [they wanted] and those who gave them less were penalized. This struck the wool bosses as very bizarre and the citizens as abominable; it was beyond all reason. Because the rich dyers acted so immoderately, they failed to profit from their trade. With this, apprentices, not the masters, had become the guild counselors, and wherever the masters went, their colleagues laughed at them. Things were so mixed up that shopkeepers had to submit to apprentices out of fear. This state of affairs was detestable, and the city was weakened from within by these revolutionary notions [*novità*].[40]

The economic directives of the Ciompi government, moreover, went beyond matters of the wool industry alone and changed the material conditions of all workers and citizens within the city walls of Florence and even those residing in the countryside. In its first acts of 21 July 1378, the new Ciompi government declared that no one was to be arrested for indebtedness for the next two years and changed the tax system of Florence toward greater equity. Second, within six months the old system of forced loans (*prestanze*), which favored citizens with the means to pay on time over the urban poor and those from the countryside, was to be abolished; now all would pay according to their wealth based on a property survey (*estimo*).[41] Third, the new government in effect abolished the Monte or communal bank of Florentine state bonds, which had given favorable rates of return to the wealthy from monies that derived from indirect taxes (gabelles) and the direct taxes taken largely from the countryside. Interest was no longer to be paid out over a twelve-year period, and gradually all the shares would be refunded.[42] Fourth, the new government stabilized the rate of exchange between the gold florin and the money of payment (in copper [*rame*] or *piccioli*) at 68 shillings a florin.[43] The inflation of the florin had been a means by which the wool guild and other Florentine entrepreneurs had lowered wages by stealth, devaluing the money that workers and artisans used for their daily transactions. In the year preceding the Revolt of the Ciompi, the rate of exchange had fluctuated between 70 and 75 shillings per florin, but since the florin's first minting in 1215, it had risen almost fourfold.[44] By stabilizing the exchange rate, the law in effect raised workers' purchasing power and thereby their wages. Finally, many shops had remained closed since the Ciompi revolt, and those that opened did little work. As a consequence many were starving. Thus in August the government implemented elementary welfare measures to assist the poor—

a point that no modern historian of the Ciompi has mentioned. It provided a bushel of grain per head to any who needed it. But the most severe problems appear to have been in the countryside: the new government sent men out to issue money to those in need who resided three miles beyond the city walls to the borders of the Florentine state.[45]

The great reversal in workers' rights came not with the defeat of the Eight of Santa Maria Novella at the beginning of September 1378 but on 19 January 1382, when the soldiers of the wool guild and patricians toppled the Government of the Minor Guilds. The new government immediately outlawed the two remaining revolutionary guilds of dyers and doublet makers and their affiliates and reestablished the status quo that the wool guild and patricians had enjoyed before the constitutional reforms of Salvestro de' Medici in June 1378. In the words of the anonymous diarist of the Machiavelli family: "The deal was done; from now on, all those artisans who previously had been underlings [*sottoposti*] would again be underlings, subject to the councils of their guilds and to the guildsmen's will."[46]

The return to patrician rule did not, however, end workers' protest in Florence. Immediately, revolts of ex-Ciompi erupted with flag-waving marches into the main square of Florence; sometimes these ex-Ciompi united with exiled magnates, sometimes with craftsmen *(artefici)* from the fourteen minor guilds. Stefani, the principal contemporary chronicler for the years following the defeat of the Ciompi and the Government of the Minor Guilds, describes nine such revolts from 24 January to July 1383,[47] and an anonymous diarist, probably a minor civil servant,[48] lists a further six during these months.[49] Still others appear in the surviving judicial registers.[50] In most of these, the rebels made their central objective clear: waving the three illegal flags of their outlawed guilds and chanting "Long live the twenty-four guilds," they sought to reinstate their recently lost rights and reestablish the revolutionary guilds of the past three years. To this extent their objectives were economic, but, as with the Revolt of the Ciompi itself, despite its remarkable forward-looking economic policies, the main aims were political. By becoming once again members of the minor guilds, they would become full-fledged citizens of Florence, possessing rights of election and holding office.

Other Workers' Struggles in Central Italy

If the remarkable revolt of the Ciompi were the tip of the iceberg of workers' protest, indicative of revolts with clear programs for economic reform either in Florence or in other northern and central Italian city-states, certainly its base remains well hidden from both narrative and archival sources. In Florence, other revolts touched working conditions and made economic demands, but they are found almost exclusively in archival and not narrative sources, and even here they remain rare. Most notable was the arrest and execution of the labor organizer and leader Ciuto Brandini, whose capture led to rioting by the wool workers of Florence in 1345. This carder from the parish of San Pier Maggiore had formed a union or fraternity *(fraternitas)* of fellow disenfranchised workers in the wool industry. It attracted workers throughout the city of Florence, collected funds from them, held regular meetings, elected officers, and in the language of the judicial inquiry "organize[d] gatherings and meetings to bring about quickly the worst possible outcome."[51]

Another protest that brought workers into direct conflict with their bosses (but went unrecorded in the Florentine chronicles) developed from 1369 to 1371. With competition from the Low Countries and shrinking markets, the Florentine wool guild sought to cut costs by lowering the rates at which the woad dyers supplied their finished cloths. These dyers protested and went on strike, but their employers finally broke the strike and penalized the dyers severely.[52] Still other protests may have brought workers into the streets against their bosses, challenging prevailing labor conditions or even the social relations of production; however, the surviving sources do not reveal them. For instance, the carders and "other rabble," who followed the mad Andrea Strozzi and then his son in March 1343, may have had their own agenda, but neither the scribes of the judicial tribunals nor the chroniclers disclosed them.[53] Similarly, the 1,300 "wool carders and others of the *gente minuta* who gathered together at the Servite church" on 25 September that year may not have been so "clueless" without "knowing what to demand," as the chronicler Stefani contemptuously scoffs.[54]

Indeed, an anonymous chronicler from Pistoia put a different gloss on Florentine workers' revolts in 1343 than they received in either the Florentine judicial records or chronicles. After the Strozzi failed in their two attempts to lead a social rebellion of wool workers for their own benefit, the wool workers appeared a third time behind their own leader, a dyer named Corazza, who led 1,300 workers to the Palace of the Priors. From fear, the priors allowed them to enter and with flattery and well-chosen words promised them whatever they wished. Did these promises concern working conditions or political rights? Unfortunately, the chronicler does not say.[55]

In other city-states, workers may also have made demands that attacked prevailing labor conditions and social relations of production but which chroniclers and scribes of judicial and other city council records preferred to pass over. For instance, in 1355, with the revolution that toppled the longest-lasting political regime of any Italian city-state, that of Siena's government of the Nine, the *popolo minuto* followed the others on the first day of the rebellion, 23 March. Two days later, however, they were the first to riot and lock the chains across the squares and streets of the city. The other enemies of the Nine, from members of magnate clans to notaries, then followed the lead of the *popolo minuto*. Perhaps the *minuti* had demands of their own that went beyond a change in regime, but their cries and chants recorded by Siena's chronicler resound in unison with the others excluded by the Nine. They cried for the death of the Nine and new life for themselves as a governing body.[56] Nonetheless, the first legislative acts of the new government of the Twelve show that the *popolo minuto* had made an impact and were not simply front-line fodder of an upper-class revolt. As with the Revolt of the Ciompi twenty-three years later, the new government guaranteed guild status to almost all working males in the city along with rights to elect and be elected to the city's highest offices. Those included in the new government of the Twelve reached down to the lowliest positions in the cloth and leather industries: dyers, leather dressers, slipper makers, purse makers, cloth cutters, finishers, stretchers of woolen cloth, sewers, wool combers, rug makers, tailors, and shearers. It even extended political rights to professions that never gained separate guild recognition in Florence: greengrocers and barbers.[57]

Similarly, economic demands may have been at stake on 16 May 1371, when the wool workers of Perugia and "foreign gangs of thieves [*forestieri masnaderotti*]" led a riot, shouting, "Long live the Church and the People," and succeeded in chasing out the city's ruling merchant oligarchy of the city, the Raspanti.[58] Further, they may have been a part of the plans when Giacomo d'Odda of the working-class neighborhood *(porta)* of Sant' Angelo "united many of the youth of this neighborhood to rid the city of all those of the Raspanti faction" once again. However, nothing in the sources or in their recorded rallying cries—"Long live the people and death to the Raspanti"—reveals any such program.[59] The same must be said for the only revolt recorded by the surviving chroniclers of late medieval Lucca, in which cloth workers and other artisans appear among its leaders and the rank and file—Nicolao di Lippo, a needle worker; Pieretto, a weaver; Stefano, called Trombante, a gold beater. In late July these workers organized secret meetings and made public addresses in Lucca's main square, where "the majority of the people of Lucca" were assembled to topple the government of the oligarchic Guinigi family. Their programs, set out in secret meetings, dealt with strategies for overturning the city's government and their rallying cry was political: "Long live the people." For this revolt, moreover, we possess detailed judicial records along with the account of the city's principal chronicler.[60]

Economic Disputes and the State

Perhaps we should conclude, along with James C. Scott, that the absence of such programs and economic demands result from a "conspiracy of silence" on the part not only of upper-class chroniclers and judicial clerks but also of the insurgents themselves. But, as we have said, far from having been reluctant to report popular riots and revolts, chroniclers filled their narratives with them. Moreover, as we shall see, these movements ranged over a wide variety of participants and matters of contention. Chroniclers (and those who kept journals or diaries, such as the court scribe of the Parisian Parlement, Nicholas de Baye) occasionally reported minor disputes between various ranks of workers and their bosses, ones that were fought out mostly in the courts rather than in the streets. Such a dispute arose in the Parisian suburb of Saint-Denis on 27 July 1409 between the town's dyers and drapers. The drapers, whose corporation had 140 members, brought to court a tiny guild of dyers with only six members. The drapers reproached them for violating their "ancient customs" by dying woolen cloths with the seeds of nuts, roots, and bark *(d'escailles de nois, de racines et d'escorces)* instead of with woad; as a result the colors ran and became rusty *(rougist)*. But the dyers, "despite their numbers," stood up to the more powerful drapers and presented a decree to the corporation of drapers, declaring that "they [the dyers] could dye however they wished and in their opinion, [their methods] made the best and most brilliant colors." The quarrel continued to bubble, leading to injurious words, bodily harm, and damage to property. Eventually the Parlement of Paris had to intervene. Unfortunately, Nicholas de Baye does not give the final resolution, but since he refers to the dyers' practices as unlawful *(les empiètements des teinturiers)*, presumably the verdict favored the more powerful drapers.[61]

In addition, chroniclers and diarists described other revolts that were essentially protests against economic policies or made use of economic measures such as the strike, but these quarrels were not ones in which workers confronted employers or questioned social relations of production or other matters originating from the point of production. The most common economic protests concerned the crown's or a city-state's manipulation of coinage, the exchange rate between gold and cheaper metals of daily market exchange; such shifts in policy could suddenly and seriously lower the standard of living of artisans and laborers. The earliest of these from my samples originated with Philip the Fair's manipulations of coinage in 1306, 1311, and 1313. The most important came in 1306, and at least eight chroniclers described the Parisian revolt that ensued. The *menu peuple* of Paris were paid in "weak money" but now had to pay their house rents in the new "strong money." The manipulation of exchange rates meant that their house rents suddenly trebled. "Little people such as fullers, weavers, seamstresses, furriers, cobblers, and many others of various different crafts made an alliance."[62] First they went after a "rich and powerful" Parisian bourgeois named Étienne Barbete, who they thought was behind the rent hikes. They set his manor outside Paris on fire and stole his hunting dogs. Then they broke into his city mansion, destroyed his fine furniture, and rubbed his cushions, chests, and other property in the mud on the side of the road. They ripped apart his mattresses, throwing the feathers "scornfully to the winds," and opened his casks of wine, which they dished out in the squares. This done, they went to the palace of the Knights Templar, where the king of France was staying with several of his barons. Since the king was well guarded, they did not dare attack him but sought to humiliate him by throwing the meat delivered to him into the mud.[63] Firmin de Coquerel of Amiens, provost of the merchants of Paris, came out to appease the crowds "with sweet words and flattery," and "the commoners returned peacefully to their houses." The next day proved more costly for the commoners: the king executed twenty-eight of them from various gates of the city. The other two changes in the value of money caused grumbling among commoners in the city *(murmur in populo)* but affected more the rich *(grandes)* in 1311 and "especially the merchants" in 1313.[64]

Seven other popular revolts against "new money" postdated the plague. The first was an early victory for Étienne Marcel, provost of the merchants of Paris, and a prelude to the mobilization of Parisian discontent that paralleled the Jacquerie. In December 1356, the Duke of Anjou (acting on behalf of his brother, the king, who had recently been captured at the battle of Poitou) issued new money, which changed the rate of exchange between gold and silver. Even the king's official chroniclers at Saint-Denis reported that "it was said that the change went against the people." With "a great number of inhabitants" the provost marched on the Louvre and approached the duke on four occasions, demanding that the new money be withdrawn. Parisian pressure prevailed: the duke ceased minting the new money, and the old exchange rates were reinstated.[65]

Another three riots clustered in Paris in the last years of my analysis: 1421, 1422, and 1425. The first of these was reminiscent of the crown's changes in 1306. In June, the king once again imposed "strong money" (meaning that commoners had to pay their taxes and rents in coins valued at 16 Parisian pennies *per gros,* while their wages continued to be paid in "weak money" at 12 Parisian pennies *per gros*). The Parisians rioted and by August had won their demands, restoring the old rates of exchange.[66] The following year the currency was manipulated again in other complex ways "that made the people unhappy"; this time their protests had no effect.[67] In November 1425, Flemish money called *plagues,* which was common currency in Paris, was clipped in value from nine to eight *doubles.* It caused a great fuss *(dont grand murmure fut),* but the people had to suffer the consequences.[68] The other two protests against monetary policies both arose in Florence. The first, as we have seen, was one of the many demands and laws made when the government of the Ciompi took office on 21 July 1378, which had the effect of raising wages. In 1380, the artisans of the Government of the Minor Guilds sought further to improve their lot by lowering the value of the florin by another six shillings.[69]

Other popular protests challenged market decisions of kings or other rulers that local populations saw as detrimental to themselves and their local economies. As with monetary policy, the demands were "economic" but the conflicts were "political"; that is, the insurgents rebelled against the state, not against bosses; against laws and not directly against wages or conditions of work. During a severe food shortage in 1343 the king agreed to assist the Duke of Burgundy and ordered the regions of Orléans, Beauce, and the Gâtinais to export their grain to Burgundy. Along with the bourgeois and the commoners, clerics studying at the University of Orléans were distraught because, they claimed, these demands would greatly diminish their own supplies. The king sent several barges down the Loire to float the grain to Burgundy. But before it could be carried away, the insurgents seized and sold it to anyone who wanted it for any price they wanted to pay. Others ran through town, the suburbs, and into neighboring villages, breaking down doors and pillaging. Not wishing to allow "such madness to continue," the provost of Orléans arrested "twelve or thirteen of the rebels."[70] But others then broke into the prison and freed the rebels along with the other inmates. When the news reached the king, he sent two knights with a large army and orders to capture the guilty and hang them immediately, which they did; among those executed was a deacon.[71] A similar protest against the royal grain policy flared at Abbeville in the north of France in 1408. Commoners assembled and rioted against the orders of the séneschal of Pontieu and the royal chief officer at Abbeville to ship grain from the city to Calais and then by English vessels on to Holland.[72] In 1410, Nicholas de Baye reported a revolt reminiscent of the sabotage of the king's export of grain from Orléans in 1343: the widow of a man who had recently been killed in a riot at Orléans addressed an appeal to the Parlement in Paris (probably to receive her inheritance). The riot had been against those who were transporting grain to sell it outside the city of Orléans "at the peril and risk of famine to the people." Had there been some collective memory of the events two generations earlier?[73] At any rate, this was another riot that touched matters of domestic economy but not relations of production and that was redressed by attacks against the state.

Matters of commerce and economic impositions of the state provoked a conspiracy in Pisa in 1360. Florence had imposed an embargo on Pisa's port, which caused incomes to sink, especially those of craftsmen (arte minuta). As a result, artisans "complained, grumbled, and cursed [the Florentines]," and "a large number of them" met in secret, swore oaths, and "drew up ordinances between them." They planned a coup d'état for Good Friday, 3 April, and afterward would sue for peace and negotiate with Florence to reopen the port. The conspiracy, however, was nipped in the bud when one of the conspirators, a priest, was caught cursing among his lay comrades. Soon afterward, four priests and seven friars were arrested, followed by a hundred artisans from the minor guilds.[74] By Villani's account, this conspiracy was considerable: "the governors of Pisa proceeded further in this affair, discovering that many others had been involved in the conspiracy." Although it never came to fruition, it "disturbed and frightened the city greatly," bringing down Pisa's government of the Seven.[75]

The first appearance of Siena's remarkable Company of the Caterpillar in the chronicles (unlike its more famous revolt in 1371) did not involve matters of wages or production within the wool industry, but it did concern economic policy. On 26 August 1370, eleven months before the disputes with their bosses erupted, "three hundred or more" of these wool workers conspired like legendary urban Robin Hoods to redistribute grain in their neighborhood (the contrada d'Ovile), the poorest of the city, "taking from those who had it and giving it to those without."[76]

As we have said, tax revolts were often prompted more by politics than economics, and those who perceived themselves thus unjustly treated turned not against their employers but against the state, whether it was a town government or the crown. Nonetheless, on rare occasions certain groups used the economic means of withholding their labor and services to attack the state and to redress the injustice of what they perceived as unjust taxation. For instance, on two occasions in the early fifteenth century, 1408 and 1415, the cardinal legates of Rome imposed taxes on parish priests of the city. "All the canons, the treasurer of the clergy, and many other priests of the city" responded by meeting in the monastery of the Rose and voting not to pay any taxes without a directive from Pope Gregory XII. In the meantime, they went on strike, refusing to ring the church bells (which inconvenienced the city not just spiritually but in ordering daily life) and to perform mass. The first strike lasted from the first to the sixth of January, when the legate broke it up, arresting many of the canons and clerics.[77] Seven years later, the legate imposed taxes on the Roman clergy again; as before they responded by shutting the doors of all the churches in Rome, declining to sing mass or ring their bells for six days.[78]

Finally, two cases from the end of our period, both from the Flemish town of Tournai, at the time under France's suzerainty, show the use of the strike and assemblies by workers for political ends rather than as a face-off between workers and bosses. On 11 November 1424 the various craft guilds of the town *(collèges des mestiers)* were marching in one of the city's ordained processions. The blacksmiths *(les febvres)* met separately and decided to go on strike *(de jamais ouvrer de leur mestier)* until one under their guild pennant, Jehan Boubriel (Jean de Bléhaires, called Blarie), banned from the city, was allowed to return. The fullers, weavers, and other laborers supported the blacksmiths, and together they built barricades around the central market using the trolleys, boxes, and benches of the fish stalls. They prepared for battle against the city council by stealing and bringing into their makeshift fortification all the shields and bolts belonging to the marketplace *(la Halle)* along with other artillery of the city.[79]

In the following year, the dean *(doïen)* of the weavers in Tournai was wounded by Andrieu de le Prée. Led by their dean, the weavers ceased working and went to court to make sure that Andrieu was given a heavy sentence. Their pressure worked: he was condemned to have his hand chopped off. But, as Andrieu was being brought past the market to mount the executioner's block *(hourt)* "with between two and three hundred weavers present to see that justice was done," Andrieu screamed "Clergy!" Suddenly several men came forward and without any hindrance swept him into the church of Notre-Dame. The weavers and their supporters retaliated, screaming "To arms, get the banners!" At which point, the whole town rose up and went armed to the market, carrying their banners. At vespers they approached the church of Notre-Dame and asked those guarding its doors to hand over Andrieu. They were given six hours to do so or they would be heavily fined and banished from the city for life.[80]

The majority of protests (14 of 16) that revolved around economic issues, whether popular protests against monetary policy, commercial decisions of various sorts that people saw as detrimental to them, or the use of the strike for redressing political grievances and miscarriages of justice, came after the Black Death.

Grain Riots and Acts of Destitution

What about supposedly that most common of revolts in preindustrial societies—the grain or bread riot—and the economics of hunger?[81] First, the chronicles as well as the archival records surveyed for Italy, France, and Flanders show that these riots were extremely rare: there were only eleven, less than 1 percent of the recorded revolts, and four of these concerned the politics of the grain trade and were staffed by clerics, students, artisans, or bourgeois. These hardly suggest revolts of destitution. Second, the only riot specially tied to bread prices in France in these samples occurred in Paris and its surroundings in 1304, when the well-to-do were compelled to lock their doors and windows.[82] But even here the conflict was short-lived; the king immediately revoked a previous edict, bread was sold at "a just price," and social harmony restored.[83] Furthermore, the more widespread and disastrous famine of northern Europe of 1315–1317, which in terms of mortality ranks as Western Europe's most severe famine for any historical period, did not spark a single grain or bread riot found in these chronicles or in the records of the Trésor des chartes.[84]

The other cases were from central and northern Italy—Siena in 1302 and 1303,[85] Florence in 1310,[86] Bologna in 1311,[87] and Rome, Siena, and Florence during the widespread famine of 1329.[88] With the possible exception of the riots in Rome, which led to King Robert's baron and senator of Rome, Lord William of Eboli, being chased from office in 1329, these riots appear as minor disturbances. The Florentine one of 1310 may not have even been a riot: Giovanni Villani comments that during a serious shortage that year "the entire city was almost moved to rioting [*onde tutta la città ne fu quasi ismossa a romore*]." The Bolognese riot of 1311 concerned only one neighborhood of the city—at the gate of Ravenna. Furthermore, the state often met these revolts of scarcity with compassion rather than executions and often nipped them in the bud with charity before they sprouted into city-wide revolts. During famine conditions in Siena in 1302, with a "tumulto" growing "that might have spread through the land," the government of the Nine quickly restored order by distributing "many barrels [*tine*] filled with grain and other provisions."[89] Similarly, during the worst wave of famines in late medieval Italy, 1327–1330, Giovanni Villani praised the vision and compassion of his city, which succeeded in avoiding rebellion. Instead of kicking beggars out of town, as he alleged had been the policy in Perugia, Lucca, Pistoia, and Siena, Florence welcomed them into the city, bought huge supplies of grain from Sicily, and took over the distribution of grain, fixing its price and the amount that could be sold per head "so that everyone would have enough bread to live on and thus to survive."[90]

Despite Villani's boasting, Siena appears to have been as compassionate, successfully preventing a bread riot from becoming city-wide during the famine of 1329. Siena's government of the Nine also imported large grain supplies from Sicily, allowed those from the impoverished countryside to crowd into the city, and doled out charity from its principal hospital, Santa Maria della Scala. Nonetheless, because "a multitude of the poor from the countryside of Siena and Florence" rushed into the city for relief, a riot erupted in Siena's main square, the Campo. The crowds "dying of hunger" ripped through the barrels of grain and bread and threw rocks at the windows of the palaces of the Podestà and the Nine, all the while screaming "Misericordia." Soon the rectors of the hospital of Santa Maria della Scala quelled the crowd by promising that the hospital would provide everyone with enough bread, and in the following days, the Nine sold bread at fixed low prices in the Campo.[91]

These mumblings and riots over basic matters of the hearth—grain and bread—cast a trend counter to that of the other economic protests examined thus far. All but two of the grain riots—Abbeville in 1408 and Orléans in 1410—came before the Black Death. This cannot be explained by any absence of shortages or severe famines in the seventy-seven years examined here following the plague's first strike. As can be seen in the *contado* of Florence, along with increased devastation from war, crop failures produced horrific conditions for numerous villages and towns during the second half of the fourteenth century. The Florentine countryside reached its nadir of population and wealth fifty years after the Black Death, and certain villages in the mountains lost greater proportions of their populations from migration than the plague.[92] Moreover, the famine of 1374–1375 raged throughout most of Italy and was reported by numerous chroniclers, but not a single bread or grain riot ensued from it.[93]

Another revolt that turned to grain, although left unreported by the chronicles, appears in the judicial records of Florence in 1368. This revolt, however, was different from the bread riots that occurred in the preplague famine years. In contrast to starving masses, mostly from the countryside, pressing into cities and screaming for mercy, this "grain riot" appears as an orderly revolt of the urban "popolo" with a clear political agenda for changing the government of Florence. On 19 August 1368 more than five hundred approached Florence's central grain market and began systematically grabbing sacks of grain on sale not for their own consumption, but to dump on the doorsteps of their rulers. Theirs were the acts of revolutionary theater.

> They then took a certain quantity of grain, beyond twenty bushels [*staia*], also on sale here in this loggia, and along with the assembled people went with this grain to the Palace of the Lord Priors, where they shouted: "Long live the People." Then they took the grain to the door of the lord priors and dumped it on the ground. Having done it, they returned to the loggia, chanting along the way, "Long live the People." They took a certain quantity of flour beyond twenty bushels on sale in this loggia and with this flour went off shouting to the Palace of the Lord Priors, threw it on the ground in front of the door of the lord priors, and threw rocks at the guards of the lord priors and those of the podestà of the city of Florence in serious breach of and prejudice to the present peace of the city of Florence. Each and every one of these acts might have overturned the peaceful state of the commune of Florence.[94]

In contrast to the starving pleas of the Sienese poor in the famine of 1329–1330, these were not the last gasps of those trying to feed themselves or their dying children; rather their revolt was directly political: grain was used symbolically to embarrass and bring down the current priors of the commune.[95]

Insurgents' chants and chroniclers' commentaries suggest that a further thirteen revolts that did not take the form of a food riot or an attack on grain shipments nonetheless had scarcity in the background and may have been triggered by destitution. In 1304, the magnate Corso Donati tried to profit from tensions in Florence created by a severe food shortage to get rid of the

Ordinances of Justice, but the people (both the *grasso* and the *minuto*) put an end to his plans by rioting.[96] In 1319, "it was said" that a riot of the *popolo* began in Genoa with the hurling of stones from machines against the city walls because of food shortages *(in urbe victualium penuria.)*[97] Scarcity was in the background of the revolt of wool carders who followed the crazed Andrea Strozzi and then his son, storming several public buildings and attempting to bring down the government of the "fat cats." Villani depicted the revolt as one over taxes and class war; the wool workers' chant was "Long live the *popolo minuto* and death to the gabelles and the fat cats [*popolo grasso*]."[98] But the criminal record pointed to the high price of bread, and in a second revolt that followed from the first, Andrea's son Pagnotto roused the crowds on street corners by insulting them: "You dogs, dogs, dogs; you who die of starvation; you who have scraped for what ought to be given to you for ten shillings a bushel;[99] even I can make only a morsel out of you, you vile bunch."[100] Three years later, Siena had its own version of the same. Spinelloccio, the son of a lord of the Tolomei clan, led the *popolo minuto* of Siena's poorest neighborhood, d'Ovile, to overthrow the government. Their chant pointed to the material cause of their discontent: "Long live the people and death to those who make us starve." The chronicler further comments that all of Tuscany was suffering great shortages and as a result the poor from Florence, Pistoia, San Gimignano, Colle, and various other places from Siena's *contado* had crowded into its city walls.[101]

Food shortages as a spark of revolt were not limited to conditions of overpopulation before the Black Death or to Tuscany. According to Matteo Villani, scarcity was felt throughout Italy in 1353. At Gaeta, these conditions propelled the "minuto popolo" to take up arms and "kill as many rich merchants as they could."[102] The same shortage caused greater disturbances in Rome. Because the government failed to move grain from its hinterland (the Maremma) to the city, the "popolo" assailed the Palace of the Senators in the Campidoglio, chasing one senator out, an Orsini, and killing another, a Colonna (members of two of Rome's most powerful families). By these means, "the people could then endure the famine more sweetly."[103] As we have seen, scarcity may have given rise to the first revolt of the Sienese Company of the Caterpillar in 1370.[104] Furthermore, food shortages formed the background *(sub colore caristie)* when the *popolo* of Naples rioted against the nobility's control of certain neighborhoods *(platea)* and the city's government.[105] After the fall of the Government of the Minor Guilds in Florence, ex-Ciompi attempted to regain their guilds on several occasions in August and September 1383 with the cry, *"Vivano le vinti quatro arti et muogano li tradeturii che ce fanno morire de fame."*[106] But this may have been just a stock slogan; according to statistics compiled by Richard Goldthwaite, grain prices did not rise sharply in 1383. Instead, they would not spike upward until the end of this decade.[107]

In 1389, "many citizens" of Padua revolted against Milanese control. The chronicler pointed to two causes, "their bad treatment" at the hands of the Visconti governors and the great shortage of foodstuffs.[108] Similarly, in 1405, the Veronesi had two reasons for revolting against their present lords and handing their city over to the Venetians—the current war and the accompanying scarcity of grain and presence of famine conditions.[109] Finally, in the same year a combination of interconnected causes—war, flooding of the Po, plague, and famine—led to rioting in Ferrara, but instead of posing a direct threat to their rulers, many Ferraresi simply left the city and crowded into Venice.[110]

Food shortages and destitution were among the causes of several tax revolts of southern France from 1378 to 1381 in Montpellier, Lodève, Le Puy, and Béziers.[111] In the most serious of the southern revolts, the 1379 revolt against royal officials at Montpellier, its local chronicler commented that "[t]he people [*pobol*] were already entirely devastated, broken by the great dearth that had run through this region for a long time" before Charles V quadrupled their hearth tax.[112] Yet revolts and social movements that arose over grain, even when combined with those that took other forms but were sparked by scarcity (among other causes), remain rare (24 of 1,112), 2 percent of the cases. One contemporary from the ruling classes saw the relationship between food shortage and rioting as pointing in the very opposite direction to that often assumed by modern historians: rather than stimulating revolt, scarcity dampened its likelihood. According to an anonymous chronicler, the Florentine *popolo minuto* in 1390 hated their bishop, Lord Nofri, because he reputedly advised the governors of Florence: "If you want to rule and maintain power, keep the people starving."[113]

In conclusion, urban revolts confronted a wide range of economic questions and used economic weapons such as the strike and workingmen's fraternities and other organizations. Yet seldom did the revolts of artisans or workers directly attack their employers. Instead, their riots turned on politics and confronted the state with assaults against the arrogance, violence, and corruption of ruling aristocrats and merchant oligarchies. Further, they were often bent on political inclusion, legitimizing workers' guilds and incorporating disenfranchised workers and artisans into governments as citizens with rights to hold the highest offices in the land. By contrast, grain riots and struggles by the destitute to acquire bread and other basic commodities, ascribed by some modern historians to have been the principal form of collective protest in preindustrial societies, are almost wholly missing from the sources of the late Middle Ages. When riots over grain occurred, rather than being spontaneous uprisings of the starving, they were attacks by groups such as clerics and students on royal policy or by artisans using grain symbolically to embarrass and bring down a city-state's government. In less than a handful of cases do we hear desperate cries from crowds clamoring for bread, and in these cases, their rage was quickly mollified by measured actions and the state's use of charity.

In a similar vein, other revolts that at first sight appear economic in character, such as ones that attacked monetary policy, trade restrictions, rising rents, or industrial practices, also confronted states, not employers. Besides, even when these "economic" protests are combined with the handful or so that rallied popular forces against landlords or urban employers, they still comprise a mere fraction of the protests and movements seen in the medieval sources. For Liège, the early-twentieth-century historian Godefroid Kurth went even further: "the workers of the Liégeois . . . made no economic demands. In their numerous struggles with the prince and the privileged classes, they battled exclusively for political rights."[114] So what were the revolts that filled the narratives of late medieval chroniclers and archival ledgers?

CHAPTER 4

Varieties of Revolt

Typologies of revolt can be devised by various means and across different grids—according to who participated, what was done, the causes, and the rebels' objectives and targets. Even the most basic of these divisions—peasant versus urban revolts—were not always clearly delineated, as we have seen with widespread revolts in Flanders, 1297–1304 and even more so in 1323–1328. These revolts and others brought commoners in towns and the countryside together against common enemies and for common goals. Nonetheless, such heuristic divisions of revolt are necessary to make sense of the enormous diversity of protests during the later Middle Ages. We have made another broad distinction in popular protest—those whose aims were principally political as opposed to ones that redressed explicitly economic grievances, in which peasants or artisans combated landlords or employers—and found the latter to be relatively rare. So if late medieval popular rebellions were seldom about economic gains and still fewer pitted peasants or workers against landlords or bosses, what forms did popular protest usually assume?

Revolts of the People

The most numerous of these urban revolts were ones in which an urban "people"—variously called the "popolo," "pedites" "habitans," "bourgeois" or "peuple"—attacked aristocratic oligarchies, governments of magnates, or the local ruling viscount or count and aspired to gain self-government or regain recently threatened liberties, such as prerogatives to set and collect their own taxes. At least 311 of these can be counted in my samples. One of the earliest of them involved the rock-and-mud–tossing *pedites*, or *popolo*, who ousted the *milites* in Piacenza in 1090. Most of these revolts occurred in the larger city-states of northern and central Italy, including at least eight in Parma, eleven in Genoa, seventeen in Bologna, twenty-two in Florence, and twenty-six in Rome. But smaller towns also had their rebellions against aristocratic regimes. On 3 May 1322 the *popolo* of Osimo in the Marche sued for peace with the church, rioted against the rectors under the jurisdiction of Count Federico of Urbino, and ran these officers out of town.[1] The "people" quickly grew tired of their new rulers and, with the help of the *popolo* of Fermo, rebelled against the church several months later; they then helped their neighbors at Fabriano to do the same.[2]

Places further south, although generally taken by historians to have had weak organizations of the *popolo*,[3] also had such revolts against dominant aristocratic regimes of either the church or local aristocracies. In fact, Rome, with its popular organizations and militias based on neighborhoods *(rioni)*, experienced the greatest number of popular insurrections against aristocratic rule, whether of the pope, his legates, or senatorial families such as the Orsini, Colonna, and Savelli. Often these revolts were successful, as when the people expelled their senators Giovanni di Polo in August 1237,[4] Lord William of Eboli during the famine of 1329,[5] and Luca Savelli in 1353;[6] or when the Roman *popolo* forced the pope and all his cardinals to flee Rome in 1405.[7] In efforts to extend their self-government and limit the arrogance and abuse of foreign cardinals, aristocratic senators, or the pope, the rallying cries of the Roman people were much the same as those of communes to the north: "Long live the People" and later in 1410, "Long live the People and Liberty."[8] Revolts of the *popolo* flared still farther south, as in Naples in 1374. Then, "the people" and groups of adolescents marched under their banners against the noble families of the neighborhoods of Capuane, Nidi, and other squares, chanting "Long live the Queen, long live the People, and death to the traitors." In battles for rule over these various squares, the people forced the nobles to negotiate and share power with thirty-six commoners from the city's three districts, who were elected by "the people."[9] The *popolo* had a strong presence in L'Aquila as well, where they led eight revolts against local counts or the kings of Naples between 1263 and 1415. By allying with either the local count or the king of Naples against the other, these revolts of the *popolo* usually ended with success.[10]

In France, the crown and the configuration of power between cities and counts meant that struggles within towns would be different from revolts of the *popolo* in Italian city-states. Nonetheless, city bourgeois or citizens as well as those further down the social ladder, the *menu peuple,* fought for political rights and supremacy. In these samples the earliest such rebellions came in Marseilles in 1257, when the bourgeois fought against the seigniorial rights imposed on them by Charles *(Kalle)*, count of Anjou and Provence and brother of Louis IX. To preserve their rights, the bourgeois rebelled against his rule, killing or throwing out his soldiers and officers. But with a large army supported by the crown, Count Charles surrounded the city and starved them into submission.[11] Nonetheless, five years later, the inhabitants *(Marsilienses)* rebelled again to restore their rights, killing his officers, but again without success.[12]

Similar rebellions between the "people" or the "bourgeois" of cities against encroachments by their viscounts took place in other areas of France during the late thirteenth century. In 1274 Countess Margaret, daughter of the Duke of Burgundy, tried to extend her suzerainty over the town of Limoges. The people rebelled but without success. Two years later, however, they revolted again and expelled her from her castle.[13] Several chroniclers reported Valenciennes' revolt in 1291 against the count of Hainault, who "tried to oppress them unjustly." By turning to count William of Flanders for protection, the people *(gentes)* "shamefully" ejected their count from town and were able to change their lordship.[14]

After the collapse of the alliance between Count Guy de Dampierre and the cities of Flanders against Philip the Fair's incursions into comitial power (1297–1304), waves of revolts by the cities of Flanders against their counts more or less structured the political history of fourteenth-century Flanders. These were revolts from Courtrai against the count in 1305, all Flanders in 1314, and Bruges in 1322, followed by most of the cities of Flanders for the next six years. Ghent under Jacob van Artevelde rebelled in 1338, as did most of Flanders in 1339, and Ghent again against the encroachments of Louis de Male in 1348–1349. Revolts took place in Ypres, Ghent, and other towns in 1359–1361; Ghent in 1364 and 1368; and then Ghent followed by most of Flanders from 1379 to their defeat at Rozebeke in 1382—a revolt that extended as far south as Douai. Before 1297, the narrative sources for Flanders also report conflicts between city dwellers and the count, even if they appear less frequently. City dwellers even went against Count Guy of Dampierre, later to be defended by artisans and peasants in the anti-French revolts of 1297–1304. In 1286, the tower where Bruges's judiciary met and that held the city's charters accidentally burnt to the ground. Count Guy took the occasion to strip Bruges of its privileges, "returning the city to its pristine state of servitude [*et voluit Brugenses in pristinam servitutem redigere*]." The people of

Bruges rose up against him and against the percolation of aldermen in a revolt called *moerlemay*, because it occurred in May. Afterward many revolts of commoners *(populares)* "followed the example of Bruges and spread throughout Flanders."[15]

In addition to counts and viscounts, commoners and bourgeois in late medieval France and Flanders also turned against their local bishops or archbishops, as in Sens in 1315, when the bishop's officers harassed those of the province. "Many of the people [*populus*]" congregated and revolted against the archbishop, who excommunicated them. In response they elected their own king, pope, and cardinals; absolved themselves of the excommunication; and ("going beyond all limits") administered the sacraments themselves or forced priests to perform them. Finally, the real king of France intervened and arrested the lay leaders.[16] In Liège the people revolted against their bishop at least seventeen times between 1253 and 1384, often with success.[17]

Revolts against the Crown

Beyond regional governors, urban protest struck against royal power in kingdoms such as France, Sicily, or Naples and against the larger international powers, the Holy Roman Emperor, and the pope. As we have seen, in struggles such as the commoners' tax revolt in Rouen of 1291, the attack was as much against the crown as it was against the local bourgeoisie, who finally repulsed the revolt and punished the insurgents. Similarly, the revolts of 1323–1328 and the strikes of Jacob and later his son Philippe van Artevelde attacked the count in the first instance but ultimately turned against the prerogatives and armies of the French crown. The principal target of a substantial number (87) of these revolts opposed the crown or royal regional officers. As we shall see, these revolts hardly showed the awe and respect for royalty that modern historians often claim was embedded in rebels' mental structures; nor did these rebels distinguish between "the good king" and his corrupt officers:[18] genuine heart-felt hatred and disrespect for a king or queen is easy to find.

Seven of these revolts were in the kingdom of Naples, three of which erupted in the years immediately before the Black Death, during the reign of Queen Joanna (1343–1381). The first of these stemmed from the mysterious murder of her husband Andrea in 1345. The rage of the populace might be seen as showing affection for the dead king, but it hardly showed any respect for the royal office or for the legitimate bloodline, which belonged to Queen

Joanna, daughter of the previous king, Robert. After catching one of the conspirators and torturing him to confess, Andrea's brother, Lord Charles of Durazzo, king of Hungary, with a great mass of the Neapolitan *popolo*, dug up Andrea's grave and found a noose around his neck. Immediately, both groups commissioned flags to rally their discontent and outrage. The nobleman's bore a silver sword dripping blood draped against a black field,[19] while the commoners depicted the dead king painted with the noose around his neck. With this banner the Neapolitan *popolo* marched eight miles out to the queen's castle at Aversa, where she and her coconspirators were guarded. With their chants, the Neapolitan crowd showed their respect: "Death to the traitors and to the queen, the whore."[20]

Two years later (25 February 1347), Tommaso of Iacca (called Cutinone) a goldsmith, was beheaded because he had made the flag depicting the hanged Andrea. Unlike its maker, however, the flag lived on to lead another riot, in which the "Neapolitan people" destroyed the gates leading to the royal castle and killed a young nobleman.[21] Further, a royal charter issued by the queen refers to "earlier revolts" and adds to the details of the one above, stating that the siege of the castle lasted two days and the royal armory was sacked.[22] In May a cobbler led a third revolt against the queen. He was hanged; again the flag of the hanged king was at the head of their antiroyal revolt.[23]

With the papal schism set off by the election in Rome of two rival popes in 1378, Joanna again became the target of popular protest because of her Provençal origins and allegiance with the French papal contender, Clement VII (Robert of Geneva), against the Italian choice, Urban VI. Civil war between the French-leaning Neapolitan aristocracy and the populace continued even after the queen's death and the succession of Charles of Durazzo to the throne.[24]

Such signs of disrespect to royals were not limited to women or to southern Italy. France was the principal theater of antiroyal revolt. Before the fourteenth century, however, such revolts occurred rarely, and when they did, they were often part of movements that sprang from local grievances, as in Rouen in 1292. Only after the bourgeois called in royal troops did this revolt develop into an attack on the royal castle and the king's officers. As with the revolts in Flanders, matters changed with the aggressive territorial aggrandizement of Philip the Fair, whose tax policies triggered revolts in various regions of France. Outside Flanders the major area of this protest was the south of France. In 1306 two clerics led an urban revolt against royal power in Carcassonne.[25] In 1310 Lyon rebelled against the king, storming his royal castle of Saint-Just.[26] In June and August 1313, armed rebellion raged throughout Languedoc, uniting the three estates against the king's subsidies on foodstuffs to raise 300,000 livres to fight his wars. By 1314, the antitax revolts against the king's efforts to wage war on Flanders had spread throughout most of his kingdom, even if these (unlike the earlier revolts in the south) were limited largely to parliamentary actions of the three estates. These protests succeeded, forcing Philip to abandon his new subsidies and his Flemish wars.[27]

A second cluster of antiroyal revolts came on the eve of the Jacquerie and centered on Paris. According to the continuator of Richard the Scot's chronicle, Étienne Marcel congregated and mobilized over 30,000 armed men to boycott and protest against new money issued by the crown in 1356, which led to popular rioting through the streets of Paris.[28] Better known is Marcel's assault on royal dignity on 22 February 1358, when he assembled and armed three thousand tradesmen of Paris, marched to the Louvre, and butchered two of Regent Charles's marshals and chief advisers in his private apartment before his eyes. Afterward, the people armed and rioted, chasing many of the king's officers from town.[29] Then, during the Jacquerie the Parisians joined the rustics with military forays into the countryside, which from the Parisians' standpoint were less an attack on the nobility per se than on the policies of Charles and his blockade of Paris.[30] Finally, following the suppression of the Jacques, the "bourgeois" and the people of Rouen besieged their royal castle.[31] Similar antiroyal attacks, initiated by town mayors, city councils, and bourgeois rabble-rousers can be found in other cities during the Jacquerie—at Sens, Senlis, Amiens, Caen, and most dramatically and disastrously at Meaux.[32]

Riots against royal power continued through the fourteenth century and intensified during the first two decades of the fifteenth. In September 1365, the weaver Jehan de Semerie led two to three hundred tradesmen *(mestiers)* in Tournai, who rioted with their trade banners against the governor and king's men under the king's banners.[33] In 1367 those of Montpellier protested against infringements made by the king's lieutenant in Languedoc of their town's franchises and liberties.[34] The cluster of revolts in 1378–1382 in France began in the south, first against Charles V's tax increases and then against those of his son, Charles VI. The king's embodiment in these towns and the countryside—his royal officers—were most often the victims. The bloodiest of the southern revolts happened in Montpellier on 25 October 1379, when townsmen massacred more than eighty royal officers, dumping their bodies ignominiously down city wells. Many of these victims were high-ranking chancellors of the household of the king's brother, lieutenant for Languedoc, the Duke of Anjou.[35] Soon afterward, nearby Clermont de Lodève followed Montpellier's example and rose up against royal authority.[36] Two years later, a wider arc of violence spread against the crown through Languedoc and the county of Foix, with revolts "in many towns but especially at Narbonne, Nîmes, Béziers, and Toulouse."[37]

Better covered in the chroniclers and better known to historians are the revolts against taxation and royal power in the north, principally in the cities of Rouen and Paris: the revolts of the *Harelle* and the *Maillotins,* or Hammer men. These two revolts of early 1382 had been preceded by several others in these cities that erupted in 1380 when the young Charles was still under the shadow of his corrupt uncles. These revolts were sparked by the crown's need to raise war revenues after Charles V's extraordinary deathbed legacy that ended the hearth tax. To circumvent the problem, the regent devised new taxes on consumption—the subsidies. Along with the brutal practices of corrupt tax officials, who, according to king's own chronicler, Michel Pintoin, "pillaged the entire diocese of Paris with all the atrocities that one enemy levies against another,"[38] the new taxes led to widespread urban revolt. Against the claims of modern historians, none of the chronicles or letters of remission show rebels making the supposed distinction between the king and his corrupt advisors, even though in this case such a distinction would have been warranted: immediately after Charles V's death, the new regent's principal advisers, his uncles, busied themselves robbing the royal till for all they could grab. Their actions exacerbated the already deep financial crisis left by Charles V, which military threats from the English were compounding daily.[39]

Tax collectors and other local royal officers were the rebel's first targets. Afterward, attacks on Jews, who had been given special protection in forty houses by the king, were an added affront to his authority and dignity. As his chronicler Pintoin emphasized with the tax revolts of 1380, few obeyed the royal ordinance to return stolen goods after the crowds had broken into the houses of Jews in the area the king had cordoned off for the Jews' protection and housing.[40] Pintoin makes the connection between the massacres of the Jews and disrespect for the king more explicit during the Hammer men's revolt on 1 March 1382, when the protest against the Charles' new taxes spilled over into anti-Semitic violence: "the wickedest went after the Jews, who the king protected; they killed some and stole their most valuable possessions. Adding to their infamy, they felt no shame in violating the house of the king, incurring for a second time the crime of treason."[41]

Still more biting and explicit were the attacks and mockery leveled against the king in antifiscal riots at Rouen, which erupted the week before the Hammer men's rage. According to Pintoin the crowd was composed mostly of apprentices and journeymen;[42] according to the local chronicler Pierre Cochon, they were a mixture of "the scum as well as notables, drapers, and people of cheap cloth."[43] At any rate, they attacked the abbey of Saint-Ouën and other large ecclesiastical foundations across the city, which possessed special privileges over Rouen, some dating to Merovingian times, others from recently granted royal charters. The insurgents not only ripped these to shreds (as often happened in popular rebellion, especially with tax revolts); they also forced the abbot and monks of Saint-Ouën to draft a new charter renouncing their royal privileges.[44] Further, the commoners engaged in street theater ridiculing the king and his authority.

> More than two hundred of the most insolent sort, workshop assistants in various crafts,[45] were emboldened no doubt by having drunk too much wine. By force, they seized a simple bourgeois, a rich vendor of cloth, nicknamed the fat one because of his obesity. Impertinently, they placed his name at the top of their acts and threw themselves headlong into this insane enterprise without any calculation of where it might end. Immediately, they made him their king. They raised him up onto a throne as though a monarch, placed it on a chariot, and paraded him through the city, parodying the acclamations that would be made to a king. When they arrived at the market square, they asked him if the *plebes* should be freed from the yoke of all the subsidies, and he granted it. This franchise of short duration was made public through the city by the cry of a herald—a scene so ridiculous that it even justifiably made prudent men laugh. A huge crowd of the most wretched sort quickly ran towards him and forced him to listen to their pleas as he sat in judgment. If anyone conceived of a riotous act and asked him his advice, he would be compelled to approve it and say: "Do it; do it." Then, driven not solely by audacity but by a beastly rage, they rose up against the royal tax collectors, killed them mercilessly, and unreasonably divided their belongings among themselves.[46]

Revolts against the king did not disappear after the cluster of revolts in 1378–1382; instead, they increased in number during the early fifteenth century. First, there was an antiroyal tax revolt in Reims in 1403[47] and then civil war between the Armagnacs and Burgundians. In the Cabochiens' or butchers' revolts of 1413, the insurgents imprisoned and mercilessly murdered many of the king's relatives. Further, in 1411, popular insurgents threatened the king's safety and ordered the officers of his relatives—the Dukes of Orléans, Berry, and Alençon—to leave the city.[48] Paris was not alone in its threats to the king and disobedience to his ordinances. In 1414 the king dispatched several officers of his court to Noyon to prepare lodging for himself and his noble entourage. The city's "inhabitants," however, held a general assembly and decided to refuse them entry, bitterly offending the king. That night a fire just happened to destroy "the beautiful mansions of the town," where the king and his men were supposed to stay. The king fined those responsible for such "disobedience."[49] In the same year, Compiègne and Soissons followed Noyon's example with similar acts of royal disrespect, but their leaders received stiffer penalties, particularly in Soissons, where the entire town rose in revolt. The king's men burnt the town and beheaded its principal leader, Enguerrand de Bournonville.[50] In 1417, the king ordered the bourgeois of Rouen to receive and negotiate a peace with the English troops in their environs. At this news, the *menu peuple* and workers *(minoris populi et mechanicis artibus)* "assembled in great numbers and madly charged through the streets and squares of the city, clamoring that they would never obey these injunctions nor allow the foreign brigands to enter their city." They stole the keys to the city gates, chased out the royal guards, killed the king's lieutenant and chief officer of the city and other royal officers, and commandeered the watch over the city night and day, swearing an oath *(sacramentis terribilibus)* to maintain the city's safety and to preserve its ancient liberties.[51] In the same year, the citizens of Amiens chased their royal officer from town.[52] In 1418, after the people of Paris "wickedly murdered" the count of Armagnac, five to six hundred of the *menu peuple* rioted through the city, killing the king's officers and his treasurers and forcing the king to retreat to Meaux.[53] Finally, in 1420, Sens unsuccessfully rebelled against royal control.[54]

Revolts against the Emperor and the Pope

North of Naples city councils rarely came under royal control, but they had their equivalent to antiroyal revolts in resisting the authority of supra-regional kings, Holy Roman Emperors, or the papacy. The chronicles describe at least twenty-two revolts against the emperor that contained some popular element or in which entire cities turned against imperial power. They happened throughout the period of our analysis, from a revolt of Parma against imperial control in 1229[55] to a revolt of the people at Viterbo in 1414 against King Ladis-

lao of Naples and his representative in the city, Giovanni Gatto.[56] They
occurred in major cities such as in Milan, when its citizens revolted against
excessive taxes imposed by Emperor Henry VII in 1311,[57] and in mountain
hamlets of Lunigiana and Garfagnana, where villagers resisted Frederick II's
policies of aggrandizement in 1247.[58] Most of these revolts were in the north
of Italy, but they also occurred in the south, as with Messina's revolt against
Frederick II and his imposition of the Constitutions of Melfi in 1232, which
stripped the city of its corporate liberties.[59] Often these revolts came with an
emperor's entry into Italy to be crowned at Rome, as with Charles IV's movements in 1354–1355. The most reported of these was a popular revolt against
Charles in May 1355, while he and his troops were sojourning in Pisa. With
the help of the Florentines the Pisan *popolo* set fire to his palace, which
revealed the emperor and his empress with no clothes as both fled in the nude
in the middle of the night. Ultimately, the emperor prevailed and punished
the Pisans, but not without severe casualties to his Bohemian soldiers.[60]

More frequent in the chronicles and widespread through Italy were revolts
against papal rule. My samples report at least ninety-seven of them from the
chronicles, but the actual number of individual revolts is more difficult to
count: for instance, revolts against the cardinal legate for Romagna swept
across the entire region in August and September 1333 and expanded into a
large number of town and village uprisings against their local aristocratic
regimes.[61] Still more difficult to count are the waves of revolts against the
papacy from 1375 to 1378 that according to a chronicler of Forlì, stretched
from Lombardy to Puglia.[62] According to a Milanese chronicler, within a few
months at the end of 1375, "all the cities and villages of Romagna, the Marche,
the Duchy of Spoleto, the Papal States [*Patrimonio*], and the Campania of
Rome, then under the dominion of the priests, threw off the church's yoke,
went under the flag of liberty, and made themselves free." Along with Giovanni de Mussis of Piacenza,[63] this chronicler counted sixty cities that revolted
during the last month of 1375 alone.[64] Others made lists of the places that
revolted in 1375, such as an anonymous chronicler of Padua, who named
thirty-eight cities and territories as well as several places left vague and open-
ended, such as "the entire province of Galeata with many walled villages
[*castri*]."[65] The anonymous diarist of the Florentine Machiavelli family was
the most meticulous, drawing up several lists of towns and villages in revolt
during the winter of 1375 through 1376 and giving the precise days, even
the hours of the uprisings. He named eighty places in revolt against papal
rule; some place names were followed by phrases such as "e ogni suo castello"
and "e suo contado," which would have included not only many villages but

also towns.[66] According to a chronicle from Rimini, by 28 March 1376, 1,577 walled towns and villages *(buone castella)* from Milan to Naples "had thrown off the rule of the rectors, not counting small or tower villages [*delle piccolo e di certe torricelle*]."[67] These were not the usual Guelf-Ghibelline factional conflicts between local nobilities. Instead, entire populations rebelled against the church because of "the loss of justice," the church's "misrule," and its "excessive taxes." In these places, the insurgents replaced papal tyranny with new governments of the *popolo* and elected officials. As in the anonymous Machiavelli's ode of praise for these revolts, "they all cried out for liberty."[68]

Revolts against Territorial Dominance

In addition to these two overarching international empires—that of the pope and the Holy Roman Emperor—the city-states of Italy themselves constituted territories, which humanists by the early fifteenth century called *imperii* or empires.[69] These city-states lorded over subject villages, towns, and even cities, and, in the case of Genoa and Venice, possessed foreign colonies. The chroniclers described at least twenty-one village revolts against their dominant city-states. These could have also been labeled as peasant revolts, however, and do not include various territorial revolts, such as revolts of villagers in the three valleys of Genoa. Further, the chronicles certainly underreported such village revolts, as can be readily seen in the territory of Florence at the beginning of the fifteenth century. According to archival petitions, as many as 282 villages rose up against Florence in the years 1402–1404 alone.[70] Although Giovanni Morelli and the Minerbetti chronicler mention that such rumblings were spreading through the *contado* of Florence, neither reported a single village by name (and thus not a single one of these revolts entered my samples).

By contrast, the Bolognese chroniclers specified several villages that in 1401 and 1402 attempted to throw off Bologna's domination and recorded the villagers' rallying calls and flags. Some carried the symbols and cried the chants of "the *popolo*, the guilds, and liberty"; others chanted against the ruling Bentivoglio and carried the flags of their enemies, the Malatesta lords of Romagna and the Duke of Milan. While the war between Milan and Florence opened revolutionary possibilities for the mountain districts of Florence in 1401–1402, village revolts against the Bentivoglio came from the plains. In less than two years the lowland village of San Giovanni in Persiceto, northwest of Bologna, rebelled four times. Other villagers from Minerbio (near Modena), Poggio

Renatico (on the borders with Ferrara), and Castello d'Argile and Sant'Agata in the plains north of Bologna also turned against Bentivoglio domination.[71]

The revolts of cities against their dominant powers during the fourteenth and fifteenth centuries clustered into specific periods and were sparked by major political upheavals. As with village revolts, these subject towns often sided with the dominant city-state's enemies or sympathized with those of the city-state's old regime, even when the new government was a more broad-based one of the *popolo*. Once the regime of the Nine in Siena had been toppled in 1355,[72] Siena's dependent towns Casole, Massa Marittima, Montalcino, Montepulciano, and Grosseto (in 1355 and again in 1356) rebelled, attacked the Sienese-controlled castles dominating their towns, and kicked out or killed all Sienese citizens and their podestà.[73] However, the Nine had not been immune to such attacks: the towns of Massa, Magliano, and Montepulciano had revolted in the years just after the Black Death,[74] and Massa would revolt at least twice again in 1368 (during a period of another regime and of renewed political turmoil in the capital city, Siena) and again in 1378.[75] In fact, from the chronicles, Siena's control over its subject towns appears to have been the most volatile in Italy. Of thirty-five such revolts, nineteen were staged by towns under Siena's control. Nor was this precarious hold over its subject towns drastically different between the long and relatively stable period of the Nine's control (the longest-lasting government of any Italian city-state) and the period of extreme political volatility that ensued after the Nine's fall until the early fifteenth century. Two city revolts occurred before the Nine's coming to power in 1287, seven during its tenure in office, and ten afterward.

Colonial Revolt

Not all colonial conflicts can readily be seen as social revolts. In some cases, it was a matter of one government struggling against another, as with the battles between the kings of Hungary and Venice over ports along the Dalmatian coast during the second half of the fourteenth century. However, chroniclers describe colonies often mobilizing their entire populations across social barriers to rid themselves of Venetian or Genoese control. As with struggles of the *popolo* in Italian city-states, negotiations and alliances with another foreign power were often the most effective means of achieving liberty, or at least better conditions of rule. The vast majority of the colonial disputes in my samples involved Venice and its sea empire (32 of 35). By comparison, Genoa seems to have been less troubled overseas, or perhaps its chroniclers publicized them less: only two popular revolts in Corsica (not counting those of the aristocracy) and one on the Island of Chios off the coast of Turkey come to light. Most rebellious of the Venetian colonies was Zara (or *Jadera*), which had been the Byzantine capital of Dalmatia. The chroniclers of Venice even knew Zara's uprisings by their number in the sequence of revolts, counting eight of them from the mid-twelfth century to 1357, when Venice definitively lost the port to the local insurgents. After Zara's fall, the whole of Dalmatia followed, and as a consequence, the doge's title was shortened with "Dalmatiae atque Croatiae Dux e de cetero" lopped off.[76] The most widely reported of these colonial revolts was the seventh, when the Zaratini allied with the king of Hungary in 1345. The Venetians squashed the revolt by sending an infantry of 3,500. They then "tore down many houses and wrought other damage" to the city by building a bastion where Zara's central fountain had once stood, "to the great hatred of those of Zara."[77]

The longest and one of the bloodiest of the Venetian colonial revolts was an uprising at Trieste in September 1368 that lasted until November 1369. When a Venetian galley came to collect the "annual tribute" for the doge, rebels killed the captain and wounded others. "Not only did the Triestini do this, but worse, they refused to raise the flag [*stendardo*] of Saint Mark, which they were obliged to fly on the principal feast days in their main square. And for this," the Venetian historian Marino Sanuto concluded, "the doge decided to avenge the injury and send an armed force to Trieste." The Venetians sent in their galleys, built a bastion, and laid siege to the city, bombarding it with their catapults *(mangani)*, "creating great damage, breaking down palaces and the city walls, and killing men and women." But at night the men and women rebuilt and fortified their walls, making them stronger than before. Over a year later, "dying from starvation" from the Venetian blockade, the Triestini finally surrendered. The Venetians then built a "very beautiful and strong castle" along the seafront at Trieste's expense.[78]

Revolts of *Minores* against Merchants and Oligarchies

Revolts in France and Flanders not only united towns and villages against their regional lords but also divided them along class lines. As in Italian towns, the *minores* revolted against oligarchic city councils or against the bourgeois more generally. Often it is difficult to know whether these *minores* were artisans, who were citizens, like the Italian *popolo,* or were more like the Italian *popolo minuto*—without guild status or any political rights. In addition, revolts of *minores* in France and Flanders were rarely limited to the city alone; often an attack on the bourgeois would quickly develop into one against the count or the crown. For example, in 1270, the *minores* of the town of Cahors revolted against the bourgeois over taxes *(tallia)*, which led to an assault on the king's chief officer *(bajulum)* in the town: "shamefully they burnt down the home of one of the richest bourgeois of the city, killing him along with his daughters and servants." Further, they chased from town the chief officer and the prior of Brive-la-Gaillarde (Corrèze), whom the king had sent to investigate the case. Eventually, the king sent in his army, imprisoned many of the *minores,* hanged more than fifty, and banished four hundred.[79]

In the same vein, exactly who were the *plebes* who revolted and murdered their mayor on the bridge at Rouen in 1281,[80] or the *menuz* who on 5 March 1356 revolted against the "gros" at Arras, killing sixteen of the "most notable citizens" on Saturday and another four on Monday, and banishing all those "who were not of the city"? As with many of the revolts of the *popolo* in Italy, often these *menuz,* after victory, became *seigneurs* and masters of their town, as happened in Arras in 1356: the king, unlike the earlier occurrence at Rouen, did not intervene to restore the bourgeois.[81] More revolts of the "people" occurred in Paris (54) than in any other city found in these samples for France or Flanders, and was second only to Florence (64 revolts). In addition to the most famous of these—the Parisian revolt of Étienne Marcel, the Hammermen sedition of 1382, and the Cabochiens' (butchers') revolt in 1413—there were revolts against royal manipulations of money in 1306 and 1356, as described above. The causes and objectives of the earliest of these Parisian revolts are difficult to discern. During Lent in 1229, "a terrible and cruel war" broke out between the clergy and the laity, which left few clerics in the city. In addition, the most eminent of the masters left town.[82] Nonetheless, in 1252—forty to fifty years before Italian chroniclers began to distinguish the *popolo minuto* from the *popolo,* first in Florence then elsewhere—the *menu peuple* of Paris and its suburbs protested against the provost of Paris and the city council. They objected to the provost's corrupt selling off of public property to his rich bourgeois cronies and his "harass[ment of] commoners" in other ways. The *menu peuple*'s protest appears to have been nonviolent: their weapon was migration from the king's territory. On this occasion the king, Louis IX, intervened on the people's side, first asking the bishop of Paris to reform matters and, after he did nothing, replacing the corrupt provost himself with a new one, Étienne Boileau (Boiliaue), who threw the malefactors out of town. Louis then abolished serfdom on the rural domains of the region of Paris.[83]

Nor were urban revolts of the *menu peuple* limited to the north of France and Flanders. In 1310 Philip the Fair imposed "a huge subsidy" on Languedoc without the consent of the three estates. A knight, Pontius of Boissaco, rode through the province of Toulouse to solicit support "in favor of the people," to repeal the tax, and to rebel against the king. He was caught and sentenced to be hanged and then decapitated in the square of Saint Stephen on 1 December 1310, with "a theater dressed in black erected for the occasion." From the neighborhood gate of Narbonne, three hundred masked and armed men began to riot: clamoring for liberty, a butcher freed the knight. The crowd then went through the streets breaking into houses and robbing. The city magistrates did not dare respond, but later many of the rebels were sentenced to be hanged in their absence; others left for Aragon.[84]

As these examples show, one category of revolt easily overlapped another. After revolts of the *popolo* or bourgeois against the arrogance and rule of local aristocracies, the next-largest category of urban popular revolt (112 cases) was one in which the protagonists were more clearly defined as disenfranchised urban laborers or craftsmen, the *menu peuple* or *popolo minuto*. For many of these (as opposed to vaguer revolts of the people), the chroniclers specified the occupational groups involved. The most important of these—the butchers and cloth workers of Bruges in 1302; the peasants and artisans throughout Flanders, 1323–1328; the Florentine Ciompi of 1378; and the *Harelle* of Rouen and the *Maillotins* of Paris in 1382—have been described many times. Many others, however, have received scant attention from modern historians. One example is a weavers' revolt in Douai in 1280, against the town council, when workers killed eleven aldermen *(eschevins)* and "many other bourgeois of the town." The count of Flanders had to intervene; three weavers were hanged and eighteen permanently exiled.[85] Similarly, the weavers of Tournai rebelled in 1281 against their town council without success,[86] but in 1307, the commoners, whom the chronicler specified as "weavers, the poor, fullers, and others," were successful. Against the introduction of a new tax *(tallia)*, they "beat up the tax collectors, then congregated and went to the city gates, where they hanged them and threw their bodies into the moat." Immediately afterward, "all the other commoners and combatants spurred one another on to greater feats of wickedness and amazingly continued to do so throughout the day." But despite these offenses, "which rightly stunned the governors, the rich, and powerful" of Tournai, sending "lords, the bishop, prelates, and parish priests fleeing as fast as they could," the conflict ended in a negotiated settlement. Even though the king of France had intervened with secret agents, the commoners imprisoned the old rectors, put them on trial, and elected new ones by an assembly of the entire town, including "magnates, the middling sorts [*mediocribus*], and the little people [*parvis*]." By contrast with the revolt of 1281, none of the commoners were tried or prosecuted.[87]

Taxes were also behind the commoners' *(minor populus)* uprising at Rouen in 1292 against their magistrates and the king's officers. They assailed the city's castle, destroyed the house where taxes were collected, and threw the money into the city's squares. But at Rouen the commoners were not as successful as at Tournai; the mayor and bourgeois of the city prevailed, "hanging very many of the insurgents and imprisoning many others."[88]

Struggles for power in Italy, in which chroniclers distinguished a lower class or *popolo minuto* from and against other commoners—the *popolo* or *popolani*—came later, and its earliest examples are from Bologna, not Tuscany. In 1289, this lower class of craftsmen called "the people without underpants [*appellati popolari, zoè popolo senza braghe*]," distinguished as "the lowest of the low [*de più ville condicione che costoro*]" opposed the chief magistrate of Bologna, the podestà, in the main square of the city, threw two rocks at him, and then escorted him to the city walls, where they kicked him out of town. As with many of these revolts, no repercussions or penalties followed.[89]

Although much rarer than in northern Italy, the *popolo minuto* can also be seen in action south of Rome, even in minor towns such as Gaeta, north of Naples. In December 1353, with food shortages throughout most of Italy,[90] the "minuto popolo" of Gaeta, "out of hatred of the good and rich merchants," took up arms and charged madly through the city, attempting to kill any upper-class citizens *(maggiori)* they could get their hands on "and in the thick of things without any mercy murdered twelve of them, great, honest, and good merchants." Others fled to places "where the madness of the people could not reach." To execute justice, King Louis of Naples, rode into town, "but only the weakest were executed; the rest bribed the courts and were let off the hook,"[91] which suggests that the low here may not have been "the lowest of the low," as in Bologna fifty-five years earlier.

Throughout the period studied here, chroniclers described several other seemingly senseless, mad revolts of outraged workers and craftsmen—urban Jacquerie—which by the prejudicial reports of upper-class chroniclers appeared to have had no aims other than killing the rich, with no causes beyond animal hatred. According to the religieux de Saint-Denis, horrible murders and rioting engulfed Paris following the assassination of the duke of Armagnac; the "rabble killed over 1,500 men and women" on 12 June 1418.

On 21 August "this madness" reached the northern suburb of Paris, the town of Saint-Denis, where the lowest of the workers *(vilibus mechanicis artibus)* rioted, "murdered indiscriminately," and burnt down houses.[92] Yet, despite chroniclers' elitist prejudices, such reports of madness and sheer hatred can be counted on the fingers of one hand.

Women, Youth, and the Elderly

Beyond class and geography, modern sociological and historical categories would direct us to look for other divisions, principally ones of gender and, after that, age. On the first, revolts made up exclusively or primarily of women are wholly missing from these sources. Indeed, women hardly appear in any of these rebellions—a point to which we shall return in Chapter 6. Furthermore, we shall see that their absence cannot be attributed to chroniclers' total neglect in mentioning women, even of female commoners. They appear in religious movements, such as the Alleluia movement of 1233 and the flagellant movements in 1260, 1349, and 1400; and as heretics.[93] Most often women were the victims of war and acts of savage repression, as with the vengeance taken by the nobility after the Jacquerie of 1358 or the Breton soldiers' sack of Cesena in 1377.

More surprisingly, riots made up of and led by youth, adolescents, and even children were more common. First amongst these were student revolts, which could spill beyond the boundaries of the school or the university, as we have seen with the student-organized riot in 1343 against the king's shipment of grain from the territory of Orléans to Burgundy. Perceived miscarriages of justice against fellow students often sparked student revolts, as in Bologna in 1325, when a student was beheaded and his comrades left en masse for Imola;[94] or in Paris in 1304, when the provost of the merchants convicted and hanged a student. The students responded by refusing to attend classes in all faculties until the provost made amends according to their will. The students won, persuading Philip the Fair to intervene, which he did by forcing the provost to found two chapels at the university with a perpetual annual income of 40 livres.[95] On occasion, these injustices involved sex, as in Bologna in 1321, when a Catalonian student had an affair with the niece of the famous law professor, Giovanni d'Andrea, and was beheaded for it.[96] Other injustices touched politics on the international stage, as in Toulouse in 1407, when a friar minor organized a revolt of over a hundred students to protest the appointment of Pierre Ravaut as archbishop of Toulouse by Pope

Benedict XIII,[97] whom they called the antipope. This appointment replaced their own candidate—provost of the cathedral and professor of law at the university, who had been elected by their chapter.[98]

The participants in these university revolts were not always exclusively adolescents or young clerics, as we might assume. They could be younger. One of the most dramatic of these conflicts had dire consequences, even for members of the royal family, and lasting effects on the typography of Paris. It was sparked by the chortling of small children, who threw rocks and mud at the Duke of Savoy's valets, which startled their horses, causing some to fall off.[99] Several days later on 14 July 1404, the soldiers retaliated: on horseback they charged the young students and beat them while the older students were leading the little ones on a solemn procession from Saint-Mathurin, north of the Seine, to Saint Catherine in the Vale of the Students. The soldiers' first victims were the youngest of the elementary classes, the *minores gramatici*. For this atrocity, the university cancelled all classes, stopped preaching in all the churches of Paris, and threatened to leave Paris. To keep them, the king sided with the university against his own kin, penalizing the duke severely by banishing him and all his immediate kinsmen from the kingdom. Further, the king ordered the duke's palace to be demolished "from roof to floor." Only by negotiations from others was his art collection saved and placed in a permanent gallery for the public along the city walls of Paris, at the duke's expense. In addition, the duke was condemned to fund two chapels and to pay two thousand livres to the university and the victims.[100]

Remarkably, children participated in other riots and demonstrations—even small children, and sometimes even as the leaders of adults. The most famous of these movements were the children's or shepherds' crusades of 1251 and 1320 through France and Germany, but protests by children appear to have cropped up more on Italian soil than north of the Alps. In 1347, with ships from Sicily in the Bay of Naples poised to attack the city, "small children [*pueri parvuli*] of Naples protested the impending war by marching through the streets of the city until they reached the royal castle." They carried the banners of the Kingdom of Two Sicilies and chanted, "Peace, peace."[101]

The importance of children in Italian city-state demonstrations and riots is suggested by a law passed in Parma in 1331 that "prohibited children and others [*pueris et aliis*] chanting the rallying cry of 'Vivat, vivat.'" Nonetheless, soon after the decree was passed, "many men, women, the old, and the young" marched on the cathedral square of Parma at night on 3 March. They chanted, "Long live the king" (King Robert of Naples, who was then titular head of Parma), and afterward, "Peace, peace," "Death to the taxes [*dacia*] and gabelles," and "Death to Riccardo," the king's notary and governor of Parma, responsible for imposing new taxes and for "much cruelty and wickedness in the administration of his office." The next day over a thousand filled the main square chanting, "Long live the king, and death to the taxes and the gabelles." But unlike most crowds with charged rallying cries, this one did not lead to violent assaults on public or private palaces or against officials. Instead, the youth, along with others, "without drawing social distinctions danced [in the streets] for the next eight days, day and night." Surprisingly, these actions frightened the despised notary and chief official of Parma, Riccardo, who fled the city. The crowds then freed prisoners and won pardons for unpaid taxes. Further, on 15 March they pressured the general council of the commune to withdraw some taxes and lower others. With this success, the youth took their tactics to the countryside, to the village of Viarolo, south of Parma. "Young children and adolescents [*pueri et juvenes*] with branches, twigs, and garlands of flowers danced and chanted: 'long live, long live; peace, peace; death to the taxes and the gabelles.'" They sought peace between Parma and Lucca, which was negotiated on 21 April. Their success led to further exuberance, marching, dancing, and chanting: "Peace, peace, peace!"[102]

Just as the youth could lead peace marches, they could also push for war. At least this is what the children of Florence did on 3 July 1323. While the famous war captain of Lucca, Castruccio Castracane, was plundering the Florentine territories of the Valdarno Inferiore, the Florentine troops stationed at Prato were "in disarray, led by an incompetent captain and because of the vices of the nobility had no intention of winning a war to honor a state of the *popolo*." Fights and divisions broke out between the soldiers of noble status, who wished to drag their heels, and the commoners, who wanted to fight. Wind of these divisions reached Florence, where the councilors met in the Palace of the People and, "led by childish ones and children [*cominciando da' pargogli, fanciugli*]," the *popolo minuto* gathered outside the council chambers in "uncountable numbers" and chanted, "to battle, to battle; kill the traitors." They then began throwing rocks at the windows of the town hall. The children and the *popolo minuto* won. From fear that the riot would spread and "from the necessity to calm the *popolo minuto*," the lord priors that evening sent a letter to the troops stationed at Prato ordering them into battle.[103]

Youth could also be behind more serious threats to ruling oligarchic regimes in Italian city-states. According to the fifteenth-century Perugian chronicle, *Diario del Graziani,* the revolt to topple the government of the Raspanti in 1383 that emerged from the working-class quarter of Sant'Angelo was also a youth movement, led by young Giacomo d'Odda and his friends.[104] Children's provocations could even reach levels of international diplomacy. In Florence, for example, the pro-Florentine Pope Martin V, then at war with Bologna in 1419, became indignant with Florence because its children were going around the city mocking him by singing and scribbling on walls: "Pope Martin is not worth a cent; the valiant Braccio conquers all."[105]

In France and Flanders, children also appeared in the melee of popular rebellion, but outside the university they stay in the background, at most as followers, not leaders. In the last stages of the 1365 tax revolt organized by craftsmen in Tournai, "many children and servants of the bourgeois joined the insurgents, disguising themselves by blackening their faces and wearing strange clothes. They then went yelling and carrying on like the others . . ." Among the jingles they sang was this:

> The gabelle is levied in Lille and Douai;
> Killing a hundred men there, it ran to Tournai.[106]

Children sometimes followed social revolts with taunts that were more ghoulish than blackened faces and innocent jingles. In 1418, a revolt of 40,000 commoners (*gens de petit estat*) of Paris (according to the chronicler Jean le Févre)[107] rose up in "a beastly rage," broke into the prisons, and massacred over three thousand prisoners, "regardless of their crimes, which included the Count of Armagnac, many bishops, and lords." Bad children (*les mauvaises effans*) then followed, playing with the body parts of the dead constable, the chancellor, and Remonnet de La Guerre. They dragged the bodies before the court of the town hall "and from the constable they stripped off a two-inch-wide band of flesh, which gave them a great laugh."[108] Similar displays of body parts entertained the children of Florence with the fall of the Government of the Minor Guilds in 1382. After the execution of the artisan prior Simone di Biagio, the children dragged his body through the streets of Florence to the house of the rebel Lord Tommaso Strozzi, where they cut off di Biagio's hands and used them to play ball. They then tried to hang his corpse but were not allowed to do it, so they dragged it to the cathedral, where Simone's eldest son had been killed. The two were put in a tomb together, but the children would not allow anyone to cover it for four days.[109]

From these examples should we agree with the French historian of early modern Europe, Yves-Marie Bercé, that "the role played by young men in outbreaks of violence is something of a biological truism"?[110] My conjecture would be no. At any rate, the late medieval chroniclers give no hint of it. The 1383 revolt at Perugia was the only one led by a youth that attempted to overthrow a regime. Otherwise, the chroniclers say little about age. On certain occasions, however, glimpses into the crowd reveal old men, even ancient ones by medieval standards, playing key leadership roles. The leader of the revolt of Flanders in 1301 was the weaver Peter the King, who Villani claimed was more than sixty at that time. In 1309 Peter (although knighted in the interim), at more than seventy now, was still active as a leader of the city's "weavers, fullers, and clippers of cloths [*rasoribus pannorum*], and all the other workmen [*et alii omnes mechanici vulgares*]." He persuaded them in that year not to go along with the bourgeois of Ghent and Bruges in agreeing to what later proved to be a disastrous peace treaty with France.[111] In the 1365 tax revolt in Tournai referred to previously, the one to spark the violence was an old man in the crowd who taunted the city's provost—"Sire, sire, this is pointless, since we'll pay nothing." He was arrested, but as he was being carried off stoked the courage of others, crying out, "What I said, I said for you as much as for myself." Then the riot began. In a revolt to overthrow the ruling regime of Siena, the Nine, in 1346, the only commoner singled out by a chronicler was the eighty-year-old tailor, Pietro.[112]

Finally, the tax sources *(estimi)* of late–fourteenth-century Florence, the earliest anywhere in the West to list ages of residents of the countryside, affords a rare opportunity for gauging revolutionaries' ages in the late Middle Ages. Linking mountain rebels who revolted against Florentine rule during the summer and fall of 1402 to their tax records fails to reveal rebels as footloose, young hotheads, moved by adolescent hormones, as Bercé would have us believe. Instead, those sentenced to death as rebels or who a year later were able to cut special deals for themselves and their communities were, with one exception, married, middle-aged *patrifamiliae* with above-average holdings and authority in their mountain villages. They had something at stake, something to lose.[113]

Tax Revolts

The typologies above have been organized around who rebelled and against whom they rebelled: rebellions of the bourgeois, the "people," specific craftsmen, the *popolo minuto* or *menu peuple,* the young and the old; revolts against aristocrats, town councils, bishops, regional lords or counts, the king, the emperor, or the pope. As the examples show, these protagonists rebelled for a variety of reasons—miscarriages of justice, corruption of officials, the arrogance of magnates, new or raised taxes, anti-Semitism, the expense and suffering of war, and the incompetence of military leaders. These revolts could be classified just as logically by causation. Revolts against the monarchy were often also tax revolts, and defiance of the king could spill into anti-Semitic riots, which flaunted his decrees and insulted him personally. The vast majority of revolts viewed by these means—to repeat—were waged for political reasons: political inclusion and participation. Such revolts sometimes involved the bourgeois concerned with threats to their franchises, as with the early-thirteenth-century revolts in Marseilles against the regional count, or the *popolo minuto* in Siena in 1355, when they joined other outsiders to topple the Government of the Nine. Even an exceptional revolt with specific economic programs, such as the Tumult of the Ciompi, was essentially a political revolt: a struggle for political recognition and rights of citizenship.

After revolts of the *popolo* against aristocrats, the tax revolt (for both urban and rural areas) ranks second in frequency (142 cases). However, these too were often combined with revolts for political inclusion, the extension of franchises, and resistance to other forms of political encroachments by the king, the count, the church, or the emperor. Such can be seen in the revolt of the *Harelle* in Rouen, where a protest spurred by the king's new subsidies spread to an attack on the principal abbeys of Rouen and especially Saint-Ouën, which held the rights of barony over the city and which infringed on the franchises of the town council. Similarly, Philip the Fair's new taxes may have sparked the revolt of Flanders in 1297–1304, but it was his encroachment onto the rights of the count and the Flemings that fuelled it. This revolt finished with weavers and fullers becoming enfranchised with rights to elect and hold office across the cities and towns of Flanders.

More than any other type of revolt, that against taxes straddled the economic and the political, but it was the political aspect—a question of rights—more than the economic (or at least dire economic straits) that provoked these revolts. In essence, the tax revolt was a protest against the infringement of political rights to set or consent to the imposition of taxes. In only five of these tax revolts (and only three of these were recorded by the chroniclers) was scarcity or poverty signaled as a precondition of rebellion. The attack at San Marco against the increase in the grain gabelle in 1266 occurred at a time when famine was spreading.[114] Similarly, the riot of the Florentine wool carders in 1343, led by the mad Lord Andrea Strozzi, occurred in a period of food shortages, but the attack on the gabelles was only part of their rallying

cries; the other shouts exalted their class over the city's "fat cats," who pre-
vented them from enjoying rights of election and citizenship: "Long live the
popolo minuto, and death to the fat cats and their gabelles."[115] A local chronicler
of Montpellier explained his city's revolt against increases in the hearth tax,
which led to dumping royal officials down wells in 1379, by pointing not only
to "the large and intolerable demands" of the crown (an increase of the hearth
tax by three times in as many years) but also to the impoverished conditions
of the region: "The people [*pobol*] were already entirely devastated, broken
by the great dearth that had run through this region for a long time."

Further, letters of remission give evidence of opposition to the salt tax in
Montpellier in 1341 during a severe food shortage *(maxima caristia)*[116] and of a
revolt at Le Puy en Velay, 1378, against increases in the hearth tax and the
gabelle on wine and other commodities. "Because of their poverty and the
desperate state of their inhabitants, these communities had not been accustomed to paying royal subsidies or the hearth tax for some time." This is one
of only three revolts found in these samples in which the insurgents pleaded
for mercy:

> Filled with laments and tears and gathered here in great numbers, they
> rose up [*insurexit*]. In front of the image of the Virgin Mary, they implored
> loudly: "Blessed Virgin Mary, help us! How can we live and feed our chil-
> dren, since we cannot bear these heavy taxes imposed on us to our harm,
> which strip and siphon off our property?"[117]

However, for the other 137 tax revolts found in letters and chroniclers (96
percent of them), no such conditions of economic destitution appear in the
background, much less as the spark of revolt. Instead, these revolts were most
often bundled together with rebellions for political inclusion, were politically
motivated attacks against encroachments into franchises, or were questions
of justice. We have already seen that the revolts in Toulouse in 1310 arose
because Philip the Fair issued new taxes without the consent of the three
estates; by 1314 this rage over the king's overstepping his bounds had spread
throughout France.[118] One of the earliest of these protests against taxation
came from the *menu peuple* of Paris, who were enraged, not with the taxes
and fines imposed on them by the city council and the provost of the merchants, so much as by the provost's corruption and his doling out special
favors so that the privileged could avoid paying taxes.[119] Later, in 1380 in the
region of Paris, Michel Pintoin pointed to the corruption and brutality of the
king's tax collectors (even before Charles VI imposed his new subsidies) as
the first cause of a new "appetite for liberty" and "incessant lust for new

things" that he saw as the firmament of that wave of tax revolts that would sweep through northern France and Flanders for the next three years.[120]

Tax revolts in Italy reflect similar political sentiments. In 1355 the *popolo* of Udine revolted against the Patriarch of Aquilea, because of "the oppression of his taxes." However, it was the "overwhelming arrogance" of his chief officer, a Lucchese who had married the Patriarch's daughter, and the "dirty things he had done to the people of Udine" that sparked them to risk rebellion. The Lucchese officer was the first to pay: while imprisoned in the town hall of Udine, the *popolo* decapitated him without trial.[121]

In 1373 revolts arose across the Papal States (*Patrimonio e Campagna*), not only because the papal legate, Gerardo, abbot of the monastery of Montemaggiore, "began to tax everyone more than usual" but also because he did so "in a manner not practiced by previous legates, taking no account of the status and condition of noblemen, communes, or clergy." In the same year a rebellion broke out in Orte, again not only or especially because the taxes had been raised, but because "a certain notary, Ceccone, had implemented them with such arrogance and unpleasantness [*per le tante soperchiarie e spiacevolezze che fece*]."[122]

Often, revolts with cries against gabelles, attacks on tax officials, and assaults on communal archives to shred tax surveys were simply a part of larger revolts for political inclusion or the overthrow of existing regimes. In 1383, the revolt of Genoa's butchers against a gabelle on meat was just the beginning of a revolt that brought down the doge and established a government of the *popolo*.[123] A revolt of the *popolo* of Gubbio in September 1376 went straight to the chancellery, where immediately the books of the gabelles were burnt. But this was more than a tax revolt; it formed part of the wave of revolts over the previous year to throw off the yoke of church rule.[124]

Finally, the supplicants in two letters of remission from the early 1380s— one from the north of France, the other from the south—show that objections to taxes did not arise simply from poverty or concerns over material conditions but turned on notions of justice. The first concerned a furrier's *valet* (a journeyman) caught up in the Hammer men's revolt against Charles VI's new taxes on commodities on 1 March 1382. When asked why he opposed the king's taxes, he turned not to matters of the hearth or destitution or to personal circumstances of family needs, as was the norm in such letters to absolve individuals' responsibility; instead, he pointed to matters of principle and fairness. In contrast to the usual rhetorical strategy of these letters—"humble supplication" at the feet of royal majesty and grace—this letter turned for a moment into a critique of royal policy and broken promises. First, the king's father, Charles V, had cancelled the taxes on his deathbed and his son, Charles VI, had broken the pledge. Second, it was not taxation per se that irked the journeyman. Instead, he opposed the particular form of the new taxes—the regressive subsidies—and reasoned that taxes should be levied "each according to his means [*taux*] and his ability [*faculté*]."[125]

The second example came in 1378 from impoverished Le Puy en Velay, where the townsmen had not been accustomed to paying taxes for some time and implored for mercy, first from their unveiled Virgin Mary, then from the king's council. Yet, even here, principles of fairness were at the heart of the commoners' rebellion: they accused their town councilors of favoring friends and the rich at the expense of the poor, and claimed they "would willingly pay us [the king] this tax if it had been assessed according to the value of their property or by another means."[126]

Revolts of Religious Belief

Another block of popular movements revolved around religious ideas branded heretical by dominant powers. Thirty-three such movements appear in my samples, some of them reported by numerous chroniclers. These movements did not simply attack clerical privileges or orthodox teachings but also could challenge social hierarchy as a whole.[127] Only one of these movements appears attached or allied to an existing city-state or town council in its revolt against the crown or a regional authority. The king, backed by the Holy Inquisition, imprisoned and fined two clerics who in 1306 led the men of Carcassonne to oppose the crown. Although the document (a letter of remission) brands the clerics as heretics, it never explains how these clerics moved the inhabitants of Carcassonne to revolt or why they did so (other than for heretical ideas). But despite their popular following and even backing from the town council, the clerics were judged in the first instance not by the royal courts but by the inquisition for heresy.[128] This revolt was tied to earlier movements in the area: a quarrel between heretics and the Dominicans, who ran the inquisition in Toulouse in 1303,[129] and a broader insurrection the next year, when heretics from Albi, Cordes, and Toulouse joined the inhabitants of Carcassonne against the office of the inquisition. Men and women "united in riot to do evil [*turba coadunata et colligata in malum*] giving rise to a serious popular insurrection."[130] They chanted cries to kill the bishops of Albi and Toulouse, "the traitors," who had condemned the heretics. The prosecutions and persecutions lasted until at least January 1308, when "many heretics" were burnt alive in the square of Saint Stephen in Toulouse.[131]

Other wars and crusades against heresy or movements organized by clerics and based on religious ideas are well known to historians. They include the radical Franciscans, Humiliati, and Cathars of the late twelfth and early thirteenth century, such as the Poveri Lombardi.[132] Another movement is that of the Albigensians accused of Catharism *(Bulgarorum haeresis)* and the crusades of the crown against them from the opening years of the thirteenth century to 1240, culminating in the massacre of 1244, when 205 heretics "of both sexes" were rounded up in the mountain village of Montségur and burnt alive at the foot of the mountain.[133] Then there were the shepherd's or children's crusades of 1251 and 1320,[134] which attacked local clergymen as readily as Jews but never the eastern infidel, and who performed their own religious rites, at least according to unsympathetic chroniclers;[135] and the community of Fra Dolcino, established in the Alps above Biella in the region of Novara from 1304 to 1307.[136]

Somewhat less well known were a heretical movement in Flanders crushed by the archbishop and the count in 1183,[137] and another in Padua in 1233, in which sixty were burnt at the stake in three days.[138] Further, in 1240 the heretics of Orvieto killed the regional inquisitor but were caught and executed.[139] In 1315 the podestà of Siena wanted to chop off the feet of six men of low status *(picolo affare)* from the countryside, next to the city walls of Siena *(la Masse)*. One of them (reminiscent of the accusations hurled against Fra Dolcino ten years before) had been preaching that he was "the true apostle of Christ, that all property should be held in common charity along with women, who could be used without any sin being committed, and other disgusting articles of heresy." He opposed the pope, his cardinals, and the other rectors of the church, holding that they failed to observe the evangelical life, and he further claimed that he was worthy of being pope. According to Agnolo di Tura, this heretical leader had a following of three thousand men and women.[140] In 1322 the spiritual Franciscans came in conflict with the church, preaching that Christ was poor and possessed no property; Pope John XXII responded by launching a crusade against them.[141]

One of the most remarkable of these lesser-known heretical movements was that exposed by the crusade launched against Federico of Montefeltro and his stronghold of supporters at Recanati in the Italian Marche.[142] On 19 October 1319, the pope excommunicated the entire commune of Recanati, who were accused of practicing sorcery and idolatry. The town responded in kind by excommunicating their bishop and followed the decree with a mock funeral procession of the bishop through the town, carrying an effigy of him made of straw. At the funeral pyre, they burnt him, chanting, "Too bad we cannot do the same to the bishop himself, the Marchese,[143] the pope, and his cardinals. It is not us who have sinned; rather all the world's evil emanates from them!"[144] On 15 May 1322, "without mercy," the forces of the Marchese burnt the town to the ground.[145] Clearly, the accusation of heresy was politically charged and the response to it spawned a popular political movement against church power.

Strikingly, other than two references to the distant Hussites,[146] only two cases of heresy that stirred a popular movement appear in these samples after the Black Death. The first (not actually called a heretical movement but condemned by the church) appeared in the immediate wake of the plague: the flagellants, who spread across large areas of Europe and were condemned by Pope Clement VI in 1349. The second came much later: in 1422, "many men and women" who according to Monstrelet held the same heretical beliefs as those at Prague held a church council in the village of Sains, near Douai. They were rounded up and led as prisoners to the court of the bishop of Arras. Compared to the horrific mass burnings of heretics common before the plague, the church's treatment may have been slightly more lenient, or at least more surgical:[147] those who repented received mercy; the others, however, after the bishop and the inquisitor had tried to persuade them to abandon their beliefs, were burnt at the stake at Arras, Douai, and Valenciennes.[148]

Anti-Semitic riots were another form of revolt prompted by religious belief and intolerance, which also had political and economic overtones. From 1200 to 1425, numerous chroniclers described four large waves of anti-Semitic hatred that swept through much of France, Flanders, and into areas not covered in this survey, Germany and Spain—the children's or shepherds' crusades of 1251 and 1320; the attacks and burning of lepers of the following year, which were centered in Aquitaine but spread elsewhere and to Jews;[149] and most devastating of all, the persecution of Jews that accompanied the fears of the Black Death in 1348 and 1349.

In this sample, none of these waves appears to have reached Italy.[150] Indeed, only one anti-Semitic riot is found in the Italian boot in my samples, and it was small and highly localized. In 1289 "citizens" of Nerito, a mountain village at over 1,100 meters in altitude on the northern slopes of the Gran Sasso (Abruzzi), dominated by the Benedictine monastery of Santa Maria, rioted against the Jews, "killing many," which greatly upset the abbot of the monastery: many of the Jews were "his vassals."[151] The chronicler does not state the motives for the attack, but it might have been in part a means of attacking the authority of their local abbot, who was also their lord.

After 1349, no chronicler of France, Flanders, or Italy reports any further waves or movements as such of anti-Semitic violence that spread across territories. In the 1380s, however, several of the revolts against Charles VI and his fiscal policies spilled over into anti-Semitic rioting in Paris and isolated attacks on Jews at Rouen. As we have seen, more than in the earlier waves of anti-Semitism that accompanied the shepherds' crusades, these postplague anti-Semitic riots were explicitly staged to insult the king by violating his special protection of the Jews. In Paris they entered the district of forty houses he had allocated to Jews for their protection, stole from them, and blatantly disobeyed the king's decrees to return their stolen goods.

Revolts against Soldiers and Foreigners

Chroniclers report a rich variety of other types of popular revolt, which occurred less often than the political revolts just described, several of which were some of the most dramatic and important insurrections in late medieval Western Europe. One such form of popular revolt was against the arrogance, cruelty, and persecution of local communities by soldiers billeted in their towns and villages or by other foreign officials and dignitaries. The most widely reported revolt—the Sicilian Vespers of 1282—was of this type. Its origins were popular and spread from the suburbs of Palermo to local populations in Val di Mazara, Trapani, and Messina, rapidly circumnavigating the island.[152] According to Henri Bresc, it was a movement for municipal liberties, "showing signs even of democracy," and gave birth to Sicily as a national identity.[153] According to the Italian versions (but not the French ones), it erupted in the village of Santo Spirito on the outskirts of Palermo during a local feast day, which was also Easter Monday.[154] At the festivities, a French officer grabbed a Sicilian woman and began "touching her indecently [*disonestamenti*] with his hands all over her, as they were accustomed to doing." The woman screamed, and Sicilian men ran to her defense, rallying others with the call "Moranu li Franchiski!" According to a Sicilian chronicler, three thousand Frenchmen were massacred in Palermo alone,[155] and according to Brunetto Latini, 6,500 throughout the island. From the French officers, the massacre spread to the Friars Minor and Dominicans, and any others who were French or even spoke French.[156]

The bloodiest of the repressions of popular revolt found in these sources—rivaling even the better-known Jacquerie—ended by totally depopulating for a year or more a major Italian commercial city, Cesena, in 1377. It came in retaliation to a popular revolt in the city, when its inhabitants felt they could no longer tolerate the abuse of Breton soldiers billeted in their town and environs.

> For two months they [the Breton mercenaries] consumed everything on the outskirts of Cesena, forcing all the peasants to take refuge inside the city because of the great beatings they were getting. And after all had been consumed outside, the troops came into the city and devoured everything there, raping [*sforzavano*] men and women, to the point where they could endure it no longer. In short, on the first of February 1377, the citizens rioted, yelling: "Long live the Church and death to the Bretons." And they killed more than a hundred of them.[157]

The cardinal legate, Robert of Geneva (who a year later would become Clement VII, France's papal candidate), ordered mercenaries under John Hawkwood to punish Cesena. The slaughter lasted five months; Cesena, depopulated entirely of its natives, became Hawkwood's military base. As the Malatestiana chronicle described it, "these Bretons devoured Cesena inside and out."[158]

Another revolt against the arrogance of foreign officers and servants that violated local sensibilities also received widespread attention from chroniclers—one of the few, in fact, that French (north and south) and Italian chroniclers reported. On 5 September, a member of the cardinal of Carcassonne's retinue at Viterbo was washing the cardinal's "pretty little dog [*cagnolino*]" in the fountain of the artisan neighborhood of Scarlano.[159] A servant woman of the neighborhood, who was coming to fetch drinking water, shouted at him. The cardinal's servant responded by running her through with his sword, which sparked the neighborhood (*contrada*) to seek revenge; from the poodle's bath, the riot spread city-wide, becoming a bloodbath of foreign church dignitaries and their retainers.[160]

While Italy was the scene of most of these antiforeign revolts, they can be found in France and Flanders as well. In 1295 the inhabitants of Rions, southwest of Bordeaux in English-controlled Gascony, were indignant over the English treachery at Podensac across the river Garonne and in response massacred the English soldiers stationed in their town. They led sixty soldiers into the main square and hanged them. Seeing the discord in the city, the French attacked and captured the town with ease, killing many and placing it under the French crown.[161] In 1347 a fight broke out in Tournai over a game of dice (*ludens ad taxillos*) between soldiers of Hainault and a resident of the town.

The soldiers dragged the resident into their lodgings and beat him to a pulp. On seeing this mismatch, commoners rioted throughout the city as far as the Escaut River; a large crowd *(maxima multitudo communiae)* gathered in front of the soldiers' lodging, hurled insults, and "did much damage." Those from Hainault, billeted in the monastery of Saint Martin, gathered and armed. The commoners encircled the monastery, scaled its walls, and broke in with swords and clubs. The provost and governors of Tournai joined the crowd, forcing the monks to open their doors. But "for the love of God," those from Hainault were not harmed and eventually were pardoned.[162] Other revolts turned on hatred of foreign governments and a foreign military presence, most emphatically in the anti-French revolts of Flanders in 1297–1304 and 1323–1328. In such movements commoners massacred thousands of French troops, in one case "slicing [them] to pieces like little tunny fish," as Giovanni Villani described the assault against the French known as the "Matins of Bruges" on 18 May 1302.[163]

Contested or rigged elections could also bring commoners armed into streets, especially in the towns of central and northern Italy. One such conflict occurred in the market town of Barberino Valdelsa within the *contado* of Florence in 1347, when some inhabitants opposed local election results, accusing the elected of being "no good" and demanding new elections. Their accusations brought many more into the streets, creating a "major riot" in the town.[164] Such disputes also extended to the election of popes, when the cardinals dallied in making their electoral choices or made the wrong choice, as the locals saw it. These conflicts were specific to two cities, Rome and Viterbo, and arose in 1155, 1268, 1282, 1404, and most profoundly in 1378, when Froissart estimated that 30,000 Romans filled the streets to demand first a Roman and then an Italian pope, which set off the Great Schism.[165] Furthermore, after the elections of popes, controversy could brew and lead to popular insurrections between supporters of rival claimants to the papacy in towns as distant from Rome as Toulouse in 1407,[166] Liège in 1383,[167] and Ghent in 1392.[168]

Peace Movements and Nonviolent Collective Protest

As shown by the flagellant movement for peace through the territories of Pisa, Lucca, and San Miniato in 1311; the children's peace march through Naples in 1347; or the youth dancing through the streets and countryside of Parma in 1331, late medieval popular movements were not always violent, nor did they always need to be to win their demands. In 1291, the four trades of Parma—butchers, ironmongers, cobblers and furriers—came together with the judges, notaries, and other professions *(misterii)* of the city, swore an oath to support one another, and passed certain laws. Instead of leading to collective violence, this agreement "suddenly ended all rioting and bickering [*omne murmuramentum*]" in the city. As later conflicts revealed, this peaceful act changed the balance of power between the magnates and the craftsmen of the city.[169] Similarly, in 1338 people from the artisan quarter of Trastevere (Rome) met at night in their church of Santa Maria and began clamoring for peace, "saying nothing more." Others joined them; went to the homes of the warring Orsini and Colonna, the two most powerful noble families of Rome; and "forced them to make peace[,] and miraculously peace was made."[170]

On occasion, the act of leaving a city-state, region, or kingdom, or even the mere threat of it, could successfully redress injustices. This happened in numerous town-gown disputes and in the protest by the *menu peuple* of Paris against their corrupt provost in 1252. In at least thirteen cases found in these samples, migration was the principal weapon of the people. In 1394, for instance, mass migration throughout Languedoc because of royal "taxes, subsidies, hearth taxes [*fouages*], criminal condemnations, and other fines" had led "to the ruin of vineyards, arable lands, and other possessions." As a result, Charles VI felt forced to reverse gears in his efforts to collect taxes, "ending all violence and oppression" toward these inhabitants: if they returned to their homesteads, he would grant them immunity from all taxes for six years, except for the *aides*.[171]

Revolts within Specialized Communities

From the chronicles, a rich panoply of other forms of popular protest also emerge within specialized communities such as the army, galleys, or monasteries. For instance, in 1379 the rowers *(le ciurme)* of Venetian galleys refused to go to war under their newly appointed captain, Taddeo Giustiniano, and protested against the doge's imprisonment of their former captain, Vittore Pisani. Before they would man their oars, they demanded that Pisani be reinstated as their leader. With the support of the *popolo* of Venice, who protested with flag-waving sermons in San Marco, they won: Vittore Pisani was reinstated and later that year commanded Venice's heroic victory over the Genoese at Chioggia.[172]

Behind their cloistered doors, monasteries and friaries[173] could also witness class struggle or at least conflict that was aligned vertically down their hierarchies, such as the one in 1315 in Limoges at the priory of the Grandmont.[174] The brothers judged their prior to be living a depraved life with ill-suited contacts *(erat prave vite et conversacionis)* and to be destroying the buildings and property of the priory. They rose up against him, brought an inquest to the secular authorities at Limoges, and among themselves elected a new prior. The takeover was not, however, so easy. The deposed prior mounted an armed defense within the walls of the priory but eventually lost.[175] According to the German chronicler Henry of Hervodia, "violent disagreements, rebellions, conspiracies, plots, and intrigues sprang up among both secular and regular clergy everywhere" after the Black Death.[176]

These protests within specialized communities, as with those of larger communities of villages, cities, regions, and kingdoms, centered on politics: they were disputes over power and its abuse. Only one of these focused on economic demands. In 1329 or 1339, Genoese sailors who had served in galleys of the king of France under the command of the Genoese Lord Aiton Doria revolted over a delay in pay and loss of interest on the sums. Their revolt spread to the coastal villages of Voltri west of Genoa and then to the seamen of Savona.[177] But the rarity of conflicts over wages or other aspects of working conditions, whether in specialized organizations such as armies or within the broader worlds of workers and peasants, should not lead us to conclude that those of lower orders or classes were too cowed to imagine collective action or saw it as a last, suicidal resort. Instead, by collective violence or peaceful means, various groups in urban society, from disenfranchised workers to well-heeled bourgeois, regularly organized and gathered to oppose different levels of the state—priors, aldermen, lords, governors, counts, bishops, kings, popes, and emperors. These rebellions present a variety of forms, including student revolts, protests against judicial sentences and cries against corrupt justice, revolts against the arrogance and violence of aristocrats, attacks on church rule, colonial revolt, disobedience to kings, refusal to allow troops to be billeted within city walls, revolts against mercenaries, peace movements, and more. Nor, as our survey shows, were class-prejudiced chroniclers or government scribes so chary as to conceal all traces of these popular endeavors. Now let us look inside these protests to analyze their leadership; the composition of the crowds' and the role of women, ideology, and repression.

CHAPTER 5

Leaders

In the 1960s and 1970s, historians and sociologists who were not specialists in the Middle Ages constructed models of preindustrial crowds and revolt to understand the distinctiveness of modern, post–French Revolutionary Europe. Foremost among these scholars were George Rudé, a historian of eighteenth-century England and France, and Charles Tilly, a sociologist of the French Revolution, who afterward branched out into various fields of historical sociology. For Tilly, the form of popular protest changed from "communal" to "associational" in the middle of the nineteenth century. Before this turning point, popular revolts were "localized, uncoordinated, dependent on the normal rhythms of congregations like marketing, church-going, or harvesting . . ."[1] For Rudé, the characteristic form of "the preindustrial crowd" was the food riot, which rose and fell with the ebb and flow of grain prices. As a result of this supposed focus on matters of the hearth, women, he claimed, largely composed the preindustrial crowd; by contrast, modern industrial revolts became the business of men. Further, spontaneity characterized preindustrial uprisings; their insurgents resorted to direct action; their leaders came, not from the crowd, but from outside it and usually from the upper classes; and the rebels' aims were backward-looking. Organized strikes were almost unheard of until well into the nineteenth century.[2] For several decades now, Rudé's and Tilly's models have stood the test of time. Modern historians such as William Redding chipped at them, claiming that the eighteenth-century bread riot was a sort of strike.[3] Feminist historians such as Eleanor Gordon and Temma Kaplan have shown a rich array of women's radical politics, street theater, and strike activities in the late nineteenth and twentieth centuries.[4] John Bohstedt has shown that women were not the sole or even always the principal rebels in food riots during the heyday of these forms of protest at the end of the eighteenth century in Britain.[5] I also have used the models of Tilly and

Rudé to highlight the exceptional character of the Florentine Ciompi—its modernity.[6] But like others,[7] I assumed that they described reasonably well other revolts of Europe's preindustrial past. I know of no medievalists to have challenged these models.

More recently, from the perspective of revolt in early modern Europe, Yves-Marie Bercé has shored up these generalizations. He also has seen grain scarcity as the usual spark or precondition of premodern uprisings,[8] "the traditional involvement" of women,[9] and leadership from the outside: clergy, mayors, or lords were the usual rabble rousers.[10] Finally, he has emphasized "the fleeting character of popular enthusiasm, the apparent spontaneity of their gatherings and the ease with which they dispersed."[11] Furthermore, medievalists Mollat, Wolff, and Guy Fourquin, whose studies remain the only book-length surveys of continental revolt in the later Middle Ages, have broadly affirmed the same. As in the previous chapters, my analysis of the structure and content of late medieval revolts—their leadership, composition, ideology, and success—will not depend on the major revolts alone (the Flemish revolts of the early fourteenth century, the Jacquerie of 1358, and the Ciompi) but will draw on over one thousand revolts and social movements, principally found in published chronicles, circa 1200–1425.

Bourgeois and Community-wide Revolts

To begin with the leaders of late-medieval popular revolt: did they come largely from outside the social ranks of those rioting, that is, from the clergy, local mayors, or the aristocracy? First, chroniclers singled out leaders (including those named for special punishments) in less than one-fourth of the revolts they reported. It is difficult to argue from silence, but given the social position and prejudices of some, such as Jean le Bel and Jean Froissart, perhaps other chroniclers believed that the lower sort, like their animals,[12] were incapable of leading themselves and thus depended on outside agitators—the king of Navarre, Robert Le Coq, Étienne Marcel, or others of the elites. If this were the case, the silence in the chronicle sources (as the letters of remission make clear for the Jacquerie) would underestimate the extent to which peasants or artisans served as the leaders of their own protests and movements.

Second, of those identified as leaders or singled out for special punishment, only a little over half (112 of 212) came from those groups that Bercé, Fourquin, and others have claimed comprised the leadership of popular revolts—aristocrats, bourgeois, or members of the clergy. But this figure is deceptive. As we saw with various forms of revolt, popular rebellion was often just that: it cut across social classes to unify villages, cities, regions, and colonies against an overlord—the count, the king, the pope, or an imperial city-state such as Venice. Thus in 1264, the *peuple* of Marseilles, in challenging their count's threats against their franchises, solicited and obtained the support and leadership of a nobleman "named Boniface." The chronicler, however, does not imply that this Boniface instigated the revolt or somehow led the people of Marseilles for his own selfish purposes.[13] In fact, he held his castle of "Chasteillon" in the territory of Marseilles and was feeling the same pinch from Count Charles as were the bourgeois and other *peuple* of Marseilles.[14] Similarly, in 1303 and again in 1406 the Calergi family, the "principal noblemen of the island," along with other rebels of the Venetian colony of Candia (Crete) led a revolt to throw off Venetian control. In the first of these revolts, the Calergi were the leaders who negotiated with the Venetians; in the second, they were the ones who were hanged. But in neither revolt do the Venetian chroniclers—Andreas Naugeri in the first, Marino Sanuto in the second—suggest that this family was pursuing its own goals, which may have differed from those of the rest of the islanders, or that they were in anyway outsiders. Instead, as with all the colonial revolts found in these collections of chroniclers, those from Candia were presenting a united front against their imperial lords. Often, as in the 1406 revolt, the colonial rebels solicited outside help from kings and emperors, in this case, the emperor of Constantinople. But again, the initiatives appear to have come from the colonials themselves, who saw their present rulers as oppressive. To throw off that yoke, they had to bargain with outside rulers, even if that support came with the promise to hand over their sovereignty to new rulers.[15]

In addition, a number of the revolts led by notable citizens or bourgeois were ones in which the main constituents of the revolt were the citizens or bourgeois of a town. Examples are Étienne Marcel's revolts against the crown's monetary policy in 1357, against the regent's marshals in January 1358, and against the crown and in support of the Jacques in May of that year. The same goes for other bourgeois revolts. Such citizens led and staffed their own protest against the royal castle at Rouen, when they feared that noblemen might invade their city following the nobles' slaughter of the Jacquerie in August 1358.[16] One of the most famous of these bourgeois revolutionaries was the Florentine Giano della Bella, who led a revolt against the Florentine magnates to curb their violence and oppression of merchants, shopkeepers, and artisans alike. The result was the passage of the Ordinances of Justice and later a new tribunal that reduced noble status from a privilege to a liability. Giano was neither a class traitor nor an outside agitator, even if his most loyal support came from craftsmen and disenfranchised workers. Rather, he led a broad coalition of the *popolo* against magnates, even if this coalition later proved fragile and led to his banishment in 1295.[17] Around the same time (1293), a Lord Nicola dell'Isola led a revolt of the *popolo* in L'Aquila and was proclaimed Cavaliere del Popolo; but despite his noble origins, the chronicler does not portray Nicola as manipulating the *popolo* to fulfill his own personal or class agenda.[18]

Other bourgeois leaders of citizen movements with followers from the artisan and laboring classes can be seen in the north of Europe. One of the earliest of these citizen movements was led by Henri de Dinant, a patrician from a rich family of bankers but not of the ruling patriciate,[19] in 1253 and again in 1254. He established a commune with its own taxes and citizen militia organized by neighborhood but was unable to topple the dictatorial control of the Prince-Bishop of Liège, Henri de Gueldre.[20] As Kurth emphasizes, this was not a "democratic movement to emancipate a class but the struggle of an entire city, not against the patriciate as a class but against the tyrannical Henri de Gueldre." Later Fernand Vercauteren showed that the movement radicalized over its two-year history, but essentially he said much the same.[21]

In Ghent, the wealthy Jacob van Artevelde led a broad front, with weavers at its head, and gained hegemony over the city from 1337 to 1345. His rule might be viewed as a case of a class outsider leading a workers' rebellion.[22] But by this time weavers had been full-fledged citizens in Flanders with considerable power in city government for almost three decades, even if they were formally admitted to the city council only in August 1338.[23] Further, weavers often employed the fullers (who were also represented in city government). Thus Jacob and later his son Philippe hardly led revolts of those on the margins or disenfranchised workers, who made up the rank and file of the Flemish revolts at the beginning of the century or later in the Italian city-states; rather, the van Artevelde–led revolts were power struggles for city control among citizens of more or less equal political standing.[24]

Clerics as Leaders

Clergy (secular and regular) apostate friars, or magicians with a religious tinge, far from being the typical leaders or primary participants singled out for punishment in these revolts, were present in only 27 of the 1,112 movements, about 2 percent of them. But even this low figure is deceptively high: a large proportion of these popular movements were not popular rebellions in the usual sense against landlords, employers, city councils, counts, or kings; they were popular religious movements: for example, the flagellants in Tournai in 1349, when an unnamed Dominican friar attracted a "crowd of men and women the size of which had never been seen before in the town," rioted through the town and created havoc with the resident Dominicans.[25] More important, apostate friars or other clerics led a variety of heretical movements or conflicts within or against the church, such as the shepherds' crusade in 1251, led by the Master of Hungary from Paris.[26] A man who reputedly learnt his magic from the sultan of Babylon led a branch of the same movement in Amiens;[27] Fra Dolcino led the supposed Cathar community in the mountains of Novara from 1304 to 1307;[28] radical Franciscans attacked their orders on questions of poverty that led to rioting in parts of Italy in 1250[29] and Provence in 1322.[30]

By contrast, civil revolts that were led by clerics or that even mentioned them were extremely rare: when flagellant and heretical movements are taken from the equation, the number of clerics appearing in these revolts falls to six (less than 1 percent of the cases). But even in this tiny group, clerics do not appear always as the charismatic leaders portrayed as the norm. Rather, the chroniclers often named them because they happened to have been arrested and may have been little more than participants. For instance, the two clerics arrested in 1306 who were accused "over a long period of time of planning a revolt of the men of Carcassonne to overthrow our royal government" were handed over to the bishop to be tried by the inquisition for heresy. A later letter of remission says that the people of Carcassonne had given them their consent, but it is not clear that these two clerics were the leaders of revolts in Carcassonne in the years 1304–1306, when "heretics" of Carcassonne rose up against the inquisition and the crown.[31] In 1307, the king fined the entire commune of Carcassonne for insurrections over the previous three years, but these condemnations did not mention the two clerics; instead, the councillors of the city received the blame for leading the revolts.[32]

In the 1360 conspiracy against the anti-Florentine government by artisans in Pisa, who were suffering because of Florence's blockade of their port, clerics and priests were the ones caught because of their haggling and vulgar language. But it is not clear that they were the leaders. Neither Villani nor the contemporary Pisan chronicler suggests that this conspiracy had any religious overtones, ideology, or ecclesiastical interests that would have led to the clerics' participation.[33] The more detailed Pisan account lists only one cleric, a Frate Bernardo del Pattieri, of twelve leaders singled out and of thirteen others later hanged or fined for conspiring. The movement's artisan direction is reflected in the fact that, of the eight hanged, six were identified by occupation—a fisherman, doublet maker, cobbler, poultry butcher, and two saddle makers; of those fined, one was a locksmith. The same goes for their chants—"Long live Ceccho Agliata and Piero Gambacorta!" "Viva lo popolo minuto!" and rather remarkably, "Long live the gabelles!" They suggest no religious sentiment or clerical influence whatsoever.[34]

In other cases, clerical leaders opposed civil authorities but their lead may not have extended to the laity whom they had hoped to move. Such appears to have been the case in Parma in 1237, when Frater Giordano, called the Hypocrite (at least by the chronicler), led a revolt "with many followers" against the Lombard "tyrant" Eccelino da Romano. According to the chronicler, this brother "wanted to overthrow the tyrant and give the city to the lower classes [*de minibus*]." He failed, and was seized and imprisoned. The bishop of Padua became indignant and went to Eccelino's court with a crowd (this time specified) of clerics and monks, protesting against this secular ruler. Believing strongly in Giordano's innocence, the bishop took action against Eccelino. On hearing this, the laity rioted against the clergy. Even though "the Hypocrite" and the bishop posed as acting on their behalf, the laity did "not want to be implicated and punished for the crimes of these clerics." Eccelino fined the bishop 2,000 marks and "forced him into silence," and many clergymen left town, fearing further reprisals.[35]

Clerics appear as charismatic leaders of the underclasses in less than a handful of cases. On the first day of a revolt of the *popolo* against the government of Reggio nell'Emilia in 1287, a monk from Bibianello[36] led armed men, broke open the prisons of Reggio, and freed all the prisoners.[37] Afterward, however, he vanished from the scene. A parish priest of Ypres emerged in the last desperate days of the revolt of Flanders, 1323–1328. On 7 September 1328 he assembled a great crowd *(magna copia)* of weavers and other commoners and preached the evils that would redound on them if King Philip of France should return to their city; his sermon succeeded in moving the city to rioting. When the king heard the news, he sent his men after the priest and burnt him along with nine of his followers.[38]

In 1233 the Dominican friar Giovanni de Scledo,[39] born of a noble family, "a man of exceptional eloquence and who gave appearances of leading a virtuous life [*innocentiaeque vitae apparens*]," first brought peace among warring factions not only in his home town of Vicenza, but also, according to the chronicler Antonio Godi, in Treviso, Feltri, Conegliano, Verona, Mantua, and Brescia, and between the lords of Camino and the Romano. At Vicenza, he persuaded the city's ruling council *(Consiglio maggiore)* to elect him "Duke, Count, and Marchese of the city." He reformed the statutes of Vicenza, locked up the city's podestà and all his guards, broke open the jails and freed his friends, divided the people into two warring groups, and burnt his enemies and others, declaring them and their books heretical in the main square of Vicenza, "and did similar things in Verona."[40] But his success was short-lived; after a month, his reforms were undone.[41] André de Ferrières, secretary of the citizen council of Liège, "pushed the people to revolt" against their prince. But should we consider the "clerk" André a cleric? He was the illegitimate son of a priest and had taken holy orders but lived outside of them in concubinage; his power came from his secular position as the city council's secretary, not from the pulpit or his religious orders. From the vague and probably biased report of the canon Hocsem, the butt of André's rage was the clergy. He wished "to fleece them of their wealth, banish them from town, and commit innumerable acts that would scandalize the faithful."[42]

The most effective rebel cleric was the only one of two in these samples to appear after the Black Death. Unlike the nameless monk from Bibianello, the priest of Ypres, or the northern Italian brother John, the Augustinian friar Iacopo Bussolari (or Bossolaro) had an impact on the lives of the *popolo* and a city-state that proved more than a flash in the pan.[43] Preaching to the people of Pavia, he convinced them in 1356 to revolt against their overlords, the Visconti of Milan. Friar Iacopo was even behind the military plans that led to the escalade and successful seizure of the Pavia's bastions from the Milanese.[44] In the following year he gained support from the marchese of Monferrato, the emperor's chief officer *(vicario)*; called the *popolo* of Pavia to assemble; and preached to them about the wickedness of tyranny. This time, his eloquence was directed against Pavia's ruling family, the Beccheria. The friar's role in revolt again went beyond words; from his pulpit he organized the assault by choosing twenty men representing each of Pavia's neighborhoods *(contrade)*, four of whom were to be his captains. These twenty were then ordered to choose 100 men, Centuriones, for the twenty-two neighborhoods of the city. In Roman fashion, he also created squadrons of Decuriones and Quinquenarii.[45] In September, Frate Iacopo used his pulpit to send his Centuriones against the head of the Beccheria family, ordering the magnate *paterfamilias* to leave the city and *contado* of Pavia. "Frightened by the rage of the *popolo*," he left, taking his whole clan with him.[46]

Later that year the Beccheria conspired with the Lord of Milan to recapture the city, but the *popolo* uncovered the plot and executed a hundred of the conspirators. After this victory, Pavia's new government of the *popolo* was reformed, and according to Villani, nothing was done without this friar's "advice."[47] In 1358, the friar again assembled the *popolo*, "men and women," and "with beautiful and crafted words" convinced them that they had not done enough by having chased their former tyrants from town; so long as the tyrants' palaces and houses remained intact they would return. On his orders, the *popolo* dismantled the Beccheria's palaces without "leaving a stone atop another." According to Villani, "it was awesome; all the people, men, women, the rich and the poor, like ants, removed these buildings leaving the squares entirely bare."[48] But by November 1359, with Frate Iacopo still at the helm, the *popolo* had reached the end of their tether and were forced to surrender to their much larger and more powerful adversary, the Visconti of Milan. Frate Iacopo was sentenced to life in prison, "which put an end to the secular storms he could stir up with his silver tongue."[49]

In the 1,112 revolts found for this study, Frate Iacopo, a charismatic cleric who successfully led a civil revolt, was unique. He might be seen as a Trecento Savonarola, especially given his rigorous campaign and draconian measures against prostitutes, marital infidelity, and the vanities of dress and jewelry.[50] Yet Frate Iacopo's religious morality differs from Savonarola's militant and heartfelt zeal; Frate Iacopo's morality appears to be only the handmaiden for political ends. From the *carroccio*, the cart symbolic of communal liberty and pride, he rode through the city castigating citizens for moral laxity to toughen them for the secular battles that lay ahead. He cajoled men and especially women to part with their jewels and fancy dresses, which he then sold to places as far away as Venice "to pay for soldiers for the defense of the *patria*."[51] From Villani's reporting and Corio's retrospection a century later, the friar used his pulpit to extol political liberty, end tyranny, and organize citizen militias. By the eyewitness reporting of Pietro Azzari, Bussolari moved the *popolo* of Pavia to combat Milan's superior forces, "preaching Roman history to them so that they would not fear death."[52] Frate Iacopo cited passages from Cassidorus and exhorted the crowds "not to wait for judgment day" but rather "from the stores of their own blood [*o frumenatii sanguinum populi*] to inflict grief" on their city's tyrants.[53] By contrast, the chroniclers mention no references in Fra Iacopo's speeches to the Bible or other religious texts. His was a secular morality and mission. God came into play only to assist "in destroying the demons of the Beccheria and the tyrants of Milan."[54]

Leadership of Peasant Revolts

The previous examples show that even when leaders from the aristocracy, notable families, or the clergy led popular revolts, these were usually revolts of the people—broad-based coalitions—as in colonial revolts against their imperial lords or the people of Pavia against outside tyranny and its own magnate clans. What about peasant insurrections, revolts in which specific artisan groups are represented, or those made up of the *menu peuple* or *popolo minuto?* First, of the sixty-nine peasant revolts, aristocrats played a role in only five, and notable bourgeois or clergy led none of them. But even in these five, we see nothing akin to the peasant revolts of seventeenth-century France, where notable aristocrats organized and led peasant revolts, as with the Nu-pieds and Croquants.[55] As in 1308, during the struggle between the parties of the Emperor and the bishop in Parma, the magnate Rolandino Scorza invaded the city with a troop of "peasants [*rustici*], ruffians, and other vile sorts." Once in the city, however, the peasants sought targets for their own advantage; they broke into public buildings and tore up documents that listed their past fines, condemnations, and taxes. At that point—the moment their revolt began—Rolandino no longer appeared as their leader but had lost all control over them.[56]

In 1375, the Marchese Francesco of Montelino organized a coup to over-throw the government of the Este of Ferrara. He led "an exceptionally large crowd of peasants [*maximam multitudinem comitatinorum*]" to break through "the big gate of Ferrara" that led to Padua. Once in the city, they were to yell "Popolo, Popolo, death to the taxes, the gabelles, and those of the Marchese." Their objective was to bring about a regime of the people *(regimen populare),* but the plot was nipped in the bud and the "principal traitors" named. First came the Marchese, but after him another twelve leaders were condemned. They included a medic, two notaries, a tailor, and three cloth cutters *(strazaroli);* only the doctor and one of the notaries bore a family name,[57] suggesting that this conspiracy had popular elements in its leadership as well as in the rank and file.

In 1376, as we saw earlier, the Counts of Bruscoli, Loiano, Panico, and Vizano organized their peasants to travel into the city of Bologna, break through the walls, storm the cardinal legate's palace, pull him out, and rob and humiliate him, which they did. The riot succeeded: Bologna was freed of church rule, and less than a month later the city became a government of the *popolo* with elected elders. By several accounts, Count Antonio of Bruscoli was the prime instigator. But neither the narrative nor the archival sources reveal exactly what was at stake for the mountain peasants who did the deed.[58]

In April 1395, "thousands of rustics [*villani*]" of the area of Puleggio di San Giorgio,[59] near Ferrara, rose up and threatened the village of Villa di Porto and Ferrara, shouting, "Long live the house of Este and death to the gabelles and the *dazi*." The revolt was easily and brutally crushed. According to Friar Giovanni of Ferrara, the outcast Marchese of the Este family, Azzo, was trying to wrest control of the city from Niccolò II d'Este and "made fraudulent promises of great gains" to be had from their revolt. According to the Florentine Minerbetti, Azzo was only vaguely behind it, but by neither source can it be said that Azzo or any other nobleman was the peasants' leader. When the revolt took place, Azzo was away in Lugo, and only heard about it after the peasants had been defeated. He then sent his forces to Ferrara, which were smashed by the combined forces of Niccolò, the Lord of Faenza; Astorgio I; and the Florentines.[60]

In 1396, the noble family of the Bertolotti led revolts against Genoese dominion along the eastern shores of the Riviera. The chroniclers do not make clear exactly who formed the ranks of this rebellion. The area, however, was one of small mountain villages with fishermen and herdsmen, and thus the action most likely was a peasant revolt.

Finally, the Florentine chroniclers said little about peasant uprisings that encircled the mountainous northern and eastern perimeter of the Florentine state, but those who noticed it claimed it was sparked by the lords of the old feudal clans—the Ubaldini and other "Ghibelline" families. The archival records, however, give greater details and show that the peasants had their own leaders, who negotiated with the Ubaldini and the enemy forces of the Milanese. According to these records, they were at least equal partners in planning uprisings and building bastions on mountaintops in the Alpi Fiorentine. Indeed, in the siege of Florence's stronghold in the north, Firenzuola, peasant leaders made the plans and ordered noble generals to follow.[61] In summary, far from being the norm, the chroniclers reported few instances in which nobles led peasant revolts, and even in cases where noble instigation or support is revealed and archival sources survive, often these noblemen were less leaders than partners in a coalition against a common enemy—in the case of central and northern Italy, the ruling elites of cities.

On the other hand, the chroniclers do on occasion point to peasants who emerge from their own ranks as leaders. In the first rural revolt in the valleys west of Genoa in 1233–1234, a Conrado da Castro led the rustics, first against the local bishop, their landlord, then against the Genoese state. After their victory, they elected one of their own, Bergondio Pugno, as their podestà.[62] In 1334, the rustic Mazarelo da Cuzano led a large force of mountain villagers to invade the city of Bologna.[63] In the Beauvaisis, two peasants— Guillaume l'Aloue and after his death, the Big Iron Man—valiantly organized and led peasant resistance against the cavalry of English nobility in 1359.[64] Moreover, for many other revolts, though the chroniclers may not have named specific peasant leaders, they make clear that the peasants themselves organized and led their revolts. Examples include the male serfs on the estates of the canons of Nôtre Dame at Orly and Châtenay, who refused to pay their rents. Afterward, their womenfolk took it on themselves to protest the canons' cruelty and petition the queen mother.

The most famous peasant leaders to emerge from the chronicles appear in the largest and most important peasant revolts of the later Middle Ages. Clais Zannekin, a native of the region of Veurne; Segher Jonssone; and Jacques Peit led not only other peasants but also artisans and commoners, who would have included bourgeois, when the 1323–1328 revolt of Flanders reached the cities. There, Zannekin had his lieutenants, such as the butcher John Bride; William, the Deacon; and John, called the Moor, who also came from peasant or artisan backgrounds.[65] Further, numerous chroniclers described the Jacquerie's principal peasant leader, Guillaume Cale, and for the most part in a favorable light. Some historians, such as David M. Bessen, wish to see the Jacquerie not as a peasant revolt or a class struggle but more as a civil war. Based on one chronicle, which mentions that some nobles may have joined the Jacques, Bessen concludes that the uprising was essentially a battle of bourgeois and noblemen settling old scores.[66] If this were true, it is all the more remarkable that nobles do not emerge as the Jacques' leaders, either from the chroniclers, some of whom were reluctant to believe peasants could lead themselves, or from the large number of surviving letters of remission. When nobles appear in these letters it is because of their overzealousness in crushing the peasants after the king of Navarre had betrayed them and had begun the counterrevolt. If Bessen is correct (and I do not believe he is), then peasants led the nobility.

With the letters of remission as a guide, it is safe to say that the chroniclers give a limited view of peasant leadership, even though they mentioned assemblies and elections at a number of villages. On the other hand, the letters uncover another layer of peasant leadership below that of the peasant Guillaume Cale. They named local leaders or captains even in petitions not initiated by these leaders, such as Hue of Sailleville, who was elected by the villagers of Agincourt; Jehan Herssent, leader of the village of Châtres-sur-Monthéry; Étienne du Wès, captain of the village of Montataire; Jean Flageolet, elected leader of several villages of Perthois; and many others, some named, some not, as with a reference to the peasant leader of Feigneux in the Beauvaisis.[67] These men organized local assemblies and directed military operations across a plethora of villages in the Beauvaisis, Picardy, Île de France, and Champagne. On occasion (according to the letters), they not only led but restrained their fellow peasants from attacking their lords. Further, although the Jacques and the Parisians communicated and for a brief moment were involved in military operations against the nobility in the Île de France and at Meaux, bourgeois leaders do not appear to have led the peasants. Jean Vaillant, provost of the Mint, led three hundred Parisians into the countryside to reinforce Guillaume Cale's peasants,[68] and Marcel Étienne's captain, the Parisian grocer Pierre Gilles, led Parisians to fight for the king's stronghold at Meaux. None of the accounts or letters, however, suggests that either bourgeois leader led peasants or other villagers.[69] Further, although Étienne Marcel may have given orders to the peasants, by his own admission and from the peasants' letters of remission, they were not at his beck and call.[70]

Leadership of Artisans' and Workers' Revolts

In revolts composed largely of artisans and workers, as opposed to vaguer and more broad-based ones organized across social classes, did aristocrats, bourgeois, or others outside the ranks of artisans lead their movements? Do the chroniclers and letters give credence to Bercé's claims for the long sweep of the premodern European past: "most of the time, rebels took traditional figures, such as the lord, the parish priest, or the mayor, for their leaders?"[71] First, as we have seen, members of the clergy rarely led revolts of any sort other than heretical movements. For revolts of artisans or the *menu peuple*, a cleric appeared as a leader in only one of their 171 revolts—the parish priest of Saint Michaels in Ypres—but even then only during the last throes of the 1328 revolt. Further, chronicles and archival sources fail to signal even their presence as participants in all but one other artisan revolt, the Pisan conspiracy of 1360, blown by a foul-mouthed cleric.

Notable bourgeois and aristocrats were more often involved with artisan revolts than clerics, but it is not always certain or even suggested by the chroniclers that those of higher status led artisans or disenfranchised workers. For instance, Siena's oligarchic government of the Nine ruled by excluding a number of groups both from below and above the social prestige of bankers and cloth merchants. As a consequence, a coalition of these forces revolted and rocked the stability of this government on a number of occasions before finally toppling it in 1355. In 1317, the four groups who plotted to overthrow the government included the noble families of the Forteguerra and the Tolomei, notaries, and butchers, but the Sienese chroniclers do not describe one group leading another with noblemen calling the shots. Instead, each of the four contingents had its own leader, who was named. In the case of the butchers, it was Cione di Vitaluccio, a butcher. A cobbler revealed the plot to the Nine, and the conspiracy was crushed. Among those sentenced to be executed were Cione and three of his corporals, all butchers.[72]

In the following year, butchers and blacksmiths who comprised part of the citizen militia opposed the Sienese war captain and the government of Siena for failing to win a battle at Massa Marittima. When they returned to Siena, these artisans were the first to arm; they led the chants against the war captain, began the stone throwing, and stretched the chains across Siena's streets and squares. The *popolo minuto* and the notaries, also excluded from government, allied with them and followed their lead.[73]

In 1319 three riots erupted against the Nine with the cry of "Long live the *Popolo Minuto* and death to the Nine." One of these broke out during a "game of fists," or the competition of combat among the three districts or "Thirds" of Siena. Again, notaries and butchers joined forces, but none of the chroniclers suggests that one ordered or followed the other. In this year the butchers, notaries, and noblemen of the Forteguerra and Tolomei clans moved their operations to the countryside and with secret pacts and assistance from the Florentines raided Val di Strove, Poggibonsi, Menzano, San Gimignano, Colle, and in 1320, Menzano again—all under the Nine's control. In the first attacks, Cione the butcher and his four corporals continued to lead their craftsmen, but this time they were caught and beheaded.[74]

Two later revolts against the Nine differed from the previous coalitions. In 1329 in Massa Marittima, the united front against the Nine splintered: the principal citizens and merchants of the city hired the Florentine mercenary Langante Foraboschi as their captain to overthrow Sienese rule. But the Florentine betrayed them, and with his assistance, the town's *popolo minuto* rebelled against the rich and the merchants, kicking them out of town.[75] In 1346, in a period of "great scarcity," "a sect" of the *popolo minuto* "ordered" a revolt against the Nine with the cries of "Long live the People and death to those who make us starve." The leader of this revolt, however, was the exception, a class renegade from the disaffected Tolomei family, Spinelloccio, the son of Lord Jacomo.[76]

In Siena's most important medieval revolt, that of 1355, which finally toppled the Nine, the old coalition of disaffected parties and crafts across Siena's political and social horizons came to the fore again. The Salimbene and Piccolomini now appeared as prominent noble enemies of the Nine, while the Forteguerra had disappeared from these ranks. A united front of the *popolo minuto* replaced the corporate bodies of the butchers and blacksmiths, but the notaries, the judges, the noble families, and the *popolo minuto* (sometimes called simply the people) continued to act as separate bodies without a clear hierarchy of command. The only group to follow any others' orders were the magnate Piccolomini, who were commanded by other magnates to revolt after the ceremonial entry of Emperor Charles IV into the city on 23 March 1355. In the next two days, the *popolo minuto* joined the revolt, sealing off streets with chains, storming the palaces of the Merchants' Court *(Mercanzia)* and the Biccherna,[77] robbing and burning treasury and judicial records in the Campo, seizing the ballot box of eligible names for office *(bossoli)* from the Dominicans, throwing them out the window of the Palace of the Nine, then tying the box to the tail of a donkey, which spewed the names across the Campo to humiliate further the governors of the Nine. While the chroniclers do not name a single leader of the *popolo minuto*, they do not suggest that they were following orders from the nobility or anyone else. They took orders from the emperor alone and only on one occasion: after the crowd presented him with the ballot box, he instructed them to throw it out the window, and they did it.[78]

According to the Sienese Donato di Neri, on 9 April, after the emperor had left town, "the noblemen, with their characteristic arrogance," threw out those who were elected to constitute the new government (the Twelve) and placed it under the control of their own committeemen *(collegio)*.[79] But a month later (22 May), "because the citizens of Siena were in such discord," the *popolo minuto* were able to engage in what was effectively a second revolt. According to Matteo Villani, "they took their own course of action and seized the government largely for themselves, much to the dislike of the others."[80] In June the *popolo minuto* brought the revolution further still, setting up what Villani called a government of the "popolazzo."[81]

By December, the fruits of the commoners' struggles could be clearly seen in the new constitution of the government of the Twelve. It granted rights of citizenship to a large swath of the Sienese population that were as extensive as the reforms of the Ciompi would be for Florence twenty-three years later. Menial tasks in the wool industry, leather manufacturing, and hardware now gained guild recognition and through it rights of election and office holding.[82] Indeed, one might conclude that these reforms went further than those of the Ciompi, which still upheld the different gradients and privileges between major and minor guilds. Further, the great majority of the Florentine population—disenfranchised workers mainly in wool production—were allotted only three guilds; these were minor guilds with less representation and offices than those established for the seven major guilds. By contrast, the workers, artisans, and merchants of Siena were distributed over twelve guilds with no differences in rank or in electoral privileges: all twelve were entitled to the same number of votes and governmental offices. The only group the new reforms disadvantaged was the bankers, who had to share their guild and offices with goldsmiths and mere polishers *(sbraghieri)*. Probably this dilution of power stemmed from the fact that the hated Nine had been principally bankers. Thus, even if the chroniclers failed to mention individual leaders of the *popolo minuto* who had led their revolt in 1355, not only in March, but during further revolts in April and June, it is clear the people had their own captains. These captains shrewdly and successfully manipulated matters for the political ends of their class and ultimately against the interests of their higher-class co-conspirators.

Outside Siena, there were few revolts of artisans or urban workers with leaders either above and outside their class or allied beside them. Lord Luca da Panzano was a leader of the failed radical phase of the revolt of the Florentine Ciompi in late August 1378, the group known as the Eight of Santa Maria Novella. But, as historians often fail to remember, while Lord Luca may have been the only leader the chroniclers named, it is doubtful that he was the movement's principal leader, the one who initiated the new radical reforms presented to the priors on the 31 August, or that he exerted more power and control than the Eight of the revolutionary council. He was not even one of the Eight. Indeed, according to the only surviving judicial inquest following the failed revolt, it was not Lord Luca but Piero di Ciro, a carder of the working-class district of San Frediano, who was the chief instigator of the revolt. "He met and assembled in the city of Florence in the Santo Spirito neighborhood of Camaldoli, in a certain field beyond the nunnery of the converted whores [*convertite*], with Angiolo di Cenne, Nofrio di Cinello, Niccolò di Bartolo, Matteo di Ser Salvi, Simone d'Andrea, Domenico di Bonacorso, and a great multitude of their followers numbering two hundred or more from the guild of the carders." These men then met at Santa Maria Novella and planned strategy. Later di Ciro and his corporals organized yet another meeting, this time "numbering five thousand or more in the church of San Marco." Further, it was di Ciro who went to the Palazzo Signoria to intimidate the city priors into supporting the Eight's reforms, a promise sealed with handshakes. In this record, Lord Luca appears in the background only as a co-conspirator.[83]

In Bologna, Count Antonio of Bruscoli, who was the principal leader of the mountain peasants' raid against Bologna's cardinal legate in 1378, may have also been a leader of a failed artisan revolt in 1399. At any rate, accused of being involved in the revolt, the old man, now eighty, was hauled before the ruling magistrates of the Bentivoglio in his underwear and bare feet and then executed.[84] In Viterbo in 1390, a citizen, Lord Andrea Capoccia, assisted in organizing the *popolo minuto* from the artisan neighborhoods of San Sisto, San Faustino, and Santa Lucia in a peace march to protest against Breton mercenaries who enforced papal rule over the city and who were besieging the countryside. From a peace movement the insurgents turned to arms and succeeded in ousting the priors of the city along with the pope's captain. However, the artisans also had their own leader, a greengrocer who initiated the peace movement and then organized his fellow greengrocers in 1390 to lead the first riots against the Church.[85]

In Paris, chroniclers and, even more so, modern historians[86] have stressed that the Duke of Burgundy, John the Fearless, and his men were behind the Cabochien revolts of the butchers and their reign of terror from 1411 to 1413. Certainly these butchers and skinners favored Burgundian leadership over the old royal reactionaries of the Duke of Orléans and his noble supporters, the Armagnacs, and they received aid from the Burgundians. After the failure of their revolt, the Burgundians ensured that the artisan leaders received safe passage out of France. In addition, the butchers' most eloquent spokesman was not a butcher but the famous surgeon Jean de Troyes. Finally, the rector of the University of Paris and others of high learning helped draft the far-reaching reforms that were momentarily promulgated against privileges of the crown and its royal officers. But butchers, lowly skinners, and a furrier (Philippe du Mont, a furrier; Thomas le Gouais and his children; butchers; the two brothers Legoix, "common butchers"; and Denys, or Denisoit, de Chaumont and Simon Caboche, animal skinners in the butchery of Paris) led the plebes (whom the religieux of Saint-Denis estimated at 10,000). These were the ones who planned tactics, organized the raid on the prisons of Paris and the massacre of Armagnacs that followed, and to some extent inspired and wrote the 258 reforms that bear the butcher-leader's name, the Ordonnance Cabochienne.[87]

Chroniclers were only slightly more ready to remember the names of rebel leaders from the ranks of artisans and workers than they were to recall those of the peasantry. In an unsuccessful weavers' revolt to overthrow the city council in 1281, "one Roussian called Li Kos" was singled out to be drawn and hanged.[88] In the 1289 revolt of "those without underwear" in Bologna, the leaders were Zanobi, the servant of Jacobo from Panico, and Michele of Vado, "who stayed with" (was the servant or apprentice of) Michele of Panico.[89] In the revolt of Flanders, 1297–1304, the butcher Jehan Biede (Bride) or Breidel and the weaver Peter the King were the principal leaders. In 1309 Breidel and Peter the King, along with John Heine, a fuller, led the weavers, fullers, and clippers of cloths "and all other workmen" in their refusal to consent to the crippling terms laid out in the peace of Athis-sur-Orge of June 1305.[90] In an unsuccessful revolt of fullers against the town council of Tournai in 1307, an unnamed "elected leader" was drawn and hanged, along with two commoners, Peter of Moussein and Alard of Bourgella, who gave advice.[91] In 1328, chroniclers named three butchers, all from the same neighborhood, who were dragged through the Campo del Mercato of Bologna for chanting "The People, People"; whether they led a revolt or not is difficult to tell.[92]

Eleven years later, the mariner Piero Capurro led his fellow Genoese sailors to mutiny against Aiton Doria because their stipends had not been paid. With fifteen of his associates (socii), Piero was captured and imprisoned, but his men went on: in his defense they organized further mutinies among the sailors of Savona as well as a "union" (unionem fecerunt) among inhabitants of the three valleys, bringing armed artisans into their camp and protesting with cries down the coastline of Genoa of "Long live Capurro."[93]

Along with Spinelloccio, son of Lord Jacobo, in the revolt of Siena in 1346, the Sienese chronicler also singled out an eighty-year-old man named Pietro, a tailor.[94] For some reason this case was tried in Florence, and the sentence survives. The court condemned to death thirty-three, three of whom (as with Spinelloccio) were nobles from the Tolomei family; the others, however, appear to be of low status: persons without family names or titles, one identified only by matronymic. The judicial list indicates that these included needle workers, carders, and other wool workers and residents of Siena's poorest artisan neighborhood, San Pietro d'Ovile. However, Pietro the tailor does not appear here.[95]

In the revolt of the Ciompi, the most famous of the artisan leaders was Michele di Lando, identified by the chronicler known as the *Squintinatore* as a wool comber, son of the woman Simona, who sold vegetables in front of the Stinche prison.[96] Chroniclers singled out other leaders who were previously disenfranchised wool workers—Simoncino, called Bugigatto, a carder; Simone d'Andrea, called Morello, a wool comber;[97] Luca da Melano; Betto di Ciardo, a burler; and others. Of the thirteen who met at the Ronco, a southern point of the Oltr'arno, to plan the first workers' assault of the Palazzo Signoria on 18 July 1378, twelve were identified by profession; all were workers or artisans—five carders, two combers, two nappers, a burler, an armorer, and a baker.[98] After their victory, the emergency council of the thirty-two syndics of the *popolo minuto* directed the new government of the Ciompi. The vast majority of those identified by occupation were disenfranchised workers of the wool industry: seven carders, four combers, a napper, a finisher, a dyer, and a weaver.[99] In the last month of life for the Florentine Government of the Minor Guilds (January 1382), a wool shearer, Jacopo di Bartolomeo Scatizza da Fiorenza, along with the armorers Simone di Biagio and Feo di Piero, conspired to reinstate the disbanded Ciompi guild.[100] From this political failure and the efforts to free Scatizza, the wool bosses and their allies began their counterrevolution, which succeeded several days later in outlawing the two remaining workers' guilds and reinstating the status quo of the old oligarchy.[101]

From archival sources, Richard Trexler has pieced together short biographies of many other leaders of the Ciompi, most of whom had previously been disenfranchised wool workers.[102] Government documents show that many of these workers were elected to Florence's highest chambers and held posts such as ambassador to foreign cities, despite the knighting of two patricians of June's constitutional revolt, Salvestro de' Medici and Giovanni di Mone. At the same time, they also knighted two from their own ranks: "Lord" Guido, a wool beater, granting him 2,000 florins from the property of rebels or from the treasury, and a carder named Chimento.[103]

The leader *(capo)* of the revolt of the Sienese wool workers, the Company of the Caterpillar, who aimed to restore peace and to steal and redistribute grain to those without it, was a cloth vendor *(ligrittiere)*, Domenico di Lano.[104] In their more extensive and violent revolt of the following year, the captain of the company was a Feraccio (identified by no family name or even a patronymic), who with his own hands murdered the Sienese captain of the people and led the riots against the Salimbene and other powerful men of the commune.[105] In the 1383 revolt of the working-class quarter of Perugia, the gate of Sant'Angelo, a later chronicler of Perugia named the adolescent Giacomo d'Odda from this working class–artisan neighborhood as the one who led fellow youths of the neighborhood to overthrow the ruling patrician faction, the Raspanti.[106]

In 1390 Viterbo was beginning to starve because of warfare and the brigandage of the Breton mercenaries employed by the Church in the territory of Viterbo. A greengrocer *(ortolano)* named Angelo di Casella went on an embassy to Montefiascone to negotiate with the cardinal of Ravenna for peace. He returned empty-handed and as a result took matters into his own hands, leading peace marches through the city and organizing fellow greengrocers to revolt against the city's papal rule.[107] After the artisan leaders of the Cabochien revolt of 1413 (listed above) had escaped into exile, other workers continued to lead riots against the Armagnacs. But the only one chroniclers named was the leader Capeluke, a public executioner in Paris. He organized the break into the prisons of Paris and its aftermath—the "inhumane" massacre of more than three hundred prisoners, who included noblemen and women.[108]

In revolts in Tournai in 1424 and 1425, chroniclers named the ringleaders. The blacksmith Jehan Boubriel (Jean de Bléhaires, called Blarie), who had been banned by the city four months earlier, returned to lead his guild *(collége)* to go on strike. He then allied his guild with the fullers, weavers, and "other laborers of the city"; erected barricades in the central market; and armed against the city's magistrates in 1424.[109] A year later, the "doïen" of the weavers, Guillemme de Brabant, because of a miscarriage of justice involving one of his guild members, led his fellow craftsmen on strike and followed it by organizing an armed revolt.[110] Then at the end of our period, from 1425 to 1428, a smelter of copper and son of workers, Michel le Maire, called "from

Ghent," led another artisan revolt in Tournai.[111] Further examples used later for other purposes show still other artisan and working-class leaders, such as the dyer Lionardo di Nichola, who in 1393 organized the last of the abortive ex-Ciompi riots of disenfranchised workers and minor guildsmen.[112]

We have witnessed the reluctance of chroniclers to name individual leaders who came from the ranks of peasants, workers, and artisans. One example is the August revolt of the Eight of Santa Maria Novella, when they singled out only Lord Luca da Panzano, leaving his eight co-conspirators unnamed, even though the judicial records pinpoint the commoner Piero di Ciro as the Eight's pivotal leader. Similarly, in the last throes of the Government of the Minor Guilds, artisans and Ciompi attempted to free Scatizza, a fellow worker who had tried to push the revolution further. The chronicler Ser Naddo da Montecatini makes clear that "craftsmen of the two new guilds" formed the bulk of the "great gathering" that then rose up in the Piazza Signoria, shouting "We are taking back our Scatizza"; however, neither this chronicler nor any of the others tells us much about the wool-worker leader Scatizza or his revolt that made him the final cause célèbre of the Florentine workers' government. Instead, Ser Naddo and the others focus on the lords, Tommaso di Marco Strozzi and Giorgio Scali, and their attempts to hold on to power during the last gasps of the government of the Minor Guilds. Yet while these chroniclers may not give these workers and artisans their due, they do not imply that these two patricians were the leaders or instigators of the protest, stirring the masses for their own ends;[113] nor as readers of these documents should we jump to the conclusion that they were.

Chroniclers' hesitation to name lower-class leaders might best be illustrated by Giovanni Villani, who goes to great lengths to describe the Flemish leader of 1301–1304, the weaver Peter the King. Villani goes beyond any Flemish or French chronicler in praising Peter's talents, especially his eloquence and power to move rebels, but he ends his portrayal by feeling obliged to justify the space he has just spent on someone of Peter's social status: "And thus it is right to preserve his memory."[114]

In some cases chroniclers' omissions impede more seriously our understanding of popular revolt and the nature of leaders and followers. For Florentine history modern historians have used the 1343 case of the crazed Lord Andrea Strozzi as a quintessential example of a class traitor and class outsider leading the dazed "leaderless" rabble by their noses, making wild promises to them, even insulting them, but ultimately using them for power plays within the political world of the elites—the only world, according to Sergio Bertelli and others, where politics mattered.[115] This view—even from this one extraordinary incident and a criminal case that followed against Pagnotto, the son of Lord Andrea, who tried to rouse the rabble again to do his bidding—is called into question, however, when a non-Florentine source is consulted. Despite the number of times modern historians have repeated the details of this revolt, not one historian to my knowledge has reported the contemporary description of the case by the anonymous Pistoiese chronicler of the *Storie Pistoresi* from 1300 to 1348, who adds further details. After the kinsmen of the crazed Andrea had captured him, put him in a cage, and dumped him far from Florence's city walls, another leader arose from the ranks of these carders and other "undisciplined and unarmed rabble [*popolazzo*]."[116] This one, a dyer, succeeded where the aristocrats Andrea and Pagnotto had failed:

> A dyer named Corazza became the leader [*corporale*] of the *popolo minuto* and those of low birth. With great daring, he went to the Palace of the Priors with 1300 foot soldiers of the *popolo minuto*. From fear they [the priors] did not block the door but let him enter. With flattery and smooth talking [*con buone parole*] the priors won him over and made him good promises, if he would not cause any further disturbances [*novità*].[117]

The Florentine chronicler Stefani may have referred to the same incident. At least, the two descriptions have in common the same estimate of the numbers of insurgents—1300 from the *popolo minuto*. However, Stefani did not connect this revolt to the previous uprising led by the Strozzi and mocked it as frivolous. Instead of being frightened (by Stefani's account), the priors put it down with ease: "They [the rebels] did not know what they wanted to do or what to ask for; they did not have a clue. On hearing this, the rectors took command . . . Having seen these events, the priors and others punished some, pardoned others, and brought law and order to keep the country from ruin."[118] More important, Stefani failed to mention the wool worker Corazza, leader of the revolt.

The Florentine judicial records suggest that Stefani was guilty of more than just sins of omission. None of the surviving sentences, books of accusations, or testimony that survive for this year[119] bear any trace of Corazza or of his revolt. Had Corazza's revolt failed so miserably as Stefani reports, Corazza would have left his mark in these records, as did the revolt's first failures under the command of Andrea and then Pagnotto. In short, the records suggest that the contemporary Pistoiese—not the Florentine Stefani writing forty years later from hearsay—got it right: no sentence or inquest survives because

Corazza and his *popolo minuto* succeeded in winning what they had bargained for (even if no chronicler recorded exactly what it was). The worker Corazza proved more successful than the aristocrat Strozzi.[120]

These examples show that chroniclers often refrained from "preserving the memories" of lower-class leaders. Certainly, archival records provide a wider view of popular leadership, showing deeper layers within villages and neighborhoods. From these sources a peasant or worker leader—a Peter the King or a Guillaume Cale—does not appear so exceptional. Despite chroniclers' prejudices, however, they do not give the impression conveyed by current historians that peasants, artisans, and workers failed to lead their own revolts and instead had to rely on the organizational skills, military expertise, eloquence, and charisma of class outsiders, their social betters from the clergy, bourgeoisie, and nobility. Chroniclers only mention such outsiders, even as mere participants, in less than 10 percent of the revolts composed largely of workers or artisans (16 of 171). Moreover, several of these were revolts in which nobles and craftsmen were united. In these, aristocrats did not stand above their artisan allies, making the plans and giving the orders, but alongside them; the artisans had their leaders, made their own decisions, and sometimes even led their aristocratic allies. Except in the extraordinary case of Jean le Bel's reporting of the Jacquerie (and Froissart's copy of it), not even class-prejudiced chroniclers suggested that the subaltern classes depended on outside social superiors to lead them. Instead, even those from the lowest social rungs—peasants, servants, men "without underwear"—are seen in their pages holding elections, organizing assemblies, planning tactics, overturning governments, and formulating future programs for reform.

CHAPTER 6

Women, Ideology,
and Repression

Historians of modern and early modern Europe have asserted that women predominated in the crowds of preindustrial revolts, that the ideology of these revolts was reactionary, and that almost inevitably, they were crushed, with brutal consequences. Does the evidence from the medieval sources back their claims?

Women

First, was "the involvement of women" in preindustrial riots so entrenched or "traditional"[1] as historians such as Bercé and Rudé have reasoned? They have asserted that because the food riot was the principal form of revolt, matters of the hearth—where women ruled—were crucial.[2] But, despite what may have become characteristic during the early modern period, food riots were extremely rare in the Middle Ages— hardly this period's characteristic form of revolt.[3] Nevertheless, were women the leaders of or the principal participants in these riots during the later Middle Ages? The answer is a resounding no. While they were no doubt part of the starving poor[4] who pressed before Florence's grain market of Orsanmichele in 1329, clamored for grain in the Campo of Siena in the same year, and screamed for mercy before the Virgin Mary in the cathedral of Le Puy, chroniclers do not name a single woman in these revolts.

One exception comes, not from a chronicler, but from a court case in Douai in 1322. Two "foul-mouthed" women *(par leurs mauvaises lanwes et par leur mauvais parlers)*—one married, the other single—"cried out in the middle of the marketplace" against the town's bourgeois and their grain dealers, inciting other commoners to threaten the grain dealers. They were not the only leaders or even the principal ones to incite the crowds in this riot: sixteen men (including a Scot, one from Arras and another from Hennin, a porter of sacks at the Friars Minor, a smith, a sapper, and two weavers) were also "big talkers [*gros parlers*]," who threatened to rob and massacre the grain dealers of Douai and tried to arouse many other commoners *(pluseurs du commun)* to dig into the mounds of grain lying at one bourgeois's house and on ships and barges docked on the Scarpe. As Georges Espinas indicates, the court record does not clarify the cause of their outrage. (It was, after all, a year of grain abundance.) The following year, however, the women's tongues were cut out and they were banished for life, while the sixteen men received sentences of banishment from life to three years and three days.[5]

Were medieval chroniclers so blind in reporting deeds worthy of preservation that women, no matter how notable the incident, remain hidden from history? The answer again is no. For other, nonrebellious crowds, chroniclers certainly took notice of them, giving women particular attention in religious movements and processions. For example, in Florence on 3 March 1382, "a great crowd of men and women [*gran popolo d'uomini e di donne*] processed through Florence carrying the city's most venerated relics, including the head of its patron, San Zanobi."[6] In addition, chroniclers often saw women as the principal objects of collective violence, as in the Jacquerie, first with the peasants' atrocities against noble ladies, then with the nobles' repression of village populations of women and children. Occasionally, crowds composed exclusively of women appear in chronicles, as in 1238, when a woman from the Rucellai family died. Women alone congregated at the family palace in Florence for the funerary preparations and mourning. We know about this crowd because a second tragedy struck: the terrace of the palace collapsed, killing twenty-six, all of them women.[7] Chroniclers even described women involved in military operations, as in 1318, when the women of Namur, "well armed and enraged, defeated the Flemings."[8] In an internecine conflict between Huy and Liège in 1328, the women of Huy joined the front lines, gathered projectiles for the soldiers of the bishop, and helped this smaller rival to prevail over its wealthier neighbor.[9] In 1352, thirty women villagers defended the mountainous northern borders of Florence: "screaming without stopping," they chased seventy well-armed Ubaldini soldiers across the hilltops and over the borders of the Florentine state.[10]

In the later Middle Ages, however, crowds of women such as those who marched on Versailles in the first months of the French Revolution just do not appear. The closest example to any such women's revolt comes from only one source and that one not contemporaneous with the events it narrated.

Moreover, it was a "revolt" that never happened. Prompted by false pretexts, it withered away with hardly a whimper. In 1302 the city councilors of Milan met to discuss whether the city should enter a league with other northern Italian cities. About two hundred "poor women," believing that the councilors had convened to raise taxes, "gathered with knives and a great clamor." They marched on the chambers of the salt tax only to discover that the tax had not been changed, and so they ended their protest. In fact, according to Corio, "certain seditious and bad men had instigated the whole affair."[11] The only other example of collective violence of any sort comprising and led by women comes just after the close of my analysis, but this "zuffa" or brawl was an internecine fight among equals and should not be labeled a social revolt, at least from the chronicler's description. In 1431 the women of the village Ambra, in the Valdambra between Siena and Arezzo, went to neighboring Cennina to collect grain. The women of Cennina met them with scythes and clubs; a "big fight" ensued. Those of Ambra won, wounding many of Cennina and leaving one dead before carrying back the harvested grain to their village.[12] Although the fight concerned collecting grain, nothing in the account suggests that it was a grain riot or arose from food shortages. In another incident, women serfs acted collectively in 1252 in defense of their husbands on the estates of the canons of Notre-Dame, but their action was a petition to the queen mother, not a riot as such.[13]

If not in grain revolts and if not as the exclusive or even principal participants in revolts, are women at least found in other revolts? The answer is yes, but their appearance remains rare. Most notably, they were present in heretical movements such as the communities of Fra Dolcino, whose girlfriend Margaret may even have been a leader. She is, however, the only one to figure in the documents on this movement. Women also appear at the end of our period, among the Hussite heretics of Sains outside Douai in 1422. They were present among the flagellants and other devotional movements in 1349. The abbot chronicler of Tournai, Gilles li Muisis, emphasized women's role in this movement, giving up luxuriant dress and jewels for the habit, covering their heads, and dispensing with "open" fornication and adultery.[14] They also appear in earlier devotional movements, such as the Great Alleluia in 1223, which had a political dimension: to bring peace to northern and central Italy.[15]

Further, women may have sparked a revolt in 1279, when the inquisition of Parma burnt at the stake Todescha, the wife of Ubertino, an innkeeper, and another woman, Olivia de Fredulfi. But despite women being the victims, no women followed the cause to vindicate their deaths; rather, "bad men, inspired by diabolic instinct," charged the Dominican convent (since they were the inquisitors) and beat up the brothers, killing one of them. As a result, all the friars left Parma for Florence the next day, and afterward a serious diplomatic quarrel brewed between Parma and the church. Churchmen and other "good men" of Parma moved "continually" between their city and Reggio, Modena, and Bologna, promising to make amends. Cardinal Latini, then legate for Lombardy, ordered the podestà (Captain of the People), twelve of its most prominent citizens, and its mayor to be tried in Florence. They went, and the city and its councilors were excommunicated.[16]

The scream of a woman hawker of watercress in Les Halles at Paris set off the revolt of the Hammer men, but it came not from any revolutionary plan or because she was a leader (even if by Bonaccorso Pitti's account alone, her scream was "Death to these taxes.")[17] Instead, she just happened to be the first one the taxmen levied with the new subsidies on 1 March 1382. Similarly, a servant woman's scream against the cardinal's majordomo washing the "pretty little dog" in the communal fountain of Pian Scarlano led to the bloodbath of foreign dignitaries on 5 September 1367. If women were among these crowds, chroniclers north and south of the Alps failed to mention it.[18] Another woman's scream in Florence's main square triggered an abortive riot on 22 December 1379, but the reason for her outburst is unreported. Afterward, the piazza was "flooded" with women and children to witness the rebels' executions. Whom they executed and whether any were women is left unreported, but "this flood" led to no new insurrection.[19]

Only in a handful (less than 1 percent) of the revolts did the chroniclers list any women or suggest that women were present in any revolutionary crowd. In 1243, with war between the papacy and Frederick II raging around Viterbo, "men and women, rich and poor, unanimously" rioted, "going to the houses of those citizens who had put their town in such danger, pulled all their belongings out, and set them on fire."[20] During the "Matins de Bruges" of 1302, when workers and artisans massacred French troops, Giovanni Villani claimed that "the women did even more than the men." They barricaded the streets and murdered the troops by showering them with stones.[21] An account by a chronicler from Arras corroborates Villani's claims, even if the women appear further removed from the theater of battle: climbing on to their rooftops, they emptied their chamber pots on the French soldiers.[22]

Women marched alongside men during the peace movement in Parma of 1331, led by youth who danced through the city and into the countryside waving flags; chanting; and carrying twigs, branches, and garlands.[23] In 1348, a chronicler hints that women, if not actually part of the crowd, at least sympathized with the rebels who resisted Count Louis de Male's reforms, which ended the weavers' privileges. After many had been executed in the main square and others drowned in the Scheldt River, the chronicler added that "the soldiers had obtained a complete victory and the town was entirely dominated; now all the men as well as the women obeyed the count."[24] Women were described as a part of the crowds of the *popolo* who gathered before Friar Iacopo Bussolari in Pavia, listening to his sermons and being inspired to revolt against the Milanese government and the arrogance and "tyranny" of their leading magnate family.[25] Women may well have been a part of the insurgents who resisted Venetian occupation in 1419 by capturing eight Venetian soldiers *(saccomanni nostri)*, drawing and quartering them, and sticking their body parts above the city walls. The Venetians reacted with a cruelty that stunned that city's chronicler, "making [it] the cruelest war he had ever heard of": of the Friulani who were captured, thirty men and twenty women were beheaded. Were these twenty women rebels or just the butts of the Venetian's "unheard of" brutality? Finally, during the English occupation of Paris in 1423, the bourgeois of the city took the major role in an attempt to depose the rule of King Henry and turn the city over to Charles. "Some were beheaded, others became fugitives, and one woman was burnt at the stake."[26]

Archival lists of rebels corroborate the impressions gained from the chroniclers: women insurgents were even rarer in letters of remission for France and judicial and legislative records *(provvisioni)* for Italy than in the chronicles. In hundreds of published letters of remission granted to rebels of the Jacquerie, Tuchins, *Harelle*, and *Maillotins*, not a single woman appears. The only exceptions are cases of wives appealing to the king on behalf of their husbands, and in these, the wives give no hint that they too had rebelled or had been adjudicated as rebels. Indeed, as part of their pleas, rebels often referred to their current state of poverty and their "responsibility" to care for wives and children, but these letters never implicated wives in their husbands' previous deeds.

In hundreds of other cases of rebellion taken from the published inventories of the royal letters in the Archives nationales at Paris (which at present extend from the earliest records of Jean le Bel's reign to 1362), the royal letters published in the *Histoire générale de Languedoc,* and those for Poitou (over 1,000 charters before 1425), only three letters from well over 10,000 point to women rebels (and two of these refer to the same case). Around 1338, after serfs from fifteen villages in the Laonnais "allied and conspired" against the Dean and Chapter of the Cathedral of Laon, the royal commissioners executed nine men and "branded many women."[27] In a second case, Jeanne, the wife of Thierry Lalemant of Orléans, had stayed in Orléans for too long and had been arrested in a "rebellion" against the town's governor that had occurred sometime before 1384.[28]

In the state archives of Lucca, Bologna, and especially Florence, I have unearthed lists of popular rebels totaling well over a thousand names; yet not a single woman appears.[29] The closest I have found to women playing even a supporting role in the Revolt of the Ciompi comes after the rebel's defeat. In August 1380, a woman from Vittorato (near L'Aquila?) guarded an illegal flag of the Ciompi for a certain rebel named Baldo from her hometown. After Baldo's death, she ran off with the flag to Vittorato.[30] The only list I know that may contain women insurgents is found for Ghent in 1358. It is not, however, a judicial record of condemnations or remissions for previous crimes of rebellion but a document granting families who had been banished during the 1353 weaver's revolt against Louis de Male the right to return to Ghent. Some of these women may have been the wives of rebels who had since died or disappeared during the previous eight years. At any rate, it gives the highest profile of possible women rebels of any document I know; even here, however, women represented a small proportion of the rebels, only twenty-five of 566 names, or 4.25 percent.[31]

No doubt, sexless terms such as *populares, popolo, pobol, gens, minuti, menu peuple*, and *communeté* on occasion included and covered up women's appearance in otherwise nearly faceless, sexless crowds. To conclude that women were the "traditional" participants or the leading force behind medieval revolts, however, would be to disregard the sources entirely. Not only was their presence extremely rare but what's more, their bravery usually turned in the opposite direction—to support the state against popular insurrections. Such was the role of a woman in Venice, who carefully dropped a building block atop the standard-bearer of an insurrectionary crowd who were attempting to depose the doge in 1310. With their flag broken, the crowd ran.[32] In 1416, the Duke of Burgundy's faction held secret meetings, especially in Paris, to plan "the most cruel and despicable plots one can imagine," but a woman revealed all, and "their evil" was nipped in the bud.[33]

Ideology

Except for the great revolts of the late Middle Ages—the Ciompi, the English Uprising of 1381, and the Hussites—little research has been done on the ideology of revolt. To be fair, few scraps remain for reconstructing the ideas, beliefs, and motives behind most late medieval revolts. Nonetheless, the general notion is that these revolts looked backward, resisted change, or attempted to resurrect some visionary but nonexistent golden age. Further, it is alleged that they looked to forces beyond the horizons of their villages, towns, or regions, such as the pope or emperor, to intervene and restore some ancient order. In places with royal power, such as France, popular rebels supposedly revered the king and blamed his advisers for misgovernment and for other causes of their discontent.[34]

First, any evidence in contemporary records pointing to popular rebels' respect for their king or blaming the king's councilors while shoring up "the good king" is extraordinarily rare, if it exists at all.[35] Only one source from the many chronicles and letters of remission describing the Jacquerie even suggests that the Jacques may have supported their king. The *Chronique des quatre premiers Valois* mocks the peasants' pride and solemnity moments before the King of Navarre butchered them: "with a fierce demeanor [the Jacques] held their ranks, tooting their horns and trumpets and crying haughtily 'Mont Joye,'[36] and they carried many insignia painted with the *fleur de lis*." Given that no other source alludes to any such flags or slogans, this may well have been this Norman aristocrat's sarcastic invention.

Later, on 31 July, the bourgeois Jehan Maillart toppled Étienne Marcel, leading his charge with cries of "Monjoye" and "Long live the king and the regent" and carrying "the banner of the king."[37] But this was the counterrevolution. Étienne Marcel had fought against the dauphin and had allied with his rival, the King of Navarre. In the punishments and remissions that followed Étienne's defeat and execution, King John II and his son accused the Parisian rebels of treason.[38] Certainly, six months earlier (22 February), when Étienne, backed by the people of Paris, broke into the dauphin's private apartment in the Louvre and murdered his two most trusted councilors before his eyes, the rebels hardly showed the royalty great respect. Even if their violence distinguished the king's evil councilors (whom they murdered) from the king (whom they spared, giving him the half-blue, half-red hood of their Parisian alliance minutes after the assassinations), their actions were taken by Dauphin Charles to have been deeply humiliating. The rebels' power play and gift of their hood were aimed at showing who was boss in Paris,[39] and the act ate at Charles as a deadly insult. He spent the next six months bitterly plotting how to redress it, and in August he succeeded, with the execution of Étienne and his most trusted men.

As we shall see in Chapter 8, the journeymen of Rouen insulted the king with a mock theater of their enthroned king for a day—the fat bourgeois— forced to do their bidding during their *Harelle*. In addition, as we have seen, the Parisians disgraced the king in several revolts of the early 1380s by violating his orders and attacking the Jews under his protection. Certainly, the cantor of Saint-Denis, Michel Pintoin, who tried to probe the psychology of the late-fourteenth- and early-fifteenth-century crowd, held no such belief in any deep-seated awe or respect commoners may have had for their king. Instead, he and his elite interlocutors, such as the provost of Paris; John Culdoe; and the king's chancellor, Lord Miles de Dormans, bishop of Beauvais (whose speeches Pintoin recorded but probably invented), pointed to the rabble's pride, "their pleasure taken to extravagant and immoderate lengths," "their seditious words," and their failure to address their demands to the king with decorum. Pintoin scorned their arrogance: "you order threats rather than pleas with respectful words."[40]

To turn to Naples, the other principal monarchy considered in this study, riots with slogans exalting the crown, the king, or the queen can be found, but does this mean that the *popolo* held the crown in awe, beyond reproach? In 1415, King Ladislao of Puglia ordered the Queen of Naples, Joanna II, not to return to her castle in Naples. The people of the city armed and revolted, answering her appeal, "My faithful ones, do not abandon me," with "Long live Joanna."[41] The Neapolitan people had not, however, always addressed their crown or queens so lovingly. This we saw earlier, when chants hurled at her namesake, the first Joanna, Queen of Naples, rang from Neapolitan crowds from 1345 to at least 1347—"Death to the traitors and the queen, the whore." Yet in 1374, the same *popolo* of Naples, in staging a three-day armed revolt in two neighborhoods against the city's magnate families, rallied their forces with cries praising the same queen whom, thirty years before, they had called whore: "Long live the Queen, the People, and death to the traitors."[42] Were the people so fickle or were they politically astute, realizing that to succeed in overturning magnate control and to govern their city they needed a powerful political ally? At any rate, the people's reverence for this queen, if it ever existed, was short-lived. In May 1379 the Provençal Joanna invited to Naples the French-supported pope, Clement VII, against the wishes of the populace, who supported the Italian pope, Urban VI. Joanna's feting of Clement at her castle, Castello dell'Ovo, brought the Neapolitan commoners once again to a boiling point. A master carpenter spoke out against her in one of Naples's major squares, the Piazza della Sellaria. "On hearing such beastly things, a nobleman, Lord Andrea, grabbed the carpenter and reprimanded him, saying that he should not say such evil things and be so disrespectful of his majesty [*della Patrona Sua*]." But the scolding only spurred the carpenter to speak more foully of the queen. Then Lord Andrea poked his finger in the carpenter's eye, blinding him. On hearing the news, the carpenter's nephew, called "lo Brigante Cosetore" (the brigand needle worker), came into the piazza, shouting "Long live Pope Urban." A great crowd followed, chanting the same, and rioted through the three neighborhoods where the French "oltremontani" nobility resided. They broke into the archbishop's palace, stole everything they could carry off, and marched on the queen's palace, chanting: "Death to Pope Clement, his cardinals and the queen, if she wishes to defend him."[43] Greatly upset, the papal claimant with all his cardinals left immediately by boat for Provence, never to return to Italy again.[44] So much for popular respect for and awe of royals.

Similarly, in other parts of southern Italy, popular forces mixed their chants of "Viva lu popolu" with "Viva lu re," if it suited their political needs, as in 1293 in L'Aquila, when the *popolo* appealed to the king of Hungary in their conflict against the king of Naples.[45] In 1351, it suited the same *popolo* of L'Aquila instead to curry the support of their local count against their king as they juxtaposed cries of "long live the count" with shouts "of the greatest curses and disgrace" against their king, the king of Naples.[46] On several occasions in the 1350s, the *popolo* in various places in Sicily allied with the king of Sicily against their local counts.[47] Such clamoring for the king, however, hardly formed any deep-seated popular ideology. As with the Neapolitan *popolo,* so with those in Sicily: the same communities could swiftly turn their backs on their king and rebel against him. Led by the peasant knight *(miles quidam rusticus)* named Rusticus, the *popolo* of the countryside *(terra)* of Catania did just this in May 1357 in a revolt against the king of Sicily.[48] Yet less than four years before (September 1353), the same *popolo* of Catania had revolted against their local count, Symon de Claromante, with cries of "Viva lu re, et lu populu." After electing one of the king's knights as their captain, they succeeded in expelling all the noblemen of this house from their lands.[49]

Popular attacks against the "tyranny" of the pope and the church or against the emperor and imperial rule far outnumbered the popular uprisings that turned to either of these superpowers for help to relieve them from their earthly woes. At least twenty-two revolts against the emperor that included popular forces, and fifty-nine against the pope, are seen in these chronicles. But as mentioned, such figures understate the number of individual revolts against these powers; often they constituted waves of revolts that spread through large areas of Italy, provoking numerous individual revolts in cities and villages. On the reverse side, only eleven popular revolts turned to the church for support and eight to the emperor. But in none of these were popular forces portrayed as naively or even humbly beseeching the intervention of one of these figures to restore lost rights (*deus ex machina*) to save them from oppression and injustice. Instead, they turned to popes and emperors as they did to other powers, whether a foreign city-state, signore, or count, as an ally against a common enemy. Thus in 1328 the Roman *popolo* joined forces with Emperor Ludwig of Bavaria to revolt against Pope John XXII.[50]

The lack of any deep-seated sentiments in such alliances can be seen in the hilltop town of Osimo in the Marche. In May 1322 the *popolo* turned to the pope to revolt against their signore, which may seem surprising: for the previous six years or more the pope had sent his forces against this town because they had formed an alliance with the Ghibelline leader in the Marche, Federico da Montefeltre. Along with the people of Recanati, the pope had condemned them as heretics—idolaters and worshipers of the devil. But with the death of Federico and the revolt of Urbino against the Ghibelline faction, the people of Osimo saw which way the wind was blowing and revolted to surrender their city to the church. The chroniclers, however, do not attribute their decision to any change of belief or to a new respect for the church; instead it was nothing more than Realpolitik. In 1319 the people of Osimo had revolted against the pope and were excommunicated, and in 1326 they would switch sides again, revolting against the Church, resulting once more in their excommunication.[51]

Nor did artisans in Rome look in awe and respect upon the pope as the ultimate arbiter of power in their city. As we have mentioned, more revolts of the *popolo* are found for Rome in my samples of chronicles than for any other city. On several occasions they ran the pope and his entourage of cardinals and other dignitaries from his palace or even out of the city. Only after they began to feel the economic pinch of his absence did they plead for his return.[52] According to Ronald Musto, one reason the popes remained for so long in Avignon was their fear of popular turmoil in rebellious Rome. "Unlike the Roman commune, it [Avignon] did not offer a persistent threat of claims to the pope's political status and personal safety, nor put forth a long list of claims to republican traditions and imperial glories."[53]

Of 1,112 revolts, in only one does a chronicler or archival document distinguish between the good king (or in this case the good queen) and his or her advisers. According to Matteo Villani, Neapolitans took up arms and protested against high taxes in 1355 "to show their power and freedom"; they chanted "Long live the queen and death to her council!"[54] But, as we have seen, there was no deep-seated love, respect, or awe for this queen, who eight years earlier they had greeted with cries of "Death to the Queen, the whore!"

The next closest case of a popular movement distinguishing between a good king and bad advisers or a bad lieutenant comes with the successful peace demonstrations led by the youth of Parma carrying their twigs, garlands, and flags and dancing in the streets in 1331. The butt of their anger was not their lord, King Robert of Naples, but his lieutenant in Parma, the notary Riccardo, who was responsible for setting taxes that the people of Parma found excessive and cruel. While they chanted for this Riccardo to die, along with his taxes and gabelles—"Moriantur dacia et gabelle et moriatur dominus Ricardus"—they also screamed "Long live the king." But nowhere does the chronicle explain this contradiction or suggest that the youth possessed any love or affection for the foreigner Robert, whom they probably had never set eyes on. Why should we assume that the people had any such deep structural need, especially in a northern Italian city-state, whose communal government was based on guilds and neighborhoods, held elections, and had councils of the people that numbered in the thousands?[55] The better assumption would again be Realpolitik: the *popolo* wanted to end a costly war with Lucca, high taxes, and the reign of the abusive Riccardo without calling down upon them the military might of King Robert. In fact, the king did not intervene, and by avoiding him, they succeeded in all three objectives without lifting a sword.[56]

Here, as in other respects, assumptions about parallels between the English Peasants' Revolt of 1381 and the continental experience are perilous. None of the revolts in Italy, France, or Flanders exempted the king so clearly from abuses while blaming his advisers as did the men of Kent and Essex in June 1381. These men branded the king's men as traitors, demanded that his closest councilors be executed, burnt John of Gaunt's palace of Savoy to the ground, and played ball with his chancellor's head (the archbishop of Canterbury), while they held the young Richard II in esteem, placing their last revolutionary hopes in him.

Of course, the city-states of central and northern Italy rarely had the opportunity to show respect to or revile kings, queens, or their representatives. But some had other titular heads whose authority would have been tantamount to kingly or hereditary rule, as with Viterbo and its lords, the prefects of Vico. On numerous occasions, the *popolo* of Viterbo revolted against the prefect, and their relish of communal freedom hardly showed any room for respect for this, their hereditary ruler. Let one revolt suffice: on 17 March 1387 the *popolo* rioted and sent the prefect into hiding. They found him, dragged him into the city's main square, and ritualistically humiliated him by pressing his mouth up the anus of his prized steed and sending him naked out of the city in a casket. Next, they went after his bastard son, who had killed the father of one of the rebel leaders. They skinned him alive *(e tagliare a pezzi vivo)* and fed his flesh to hungry dogs.[57]

Do these late medieval popular movements show popular movements as reactionary, a yearning for a lost golden age? Perhaps the most successful of any attempts to turn the clock back were the revolts in Paris against the regent and (soon-to-be king) Charles VI in 1380. In a remarkable ordinance of January 1381, Charles agreed "to restore all the customs and liberties to Paris and everywhere else in the kingdom, to what they had been at the time of Saint Louis and Philip the Fair, ending in perpetuity all the taxes, aids, tailles, and any other fiscal impositions." Further, he agreed to refrain from all murders and other crimes in the future, such as those that had been committed by his royal officials in their zeal to collect taxes and line their pockets.[58] But does such success in constraining a king's powers reflect a "reactionary" turn of the people, a yearning for some mystical world of lost rights? Cases in which chroniclers or other sources pointed to popular revolts that even mentioned ancient rights, much less lost ones, are extremely rare. The closest to any sense of lost rights comes with the view of the *Chronographia Regum Francorum,* regarding the Revolt of Flanders, 1323–1328. It held that Clais Zannequin mobilized his crowds *(multos populares)* along with those from Bruges in 1324 "by saying that those governing the country no longer ruled according to ancient customs [*secundum usus antiquos*]."[59]

More often, revolts were fought over threatened or recently lost rights to govern and tax according to previous conditions or liberties granted to corporate bodies of elected officials. The tax revolts of Flanders, from Peter the King in 1301 to Philippe van Artevelde in 1382 were grounded in this sense of franchises and their violation by overlords, the count of Flanders, or the king of France. In France, such threats of encroachment on rights can be seen throughout the period of my analysis. As seen in Chapter 4, news that the constable of France was sending troops to Rouen sparked workers and commoners *(minoris populi et mechanicis artibus)* in 1417 to amass in large numbers and riot through the city's streets, proclaiming that they would not obey the royal injunction or allow "the foreign brigands" into the city. Taking over the guard of their city from the royal officers, they pledged to preserve the ancient rights of the city *(in libertate antiqua).*[60] Violations of ancient rights also provoked those in the countryside to riot, as at the village of Seraing on the outskirts of Liège. The lords and aldermen of Liège passed a law in 1395 prohibiting the villagers from cutting down trees in their wood; the villagers resisted, claiming that they possessed such rights by ancient custom *(antiquissima consuetudinie)*. Certain bourgeois *(Burgimaestri)* and commoners *(populares)* joined their cause, sparking further riots against the Episcopal lords and aldermen, which led to the bishop fleeing Liège with his entire ecclesiastical court for Diest. Only after many meetings and negotiations and the promise that the bishop would pay a 4,000-franc fine to the villagers was he allowed to return.[61]

Chroniclers may have sometimes mocked the populace for their ardor in attempting to preserve their rights and customs, as with the Neapolitan tax revolt of 1355. Matteo Villani sneers that all the huff was only over allowing the price of salt to fluctuate according to market conditions *(consentita loro migliore mercato: con concenevole prezzo di cotanto movimento)*. They "puffed themselves up with such anger just because they did not want to let go of ancient custom *[ex antica consuetudine]*."[62] But I know of no cases when a chronicler suggested that the populace was naively yearning for some lost mythical golden age as opposed to the restoration of concrete economic and political rights.

Another means for trying to interpret the ideology of the crowd is to look at revolts in which chroniclers stated the rebels' cause or it was implied in the rebels' chants. These chants and causes point to miscarriages of justice (as we have seen in various student revolts of the early fourteenth century), the arrogance of nobles, the excesses and cruelty of rulers, the loss of a battle or the ineptitude of the military captains (as in the revolt of the Sienese artisan militia after the Nine's failure to take Massa Marittima in 1322), food shortages (in rare instances), and wasteful violence in factional conflict among the elites, as well as protests for peace.

As we shall explore further in the final chapter, religion played a role especially in revolts labeled heretical by the church or secular powers, but religious aspirations or ideals were certainly not a constant underlying theme or cause of preindustrial revolts, as some have assumed.[63] Further, some revolts may have had religious undercurrents, but more often it appears rebels took advantage of opportunities opened by a religious conflict rather than religious sentiment being the spur of action. For instance, because Ferrara had been excommunicated, its *popolo* revolted against the signoria, chased out the podestà, and opened the city to the papal legate and his troops. The chronicler does not, however, point to any underlying religious motivation or sudden desperate need for church services and other rites. Rather, the rebels seized the moment when they could ally with a powerful force, which just happened to be the church at this moment, to throw out their rulers for a variety of other reasons.[64] With other revolts, it is difficult to know whether religious solidarity and belief or a sense of secular justice were the motives, such as when the people of Parma attacked the Dominicans in 1279, after their inquisition had burnt two women at the stake.[65]

Nonetheless, when chroniclers reported the crowd's sentiments or motivations, the cause most often heard was that of "liberty" *(libertas)* and the desire to rid themselves of "tyranny." Despite the multifaceted meaning of this ambiguous word (tyranny), context often made its meaning relatively clear. Almost invariably it was a matter of political, not economic liberties, expressed in opposition to a political "tyrant." Those shouting it were bent on overthrowing their present regime, lifting "the yoke" of their oppression. The expression of these desires, moreover, cut a decisive chronological division to which we shall turn at the close of this book.

Do the majority of revolts across Italy, France, Flanders, and the Liégeois support Rodney Hilton's claims that the class consciousness of popular rebels of the later Middle Ages was a "negative" one, defined by hatred of the nobility or, for that matter, any other upper class?[66] Certainly, the ferocious rage of the Jacquerie and the massacre of their lords support this view, that is, if the chronicles are believed and letters of remission discounted. The letters claimed that rebels often acted with restraint, even against the orders of Étienne Marcel, and at least occasionally refused to kill their lords.[67] Villagers formed assemblies, but after deliberating, the letters reveal, they could decide not to rise up against their lords or pillage their property.[68]

Other Jacquerie-like massacres of nobles or other ruling classes can be found in these documents, such as the revolt of the "minuto popolo" in 1353 against "the good and rich" citizen-merchants in Gaeta, which Matteo Villani attributed to blind fury.[69] Similar hatred wafts from a letter of remission of the *plebes* who attacked the nobility in the small towns of Gimont and Simorre in the district of Toulouse in 1364.[70] "Like madmen," they assembled to battle against Pierre Raimond of Rabastens,[71] then knight and lord of Sauveterre. They invaded his village, sacked and burnt his castle; took his lady and three children, their servant, and movable goods; and led them to the village of Simorre. There they burnt some of the servants, hanged others from trees, "and committed many other very great, inhumane, and detestable acts of evil, outrage, and injury to this couple and their family."[72]

Our samples give further examples of wild hatred of groups that led to bloody massacres, but the objects of these massacres were not usually those of a class. Rather, hatred of the foreigner more than class fed these rebellions, even if class and foreign status often overlapped. Most famous of all—and probably the most bloody in terms of casualties—were the revolts of the Sicilian Vespers of 1282, which began as a popular revolt in Palermo against French soldiers and spread to massacring the French regardless of rank throughout the island. According to chroniclers, they killed any who spoke French in Messina, which included Franciscan and Dominican friars.[73] The "Matins de Bruges" in 1302 also was an assault against a foreign enemy, in which both men and women joined the massacre, "slicing the French like tunny fish" (but not the local patricians, who had provoked the revolt in the first place). Similarly, the massacre of foreigners in Viterbo sparked by the bath of the cardinal's pretty little dog was not so much or initially an attack on the nobility but on the foreign servants of cardinals and the pope. The butcher-led revolt against occupying troops in Cesena in 1377, fueled by their arrogance and consumption of everything in sight, focused on a lower social stratum—the foot soldiers, who were Bretons. The populace slaughtered more than a hundred of them, which was nothing compared to the church's brutality that soon followed.[74] Forty-four such assaults on foreigners can be found in these sources. They were not always matters of class antagonism, however: their victims spanned social horizons from a king's chief officer to domestic servants.

Should the more than 100 examples of the rise of the *popolo* and their assaults on magnates in northern and central Italy be described as "negative class consciousness"? More than blind rage against a class, most of these movements were instances of "the people" struggling to enter governments alongside noblemen, to control noble violence and tyranny but not to indulge in it themselves, by slaughtering the old elites. Once in power, more often than not, the *popolo* shared offices with their old enemies. Even when the *popolo* succeeded in running magnate families out of town, the chroniclers—including those from noble families—give little evidence of blind rage and massacres. More often, the people's desires were for peace and an end to factional and wasteful violence.[75] Only certain leading families were targeted, as with Friar Iacopo Bussolari's popular revolt, which resulted in dismantling the palaces of only one noble family, or the raids by the four craft professions of Parma, which targeted only those magnates guilty of egregious crimes against commoners.

What about the Ciompi? A chronicler such as the Machiavelli diarist or the wool shearer Pagnolo di Ser Guido provides catalogues of the *popolo min-*

uto's atrocities against the rich (whether *popolani grassi* or magnates), listing the palaces robbed and burnt.[76] But as is well known, the Ciompi did not turn blindly against their social superiors. Instead, they astutely welded alliances with members of both the magnate and *popolani* classes, rewarding some, such as Salvestro de' Medici and Giorgio Scali, with knighthoods and perpetual rents from shop stalls. Although the radical wing of the Ciompi—the Eight of Santa Maria Novella—at the end of August tried to ram through petitions to end the special privileges to Salvestro de' Medici and other fat cats rewarded by Ciompi rebels only six weeks earlier, they also combined forces with disgruntled noblemen, most prominently, Lord Luca da Panzano. After the fall of the Ciompi, members of two of the three new revolutionary guilds prudently allied with minor guildsmen to stay in power and to maintain their newly won economic and political privileges. Those who lost the late August rebellion, however—the Ciompi or *Popolo di Dio*—now formed alliances with those from a social class that less than two months earlier had been their most deadly enemies, the exiled magnates. Now they had a common enemy. Certainly, such flexibility and abrupt changes in alliances should throw into question any notion that the Ciompi's rise to power was fuelled by a blind rage against noblemen or *popolani grassi*, that their class consciousness had been fixed only as the negation of the class it opposed, especially given their positive and detailed economic and political reforms. More astonishing still are peasant uprisings. Far from rallying peasant forces to slaughter their lords (feudal or otherwise), these uprisings rarely opposed the lords. Instead, especially in Italy, peasants allied with lords in struggles against expansive city-states, often republican ones composed in part of artisans. Was this a negative class consciousness? If so, what class was being negated?

Given these alliances and shifting allegiances, should we assume, as many historians of the Ciompi have, that these and other insurgents of the fourteenth and fifteenth centuries had no "cohesion" and no class consciousness?[77] First, it is almost impossible to find a group, profession, or class in these documents acting on its own, at least with any success.[78] Instead, broad coalitions structured most late medieval popular revolts. In the revolt of Flanders in 1297–1304, peasants, artisans, some patricians, and the count united against pro-French patricians and the French crown. In 1323–1328, peasants, artisans, and again some of the bourgeoisie united, even if this time the count sided with the crown. Similar alliances were forged in Italian city-states. In 1291, for example, the four major crafts of Parma—butchers, blacksmiths, cobblers, and furriers—swore a solemn oath of allegiance with notaries and judges to protect themselves against the tyranny and violence of their magnates.[79] This allegiance would endure for at least the next forty years. In Siena, the merchant oligarchy of the Nine in the early fourteenth century provoked opposition that bound together butchers, blacksmiths, notaries, and the noble family of the Tolomei. With the oligarchy's fall in 1355, the alliance went further, adding other magnate families such as the Piccolomini, Salimbene, and Giovanni, along with the *popolo minuto*. The latter gained rights of citizenship and eligibility to hold elected offices, which lasted much longer than the gains of the far better-studied Ciompi and their artisan comrades. In France, opposition to royal taxes, especially when they were raised without the consent of the three estates (as Philip the Fair did in 1314) or against previous royal promises (as Charles VI tried in the early 1380s), brought a wide array of forces into the streets—*menu peuple*, bourgeois, and noblemen. But such alliances show commoners simultaneously acting as a political class with their own leaders and negotiating for their own rights. Examples include the *popolo minuto* in Italy or the weavers and fullers in Flanders who fought for and gained rights of election and citizenship. We will see that these groups, at least in northern and central Italy, had their own symbols, insignia, chants, and flags that united and identified them across occupations, craft guilds, and neighborhoods but also distinguished them from others, whether they were nobles or higher echelons of craftsmen who already possessed rights of citizenship.[80]

Although chroniclers may have viewed commoners contemptuously from their upper-class perches, they often saw commoners as a definable body—a class—if not in a strict economic or Marxist sense, then in a larger political and social sense of those in inferior occupations or those excluded from power. The commoners acted collectively in pursuit of new rights and redressed injuries to their members inflicted by those of higher social and political status.[81] Thus those who refused to pay their rents protested against the king's monetary policy, and insulted him by blockading his residence and throwing his meat in the mud in 1306 were seen as *menu peuple*. The *Chronique anonyme* defined them further as "fullers, weavers, seamstresses, furriers, cobblers, and many others of various types of work."[82] Another chronicler defined them similarly, as fullers, weavers, tavern keepers, and many other workers *(ouvriers)* in other crafts.[83] In official documents and letters, the authorities could pinpoint who these commoners were, as with the fines meted out after the revolt of the Cockerulle in Ypres, 1281: Count Guy de Dampierre spelled out the condemned commoners as "weavers, fullers, wool beaters, and their adherents."[84] Finally, the *popolo minuto* of Florence in July 1378 defined three new guilds for themselves, which redefined the old notion of the craft guild. The new guilds consciously cut across shop and skill divisions, putting barbers together with tailors, and doublet makers and soap makers with wool shearers.[85] This class, moreover, possessed their own flags: the "armed arm" *(braccio armato)*, the people, and the angel. Their shouts, which lasted long after the Ciompi's fall, continued to call for political and economic representation and rights: "Long live the twenty-four guilds." As this chant indicates, theirs was not a "negative sense" of class. They were not out to annihilate the nobility or the *popolani grassi,* but to join them, winning rights of citizenship and rights to elect and be elected to the highest offices in the commune[86]—what members of the elites such as Bonaccorso Pitti called "honors."[87]

Repression

Social scientists such as James C. Scott, along with many medievalists, view open collective rebellion on any scale as extremely rare and risky in preindustrial societies. According to them, almost inevitably such open attempts to combat the ruling elites resulted in repression. This repression by the state, landlords, or bosses, moreover, was often disproportionate to any previous offenses committed by the crowd. The number of revolts seen in my sample, however, is hardly miniscule. The quantity of revolts is all the more remarkable in that their reports come predominantly from chroniclers whose records are fragmentary, who provide a comprehensive view of few cities or territories in Europe, and who almost invariably disapproved of the popular movements they reported. Even if some, like Jean de Venette, might occasionally express sympathy with the insurgents, especially after they had been cruelly repressed, they certainly did not wish their readers to conclude that such misadventures could be profitable. Yet despite this bias in the sources, did these rebellions inevitably or generally fail, leading "only to repression and not to revolution," as Guy Fourquin has put it?[88]

Certainly, the sources unveil cruelty against rebels beyond even what the upper-class-bound sources saw as just or humane. In terms of the fame of such cruelty, the Jacquerie of 1358 leads the list. Although Jean le Bel and Froissart may have reveled in the gore and glory that the knights at Meaux achieved (protecting royal ladies by butchering thousands of artisans and peasants), others, such as Jean de Venette, saw the nobles' vengeance running beyond reasonable bounds.

For the knights and nobles recovered their strength and, eager to avenge themselves, united in force. Overrunning many country villages, they set most of them on fire and slew miserably all the peasants, not merely those whom they believed to have done them harm, but all they found, whether in their houses or digging in the vineyards or in the fields.[89]

Examples as grisly as the Jacques' repression can be seen with other late medieval revolts. If not in absolute terms of numbers killed, then relative to its population, the massacre and destruction of Cesena in 1377 may have been the worst of the Middle Ages. The rage of the soldiers completely depopulated a medium-size Italian town for a year or more. Here, a chronicler's lament speaks for itself:

On 2 February, another riot rose up; this time leaving dead certain citizens. The Bretons returned within the walled-town. The cardinal [Robert of Geneva] immediately sent for the English troops to come from Faenza, who had just defeated that city, and they came to Cesena. When they arrived, they broke down the walls and marched into the city as an armed force, and whoever they found, men, women, or babes at their mothers' breasts, they killed them all, filling all the squares of Cesena piled high with the bodies of dead men and women. And they threw others into the swamps . . . drowning more than a thousand. Some fled by the city gates, but the Bretons pursued them, killing or robbing some, raping others. They brought the beautiful women back into the city, where they raped then killed them. By these means, not a single man or woman remained in Cesena. They put more than a thousand baby girls and boys to their knives. They then robbed the city, carting off the most valuable property to Faenza, where they sold it to those from Forlì, Ravenna, Rimini, and Cervo . . . And thus the entire city had been laid to waste. All the monks and nuns had been captured, robbed, and murdered. And eight thousand, among the rich and the poor, left for Rimini, all forced to beg for charity, except a few artisans whose skills were needed. And thus by 13 August these Bretons had completely consumed Cesena inside and out.[90]

The sources tell other sad tales of mass slaughter and cruelty. From the late twelfth to the fourteenth century, heretical communities often ended with mass executions by burning: Flanders in 1183,[91] Vienne in 1239,[92] the crusades against the Albigensians from 1207 to 1240, and the slaughter of Fra

Dolcino and his followers in 1306. One chronicle concentrated his account on "the terrible justice" inflicted on Fra Dolcino rather than on his heretical views. It described how his girlfriend Marguerite was sliced up, piece by piece, before his eyes; the same was done to him, and all their pieces were then burnt.[93] In the mountain village of Montségur, southwest of Carcassonne, the inquisition rounded up 205 heretics of both sexes and burnt them at the foot of the mountain.[94] But this approach to stamping out heresy began to change in the fourteenth century, when the church pursued a more surgical strategy, targeting smaller numbers of key individuals and leaving the mass of followers alone, or attempting to convert them, as happened outside Douai in 1422.[95]

To set an example for others, dominant powers on occasion brutally suppressed villages, towns, or colonies that attempted to slip from their control. Such was the case in 1391, when the mountain village of Raggiolo sought help from its former feudal lords and regained control of its castle from the Florentine republic. Its victory, however, was brief. Florentine troops stormed the castle, won it over, and burnt it to the ground. Frightened by the soldiers' violence, the women and children carried away their most valuable possessions and took sanctuary in their parish church. The Florentines unhesitatingly burnt it to the ground, filled with those women and children, "killing and devouring them all." The troops then set fire to the rest of the village, "littering its streets with many charred bodies." Fifteen surviving "rebels" were led back to Florence, where they were either hanged twice by the neck or sentenced for life. In either case, the commune of Florence confiscated all their goods. The Minerbetti chronicler ended his report:

> And thus the village of Raggiolo, which formerly had counted 150 households or more, was entirely destroyed along with its castle, and all the houses together with its church were burnt to the ground. The place now remains uninhabited and broken. As a good example to the surrounding villages, the Florentines were more evil than they needed to be to show that they would do the same to others.[96]

As grisly as the stories are, mass slaughter of the innocent was the exception. In contrast to the disproportionate punishment of the peasantry following the Jacquerie or Robert of Geneva's retaliation against the populace of Cesena, repression of the most important urban revolt of the later Middle Ages—the Revolt of the Ciompi—appears remarkably light. Victor Rutenburg and Niccolò Rodolico claimed that the fall of the Ciompi resulted in "systematic repression," mass exile, and mass emigration,[97] but they supply scant evidence of it.[98] In September 1378, only forty-four Ciompi were sentenced to exile, and sixteen days after their defeat, the government invited back all members of the *popolo minuto* who had not been condemned as rebels "to live and work" in the city.[99] With the fall of the Government of the Minor Guilds in January 1382, the reprisals against the defeated were only slightly more severe; three were beheaded and eighty-five fined or sent into exile. But while some were sentenced for life, others were exiled for only a year.[100] Indeed, less than a month after the change of regime, the government even reissued crossbows to the Ciompi who had been chased from Florence in September 1378.[101] On 7 February—seventeen days after the fall of the Government of the Minor Guilds and the suppression of the two revolutionary guilds—the Sienese diplomat Giacomo Manni observed, "very little harm has resulted from so much turmoil and revolution: only fifteen people have been killed, of whom three were executed [by the government] and twelve killed in private vendettas."[102]

Instead of mass arrests, executions, sentences of exile, and savage destruction of innocent civilians and their property, governments usually limited executions or ceremonial displays of cruelty to the few. To take a colonial case, the Greeks on the island of Crete in 1342, led by the feudal clan of the Calergi, revolted and destroyed the castles lining the mountain crest belonging to the Venetians. The Venetians repressed the revolt but restricted their punishments to the leaders, "beheading some, hanging and drowning those they wished to give the cruelest death." But others were pardoned "so that the Greeks would once again become our loyal subjects."[103]

Governing bodies that discovered conspirators and nipped their plots in the bud often meted out special ritualistic punishments to the traitors. The most severe of those recorded for late medieval Siena came in 1324, when scions of the Tolomei clan and butchers of Siena allied to overthrow the Nine. Four butchers were interrogated, tortured, and beheaded, while forty other artisans were sent into perpetual exile along with two leaders from the Tolomei family, whose palaces were destroyed.[104] Leaders of artisan revolts also could receive ritualistic death sentences. After a failed weavers' revolt in Tournai in 1281, its leader, a Roussian called "Li Kos," was drawn between horses and hanged.[105] In the same town in 1307, the fullers revolted, for which two of their leaders were drawn and quartered and then hanged; a third who gave advice was also beheaded.[106] No matter how gruesome, these were hardly mass executions or wholesale destruction of civilian populations. Such punishments pale in comparison with the degradations heads of state dealt out to conspirators in Italy's "age of conspiracy" during the second half of the fifteenth century,[107] and even more so in comparison with the horrific carnage monarchies could inflict by the sixteenth and seventeenth centuries.[108]

The ceremony of absolution and grace following a revolt could be as vital to state power and authority as the execution of a few leaders. When the king finally broke the revolt of the Parisian Hammer men on 11 March 1382, he negotiated a peace by absolving almost all those guilty of rioting, hanging only seven at various gates of the city. Even such limited ritualistic sentences could, however, be explosive and counterproductive. According to the *Chronographia Regum Francorum*, these executions "caused [the Parisians] a great deal of shame and left them indignant. When their guilds were asked to assemble and decide on what taxes they would pay the king, either the tailles or in some other form, they responded that they would by no means consent."[109]

As the 1382 case illustrates, even the kings of France, once they had ended a revolt, could not impose their punishments arbitrarily or absolutely but felt obliged to negotiate with the rebels. In 1278, after the Parmensi had retaliated against the inquisition's burning of a woman by beating up Dominicans, the cardinal legate Latini excommunicated the city of Parma. He was finally forced to enter negotiations with the city council, however, so that they would cooperate in meting out punishments to those "bad men, instigated by the spirit of the devil."[110] A tax revolt in Tournai in 1307 did not conclude with the same dire consequences for the rebels as the weavers' revolt in that city in 1281 or a fullers' revolt later that same year. This, even though the rebels—"commoners [*communitas*], that is, the weavers, the poor, the fullers and others"—conspired against their city governors, assembled with their elected captains, beat up the tax collectors, hanged them on the city's gates, and then threw their bodies into the moat. Immediately afterward, "all the other commoners and combatants spurred one another on to greater feats of wickedness and amazingly continued to do so throughout the day." Eventually, an outside negotiator, the soldier Matthew de Haudion, had to be brought in to broker a peaceful solution between the commoners and the city council. Overwhelmingly, the resolution favored the rebels, as the abbot of Saint Martin, Gilles li Muisis (certainly no friend of the lower classes or sympathetic to popular unrest), reported.

> The next morning, they called an assembly of almost the entire city—the magnates, the middling sorts [*mediocribus*], and the little people [*parvis*]; hardly anyone dared not to attend. And on that day they chose thirty

electors and that night and the following day appointed prefects, judges, and others, who would be so elected every year on the feast day of the Blessed Lucy [13 December]. With this law passed, many who had been exiled for life, for years, or had left because of fines returned timidly, and the commune came forth and received and applauded them. And the governors by common consent chose inquisitors to examine the old rectors and record in writing everything said. And because new taxes had sparked off this rebellion, they were rescinded, and the order was read out and made known to all the commoners in a public forum.[111]

Thus not only were the taxes rescinded—the object of the revolt—but the city councilors were expelled from office. Even more profoundly, the agreement marked the end of the old patriciate regime and instituted a new system of government based on guild representation and elections that now gave political rights to commoners.

Another negotiated settlement, this time from the south of France, also favored popular rebels. In this case those on the losing side were even grander—the king of France and his lieutenant in Languedoc, the count of Armagnac. In 1356, this royal lieutenant levied a new tax through the Estates of Languedoc on the commune of Toulouse to raise war revenues. A year later, the "peuple menu" rose up against the count, claiming that he was the stumbling block for achieving peace *(stubatore della pace)*. They refused to pay the tax, assailed the royal officers on guard, burnt the gates of the royal palace of Toulouse (la Salle Neuve royale), and threw the furniture and plates from the windows. The noblemen of Toulouse intervened to negotiate between the two sides. In return for assurance that the count "would not be harmed, that his army be given safe passage in the region, and that the people would quit their revolt," the count promised that he would not punish the people of Toulouse for what they had done to him. Furthermore, he would not levy the disputed new tax, or for that matter, any other tax on the city.[112]

Even more surprising than these negotiated settlements that favored popular rebels is the general picture cast by more than a thousand popular movements in my samples. From the chroniclers' descriptions, no reported punishment followed the vast majority of revolts. In 70 percent of cases found in chronicles (726 of 1,012),[113] either the chronicler did not mention any repression or the rebels won their demands. The percentage would be much higher if letters of remission, criminal records, or *provvisioni* were counted, such as the numerous cases of villages reaping "handsome pacts" from the Florentine state after their tax rebellions in 1402.

Of course, a definition of victory depended on time. For instance, the Revolt of the Ciompi in July 1378 was a victory. After all, they ousted the present government and founded their own, even if, with another revolt that failed in late August of that year, part of the rebels' original demands were lost when one of the three new revolutionary guilds was outlawed. Ultimately, in January 1382, after three and a half years and another failed revolt to free the wool shearer "lo Scatizza," the other two guilds were destroyed, and Florence returned to the status quo of the old patrician guild republic. Similarly, the first revolts against the regent Charles VI in January 1380 were successful. As the king's own chronicler had to admit, in a speech he probably invented for the king's chancellor, Lord Miles de Dormans, bishop of Beauvais:

> Therefore, because of his paternal munificence, he [the regent] withdraws the subsidies and all those taxes on importing and exporting merchandise that used to be levied on subjects of the realm and foreigners. Henceforth, no one under any pretext can be forced to pay any of these taxes; each will have the right to buy and sell freely. The king has also decreed by his special grace that tomorrow he will have this edict posted on every street corner of the city.[114]

Furthermore, that royal ordinance survives, detailing the concessions Charles VI was forced to grant to the Parisian crowd as well as his subjects throughout northern France (Langue d'oïl).[115] Three years later, after numerous other revolts—some partially successful, such as the *Maillotins* of 1382, others not, such as the *Harelle* of Rouen and ultimately the victory over Philippe van Artevelde's army at Rozebeke on 27 November 1382—Charles's hand had changed. Strengthened by his military success in Flanders, he now marched back to Paris and withdrew the concessions he had legislated in 1380; finally, he succeeded in levying some (but not all of the originally proposed) "dreaded subsidies" in the north of France and Flanders. This subsequent history and turn in military fortunes does not, however, erase the fact that the Parisian crowd had previously won its demands.

In judging whether a revolt was successful or not, however, time remains a crucial variable. The revolt of the *Harelle* succeeded in defying and mocking royal power. They stripped the major abbeys of their privileges and cajoled notaries to draw up new charters that returned the rights of the barony to the commune. The charter drawn up at Saint-Ouën, which still survives, established these new rights and relations between the secular and clerical powers of the city.[116] But the revolt's success ended abruptly with the king's march into the city on Palm Sunday (30 March), only five weeks after the revolt.

Thus it is probably not just to label this colorful revolt—the best known of Rouen's many late medieval revolts—a success, and I have not done so.[117]

Another case, a revolt of the *popolo* in 1382 at Arezzo, is more difficult to classify. In 1382 the *popolo,* led by one called "Priore" from Lucca, rose up against Arezzo's magnate government, which at that time divided control equally between Guelf and Ghibelline factions. The *popolo* won, at least temporarily, and were able to force the nobles to obey their laws. However, the nobles colluded and defeated the *popolo,* captured Priore, and dropped him down a well. The chronicle does not specify just how long the *popolo* were able to enjoy their victory and impose their laws. Cautiously and perhaps mistakenly, I have not classified this revolt of the *popolo* as victorious.[118]

In the preceding pages, we have witnessed the success of a number of revolts. For instance, almost invariably, when students refused to attend their classes or migrated to other towns, city governments and their economies felt the commercial pinch, pleaded for them to return, and made concessions. Another group of revolts that often won was the early rise of the *popolo* in the thirteenth century against governments of *milites* or magnates, as when the *popolo* of Piacenza, with stones and mud, chased their ruling knights from the city and intimidated them in exile on their rural estates.[119] Such revolts did not simply rotate political elites; they resulted in fundamental constitutional changes, establishing new systems of election and political representation based on neighborhood districts and craft guilds and not on bloodlines.[120]

Throughout my period, revolts of the *popolo* succeeded in deposing governments of magnates or of outside elites—those of the church or the emperor— even if the *popolo* changed in social character from the starving *pedites* of Piacenza in 1090 to well-heeled citizens, who included merchants and bankers, backed by well-armed neighborhood militia. For instance, in 1416 Bolognese citizens rose up, chased their papal legate out of town, and changed their government from church rule to a citizen government with the traditional nine lord elders. Powerful citizens with old family connections were not, however, the only ones to assume the highest offices as the new lords. Craftsmen still counted; one of the new nine "segnori" was a butcher and another a doctor, and only three possessed family names.[121]

Factional struggles between elites, such as those who backed the church or the emperor or various stripes of Guelfs and Ghibellines,[122] often created power vacuums in which the "small people [*le petit peuple*]" could emerge and get their way, as in Genoa in 1415. With internecine battle in Genoa, its Guelfs appealed for help from the king of France while the Ghibellines negotiated with the newly elected emperor, the king of Hungary. Neither group of elites prevailed. Instead, a popular movement of "the small people and artisans" emerged victorious from the conflict, installing their popular hero Tommaso Campofregoso as doge. He ruled Genoa with a popular government until 1421, when a new revolt placed Genoa under Milanese rule.[123]

Successful protests of the stratum beneath the *"popolo,"* citizens, or bourgeoisie—the *popolo minuto* or the *menu peuple*—appear first in France and Flanders. As we have seen, these protests could occasionally achieve their ends without recourse to violence, as in 1252 when the "little people" of Paris and its environs protested against the corrupt practices of the city's provost. By threatening to emigrate, they forced the king's hand and changed the government of Paris.[124] The first outright victory of this lower stratum in Italy appears in Bologna in 1289, when "the people without underpants" (servants, apprentices, "and others of the lowest sort") booted Bologna's highest officer, the lord podestà, out of office and led him personally to the city's gates. No retaliation followed, either from the city government, the forces of the podestà, or any faction of the ruling elites. Instead, a new podestà had to be found.[125] In 1298 a conflict erupted between weavers and drapers in Huy. The drapers allied with the patriciate aldermen *(scabini)* and other "rich men" of the city, but the workers prevailed. In 1299 they destroyed their adversaries' houses and ran them from town "with all their goods, furnishings, wives, and families" to Liège, where they were forced to remain for two years.[126] Other rebellions of workers, artisans, peasants, and "the people" against city-state oligarchies, counts, kings, the church, and emperors can claim success in these documents: the "Matins de Bruges" in 1302; Flemish peasants and artisans, who defeated the cavalry of the French king later that year; and the butchers of Bologna, who chased out the papal legate and governor of the city in 1306.[127] The chronicles are filled with many other successes in popular revolt staffed and led by the lower orders: Bruges (in 1324 and 1360);[128] Ypres (1360);[129] Milan in 1253, 1256, and 1257;[130] Modena in 1263;[131] Florence (1323, 1343, 1378);[132] Siena (three times in 1355; four in 1368; and 1371);[133] Rome (1358);[134] Viterbo (1281, 1387, 1390, and 1391);[135] Arras (1356);[136] Bologna (1398 and 1399);[137] Paris (several times in 1380; 1381; 1411; and at least twice in 1413 and 1418);[138] Tournai (1364; twice in 1423; and in 1424);[139] Liège (1253; twice in 1302; 1312; 1327; 1345; 1346; 1395; and 1415);[140] Huy (1285 and 1299);[141] Louvain (1378);[142] Enna (1354);[143] Catania (1354 and 1357);[144] Siracusa (1355);[145] Messina (1284);[146]

the peasants of L'Aquila (1257 and 1267); its *popolo* (1263, 1293, 1330, and 1370);[147] and so on.

From the mid-thirteenth century to the end of our analysis, the growth of guild communities and neighborhood and peasant militias, as well as a strengthening notion of the commune in urban and rural areas, shifted the balance of power between patrician-controlled state-cities and kingdoms, on the one hand, and bourgeois, peasants, and artisans, on the other. The victories of popular revolts—which lowered taxes, blunted the arrogance of magnates, ended regimes based on war and violence, and brought to power heretofore disenfranchised social classes—were both the cause and the fruit of this shift in the balance of power.

Far from being a rare and risky business, as current theoretical and historical analyses portray it, popular revolt had a remarkable success rate, even in sources written by churchmen and secular elites, who sought to leave "good examples" to their elite audiences. Certainly these writers had no intention of stretching facts to crown a peasant or artisan revolt with success. Ultimately, the successes of these lower and middling classes would lead to another shift: during the fifteenth century and into the early modern period, states (in some cases the direct heirs of previous popular revolts) would adopt more authoritarian and hierarchical structures to survive and maintain their rule and stability. They formed larger territorial states in Italy and more coherent monarchies north of the Alps.[148] So far, historians have focused on the external threats to stability—foreign wars and the concomitant acceleration of new military technologies—to explain the growth of the early modern state, new bureaucracies, and new forms of authoritarian rule.[149] The stimulus from below has yet to receive its fair hearing.[150]

CHAPTER 7

Communication
and Alliances

Two works compare popular movements and protest across large parts of Western Europe—Mollat and Wolff's *Ongles bleus* and Rodney Hilton's *Bond Men Made Free*. Both argue for change over time but treat Western Europe as a whole, without exploring differences north and south of the Alps, between northern France and the Midi, or between political regimes, such as republican city-states and signorial governments in Italy or the urban cultures of Flanders in contrast to cities in the Midi. This chapter begins to explore possible geographic differences. To be sure, the lens could be focused on the smallest political regions, and useful contrasts might be drawn between political protests in Florence and Siena,[1] between Toulouse and Carcassonne, or between a territorial state such as Milan and the kingdom of Naples. But at this point in research, it is better to draw the camera back in search of generalizations over wider areas. For instance, do patterns of revolt, modes of communication, symbolic action, or the ritual of revolt show closer kinships between the city-states in Flanders and Tuscany than between city-states and their neighboring political regions? Do types of political regimes—such as monarchies versus republican city-states, or other geographic distinctions, such as urban versus predominantly rural and feudal regions—divide the geography of revolt better than propinquity? As we shall see, some of the differences can be explained by pointing to the unique character of Italian city-states, with their large rural belts *(contadi)* and their control over smaller cities incorporated by purchase or war in the fourteenth and fifteenth centuries. Exploration of other differences must await studies of issues other than popular revolt to provide keys for understanding historical questions that arise from the study of popular revolt.

Revolts and Differences of Political Regime

First, the political regime—whether it was the republican city-state, a signo-rial government, the rule of a count, or a monarchy—did not determine in any clear direction either the character of social revolt from one region to the next or its frequency. For instance, Milan had fewer social revolts than any large city in my samples from Italy, France, or Flanders, especially revolts that originated from specific artisan associations or the *popolo minuto*. In the mid-thirteenth century, Milan experienced its fair share of revolts of the *popolo* against the nobility, their vassals *(coi cattanei e valvassori)*, and the archbishop as their captain. These revolts flared in 1241, 1253, 1256, 1257, and 1264.[2] Further, as we have seen, in 1311 "the citizens" of Milan rose up against excessive taxation levied by the emperor. The leaders of this tax revolt, how-ever, were the two most powerful members of the Milanese nobility. One betrayed the other, and the revolt turned into a civil war between elites. Even in the movement's origins as a tax revolt, the chroniclers provide no evidence of any broad-based support from the *popolo* or lower orders.[3]

After a rebellion in Piacenza against the rule of Maffeo Visconti and his sons in 1322, the nobles and *popolo* of Milan colluded with the church to depose the Visconti. They then elected twelve of the "best" or most important citizens from the nobility and *popolo* of Milan to make peace with the cardinal legate and then revolt. Again, neither craftsmen nor workers appear. The rebels' chant was, "Peace and long live the church," but they said nothing more; nor did any standards of the guilds or the *popolo,* much less of the *popolo min-uto,* appear in these revolts.[4] Five years later, with the backing of the newly crowned emperor, Ludwig of Bavaria, the *popolo* of Milan rose up against the Visconti and imprisoned Galeazzo and his son Azzo. According to the Floren-tine, anti-Milanese Giovanni Villani, "almost all the people of Milan detested the Visconti's tyrannical rule, because of the excessive burdens and taxes imposed on the people." Yet, once again, the chronicles show no evidence that this "revolt of the *popolo*" extended below the social ranks of merchants and shopkeepers.[5] The next revolt inside Milan occurred almost sixty years later, when a civil war erupted within the Visconti ruling family in 1385 between Bernabò and his nephew, Giangaleazzo, the future count of Virtù. In this family affair, the "popolo" assembled and supported Giangaleazzo because of his uncle's excessive taxes. Other cities and villages within the Milanese ter-ritories also rose up, but again, the chronicles do not describe a broad-based popular movement—one with specifically identified craftsmen, their chants, and their demands.[6]

With the death of Giangaleazzo in the summer of 1402, his empire began to crumble as successful revolts for independence arose in Brescia, Crema, Como, Piacenza, Lodi, and elsewhere.[7] This spirit of rebellion reached Milan itself by the following summer, but it was the Visconti and their partisans who led the revolt to take control from the hands of the foreigner Francesco Barbavara. Nonetheless, this revolt from above is the only one in which a chronicler (though not a contemporary) points to a substantial popular backing. Corio claimed that fifteen thousand "plebs" filled the ranks behind the Visconti's general, Antonio Porro, chanting "Death to the Barbavara; death to the traitors."[8]

The following year witnessed the last of the Milanese revolts before the end of my analysis. After the death of the duchess, the *popolo* sought control over all the city's fortifications and drove out the German soldiers. But as the Minerbetti chronicler reported, Lord Francesco Visconti was the leader, "the most loved by the citizens."[9] With the disruption and chaos following Giangaleazzo's death, political revolutions ensued, but they were not social ones that fundamentally changed systems of rule or brought into office craftsmen or new social classes.

The Visconti's successful control over its *popolo* and the quiescence of its artisans and workers is striking even in comparison with Venice, the Italian city most renowned for its social control over its masses and for political stability.[10] Not only did the *Serenissima* experience more than its share of revolts from colonies and places under its dominion in Terraferma; artisans and workers within Venice's city walls also led or joined revolts against the government. Examples include the rock-throwing "plebs" who stormed the Ducal Palace in a revolt against the doge's new grain tax in 1266;[11] the sedition of "plebs" and "gente vile" to gain offices and rights within the government in 1296;[12] and the galley men or rabble *(le ciurme)* who mutinied against their captain, the nobleman Taddeo Giustiniano, and led a popular revolt, largely of sailors, to free the Venetian war hero, Messer Vettore Pisani.[13] Moreover, craftsmen and workers may well have been among the crowds of the *popolo* who tried to oust doges and revolt against the privileges of the Venetian patriciate and nobility in 1275, 1328, 1310, and 1355.[14] In 1275 one of the chief conspirators was a goldsmith,[15] and the patrician Andreas Naugeri described the conspirators led by the noble youth

Michele Sten in 1355 as the *popolo,* who despised the Venetian nobility
with "grandissimo odio."[16]

Did the relative social peace of Milan and failure of artisan groups to press
for their own demands over most of the 225 years of my analysis[17] result from
Milan's form of government? This was a despotic regime (to use Burckhardt's
term), one dominated by a single ruling family with little power distributed to
representative councils of the nobility, the merchant class, or of craftsmen.
On this score no such generalization should be hazarded. In terms of number
of revolts, monarchical states or cities without republican forms of government ranked alongside or even surpassed independent city-states with republican traditions, such as Lucca, or Pisa, Arezzo, and Pistoia before Florence
incorporated them. Rome, where the *popolo* supposedly was weak, ranks near
the top with forty-five popular revolts. Naples, despite possessing few published chronicles, can count at least eighteen, and Paris was one of the most
insurrectionary cities in Europe, with fifty-four revolts in my samples. By
contrast, some city-states with well-established republican governments were
relatively peaceful, with only eighteen for Pisa, four for Arezzo, four for Lucca,
and one for Pistoia. The Pistoiese revolt, moreover, is questionable: the city's
most powerful nobleman, Riccardo Cancellieri, led it in 1402, and it is probably better classified as an internecine conflict between Pistoia's two rival
noble families. Its popular element came later and was confined to mountain
peasants, who raided neighboring villages once Riccardo moved the center of
his resistance to the hilltop village of Sambuca and when Florence intervened
to stabilize the region.[18]

The opposite claim, however—that monarchies and signorial city-states
were the true cradles of popular revolt—is even less sustainable. Cities such as
Florence, Siena, Bruges, and Ghent, with their largely independent city councils and elected officials from the merchant class and craft guilds, mounted
the greatest number of popular revolts and the most sophisticated ones. In
these, workers and artisans played important roles and made social and political demands on their own behalf. Nor did cloth production fix a city as a
hotbed of popular revolt: Lille appears only once in my samples (a tax revolt
in 1299), and Douai, despite having the earliest references to industrial strikes
of any city in Europe, appears only six times.[19] By contrast, Liège, with an
unimportant cloth industry, ranked as one of the most revolutionary towns
of the Middle Ages.

A line might also be drawn between revolts in northern France and Flanders, on the one hand, and southern France, on the other, with its different

traditions of Roman law and city government. But, while some regions of France, such as Poitou,[20] appear to have had fewer popular insurrections than other areas, it would be difficult to claim that northern cities such as Paris, Rouen, and Amiens were more prone to rebellion than the southern ones of Montpellier, Toulouse, and Carcassonne. Although Paris leads the list for France, Toulouse comes second, with fifteen revolts, and Carcassonne, with eleven, is tied for third with Rouen. However, the chronicle tradition, especially as represented in the multivolume collections begun in the nineteenth century, is much stronger for northern France. These collections contain no less than eighty chronicles for northern and central France, with revolts in the period 1200–1425; most of these, in fact, were written in the Île de France and Normandy. By contrast, these collections contain no chronicles from Languedoc that describe revolts in the same time span, and from publications outside these editions, I have found only four chronicles that mention revolts in the south.[21]

Interregional Communication

Despite possible differences in popular revolt among city-states of Italy, between the north and south of France, or between urbanized and predominantly rural regions, the differences between the north and south of Europe (or at least between Italy, on the one hand, and France, Flanders, and the Liégeois, on the other) are the most striking. Popular revolt in the north tended to be more interregional, even international, than in Italy. To be sure, Italian elites had their interregional organizations, such as the Guelf and Ghibelline parties, with their networks of association and protection for exiles that crisscrossed the peninsula, extending even north of the Alps. Noble podestà, with their judges, notaries, and police, also circulated through northern and central Italy, moving from town to town on six-month terms of office. Yet revolt among commoners in Italy tended to be an isolated event, limited by a city's walls.

By contrast, state and municipal archives north of the Alps still hold letters and other evidence of communication between insurgents of different cities who were attempting to rouse support, even across national boundaries. As early as 1274, the weavers and fullers of Ghent coordinated protests with Bruges and other cities in Brabant. When the patricians of Ghent denied these cloth workers their demands, the workers immediately pressured their employers by leaving Ghent en masse to fill jobs they had prearranged with artisans in other places throughout Brabant.[22] In the Flemish revolts of 1302, towns on either side of the French border communicated with each other. In their treaties with the king of France, towns such as Douai knew exactly what the king had offered the rebels of Lille and bargained for the same.[23] Furthermore, the revolts of Flanders of 1297–1304 and of 1323–1328 not only coordinated the efforts of city craftsmen with those of commoners who resided in these cities' rural belts, but also integrated commoners' efforts across maritime Flanders. Despite important battles such as the "Matins de Bruges" in 1302 or the peasant victory over the French cavalry at Courtrai (later to gain fame as the battle over the golden spurs), these two waves of Flemish revolts were not revolts of Bruges, Ghent, Ypres, or Courtrai per se but were regional, even international revolts that crossed the borders of Flanders, Hainault, and Liège as well as the Flemish-French frontier.[24] The same happened again with tax revolts against Charles VI in the early 1380s.[25]

In the territory of Liège as early as 1265, the citizens of its principal towns—Liège, Huy, Sint-Truiden, and Dinant—allied and formed an interurban federation to oppose new taxes from their prince-bishop and destroyed his palace.[26] Later in the century, the youth of these cities formed antiprince and antipatrician alliances (called the white hoods), which looked to the cities of northern France for inspiration. They also called themselves "Les enfants de France."[27]

Evidence from chants and rebels' letters shows that the Jacquerie of 1358 and the array of riots from Paris through Normandy to Orléans, Clermont-Ferrand, Saint-Flour, and as far south as Montpellier, were also international in character. Popular rebels solicited aid and counsel, not only across vast regions of France, but also across the national borders of France, Flanders, and England. Even before violence broke out in the countryside, Étienne Marcel and the aldermen of Paris had written letters to the major cities of France *(les bonnes villes)* requesting that they wear the Parisian hoods (half red and half blue) in sympathy and alliance with the capital.[28] Later, Marcel wrote to communes in Picardy and Flanders soliciting counsel and aid in joining the uprising of the Jacquerie. Then with the prospect of the Jacques' failure, he tried to maintain support from these cities by distancing himself from what cities and foreign elites now saw as the peasants' atrocities. Finally, in late June and July, he wrote again to Flemish cities in a last desperate plea for intervention. Some of these letters survive.[29] In them, Marcel further describes having sent town criers from Paris to sixty villages in the Beauvaisis, Artois, and Picardy, begging the Jacques to restrain their violence against the lords.[30] Marcel's ties with Flanders are evident in his adopted war cry—"Gand!"—used to remind his followers of Jacob van Artevelde's victory over this town's overlord twenty years before.[31] This tradition of letter writing and mutual encouragement between insurgents across national boundaries continued with the next conjuncture of revolts in northern France and Flanders. Artisans from Liège wrote letters to Ghent praising their cause and, beyond words, also supplied them with grain.[32] After the battle of Rozebeke, "very seditious and evil letters" were found in Courtrai, which the Parisian rebels had sent to their Flemish comrades.[33]

Lines of communication did not flow exclusively between rebellious bourgeois or artisans in the north. According to *La chronique des quatre premiers Valois*, the Jacques' leader Guillaume Cale initiated proceedings between the Jacques and Étienne Marcel's bourgeois.

[Cale] sent some of his wisest and most notable men to see the provost of the merchants of Paris and wrote to him that he was at his service and would aid and help him if the need arose. This filled the leaders of the three estates with joy, and they wrote to Guillaume Charles [Cale] that they were all ready to give him help. As a result of their cooperation, the Jacques were able to push as far as Gaillefontaines.[34]

Complex tactics and negotiations were also evident when Étienne Marcel; his lieutenant in the field, the grocer Pierre Gilles; the mayor of Meaux, Jehan Soulaz; and the peasants mobilized their forces to besiege in unison the dauphin's stronghold of the Marché at Meaux.[35] Letters of remission show further interaction between the Parisians and the country rebels during the Jacquerie. The villager Jean Hersent of Châtres-sur-Montehery (today, Arpajon, south of Paris in the Île de France) announced Étienne Marcel's orders to assemble all the men of the region to arm themselves:

By virtue of the command given to him by the former Étienne Marcel, then provost of the merchants, this Jehan proclaimed in this village of Châtres that all manner of people allowed to bear arms [should] join together at Chaillilez-Loncjumel[36] to present themselves and their weapons and to parade in front of certain officers [*commissaries*], whom the provost of the merchants had appointed for this task, and to follow these officers' orders.[37]

Paris was not the only town with revolutionaries who traveled freely between city and countryside, spreading seeds of rebellion for a common cause.

Another letter of remission reports that a Pierre de Montfort gave speeches "to rouse and sow discord between the commoners [*menu commun*] and the big fish [*les gros*] of the town [Caen];" he also "drew in people from Picardy" to Caen to join the revolt.[38]

The revolts of 1380–1383 in France and Flanders against Charles VI's subsidies had wider networks of communication and assistance than the Jacquerie and the bourgeois rebellion of Étienne Marcel. The religieux of Saint-Denys claimed that Paris "set the example of revolt" and "other cities imitated the capital."[39] Letters between Paris and Rouen in 1382 corroborate the chronicler's claim. According to the chronicler of the duke of Bourbon, the Parisians' example inspired revolts in smaller towns, such as Clermont-en-Beauvaisis.[40] But, as attested by the chants of insurgents and the accounts of other chroniclers such as Froissart, Philippe van Artevelde's Ghent was even more important than Paris as a revolutionary beacon in the 1380s—the true epicenter of revolt across regional, national, and linguistic borders: in the streets of Rouen, Amiens, and Paris they shouted "Vive Gand!"[41]—reminiscent of Étienne Marcel's cry almost thirty years earlier. The chronicler of Saint-Denis also pointed to the crucial importance of letters, messengers, and rabble-rousers who crossed regional, national, and physical boundaries to solicit aid, recruit forces, and set examples. On the outbreak of rebellion in Rouen in 1382, he speculated: "If public opinion is to be believed, it came from the Flemish, who had labored under a similar plague of rebellion [*peste rebellionis*], spread by their messengers and leaders and by the example of the English, who, at the same time, were rebelling against their king and the magnates of the realm."[42] In 1382 the Parisian rebels exchanged their crimson-and-blue hoods used on the eve of the Jacquerie for white ones to show solidarity with the Gentenars in their struggle against their count and the French crown. According to Froissart, communication of these rebels' defeat at Rozebeke in 1382 also affected rebels back in Paris and in other *bonnes villes* of France.

> For if the villains had achieved their purpose, the commoners would have engaged in rebellion everywhere, committing unprecedented ravages and atrocities against the nobly born. The citizens of Paris with their long hammers became more cautious. How did they like the news of the defeat of the Flemings and the death of their leader? They were not cheered by it. Neither were the Good men in a number of other towns.[43]

Similarly, in the south of France, the steep increases in the hearth tax that Charles V imposed toward the end of his life, followed by the subsidies of his son, spurred revolts in Montpellier, Clermont de Lodève, Le Puy, Alès, Béziers, and the surrounding countryside.[44] A letter of remission to the inhabitants of Clermont shows a contagion of southern rebellion, with one place influencing another: "Finally, the lord of Clermont realized the seriousness of these crimes, that such crimes were now common in his territory and were beginning to increase and to inflame others, and would lead to evil consequences." According to this letter, the influence and communication went beyond the immediate region of Montpellier. The residents of Clermont "wished to follow in the footsteps of Montpellier, perpetrating murders and other nefarious crimes against [the] venerable and renowned men of our councils of the district of Rouergue and other officials and councilors of our kingdom."[45]

Another wave of revolts in the Beauvaisis followed on the heels of the Cabochien rebellion of Paris in 1413. First Noyon, then Compiègne "had persisted in stubbornly resisting the orders of the king. Seeing these examples and that none had been executed by the king, those of Soissons rebelled against Charles."[46] The later rebels were not as lucky. Nonetheless, interregional communication, cooperation, and inspiration remained rife in northern France after the international "cluster" of revolts in the early 1380s.[47]

Such "contagion" of revolt may seem natural, even inevitable, but the city-states and monarchical zones of Italy provide little evidence of it, especially with popular revolts composed mostly of artisans and workers. Certainly, city elites pooled resources to repress popular revolts; even cities that were traditionally political rivals, such as Guelf Florence and Ghibelline Siena, came to one another's aid to stamp out political opposition when it erupted from below.[48] Florence might send its forces a considerable distance, even beyond its immediate sphere of territorial security, to help suppress a political uprising from below. One example occurred in 1395, when Florentine troops helped the marchese of Ferrara to squash a peasant uprising.[49] In numerous popular revolts of Italian city-states from the thirteenth to the early fifteenth century, however, scant evidence appears of pleas for assistance: town criers sent from one city to another to shore up popular support; or interregional coordination, when the rebels were artisans or the insurgent *popolo minuto*. True, Victor Rutenburg has suggested that the postplague revolts in Siena and Florence were interregional. He maintains that the Sienese revolt of the Company of the Caterpillar (Bruco) had "an echo" several years later in the Revolt of the Ciompi and that "the experience of their Sienese comrades prepared" its way, but he supplies no evidence for this claim other than *post hoc ergo propter hoc:* Florence's Ciompi happened after Siena's Bruco.[50] Further, one or two wool workers can be identified as from Siena in lists of condemned Florentine Ciompi.[51] But is this proof of influence or of any cross-fertilization of revolutionary ideals or personnel from one city to another? Such men may have been recent immigrants or outside agitators, but they could have been long-term residents of Florence, even natives of the city, whose parents had emigrated from Siena. No one has supplied evidence that these workers had belonged to the earlier Company of the Caterpillar or had participated in Siena's revolt seven years before. Neither the Revolt of the Ciompi nor other Italian popular uprisings of commoners supplies anything akin to the concrete evidence of communication north of the Alps between distant villages and Paris during the Jacquerie. Totally unknown in Italy was the coordination among weavers and fullers of various cities during the many Flemish revolts of the fourteenth century. Nor were there signs of sympathy given by one group of rebels to another in Italy, especially over considerable distances and across linguistic and national borders, as with Parisians wearing the white hoods of Ghent or yelling "Gand!" to show their solidarity during the international rebellion against Charles VI and his subsidies.[52]

There were exceptions to the isolation that marked Italian popular uprisings, but these come mainly from rebellions organized on high by emperors, popes, or city governments. Even here the influence from one place to another was often slight. In 1329 the Pisans threw off the rule of the Emperor Ludwig of Bavaria by rising up against his *vicarius* and sending his officials out of town. Neighboring Lucca's success against the emperor earlier that year had inspired them, and Lord Marco Visconti came from Lucca with his troops to assist the Pisans.[53] In 1337, the citizens of Orvieto overthrew the signoria of the Monaldeschi family, "who had ruled over them in such a tyrannical fashion." According to Giovanni Villani, the *popolo* of Fabriano in the Marche then "in a similar fashion" chased out their tyrants and set up a government of the people, perhaps suggesting that Orvieto's revolt had inspired Fabriano's. However, none of the chronicles state that the *popolo* of these communes were in communication or that Orvieto provided any support.[54] In 1387, "on hearing the news" that "those of Amelia, Terni, and other places nearby" had risen up against the papal prefect with the cries of "Long live the church," Narni also overthrew church rule.[55] In 1390, on hearing the news of Padua's rebellion against Milanese rule and chasing out the Count of Virtù's guardsmen, "almost all the citizens of Verona set their hearts [*dirizzarono li animi loro*] on rebelling against him, since they greatly loathed him and his wicked tyranny." On 24 June "the entire *popolo*, citizens and the others, took up arms and threw out all the Milanese guards and officials,"[56] but the meticulous

Minerbetti gives no hint that the Veronesi received anything from Padua except perhaps inspiration from their example. Besides, all of the above were revolts of established governments or of prominent citizens—hardly ones led and staffed by artisans.

More exceptional was the apparent coordination of revolts that formed the Sicilian Vespers of 1282, which began as a popular rising outside Palermo on Easter Monday and quickly spread through the island to Trapani, Val di Mazara, Messina, and elsewhere. It is only one of two revolts with a popular base in which letters sent from one town to another survive.[57] But in both cases, the letters came from the leaders of city-states, not from artisans, peasants, or workers. Further, although no evidence of direct communication survives, the contagion of anti-French sentiment had spread as far north as Orvieto by May. The Orvietani massacred three thousand French soldiers and officers, leaving a "bloody heap," which a generation later was immortalized in Dante's *Divine Comedy.*[58]

The most extensive coordination of rebels across cities and territories of any revolt in Italy between 1200 and 1425 came with the revolt against church rule that spread from Milan to Naples in 1375–1376.[59] The rebels even produced a flag to unite them, "a huge banner or standard with the letters LI-BERTAS stitched in gold."[60] But this series of revolts was the exception that proves the rule: its coordination came not from the popular insurgents themselves, much less artisans and workers, but, as one chronicler after another noted, was carefully manipulated by the governments of Florence and Milan. These governments sent their spies, military advisers, and soldiers to assist cities and villages throughout central Italy "to throw off the yoke of the evil Pastors." According to a Milanese chronicler, the revolt's success rested on the Florentines' "especial astuteness and wisdom and on the advice and aid sent by Bernabò and Galeazzo Visconti."[61] According to Ser Guerriero da Gubbio, the Florentines "worked undercover [*lavoravano a la coperta*] against the church in 1375, cutting many deals." He suggests that they were behind the first revolts against the papacy in November of that year at Orte, then at Viterbo, Città di Castello, and Perugia.[62] The Florentine diarist of the Machiavelli family gloats that the battle cry against the church at Perugia was "Death to the Abate [the pope's legate at Perugia] and long live the *popolo* of Florence!" and at Spoleto in the same year it was "Long live Florence and Liberty!"[63]

The prior planning of Florence and Milan was not the only reason for the brushfire speed by which this most extensive of Italian revolts spread across large parts of the peninsula. The revolt had other nodes, and its contagion—

one city-state imitating another—is seen explicitly in this wave of revolts like none other described for Italy in our period. According to an anonymous chronicler of Padua, who listed thirty-six places not counting their constituent villages within their *contadi,* "one followed the other; they were all of one piece [*omnes infra unum est*]."[64] According to Corio, in less than a month, "almost all the cities of Romagna, Assisi, Viterbo, Città di Castello, Narni, Gubbio, the Ducato [of Spoleto], the papal states [Patrimonio] and the Campagna imitated Perugia's example by rising up and refusing obedience to the Holy See." In a "short time" these led to further revolts in "Urbino, Fermo, Sassaferrato, and other places and strongholds in the Marche of Ancona."[65] In February 1376, inhabitants of Fermo assisted those of Ascoli in throwing off church rule,[66] and Rodolfo of Camerino fomented rebellion in Macerata against the church "and occupied many lands that had been under church control."[67] In March, Florence assisted Bologna in its revolt against the church. And the example of Bologna set off revolts in Imola and Cento.[68] At Cento, their cry against papal rule was "Long live the commune of Bologna and the church." "And they said that they wanted to do what the Bolognese had done."[69] Yet, to repeat, even if commoners joined the forces that defeated the papal legates and established governments of the people, it was military leaders and governments—not artisans, workers, or peasants—who initiated and directed this communication, thereby enabling the contagion to spread.

Finally, as in so many other ways, Cola di Rienzo's revolt and brief rise to power as "tribunus" and "liberator of the sacred Republic of Rome" was another exception: it was international in its appeal and cause. Cola sent letters to the papacy in Avignon and to Emperor Charles of Bohemia in Prague. He made appeals to other Italian city-states from May to December 1347; to Viterbo, Perugia, Lucca, Florence, and Sabina (these still survive).[70] By Villani's account, Cola also sent letters to all the heads of cities in Italy.[71] But again, it would be wrong to call this revolt one of workers and artisans.[72] His was a bourgeois revolt against the arrogance of the Roman nobility. As Cola's principal chronicler put it, those who followed him were the "popolari discreti," "buoni uomini," "many well-to-do and rich merchants [*moiti discreti e ricchi mercatanti*]," and even what the Anonimo romano called the *cavallerotti:* those from good families, including the lower echelons of the nobility, who ruled smaller regional city-states.[73] The nearly complete absence of Italian rebels' cross-territorial communication does not result from any parochialism on the part of Italian chroniclers, as opposed to the "internationalism" of northern chivalric writers such as Jean le Bel, Froissart, or Monstrelet. Far from it: as we have seen, Italian chroniclers relied on extensive webs of international merchant exchange; they reported revolts north of the Alps more often than any northern chivalric writer mentioned those in the south.

City and Countryside

A second difference between revolts north and south of the Alps hinges on the first—the interconnections, support, and communication between commoners of the city and those in the surrounding countryside. Rebellions in Flanders through the fourteenth century combined the forces of rural artisans, peasants, and townsmen in Bruges, Ghent, Ypres, Courtrai, and smaller towns to challenge new taxes and the power of urban patricians, counts, and kings of France.[74] In the longest and most widespread of these rebellions (1323–1328), not only for Flanders but for medieval Europe, peasants took the initiative and their principal leaders were from the countryside—Clais Zannekin, Segher Jonssone, and Jacques Peit. In Liège, after a successful revolt in 1312 against the patricians, which massacred over two hundred and chased the others from office, artisans sought to consolidate their position in the city by inscribing large numbers of peasants and artisans from the surrounding countryside into the commune as "bourgeois forains," which gave them protection and the chance to escape the authority of their lords.[75] More than a division between city and countryside, the popular rebellions of fourteenth-century Flanders and the Liégeois split along other axes: weavers fought fullers, and cloth workers from the principal cities attempted to squash competition from workers and drapers in neighboring smaller towns, as with the Cockerulle of 1281, when the drapers and weavers of Ypres attacked the cloth workers of Poperinge.[76]

In France as well, peasants and commoners from the cities joined together in battles against royal taxes and the nobility, even if these alliances were not always stable or reliable, as seen with the Jacquerie. Nonetheless, unlike the bulk of Italian popular revolts, each side looked to the other for support and advice. While Compiègne refused the Jacques entry into their town, Amiens, Senlis, and Montdidier joined villagers in attacks on noble strongholds in the surrounding countryside.[77] In Amiens, engagement with the Jacques was heated, splitting the town into two camps. The mayor supported the Jacques and sent guild militia to assist their attack on the nobility, but others on the city council decided against it and called them back.[78] The aristocracy viewed the towns as equally culpable for the atrocities of the

Jacquerie. After slaughtering the peasants, aristocrats charged the city walls of Senlis but were repulsed by townsmen, who rolled carts into the invading cavalry and poured boiling water on them.[79]

Similarly, in the south of France, the Tuchins (whose activities ranged from opportunistic banditry to major assaults against the Duke of Berry and the crown) formed bands made up of both city and country dwellers.[80] Sometime before April 1384, when they were awarded a general letter of remission, the Tuchins' bands of rural bandits and rebels allied with commoners *(popolares)* of Nîmes against the local nobility and took over the city.[81] As we have seen, the wave of revolts against royal taxation from 1378 to 1382 began in major towns, such as Montpellier, but spread to satellite towns, such as Lodève, and then throughout the countryside.[82]

Accounts of commoners in the cities and countryside of Italy reflect few examples of such coordination, cooperation, or revolutionary contagion. Unlike for revolts north of the Alps, no written communiqués between city insurgents and peasants or any references to them seem to have survived. Neither were town criers sent to gain support and instigate revolt in the countryside. Generally, alliances in Italian social rebellion stopped at city walls. Of more than fifty Italian peasant revolts, there were only a few exceptions, most of which we have already described. In the winter of 1305, peasants *(rustici)* joined unskilled laborers of Modena to invade the communal palace, rip up official documents, and bring down the marquis's rule.[83] On 10 September medical doctors, notaries, tailors, and other artisans conspired to topple the signoria of the Marchioni of Ferrara. They planned to have great numbers of peasants from the surrounding countryside break down a city gate and serve as the shock troops of this revolt. The plot was discovered, however, and the principal conspirators hanged. Moreover, the chroniclers give no evidence that these artisans consulted any peasants or held joint meetings. Their assumption seems to have been that their rallying cry alone, "Death to the gabelles and taxes," would have sufficed in currying peasant favor to follow the citizens' beck and call.[84] In 1355, on learning of the Pisans' defeat at the hands of Emperor Charles IV, the peasants of Lucca's *contado* (then under Pisan rule and heavily taxed by Pisa), invaded the city. With assistance from commoners inside (although without any evidence of prior planning or even a coordinated attack), the peasants threw out the Pisans. Once in the city, however, the peasants turned against the city and butchered its leading citizens.[85]

A more profound exception to the general lack of city-country cooperation in Italian uprisings may have been the tax revolt and peasant invasion of

Parma in 1385, at least according to a nineteenth-century source citing chronicles that no longer survive. The peasants planned their attack together with
artisans within the city walls; their common battle cry was "Long live the
plebes and down with the taxes."[86] However, the surviving contemporary
chronicles make no mention of the artisan dimension of what was essentially
a peasant revolt to terrorize the town. Finally, in 1388, on news of Padua's
loss of the villages of Santa Maria di Lugo and Bovolenta, crowds of peasants
who happened already to have been in the city of Padua "began to riot and
assemble." According to the Catari chroniclers, the citizens joined the peasants
(villani) from fear; otherwise peasants would have sacked their homes[87]—
hardly an alliance born from mutual sympathy or planning. In the same year,
peasants *(rustici)* invaded Treviso to sack the town, crying out in the central
square, "Long live Saint Mark and the Lord Count of Virtù." Several commoners *(aliqui popolares)* followed, sent the city guards *(stipendiarijs)* fleeing,
wrested control from the Carrara family, and handed the city over to the
Venetians.[88] But again the sources provide no evidence of communiqués or
common meetings, either in public or in secret, between townsmen and
peasants.

Late-fourteenth-century Genoa provides the greatest number of peasant
revolts and further exceptions. Most of them emanated from the three valleys
surrounding Genoa—Voltri, Polcevera, and Bisagno. These peasants supported
the Ghibelline party and waged an almost continual war against Genoa's
doges from the 1380s to the 1420s. In 1383, they invaded the city, met with
commoners in the Dominican church, and with cries of "Vivat il popolo!"
rioted against taxes.[89] In 1393, the commoner Antonio Re organized and led
countrymen of the three valleys to invade Genoa and ally with popular forces
of the city in support of Battista Boccanegra, but the doge's men prevailed.[90]
In 1400, under the leadership of Raphael Carpaneto, those from the three valleys joined commoners *(popolares)* of Genoa to oppose the government and
later that year joined the urban *popolo* again to break down a prison door.[91]

Elsewhere, on the rare occasions when citizens organized revolts with peasants, they failed to gel. In 1412, for example, two immigrant brothers from
Quinto in Verona's *contado*, a Veronese priest (who was also an immigrant, this
one from Bruges), along with "seventy or eighty of the lowest classes [*del
popolo di bassi condizione*]" conspired to overthrow the Venetian rule of Verona
and hand the city over to the emperor and the Scala family. They gathered
peasant support *(villani)* in Ponte Nuova along the Adige and charged into
the suburbs of Verona, but, the chronicler says, "it pleased God . . . that these
rebels did not succeed in moving any craftsmen [*de' mestieri*] or citizen [*del*

buon popolo] to action." As a result, the Venetians easily crushed the revolt, chasing the peasants from town and drowning many of them in the Adige.[92]

As examples in Chapter 2 show, the vast majority of Italian peasant revolts received no assistance from urban commoners and actually pitched the interests of the countryside against the city. While integration and cooperation between peasants and urban commoners may have been exceptional in Genoa, the city's earliest and most widespread peasant revolt set urban forces against the peasantry, when the peasants of the valleys of Onéglia and Arroscia revolted against their lords.[93] In Italy, the division between city and countryside was wider than that between classes. As numerous revolts in Florence attest, peasants more readily allied with their former feudal lords—the Pazzi, the Ubertini, and the Ubaldini—than with artisans in struggles against city rule.[94] Peasants regularly formed the shock troops when lords from the countryside or other city-states wanted to attack and take over other city-states. This occurred in 1356, when Rolandino Scorza commanded peasants to invade and ransack Parma.[95] Peasants also organized their own raids and invasions of cities, as did those from the *contado* of L'Aquila, whose "great hatred" reached a boiling point in 1370 over taxation, bad government, and the city's excessive expenditure on wars.[96] On occasion, peasants invaded cities apparently just to loot. In Bologna in 1334, for example, mountain men ventured into the urban parish of San Donato, which brought the local commoners into the streets to defend their homes. Even when peasants were on the front line in an urban revolt such as the 1376 attack against church rule in Bologna, their feudal lords—not urban commoners or merchants—supported and organized their invasion. In this successful revolt, which led to a new elected government of the *popolo*, neither the chronicles nor the archival records reveal any interaction between the mountain-men invaders and the city artisans or the *popolo*. Nor did these urban forces appreciate or reward the mountaineers for liberating them from church rule; instead, a month later they condemned them to death and ordered all their property to be confiscated.[97]

For their part, artisans were unable or unwilling to draw support from the countryside in their struggles to topple oligarchies. The Revolt of the Ciompi is a case in point. In the archival lists of condemned insurgents, few names with rural residences appear, and where they do appear, their occupations suggest that they were émigrés to the city. Immediately following the constitutional reforms in June 1378, the new government clamped down on those from the countryside in one of its first decrees, ordering "contadini" to leave the city immediately, on pain of losing a foot, because of looting and "other mischief."[98]

The Ciompi government, however, later proved sympathetic to the peasant population. Among its decrees was a law abolishing the system of forced loans *(prestanze)* that had benefited the city at the expense of the countryside, to be replaced after six months with a new tax, the *estimo*, based on a more progressive system of assessment across city and countryside.[99] In August, the Ciompi government lowered the salt taxes for those in the *contado*, putting their rates below those of city dwellers.[100] Further, the Ciompi instituted a remarkable welfare system, which targeted the poor from the countryside.[101] But despite these progressive policies, peasants refrained from aiding the Ciompi in the revolts of June or afterward: not a single peasant is listed in the thirteen uprisings that took place from the fall of the Government of the Minor Guilds in January 1382 to 1393, uprisings that strove to resurrect that revolutionary government that had also made reforms on the peasants' behalf. Instead, peasants comprised the shock troops organized by the wool merchants and other oligarchs to defeat Florentine workers. Peasants can also be seen liberally sprinkled through the judicial lists of conspirators who strove to bring down the government of the minor guildsmen.[102]

For Siena's revolt against the Nine and establishment of the guild-based government of the Twelve in 1355, it was much the same. Of the broad coalition of social and political classes that toppled the Nine, the two groups altogether missing were the peasantry and residents of Siena's subject towns. Moreover, the principal threat to the new government's stability came from its *contado*. Immediately after taking office, the Twelve, with their guild-based militia, were forced to march out in all directions to suppress revolts from small towns and villages of the surrounding rural districts. In 1355, Massa Marittima, Grosseto, Montalcino, Montepulciano, Monteritondo, and Casole all rose up individually against the new government.[103]

In turn, when peasants revolted across the mountainous periphery of the Florentine territory in 1402 (the Mugello and the Alpi Fiorentine) and again in 1426–1427 (the Casentino and the hills of Arezzo) against Florentine republican taxation and oppression, no urban artisans or workers supported their cause. They were not even joined by artisans of small towns such as Firenzuola and Scarperia, as the peasants had hoped and planned.[104] In 1413, peasants in several villages of Friuli rose up against the armies of the king of Hungary, but as in republican Tuscany, no townsmen from the capital, Udine, or elsewhere came to their aid.[105]

Unlike the English Peasants' Revolt of 1381,[106] or uprisings in Flanders and France in the fourteenth century, where artisans joined or coordinated their revolts with those from the countryside, the rural tax rebellions that swept through Italy during the late fourteenth and early fifteenth centuries were almost invariably purely peasants' revolts, with no evidence of participation or assistance from urban workers or artisans. In sheer numbers, the revolt of rustics from Puleggio di San Giorgio in Ferrara's hinterland in April 1395 may have produced the largest peasant uprising in Italy during the fourteenth century. Although encouraged by a rival faction of the Este, these rebels received no backing from the city and were massacred in the thousands by armies that included the city's militia.[107]

Hatred between city and countryside flowed in both directions. With the collapse of Milan's empire following the death of Giangaleazzo Visconti in 1402, Brescia's mountain peasants *(montanari)* invaded the city to throw out the Milanese governors and their Ghibelline supporters. The invasion, however, soon turned into a massacre of innocent townspeople: "having sacked the city, they set it on fire" and afterward turned the city into a bloodbath. As we have seen, they not only killed officers, but also, "without any regard for sex or age, they slaughtered the townsmen as though sacrificial lambs."[108] The antipathy and suspicion between city and countryside is further shown outside of Siena in 1414. A passing Sienese army of cavalry and foot soldiers (who were most likely artisans of the citizen militia) was enough to provoke peasant rioting in Montécchio (about 7 km south of Siena), and "many other peasants [*molti contadini*] throughout the land [*paese*] came down on" the soldiers.[109]

Finally, while Genoa's three valleys may provide the greatest number of exceptions to the Italian rule of city walls blocking any sympathy and solidarity between peasants and artisans, the rural folk of these valleys, despite their efforts, did not always gain urban support. In 1394, they invaded Genoa and penetrated as far as the church of San Bernardo, but only "a few inhabitants of the city" joined them; their leader Raffaele Carpaneto was captured, and they were sent running.[110] In 1401, inhabitants of the valley of Bisagno invaded the city and briefly occupied two churches; their actions "against the will of the priors and citizens," however, found no common cause with artisans and workers, and their revolt failed.[111] In 1419, those from the valley of Bisagno again waged war against the doge but failed to receive urban backing; instead, the city retaliated by sending missions into the valley to conduct raids in revenge.[112]

Uprisings along the eastern Riviera were almost continuous during the last years of the fourteenth and early fifteenth century.[113] The Guelf-Ghibelline split had become a city-country division. According to Genoa's chronicler, "the Genoese, who were Guelf, no longer dared step outside the city from fear of the inhabitants of the *contado,* almost all of whom were rural Ghibellines."[114] In 1399, "from hatred of the Genoese noble families, the Spinola and Doria," the people of Sigestro revolted.[115] Twice in 1403, the rural populations of Chiavari and the Sturia Valley rose up against Genoese taxes.[116] The following year tax revolts erupted against the city at Rapallo and Triora in the high valley of Taggia.[117] In 1405, the people of the village of Framura killed their podestà, a citizen of Genoa,[118] and in the same year those of the valleys of Sauli and Bisagio rebelled against Genoese taxes.[119] In 1415, the peasants of Orsi *(quorumdam ruralium)* killed their podestà and notary (again, Genoese citizens sent out to rule them).[120] In 1419, the most extensive revolt within Genoa's territory ensued: rustics of the Lunigiana and along the Riviera as far south as Livorno and north to Rapallo rebelled against the Genoese state. Again, commoners of the city failed to support them.[121]

An explanation for these differences north and south of the Alps must relate to the unique character of the Italian city-state, with its large surrounding countryside. After the Black Death, city-states increasingly engulfed other, previously independent city-states, incorporating them and their *contadi* into ever-larger territorial states.[122] In late medieval Italy, being a citizen and residing within city walls often put an individual at the top of a political hierarchy in terms of law, governance, and taxation (at least in theory). After antimagnate legislation spread across city-states of central and northern Italy in the late thirteenth and early fourteenth centuries, a lowly artisan could be— before the eyes of the law and by the tax system—above the aristocrat who resided in the countryside. The ancient privileges of the rural aristocrats had come under threat. Branded as magnates and supermagnates, barred from holding offices, and subject to stiffer juridical penalties and special taxes, many of the old aristocratic families of the countryside were condemned as rebels and hunted as exiles by the second half of the fourteenth century. Added to their decline in political rights, small towns and rural areas also suffered economically, especially after the Black Death, as banking, commerce, industry, minor crafts, and other services became increasingly concentrated in capital cities such as Florence.[123] Consequently, during the later Middle Ages the social, economic, political, and class distinctions between the urban commoner and the peasant widened more in Italy than elsewhere.

In areas such as Lombardy, Friuli, and the Romagna, rural aristocrats may have fared better than in Florence, which, according to Stephan Epstein, lorded over its territorial state with the most authoritarian measures and unequal taxes of any city-state.[124] But even in these mountainous regions (as in the Kingdom of Two Sicilies),[125] the old feudal families maintained their power and prestige by becoming urbanized and moving their strongholds to cities such as Faenza, Forlì, Udine, Naples, and Palermo. Thus, here too, cities became the privileged places of power and prestige.

By contrast, legal and cultural divisions between city and country were less pronounced north of the Alps. In Liège, for instance, after the victory of the tradesmen and the ousting of the patriciate in 1312, the law made no distinctions between those living within its walls and those residing in city's domain or "franchise." All paid the same taxes and possessed and fought to retain the same liberties. All were considered "citizens" and called "bourgeois."[126] Moreover, in France and Flanders, the king or the count was the ultimate arbiter over relations between city and countryside, and the ruler's political and economic interests often rested as much or more in the country as in the major cities. Often, as with Louis de Male, rulers privileged those from small towns and the countryside over citizens of the principal cities—Bruges, Ypres, and Ghent.

In Italy, however, privileged artisans of cities had less incentive to find common cause with peasants than their counterparts north of the Alps. The urban privileges of Italian citizens engendered hatred across city walls that was as strong, if not stronger than, divisions of social class within city walls. This can be seen in the poisoned sarcasm city writers such as Boccaccio, Sercambi, Sacchetti, Sermini, and Poggio Bracciolini poured out against peasants.[127] Let us now turn to another division between north and south in which an explanation appears far from straightforward.

CHAPTER 8

Flags and Words

Workers and craftsmen in the city-states of Italy were obsessed with and utterly dependent on their flags and banners when engaged in revolt. This phenomenon has been best studied for Florence, but only for one brief moment in its history: that surrounding the failure of the Eight of Santa Maria Novella and the collapse of the first phase of the Ciompi government in early September 1378.[1] Chroniclers described in detail the backgrounds and figures on the banners that workers and artisans paraded through the city during the revolt and subsequent government by the Ciompi. Along with the flags of the established guilds, the sixteen neighborhoods of the city, and the prize of all flags—that of the Gonfaloniere di Giustizia, bearing the symbol of liberty[2]—the new revolutionary guildsmen marched behind their own flag, "the one with the figure of the Angel" holding a sword in one hand and a shield in the other.[3] Further, sometime toward the end of July, the workers created three new revolutionary guilds; each had its own banner.[4]

Florence and Flags

The first sparks of the Revolt of the Ciompi came with threats against the flag of the aristocratic Parte Guelfa. Michele di Lando's leadership of the Ciompi did not depend on a fiery speech but was achieved merely by having the prized banner of justice "thrust into his hands." With it, the *popolo minuto* immediately recognized him as their leader and followed:

[22 July 1378] Then one Michele di Lando, a wool comber, son of the woman Simona, who sold vegetables in front of the Stinche prison, came out into the piazza [of the Signoria] without any weapon at his side or on his back; and the banner of justice [*confalone della giostizia*] was taken and thrust into his hands. And he took it into his hands to preserve it for the *popolo minuto*. Then he ordered that the governors [*signori*] be told to clear out of the Palace [of the Signoria].[5]

Even before the Ciompi created their new guilds, the carders already possessed a symbol with a folk memory. In his efforts to gain the favor of workers and minor artisans in 1342, the Duke of Athens granted carders the right to carry a shield *(pavese)*, on which was painted an angel.[6] With his fall in the following year, disenfranchised workers preserved it, hiding it illegally for the next thirty-five years.

Control of flags was critical to the Ciompi government. When decrees were passed to seize all arms, only men guarding the flags were allowed to carry weapons. The anonymous diary by one of the Machiavelli family describes the tensions flags could create, even on what proved to be an uneventful day in the life of the Ciompi, 24 July.

> the Piazza was filled with all the guildsmen, and the *popolo minuto* was armed with every sort of weapon; the Palace was filled to the brim, all the way up to the great bell and stuffed with all the banners of all the guilds, pouring out the windows, hanging over the rostrum. Banners and flags of all the guilds and of their captains were everywhere, and yet there was no conflict.

On this day all the shops and warehouses of the city remained closed until the banners were safely returned.[7]

More remarkable still is the fall of the Ciompi government at the end of August. According to the anonymous patrician's diary, the collapse of the radical wing of the Ciompi came from the disobedience and treachery of the *popolo minuto*;[8] by the report of the lone chronicle sympathetic to the Ciompi, known as the "First Anonymous Chronicle," the cause was the treachery of the standard-bearer of justice, Michele di Lando, in cahoots with the guild community. But by both accounts, the actions were embedded in conflicting rights to carry flags. Symbolic action here reached its extreme. No matter how they were deprived of or tricked out of holding their flag, the *popolo minuto* were totally incapacitated without it—unable to march, arm, or defend themselves.

> At three in the afternoon of the same day [29 August] the priors asked for all the guild banners because they wanted them in the palace, solely so that the "popolo" would not have a banner to run to. Consequently, all the guild banners were removed because they knew the plot had been

hatched, and it had been arranged that as soon as the *popolo minuto* had handed over their flags, they would all be cut to pieces and driven out, and that all the crossbowmen would have their bowstrings cut. But when they asked for the emblem of the angel, the people did not want to give it to them, saying: "If anything happened, what could we run to?"[9]

Florentine insurgents' dependence on flags did not die with the fall of the Governments of the Ciompi or the Minor Guilds, nor did they depend on a single chronicler's possible obsession with flags. The judicial records point to the carrying of the banned Ciompi flag as a revolutionary act in and of itself, and chroniclers describe various attempts of exiles, minor guildsmen, and Ciompi to revolt and resurrect their three revolutionary guilds. In all these attempts flags are in prominent view. Immediately following the fall of the Government of the Minor Guilds, the chronicler Stefani described an attempted coup: "like animals, the ragtag band of rebels did not wait for their ranks to form but dribbled into the square . . . hopping this way and that . . ." But despite their lack of order, the insurgents had their flag of the angel, which they unfurled and marched behind. After they had been defeated, the Emergency Council of Florence came into the square to counterpoise the previous revolutionary flag display with the banners of the establishment, that of the Guelf Party and of the Ordinances of Justice, cleansing the piazza of the previous pollution. With these, they continued to march around Florence's main square until dusk. Next, "the priors sent for the banners of the guilds and had them put on the rostrum and then unfurled them from the windows of the Palace. And for this they closed all the shops of the guilds so the craftsmen could no longer assemble."[10]

In August 1380, the discovery that a certain Baldo from the parish of Sant' Ambrogio possessed a flag was the key to uncovering a plot hatched by ex-Ciompi and Florentine exiles *(sbanditi)* and led to the arrest and torture of some of the ringleaders. After Baldo's execution, his girlfriend ran off with his flag to their hometown of Vittorato.[11] The discovery of illegal flags—this time the making of new ones—revealed another plot of wool workers in November 1382. The father of an apprentice at a linen shop leaked to the government that a Ciompi conspirator had bought linen to make revolutionary flags. Led by four—a vintner, who was the principal leader; a hat maker; a carder; and a tanner—"all those of the doublet makers and the dyers along with some of the Ciompi" were to assemble first at the Ponte alla Carraia and then in the Piazza di Santa Maria Novella. There, under three banners—two of the recently disbanded guilds of the doublet makers and dyers, and a third one of the Guelf Party—they would riot, attack palaces of the rich, and seize the Palace of the Podestà.[12] In December 1382 a group from one of Florence's poorest neighborhoods, San Paolo, gathered and plotted to restore their lost guilds and rights. The plot was uncovered this time by the discovery of four flags that were to lead the revolt: "one of the People, another of the Guelf Party, another of the armed arm [*braccio armato*]—the flag of one of the two disbanded guilds—and finally, that of the *popolo minuto*'s angel."[13]

From the defeat of the Eight of Santa Maria Novella at the end of August 1378 to the beginning of 1383, the judicial records reveal still further conspiracies and revolts of workers and artisans. The rebels unfurled their illegal flags to lead demonstrations and attacks on key government buildings, such as the communal prison (the Stinche), the palace of the Captain of the People, and the Palace of the Priors, accompanied by cries to resurrect their disbanded guilds. They flew three, sometimes four flags, which might include those of the Guelf Party, the commune and people of Florence, the angel, the angel against a background of the arms of the city's squares *(ad arma camporum civitatis)*, and the flags of the workers' two other disbanded guilds.[14] They invented still others. The most elaborate of these appeared in the hands of the Ciompi exiles in Bologna who allied with bandit magnates to plot Florence's overthrow at the end of 1379. Their new flag of alliance (called a "banderia falsa" in the judicial records) consisted of two halves. On top was the symbol of the Florentine elites, that of the Guelf Party, encircled on this new flag by lilies. On the bottom half the "minuti" embroidered their symbols—two arms, one holding balances, the other holding a broken sword. The motto read, "with this noble insignia above I will take vengeance on any who dares to wrong me *(con quello nobele segno che de sopre porto faro vendetta che me fatto torto).*"[15]

Flags Elsewhere in Italy

Workers' and artisan insurgents' reliance on flags was not unique to Florence. Flags were flown in popular revolts from Italy's northern territories to the Kingdoms of Naples and Sicily and, even further afield, in Venice's colonies.[16] From my survey of chronicles, they appear in more than sixty Italian popular revolts between 1200 and 1425. The presence of guilds with their guild banners might explain some of the popular flag waving, but not all of it. Flags led revolts not only in other guild-based communes but also in signorial states: those controlled by the pope; and those of the crown, such as at Palermo, Enna, Siracusa,[17] Messina, Naples, and L'Aquila. For instance, in Messina the *popolo*, led by butchers, "solemnly raised the banner of the commune" and charged against the French in 1282.[18] In a riot in L'Aquila of 1415, "many people loaded with rocks" gathered in the main square and chased their lords from office. At the center of the battle, their flag "was passed from one to another."[19] In Rome, the captains of the neighborhoods *(rioni)* were called "banderesi," or standard-bearers; throughout the fourteenth and fifteenth centuries, flags led their revolts against patrician senators, popes, and emperors. For instance, in 1407 the *rioni* of Rome—those of the Ponte, Parione, Sant'Eustachio, Sant'Angelo, Ripa, and Campiteli—assembled at night at the top of the steps of the Campidoglio to battle against the rule of the king of Naples. An eyewitness Roman diarist described them as they formed their armed assembly: "illuminated with their candles, they waved the banners [*vesilos*] at the head of each *rione*." Ready to engage in battle against the king's men, they chanted "death to this traitor, the king, and to all his men."[20] Earlier (as we shall see) Cola di Rienzo had been the most prolific creator of political flags, which he used at Rome and gave to other Italian city-states as a symbolic embassy.

In 1405, the *popolo* of Padua rebelled against their signore, Lord Jacobo Carrara, and filled the town square with armed men who hung their "banners and flags" in the piazza. The chroniclers do not make clear, however, whether these were neighborhood banners, those of the guilds, or those of the commune of Venice, which ultimately conquered the city.[21] In the same year, because of the war, Jacobo del Verme's blockade, and the consequent food shortages, the *popolo* of Verona also revolted against the signoria of the Carrara and took over the town square with their flag and cart *(carro)*, a symbol of the *popolo*. Eventually, they too gave their city over to the Venetians by raising the cry "Long live San Marco!" and handing over "the banner of the *popolo* and its staff with all the other symbols [*signali*] of its government."[22] In 1412, two brothers, citizens from the Veronese *contado*, led peasants into Verona to overthrow the government of the Venetians. Although their forces were composed of peasants *(villani)* and those of the lower classes, they carried their flag and with chants for the emperor and the Scala family tried (but failed) to whip up support in the city and countryside.[23]

In city-states that had been guild-based republics, the presence of flags may have been more common than in other regions of Italy. But in republics popular insurgents also relied on flags other than those of guilds. In 1316, when the nobleman Guittuccio of Bisenzio captured a ship launched on the lake of Bolsena to protect Orvieto's fishermen, the *popolo* of Orvieto rioted, broke into the jail where Guittuccio's children were held, and "cruelly killed them." They then marched into the town square behind the flag of the people, with the Captain of the People on their shoulders.[24] In 1324 the *popolo* of Orvieto revolted to halt the long-standing internecine violence between the ruling clans of the Monaldi and Monte Mare. The people's flag was the banner of justice, which they handed over to a new ruler and peacemaker.[25]

In 1369, an armed riot broke out in Lucca between popular forces led by weavers and needle workers against the oligarchic rule of the Guinigi family. The insurgents marched with the flags and pennants of their neighborhoods *(gonfaloni)*. Although the pro-Guinigi chronicler Giovanni Sercambi ridiculed this revolt as trivial, he hints that another, less violent battle had been brewing before it exploded, one that involved pictorial symbols: "the people" (who in this case included lowly members of the cloth trade) "wished to have the coats of arms of the People painted everywhere."[26]

In the same year, merchants of the middle sort *(cittadini merčanti uomini di mezzo)* and artisans *(artefici)* of Pisa grew tired of the factional warfare between the upper classes of the Raspanti and Bergulini, who dominated the ruling council of elders. For their protection against upper-class violence and robbery by foreigners, these merchants and artisans formed a society or company called San Michele, with a membership of over four thousand men. Enraged by the city's high taxes, they plotted with the exiled Gambacorti (who in the past had taxed them less) to topple the government. Led by one of the company's officials, *(giurati)* named Piero Pilati, they chanted "Long live the People and the Emperor" and rioted under their recently minted company banner, the imperial black eagle on a gold field. With it, they marched into the Square of the Elders, chased out the Raspanti, and put those from their company and the Gambacorti into office.[27]

The destruction or desecration of flags could be as important to a new regime as the creation of its own symbols of power. In 1345, artisans *(populari et artefici)* rose up against Orvieto's oligarchic government of the Seven. The violence exploded when one from the ruling Seven came into the town square with his friends, bearing a flag with his family coat of arms. The artisans attacked the Seven's guild banners, dashing them to the ground.[28] When the Lucchese revolted in 1392 and threw out the ruling Guinigi, the insurgents' first act was to throw the Guinigi's banner of justice out the window of the town hall "onto the ground."[29] Siena's revolt that toppled the Nine in 1355 began with the ritual ripping to pieces of flags[30] and ended with the rebels destroying all the Nine's symbols of power—the governmental coats of arms painted on all their houses. "They did this because they now saw themselves as the regime of the people and did not wish for the Nine to retain these accolades, now that they had been deprived of governing." The *popolo minuto* went further in humiliating the Nine: they grabbed the Nine's cabinets containing the ballot box of names eligible to hold office, which was stored in the church of the Dominicans. They took the cabinet to the Communal Palace, smashed it by throwing it from a window into the Campo, and then tied the battered box "to the tail of a donkey that dragged it, spewing the ballots out all over the city." Sweeping them up, the insurgents cried "Death to the Nine."[31] In May the new government of the Twelve was established, with offices distributed according "to their twelve lowly professions [*loro minuti mestieri*]."[32] At the outset, they invented new banners to be given to a "lowly artisan [*vile artefice*]" in each of the twelve guilds, with orders "that all the others of that guild must join and follow the flag. And so began their new regime [*reggimento*]."[33]

In 1371, the revolt of the Company of the Caterpillar, which began as a protest against the wool bosses over low wages, became an armed insurrection against Siena's ruling regime of the Twelve. Like the Revolt of the Ciompi seven years later, it was also a battle over flags. After targeting certain palaces and individuals, who "had done many nasty things at the beck and call of the Twelve," the insurgents went to the house of the Salimbene and took away the banner of the people. Further, they grabbed the banners from the standard-bearers and hung them from the windows of the Palace of the Commune.[34]

Similarly, in Bologna flags led rebels against the church in 1376. Immediately afterward, the handing over of the banner "with the symbol of the *popolo*" to the standard-bearer of justice marked the creation of the newly elected republic.[35] In the following year the *popolo minuto*, with chants of "Long live the people and the guilds," revolted against the new republic, took the flag of the city from the council of elders, and marched out to destroy various houses belonging to city elites, including that of Bologna's famous legist, Roberto de Saliceto.[36] In a revolt of 1402, other Bolognese insurgents carried flags as they entered the main square, shouting "Long live Liberty, the People, and the Guilds."[37] In neighboring Reggio nell'Emilia, a revolt of the *popolo* against the reigning magnate family, de Panceriis, was fought over a flag: "For the people said that these ones [de Panceriis] had the flag of the people in their palace, denying them [the people] their rightful possession of it. Thus they had no other recourse but to revolt."[38] The flag of the people of Genoa is seen in a revolt as early as 1241, when their banner of Saint George led them against the noble family of the Doria.[39] As we have seen, the war against the papacy that raged through central Italy from 1375 to 1378 produced the first interregional flag of Italian rebels, the "large flag" with the golden letters

"LIBERTAS" against a red background. Moreover, its life continued after this conflict: in addition to becoming the most venerated flag of the Florentine republic by the time of the Ciompi, it led revolts in Milan, Macerata, Ascoli, and other places in central Italy.[40]

Evidence of insurgents' flags at Parma extends over a longer period than that found for Florence. From as early as 1316 until 1409, popular groups within Parmense society battled against the oppression and arrogance of their magnates.[41] The principal force behind these early-fourteenth-century revolts were the four professions—the butchers, cobblers, furriers, and blacksmiths. Each profession had its own flag. Behind these came artisans of other guilds, the colleges of the commune, the neighborhoods, and the societies of archers, all carrying their own flags. On occasion, they sanctioned their revolts still further, as in 1316. Before charging against the palace of the magnate clan of Opizzone de la Porta, the *popolo* gathered and took the banner of the Virgin Mary from the cathedral of Parma. They placed it above all their other flags, which had been put atop a bull *(desuper taurellum)*.[42] Throughout the fourteenth century these organizations regularly carried their flags through the city and into the countryside to hunt down magnates who had injured individual commoners or threatened the stability of the commune.

Guilds and local neighborhood militia were not the only ones to lead protests with flags flying. As we have seen, the children and youth of Parma demonstrated against war, taxes, and the king of Naples's chief officer in March 1331 with twigs, branches, garlands of flowers, and all the flags and banners of the city. A month later, the youth used the same display of flags, branches, and garlands to move their antifiscal protest into the countryside. There they succeeded again, this time in lowering taxes and bringing a peace settlement with Lucca.[43]

Children carried flags and protested in other cities, where the presence of guilds was weaker. In 1347, with the ships of Sicily in the Bay of Naples, small children demonstrated for peace in the streets and squares of Naples, ending their protest in front of the royal palace, where they chanted "Pace, pace!" and waved banners of the Kingdom of two Sicilies.[44] Naples provided other examples of flags without any guild association leading popular revolt during the fourteenth century. After Queen Joanna had her husband Andrea killed, "a great number of the *popolo* of Naples" exhumed his body and found, despite the queen's efforts to cover it up, evidence of his murder—a noose still wrapped around his neck. Immediately, they employed a goldsmith to embroider "a large flag" of the dead Andrea with the noose, which they then unfurled in a charge against the royal palace.[45] Andrea's brother, the duke of Durazzo, outraged over the murder, also led his forces to capture the conspirators. The duke's men wore black and produced their own flag, a black one with a silver sword in the middle, dripping with blood.[46] The flag of the people bearing Andrea's head with the noose seems to have had a more portentous future: it led at least three further revolts against the queen and the Neapolitan nobility in 1346 and 1347.[47] In retaliation Joanna sought the identity of the flag-maker and beheaded him in February 1347.[48] But the flag lived on, used later that year in a popular revolt against the nobility.[49] In May the rebels may have created yet another flag: a cobbler who was captain of his guild was executed for leading the Neapolitan *popolo* against the queen's castle. They broke down the castle's principal gate and hurled great abuse against her, "which decency does not allow retelling." At the cobbler's execution, the Neapolitan *popolo* revolted against the queen again, suspending a flag "showing King Andrea with his many traitors, guilty of bringing about his death."[50] This may have been one of the flags that the *popolo* stood behind in their turf war against noble youth in 1374, when for three days the people occupied the Carmelite church.[51] For other disputes, the populace of Naples manufactured other flags. In 1386 open battle broke out between the Neapolitan *popolo*, who supported the Italian pope, Urban VI, and the elites, who supported the French claimant, Robert of Geneva. The *popolo* marched into the square carrying the flags of Pope Urban.[52]

In Italy's northern corners, popular groups also invented and carried flags to lead uprisings. For example, the Genoese *popolo* produced a new flag in the heat of a tax revolt in 1383. According to the Stella chronicle, a group of citizens congregated and marched through the city "looting and murdering" behind a flag of a lion's head with a black mane.[53] To the east, Venice and its colony at Trieste provide examples of the totemlike power flags could have over popular insurgents, equaling that seen during the last days of the Ciompi. In the so-called Tiepolo conspiracy of 1310, crowds composed "mostly of the *popolo* of Venice" rebelled and sought to kill the doge, but a woman saved the day. While the crowd marched under her balcony, she dropped a big stone block on the head of the flag-bearer. The chronicler does not say whether he died; more important his flag fell to the ground with its staff broken. Without their flag, the rebels ran for their lives.[54] Afterward, the Council of Ten passed a special ordinance rewarding the heroine, allowing her to remain in her house at a fixed rent for life and granting her the honor of flying the flag of San Marco on feast days.[55]

In 1368, the Venetians sent a small galley to Trieste to collect the annual tribute owed to the doge. A band of colonial rebels attacked the vessel, killed its captain, and wounded others. According to the early-sixteenth-century chronicler Sanuto, who copied a contemporary chronicler, "what was worse," the Triestini later refused to raise the flag of San Marco on feast days. This, not the killing of a colonial captain or their refusal to pay taxes, rallied the Venetians to invade.[56]

Popular obsessions with flags, banners, and other symbols of revolt and allegiance in Italy did not stop at city walls. In 1344 peasants besieged the market town of Cennina in the Valdambra and other nearby villages on the frontiers of the Florentine state "with tambourines, drums, trumpets, and raised banners."[57] In a revolt against Bologna in 1402, the peasants of San Giorgio in Persiceto "hoisted the flag of the feudal lords and rivals of Bologna, the Malatesta."[58] In the same year, more than eighty residents of the Florentine village of Gangalandi assembled in their square "with their banners and flags raised" before heading off to rob and destroy the goods of a certain ex-official of their commune who had run off with their money.[59] In the same year, the highland peasants of the Alpi Fiorentine rebelled against Florence's new town and frontier of defense, Firenzuola, and "on many occasions rode from Bologna to Firenzuola with raised banners to make war against Firenzuola."[60] Two decades later, Florence tried to strengthen its ideological hold over its territory by painting the symbols of the commune and the Guelf Party—the lily, the Marzocco (lion), and the red eagle holding a green dragon under its feet—on the walls of town halls, the towers of the podestà, and the churches in almost every village and market town in its territory. In new waves of tax revolt that exploded across the mountains of the Casentino from 1424 to 1427, these symbols of Florentine authority and domination were the first targets of peasants' attacks.[61]

The village of Pontenano went further in 1426, electing their own revolutionary council and assembling in front of the parish church. An old man from the crowd yelled, "I have a flag which I'll run and get that I've kept hidden away in my chest for forty years" (that is, since 1384, forty-two years before, when this village, along with the rest of the *contado* of Arezzo, had lost its independence to Florence). The old man handed the flag over to the parish priest and leader of the revolt, who hoisted it above the campanile of the church. Thus, individual and collective memory of past symbols with revolutionary portent stretched even further back in time here than in guild-conscious Florence of the Ciompi. Moreover, symbolic action and disgust with Florentine domination in this isolated village at the tail of the Pratomagno Mountains extended beyond defacing the inanimate insignia of Florentine control. These mountain men dressed up a donkey as Florence's honored Marzocco, led it in mock fashion around the village square, and then beheaded it to insult their Florentine rulers. The symbolism was not lost on the Florentine elites down the slopes. The incident was recounted in the minutes of the secret deliberations of Florence's highest chamber, the *Tre Maggiori*. In retaliation, a councilman proposed that Pontenano be leveled to the ground "so that no stone should remain atop another and no rooster or hen ever crow there again; all properties should be confiscated, its church deconsecrated, so that no one would ever be allowed to live there again."[62]

As these examples show, images other than flags also had power and nearly magical significance for rebels and rulers alike. Rebels were bent on defacing the shields and plaques city-states had plastered on public and private buildings, such as the Marzocco, which by 1427 had been painted in prominent places in nearly every Florentine village. In the same vein, the Nine's crests of the *popolo* were destroyed by the *popolo minuto* in Siena in 1355, and the Guinigi's shields of the commune were defaced by needle workers and others in Lucca in 1369. These examples also illustrate that such reliance on flags and pictorial symbols of power, along with the need to destroy competing symbols, were not limited to peasants, workers, and artisans. One of the first acts of the Florentine wool bosses in their counterrevolution of January 1382 was to storm the guild halls of the two remaining revolutionary guilds. "To show their contempt" they wrecked the furniture, threw the guild records out the windows, and destroyed their coats of arms.[63] As we saw earlier, immediately following the ex-Ciompi's first abortive revolt of January 1382, the wool bosses and other elites also felt the need to cleanse the ritual air of Florence's main square after it had been polluted by the Ciompi's illegal symbols. At the end of October 1393, Florentine elites did the same after one of the last of the ex-Ciompi's and minor guildsmen's revolts had been ushered in by a flag display. After suppressing the revolt and "slicing to pieces" the leader of this *brigata* of *gente minuta*, Lionardo di Nichola (a dyer from the artisan neighborhood of Campo Corbolini), the authorities "instantly" called out all its officials *(vicherie* and *gonfalonieri)* into Florence's main square to parade fully armed, chanting "Long live the People and the Guelf Party" and flying the neighborhood banners of Florence.[64]

States' obsessions with symbols of power can also be seen in Florence's insistence that its country towns and villages present the commune annually with a *palio,* or silk banner, as a token of loyalty. No matter how generous an offer of tax exemptions Florence might make to draw a new and strategic borderland village into its domain, the one obligation that remained inviolable was the presentation of this "gift," symbolic of a community's allegiance to its new lords. In 1403, Florence granted one of the most liberal and sweeping tax exemptions ever seen in documents of "submission" to the mountain village of Pietramala. Until this time, this village at the base of a strategic mountain pass had been in the territory of Bologna. To entice it to shift allegiance to Florence, "every man and woman" was exempted from paying all taxes and gabelles for fifteen years, and eight men of Pietramala were granted perpetual exemptions from all taxes, not only for the duration of their own lives, but also for their descendants down the male line *in perpetuum*. Florence further protected these men from paying any debts they might have incurred to the commune of Bologna or to any corporate body or individuals from Bologna and extended fifteen-year tax exemptions to anyone from the *contado* of Bologna who decided to settle in Pietramala. In return Florence demanded only one gesture from the peasants: every year on the feast of John the Baptist they were to make the ceremonial offer of a silk banner *(palium)* worth five gold florins.[65]

Flags and Symbols North of the Alps

Do these examples show only what we might expect from Huizinga's classic, *The Waning of the Middle Ages*, namely that the totemic power of symbols ("thought crystallizing into images") extended beyond northern France and Burgundy and ran down the boot of Italy during the later Middle Ages?[66] The chronicles cast another image: instead of a borderless European culture of flags and symbols in popular revolt, Italy appears distinctive. In France and Flanders, chroniclers and archival sources such as letters of remission rarely mention flags, at least before 1425 (when my analysis stops). Tournai was somewhat exceptional, with flags raised on four occasions during tax revolts in 1307, 1365, 1423, and 1425. All of them, however, were guild flags; none were specially commissioned flags for the revolt of any popular group.[67] More extraordinary is the fact that only two references to flags can be seen in numerous chronicle reports of the two largest, longest, and most important popular rebellions of the Middle Ages—the revolts of Flanders in 1297–1304 and 1323–1328.[68] One of these references, moreover, concerned the destruction of flags rather than commoners inventing their own flags or flying traditional ones.[69] In the Low Countries, symbols certainly mattered, but they had neither the resonance nor the frequency seen in the popular revolts in

Italy. An exceptional case rested on the folk memory of aristocrats rather than the populace. The chroniclers explained why the French noblemen were so intent on brutally destroying Courtrai after Philippe van Artevelde's defeat in 1382: the nobles remembered the peasants' and artisans' insults of 1302, when they had hung the noblemen's spurs in Courtrai's cathedral as trophies of their military success and mocked their coats of arms.[70]

Although more insurrections appear in Paris than in any other city except Florence in this study, and despite the importance of Paris's guilds[71] and neighborhood militia, which were divided into units of householders—*dizeniers, cinquanteniers,* and *soixanteniers*—flags do not appear as a rallying force to organize or inspire popular troops. They do not even appear in Étienne Marcel's guild-based revolts in 1357 and 1358 or that of the Hammer men of 1382, despite the large numbers of archival records (letters of remission) and narrative sources covering these events.[72] Moreover, in the very few instances when popular rebels in France are described as flying flags, the flags are not of their own making, nor do they form a part of an ongoing popular tradition. Instead, the flags' insignia were those of the crown. As we have seen, a single source mocked the Jacques' last standoff, claiming that they "haughtily" cried out "Mont Joye" and carried "insignia painted with the *fleur de lis.*"[73] But no other sources alluded to rebels' carrying banners of any sort, nor do any of the surviving letters of remission issued to the Jacques or to the noblemen who butchered them describe any such symbols borne by the populace. Only with Jehan Maillart's counterrevolution, which brought down Étienne Marcel on 31 July 1358, do multiple chroniclers describe a bourgeois force in Paris bearing flags and insignia, and these were the king's.[74]

The most detailed image of an insignia associated with a popular force in late medieval France was worn not by urban craftsmen or bourgeois but by peasants. In this case, the insignia did not rally a revolt against the state but on its behalf. In 1411, by order of the provost of Paris, peasants between the Seine and the Oise abandoned their fields and took up arms to repulse the English. As a sign of their comradery, they "placed a white cross with the *fleur de lis* in the middle on their shoulders" and carried a flag with the inscription "Vive le roi!"[75]

The almost total absence of any evidence of popular forces inventing or carrying their own insignia and flags is all the more surprising given the importance of such emblems for the aristocracy and especially the king. Rulers relied on banners for military formation and action, and the king's special flag, the *oriflambe,* could bestow supernatural power which the royal troops at the battle of Rozebeke (1382) invoked to ensure victory over Philippe van Artevelde. According to Froissart, this flag was thought prevously to have been brought out only against the infidel.

> This *oriflambe* is a greatly revered banner and standard, sent down mysteriously from heaven. It is a kind of banner and brings great aid on the appointed day to those who see it. And once again its virtues were proven: all morning the fog had been so thick that one could hardly see another, but as soon as the knight bearing it had unfurled and hoisted it, the fog broke and the sky became as pure and clear as it had ever been that year.[76]

Yet the records show that popular insurgents north of the Alps displayed no such dependence or mystical belief in banners as they certainly did in Florence, the Veneto, and elsewhere in Italy.

In contrast to the nonuse of flags, hoods *(chaperons)* were the accessories of choice of northern insurgents, but references to them are still rare and quite different from the magic of the *oriflambe* or artisans' flags south of the Alps. First, as with any club clothing even today, hoods certainly carried symbolic weight. This was not lost on the dauphin on 22 February 1358, when Marcel's men murdered his two trusted marshals before his eyes and then threw him a hood with the Parisians' colors. In 1376, the commoners of Tournai retaliated against the special laws and violence of the lords of Mortaingne by passing a law prohibiting anyone from their territory carrying weapons or wearing their clan hoods.[77] But in comparison with the magic of flags in Italy, the hood's purpose appears more practical, as Jean de Venette described it when Marcel's bourgeois took up the red-and-blue ones in 1357: "they were worn to show who was on the rebels' side."[78] Sixty-six years later, Enguerrand de Monstrelet said much the same for the hoods worn by the Cabochien rebels in 1413: "all Parisians took to wearing the white hoods so that they could better recognize who was of their party and allied with them." Now, however, it was the king who gave them out.[79]

A second point of difference from Italy's flag culture is that none of these hoods are described with any figures or designs to match even the simple detail of the peasants' patches of 1411, much less the more complex images like Andrea's portrait with a noose round his neck, Genoa's Saint George or the lion's head with a black mane, or the Ciompi exile banner in two parts with several figures and a motto. To sustain his revolt and popular control over Rome, Cola di Rienzo created still more elaborate flags, such as the one he invented for Florence—"an old woman seated as the figure of Rome with a young woman in front, standing erect with a map of the world in her hand"—or the one for Perugia, bearing the arms of Julius Caesar on a vermilion field and with a golden eagle. Further, he ordered three new flags for Rome. The first was the banner of liberty: "it was very large, red with gold lettering, on which Rome was depicted sitting between two lions, with the world in one hand and a palm in the other."[80]

Moreover, unlike the flags that lived on as symbols for various rebel groups in Italy, the hoods of Paris had little stability or folkloric tradition from one revolt to the next. Even contemporaries could not keep straight the colors of the Parisian hoods. In 1357, the bourgeois hoods were red (or vermilion) and blue;[81] and in January 1358 they appear to have been the same.[82] By February, however, when Marcel's men murdered the two constables and chief advisers of the regent Charles in his own apartment, the colors may have changed. While some chroniclers described them as half vermilion and half blue, at least three contemporary chroniclers described other colors: one said they were red,[83] another claimed they were white,[84] and still another said red and black.[85] Moreover, by the revolt of the Jacques several months later, the Parisians may have changed colors again, this time to red, to be in sympathy with their country comrades. With the revolt of the Hammer men in 1382, the Parisian rebels wore white hoods in sympathy with van Artevelde and Ghent against the count of Flanders and the king of France.[86] Afterward, the colors may have been more stable. At any rate, during the Cabochien revolts in 1413, "all Parisians wore white ones," but here the previous meaning of the hoods' color had been turned on its head. In 1382, the Parisians wore them to oppose the king and his taxes and to be in alliance with his enemies, the Gentenars. Now, the same king (Charles VI) handed out white hoods to the crowds of his own party to distinguish them from the Burgundian party, who wore blue and green.[87] Folk memory of flags also appears to have been short. None of these sources shows any recognition by Parisians or other northern French rebels that the white hoods had originally been in fact the color of Parisian rebels in the late thirteenth century, when the rebels of the Liégeois and Flanders adopted them to be in solidarity with northern France.[88] Thus in 1382, instead of adopting the colors of Ghent, the rebels of Paris, unknown to themselves, were returning to their own "true colors."

Compare this history with examples from Italy: the *popolo minuto* of Florence kept their illegal flags of the angel hidden in trunks for thirty-five years; the illegal flag of Andrew with the noose, which cost its maker his neck, led the Neapolitan *popolo* in at least three and possibly four or more revolts. When Cola di Rienzo came to power on 18 May, in addition to his three newly invented flags, he also revived a fourth one to lead his procession, one of Saint George. This flag was so old that it had to be carried in a box at the end of a pole.[89] Moreover, the flag of liberty—"the large one in red with the letters LIBERTAS stitched in gold"—took on a new life long after the end of Cola's tribune, a fact that historians have yet to recognize.[90] Twenty-nine years later, the flag led insurrections through much of Italy from Milan to Naples in 1375–1378. Then, in 1378 the flag became the most coveted banner by all sides during the Revolt of the Ciompi. As we have seen, flags lived on even in the countryside, as when the old villager living in the hills of Arezzo in 1426 pulled from his trunk the illegal revolutionary flag he had hidden for forty-two years.

Political Theater

Rebels resorted to symbolic acts by means other than flying flags and wearing hoods. As we have seen, the peasants of Pontenano dressed a donkey as Florence's symbol of virility, the Marzocco, and then decapitated it to insult their new rulers. I have thus far seen more of these displays for Italy than for the north, but my numbers are too small to draw clear distinctions. Nonetheless, several examples are worth retelling. As we have seen, after Pope John XXII excommunicated Federico da Montefeltro, leader of the Ghibelline party in the Marche and ruler of Recanati, the *popolo* retaliated in October 1319, excommunicating their bishop. They then made an effigy of the bishop in straw, complete with miter and crosier in hand, and carried it through the streets of Recanati in a solemn funeral procession, with candles and bells ringing. When they reached the main square, they ceremoniously burned the puppet, chanting regrets that they could not burn the bishop in the flesh, along with the pope and all his cardinals.[91] From this theater sprang the pope's crusade against Federico, not only against the "heretics" of Recanati, but also against the towns of Urbino and Osimo and their surrounding villages. Perugia and Foligno witnessed similar mock funerals and burnings of effigies of the pope and cardinals in 1254 and 1282.[92]

The north of Europe can also point to rebels' use of effigies and theatrical performance to enhance their rebellions. In 1360, fullers, weavers, and other artisans in Ghent and Bruges rebelled against Count Louis of Male and threw out his chief officer. While the city bourgeois were negotiating a truce with the count, the tradesmen went further in their insults by suspending an effigy of the count from the window of his palace, "which greatly upset [Louis] and his followers, though he was resigned not to show it."[93] The most dramatic and intricate of these theaters of revolt took place in Rouen in 1382, when two hundred or more journeymen seized a simple bourgeois called "Fatso" *(le Gras),* lifted him onto a mock throne, and paraded him through the city as their monarch. Afterward, they enacted another drama, this time with the potential of real political and economic change. After burning the monastery of Saint-Ouën's ancient charters, they stripped the abbot of his vestments and forced him to sign new privileges that benefited the commune of Rouen, restoring its rights of barony over the region.[94] From my samples, however, I have found no further striking examples for regions north of the Alps: given the literature on symbolic action and the importance of the late medieval and early modern "theater state" from Huizinga to the present, this strikes me as surprising.[95] To show that these differences between Italy and the lands north of the Alps did not result from Italian chroniclers possibly being more meticulous in their descriptions of popular revolt than those of the north, let us turn to another way of mobilizing popular protest that also goes against the grain of expectations.

Words of Protest

North and south of the Alps insurgents held assemblies, met in secret, elected leaders, and spoke; they negotiated and planned tactics and yelled chants in unison. Surely one of the great myths about popular insurrection championed by historians from Jean le Bel to Yves-Marie Bercé is that preindustrial popular revolts were spontaneous, surging forth from mad passion without prior planning.[96] Letters of remission issued to rebels after the Jacquerie—a revolt that chroniclers as well as modern historians have singled out for its ferocity and madness—show that almost every village in the revolt held assemblies, elected captains, and discussed tactics. As we have seen, on occasion these meetings resolved not to follow orders from Paris and urged restraint in attacking local lords. Similarly, chronicles and archival documents reveal that the Ciompi organized secret meetings, such as the one at the Ronco on the eve of the July assault on Florence's Palazzo Pubblico, when the hapless Simoncino was caught and tortured into revealing the insurgents' plans. The radicals of the Eight of Santa Maria Novella, who imposed new demands on the priors of Florence in late August, met on several occasions in various churches of Florence, where they discussed and agreed on a list of specific proposals and governmental reforms.

The sources point to many other assemblies of peasants, workers, and artisans to discuss and plan revolts. Thus the Parmense peasants, in a failed tax rebellion of 1385, held secret meetings in the countryside with artisans to decide on tactics, particularly when and where to burst through the city's walls. In 1402, peasants from the mountain villages of Florence's Alpi Fiorentine made several trips to Bologna to discuss tactics with Milanese generals on when and how to lay siege to Florence's stronghold of Firenzuola and how to control the mountain passes. Ultimately, these peasants gave orders to generals as esteemed as Milan's famous condottiere, Jacopo del Verme.[97]

Hence words were essential for all these revolts, but surprisingly, the studied use of rhetoric to move crowds with fiery speeches and flattery on street corners or village byways appears to have been more the stuff of revolts north of the Alps than in the south. The map cast by rabble-rousing speeches is the opposite of that cast by flags. Popular insurrections in the north are teeming with homespun rhetoricians from the laboring classes and the bourgeoisie, who moved or restrained crowds with "their sweet words" and eloquence. One of the earliest and most renowned of these orators was the weaver Peter Coninck (or "the King"). He led peasants and artisans, first in Bruges and then across Western Flanders, to one victory after another during the revolt of Flanders in 1301–1304 and again in 1309. According to the *Annales Gandenses,* he "obtained such power over weavers, fullers, and other commoners because he was so eloquent [*facundus*], winning them over with his smooth and sweet words [*mitibus et dulcibus verbis*]."[98] The *Chronique artésienne* described him more fully.

> In these times there was a man from Bruges called Pierron le Roy, small in stature, poor in lineage. He was a weaver and had spent his entire working life at the loom. He had never been wealthy. At the beginning of the war neither he nor any of his family was worth 10 pounds. But he had such a way with words and knew how to speak so beautifully that it was astonishing. Thus every weaver, fuller, and cloth-beater loved and believed in him wholeheartedly: he knew what to say to get them to do what he commanded.[99]

This Peter was the only rebel orator, regardless of class, whose fame crossed the Alps in the later Middle Ages. The Florentine banker and chronicler, Giovanni Villani, was stationed in Bruges when Peter rose to prominence and was probably an eyewitness to the "Matins de Bruges." His description of Peter is the most detailed of all the chroniclers'.

> Prominent among them [the leaders of artisans and of the lower classes *(popolo minuto)*] of Bruges were Peter the King, a weaver, and Jean Bride, a butcher,[100] along with more than thirty of the most important people from these crafts and guilds. I note that this Peter the King was the leader and rabble-rouser of the commoners. Because of his boldness he had been nicknamed Peter the King, which is Connicheroi in Flemish [Peter van Coninc], that is, Peter the King. This Peter was a poor man, a weaver of cloth, small in stature, lean, blind in one eye, and more than sixty years old. He knew neither French nor Latin but in Flemish spoke better, more ardently and fluently than anyone in Flanders. And by his speeches he moved the entire country towards the momentous things that followed. And thus it is right to preserve his memory.[101]

The Sienese chronicler Agnolo di Tura copied almost verbatim Villani's praise of the weaver's oratorical skills,[102] and another Sienese chronicler also took notice of this Peter's power with words.[103]

Not all those who moved the subaltern classes in the north to riot belonged to the lower classes, nor did they always strive to spark rebellion; often orators spoke out to restrain crowds. But either way, words, fiery speeches, and eloquence were vital to the movements of crowds in the north in a way hardly seen in chronicles or archival records in Italy. Examples can be easily culled from the thirteenth century to the end of our analysis. Chroniclers called Henri de Dinant, who enticed the lower orders of Liège to follow the bourgeois and revolt against patrician rule in 1253 and 1254, "demagogus" and praised his eloquence that moved crowds to revolt.[104] By one account the intoxication of his verbal "skills and eloquence" drove the commoners *(popolares)* to madness.[105] During a rent strike and protest against the king's monetary policy at Paris in 1306, Firmin de Coquerel of Amiens, provost of Paris, "appeased the crowds with sweet words and flattery so that the commoners returned peacefully to their homes."[106] After a tax revolt in the city of Tournai in 1307, the soldier Matthew de Haudion presented a negotiated peace before the masses, who had assembled in two parish churches of the city, and persuaded them to follow his advice with "wise and elegant words." "Immediately and in unison, without a single dissenting voice, they chanted, 'Well said, well said, well said.'"[107] In 1323, we have seen that two women and sixteen men "with their big and bad words" sought to incite "commoners and the good people of Douai" to kill the city's bourgeois grain dealers and scoop out the mounds of grain lying in boats and barges.[108] In 1327 and again in 1331, Pierre Andricas, a magistrate and furrier, "big-headed and eloquent," "preached" to the people of Liège. By his "eloquence and deception," he "inflamed" them to revolt against this city's patrician and Episcopal rule.[109] During the same period, the wayward cleric André de Ferrières achieved the same with his street-corner harangues.[110] The *Chronicle of the Four Valois Kings* described Guillaume Cale, principal leader of the Jacquerie, as "a knowledgeable man, well spoken, handsome, and well formed."[111] In the period of the Jacquerie, chroniclers stressed the eloquence of leaders such as Robert Le Coq and others in letters of remission.[112]

Most extraordinary of these was the rabble-rouser Pierre de Montfort, who "wore on his hat [a model of] a plough made of wood in the place of a feather." He traveled through Picardy rousing commoners to revolt and in Caen gave speeches to stir up dissent among commoners and bourgeois against the crown. Ultimately, he used his speeches to convert those in Caen and the surrounding countryside to join "the side of the Jacques."

> Pierre de Montfort on many occasions while alive tried to provoke rioting [*comocions*], conspiracies, and discord among the people of this town by rousing and inducing the common people to subvert and obstruct what the judges and good people of this town ordered and commanded and to curse the subsidies and aids that had been collected for soldiers and others for the protection and defense of this town and country. For this purpose he gave many evil and indecorous speeches, as is apparent, to rouse and sow discord between the commoners and the big fish of the town and to have them [the commoners] commit many crimes, for which they were not punished. Similarly, he drew in people from Picardy, who were put to death and perished in the marketplace of this town, where he had been one of the principal leaders [*facteurs*].[113]

In a letter of remission from the regent Charles to the people of Paris that pardoned them for their crimes during the uprisings of 1358, he ended the long list of their acts of treason by pointing to the *grans paroles* that the commoners had slung against the crown.[114]

In a retrospective on the Tuchin bands, which arose in Languedoc and the Massif Central around 1364, Michele Pintoin, chronicler of Saint-Denis and King Charles VI, claimed that these rebels had been "spurred on by terrible speeches . . . which moved them to submit no longer to shouldering the yoke of the subsidies."[115] In the same year, during a tax revolt at Tournai, its bishop came into the streets and calmed the crowds at least until nightfall.[116] During the Parisian riots of 1380 against the first attempts of the regent Charles to impose new subsidies, John Culdoe, provost of Paris, gave a speech that roused the Parisian masses to a frenzy, even if he did so reluctantly. "He showed in many ways that the commoners [*plebs*] had been taxed intolerably. When he finished speaking, the crowd arose with a terrible cry, shouting that they would not pay the taxes any longer, that they would die a thousand times rather than suffer such dishonor and harm." He then gave another speech to the crowds, "flattering them with sweet words, and when they insisted with greater rage, he calmed them down with a prudent speech and obtained what he had asked of the new king."[117] When the crowds later pressured the king to make up his mind about these taxes, the king sent his chancellor Lord Miles de Dormans, bishop of Beauvais, a man known for his eloquence, to calm the plebes.[118]

During the Hammer men's revolt of 1382, Pierre de Villiers[119] and Lord Jean des Marès,[120] "men of advanced age, great prudence, and highly respected by the plebes, often tried to change popular opinion, arguing that their words would provoke the king's anger."[121] Jean des Marès, "whose eloquence had often swayed them and whose advice they followed, went through the streets of the city in a litter, because he could not walk," persuading the crowds (at least temporarily) that the king had been appeased.[122] This people's orator then persuaded the king to make certain pledges to the Parisians.[123]

Of those who moved the masses with their words, the religieux de Saint-Denys's greatest admiration went to the Ghent leader Philippe van Artevelde, even though he was the mortal enemy of the French crown. Philippe's speech enjoining the Gentenars to fight to the end against the French is one of the great set speeches of the Saint-Denis chronicle.[124] Froissart describes sermons the Franciscans and Dominicans delivered to the people of Ghent at this time that inspired them to rebel against their count, telling the crowd how they were "like the people of Israel, who king Pharaoh held for so long in bondage." These clerics exhorted the people to action with examples from the Maccabees and the Romans.[125] Further, according to Froissart, after addressing the crowds Philippe mounted a wagon and stirred the masses with yet more moving speeches to make them lust for battle.[126]

After a wave of revolts in 1378–1382, words continued to inflame crowds in the north. At least three chroniclers recorded in full the lengthy speech the revolutionary Gilles de Laveux made to the citizens of Liège against the corrupt justice of the patrician government, which ultimately forced the nobles from office in 1386. These chroniclers claimed that "his words were drowned in thunderclaps of applause."[127] Simon Caboche, "this common skinner of animals," moved crowds by his speeches: "by these words and other similar ones, this commoner, whose crude features contrasted with the sparkle of his arms, sought to prevent the king from meeting with his princes."[128] Caboche and his journeymen persuaded Master Eustache de Pavilly of the order of Notre-Dame du Carmel—"a learned professor of theology and orator of strong eloquence, who possessed the art of persuasion at the highest level"—to assist them in their battle of words. According to Pintoin, his job was "to harangue the king and justify all the crimes committed by these insurgents."[129] The master surgeon Jean de Troyes, labeled "the orator of the crowds," in turn justified these insurgents' positions to the *menu peuple,* who numbered nearly ten thousand, assembled before him at the Hôtel de Saint-Paul on the afternoon of 12 May 1413.[130]

During the Armagnac and Burgundian civil war, other orators roused insurgents in other cities to disobey the king and unite in arms. Enguerrand de Bouronville, called "eloquissimus," "spoke the words for all," stirring the residents of Soissons in 1414 to disobey the king's orders.[131] In a revolt of Tournai in November 1424, the blacksmith Jean de Bléhaires (called "Blarie") "with big and arrogant words inflamed the passions of the crowd and fomented social hatred." According to the early-twentieth-century historian of Tournai, Maurice Houtard (equipped with archival sources that went up in smoke with a German firebomb in 1940), Jean was "the demagogue par excellence."[132] Finally, Regnault le Moqueur, a poor man, manual worker, and laborer in the vineyards, "on many occasions" delivered "many words, evil speeches, and threats against . . . the governors, council, and many notables of Châlons-en-Champagne for five or six years before his condemnation in 1418. He and his accomplices "threatened and scorned the present rulers and their government, their decisions and deeds, saying they would kill them and spill a great amount of blood. And they sounded off with many other wicked words intended to persuade the people to believe that they had been badly governed and advised."[133]

For France, Flanders, and the Liégeois, the list of crowd orators and their importance for popular protest could continue with other nameless "demagogues," such as those who harangued crowds in cemeteries in West Flanders during the peasant and artisan wars of 1323–1328, "announcing the coming of a new age and with the heat of their convictions and enthusiasm cap-tur[ing] the hearts of the plebes."[134] What about Italy, the country that sup-posedly led the West in an educational revolution that placed rhetoric as the queen of the *studia humanitatis?*

The notary of low birth, Cola di Rienzo, leader of Rome's most famous pop-ular revolt in 1347, must be placed at the pinnacle of the people's orators. He used more references to antiquity and classical forms of rhetoric than any other popular leader of the Middle Ages. According to the Anonimo romano, "in his youth he was nurtured on the milk of eloquence, good grammar, the best rhetoric, and the great books. He studied Livy, Seneca, Cicero, and Vale-rio Massimo and loved recounting the magnificent deeds of Julius Caesar."[135] At twenty-nine, he won the admiration and friendship of Pope Clement because of "the fine style" of his language.[136] According to Giovanni Villani, "he held a public meeting [*parlamento*] in Rome attended by many of the people [*popolo*]. Here, he described his embassy with savvy and ornate words as if he were a master of rhetoric."[137] But Villani heaped even greater praise on the homespun rhetorician of the north, the weaver Peter the King. Both Villani and the Anonimo romano spent many more words describing Cola's flags; his use of pictorial devices, including fresco cycles in various parish churches of Rome;[138] his reenactment of ancient Roman ceremonies; and his processions. It was these more than his words per se that moved the crowds to establish his tribune. Cola's rhetoric was theater graced by flags and picto-rial ceremony.

Other than Cola, who is there? Almost exclusively, they were preachers. In 1233 the Dominican friar Giovanni de Scledo, "a man of exceptional elo-quence" born of a noble family, first brought peace among warring factions not only in his hometown of Vicenza but also, according to the chronicler Antonio Godi, in Treviso, Feltri, Conegliano, Verona, Mantua, and Brescia and between the lords of Camino and the Romano.[139] His success, however, was short-lived; after a month, his reforms were undone.[140] Another preacher was the Augustinian Iacopo Bussolari, who "from his pulpit used examples from Roman history to preach against the crimes and wickedness of tyranny." "Blessed were the ones who could touch him" as he rode through the crowd on the city's cart—the *carroccio*—symbol of ancient communal pride.[141] With "well-chosen words [*molto bene le sue parole*]," he roused the *popolo* to throw off "Milanese tyranny" in 1356, and in 1358 organized from his pulpit a network of centurions to patrol the city and countryside and hound out the principal magnate family of Pavia, "the tyrants of the Beccheria."[142] A less significant exception was the crazed and unsuccessful Andrea Strozzi and his son Pagnolo, who with street-corner speeches insulted workers but momentarily roused them to revolt in 1343.

What about the Revolt of the Ciompi—Michele di Lando and Salvestro de' Medici? Modern historians continued to point to their eloquence and demagoguery, listing them alongside Peter the King and Jean de Troyes.[143] For neither Florentine, however, is there a shred of evidence in chronicles or archival documents that they rallied crowds with moving words. Michele assumed center stage on two crucial occasions, with the founding of the Government of the Ciompi on 20 July 1378 and on 31 August with its fall. On both, he said nothing or very little, other than the chants yelled in unison with his followers. There is no indication that he even led the chants. By the accounts of the conservative member of the Machiavelli family and the radical "First Anonymous Chronicler," Michele simply was handed a flag "to save it for the *popolo minuto*," and by that passive act he took authority, led the *popolo minuto*, and was baptized as its leader.[144] Only by the report of Ser Nofri, the ex-government's notary, does Michele have anything to say. It is a "speech" that amounts to twelve words (in Italian): "Do you wish for me to do your bidding? All right, give me the flag and follow."[145] Salvestro de' Medici's only recorded speech was a short one too, offering his resignation on 18 June 1378. While he persuaded his fellow committeemen to beg him to stay in office and resubmit his petitions against the privileges of the Guelf Party, his "speech" was hardly delivered to the masses; rather, it was a shrewd political maneuver staged within the assembly of the *popolo* among a small coterie of supporters. Salvestro was the consummate committeeman, not a crowd rouser.

Similarly, in 1282, Dino Compagni wrote of his experience during the rise of "the second *popolo*" of Florence. With six friends, he tried to persuade his fellow citizens of the need for change. They met at the church of San Procolo (Brocolo), where they "discussed their liberty and the injuries they had received." But, like Salvestro de' Medici and unlike rabble-rousers north of the Alps, Dino did not then go into the streets and squares of Florence, addressing his "sweet words" to larger gatherings of the masses. Instead, the people he and his friends tried to persuade amounted to three key individuals— "the citizen heads of the guilds." These were members of Florence's most elite guilds: the international merchants, the Calimala; the wool guild; and the bankers; one was even of the powerful magnate clan of the Bardi.[146]

This is not to say that late medieval Italian revolutionaries did not use words to persuade comrades to join them. As much as, if not more than, those north of the Alps, Italian chroniclers record the slogans that motivated people to rise up and follow leaders. As we have seen, laws in Italy banned chants. In 1331, for example, Parma's city council "prohibited boys and all others from yelling 'vivat, vivat.'"[147] Also in Pisa in 1369, after the revolutionary government of the Company of San Michele had come to power with chants of "Viva lo Popolo, e lo' mperadore," it promptly outlawed others from yelling the same under penalty of death.[148] No doubt, words smarted as much south of the Alps as did "grans paroles" in the north. We get glimpse of the stinging power of words in 1419, when children's jingles mocking Pope Martin V caused a diplomatic row between Florence and the papacy.[149] As we have seen, revolutionaries north and south of the Alps regularly met secretly or openly in assemblies, discussing tactics, drawing up demands, and stating their reasons for rebellion. Nonetheless, against the long list of orators across social classes who either roused or restrained crowds in the north, few such orators can be heard in the sources for Italy. Instead, Italian rebels relied intently on their flags and other pictorial symbols, which they often invented themselves and which could have long histories.

Guilds and Confraternities North and South of the Alps

Did the differences between north and south rest solely on the chroniclers' modes of representation? If so, it would nonetheless be significant and worthy of explanation. We have seen, however, that Italian chroniclers such as Giovanni Villani gave more attention to the Fleming Peter the King and his eloquence than did any of the contemporary Flemish chroniclers; further, Villani, who was an eyewitness, did not mention any flags in his account of the Flemish revolts from 1297 to 1302. Later, the Florentine patrician Bonaccorso Pitti was an eyewitness of the revolt of the Hammer men in Paris but reported no flags in the Parisian revolt of 1382, even though less than four years before he had experienced the rage of his own Florentine, flag-waving Ciompi.[150] The stress on words in the north and on flags in the south is all the more surprising given that these two Florentines and others, such as Giovanni's brother Matteo and the Sienese chroniclers Agnolo di Tura and Donato di Neri, imagined the northern revolts in their own Italian terms, calling commoners the *popolo minuto* and rich bourgeois *popolo grasso*. Matteo Villani went furthest in reshaping a foreign uprising to fit his Florentine frame of mind: for him the Jacquerie was exclusively a revolt of Paris and the bourgeois, not unlike Florence's revolt of the *primo popolo*. In his lengthy account of these northern events, he does not even mention a peasant.[151] Yet, despite their efforts to fit foreign events into Italian city-state molds, these chroniclers failed to see any flags in the northern revolts, much less emphasize a totemic obsession with them, as they did with the popular revolts they reported up and down the Italian boot during the later Middle Ages.

In conclusion, chroniclers and archival sources portray the symbolic action of popular revolt and the ways leaders moved masses north and south as mirror opposites of one another. They also are the opposite of what we might have expected from two grand masters of culture and ritual life of the later Middle Ages—Jacob Burckhardt and Johan Huizinga. How do we explain that words moved crowds in the north, flags in the south? Did the difference rest on the importance of guilds, confraternities, and religious processions, or on the use of pictorial devices in religious sermons in the south and their absence in the north? All these factors may provide keys for understanding the differences, but all will require new systematic research of sources not consulted for this study.

Guilds were important in places such as Paris but much less so in towns such as Troyes and Rouen.[152] Religious confraternities, even those of crafts and journeymen, were certainly not absent in the north and may have been as rich a part of the cultural and religious life in places such as Normandy, Liège, and southern France as they were in late medieval Tuscany.[153] In 1267–1268, Alphonse of Poitiers ordered an inquest of the Confrérie du Carmel in Toulouse under the suspicion that it was inciting disorder. The organization counted a membership of around five thousand men and women.[154] In 1408 Liège passed a law requiring all the trade confraternities of the city and other *bonnes villes* of its district to display their flags whenever the city council ordered them to process.[155]

Nonetheless, chronicle reports suggest that religious processional life may reflect a similar north-south divide in the use of and dependence on flags and pictorial devices, as found in popular revolt at least until the fifteenth century.[156] Peter Arnade has concluded that "in contrast to their Italian counterparts, religious confraternities in Low Country cities had but modest public visibility."[157] And according to David Nicholas, "it is hard to believe that if guild or parish festivals were as important a part of the urban scene at Ghent as, for example, in most Italian cities, so few traces would survive in the written record."[158]

As in rebellion, so in religious movements, the Italian "popolo" and even groups in the countryside invented their own flags, some of which possessed intricate pictorial detail. For example, the Alleluia movement of 1233, the flagellants of 1260, and other devotional groups in Italy created and carried flags. After describing the Alleluia movement throughout all Italy, Salimbene turned to his town of Parma.

> I saw in my town of Parma that each neighborhood [*vicinia*] wanted to have its own flag [*vexillum*], which they made in order to go on holy processions; on one flag for the neighborhood of the parish church of the Blessed Bartholomew, [its flag] was embellished with the image of their saint and the word "Gratia"; others were made in a similar fashion. And great numbers of men, women, boys, and girls bound together in their confraternities [*societatibus*] and processed with their flags from their villages to the city to hear the preachers and to praise God.[159]

In a similar vein, a notary of Reggio nell'Emilia described the flagellants of 1260:

> rich and poor alike from the *contado* and Episcopate of Reggio came whipping themselves through the city, carrying the flags of all the companies [neighborhood militias or confraternities?]. On Tuesday after All Saints' Day most of them then went to Parma. And on the next, those in Reggio made flags of each of the neighborhoods [*cuiuslibet visinancie*], which they used to process around the city, and our podestà did the same, whipping himself.[160]

In April 1334, the Dominican friar Venturino came to Rome, leading groups of penitents from all over Lombardy to celebrate Easter. They carried "a long and large green banner with several points, in which was painted the figure of Saint Mary" flanked by saints, angels, and prophets, which the chronicler describes in detail.[161] Further, Venturino (nearly two centuries in anticipation of San Bernardino) made use of Jesus's initials to draw his crowds: "He wore a linen cap bearing the letters HIS [Jesus] on its front."[162] Finally, at the end of our period, the great rhetorician and preacher, Bernardino da Siena, modeled a new style of preaching but continued to depend on flags and heightened the use of other pictorial devices he had invented, most prominently, his own Jesus monogram.[163]

Contrast these experiences and practices with the many descriptions of the children's crusades in 1250 and 1320. Only one source suggests that any flags were in evidence, and that one imposed on the troops by their leader Rogier does not describe any pictorial symbols or indicate whether it was traditional or newly invented.[164] Further, from the many descriptions of the postplague flagellants of 1349, two chroniclers in my sample mention flags, but in both cases it was the German flagellants who carried them, along with crosses, crucifixes, and candles.[165] Otherwise, no flags or ornaments beyond the distinctive wardrobe worn by the flagellants were on display, even in the meticulous description of various penitent groups observed and described in an entire chronicle dedicated to them by the abbot and chronicler of Tournai, Gilles li Muisis.[166] In summary, icons and totemic imagery no doubt held people across societies and classes spellbound throughout medieval Europe, but the evidence from popular rebellion suggests that such symbols sank deeper roots into the popular culture and psyche of Italy than north of the Alps—just the opposite of what we might have expected from the pages of Huizinga. By contrast, more often "sweet words" were the stimuli that sparked rebels to action in the north.

CHAPTER 9

The Black Death and
Change over Time

Thus far this book has said little about change over the 225 years of its analysis. Little has been mentioned besides an increase in tax and peasant revolts and a decline in heretical and religiously motivated movements after the Black Death. The significance of the Black Death for a supposed clustering of popular revolts a generation afterward continues to puzzle historians. It prompted Mollat and Wolff's investigation that became *Ongles bleus.* One of their conclusions compares the clustering of revolts of the late thirteenth and early fourteenth centuries with those of 1378–1382. Here, as with their title, they borrowed from the great historian of the Low Countries, Henri Pirenne, distinguishing the first cluster of revolts as "revolutions of the crafts," or of skilled craftsmen. The second group of revolts, they argued, stemmed from misery, and the poor or nascent proletarians filled the rebellious ranks.[1]

From Artisan to Protoproletarian Rebellion?

If such a transition held, it would be difficult to square it with the general economic trends in postplague Western Europe. The ecological plight of overpopulation and the widest and most desperate waves of famine occurred not after the Black Death but before it, in the second and third decades of the fourteenth century.[2] After a decade or so of economic dislocation created by the plagues, the European economy not only began to recover but the conditions of those at the bottom improved the most rapidly: the abrupt demographic decline meant that their labor power came into greater demand.[3] From my databases of revolts, the rare cases of utter desperation and wild scrambles for grain came from Central Italy—Rome, Siena, and Florence—before the Black Death, with famines in 1327–1330 and the mid-1340s.

205

Furthermore, the idea that the insurgents changed from respectable trades-men to nascent proletarians after the Black Death seems odd given the forms that revolts took before and after this demographic catastrophe. The earliest protests of the mid-thirteenth century were as "modern" as any on record in the West until the nineteenth century. In northern France and Flanders, abundant evidence of workingmen's associations, assemblies, strikes, and even the destruction of tools appears in local ordinances, court cases, and chronicles.[4] Riots composed of, organized by, and led by textile workers were commonplace before the Black Death.[5] Nor did such activity emerge only in major textile centers such as Douai, Tournai, Bruges, and Ghent; they also were notable in provincial market towns such as Clermont-en-Beauvaisis, Poperinge outside Ypres, Damme outside Bruges, Dendermonde outside Ghent, and Nieuwpoort.[6] Moreover, the records of northern France and Flan-ders show *menu peuple*, or "those of little wealth," revolting against city oli-garchies and mayors,[7] against changes in monetary policy, rises in house rents,[8] the privileges and impositions of the French crown,[9] and, above all, against the imposition of new taxes.[10] Along with this remarkable array of urban revolts, early fourteenth-century Flanders witnessed the largest and most widespread peasant revolts before the German Bundschuh of the six-teenth century. But the Flemish revolts of 1297–1304 and 1323–1328[11] lasted longer, won more battles, and were better integrated and coordinated with urban insurgency than any revolt seen two hundred years later in the German-speaking areas.[12] Curiously, this rich vein of popular protest begins to decline with the famines of 1314–1317.[13] Indeed, in contrast to models drawn by historians and sociologists for supposed "preindustrial riots," these famines did not spark a single grain revolt in northern France or Flanders and few others of any description.[14] The revolts against Philip the Fair's tax policies in 1314 were not tied to famine; rather they came from the top of society and were fought more in regional assemblies than in city streets or village byways.[15]

Eight years after the great famine, when abundance of grain had returned to the Low Countries,[16] Flanders erupted again, experiencing its longest and most widespread revolt (1323–1328). Beginning with the free peasants of western Flanders, the movement stirred commoners from the principal cities of Flanders to combat the nobility, patricians, and the French crown. Politi-cally, this revolt differed from the rebellions of 1297–1305. As we have seen, the new count, Louis of Nevers (1323–1346), grandson of the anti-French Guy of Dampierre, "was the most dependent of his dynasty on the French crown."[17] In 1323 he renounced his grandfather's resistance to the French crown and sought to enforce the financial penalties owed by Flanders to France. As with the Flemish revolt at the turn of the century, this second wave of rebellion arose from international politics, new fiscal demands, and the indignity of paying ransoms for nobles and welcoming back many who had been their lords and enemies during the previous rebellion.[18]

From the 1320s to the Black Death, the face of popular rebellion changed in France and Flanders. The number of strikes and other industrial actions as well as revolts by weavers, fullers, and cloth beaters against city councils and royal authority declined sharply, as evinced by the chronicles and archival sources on the Flemish cloth industry published by Henri Pirenne, Georges Espinas, and others. Because of their victories at the beginning of the fourteenth century, weavers and fullers in most cities of Flanders gained rights as citizens and entered town councils, unlike cloth workers in most Italian city-states.[19] Thus in the two decades before the Black Death, revolts of weavers and fullers resembled more those of the shopkeeper-merchant *popolo* in Italian city-states during the fourteenth century or internecine conflicts of middling groups than revolts of workers, or what in Italian would be the *popolo minuto* or *sottoposti*—underlings of the wool merchants, stripped of political and economic rights.[20]

In the postplague period, the social status of "rebels" became still more elevated, as weavers won over fullers in the revolts against Count Louis de Male in 1359–1361 and more so with those led by Philippe van Artevelde in 1379–1383. It is difficult to see this later wave of "revolt" as popular. As David Nicholas has cogently demonstrated, the well-heeled Van Arteveldes (both father and son) were hardly men of the people, and their "revolts" resembled internecine city-state conflict along the lines of the wars between Florence and Milan in the later fourteenth century more than the social revolts of Flanders in the early fourteenth century.[21] Ghent's struggle against Bruges opened with its white-hooded thugs assaulting manual laborers of Bruges, who were digging the canal of the New Leie to divert trade from Ghent. As Wim Blockmans and Walter Prevenier have remarked, the cluster of Flemish conflicts of 1379–1385 "this time . . . did not begin in [sic] a clash of count and cities, but as a feud between the two greatest cities, Ghent and Bruges."[22] After achieving hegemony in Flanders, the van Artevelde "revolt" became an international war against the French king. In short, for Flanders the transition was the opposite of that argued by Vanderkindere, Pirenne, and Mollat and Wolff. The successes of the struggles of disenfranchised workers of the late thirteenth century meant that the protagonists of revolts in the postplague period were mostly of the middling sort, and with the van Arteveldes (both father and son), merchant elites, not a proletariat or starving *misérables*. The only place where an economic downturn and worsening in material conditions for urban artisans conditioned a postplague wave of revolts was in southern France—Le Puy, Montpellier, Lodève, and Alès. Even here, however, the spark was a rise in royal taxes, which commoners saw as unfair, not in bread prices. The rebels' demands and targets were political: aggrieved by taxes and corruption, they attacked town councilors and murdered royal officers.

The social transformation of popular revolt from the thirteenth century to the postplague fourteenth century, from respectable tradesmen to a nascent proletariat, works slightly better for central Italy than for northern Europe. For the late thirteenth century and first decades of the fourteenth century, nothing akin to the Flemish or northern French strikes or revolts led and staffed by textile workers is sighted in Italy—not even in places such as Florence with well-developed cloth industries and large numbers of workers without guild recognition or status as citizens. The major contenders of class struggle in the south, the *popolo*, pitched the interests of merchants, shopkeepers, and well-to-do artisans against landed and mercantile aristocracies including those of local bishops. In Florence, Milan, Pisa, Bologna, Genoa, Savona, Siena, Arezzo, Rome, Viterbo, Naples, Ancona, and many other smaller city-states, revolts of the *popolo* toppled aristocratic regimes and ushered new social classes into power.[23] The readiness of commoners—the *popolo minuto*—to arm themselves and defend the rule of the *popolo* shows that those beneath the status of shopkeeper played their part. But a chronicler such as Giovanni Villani, well informed about the world of labor and attentive to its conflicts, not only in Florence but across Italy and in Flanders, first mentions the term *popolo minuto*, distinguishing it from the *popolo* only in 1295. Moreover, his earliest references to the *popolo minuto* pertained more often to political and social groups in Flanders than in Florence. Rebel leaders of the *popolo*, men like the wealthy Florentine major guildsman Giano della Bella, were hardly commoners;[24] they were a world apart from self-taught Flemish rebel leaders like the weaver Peter the King or the butcher Jean Bride, who organized thousands of textile workers and peasants to oppose patrician regimes and the king of France.

The only possible exception was the revolt of "the people without underpants" at Bologna in 1289. Called variously *populares, populares populus,* and *de villiori condicione,* it is difficult to know exactly what stratum of the population these insurgents represented. The few who were listed appear as servants or apprentices *(qui staba cum . . .)*, yet they were also identified as part of the guild community [*una parte delle compagnie de l'arte de l'arme del puovello*]. No matter how "vile" these rebels may have been, their revolt was still unlike many found in northern France and Flanders of the late thirteenth century. The latter often involved industrial action and led to the political enfranchisement of new social groups as citizens. The men of Bologna opposed city authority and the judgments of their podestà but did not oppose or change the social or constitutional structure of their city.[25]

In the early decades of the fourteenth century, revolts of artisans began to mount in Italy just as they were beginning to decline in the north. But these Italian ones were not associated with the cloth industry. Instead, they tended to occur among the highest echelons of artisans.[26] Butchers and blacksmiths protested the decisions of the military elites and war policy in Siena and challenged the Nine's rule in 1318.[27] In coalition with notaries, judges, and younger sons of the magnate Tolomei, artisans also threatened the Nine in 1311, 1317, 1318, 1319, and 1320.[28] Further riots erupted from fistfights and martial arts competitions, again threatening the Nine in 1324.[29] In 1306, butchers led a riot against the cardinal legate of Bologna, Napoleone Orsini. The seven guilds followed, took over the town hall, and ran the cardinal and counts of Panico out of town.[30] In 1328, butchers again tried to overturn the government with cries of "Puovolo, puovolo," but failed: four were dragged to death across the merchants' square.[31]

For Parma, the presence of butchers as a political pressure group began earlier. In 1252 they did not revolt as such but helped Lord Ghibertus de Gente take power in the city.[32] As we have seen, in 1291, four crafts—butchers, ironmongers, cobblers, and furriers—combined with notaries and judges along with other crafts of the city, promising to support one another against the city's magnates.[33] Afterward, twice in 1316 and twice in 1330, these four societies of elite craftsmen assembled their forces, raised their flags, and sacked the houses of magnates—the Opizzone de la Porta, de Zabulis, and de Saca clans—who had injured fellow craftsmen.[34] As we saw earlier, while serving in Flanders, Genoese sailors revolted against their captain over a delay in wages; their revolt spread to seamen of Savona and to the coastal villages west of Genoa.[35] In 1340, a butcher was one of the ringleaders of a conspiracy of the *popolo* to burn down the palace of the Genoese doge.[36]

While craftsmen in Florence were certainly among the forces that ousted magnates with the rise of the *primo popolo* in 1250, specific groups of cobblers, ironmongers, or butchers do not appear in the organization of the city's social movements during the late thirteenth or fourteenth centuries. The most one can point to are two bands of craftsmen, who in the summer of 1333 held street parties "with continuous games and amusement," to the chagrin of their social betters. One party comprised three hundred artisans all dressed in yellow and took place in the Via Ghibelline; in the other, five hundred dressed in white and held their festivities along the Corso de' Tintori (the street of the dyers).[37]

In 1342 Florence began to lead the way toward something new in Italian social history—social and political movements of workers. The disenfranchised and low-paid artisans of the wool industry finally appeared a hundred years after workers in cloth-manufacturing cities of the north such as Douai had gone on strike, formed associations, and had led protests against their city councils. In Florence, moreover, they surfaced initially not as the agents of rebellion but as the beneficiaries of a revolution from the top down. To break the dominance of the merchant oligarchy—the *popolani grassi*—the newly appointed governor of Florence, Walter of Brienne, the duke of Athens— favored the merchants' enemies—the disenfranchised wool workers—on the one hand, and certain disaffected magnate families, such as the Buondel-monti, on the other. As a consequence, the duke gave the *popolo minuto* their own militia banners and several political offices.[38] In November of that year the dyers petitioned a new governmental committee *(il Consiglio dei Saggi)* established by the duke to raise their wages from the wool bosses. In the same month, they petitioned to elect their own guild consuls, which in effect meant that they could organize a new and separate guild independent of the bosses' wool guild *(Arte della Lana).* The soap makers, wax makers, and those who extracted the red dye from madder *(robbiaioli)* then also entered this new guild.[39] Further, on 26 April 1343, the "sottoposti" throughout the wool industry were able to limit the arbitrary powers of the much hated *forastiere,* a judge appointed by the *Arte della Lana* to adjudicate cases involving quarrels among wool workers and cases of indebtedness, in which the workers had no rights of appeal.[40] Thus with the help of Florence's "despotic" leader, the disenfranchised workers of Florence were able to gain many of the rights that thirty-five years later they would have to struggle themselves to regain through the Revolt of the Ciompi. For the time being, as with the government of the Duke of Athens, these rights and privileges were short-lived. While chroniclers of Florence and elsewhere presented the duke's government as tyrannical and its overthrow as "a triumph of liberty,"[41] Ernesto Screpanti rightly sees this exuberance for "liberty" as that of the particular social class of merchant elites: "in reality it was the victory of bourgeois reaction."[42]

In the wake of the duke's overthrow, a series of workers' revolts aimed to regain their lost liberties. First, a maverick of the Florentine elite, Andrea Strozzi, ignited discontent among wool workers and roused them to revolt.[43] After his shamed kinsmen had caught, caged, and dumped him safely beyond Florence's walls, his son Pagnotto, with street-corner speeches and insulting taunts stirred wool workers to riot again.[44] As we have seen, historians have overlooked the evidence of a chronicler from Pistoia, which reveals that the dyers and fullers of Florence in 1342–1323 had their own leader, a dyer named Corazza, who launched a third revolt of thirteen hundred wool workers that this time was successful.[45] Two years later, a wool carder, Ciuto Brandini, organized an association of Florentine textile workers (*fraternitas*) with a strike fund (*postura seu collectio*).[46] On the eve of the Black Death, peasants of the Florentine *contado* collected funds, passed statutes, and went on their own strike.[47] Florence was not the only city-state to witness workers' movements on the eve of the Black Death. In 1346, textile workers came close to toppling the oligarchy of the Nine in Siena.[48]

Why did riots of workers suddenly appear in Tuscany a hundred years after they had flourished in Flanders and the north of France? Why not earlier, especially around 1300, when the *Arte della Lana* outlawed their guilds, reduced them to *sottoposti* without rights of free assembly or of determining their working conditions? No one has attempted an answer; no one has even posed the question. One point, however, can be drawn from this comparative analysis: popular protests north and south of the Alps before the Black Death were not marching to the same drummer; instead, their trajectories proceeded in opposite directions.

The Immediate Aftermath of the Black Death

The Black Death realigned the trajectories of social conflict north and south of the Alps to progress along similar tracks, despite the lack of any evidence of joint organization or communication linking such distant insurgents. First, for the Black Death and its immediate aftermath, 1348–1352, social movements with concrete aims to redress economic grievances, challenge political authority, or question prevailing social hierarchies are difficult to find in either the north or the south. In Tuscany, the Black Death abruptly killed off workers' new zeal to topple governments or protest against burgeoning capitalist exploitation. In Barberino Valdelsa, south of Florence, tempers rose at the end of the summer of 1348, leading to a barroom brawl and a minor riot of a handful of men and the bartender, who happened to be a lady (and a noble one at that).[49] But the cause of the conflict predated the plague, stemming from attempts to overturn corrupt election results of the previous year, when a much larger riot had engulfed this walled town.[50] Two years later, city chroniclers reported a conspiracy to topple the government of the Bentivoglio in Bologna.[51] But it amounted to little, was quickly repressed, and left no trace in this city's rich judicial archives.[52] Further, it was a revolt of the people (*puovolo*) and not of specifically named craftsmen or the *popolo minuto*. In 1348, Venice's colonies at Constantinople and Capo d'Istria revolted.[53] Supported by the Florentines and enticed by handsome tax immunities, the rural subjects of the Guidi at the castle of San Niccolò in the Montagna Fiorentina revolted against their feudal lords in 1349.[54] To what extent this was a social revolt or simply part of Florence's program to wrest lands and political control from its ancient feudal enemies and consolidate its territory along the sensitive mountain borders, we will never know. Siena had problems controlling its subject towns in the immediate aftermath of the plague: Massa Marittima in 1349,[55] Magliano in 1351,[56] and Montepulciano in 1352.[57] All of them failed, and in the case of Montepulciano, it was a revolt not of the "people" but of the "gentiliomini."

According to Matteo Villani, the "general loss" brought by the plague enriched the *popolo* of Rome, so their princes and other big lords (*gentilotti*) began to accept bandits into their districts, "who robbed, killed, disrupted, and did wicked deeds" throughout the land. The Romans were unhappy with their senator from the Orsini family and in 1351 "made war on his castle." But this was less a social revolt than civil strife between the two principal families of Rome: the Orsini and their rivals, the Colonna, supported by Jacopo Savelli. With this civil war raging, the people became worse off, "robbed by criminals inside and out of the city; foreigners and pilgrims entered Rome like sheep among the wolves." Finally, "many upstanding citizens [*molti buoni popolani*] met in Santa Maria Maggiore and decided they wanted a leader of the people and elected Giovanni Cerroni, an old citizen of of Rome [*antico popolare di Cerroni di Roma*]." The *popolo* gathered unarmed in the Campidoglio to face the armed troops of the princes, who asked "what was the meaning of this movement?" The people responded, "to have Giovanni Cerroni as their rector and to have full powers to rule and govern with jurisdiction over the people and Commune of Rome." Without any blood being spilt, the princes agreed and the pope ratified the decision. Although the change resulted in a new governor for Rome, it was a peaceful constitutional change, hardly a revolt of the lower orders.[58] In 1351, the *popolo* of L'Aquila sided with their local count to oppose their king.[59]

In France, revolts, even minor skirmishes, are even harder to find from the Black Death to Étienne Marcel's movements against the regent Charles and the Jacquerie of 1358. From my sample of chronicles only one revolt appears for these years and that one of elites rather than of the *menu peuple*. In 1351 the merchants of Rouen rebelled against the imposition of a new royal tax, which "the people called gabelles." They threw the cabinets in which the taxes were collected *(les buffés)* into the Seine. Thirty-six men from the cloth industry in this city were hanged from the gallows. From the chronicle it is not clear whether they were drapers or included cloth workers.[60]

Below this level of silence, royal letters of remission corroborate the impressions cast by the chronicles: the pickings are slim. In January 1350 the king granted a remission to the aldermen, the constable of the crossbowmen, and the inhabitants of the city of Arras, all accused of damaging fish ponds, demolishing buildings, felling trees, and violating the king's safeguard against the abbeys of Mont-Saint-Eloi and Saint-Vaast. What was at stake is difficult to know but, like earlier assaults against these abbeys outside the city walls of Arras, it may have concerned competition over cloth production. Nonetheless, if it were clearly a revolt of craftsmen or of the dispossessed, no notice of it is found in any of the major chronicles.[61] In July 1353, thirty-one peasants of Donnery (Ferrières-en-Gâtinais) were granted a remission for killing a man during a fight, but it was an internecine brawl between two villages, the inhabitants of Donnery and those of Aschères-le-Marché.[62] Finally, though not an armed revolt, a remission of 1351 reflects directly on the social and demographic consequences of the plague and shows the peasants of a village in Languedoc using the changed circumstances to their advantage: "because of the depopulation and deterioration of these difficult times brought on by the plague and the death that reigned in the year forty-eight and because of the various royal subsidies and other taxes, many of the inhabitants of this village have moved away to other places within the surrounding barony." The peasant petitioners then claimed that for the past four years they had been unable to pay these taxes and threatened that if their taxes were not lowered, many others would leave.[63]

Flanders may pose a more serious exception. In 1348 the new Count of Flanders, Louis de Male, attacked the prerogatives of the city councils and of weavers in Bruges, Ghent, and Ypres, which in turn provoked "the aldermen, captains, and governors" to call assemblies and to arm against the new count's incursions into their rights.[64] Louis's armies quickly and easily suppressed these responses and followed them with tough decrees. In Bruges, under pain of death, all the weavers and fullers were forbidden to carry weapons in public buildings and markets *(in domo civili, quae dicitur "Hala")* or to buy or borrow weapons. Not until 1359, however, did the weavers and other craftsmen of Ghent, Ypres, and elsewhere in Western Flanders organize a successful rebellion that overturned the count's repressive measures.[65] Even Henri Pirenne, who more than most historians emphasized the "democratic" thrust and "class conflict" inherent in late medieval Flemish history, did not consider Louis de Male's onslaught on the prerogatives of weavers in Ghent as part of this rich revolutionary history. Instead, he characterized the events of 1348–1349 as an internecine conflict between weavers and other craftsmen: "The fullers along with most of the small tradesmen and all the rich bourgeois broke away from the weavers to join the count's army, leaving the weavers to face their final catastrophe alone." On 13 January 1349, "in an unequal struggle, the count and his allies cut the weavers to pieces."[66]

Flagellants and the Burning of Jews

Despite the rarity of social revolts provoked by peasants, artisans, and workers, the Black Death did give rise to mass movements and immediate violence: flagellant groups and the burning of Jews swept across German-speaking areas, Spain, France, and the Low Countries from September 1348 to 1349. Italy may have been somewhat exceptional,[67] but even here Jewish communities in Mantua and Parma were attacked, and, as Cecil Roth speculated, these may not have been isolated cases.[68] Furthermore, in Sicily the Catalans took the place of the Jews, as widespread massacres against these foreigners spread from Palermo to Agrigento, Xacre, Trapani, and almost all of Val de Mazara in 1348.[69]

Stories of flagellant movements and persecution preoccupied chroniclers and contemporaries across Europe in the wake of the Black Death.[70] Jean le Bel described groups of "great devotion, making great penance," which originated in Germany. "Carrying crucifixes, banners, and standards as in solemn processions, they went down roads, two by two, loudly singing songs in praise of God and Our Lady, and twice daily stripped to their underwear [*se desvestoient jusques au petits draps*], beat themselves as hard as they could with whips and spike-tipped cattle-prods until blood spilled down their shoulders covering completely their flanks, all the while as they sang their songs." Three times a day, they threw themselves on the ground with one passing the others in great humility.[71] Then Jean le Bel described the massacres against the Jews.[72] *Les Grandes Chroniques de France* gave further details, pinpointing

August 1349 as the month when the flagellants "moved" through France, beating themselves with whips of three lashes, each lash having a knot, and each knot with four spikes like a cattle-prod. They wore a vermilion cross on hats of felt and on their shoulders, front and back.[73]

The closest attention to the waves of these penitential groups comes from the abbot of the monastery of Saint Martin at Tournai, Gilles li Muisis, who dedicated a second chronicle largely to the processions and devotions of 1349. These social-religious movements involved more than flagellants. First, he reported news of the rioting against Jews accused of poisoning wells and rivers to kill the Christian people, then the great movements *(rumores)* from Hungary and Germany into neighboring Brabant, "here two hundred, there, three hundred, another place, five hundred, and more from cities, towns, and villages where people gathered, encouraged to join the swell of people." For thirty-three days, they processed across large tracts of Europe, barefooted, stripped to their thighs, wearing hoods and beating themselves with special whips *(scorpionibus)* to draw blood. Finally, they reached Flanders, where the chronicler saw and heard them.[74]

Before the flagellants arrived, the Tournai chronicler also reported "a major disruption [*maxima commotio*] of men and women" in that year. It took place in the parish of Mary Magdalene in Tournai, when a vision of Christ on the cross sweating profusely appeared in the church and was seen by many. He reported other visions that provoked mass excitement, such as an image of the Virgin in the lepers' house just outside Tournai's city walls, "which many attested was sweating and had tears in her eyes." These visions sparked rioting throughout the city; great numbers rushed into these buildings to witness the miracles. Moreover, the chronicler claimed that "the same happened in many other towns and villages and for the most part the people believed and meditated on these miracles."[75] At the same time, "lascivious women wore every sort of ornamentation and tight clothing that revealed their nudity," and in general people ate and drank gluttonously and rioted in game playing *(surrexerunt ludere)*.[76]

Then, at lunchtime on the feast of the Assumption, the first group of penitents arrived in Tournai: about two hundred men from Bruges gathered in the main square, "causing a great riot through the city"; everyone came to see them. Men and women joined in the rites of penance. Some approved; others did not. On the next Tuesday the Franciscan Friar Gerrard de Muro preached at the chronicler's monastery, announcing that death loomed for all because of the sins of mankind. But at the end of his sermon, he refused to pray because of the penitents. Most in the audience became indignant. For the rest of the week "the people" increasingly spoke out against him. During this week, a large band *(societas)* of 450 came from Ghent, another of about 300 from Sluys, and 400 from Dordrecht. They too performed acts of penitence twice a day in the city square and in the courtyard of the monastery of Saint Martin. On Saturday, the feast day of John the Baptist's decapitation, a band of about 180 came from Liège and remained, performing their acts of penitence until Sunday. A Dominican friar preached the word of God on the spot where Friar Gerrard had preached at the monastery of Saint Martin, provoking yet another major riot throughout the city. A great mass of men and women, "the size of which had never been seen before in Tournai," converged on the monastery's square, which could hardly hold them. Friar Gerrard preached that a terrible grain shortage was about to ensnare them that would lead to death, gloom, and doom. In the middle of his sermon, a group called the red knights began performing their acts of penitence, interrupting the Dominicans, who were preaching against these acts of this rival penitent devotion. Others tried to stop the Dominicans, calling them scorpions and antichrists. "Then the blood of those called the red knights came forth seen as the blood of Christ drawn from their flagellation. And nearly everyone turned against the mendicants"; rioting spread with attacks against all the clergy.[77]

The next Tuesday the deacon and chapter of Tournai organized a public procession of citizens, who marched barefoot and shirtless. A Brother Robert, this time of the Augustinians, preached the word of God without placating the penitents. He also spoke out against the Dominican friar who had preached there the previous Sunday, but before he could finish, the crowd exploded, yelling that he was "badly informed." Again rioting spread throughout the city, with attacks against the mendicants and other clergymen.

Still other penitent groups came to Tournai, but not all of them were flagellants. One group of about sixty performed the ritual of washing feet in public, which gathered large crowds backed by the city; the city's councilors granted them a license to come and go as they pleased for thirty-three days. According to li Muisis, it was difficult to believe "just how devout men and women of the laity became at this time." They suddenly changed their ways. Women put aside their jewels and slinky gowns and took up the habit; the open adultery and fornication seen earlier that year suddenly ended. According to li Muisis, these Tournai experiences—rival penitent groups, conflicts between mendicants and lay groups, and major rioting *(in maximam seditionem commoverunt)* sparked by competition among this panoply of penitent societies—was not peculiar to Tournai. They spread through Flanders, Hainault, Brabant, and other regions of the Low Countries and into France, where the church and the king of France condemned them. By Easter week, the city council of Tournai read out Clement VI's papal bull against the flagellants and announced that all their public displays were to cease. But a major riot broke out, and the penitents continued to perform their acts and to preach.[78]

Almost daily reports from li Muisis of the roller-coaster emotions that rushed from free love to various forms of ritualistic purging and devotion hardly shows the immediate postplague period as peaceful, even in Flanders, where less evidence of mass persecution and burning of Jews appears than in Germany, Southern France, or Spain. This violence, however, differed markedly from organized protests of peasants, laborers, or bourgeois against city councils, counts, or kings seen before the plague. First, although these ritual groups with their distinctive garb and penitential practices may not have sprung forth spontaneously or "literally had no head," as the German chronicler Henry of Hervodia claimed,[79] even the meticulous li Muisis gives little indication of their prior planning, assemblies, or elected leaders, if any such elections in fact took place. Few individual leaders emerge from the chronicles, condemnations, or other official documents.[80]

Furthermore, while mendicants battled among themselves and with penitents, the violence that fills chronicles of the years 1348–1349 reveals few hints of any class cleavages. Rather than struggling for concrete goals or redressing specific political, economic, or social grievances, this violence targeted forces outside society to resolve anxieties, fears, and anger. In the case of accusations of poisoning wells and mass burnings down the Rhineland and into Austria, eastern France, and Spain, the scapegoats were the Jews; in Narbonne, it was the poor from foreign lands. In the case of the preachers and the maverick penitential movements, it was the heavens. Some combined the two. Thus, after reporting the torturing and sentencing to death by hot pincers, disemboweling, and burning of many poor beggars accused of spreading poisonous substances into rivers, houses, churches, and foodstuffs in April 1348, a burgess of Narbonne, deputy of Aymer, Vicomte of Narbonne, concluded: "we believe that it is certainly the combined effects of the planets and the potions which are causing the mortality."[81]

After the Black Death: Italy

By 1353, the number of social protests and revolts with concrete political ends began to rise in Italy again. The Roman *popolo* chased the ruling senator, Luca

Savelli, out of town.[82] Provoked by food shortages, the *popolo minuto* of Gaeta rose up against merchants with jacquerie fury, attempting "to kill as many of them as they could."[83] In Viterbo a revolt in the artisan neighborhoods of Pian Scarlano and Pian San Fautino erupted against the city's prefect. It was one of the rare revolts in which churchmen participated and may have had a leadership role, but the prefect won, and "many heads rolled." The chroniclers mentioned none of the insurgents by name but specified that three (by one account) or four (by another) were churchmen.[84]

In 1354 the number of protests increased. Citizens of Pavia rose up against Milanese rule and killed their podestà.[85] At least two revolts of the *popolo* flared in Bologna. In the first, butchers led by the Bentivoglio[86] attempted to overthrow the existing regime.[87] In the second, the citizen militia refused to obey when the regime ordered two divisions of two thousand men each to attack neighboring Modena. The people were aggrieved on two counts: too much was being demanded of them *(troppo aspro servaggio)* for no pay, and the Modenese were their neighbors and "old friends." Called to form their ranks, the militia refused, even after grave penalties were decreed. The *popolo* then armed and rioted through the streets of Bologna, chanting "Popolo, popolo," fought the mercenary guards, and then returned to their houses with impunity.[88]

In 1355, Italy exploded in popular rebellion from Naples to Venice. The best known event was the toppling of the longest-serving oligarchy in Italian history: Siena's Nine fell at the hands of a broad coalition of social groups previously denied offices, from the *popolo minuto* to magnate families of the Salimbene and Tolomei. But this was not Siena's only revolt of the *popolo minuto* in 1355. On three more occasions—25 March, 18 May, and 27 May—they pushed the revolution further, widening their liberties.[89] As we have seen, the fall of the Nine sparked other revolts in Siena's *contado* at Massa, Casole, Grosseto, Monteritondo, and Montepulciano.

The Emperor Charles IV's stay in Tuscany triggered other revolts. After Siena, he went with his troops and servants to reside in Pisa but by May had overstayed his welcome. At night, the *popolo* set ablaze the Palace of the Elders, where the emperor and empress were lodged, sending them naked onto the streets. The *popolo* armed. Led by the Gambacorta, all their companies yelled chants against the emperor, charged through the city, and barricaded streets in battles against the German troops, killing many soldiers and throwing their bodies into the Arno. But the emperor eventually prevailed, and the houses of the Gambacorta were burnt down.[90] Immediately, news reached Lucca (then under Pisan control) and the next day peasants of the Lucchesia, "because of heavy taxes" imposed on them by the Pisans, took advantage of Pisa's defeat, rose up, encircled the city, and then in unity with workers and artisans *(il popolo vile)* threw out the Pisan officials. Having "defended their liberty," they then turned against the leading Lucchese citizens, burning down their palaces.[91]

While Tuscany may have been the scene of the best-remembered revolts of 1355, others sprang up across the peninsula. In Naples, the *popolo* rebelled against the queen's councilors, high taxes, and loss of their city privileges *(la potenzia e lla franchigia di quella città)*. They won back their "ancient rights" to have salt sold according to the market and not at a price fixed by the government.[92] In Piedmont, Asti, Alba, Valenza, Tortona,[93] and "many other places," the *popolo* revolted against Milanese rule.[94] Popular forces in Venice conspired on several occasions in 1355. Mariners and others plotted to kill the doge.[95] Citizens and commoners *(cittadini e popolari)* met secretly to redress injuries they had suffered from the Venetian nobility. Further, from hatred of the nobility and to stir internecine bitterness, commoners posed as young noblemen, knocked on the palace doors of "the first citizens of the city," and yelled: "Because I hate you so, I have screwed your wife, sister, and daughter."[96] Again in 1355, the *popolo* of Venice plotted to ring the city bells and charge through the streets, yelling, "Long live the People!" and after that to disband the council of the noblemen and turn all offices over to commoners. The plot was discovered and the doge, who supported the rebels, was beheaded.[97]

Further north in Udine, because of heavy taxes imposed by the Patriarch of Aquilea and the arrogance of his deputy in the city, who was his son-in-law, the *popolo* revolted, capturing and beheading the son-in-law without trial.[98] Finally, popular revolts spread to parts of central Italy other than Tuscany. In the *contado* of Ancona, thirteen incastellated villages revolted against the city.[99] In Fermo, the *popolo* revolted against the rule of the Malatesta,[100] and because of increased taxes in Rimini, the peasants with pickaxes and scythes invaded the city but without success.[101]

For the remainder of the decade, popular rebellion was rife throughout Italy. In 1356, Cortona rebelled against Perugian control;[102] Conegliano against Venetian dominance;[103] Simone Boccanegra led a revolt of the *popolo* against the doge in Genoa;[104] inspired and organized by Frate Bussolari, Pavia rebelled against Milanese "tyranny";[105] the old alliance of butchers, notaries, and the Tolomei raised its head again in Siena but this time against the new government of the Twelve;[106] and Grosseto rebelled against Siena for the second time in less than a year.[107] The following year saw a spate of rebellions through Venice's colonies at Spaleto, Tragurino, Sberzaro, Brazensio, Liesne,[108] and Zara. Venice lost control over Dalmatia.[109] The inhabitants *(terrazzani)* of Borgo San Sepolcro revolted against their Ghibelline lords and reformed their government as one of the *popolo.*[110] Further revolts of the *popolo* against heavy taxation succeeded in ousting signorial governments—tyrants, according to Villani—at Ravenna and Bologna.[111] In 1358 Roman merchants and artisans resisted new gabelles imposed by the Avignon prelates on wine and other commodities.[112] On learning of the "shame" of their army's loss at Cortona, the *popolo* of Perugia revolted against their government.[113] On four occasions, the *popolo* of Pavia, inspired by Frate Bussolari, assembled and revolted against their magnates and Milanese attempts to regain the city.[114] In 1359 Montalcino rebelled against Siena,[115] and La Serra and a number of other incastellated villages rebelled against the Aretine dominance of the Tarlati lords, "throwing off their long servitude under the yoke of this tyranny."[116] The *popolo* of Perugia rioted against the corruption of Leggieri d'Andriotto and other "grandi cittadini" of the ruling class called Raspanti.[117] Finally, the *popolo* of Pavia once again assembled under the leadership of Frate Bussolari and attempted to resist Milanese encroachments on their independence but finally failed.[118] These and other revolts contrast with the near absence of popular protest in the seven years immediately following the Black Death and show that the cluster of revolts in 1378–1382 may not have been so remarkable in number or character as the historiography now contends.

After the Black Death: France and Flanders

Despite this postplague social ferment in Italy, the most famous of the revolts of the 1350s arose in the north. First, the Parisian bourgeois rebelled under the leadership of Charles Taussac, a Parisian alderman, against the king's change in monetary policy and new taxes in 1357.[119] Then, with Étienne Marcel at the helm, matters became more confrontational, leading to the crowd's siege of the Louvre and the murder of the regent's two marshals in his private apartments on 22 February 1358.[120] These events were followed by the aristocracy's violent reaction in the Île de France—the capture of river ports on the Seine and the blockade of Paris—which led to further rioting in Paris and the beheading of royal officers.[121] In late May the peasants' revolt or Jacquerie spread through hundreds of villages in the Beauvaisis, Picardy, the Île de

France, and Champagne, as far east as Bar on the borders of France. Besides the bourgeois rebellion of Paris, the Jacques inspired revolts against the nobility in cities such as Amiens, Caen, Rouen, Sens, Senlis, Montdidier, and ultimately and fatally at the king's stronghold at Meaux.[122] Behind these revolts were certainly the realities of the Hundred Years' War and the difficulties of financing increased warfare and raising King John's ransom with a tax base greatly diminished by two strikes of plague. But other causes seem to have been paramount, especially for the Jacquerie. In the Jacquerie's many chronicle accounts and letters of remission, taxes are not mentioned once as a cause;[123] instead, chroniclers pointed to betrayal by the local nobility.[124]

The battlefields of the Jacquerie were not the only places in France to see revolts during the late 1350s. Before the protests of the Estates General and the provost of Paris in 1357, the Rouennais refused to pay taxes to King John in 1355,[125] and on 6 March 1356 the commoners *(minor populus)* of Arras revolted against the king's subsidies and the salt tax, killing fourteen of the wealthiest bourgeois in the city. News of their revolt spread to Normandy, where further revolts against the same taxes followed.[126] Nor was the south of France spared from social tensions and revolts. Royal officers *(élus)* were attacked in the county of Forez; a tax revolt erupted at Montbrison with cries and attacks against royal officers; and in various places in Languedoc, crowds attacked tax collectors and houses of royal officials on 9 May 1357.[127] As we have seen, in May the count of Armagnac, the king's lieutenant for Languedoc, came to Toulouse to collect the taxes needed to wage war against the English. The people rebelled and laid siege to his palace, forcing the local aristocracy to intervene. The crowds won: in return for the count's safe passage through his realm, the new taxes were rescinded.[128] A year later, fullers, weavers, and cobblers waged war against the count of Flanders, humiliated him, and took over city councils in Ypres, Bruges, and Ghent. By August 1361 the weavers had been restored to power in all the cities of maritime Flanders,[129] and, in contrast to the previous thirty years, weavers and fullers now joined forces against patrician oligarchs and the count.[130]

Little, if anything, has been said about popular revolt in France between the Jacquerie and the cluster of revolts in France and Flanders at the end of Charles V's life and the opening years of the reign of the young Charles VI.[131] Was this the calm before the storm, a period of social peace and effective control by elites and the crown? Did the cruel and disproportionate repression of the Jacques kill off all desire and capacity of urban and rural groups to rise up for a generation? Curiously, on the very battlefields of the Jacquerie and less than a year since its bloodbaths, peasants assembled, armed, and took it upon themselves to resist incursions from armies of the nobility, who were now the English instead of the French. Most famous of these peasant initiatives was at Longueil-Sainte-Marie, near Compiègne in the Beauvaisis, where a peasant, Guillaume l'Aloue, assembled two or three hundred rustics and defeated an English cavalry of 600. Soon afterward, the peasants, under the leadership of another peasant called Grandferre, resisted a second assault from the English nobles.[132] While this peasant resistance entered French folklore, it was not an isolated incident. A year later, again near Compiègne, villagers of Thouri-en-Beauce resisted English troops.[133] In the same year, the villagers of Châtres fortified their church and prepared to combat the English; however, they were slaughtered because their captain and more powerful villagers betrayed them.[134]

True, for the north of France it is difficult to point to insurrections during the 1360s and early 1370s. But their absence reflects the very opposite conditions ascribed by historians such as Mollat, Wolff, and Bertelli to explain the rise of popular rebellion a generation after the Black Death—misery.[135] The continuator of Guillaume de Nangis paints a gloomy picture of death, destruction, oppressive taxation, and betrayal in northern France during the 1360s from Poitou to Brittany and from Normandy to Paris: "Thus at this time the people . . . were as grievously oppressed by their friends and protectors as by their enemies." To capture the picture of social and political relations in the region of Paris around 1363, he then tells the story of the strong dog employed to protect the sheep but who befriends the wolf. While the dog feigns protecting his flock, in reality he is in cahoots with the wolf; the two team up and devour the flock.[136]

Nonetheless, the continuator of de Nangis points to a silent revolt taking place among peasants at the same time. Against the raids of brigands and "extraordinarily onerous taxes," villagers responded with their feet, abandoned work in the fields, and headed for Paris.[137] Perhaps further research into the rich archive of the Trésor des chartes and its letters of remission will reveal that these years of misery and betrayal were not as rebel-free as silences in the chronicles suggest.[138] From a cursory look, several popular disturbances can be reported: in 1362 the town council and inhabitants of Fanjeaux disobeyed royal commands and refused to open their gates to the king's treasurer and his troops;[139] in 1363 the villagers of Givry and Sambles (outside Châlons-sur-Saône) attacked ducal officers who came to maintain order;[140] and again in

1363 villagers at Réalmonte hurled insults at a collector of the gabelles, which led to a fight that left one villager dead.[141]

The silence of Langue d'oïl, however, cannot be read for Flanders or France writ large. Tournai was especially tumultuous. In 1359, the regent's uncle and chief adviser, Louis of Anjou, came to Tournai to raise new taxes. The town's provost greeted him and agreed to do his bidding, but the commoners had ideas of their own and forced Louis to seek refuge in the town's bell tower, for which deeds, the chronicler adds, "the town would pay."[142] Five years later Louis issued a letter of remission, describing the incident in his own words: "several inhabitants came into the abbey of Saint-Martin (where Louis was hosted) with hostile intent and rioting. They broke down the doors to our room, tore the curtains of our bed to bits, and committed other offences against us and our men, which cannot be retold. For this reason we ordered a counter-offensive against the Tournaisians by Sire de Chin."[143] In 1364, taxes again provoked a popular revolt at Tournai. This time it succeeded and spread to Valenciennes, and "by their examples" spread further still "to all the towns of Hainault."[144] In February of the following year, commoners led another tax revolt, this time against the town council and its provost,[145] but it did not end with attacks against these notables. Tournai's weavers led a troop of two to three hundred artisans under their banners against the French crown.[146] In 1368, the Tournaisians aided those from neighboring cities in Flanders in a conspiracy against Louis de Male, and in 1369 they rebelled twice against the king's imposition of a new tax on wheat.[147] Further, weavers revolted in Ghent in 1362, 1365, and 1373[148] and in Ypres in 1367, 1370, and 1377.[149]

By the end of the decade, tax protests arose on a large scale in the traditional regions of antiroyal rebellion, especially in Normandy. In 1369 the king called on the bourgeois of his principal towns to raise taxes to finance the war against the English. Through the abbot of Fécamp, he imposed new subsidies on wheat, beer, cider, and wine along with other gabelles. When "the people throughout the realm" heard the news, they put the abbot's life in danger, claimed they had not consented to the tax, and refused to pay.[150]

The south of France was even more important as a theater of class struggle during the 1360s. The combination of political instability, roaming brigands, war, and new taxes weighed heavily on the mountainous areas of the Massif Central. Soldiers, peasants, and townsmen formed bands called Tuchins to redress personal grievances and pursue economic advantage but also to challenge the crown and its rising taxation in this milieu of hardship, war, and half-hearted truces between the French and English.[151] This was especially true farther south, in the regions of Toulouse, Carcassonne, and Beaucaire, where groups also called Tuchins later took over villages and even the city of Nîmes.[152]

Still other revolts raged through southern France in the 1360s. The inhabitants of Mirepoix, southwest of Carcassonne, received a pardon for being rebels and conspiring against the crown in 1360.[153] In the same year the town council of Servian (about 10 km northeast of Béziers) defied royal orders to repair their fortifications.[154] In 1362 the town councilors and inhabitants of Clermont de Lodève were found guilty of rebellion against the crown and fined 800 florins.[155] Again that year, the king's lieutenant in Béziers brutally repressed those of the small market town of Gignac who had rebelled against the reorganization of their district, when the town lost its administrative jurisdiction (*la viguerie de Gignac*) and became absorbed into the viguerie of Béziers. The crown fined the town councilors and inhabitants 3,000 florins.[156] In 1363 about sixty men, including town councilors, rioted in Béziers to free an apothecary from arrest. They threatened the king's lieutenant at Béziers and were charged with treason (*crimen lese majestatis*).[157] In 1364, three hundred men of Carcassonne, "armed with various weapons and with the consent and guidance of their town councilors," made war on the royal castle of their region, setting fire to its gates and entering it. Seven insurgents were arrested. A few days later, organized by the town council, two thousand men of Carcassonne marched to the prison, killed the royal officers, and liberated the seven.[158] In the same year "plebes" from the market towns of Gimont and Simorre in the region of Toulouse staged their own Jacquerie, deposing aristocratic rule in the region and butchering their lords. For the next thirty years the crown was unable to bring the insurgents to trial or to collect a 25,000-franc fine levied on them. Finally, with a letter of remission, the king and his lieutenant admitted failure and gave up trying to get it.[159]

In 1364 in the region of Albi, the crown charged peasants and townsmen as accomplices in aiding the great companies of mercenaries (*magne societatis*) who had "captured, ransomed, robbed, tortured, killed, set fires, devastated the countryside, raped virgins and married women, and committed many other crimes."[160] Further, the councilors and inhabitants of several rural communes of the Albigeois were charged with molesting royal officers.[161] In 1369 inhabitants of Montauban revolted against the crown.[162] Evidence of tax rebellion also appears in English-controlled Gascony during the 1360s, where the barons led a revolt and refused to pay new hearth taxes imposed by the Prince of Wales. In 1370 Edward III was forced to abolish these taxes and pardon the rebels.[163] By contrast, the decade of the 1370s appears quieter in the south, that is, until 1378, when this region led the rest of France and Flanders in a new round of tax rebellions against the crown.

The Supposed Cluster of Revolts, 1378–1382

As important as the battlefields of the Hundred Years' War were to instability and revolt, they were hardly the only areas of Europe to see popular rebellion rise during the latter half of the fourteenth century. Rebellion was more rife in Italy than in France or Flanders from the late 1350s to 1378. In Siena, no fewer than six governments were toppled and replaced with new regimes within five months alone between September 1368 and January 1369.[164] In all these permutations, artisans and workers played a key role, and for their efforts they secured governmental offices and privileges. Revolts in Siena culminated in 1371 with the uprising of the wool workers organized around their neighborhood association, the club of the Caterpillar, first against the wool bosses to secure higher wages, then to release three of their comrades, and finally to overthrow the Government of the Twelve.[165] After this failure, rioting and serious threats to political stability from lower classes in Siena died down or disappeared altogether, but unlike in Florence and most other Italian city-states, these social classes maintained a presence in Siena's various governments well into the fifteenth century.

Perhaps the most lasting of the conclusions drawn in Mollat and Wolff's *Ongles bleus* has been their emphasis on the sharp pan-European cluster of revolts a generation after the Black Death—the years 1378 to 1382.[166] For France and Flanders, the tax revolts in the south, the *Harelle* in Rouen, the *Maillotins* in Paris, and the "troubles" of the Low Countries all support their case.[167] But popular insubordination and rebellion continued to boil from the mid-1350s to the 1370s and did not suddenly appear exactly a generation after the Black Death. In Italy, in fact, the numbers of revolts continued to build during the 1370s and then temporarily dipped during the so-called cluster of 1378–1382. The Florentine Revolt of the Ciompi in 1378 was an outlier.

Because of the Revolt of the Ciompi, historians have paid greater attention to popular revolt in Florence than elsewhere in Italy. However, insurrections were more numerous in other regions of central Italy in the 1360s and 1370s. These included tax revolts at Bologna and Ravenna in 1357;[168] insurrections of artisans and workers in the wool industry at Lucca,[169] Perugia,[170] and Siena;[171] and various attempts by underlings *(sottoposti)* to change the political control of their city-states: in Lucca, 1369;[172] Siena, 1368 (at least four times);[173] Cortona and Perugia, 1371;[174] and Bologna, 1377.[175] But by far the most numerous of these revolts stemmed from popular outrage over the violence, arrogance, and injustice of aristocratic behavior and rule, whether it came from the church's "pastors," a foreign military presence, or the old local patrician families. We have already seen a number of these, including the people's bloodbath of cardinals and their retainers at Viterbo in 1367, Gubbio's ousting of its papal ruler in the same year,[176] the papal legate's defeat at the hands of the Perugian *popolo* in 1369, and the butcher-led assault on the abusive Breton mercenaries billeted in Cesena in 1377.

The most important sweep of revolts in Italy occurred in the mid-1370s. In sheer numbers, these revolts dwarf those of Florence as well as the supposed cluster of Europe-wide revolts listed by Mollat and Wolff. In one month alone, December 1375, sixty cities in the Marche, Tuscany, Umbria, Emilia-Romagna, and the Papal States revolted, and almost all of them succeeded in "freeing themselves from the yoke of church rule," that is, one-third more than Mollat and Wolff found for all of Europe in 1378–1382.[177] The *Cronaca malatestiana* of Rimini counted even more; by 28 March 1376, 1,577 walled towns and villages had thrown off the rule, "not counting small or tower villages."[178] According to Gene Brucker, this war against the papacy was "one of the most radical revolutions in Florentine history . . . a revolution of internal politics, a critical phase of the struggle between an old order and the new."[179] Screpanti has gone further, seeing it as a class struggle in central Italy "against the old aristocratic classes and the papacy, a war against nascent capitalism and the dying medieval order."[180] As the conservative anonymous diarist of the Machiavelli family observed for Bologna in 1376, "the aristocrats [*grandi*] were hounded out of office and in their place merchants and artisans remained as lords."[181]

By contrast, only a handful of riots in Italy erupted during the supposed cluster in 1378–1382: the Florentine Ciompi; a revolt of the *popolo* in Genoa, which may not in fact have involved artisans or workers; the undefined crowd in Rome that pressured the cardinals to elect an Italian pope in April 1378; a small tax revolt against the imposition of a land tax *(aestimum)* in Parma in 1380;[182] and an insurrection of "the people" to overthrow the ruling family in Treviso around 1380 (the chronicler is vague). Only one official, however, was singled out and killed, a Pirinzolo who during Treviso's last war had allegedly captured Trevigian women, forcing them "to pull up their slips to their groins" so that he could "ruminate on their private parts [*ad propria remandere*]."[183]

Nor did 1382 mark a sudden or long-term decline in popular rebellion in Italy or north of the Alps. True, the experience with radical politics had largely ended more or less definitively even before the cluster began for one of the most revolutionary of Italian city-states, Siena. For the city of Florence, only minor and unsuccessful ripples of popular revolt followed the fall of the Government of the Minor Guilds in January 1382. The last decades of the fourteenth century and the opening years of the fifteenth century, however, saw a dramatic surge in revolts in other places in Italy: those of the *popolo* of Rome against the papacy multiplied; peasant revolts spread through the mountains of Florence and Bologna and in the valleys of Genoa; and popular movements brought down governments in Bologna, Genoa, Padua, Udine, and elsewhere.

Similarly, Charles VI's victory at Rozebeke in 1382 may have marked a temporary lull in the pace of popular rebellion in France and Flanders, but neighboring Liège hardly missed a beat. In fact, the years 1378–1382 were peaceful there. Its great revolt, which definitively dispelled patrician rule and established a government of tradesmen that would endure into the early modern period, came immediately after the cluster, with popular riots from 1384 to 1386.[184] Certainly by the fifteenth century, popular revolt was on the rise again in France, with the Cabochiens and other revolts made possible by cracks in royal authority, the king's bouts with madness,[185] and the civil war that raged between Burgundians and Armagnacs. Tax revolts, movements of butchers and other artisans, the flouting of royal orders, and the murder of royal officers occurred in the early fifteenth century at Reims (1402), Troyes (1402), Toulouse (1407), Liège (1403, 1408, and 1415 twice), Orléans (1410), Soissons (1412, 1413, and 1414), Noyon (1413), Carcassone (1415), Amiens (1416), Rouen (1416, 1417, 1418, and 1419), Sens (1420), Tournai (1423, 1424, and 1425), and most spectacularly, Paris (1404, 1409, 1411, 1412, 1413, 1415, 1416, 1418, 1419, 1421, 1422, 1423), as well as at smaller places across France and Flanders.

Despite the absence of any evidence of communication between popular rebels north and south of the Alps and a wide variety of popular revolts with different aims and causes, rebellion in postplague Europe (or at least much of Western Europe) began to reflect a common community. The Black Death brought a hidden sense of unity.[186] In contrast to the preplague Middle Ages, the pace and character of popular revolt now traveled more or less along the same chronological tracks: first a lull during the years immediately following the plague, then a rush from 1355 on. How do we explain the change?

CHAPTER 10

A New Appetite
for Liberty

Despite small differences in the clustering of popular revolts, the incidence of rebellions rose more or less in tandem north and south of the Alps after the Black Death, in contrast to the preceding century. After a lull in popular revolt and a turning in many parts of Europe to violence without social aims in the years immediately following the Black Death, the number of insurrections with concrete goals began to climb by the second half of the 1350s and, with fits and starts, remained fairly steady throughout the remainder of the century and into the next. In my samples, 470 revolts appear between 1200 and 1348, or 2.73 per annum, and 621, or 8.06 per annum, after the Black Death to the end of my analysis in 1425—nearly triple the numbers from the preplague period. If the years 1354–1383 are compared with the preplague period, the increase is higher: 300 revolts, or 10 per annum. Revolts are difficult to quantify with precision, however, especially waves of revolts, such as those against the papacy that spread through central Italy from 1375 to 1377. Chroniclers most often spoke of them collectively yet counted hundreds of places that were in revolt in only a few months. If these revolts are counted only for cities individually named (not including villages), the sums for 1375 would then spike upward, pushing the postplague cluster of 1354–1383 to 12 a year, more than quadrupling the preplague rate.[1]

On the one hand, it might be argued that chroniclers after the plague paid greater attention to popular uprisings than they had before—Matteo Villani counted 35 revolts, the anonymous Minerbetti 24, and the Stella of Genoa 42—even if preplague chroniclers such as Giovanni Villani described just as many (35). Nonetheless, as historians have often assumed but have never quantified, popular rebellion undoubtedly increased in frequency during the second half of the fourteenth century, even if it would be hazardous to place too much stock in the precise magnitude of that increase, given the wide variety of revolts, the numbers involved, the areas covered, and the records available. As with much of the analysis presented thus far, the quantitative must be mixed with the qualitative, and my argument rests essentially with the latter. On the other hand, it would be wrong to think that the change in the number of revolts or their ideology resulted simply from a sudden trans-formation of the sources. Before and after 1348, my sample relies on essen-tially the same diverse mix of religious, merchant, and royal chroniclers. By the end of my period (1425), the humanist history had yet to displace the late medieval chronicle. Of the 298 narrative sources used for this study, only three humanist histories appear, two in the south (both of Leonardo Bruni) and one in the north (that of Michel Pintoin).

Structural Explanations: Demographic, Economic, and Political

Given the widely different political histories of the north, which was domi-nated by the Hundred Years' War, and Italy, where politics turned increasingly on territorial conflict and consolidation, how do we account for the rise of insurrections across much of Europe from the late 1350s to the 1370s? Most explanations of the postplague increase in popular rebellion have fixed on England and demography. With a sudden shrinkage in the tax base, govern-ments were forced to raise taxes sharply to pay for more costly wars.[2] At the same time, the dramatic demographic collapse meant that laborers were in a better bargaining position vis-à-vis their bosses, landlords, and the state. This was especially true for peasants, since many left the countryside for higher wages in the cities, leaving the countryside more in need of labor than the towns.[3] Thus, the land-to-labor ratio changed dramatically, with rents during the century after the Black Death declining by one-third to one-half.[4] Cer-tainly, labor legislation in Tuscany pointed in this direction: Florence directed almost all its appeals to attract foreign labor during the late fourteenth and early fifteenth centuries exclusively at agricultural labor and to those who would reside in its *contado*.[5] Moreover, while the English Ordinances and Statutes of Labourers (1349 and 1351) legislated against wage hikes and price rises demanded by artisans, their major focus was on the countryside, and the majority of the resulting prosecutions concerned landlords and rural laborers.[6] According to Bertha Putnam, the areas of greatest revolutionary activity in 1381 coincided with the areas having the greatest enforcement of the labor laws.[7]

On first observation, the statistics from my samples of popular revolt lend support to this demographic explanation: while revolts increased by 2.9 times per annum after the Black Death, tax revolts increased almost fourfold and peasant revolts six times. However, the majority of these peasant revolts did not occur immediately after the Black Death or even after the first three or four plagues; instead, 34 of the 49 postplague peasant revolts (69 percent) came after the supposed "cluster of revolts" 1378–1382. Furthermore, while plague mortalities, except for a few pockets, were relatively evenly distributed over France, Flanders, and Italy (at least by the time of the third or fourth wave of plagues), peasant revolts were not. Instead, postplague peasant revolts were primarily Italian, in fact northern Italian; only five in my sample came from France (8 percent), none from Flanders, and one from Liégeois.

Moreover, as I argued in *Creating the Florentine State,* taxes per se or their economic burden were not the principal reason for peasants risking their lives and homesteads in revolts that spread across the mountainous frontiers of Florence; rather perceived injustice was at the core of peasant discontent, as with Florence's unfair taxation, which hit mountain communities as much as thirty-two times harder than villages close to Florence's city walls.[8] After the peasants won their cause, taxes were not the only issue in their petitions and negotiations with the Florentine state. As we have seen with revolts elsewhere, politics were central: the rebels gained liberties, such as the rights to carry weapons throughout the Florentine territory and to choose who could settle in their villages. In a rebellion of the Romagnol market town of Rocca di San Casciano, the insurgents stated their reasons for revolt more explicitly: they wanted the right to set and collect their own bread gabelle, which Florence had assured them of when they agreed to recognize Florence's suzerainty but which Florence then illegally reneged on. As a consequence, those of Rocco turned to their former feudal lords of the Romagna to "free" them from Florence, proclaiming: "one day, we will escape from this tyranny once and for all."[9] Similarly for peasant revolts in late-fourteenth-century and early-fifteenth-century Genoa, high taxes were not the principal cause; instead, these peasant uprisings hinged on other political issues—to oust magnate doges and to install new governments of the *popolo.*

In addition, the demographic context of the best known of the late medieval revolts south of the Alps—the Revolt of the Ciompi—was just the opposite of what is usually assumed to have been universal with postplague rebellion, even though this revolt occurred after the Florentine population had shrunk to half its preplague figure. The bargaining position of wool workers would have been at its best in the early 1360s. Not only was wool production expanding, but also the war with Pisa (1362–1364) attracted wool workers into military service with its higher wages. In these years, Michele di Lando, for instance, left the wool industry to serve in the Florentine campaigns in Pisa.[10] By 1365, however, the consuls of the *Arte della Lana* were complaining of a scarcity of wool workers, especially of weavers.[11] Yet for these years the chronicles and criminal records show no unrest.[12] In the 1370s the tide turned: Florence's wool industry declined from peak productions of around 30,000 cloths per annum in 1373 to fewer than 24,000 cloths in 1378 on the eve of the Ciompi—a slump of at least one-fifth.[13] The later figure, moreover, is a hypothetical one, taken from what the Ciompi demanded of the wool bosses to guarantee employment in a declining industry. The actual figure must have been considerably lower.

The same years, however, saw an increase in population, most likely from immigration from the countryside, especially after the famine and plague of 1373–1374. From the aftermath of the plague of 1363 to 1379, the Florentine population increased by about 10,000, or roughly 20 percent, despite famine and plague. Since 1348, Florence's population had increased by 40 percent or more.[14]

Thus the years leading up to the Revolt of the Ciompi, from around 1374 to 1378, were a period of labor surplus, not scarcity, as far as wool production goes. As a consequence, many workers in the wool industry were forced to seek employment in the communal army, joining Florence's war against the papacy in 1375 to avoid indebtedness for which they would face imprisonment. As Brucker and Trexler have shown, the "War of Eight Saints" provided the training grounds for future Ciompi militants and leaders, giving many on the lowest rungs of the industry, such as carders and combers, jobs as crossbowmen. Many rose through the ranks to become "corporali" and later used these skills to lead the Ciompi rebellion.[15] This experience resulted in large part from the decline in wool production, which outpaced the city's demographic fall. Thus a key demand of the Ciompi was that their bosses produce at least 2,000 cloths per month to secure jobs in this declining industry.[16] Nor was Florence the only place where a labor surplus rather than scarcity created conditions for a postplague popular revolt. An influx of immigrant labor into the region of Barcelona caused wages to fall and, according to Philippe Wolff, was a factor that led to the rebellion of Barcelona in 1391.[17]

The demographic-economic model further fails to explain the rush to rebellion in the second half of the fourteenth century. The vast majority of these revolts (especially in Italy) turned on politics; they were neither tax revolts, as in the north, nor disputes at the point of production, as with the exceptional

Ciompi. Instead, across large areas of Italy, commoners battled to end aristocratic abuse and to demand a share of governmental offices and political control, as seen with the sweep of revolts against papal authority in the mid-1370s. Such revolts against aristocratic arrogance were also rife in the north, without any direct connection to demography. For instance, in 1384 the sons of the noble family of the Hers humiliated and killed a townsman (*quemdam oppidanum*) of Sint-Truiden by turning their hunting dogs on him. Those of the town responded collectively, marched to the sons' castle, and burnt it to the ground.[18] More important, the final and definitive assault that would establish a government of craftsmen in Liège and bar patricians from the city councils as of 1386 erupted not from grievances about taxes or from underlings flexing their demographic muscle but from commoners' growing indignation over patrician injustices—in this case, the patricians' sale of justice. As the firebrand Gilles de Laveux prompted the crowd, "You all are as sure as I am that their sentences depend not on justice but on who can put up the most money."[19] Taxes were not mentioned, nor were demands made about wages or working conditions to bring economic relations in line with new demographic realities. Gilles did, however, make concrete demands that were shortly instituted: a committee of tradesmen throughout the *bonnes villes* of the Liégeois was established to review patrician justice over the previous twenty years and to adjudicate cases of upper-class corruption.[20]

Can a general theory of politics then explain the surge in revolutionary activity during the half-century or so after the Black Death? Did this myriad of different forms of revolt result from crises in state structures and finances? Was war the midwife of revolution?[21] To be sure, postplague revolts such as the Jacquerie did follow political and military crises, as with France's defeat at Poitiers in 1356, mounting fiscal pressure, and civil war between the young Dauphin Charles and rival claims to the throne made by his cousin, Charles of Navarre. Revolts in Paris and Rouen, 1380–1382, erupted against a similar backdrop: the regency and succession of a young, inexperienced king accompanied the depletion of royal coffers caused by war and corrupt officials. But during the latter half of the fourteenth and early years of the fifteenth centuries, states became generally stronger, more centralized, and better adept at managing funded debts. As a result, the political map of northern Italy changed more dramatically than at any time before unification in the mid-nineteenth century. From a mosaic of small and middle-size city-states, five or six large territorial states crystallized.[22] Yet despite this strengthening of states, the pace of revolts continued to increase, whether popular revolts failed or not. Indeed, revolts raged in places such as Florence, Flanders, and Paris more than in places with weaker states, such as Pisa or Siena, where after 1371 the history of popular insurrection had all but finished.

Finally, such a structural explanation gives little or no agency to those who organized and led these revolts—the insurgents themselves, whether workers, peasants, or bourgeois. Their efforts and organization, after all, were essential elements contributing to these states' crises. For instance, the Jacquerie and Étienne Marcel's revolts against the crown did not spring immediately or automatically from the French defeat of 1356. Instead, protests that were mounted by the Parisian crowds and the Estates General against royal monetary policy and the provisioning of troops, along with their active military resistance to the Dauphin Charles, were themselves part of the mix that intensified the state's troubles, creating revolutionary conditions by the summer of 1358.

The same applies to the most widespread sweep of revolts during the Middle Ages: those throughout much of Italy against the papacy from 1375 to 1378. If it were chinks in the armor of papal authority that sparked revolts against their rule in Italy, we should have expected the big wave of revolts to have arisen at other junctures during the fourteenth century. Better moments would have been at the beginning of the Babylonian captivity of the papacy in 1304, or with increased papal weakening and dependency on the French crown that endured to at least 1309, or with the death of Cardinal Albornoz in 1367 and the end of his papal consolidation in much of central Italy. Or revolts should have sprung up in 1370, after Urban V's failure to return the papacy to Rome, or in 1378 with the Great Schism, which divided papal rule and loyalties across Italy and Europe. Instead, the revolt occurred under the aegis of the statesmanlike Pope Gregory IX, whose aggressive policies of centralization were pursued by the ruthless but effective Robert of Geneva in alliance with the most powerful military force in Italy, that of the English condottiere John Hawkwood.[23] More than any sudden military or fiscal crisis from forces outside the Papal States and its ambit of control, the actions of a broad alliance of social classes from within brought this strong papacy to its knees. To these actors we now turn.

Religion

The great increase in popular rebellion from the mid-1350s to the fifteenth century—including tax revolts, protests against labor exploitation, and the larger spectrum of popular protest that arose from various causes and combated various levels of the state—depended on a new self- and class-confidence, that commoners could change their social, economic, and political worlds, the here and now, in concrete and practical ways. Of course, it cannot be said that such revolts were altogether new for the Middle Ages. As I said at the outset of this book, many of the most "modern" revolts of the Middle Ages clustered during the late thirteenth and fourteenth centuries, before the Black Death. Nonetheless, the near total lack of records of religious revolts from 1349 to the 1420s is striking. Before the plague and especially in the first two years of its immediate impact, revolutionary religious movements were rife in Europe. The Albigensians of the early thirteenth century, the massacres of Montségur in 1244, the shepherds' crusades of 1250 and 1320, and Fra Dolcino's radical communities in the hills of Novara in 1305–1307 are the best known. Further heretical movements spread in Toulouse, Carcassonne, and other places in Languedoc at the beginning of the fourteenth century; radical Ghibellines in Umbria and the Marche from 1319 to 1322; the spiritual Franciscans in Provence and various places in Italy in 1322; and flagellant and other penitent movements of 1348–1349. Except for perhaps the Flemish revolts of 1297–1304 and 1323–1328, these religious movements were the most significant revolts of late medieval Europe before the Black Death in terms of numbers mobilized and territory covered. In addition, even these two Flemish revolts had a religious impulse. According to Pirenne, monks and priests were the ideologues of the revolts of 1323–1328, preaching an evangelical ideal that mixed "communist aspirations with class hatred."[24] The rebels refused to pay tithes, attacked clerics, and seized the harvests of abbeys, which they redistributed among the peasants.[25] Anticlericalism was a key component of these peasants' efforts to establish their own governments in opposition to the lords of large ecclesiastical estates, a sentiment that became even more intense after the pope's interdiction of the rebels.[26]

By contrast, although persecution of individual heretics continued after the plague, heretical movements disappear from the chronicle accounts with one exception, a supposed Hussite group, which had established a small community in the village of Sains on the outskirts of Douai in 1422.[27] By the second quarter of the fifteenth century, things would change with the Hussites capturing more attention than any other popular movement in Europe in the fifteenth century. Their cause was God's cause and the Hussite armies waged holy battle as the warriors of God.[28] By the sixteenth century similar revolts "mandated by God and waged in Christ's name" would spread elsewhere in Europe.[29] But from 1350 to the end of my analysis in 1425, the presence of clerics (official or apostate) in revolts or revolts that turned on religious doctrine were extremely rare in France, Flanders, and Italy. Although some have

claimed that priests filled the ranks of the Jacquerie,[30] the chroniclers mention none. Moreover, in letters of remission that have been printed or mentioned by historians, the names of only two priests emerged: a canon from
Meaux[31] and the hapless rural curate of Blacy, forced by his parishioners to
do their bidding. In any case, the text of his remission claims that the rural
clergy "were favorably disposed and obedient to these lords in this region."[32]
None of the accounts of the Jacquerie make even the slightest hint of any
religious purpose, inspiration, or ideology.

Similarly, in postplague Italy any inkling of religious or heretical ideas or
the presence of clerics in popular revolt is rare (in contrast to generalizations
about preindustrial revolts).[33] Two exceptions prove the rule. A number of
clerics (according to Matteo Villani) were among the conspirators who plotted to overthrow an anti-Florentine government in Pisa in 1360. The revolt,
however, had nothing to do with religion. In fact, it was one of the rare revolts
of the later Middle Ages to revolve around economic grievances: Florence's
blockade of Pisa's port brought business losses for shopkeepers and artisans.[34]
The other exception was the four revolts of Pavia from 1358 to 1360, inspired
and led by Friar Iacopo Bussolari against Milanese rule and the "tyranny" of
Pavia's magnates. But nothing in the accounts of Bussolari's sermons gives any
trace of a religious message. Instead, his use of classical examples, his morality, and his ideology were secular—the evils of tyranny as against their alter-
native, liberty.

By some accounts, the Revolt of the Ciompi might be taken as a more fundamental exception. Historians have argued that behind these worker insurgents was the heretical and radical ideology of the Fraticelli, derived from
Franciscan ideals of poverty and equality.[35] While it cannot be denied that
these ideals or the general anticlericalism brought on by Florence's previous
three years of war with the papacy may have influenced the Ciompi, it is difficult to point to them or to any Fraticelli ideology during the events of the
Ciompi revolt: not one of the new government's demands touched matters
of the church or religious doctrine. Instead, the workers' petitions addressed
economic and political issues and demanded concrete social change. Moreover, not a single apostate cleric can be spotted in the leadership or even the
rank-and-file from lists of the original conspirators of the Ronco, the thirty-
two syndics of the *popolo minuto*, numerous Ciompi sentences after the defeat
of the radical Eight of Santa Maria Novella on 1 September 1378, or those
adjudicated after the fall of the Government of the Minor Guilds on 17 January 1382. Only during the period of counterrevolution, when exiled oligarchs

of the Guelf Party, sometimes allied with disenchanted Ciompi, regularly attacked the government of artisans, did a lone cleric appear among the insurgents—a priest from San Lorenzo.[36] Further, as far as any Fraticelli influence goes, the best that can be extracted from the sources is the participation of a Guasparro del Ricco, a school teacher, who twenty-five years before the revolt of the Ciompi had been condemned for heresy.[37] The sources, however, say nothing about his religious views at the time or suggest any Fraticelli doctrines or networks.

If there had been a strong underlining of Fraticelli ideology behind the Ciompi revolution, certain enigmas need to be explained. First, as with a number of other thirteenth- and early-fourteenth-century heretical movements, the Fraticelli gave wide scope to women, even equality in many realms, allowing them, for instance, to preach. Given these views one might expect to find women among the Ciompi rebels, even at the forefront, but not a single woman appears among the participants (let alone as a leader) mentioned by chroniclers or listed in the judicial inquests and sentences. Second, had these Franciscan radicals been so instrumental, it is strange that of all the churches used for Ciompi meetings either in secret or in the open—the canonical San Lorenzo, San Barnabà, the Dominican Santa Maria Novella, San Marco, the Hospital of the Priests in the Via San Gallo, the grounds of the monastery of the converted whores in Santo Spirito (delle Convertite), and various parish churches—the Franciscans' temple, Santa Croce, does not appear once as a stronghold or as a place where rebels convened their meetings. Instead, even rebels residing in the neighborhood of Santa Croce used the church of Sant'Ambrogio,[38] while the Ciompi's enemies—wool bosses and other patricians—met at Santa Croce to rally their counterrevolutionary forces.[39]

Liberty

To be sure, rising taxes and the economics of labor scarcity were conditions underlying some of the postplague rush to revolt, north and south of the Alps. But these objective causes are insufficient in explaining the great variety of revolts in widely different social, economic, and political circumstances. By 1355 a new spirit for societal change and a desire for liberty had sunk deep roots beneath the bourgeois or *popolo*, the class that, along with the nobility, had defined liberties as special corporate privileges since the central Middle Ages. The change came not in 1348, with the Black Death itself, but seven to ten years later, when the horror of the plague had subsided even though the disease returned periodically. Unlike many other infectious diseases, this plague did not linger, slowly weakening and destroying populations, permanently scarring the survivors.

Furthermore, from the second plague of 1358 on, the death tolls of the new disease declined steeply. Through the fourteenth century, the disease rapidly became primarily one of children. With the first strike of plague, 1347–1351, chroniclers and doctors alike claimed that this epidemic was different from all previous ones in world history: for this one there were no remedies; the only recourse was to pray for God's forgiveness. However, by the time of the second plague or soon afterward, doctors' attitudes toward plague and its cure had made an about-face. In the 1360s, physicians such as John of Burgundy began to boast of their credentials derived from "long experience" in treating plague victims and their success "in liberating" them from death.[40] In 1363, Guy de Chauliac treated himself for plague and with his recipes had succeeded in "evading God's Judgment." Numerous other doctors bragged of their successes in curing patients through their surgical procedures and pharmaceutical recipes. In 1382, the pope's doctor, Raymond Chalmelli de Vinario, looked back over his experience with four plagues and reported the steep fall in rates of mortality and morbidity: "In 1348, two-thirds of the population were afflicted, and almost all died; in 1361, half contracted the disease, and very few survived; in 1371, only one-tenth were sick, and many survived; in 1382, only one-twentieth became sick, and almost all survived." He attributed the difference to his generation of doctors and praised them for going beyond the ancients in the art of healing.[41] A doctor from Padua during a plague in the 1390s, after healing himself and his wife of plague, claimed he had "triumphed over the plague."[42] With his plague tract written in the vernacular and dedicated to his fellow citizens of Padua, they too could now be empowered to do the same (even if it were the body's immunity and not the doctors' recipes that was making the difference).[43] The plague experience over the last decades of the fourteenth century gave doctors and their patients a newborn confidence that their actions (and not just their prayers) could change their fate and the world around them.

Postplague popular revolt reflects an analogous about-face from utter despondency and fear to a new confidence on the part of peasants, artisans, and workers that they too could change the world, fundamentally altering the social and political conditions of their lives. In 1348 and immediately afterward, popular movements and violence either turned inward, with penitent movements marching through large tracts of Europe, from Hungary to the Netherlands, whipping themselves, or outward, with cries to the heavens and massacres of the outsider. In German-speaking areas and in parts of Spain and France, they burnt Jews; in Sicily, they murdered Catalans. But by the mid-1350s in Italy and 1358 in northern France, the pattern of social violence changed: the bourgeois and those below them now saw the causes of their anxieties, inequality, or loss of liberty as coming from within the class structures of the societies in which they lived. They assembled and combated the injustices they now saw lodged within these social and political worlds.

Except for heretical movements, chroniclers provide little insight into rebels' ideologies. On occasion, their chants, flags, and other pictorial emblems, along with chroniclers' explanations, give us further clues. After the Black Death, one word became dominant when chroniclers pointed to rebels' motives—*libertas*. Chroniclers such as the Florentine Matteo Villani viewed it as a virtue (unless somehow perversely rebels used it against his own city-republic),[44] while others, such as the king's official chronicler at Saint-Denis, likened it to lust. Liberty as a cause or as the cry of rebels was not unique to the postplague experience, but the chronicles in my sample reported it as the rebels' cause in only sixteen revolts before the Black Death and as their chant only twice. Afterward, it soared to forty-eight rebellions—a fourfold increase, almost eightfold per annum. Further, as a rebels' chant, "libertas" sprang to their lips in seventeen revolts, not counting the waving of the first interregional rebel banner—the "huge one" with liberty's letters stitched in gold—unfurled in hundreds of revolts from Milan to Naples against the "tyranny of the church fathers" in 1375–1376.[45]

In preplague appearances, moreover, chroniclers used the word *libertas* to describe only one insurrection of commoners, and even that one is questionable as a commoners' revolt. Of the many flags that Cola di Rienzo invented to propagandize his new dictatorship *(tribuno)* over the Roman *popolo*, one bore the word "libertas." But was this notary and friend of the pope, despite his lowly origins, a commoner by the time of his seizure of power and his self-proclamation as Rome's new Augustus?[46] The other preplague examples of chroniclers' or rebels' use of the word liberty pertained to the bourgeois or upper echelons of societies, who defended their franchises or corporative privileges, whether of cities, territories, or noblemen or to communities as a whole but under the aegis of upper classes.[47] Their cries demanded privilege, not equality.[48] In 1232 Messina revolted against Frederick II's new Constitutions of Melfi, which eroded the city's corporative privileges.[49] In 1253, led by the patrician Henri de Dinant, the bourgeois with a popular following fought against Episcopal rule to gain a share in governing Liège and its satellite town of Awans.[50] With the rise of the "second *popolo*" in Florence, 1282, the merchant Dino Compagni and others met in the church of San Pancrazio to persuade prominent citizens of the need for change: "They spoke of their liberty and the injuries they had received."[51] "The injured," as we have seen, were hardly commoners; instead, they belonged to Florence's most elite merchant guilds. In 1303 liberty was signaled as a cause when the most important noble family of Crete *(case de' Calergi primarj nobili dell'isola)* sparked a rebellion to free the island from Venetian domination.[52] In 1310 the knight *(miles)* Pontius de Boissaco led a revolt in Toulouse against Philip the Fair's new taxes. After he had been captured, his supporters rebelled to free him, "proclaiming liberty."[53] In 1317 the *popolo* of Ferrara, led by the prominent citizen Raynaldus de Bochenpanis, revolted against King Robert of Naples, who ruled the city on behalf of the church. The citizens said they wished to place their city "in liberty." Curiously, they then handed it over to the city's traditional ruling family, the Marchese d'Este.[54] In 1337, the town of Conegliano "put itself in liberty" because of its dissatisfaction with the rule of the Scala dynasty.[55]

Perhaps most telling of all these preplague revolts fought in the name of liberty was that of the Florentines against the "tyranny" of the Duke of Athens. Once the chroniclers' ideology is stripped bare, the duke's greatest crime appears to have been his efforts to make Florence more egalitarian by granting disenfranchised workers such as dyers the rights to form their own guild, which bestowed on them the rights of citizenship and eligibility for election to political offices. By extending workers' rights, he had thereby encroached on the privileges of these workers' bosses—those of the wool guild—and Florence's merchant elites—what the chroniclers called their liberties. The merchant chroniclers Giovanni Villani and Marchionne di Coppo Stefani hailed the toppling of the duke as "a return to liberty" and the chant of the merchant-led insurgents was "Death to the tyrant, long live the People and the Commune of Florence and Liberty."[56] The merchants' revolt for liberty succeeded: regaining their liberty meant keeping the vast majority of Florence's workers and artisans as dependents *(sottoposti)* without rights as citizens or liberties to practice their crafts as independent artisans and proprietors.[57]

After the plague, not only did the presence of the word liberty increase vertiginously to describe and explain popular revolts; its meaning began to shift as well, from the privileges of a few or of a special community (and usually an elite one) toward an implicit sense of equality. Earlier in the fourteenth century, radical thinkers such as Marsilius of Padua and heretical Franciscans expressed such notions,[58] but these were yet to be heard in the cries of the disenfranchised before the second half of the fourteenth century. Insurgents began to juxtapose liberty with tyranny in revolts such as those at Pavia from 1356 to 1360. Friar Bussolari's secular sermons were not addressed to any special corporation or class at Pavia but to the city collectively against "tyranny" from outside or above, first from Milan, then from the city's magnates.[59] The same was true for smaller communities, as when the peasants of the Aretine village of La Serra, who still owed feudal dues and services, broke from "the yoke" and servitude of their Tarlati lords in 1359. The waves of revolts throughout most of central Italy from 1375 to 1378 were the most spectacular of these revolts for liberty against outside tyranny. Under the banner of their newly invented flag of Liberty, more than sixty cities and 1,577 villages successfully rebelled against the church's "tyranny," deposed aristocratic governments, and established new regimes of the *popolo*.

Furthermore, after the Black Death, free peasants, artisans, and workers took liberty as their battle cry—and not only for their own liberties. Now in the name of liberty they fought for the rights of wider communities, as in 1355 when the peasants *(contadini)* of Lucca led the struggle to free Lucca from Pisan domination.[60] Similarly, in 1402, when the peasants *(villani)* of the villages of Castel d'Argile and Sant'Agata rebelled against the Bolognese rule of the Bentivoglio, their battle cry was "Long live the people, the guilds, and liberty."[61] According to Matteo Villani, the *popolo minuto* of Siena continued the revolt after the fall of the Nine, so that they too could rule "in liberty," and with the formation of the government of the Twelve, so began the "liberty of that government of the rabble [*regimento di quello popolazzo*]."[62] In the last moments of the Ciompi government on 31 August 1378, when their flag of the angel was taken from them, they asked for the one of liberty, which forty-five days before had led them and other *sottoposti* to storm the Palazzo Signoria and establish a government that included all working men in Florence. Workers had co-opted the symbols and word of upper-class privilege not just for their own ends but for the guild community at large. After an abortive uprising of artisans and workers in Florence in 1393, whose cries were "Long live the Twenty-Four Guilds," the crowd hurled abuse at the Captain of the People, who had sentenced the rebels to death. In the name of liberty and against tyranny, their chants called into question one of the pillars of the late medieval city-state republic and its jurisprudence, which rested on foreign noblemen taking over a city's judiciary and police for six-month stints: "We will execute you on our grounds. We are the citizens and you the foreigners. Today we will take back our state and free it from the hands of tyrants."[63]

Such cries and appeals to liberty also began to be heard north of the Alps after the Black Death. As in Italy, they now came from the *menu peuple* and crowds that the chroniclers called the rabble. The king's chronicler at Saint-Denis, Michele Pintoin, described the revolt known as the *Harelle* that erupted in Rouen in 1382 as perpetuated by "these most untrustworthy men [who] hoped they could gain their liberty in spite of the king" and as a result "fell into daring crimes" to achieve their ends.[64] Others, such as the local chronicler of Rouen, Pierre Cochon, said much the same. The "rabble" of Rouen seized the abbey of Saint-Ouën in 1382 and forced the abbot and monks to rip to pieces the ancient privileges of barony over Rouen granted to them by the king. This crowd of journeymen—not the mayor, aldermen, or the bourgeois of the city—now acted on behalf of the commune, fighting for the corporative rights of the city as a whole. They forced the monks to draw up a new charter "of the rights and liberties of Normandy of everything that they [the rabble had] demanded from the monks" and by this charter "restored the ancient rights to the commune of Rouen."[65] Earlier, Pintoin had seen these impulses at work in tax riots at Paris against the crown in 1380. Again it was the *plebes* or *menu peuple* who pressed for the city's "liberties" and not the old forces of corporate privilege—the provost of merchants, the bourgeoisie, or the Third Estate. Now, the "vilest sort" pressured the provost of merchants to speak on behalf of the *menu peuple* and to negotiate with the king's men on behalf of the city: "All [the plebes] were of the same mind, to throw off this yoke and reclaim their liberty . . . they all would rather die a thousand times than lose their ancient liberties."[66]

According to another official chronicle of the king, the *Chronographia Regum Francorum*, this rabble went further and rebelled not only for the corporative rights and liberties of their city, Paris, but for all of France: "they would defend their liberties, those of the city, and of all the kingdom of France."[67] In the short run, they won, forcing the king to "restore all the customs and liberties to Paris and everywhere else in the kingdom to what they had been at the time of Saint Louis and Philip the Fair, ending in perpetuity all taxes, aids, tailles, and any other fiscal imposition."[68] This was no privilege of a caste, class, or special community. It was, in effect, the rights of all Frenchmen. In fact, the one group not included in the new charter were foreign merchants— "Genoese, Lombards, and others across the Alps or born outside our kingdom." The king could continue taxing them as before.

For Pintoin this appeal went further still, crossing the frontiers of France. He saw the underlying cause of the nearly simultaneous revolts in Paris, Rouen, Ghent, Flanders, and England at the beginning of the 1380s as the same: all stemmed from a new sentiment among the *plebes*. With scorning disapprobation he lamented: "the appetite for liberty was burning . . . the lust for new things incessant."[69] Despite the absence of communication between rebels from one city-state to another; the great diversity in the forms of rebellion; the differences in local economic, social, and political contexts; and the variety of sparks that lit these social revolts, Pintoin's eloquent condemnation of revolts in late-fourteenth-century France and Flanders can equally well be applied to postplague rebels in Italy from 1355 to the early fifteenth century. The *popolo minuto* now led struggles for "liberties" that were no longer limited to privileged corporate groups in medieval society. As Pintoin feared and the trajectory of social protest over the later Middle Ages shows, "libertas" as the battle cry of "the vilest sort" expressed a new political ideology,[70] and one that was hardly historically constant for subaltern classes through the Middle Ages. Rather it became their ideological hallmark seven to ten years after the Black Death and remained well entrenched into the fifteenth century.[71] From utter despondency in the wake of Europe's most monumental mortality, peasants, workers, artisans, and petty shopkeepers became emboldened with a new self- and class-confidence. After the Black Death both north and south of the Alps, they organized collectively, and with increased frequency they revolted to change the here and now, to gain liberty, to preserve their dignity, and to expand their rights and those of their communities, thus shaping their future welfare.

NOTES

SOURCES

INDEX

Notes

1. Introduction

1. Among those works that spurred on international comparative study of revolt, not only for Europe, but also for Asia and North and South America, see Moore, *Social Origins of Dictatorship and Democracy* (Boston, 1966); Hobsbawm, *Primitive Rebels: Studies in Archaic Forms of Social Movement in the 19th and 20th Centuries* (New York, 1966); Rudé, *The Crowd in History, 1730–1848* (New York, 1964); Thompson, "The Moral Economy of the English Crowd in the Eighteenth Century," *Past & Present*, 50 (1971): 76–136; Theda Skocpol, *States and Social Revolution: A Comparative Analysis of France, Russia and China* (Cambridge, 1979). For an evaluation of the impact of E. P. Thompson on global and transhistorical questions of preindustrial insurrection, see *Moral Economy and Popular Protest*, ed. Adrian Randall and Andrew Charlesworth (Houndmills, 2000).

2. These were peasant revolts against *malos usos*, or bad practices of the nobility that imposed a new form of serfdom. It culminated in widespread insurrections in the mid-fifteenth century.

3. Léon Mirot, *Les insurrections urbaines au début du Règne de Charles VI (1380–1383): Leurs causes, leurs conséquences* (Paris, 1905). The only book after Mirot's that I know on the Hammer men was privately published: Régis de Chauveron, *Des Maillotins aux Marmousets: Audouin Chauveron, Prévôt de Paris sous Charles VI* (Paris, 1992).

4. Archives nationales, JJ 71, f. 65, no. 86; and JJ 75, f. 186[r-188r], no. 316.

5. See *Popular Protest in Late Medieval Europe: Italy, France, and Flanders*, ed. and trans. Cohn, Manchester Medieval Sources Series (Manchester, 2004), doc. no. 66.

6. Ibid., doc. no. 77.

7. Ibid., doc. nos. 86–90.

8. *Choix de pièces inédites relatives au règne de Charles VI*, ed. L. Douët D'arcq, 2 vols., Société d'histoire de France (hereafter, SHF), CXIX (Paris, 1864), I, pp. 399–400.

9. M. Villani, *Cronica con la continuazione di Filippo Villani*, ed. by Giuseppe Porta, 2 vols. (Parma, 1995), II, pp. 185, 214–216, 274–275; and *Popular Protest*, doc. no. 99.

10. According to E. B . Fryde in "Peasant Rebellion and Peasant Discontents," in *The Agrarian History of England and Wales*, III: *1348–1500*, ed. Edward Miller

(Cambridge, 1991), p. 760, the *Anonimalle Chronicle* was probably written by William Pakington, the keeper of the king's wardrobe.

11. *Chronique du religieux de Saint-Denys,* ed. M. L. Bellaguet, 6 vols. (Paris, 1839–1852), I, pp. 132–135. Pintoin was in London as an ambassador for his abbey at the time of the uprising. I know of no historian to cite Pintoin's eyewitness account of the public execution of the archbishop of Canterbury and the plebes' football match, when they kicked "the sacred head of the archbishop through the streets of the city."

12. *Corpus Chronicorum Bononiensium* (*Cronaca A* [called *Rampona*], *Cronaca B, Cronica* [called Varignana] . . . *da Villola,* and *Bolognetti*), ed. Albano Sorbelli, *Rerum Italicarum Scriptores* (hereafter, RIS), 18/1 (Città di Castello, 1910–1938), III, p. 352; *Cronaca di Ser Guerriero da Gubbio dall'anno MCCCL all'anno MCCCCLXXII,* ed. Giuseppe Mazzatinti, RIS, XXI/4 (Città di Castello, 1902), p. 21.

   I know of only three Tuscan chroniclers to have noted it: *Monumenta Pisana, 1089–1389 auctore anonymo, Cronica di Pisa,* in Lodovico Muratori, *Rerum Italicarum Scriptores,* 25 vols. (Milan, 1723–1751) (hereafter, Muratori), XV, col. 1074; Laurentius Bonincontri Miniatensis, *Annales ab anno MCCLX usque MCCCCLVIII,* Muratori, XXI, col. 36; and *Cronaca senese di Donato di Neri e di suo figlio Neri* in *Cronache senesi,* ed. A. Lisini and F. Iacometti, RIS, XV/6 (Bologna, 1931–1937), I, p. 671.

13. *Cronicon Siculum incertis authoris ab a. 340 ad a. 1396,* ed. Joseph de Blasiis, *Monumenti storici, ser. 1:* Cronache (Naples, 1887), pp. 30–31; Bonincontri, *Annales ab anno MCCLX usque MCCCCLVIII,* col. 18; Georgius and Iohannes Stella, *Annales Genuenses,* ed. Giovanna Petti Balbi, RIS, XVII/2 (Bologna, 1975), p. 170; *Cronaca del Conte Francesco di Montemarte e Corbara, 1330–1400,* in *Ephemerides Urbevetanae,* ed. Luigi Fumi, RIS, XV/5 (Città di Castello, 1903–1920), I, p. 243; *Cronaca malatestiana del secolo XIV (AA. 1295–1385),* ed. Aldo Francesco Massèra, XV/2 (Bologna, 1922–1924), p. 45; *Cronaca senese di Donato di Neri,* vol. I, p. 671; Niccola della Tuccia, *Cronache di Viterbo e di altre città,* in *Cronache e statuti della città di Viterbo,* ed. Ignazio Ciampi, Documenti di Storia Italiana, V (Florence, 1872), p. 38; *Diario d'anonimo fiorentino dall'anno 1358 al 1389,* ed. Alessandro Gherardi, in *Cronache dei secoli XIII e XIV,* Documenti di Storia Italiana VI (Florence, 1876), p. 334; *Chronicon Comitum Flandrensium,* in *Corpus Chronicorum Flandriae,* ed. J.-J. de Smet, (Brussels, 1837), I, p. 234; *Chronographia Regum Francorum,* ed. H. Moranvillé, SHF, CCLII (Paris 1891–1892), II, p. 363; and *Chroniques de Jean Froissart,* ed. Gaston Raynaud, SHF, CXLVII (Paris, 1894), IX, pp. 51–52.

14. See *Le croniche di Viterbo scritte da Frate Francesco d'Andrea,* in *Archivio di R. società Romana di storia patria,* XXIV (1901), pp. 335–337; Niccola della Tuccia, *Cronache di Viterbo,* p. 35; *Cronaca senese di Donato di Neri,* p. 616; *Cronaca di Ser Guerriero da Gubbio,* p. 16; *Istoria della città di Viterbo di Feliciano Bussi* (Rome, 1742), pp. 204–205; Pompeo Pellini, *Dell'Historia di Perugia* (Venice, 1664), I, p. 1031; *La chronique romane,* ed. Thomas and Desmazes Pegat, in *Le Petit Thalamus de Montpellier,* Société archéologique de Montpellier (Montpellier, 1840), pp. 380–381; *Chronique des règnes de Jean II et de Charles V,* ed. R. Delachenal, SHF, CCCXLVIII, (Paris, 1910–1920), II, p. 32; *Cronaca di Pisa di Ranieri Sardo,* ed. Ottavio Banti,

Fonti per la storia d'Italia, no. 99 (Roma, 1963), pp. 224–225; *Cronaca di Niccolò di Borbona delle cose dell'Aquila, dall'anno 1363 all'anno 1424,* Muratori, ed., *Antiquitates Italicae medii Aevi,* 6 vols (Milan, 1738–1742), VI, col. 856; *Chronicon Cornelii Zanteliet S. Jacobi Leodiensis monachi,* in *Veterum Scriptorum et Monumentorum Historicorum, Dogmaticorum, Moralium amplissima Collectio,* ed. Edmund Martène, V (Paris, 1729), col. 311.

15. *Ongles bleus, Jacques et Ciompi: les révolutions populaires en Europe aux XIVe et XVe siècles* (Paris, 1970), translated as *The Popular Revolutions of the Late Middle Ages,* trans. by A. L. Lytton-Sells (London, 1973); R. H. Hilton, *Bond Men Made Free: Medieval Peasant Movements and the English Rising of 1381* (London, 1973). Also, Guy Fourquin *(Les soulèvements populaires au Moyen Age* [Paris, 1972], translated as *The Anatomy of Popular Rebellion in the Middle Ages,* trans. A. Chesters [Amsterdam, 1978]), considered revolts across Europe but in a more theoretical way to draw definitions of revolt, riot, etc. One of the most directly comparative works to examine differences across national boundaries is an article by E. B. Fryde, "The Financial policies of the Royal Governments and Popular Resistance to Them in France and England, c. 1270–c.1420," *Revue belge de philologie et d'histoire* 57 (1979): 824–860, but it concentrates more on finance and government than on forms of rebellion. For a useful overview of the Marxist versus non-Marxist debates on late medieval and early modern revolt, see Rinaldo Comba, "Rivolte e ribellioni fra tre e quattrocento," in *La storia: I grandi problemi,* ed. Nicola Tranfaglia and Massimo Firpo (Turin, 1988), vol. II, part 2, pp. 673–691. For surveys and comparisons within France, see Charles Petit-Dutaillis, *Les communes françaises: caractères et évolution des origins au XVIIIe siècle* (Paris, 1947); André Leguai, "Les révoltes rurales dans le royaume de France du milieu du XIVe siècle à la fin du XVe," *Le Moyen Âge 88* (1982): 49–76; and, "Les troubles urbains dans le Nord de la France à la fin du XIIIe et au début du XIVe siècle," *Revue d'histoire économique et sociale* 54 (1976): 281–303; and Bernard Chevalier, "Corporations, conflits politiques et paix sociale en France aux XIVe et XVe siècles," in *Les bonnes villes, l'état et la société dans la France du XVe siècle,* ed. Chevalier (Orléans, 1995), pp. 271–298. For comparisons of peasant revolts in the late medieval German empire, see Peter Blickle, "Peasant Revolts in the German Empire in the Late Middle Ages," *Social History* 4 (1979): 223–239. His examples, however, pertain largely to the second half of the fifteenth and early sixteenth centuries.

16. As a research tool, Mollat and Wolff's book is seriously hampered by the absence of notes and few indications of the sources. The French edition contained references only to selected secondary works with no citations of archival or published primary sources; the English edition eliminated even this limited bibliography.

17. For a recent assessment of Pirenne's lasting importance for our understanding of the Low Countries, see Marc Boone, "Urban Space and Political Conflict in Late Medieval Flanders," *Journal of Interdisciplinary History* 32 (2002): 621–640, esp. 621–622.

18. Mollat and Wolff's own evidence of preplague revolts of misery weakens their generalization, not only for Flanders, but also with bread riots in Barcelona in the 1330s and those in Florence in the mid-1340s, the rare instances of the poor revolting because of conditions of misery.

19. In addition to Fourquin, *The Anatomy of Popular Rebellion*, pp. 20–21, 24–25, 83, 101–102, and 109, see Mollat and Wolff, *Popular Revolutions*, for such distinctions: "A revolution is something planned and prepared; it has a program. A revolt is a spontaneous reaction, a reflex of anger or self-defense, sometimes of both" (p. 91). Further, while S. H. Rigby (*English Society in the Later Middle Ages: Class, Status and Gender* [Basingstoke, 1995], p. 323), emphasized "local friction and piecemeal conflict" over "the class harmony favored by medieval preachers," he pegged the Peasants' Revolt of 1381 as "hardly revolutionary," even though their demands questioned social hierarchy and challenged its central economic institution of serfdom. With such stiff requirements, what would constitute a revolution? As historians of the French and Russian Revolutions know, these events hardly swept aside all residues of previous *anciens régimes* in terms of institutions or personnel; for the French Revolution, see Hobsbawm, *The Age of Revolution 1789–1848* (New York, 1962), esp. pp. 99–100; for the Russian, Charles Bettelheim, *Les luttes de classes en URSS: première pèriode, 1917–1923* (Paris, 1974), on the rise of the "New Economic Policy," esp. pp. 467–472. František Graus, *Pest-Geissler-Judenmorde. Das 14. Jahrhundert als Krisenzeit* (Göttingen, 1987), pp. 527–528, has voiced similar criticisms of such distinctions being imposed on the late medieval past.

20. According to the sociologist T. H. Marshall ("The Nature of Class Conflict," in *Class, Status and Power*, ed. R. Bendix and S. M. Lipset [London, 1954], pp. 81–87 [first published in 1938]), the dominant ideologies of preindustrial societies saw their role as creating social harmony. See also Rigby, *English Society in the Later Middle Ages*, p. 306.

21. See for instance the theoretically informed analysis of late medieval English conflict, Rigby, *English Society in the Later Middle Ages*.

22. *Cronicon Siculum incertis authoris*, p. 8.

23. *Les Grandes Chroniques de France*, 10 vols., SHF, CDXXIII, ed. Jules Viard (Paris, 1920–1953), VII, pp. 167–169; *Extraits des chroniques de Saint-Denis*, in *Rerum Gallicarum et Francicarum Scriptores* (hereafter RGFS), XXI, ed. J. D. Guigniaut and N. de Wailly (Paris, 1855), p. 117; *Extraits d'une chronique anonyme finissant en MCCLXXX*, in ibid., p. 141, and Marc Bloch, "Blanche de Castille et les serfs du chapitre de Paris," *Mémoire de la Société de l'histoire de Paris et de l'Ile-de-France*, XXXVIII (1911): 224–272; reprinted in *Mélanges historiques*, ed. Charles-Edmond Perrin (Paris, 1963), I, pp. 462–490.

24. *Chronicon Girardi de Fracheto et anonyma ejusdem operis continuatio*, RGFS, XXI, p. 42; and André Artonne, *Le mouvement de 1314 et les chartes provinciales de 1315, Bibliothèque de la faculté des lettres de l'université de Paris*, XXIX (Paris, 1912). According to Elizabeth R. Brown, in "Reform and Resistance to Royal Authority in Fourteenth-Century France: The Leagues of 1314–1315," in *Parliaments, Estates*

and Representation, I (London, 1981), pp. 109–137, the dominant force in these alliances was the nobility.

25. Thus for instance at a supper-party dispute between two groups of students at Orléans in 1408, one group armed itself with mail coats, padded jackets, swords, daggers, battle-axes, *guisarms,* and a weapon called a falcon's beak, then invaded a dinner party of other students and killed the host; *Choix de pièces inédites,* II, pp. 29–31.

26. *Vie de Saint Louis par Guillaume de Nangis,* RGFS, XX, ed. P. C. F. Daunou and J. Naudet (Paris, 1840), p. 319. In the early thirteenth century, the term *bourgeois* was vague and "extremely complex": it could refer to all the inhabitants of an urban agglomeration; see J. L. Charles, *La ville de Saint-Trond au Moyen Age: Des origines à la fin du XIVe siècle* (Paris, 1965), p. 281. Later in the thirteenth century, chroniclers and other commentators began to distinguish the *bourgeois* from the *menu peuple* or *populares.*

27. On Giovanni d'Andrea's works and life, see G. Tamba, "Giovanni d'Andrea," *Dizionario Biografico degli Italiani,* 55 (Rome, 2000), pp. 667–672.

28. The fullest narrative source of this incident comes from the Sienese chronicler, *Cronaca senese attribuita ad Agnolo di Tura del Grasso detta la cronaca maggiore,* in *Cronache senesi,* p. 385. Also see *Cronaca gestorum ac factorum memorabilium civitatis Bononie a fratre Hyeronimo de Bursellis (ab urbe condita ad a. 1497),* RIS, XXIII/2, ed. Albano Sorbelli (Città di Castello, 1911–1929), pp. 37–38.

29. On the other hand, social groups could achieve rapid and fundamental constitutional change without resorting to popular protest, whether violent or peaceful, such as in 1202 when "a popular party won a landslide" in the city council and effectively pushed out the old patrician families; see John H. Mundy, *Liberty and Political Power in Toulouse 1050–1230* (New York, 1954), p. 67. Another example comes with the "Victory of the tradesmen" of Sint-Truiden, who obtained a charter of rights in 1366 in what appears to have been a transformation without violence; see Charles, *La ville de Saint-Trond au Moyen Age,* pp. 313–314.

30. Salimbene de Adam, *Cronica,* ed. Giuseppe Scalia, Scrittori d'Italia, no. 232–233 (Bari, 1966), I, p. 99.

31. *Diario di Ser Giovanni di Lemmo da Comugnori dal 1299 al 1320,* in *Cronache dei secoli XIII e XIV,* p. 175.

32. On the *popolo,* see Jones, *The Italian City-State: From Commune to Signoria,* Oxford, 1997, esp. pp. 586–587. Literally, it was a party of sworn associates of social groups beneath the magnates but did not include peasants, workers, or the "plebeian mass." In the pages that follow his description, Jones emphasized the elitist dimensions of the *popolo* without consideration of place or time, as if artisans were not a part of the *popolo,* which they were.

33. Earlier, the arch-Ghibelline Federico, count of Montefeltro, killed the nephew and soldiers of the Marchese of Ancona in Urbino. On October 1319 Pope John XXII brought sentences against Federico and the town councils of Osimo and Recanati, charging that Federico and those under his jurisdiction were heretics

and idolaters. The pope initiated a crusade to oust Federico, granting pardons from sins and fines to those in Tuscany who took up arms against him.

34. *Cronaca senese attribuita ad Agnolo di Tura*, p. 392; also Giovanni Villani, *Nuova Cronica*, ed. Giuseppe Porta, 3 vols. (Parma, 1990–1991), II, p. 342.

35. *The Anonimalle Chronicle*, ed. V. H. Galbraith (Manchester, 1927), pp. 41–42.

36. *Chroniques de J. Froissart*, IX, p. 51.

37. See Frank J. Swetz, "*Figura Mercantesco*: Merchants and the Evolution of a Number Concept in the Latter Middle Ages," in *Word, Image, Number: Communication in the Middle Ages*, ed. John J. Contreni and Santa Casciani (Florence, 2002), pp. 391–412. Swetz argues that a new concept of numbers and precision with figures spread with mercantile manuals in the thirteenth century.

38. *La chronique des quatre premiers Valois*, ed. Siméon Luce, SHF, CIX (Paris, 1862), pp. 69–77; *The Chronicle of Jean de Venette*, trans. Jean Birdsall, ed. Richard Newhall (New York, 1953), pp. 76–77; "The testimony of Bascot de Mauléon in 1388," in *Chroniques de J. Froissart*, SHF, CXLVII, ed. Léon Mirot (Paris, 1931), XII, p. 97; and *Popular protest*, doc. no. 102. Kenneth Fowler (" 'A world of visual images': Froissart's legacy to Burgundy," in *The Burgundian Hero: Proceedings of the Annual Conference of the Centre Européen d'Études Bourguignonnes (XIVᵉ–XVIᵉ Siècles)*, ed. Andrew Brown, Jean-Marie Cauchies, and Graeme Small [Neuchâtel, 2001], pp. 24–25), accepts the essential truth of Froissart's interview with Bascot but questions whether it ever took place or if any such Bascot ever lived.

39. See Luce, *Histoire de la Jacquerie d'après des documents inédits*, 2nd ed. (Paris, 1894), pp. 175–234: Appendix of place names mentioned in the Jacquerie remissions; and *Recueil de pièces servant de preuves aux mémoires sur les Troubles excités en France par Charles II dit le Mauvais, Roi de Navarre et comte d'Evreux*, ed. Denis-François Secousse, 2 vols. (Paris, 1755), I, pp. 83–132. Fourquin (*Les campagnes de la région parisienne à la fin du Moyen Age* [Paris, 1964], pp. 229–240), cites these and a few others. According to my student Douglas Aiton, more than 200 survive in the Trésor des chartes; the vast majority has yet to be transcribed or cited. Further, these show the Jacquerie making a wider sweep of northern French villages than has previously been charted.

40. *Histoire générale de Languedoc*, ed. Cl. Devic & J. Vaissete, etc., new ed. (Toulouse, 1885) (hereafter NHGL), X, cols. 1351–1355.

41. Marino Sanuto, *Vitæ Ducum Venetorum italice scriptæ ab origine urbis, sive an CCCXXI usque MCCCCXCIII*, Muratori, XXII, col. 865.

42. William H. TeBrake, *A Plague of Insurrection: Popular Politics and Peasant Revolt in Flanders, 1323–1328* (Philadelphia, 1993). On these revolts, also see Walter Prevenier and Marc Boone, "The 'City-State' Dream," in *Ghent: In Defence of a Rebellious City*, ed. Johan Decavele (Antwerp, 1989), pp. 81–87; and *Popular Protest*, doc. nos. 11–13 and 18–20. An exception might be made for the Hussite movements, 1409–1437. Except for the Taborite experiment in the summer of 1420, however, it is difficult to see the Hussites as a popular movement. See John Klassen, in "The Disadvantaged and the Hussite Revolution," *International Review of Social History* 35 (1990): the Hussites constituted "a coalition of all the classes and

groups in late medieval Bohemia" (p. 264); "Economically, socially and politically Hussite society was not that different from the rest of Europe . . . the nobility was the big winner" (p. 249).

43. Scott, *Weapons of the Weak: Everyday Forms of Peasant Resistance* (New Haven, 1985).

44. *Cronaca senese attribuita ad Agnolo di Tura*, pp. 547–548.

45. *Recueil des documents concernant le Poitou contenus dans les registres de la Chancellerie de France*, ed. Paul Guérin, in *Archives Historiques du Poitou* (hereafter, AHP), 21 (1891), pp. 69–72.

46. For a discussion distinguishing the two, see Scott, *Weapons of the Weak*, pp. xv–xvii.

47. NHGL, X, col. 1329–1331; and *Popular Protest*, doc. no. 67.

48. This sense of relativism in understanding social relations is well illustrated in Sir Edward Evan-Pritchard, *Kinship and Marriage among the Nuer* (Oxford, 1951).

49. *Chronique latine de Guillaume de Nangis de 1113 à 1300 avec les continuations de cette chronique de 1300 à 1368*, ed. H. Géraud, 2 vols., SHF, XXXIII and XXXV (Paris, 1843), I, p. 214.

50. Ibid., pp. 278–279. Another Parisian chronicler (*Extraits d'une chronique anomyne française, finissant en MCCCVIII*, RGFS, XXI, p. 133), reveals more on what the count's oppression may have been: "he wished to enslave [those of Valenciennes] and to suppress all the ancient customs held by the city," but the source goes no further in identifying who led or staffed the revolt. According to Henri Pirenne, in *Histoire de Belgique: des origines à nos jours*, 3rd ed., (Brussels, 1922–1932; first edition, 1900), I, p. 397, the count supported the "povre peuple" against the town's rich bourgeois. Pirenne dates the revolt to 1290.

51. *Chronique latine de Guillaume de Nangis*, I, p. 282; and *Popular Protest*, doc. no. 10.

52. On the difficulties of pinning down the meanings of terms such as *le petit peuple, menu peuple*, and *pauvres*, see František Graus, "Au bas Moyen Âge: Pauvres des villes et pauvres des campagnes," *Annales: E. S. C.*, 16 (1961): 1053–65; and Claude Gauvard, "Le petit peuple au Moyen Âge," in *Le petit peuple dans l'Occident médiéval: Terminologies, perceptions, réalités*, ed. Pierre Boglioni, Robert Delort, and Claude Gauvard (Paris, 2002), pp. 707–722. For the term's double significance of class and geography—those residing within city walls—and its evolution during the thirteenth century to meaning "merchant aristocracy," see Fernand Vercauteren, *Luttes sociales à Liège (XIIIme et XIVme siècles)*, 2nd ed. (Brussels, 1946), pp. 25–6. For the "classical" sense of *populares*, meaning everyone in a community, see Jan Rogozinski, *Power, Caste, and Law: Social Conflict in Fourteenth-Century Montpellier* (Cambridge, Mass., 1982), pp. xviii–xix. Certainly, chroniclers cut sharper distinctions than medieval political theorists, who rarely went beyond Marsilius of Padua, for whom the *populus* included "the whole body of citizens, defined negatively as everybody other than children, slaves, aliens and women." See Hilton, "Popular Movements in England at the End of the Fourteenth Century," in *Class Conflict and the Crisis of Feudalism: Essays in Medieval Social History* (London, 1985), p. 153. Nonetheless, Hilton defined the "people" as those who were ruled (pp. 153–154).

53. *Chronicon Placentinum ab anno MXII ad annum MCCXXXV*, in *Chronica Tria Placentina a Johanne Codagnello, ab anonymo, et a Guerino*, ed. B. Pallastrelli, Monumenta historica, III (Parma, 1859), pp. 1–2; *Iohannis Codagnelli Annales Placentini*, ed. Oswaldus Holder-Egger, *Scriptores Rerum Germanicarum in usum scholarum ex Monumentis Germaniae Historicus separatim editi* (Hanover, 1901), pp. 1–2); and *Annales Placentini Guelfi*, in *Monumenta Germaniae Historica, Scriptores* (hereafter MGH:SS), XVIII, ed. G. H. Pertz (Hanover, 1863), p. 411.

54. Ottokar, *Il Comune di Firenze alla fine del Dugento*, 2nd ed. (Turin, 1962; first published in 1926).

55. Cristiani, *Nobiltà e popolo nel comune di Pisa dalle origini del podestariato alla signoria dei Donoratico* (Naples, 1962).

56. Heers, *Family Clans in the Middle Ages: a Study of Political and Social Structures in Urban Areas* (Amsterdam, 1977 [Paris, 1974]); also see John Koenig, *Il "popolo" dell'Italia del Nord nel XIII secolo* (Bologna, 1986), p. 22, on Heers, P. J. Jones, and Sergio Bertelli, who have followed in the footsteps of Ottokar.

57. Salvemini, *Magnati e popolani in Firenze dal 1280 al 1295* (Florence, 1899).

58. See for instance Carol Lansing, *The Florentine Magnates: Lineage and Faction in a Medieval Commune* (Princeton, 1991); Koenig, *Il "popolo" dell'Italia del Nord;* and Paolo Grillo, *Milano in età comunale (1183–1276): Istituzioni, società, economia* (Spoleto, 2001).

59. For such cases, see *Popular Protest*, doc nos. 28–29.

60. *Storie Pistoresi [MCCC–MCCCXLVIII]*, ed. Silvio Adrasto Barbi, RIS, XI/5 (Città di Castello, 1907), p. 52.

61. *Cronaca volgare di Anonimo fiorentino dall'anno 1385 al 1409 già attribuita a Piero di Giovanni Minerbetti*, ed. Elina Bellondi, RIS, XXVII/2 (Città di Castello, 1915–1918), p. 323.

62. Bernardino Corio, *Storia di Milano*, ed. Angelo Butti and Luigi Ferrario (Milan, 1855–1856), II, pp. 465–466.

63. *Cronaca di Alamanno Acciaioli*, in *Il Tumulto dei Ciompi: Cronache e Memorie*, ed. Gino Scaramella, RIS, XVIII/3 (Bologna, 1917–1934), p. 21; and Ernesto Screpanti, *L'Angelo delle liberazione e il Tumulto dei Ciompi, Firenze, giugno-agosto 1378*, (unpublished Ms.), p. 122.

64. *Chronicon Parmense ab anno MXXXVIII usque ad annum MCCCXXXVIII*, ed. Giuliano Bonazzi, RIS, XI/9 (Città di Castello, 1903), pp. 145–146; and *Annales Parmenses maiores a 1165–1355*, in MGH:SS, XVIII, p. 745; *Corpus Chronicorum Bononiensium*, II, p. 294; G. Villani, *Nuova Cronica*, II, p. 185. Neither of the two non-Parmense chronicles mentions the invasion of peasants and the ripping up of communal charters.

65. Petrus Azarii, *Liber gestorum in Lombardia*, ed. Francesco Cognasso, RIS, XVI/4 (Bologna, 1925–1939), pp. xxiv and 83.

66. *Le Cronache di Todi (secoli XIII–XVI)*, ed. G. Italiani et al. (Florence, 1979), pp. 133 and 136. For similar conflicts in thirteenth- and fourteenth-century Lazio, see Jean-Claude Maire Vigueur, "Comuni e signorie in Umbria, Marche e Lazio," in *Storia d'Italia*, ed. G. Galasso, VII/2 (Turin, 1987), p. 490.

67. Edited by Colette Beaune (Paris, 1990).

68. Edited by Laura Artioli, Corrado Corradini, and Clementina Santi (Reggio nell' Emilia, 2000).

69. In the case of three histories (by Bernardino Corio, Marin Sanudo the elder, and Pompeo Pellini), I relied on sixteenth-century sources for collecting these revolts. These historians utilized (and often cited passages in full from) contemporary chronicles that no longer survive.

70. The exact number of separate and independent chronicles is difficult to pin down precisely: some overlapped others, as with the chronicle of Jean Juvenal des Ursins, which until 1418 was almost entirely a French translation of the chronicle of the religieux de Saint-Denys. On the other hand, a work such as *Istore et croniques de Flandres, d'après les textes de divers manuscrits,* counted as one chronicle, was in fact an interspersing of several chronicles. The number of 298 is my best approximation.

71. *Chronicon Cornelii Zanteliet,* col. 118.

72. Under this rubric I have included a wide diversity of history writing from the single lines of dates and brief comments of ecclesiastical annals to "universal chronicles" and early humanist histories, which in several cases contain a thousand pages or more. Also, I have included under this rubric personal memoirs or *ricordanze* and journals that mixed catalogues of family, legal, or business affairs with eyewitness reports of revolts. Examples are Bonaccorso Pitti's *Ricordi* and Nicholas de Baye's journal taken largely from his activities as scribe to the Parlement of Paris from 1400 to 1417. On those who have recently questioned the utility of chronicles, see for instance Harriet Merete Hansen, "The Peasants' Revolt of 1381 and the Chronicles," *Journal of Medieval History,* 6 (1980): 393–415; and to a certain extent, Andrew Prescott, "Writing about Rebellion: Using the Records of the Peasants' Revolt of 1381," *History Workshop Journal,* 45 (1998): 1–27. Against this grain, John Hatcher, in "England in the Aftermath of the Black Death," *Past & Present* 144 (1994): 3–35, has argued that literary works, including chronicles, can provide a more precise picture of medieval society and economy than statistics reconstructed from manorial rolls and other nonnarrative records. Still others, such as Ronald G. Musto (*Apocalypse in Rome: Cola di Rienzo and the politics of the New Age* [Berkeley, 2003]), rely heavily—even principally— on chronicles while recognizing the chronicles' rhetorical schemes and use of classical models for shaping their stories. Steven Justice (*Writing and Rebellion: England in 1381* [Berkeley, 1994]), has argued forcefully that a history of rebellion based on manorial records or judicial records alone impoverishes our perceptions of these events and that judicial records are as prejudicial, if not more so, than chronicles in treating popular revolts.

73. *Corpus Chronicorum Bononiensium,* III, p. 452.

74. *Chronicon Girardi de Fracheto,* p. 28.

75. *Cronaca di Ser Guerriero da Gubbio dall'anno MCCCL all'anno MCCCCLXXII,* ed. Giuseppe Mazzatinti, RIS, XXI/4 (Città di Castello, 1902), pp. 16–17.

76. Recently, scholars have called into question the Carmelite friar as the author of this continuation of Guillaume de Nangis; see *Dictionnaire des lettres françaises: Le Moyen Âge,* ed. Geneviève Haenohr and Michel Zink (Paris, 1992), pp. 290–291.

77. *Chronique de Jean le Bel,* ed. J. Viard and Eugène Déprez, SHF, CCCXVII (Paris, 1904–1905), 2 vols., I, pp. 255–262; and *Popular Protest,* doc no. 91.

78. See for instance *La chronique normande du XIVe siècle,* ed. A. and E. Molinier, SHF, CCV (Paris, 1882), pp. 127–132; *La chronique des règnes de Jean II et Charles V,* I, pp. 177–188; *The Chronicle of Jean de Venette,* pp. 76–77; and *Popular Protest,* doc no. 94, 95, and 97.

79. See various letters of remission published in Luce, *Histoire de la Jacquerie,* for instance, pp. 230–231, 253–254, 270–272, 291–292, and 333–335; and *Popular Protest,* doc nos. 103–120. Of course, postmodernists and deconstructionists would pose broader theoretical and linguistic questions, claiming that the historian is trapped in a "prison house of language," that any "realities" outside the texts cannot be visualized. But this reasoning applies equally well to all the documents used in this book (chronicles, memoirs, letters of remission, judicial records, *provvisioni,* etc.) and not just to chronicles; see Gabrielle M. Spiegel, "History, Historicism, and the Social Logic of the Text in the Middle Ages," *Speculum* 65 (1990): 59–86, esp. pp. 63–64 and 68–69.

80. *Venetiarum Historia vulgo Petro Iustiniano Iustiniani filio adiudicata,* ed. Roberto Cessi and Fanny Bennato, Monumenti Storici, Deputazione di Storia Patria per le Venezie, 17 (Venice, 1964), p. 176; Andrea Danduli, Dux Venetiarum, *Chronica per extensium descripta, aa. 46–1280,* ed. Ester Pastorello, RIS, XII/1 (Bologna, 1938–1958), p. 314; and Sanuto, *Vitæ Ducum Venetorum,* col. 564.

81. A. Carile, *La cronachistica veneziana (s. XIII-XVI)* (Florence, 1969); Paolo Sambin, "Di un'ignota fonte dei Diarii di Marin Sanudo," *Atti dell' Istituto Veneto* 104 (1944–1945): 21–53; Ser Pietro Dolfin's *Annales Veneti,* 1427–1506, survives.

82. See for instance Lauro Martines, *Power and Imagination: City-States in Renaissance Italy* (New York, 1979), p. 133.

83. *Le Croniche di Giovanni Sercambi, Lucchese,* ed. Salvatore Bongi, Fonti per la Storia d'Italia dall'Istituto Storico Italiano, nos. 19–21, 3 vols. (Lucca, 1892), I, pp. 204–205; and *Popular Protest,* nos. 80–81.

84. On the rhetoric of letters of remission, see my remarks in *Popular Protest,* pp. 149 and 179; and on judicial records, *Creating the Florentine State: Peasants and Rebellion, 1348–1432* (Cambridge, 1999), pp. 138–139.

85. Similarly, poets such as John Gower (*Vox Clamantis,* book I) saw peasants as oxen and the Peasants' Revolt of 1381 as inspired by the devil; see Hilton, "Ideology and Social Order" in *Class Conflict and the Crisis of Feudalism,* p. 248; and Paul Freedman, "Peasant Anger," in *Anger's Past: The Social Uses of an Emotion in the Middle Ages,* ed. Barbara H. Rosenwein (Ithaca, 1998), pp. 177. According to Froissart, when the Kentish peasants saw the royal barge approaching the southern shore of the Thames on 12 June 1381 "they raised a terrific noise as if all the devils from Hell had been released among them," cited in Fryde, *The Great Revolt of 1381,* Historical Association, no. 100 (London, 1981), p. 18. I wish also to thank S. H. Rigby for the reference to *Vox Clamantis.*

86. These were elected citizens of Lucca, preferably knights, who presided over the court of the Vicariates and exercised civil and criminal justice; see Catherine

Meek, *Lucca, 1369–1400: Politics and Society in an Early Renaissance City-State* (Oxford, 1978), p. 15.

87. The leading family of Lucca's ruling elite; see ibid., pp. 180–183.

88. Archivio di Stato, Lucca, Sentenze e Bandi, no. 43, np, 1370.vii.20.

89. Cohn, *Creating the Florentine State.*

90. Baron, *The Crisis of the Early Renaissance,* 2 vols (Princeton, 1955; revised ed., 1966); Lanza, *Firenze contro Milano: Gli intellettuali fiorentini nelle guerre con i Visconti (1390–1440)* (Rome, 1991).

91. *L'Istoria di Firenze di Gregorio Dati dal 1380 al 1405,* ed. Luigi Pratesi (Norcia, 1902), pp. 49–50.

92. Fourquin, *The Anatomy of Popular Rebellion,* p. 163.

93. Archivio di Stato, Bologna, Curia del Podestà: Guidici ad Maleficia: Sententiae, no. 22, 98r–99r, 11–16 April 1376; and *Popular Protest,* no. 88.

94. *Cronaca gestorum . . . a fratre Hyeronimo de Bursellis,* pp. 53–54; and *Cronaca B* and *Cronica Bolognetti* in *Corpus Chronicorum Bononiensium,* III, pp. 306–308; *Cronaca A,* in ibid., III, pp. 312–313; and *Popular Protest,* no. 89.

95. *Annales Forolivienses ab origine usque ad annum MCCCCLXXIII,* ed. Giuseppe Mazzatinti, RIS, XX/2 (Città di Castello, 1903), p. 68; *Monumenta Pisana,* col. 1070; *Cronaca malatestiana,* p. 916; *Cronaca senese di Donato di Neri.* p. 660; and *Diario d'anonimo fiorentino,* p. 329.

96. *Cronaca gestorum . . . a fratre Hyeronimo de Bursellis,* pp. 53–54; and *Corpus Chronicorum Bononiensium (Cronaca A),* pp. 312–313. Also, see Oreste Vancini, *La rivolta dei Bolognesi al Governo dei Vicari della Chiesa (1376–1377): L'origine dei tribuni della plebe* (Bologna, 1906).

97. On these revolts, see Chapter 4.

98. In a study of these sources, Graeme Small has found only nine towns in Flanders and France that possess surviving council minutes before the Black Death. Bronisław Geremek, in *Le Salariat,* pp. 102–104, has found several examples of labor disputes in late medieval Parisian civil and ecclesiastical cases (series X, Y, and Z).

99. Luce, *Histoire de la Jacquerie;* Fourquin, *Les campagnes de la région parisienne,* pp. 229–240.

100. Marcellin Boudet, *La Jacquerie des Tuchins, 1363–1384* (Riom, 1895).

101. Mirot, *Les insurrections urbaines.* The most systematic study of these documents for the Middle Ages—Gauvard, *"De Grace especial": Crime, état et société en France à la fin du Moyen Age,* 2 vols. (Paris, 1991)—hardly mentions collective protest or revolt.

102. See Michel François, "Note sur les lettres de rémission transcrits dans les registres du Trésor des chartes," *Bibliothèque de l'École des chartes,* CIII (1942): 317–324.

103. NHGL, X, cols 1716–1718.

104. François, "Note sur les lettres de rémission," p. 318.

105. The published inventories of the Trésor des chartes are *Registres du Trésor des chartes, I: Règne de Philippe le Bel: Inventaire Analytique,* ed. Robert Fawtier (Paris, 1958); *Registres du Trésor des chartes, II: Règnes des fils de Philippe le Bel,* ed. Jean Guerout and Fawtier (Paris, 1966); *Registres des Trésor des chartes, III/1 (JJ 65A à 69)*

and III/2 *(JJ 70 à 75)*, ed. J. Viard and Aline Vallée (Paris, 1978–1979). In addition, the Archives nationales possess several handwritten analytical inventories that extend into the early 1360s. Published regional inventories include *La Gascogne dans les registres du Trésor des chartes*, ed. Charles Samaran (Paris, 1966); *Le Languedoc et le Rouerge dans le Trésor des chartes*, ed. Yves Dossat, Anne-Marie Lemasson, and Philippe Wolff (Paris, 1983); and *Les pays de la Loire moyenne dans le Trésor des chartes: Berry, Blésois, Chartrain, Orléanais, Touraine, 1350–1502 (Archives nationales, JJ 80–235)*, ed. Bernard Chevalier (Paris, 1993).

106. See *Recueil des documents relatifs à l'histoire de l'industrie drapière en Flandre*, begun by Georges Espinas and Henri Pirenne in 1906 and afterward directed by Henri-E. de Sagher, 4 vols. (Brussels, 1906–1924). The number of insurrections could no doubt be increased by searching through collections of other published archival documents such as chartularies, decrees, and discussions of town councils and other registers, but such coverage would probably require a team of international researchers.

107. Moreover, from an exhaustive analysis of archival materials, Robert Favreau *(La ville de Poitiers à la fin du Moyen Âge: une capitale régionale*, 2 vols. [Poitiers, 1978], I, p. 200), finds no popular insurrections for Poitiers in the fourteenth century.

108. Robert Boutruche, *La crise d'une société: Seigneurs et paysans du Bordelais pendant la Guerre de Cent Ans* (Paris, 1963), pp. 165–179.

109. See for instance the exploits of the *maladrini* led by Mazziotto in 1371, which infested large areas of southern Italy—Campagnia, the Molise, Valle Beneventana, and Terra de Lavoro—and other bands in 1379; *I Diurnali del Duca di Monteleone*, ed. Michele Manfredi, RIS, XXI/5 (Bologna, 1958), pp. 13 and 22.

110. See *Cronaca aquilana rimata di Buccio di Ranallo*, ed. Vincenzo de Bartholomaeis, Fonti per la Storia d'Italia, no. 41 (Rome, 1907), for revolts of the *popolo* in L'Aquila in 1293 (pp. 31–34), 1329 (pp. 74–75), 1351 (p. 207), and 1354 (p. 219); and *Cronaca di Niccolò di Borbona*, cols. 853–876, for a peasant revolt in L'Aquila, 1370, cols. 855–856; and revolts of the *popolo* in L'Aquila in 1391, 1392, and 1415, cols. 859–860, and 864.

111. The Angevin chancellery archives contained 376 parchments and over 100 volumes in paper. Since 1949, Riccardo Filangieri and his successors at the Archivio di Stato, Napoli, have reconstructed fragments of these registers from earlier transcriptions and microfilms. Caggese *(Roberto d'Angiò ed i suoi tempi*, 2 vols. [Florence, 1922–1930], I, pp. 319–332), supplied many examples of popular insurrections from these archives and argued that these movements peaked during the reign of Robert. Also, see *I Registri della Cancelleria Angioina ricostruiti da Riccardo Filangieri*, II: (1265–1281) (Naples, 1951); and *Popular Protest*, doc. nos. 52–53. Using Caggese's summaries, Hilton *(Bond Men Made Free*, p. 110), described southern Italy in the Middle Ages as "a continuous Jacquerie" of peasant insurrection. Closer inspection suggests that the rebels were often townsmen *(popolani)* and in some cases citizens of high social standing.

112. Fournial, *Les villes et l'économie d'échange en Forez aux XIIIe et XIVe siècles* (Paris, 1967), pp. 292–293, 374–375, and 472–475; Chevalier, "Corporations, conflits

politiques et paix sociale," pp. 275 and 285; and Leguai, "Les révoltes rurales," pp. 63–65. In addition, Daniel Borzeix, René Pautal, and Jacques Serbat, in *Révoltes populaires en Occitanie: Moyen Âge et Ancien Régime* (Treignac, 1982), pp. 13–65, list at least 65 popular revolts from archival sources for Languedoc from the late eleventh century to 1419, few of which appear in my samples.

113. Martines, *Power and Imagination,* p. 59. Others on the left had said much the same: František Graus, in "The Crisis of the Middle Ages and the Hussites," *The Reformation in Medieval Perspective,* ed. Steven E. Ozment (Chicago, 1971), p. 91, claimed that riots and revolts before the Hussites and Joan of Arc "never achieved any clear concept of their purpose, and usually remained local," the English Peasants' Revolt of 1381 included.

114. Bertelli, "Oligarchies et gouvernment dans la ville de la Renaissance," *Social Science: Information sur les sciences sociales,* XV (1976), p. 623. Also see Patricia Crone, *Pre-Industrial Societies* (Oxford, 1989), p. 72–73. Also see Rogozinski (*Power, Caste, and Law),* who claims that tax revolts and litigation in Montpellier in the 1320s and 1330s were "factional" conflicts among elites; his evidence, however, shows that pressure from the "many inhabitants of low condition" and "mob violence" contributed to the fight against corruption of town councilors and led to greater fiscal equality, reliance on the proportional property tax (the taille) as opposed to indirect taxes, and to the increased influence of the popular assembly (pp. 49, 91–92, and 115).

115. Léopold Genicot, *Rural Communities in the Medieval West* (Baltimore, 1990), pp. 79–80.

116. This study also overturns the notion of the peaceful, idyllic workplace held by historians of the nineteenth century. For this literature, see Geremek, *Le Salariat dans l'artisanat parisien aux XIIIᵉ et XVᵉ siècles: Étude sur le marché de la main-d'œuvre au Moyen Âge,* trans. Anna Posner and Christiane Klapisch-Zuber (Paris, 1968), p. 145.

2. Peasant Revolts

1. TeBrake, *A Plague of Insurrection,* p. 7; R. B. Dobson, *The Peasants' Revolt of 1381,* 2nd ed. (London, 1983), p. 27; Hilton, *Bond Men Made Free,* pp. 11–12; and Hilton, "Peasant Movements in England before 1381," in *Class Conflict and the Crisis of Feudalism,* p. 122. For the citation, see Bloch, *French Rural History: An Essay on Its Basic Characteristics* (London, 1966 [Antwerp, 1931]), p. 170.

2. Jacques Le Goff, *La civilisation de l'Occident médiéval* (Paris, 1964), p. 373.

3. Scott, *Weapons of the Weak,* p. xv.

4. Scott, *Weapons of the Weak,* pp. 29 and 36–37. Also see Scott's *Domination and the Art of Resistance: Hidden Transcripts* (New Haven, 1990), which generalizes some of his earlier conclusions about peasant resistance over to subaltern classes across history and into the Middle Ages.

5. Curiously, Scott (*Weapons of the Weak,* p. xvi) begins by citing Marc Bloch's dictum before launching into his diametrically opposed view.

6. Rigby *(English Society in the Later Middle Ages,* p. 124) prefers the metaphor of a "trigger" over that of a spark. The former emphasizes more human agency, even if for the Middle Ages it may seem somewhat anachronistic.

7. Thomas J. Figueira, "A Typology of Social Conflict in Greek Poleis," in *City-States in Classical Antiquity and Medieval Italy: Athens and Rome, Florence and Venice,* ed. Anthony Molho, Kurt Raaflaub, and Julia Emlen (Stuttgart, 1991), pp. 289–329.

8. Karl Polanyi, *The Great Transformation* (Boston, 1957; first published, 1944), p. 52.

9. For the relative autonomy of the state as opposed to seeing it simply as an instrument of the dominant classes, see Ralph Miliband, *Class Power and State Power* (London, 1983). This is especially true for a state such as Florence in the period of the guild republics, when artisans sat in legislative councils alongside merchants and magnates, even if they exercised less power than their social superiors. Further, as Jane Whittle and S. H. Rigby, in "England: Popular Politics and Social Conflict," in *A Companion to Britain in the Later Middle Ages,* ed. Rigby (Oxford, 2003), p. 69, have shown for England in the revolts of 1381, 1489, and 1497, "It is difficult to argue that the government was attacked simply because it represented the ruling class. The interests of the government and manorial lords were not identical; in fact, they could be in direct opposition: paying tax impoverished the peasantry, reducing their ability to pay rent to landlords." The history of Italian city-states highlights such conflicts of interests among merchants, feudal landlords, peasants, and artisans.

10. See below.

11. NHGL, X, cols. 1818–1820. Rabastens was captain for the king of France in the Agenais in March 1370.

12. On the coast, 44 km southwest of Savona.

13. *Annali genovesi di Caffaro e de' suoi continuatori dal MCLXXIV al MCCXXIV,* ed. Luigi Tommaso Belgrano and Cesare Imperiale di Sant'Angelo, vol. III (Genoa, 1901), p. 69. Also see Steven A. Epstein, *Genoa and the Genoese, 958–1528* (Chapel Hill, N. C., 1996), p. 122.

14. *Cronaca aquilana rimata di Buccio di Ranallo,* p. 20.

15. M. Villani, *Cronica,* I, pp. 49–50. As seen in tax registers of the late fourteenth century, these *fedeli* were peasants often with small holdings, who owed feudal dues in addition to their rents; see Cohn, *Creating the Florentine State,* p. 21.

16. Ibid., II, pp. 387–388.

17. *Cronaca . . . Minerbetti,* p. 309.

18. Cohn, *Creating the Florentine State,* p. 191.

19. Rodolico, *Il Popolo Minuto: Note di Storia Fiorentina (1343–1378)* (Florence, 1899; new ed., 1968), doc. no. 25, pp. 114–115; and *Popular Protest,* doc. no. 51.

20. The territory beyond the city walls of Florence was divided into the *contado* and the *distretto.* The *contado* was for the most part the original countryside around Florence before it began conquering other city-states that possessed their own belts of countryside in the fourteenth century. The two zones were subjected to different laws and systems of taxation. For a more detailed discussion, see Cohn, *Creating the Florentine State,* pp. 7–8, 15–16, 178, and 198–199.

21. *Registres des Trésors des chartes,* III/3, JJ 76 à 79b.

22. A standard set of servile obligations: *formariage* obliged a serf to pay a fee to marry someone who belonged to another lord.

23. Archives nationales, JJ 71, f.65, n 86; and JJ 75, f. 186r–188r, no. 316. In addition, the king granted the return of property to the heirs of those executed and a general amnesty to the villages where the revolts had occurred.

24. NHGL, X, cols. 1074–7.

25. Michele da Piazza, *Chronica,* ed. Antonino Giuffrida (Palermo, 1980), pp. 92, 115, 155–159, 175–177, 192, 199, 247–251, 298, 358, and 360–361.

26. Most recently, see the contributions to *Protesta e rivolta contadina nell'Italia medievale,* ed. Giovanni Cherubini, in *Annali dell'Istituto "Alcide Cervi,"* no. 16 (1994). If the peasant revolts that took place within the *contado* of L'Aquila are added, the proportion of urban-centered revolts rises to almost four-fifths.

27. David Nicholas, *Medieval Flanders* (London, 1992), pp. 211–212; and Peter Stabel, *Dwarfs among Giants: The Flemish Urban Network in the Late Middle Ages* (Leuven, 1997), pp. 95–106.

28. For a recent detailed overview of these revolts from 1127 to the sixteenth century, see Jan Dumolyn and Jelle Haemers, "Patterns of Urban Rebellion in Medieval Flanders," *Journal of Medieval History* 31 (2005): 369–393. I thank Peter Arnade and Jelle Haemers for sending me the article.

29. Certainly, as Pirenne *(Histoire de Belgique,* I, p. 373) cautions, it would be wrong to consider Peter the King as the precursor of William of Orange. Whereas the revolts of the Low Countries during the sixteenth century were "national and religious," those of the early fourteenth century were social. Nonetheless, the various social groups of 1302 were united by an anti-French sentiment. Pirenne, *(Histoire de Belgique,* I, p. 392) dates the birth of "a conscious Flemish national sentiment" to the battle of Courtrai, 1302.

30. For the background to the revolt of 1302, see Nicholas, *Medieval Flanders,* pp. 187–192; and Prevenier and Boone, "The 'City-State' Dream," pp. 81–82. The principal chronicles for this revolt are *Chronique des Pays-Bas, de France, d'Angleterre et de Tournai,* in *Corpus Chronicorum Flandriae,* ed. J.-J. de Smet, vol. III (Brussels, 1856), pp. 121–122; *Chronica Aegidii Li Muisis, abbatis XVII Sancti-Martini Tornacensis,* in ibid., II, pp. 192–193; *Annales Gandenses,* ed. Hilda Johnstone (London, 1951); and G. Villani, *Nuova Cronica,* II, pp. 88–90.

31. See TeBrake, *A Plague of Insurrection;* Nicholas, *Medieval Flanders,* pp. 211–216; and for the chroniclers, *Chronicon comitum Flandrensium,* pp. 34–261; *Chronica Aegidii Li Muisis,* p. 212; *Anciennes chroniques de Flandre,* RGFS, XXII (Paris, 1894), pp. 418–419; G. Villani, *Nuova Cronica,* II, p. 413; *Chronique des Pays-Bas,* III, pp. 143–144.

32. David M. Bessen, "The Jacquerie: Class War or Co-opted Rebellion?" *Journal of Medieval History* 11 (1985): 43–59; and Raymond Cazelles, "The Jacquerie," in *The English Rising of 1381,* ed. R. H. Hilton and T. H. Aston (Cambridge, 1984), pp. 74–84. For other titles by Cazelles on this position, see Cohn, *Popular Protest,* pp. 143–150.

33. For my arguments, see *Popular Protest* as well as older titles, such as works by Luce, principally *Histoire de la Jacquerie* and later, Leguai, "Les révoltes rurales," pp. 50–59.

34. The only nobles to receive letters of remission in the wake of the Jacquerie were those who used what even contemporary authorities judged as excessive force in their slaughter of peasants. Only one rural cleric appears, a reluctant one, forced by his parishioners to accompany the peasants; see Luce, *Histoire de la Jacquerie*, pp. 270–272.

35. The esteemed and often cited essay by Jean Flammeront, "La Jacquerie en Beauvaisis," *Revue Historique*, IV (1879): 123–143, almost succeeds in turning back the clock on this question; see my remarks in *Popular Protest*, pp. 147–149.

36. See for instance the letters of remission granted to individuals, villages, and groups of villages in Luce, *Histoire de la Jacquerie*, pp. 253–254, 266–268, and 293–294.

37. See *Dictionnaire des lettres françaises*, pp. 288–289.

38. *Richardi Scoti chronici continuatio*, pp. 126–127.

39. In the "Version non normande," *paisans* is the word.

40. *La chronique normande du XIVᵉ siècle*, pp. 127–132.

41. In discussing the English Peasants' Revolt of 1381, Rigby *(English Society in the Later Middle Ages*, p. 124) points to a similar "crisis of legitimacy" with England's fall in fortunes at that point in the Hundred Years' War.

42. For 996, see Hilton, *Bond Men Made Free*, pp. 70–71; and David Bates, *Normandy before 1066* (London, 1982), p. 35. For the early Middle Ages, see Christopher Wickham, *Framing the Early Middle Ages* (Oxford, 2005), pp. 578–588.

43. Evidence of such mass meetings, *coniurationes*, or assemblies of the disenfranchised to gain power can be seen in revolts as early as the crisis years in Flanders of 1127–1128; on these revolts, see Dumolyn and Haemers, "Patterns of Urban Rebellion," p. 370, 373–374.

44. One example comes from the neighboring Liégeois: the villagers of Seraing, outside of Liège, successfully revolted against the aldermen of Liège in 1395, when they attempted to withdraw these villagers' right to gather wood in their forest; *Chronicon Cornelii Zanteliet*, pp. 344–345.

45. David Nirenberg, in *Communities of Violence: Persecution of Minorities in the Middle Ages* (Princeton, 1996), pp. 48–50, argues that the 1320 crusade was "a revolt against the monarchy," and that the attacks on the Jews were meant as attacks on the king himself, since the Jews were under his protection. But Nirenberg cites no text, nor have I found one, that makes such a link (as would later happen with the anti-Semitic attacks in Paris in 1380 and 1382). Indeed, the chroniclers purport the opposite: at least by 1321, the king was profiting from the pillaging and burning of Jews. He was said to have gained 150,000 *livres* from the goods and incomes of Parisian Jews alone (Malcolm Barber, "Lepers, Jews and Moslems: The Plot to Overthrow Christendom in 1321," *History* 66 (1981), p. 5). Further, Nirenberg (ibid.) argues that this movement was "a rebellion against fiscality," but cites no source to back his claim.

46. See Luce, "Notice sur Guillaume l'Aloue," *Annuaire-Bulletin de la Sociéte d'Histoire de France* (1875): 149–156; and Henri Denifle, *La Guerre de Cent Ans et la désolation des églises, monastères & hôpitaux en France,* 2 vols. (Paris 1897–1899), II, 219: "Les habitants de Longueil-Saïnte-Marie s'organisèrent plus tard sous la direction d'un simple paysan Guillaumne l'Aloue et de son valet le Grand Ferré . . . Plusieurs fois ces braves patriotes infligèrent de graves échecs aux Anglo-Navarrais de Creil, bien qu'ils n'aient guère eu d'autres armes que leurs bras robustes et rarement des haches. Guillaume l'Aloue et le Grand Ferré se battirent et moururent héroïquement."

47. *Chronique normande du XIVe siècle,* pp. 146–147; *Chronique de Guillaume de Nangis,* II, pp. 288–289; *Richardi Scoti chronici continuatio,* pp. 140–141; *Chronographia Regum Francorum,* ed. H. Moranvillé, SHF, 252 (Paris 1891–1892), II, p. 288; *Istore et croniques de Flandres, d'après les textes de divers manuscrits,* ed. M. le baron Kervyn de Lettenhove, 2 vols. (Brussels, 1879–1880), II, pp. 95–96.

48. Despite variations, the story was not an invention of patriotic chroniclers. Not only is it found in a number of chronicles, it also was briefly retold in a letter of remission issued by Charles V in April 1376 to Henri Stadieu, who "sixteen or seventeen years earlier" had killed a valet under the orders of Guillaume l'Aloue (transcribed by Luce, "Notice sur Guillaume l'Aloue," pp. 153–155).

49. ~~*Chronique de Guillaume de Nangis,* II, pp. 304–305.~~

50. Ibid., II, pp. 306–307.

51. *Chronique du religieux de Saint-Denys,* IV, pp. 453–458.

52. Boudet, *La Jacquerie des Tuchins.*

53. *Chronique du religieux de Saint-Denys,* I, pp. 306–313.

54. In addition to the accounts of Jean le Bel and Froissart, see *Croniques de Franche, d'Engleterre, de Flandres, de Lile et espécialment de Tournay,* ed. Adolphe Hoquet (Mons, 1938), pp. 118–119.

55. Boudet *(La Jacquerie des Tuchins,* p. 2) thought the name was a corruption of "Tue-chiens"—those so hungry that they were forced to eat dogs. More recently, historians have argued that the name derived from "touche," meaning a wood or a part of a wood, where these supposed marginals were forced to hide. See André Leguai, "Les révoltes rurales dans le royaume de France du milieu du XIVe siècle à la fin du XVe," *Le Moyen Âge,* 88 (1982), p. 59; Robert Fossier, *Paysans d'Occident (XIe–XIVe siècle)* (Paris, 1984), p. 196; and Vincent Challet, "La révolt des Tuchins: Banditisme social ou sociabilité villageoise?" *Médievalés* 34 (1998), p. 101. Yet some still maintain that "Tue-chiens" is the correct derivation; see Borzeix et al., *Révoltes populaires en Occitanie,* p. 45.

56. *Chronique du religieux de Saint-Denys,* I, pp. 306–313. Challet, "La révolt des Tuchins," p. 102. Leguai ("Les révoltes rurales," pp. 59–63) maintains that the Tuchins were initially unemployed workers and ruined peasants before becoming more or less bandits in the Haute Auvergne. However, he does not note any source for this conclusion.

57. In addition to the letters transcribed by Boudet and in NHGL, X, see *Popular Protest,* doc. nos. 61–65.

58. See for instance NHGL, X, col. 1867–8.

59. See for instance Boudet, *La Jacquerie des Tuchins*, pp. 125–127 and 127–129.

60. For the Ubaldini and other noblemen who engaged in highway robbery on Florence's mountain passes, see Cohn, *Creating the Florentine State*, pp. 22, 148–149, and 174–175; for *maladrini* such as the famous Mazziotto Maladrino, who plagued the kingdom of Naples in the 1370s, see *I Diurnali del Duca di Monteleone*, pp. 13 and 17. However, unlike these Italian bandits, the Tuchins were from both towns and the countryside; see Challet, "La révolt des Tuchins," pp. 104–109.

61. NHGL, X, col. 1701–3.

62. Ibid., X, cols. 1716–8.

63. On the Tuchins in the region of Toulouse and the 800,000 franc fine and its consequences, see Wolff, *Histoire de Toulouse* (Toulouse, 1958), p. 156; and Wolff, *Commerces et marchands de Toulouse (vers 1350–vers 1450)* (Paris, 1954), pp. 46–47, who also distinguishes the Tuchins of the Haute Auvergne from those further south in Languedoc.

64. In addition to the remission above, see NHGL, X, cols. 1688–1689, 1689–1690, and 1757–1758. For a brief account of the Tuchins in Nîmes in 1382, see *Histoire de Nîmes*, ed. Raymond Huard (Aix-en-Provence, 1982), pp. 135–137.

65. NHGL, X, cols. 1796–9.

66. *Registres des Trésor des chartes*, III/3, JJ 77, no. 6641, JJ 77, f.45, no. 81.

67. NHGL, X, cols. 1349–1350.

68. See for instance the revolt of Gallicano against Lucca in 1372 (*Le Croniche di Giovanni Sercambi*, I, pp. 205–206) and revolts of *terrae*, such as *terra Nothi* against the Palici lords in mid-fourteenth-century Sicily (Michele da Piazza, *Chronica*, p. 115).

69. See for instance the occupations and holdings of those from Cortona in the Catasto of 1427 (Archivio di Stato, Firenze).

70. Further, I could have increased substantially the database's number of peasant revolts by including those found in judicial and *provvisioni* records that I collected earlier for *Creating the Florentine State*, but I did not.

71. *Annali genovesi di Caffaro e de' suoi continuatori.*

72. Stella, *Annales Genuenses*. Also see Epstein, *Genoa and the Genoese*, pp. 199–200.

73. *Annali genovesi*, III, pp. 70–72.

74. An exception might be the "great revolt of 1238," in which Savona, Albenga, Porto Maurizio, and Ventimiglia expelled their Genoese podestà, but I have not classified these towns' rebels as peasants; see Epstein, *Genoa and the Genoese*, p. 123.

75. See for instance the revolt instigated by Raphael Carpanetus on 12 January 1400, which brought his men from the three valleys into the city of Genoa; Stella, *Annales Genuenses*, p. 243.

76. Ibid., pp. 185–186.

77. See Chapter 5, note 93. Stella dates the incident to 1339, but this was a period when the chronicler was relying on collective memory. Perhaps he misdated the incident to 1329, when these galleys would have been returning to Genoa after serving the king of France in suppressing the Flemish revolt of 1323–1328.

78. Ibid., p. 244. This area does not appear among the feudal estates of the Spinola and Doria families mentioned by Emanuel P. Wardi, *Le Strategie familiari di un doge di Genova: Antoniotto Adorno (1378–1398)* (Turin, 1996), pp. 39–80.

79. *Annales Veteres Mutinensium ab anno MCXXXI usque ad MCCCXXXVI. . .cum additamentis Auctore Anonymo,* Muratori, X, col. 60. An *agricola* can mean either a cultivator of the soil or a peasant.

80. Ibid., col. 77.

81. *Corpus Chronicorum Bononiensium (Cronaca B),* II, p. 435.

82. *Annali genovesi,* III, p. 173.

83. *Die Chronik des Saba Malaspina,* ed. Walter Koller and August Nitschke, MGH: SS, XXXV (Hanover, 1999), pp. 120–121.

84. *Chronicon Lauretanum MCLXXXVII–MCCLXXI* (Bibliotheca Nazionale di Napoli IX, C. 24), in Vincenzo Bindi, *Monumenti storici e artistici degli Abruzzi,* 4 vols. (Naples, 1889), II, pp. 587–589.

85. *Cronaca aquilana rimata di Buccio di Ranallo,* p. 20.

86. *Cronaca malatestiana,* p. 20.

87. M. Villani, *Cronica,* I, pp. 653–655.

88. Ibid., II, p. 447.

89. *Chronicon estense gesta Marchionum Estensium,* Muratori, XVI, cols. 511–512.

90. See Chapter 1, note 93; *Cronaca gestorum . . . fratre Hyeronimo de Bursellis,* pp. 53–54; and *Corpus Chronicorum Bononiensium (Cronaca A, B,* and *Cronica Bolognetti),* III, pp. 306–308 and 312–313.

91. Conforti Pulicis Vicentini, *Annalium Patriae Fragmenta ab anno MCCCLXXI usque ad annum MCCCLXXXVII,* Muratori, XIII, col. 1262; and *Additamenta recentioris scriptoris ad hanc historiam,* Muratori, XII, col. 752.

92. According to Corio, *Storia di Milano,* II, pp. 324–325, the peasants rebelled because of the town's failure to supply them with salt.

93. According to *Additamenta recentioris scriptoris,* col. 752, three hundred citizens of Parma defeated and chased the peasants out of town.

94. Angelo Pezzana, in *Storia della città di Parma,* I: 1346–1400 (Parma, 1837), pp. 153–154, relied on contemporary chronicles of Parma by Giovanni del Giudice and Giovanni Balducchini, which are unpublished and appear no longer to exist; at least they are not inventoried under chronicles in the *Repertorium fontium historiae medii aevi,* II (Rome, 1962).

95. Galeazzo and Bartolomeo Gatari, *Cronaca carrarese confrontata con la redazione di Andrea Gatari (1318–1407),* ed. Antonio Medin and Guido Tolomei, RIS, XVII/1 (Città di Castello, 1942–1948), I, pp. 326–329. Also, see Roberto Cessi, *Il tumulto di Treviso (1388)* (Padua, 1908).

96. Raphayni de Caresinis, cancellarii Venetiarum, *Chronica, aa. 1343–1388,* ed. Ester Pastorello, RIS, XII/2 (Bologna, 1922), p. 72.

97. *Cronaca . . . Minerbetti,* p. 127; and *Croniche fiorentine di Ser Naddo da Montecatini,* in *Delizie degli eruditi toscani,* ed. Fr. Idelfonso di San Luigi, 24 vols. (Florence, 1770–1789), XVIII, pp. 120–121; and Cohn, *Creating the Florentine State,* pp. 125–126.

98. Cohn, *Creating the Florentine State*, Ch. 3.

99. On divisions within the ruling class as a strong precondition of popular uprisings from the Revolt of the Ciompi to the French Revolution, see Cohn, *The Laboring Classes in Renaissance Florence* (New York, 1980), p. 132; and *Popular Protest*, pp. 206–208.

100. Azzo IX, Marchese d'Este, 1344–1415. Ferrara was then under the Signoria of Niccolò II d'Este.

101. Fr. Johannes Ferrariensus, *Annalium Libris Marchionum Estensium Excerpta [AA. 00–1454]*, ed. Luigi Simeoni, RIS, XX/2 (Bologna, 1920–1936), pp. 15–17.

102. *Cronica . . . Minerbetti*, p. 194; and *Popular Protest*, doc. no. 197.

103. They were the ruling family of Ferrara for most of the period from 1212 to 1597.

104. Various excise taxes on commodities.

105. *Cronica . . . Minerbetti*, p. 194. Also, see *Annales Estenses Jacobi de Delayto cancellarii D. Nicolai Estensis . . . an MCCCXCIII usque MCCCCIX*, Muratori, XVIII, cols. 923–924.

106. *Cronica . . . Minerbetti*, p. 194.

107. Corio, *Storia di Milano*, II, p. 467.

108. On the region of Friuli, see Edward Muir, *Mad Blood Stirring: Vendetta and Factions in Friuli during the Renaissance* (Baltimore, 1993).

109. 15 km from Treviso.

110. 10 km from Padua.

111. Sanuto, *Vitæ Ducum Venetorum*, cols. 877–878.

112. See *Protesta e rivolta contadina nell'Italia medievale*, where Italian historians presume that "true" peasant revolts were common only north of the Alps, and especially not in the commercial regions of Italy.

113. See for instance Archivio di Stato, Firenze (hereafter, ASF), Provvisioni registri (hereafter, Provv. reg.), no. 92, fols. 87v–90v; for other examples and most of what follows, see Cohn, *Creating the Florentine State*, Chapters 4–6; and *Popular Protest*, doc. nos. 198–9.

114. On this condottiere, see Michael Mallet, "Dal Verme, Iacopo" in *Dizionario biografico degli Italiani*, 32 (Rome, 1986), pp. 262–267.

115. ASF, Atti del Podestà, no. 3886 (hereafter AP), 9r–10v.

116. Giovanni di Pagolo Morelli, *Ricordi*, in *Mercanti Scrittori: Ricordi nella Firenze tra Medioevo e Rinascimento*, ed. Vittore Branca (Milan, 1985), pp. 262–263.

117. As mentioned in Chapter 1, this might not be true for southern Italy.

118. Hilton, *Bond Men Made Free*.

119. Hilton, "Peasant Movements in England before 1381," in *Class Conflict and the Crisis of Feudalism*, pp. 122–138, p. 131. Rosamond Faith, in "The 'Great Rumour' of 1377 and Peasant Ideology," in *The English Rising*, pp. 43–83, describes a notable exception on the eve of the Great Revolt: an organized refusal of peasants to work at harvest time that involved at least forty villages in Wiltshire, Surrey, Sussex, and Devon.

120. Fryde, in *The Great Revolt of 1381*, p. 7, points to Cade's rebellion in 1450 and the Cornish revolt of 1497. Whittle and Rigby, "England: Popular Politics and Social Conflict," pp. 69–70, add the Yorkshire tax revolt of 1489. Fryde, in "Peasant

rebellion and discontents," pp. 797–808, lists others: Yorkshire and Cheshire in 1391–1393, Essex and Cheshire in 1400, and Cheshire and York in 1403. But the ones in Cheshire and York appear more as disturbances of unemployed soldiers rather than peasant uprisings (pp. 798–799). Dyer, in *Making a Living in the Middle Ages,* pp. 291–292, includes as a peasant revolt the Welsh revolt of 1400 against English rule, led by the gentry and their proclaimed prince, Owain Glyn Dwr, which lasted for nine years. It began as an uprising of the nobility and ended with international alliances, but became (according to R. R. Davies, *The Age of Conquest: Wales 1063–1415* (Oxford, 1987), pp. 443–459) "a national revolt." Also see Davies, *The Revolt of Owain Glyn Dwr* (Oxford, 1995).

3. Economic Revolts

1. Hilton ("Popular Movements in England at the End of the Fourteenth Century," pp. 157–158) has argued that peasant movements were "more important than movements of urban artisans or journeymen," by which he meant that peasant movements were more frequent and more threatening to the political stability and economic structure of England. While this may have been true for England, the samples show overwhelmingly the opposite for Italy, France, Flanders, and the Liégeois. Here as with many other aspects of popular revolt, England's experience appears strikingly different from that of the continent.

2. Mollat and Wolff, *Popular Revolutions,* p. 272; Léon Vanderkindere, *Le siècle des Artevelde: Études sur la civilisation morale et politique de la Flandre et du Brabant,* 2nd ed. (Brussels, 1909). Pirenne, *Histoire de Belgique,* II, pp. 28 and 121; Pirenne, *Les anciennes démocraties des Pays-Bas* (Paris, 1910), p. 168: "an equivalent in the richness of their vicissitudes, energy, and duration was found in the republican municipalities of Italy."

3. *Recueil des documents rélatifs à l'histoire de l'industrie drapière en Flandre,* II, p. 22: 1245–1247: Douai: document no. 218. In 1266 this legislation was renewed with penalties also extended to those who "forced, aided, or gave counsel" to strikers. However, the fines declined from 60 to 50 shillings, ibid., p. 109, document no. 259. When weavers and other workers of Douai went on strike in 1276, the consequences were more severe: twenty-three were put on trial, twenty-one were banished, and three weavers were decapitated; see Georges Espinas, *La vie urbaine de Douai au Moyen Age,* 4 vols. (Paris, 1913), II, pp. 1112–1113. For a recent survey and appraisal of these early industrial conflicts, see Prevenier, "Conscience et perception de la condition sociale chez les gens du commun dans les anciens Pays-Bas des XIIIᵉ et XIVᵉ siècles," in *Le petit peuple dans l'Occident médiéval: Terminologies, perceptions, réalités,* ed. Pierre Boglioni, Robert Delort, and Claude Gauvard (Paris, 2002), pp. 175–189. Also, see *Popular Protest,* doc. nos. 2–4.

4. In addition to the evidence of Douai's ordinances, the municipal tribunal adjudicated at least two major strikes of cloth workers and other artisans in 1276 and 1280, which were also attacks on the city's patrician magistrat; see Espinas,

La vie urbaine de Douai, II, pp. 1111–1113. On the economics of these thirteenth-century revolts going back to the massacre of patricians by fullers, weavers, and other "poor people" in Valenciennes in 1225, see John H. Munro, "Medieval Woolens: Textiles, Textile Technology and Industrial Organization, c. 800–1500," in *The Cambridge History of Western Textiles*, I, pp. 222–223, ed. David Jenkins (Cambridge, 2003).

5. *Recueil des documents rélatifs à l'histoire de l'industrie drapière en Flandre*, I, p. 313, no. 128 and pp. 328–330, no. 132.

6. Ibid., III, pp. 235, 238, and 244. In addition, trades such as the furriers of Paris (1319) had their own mutual societies, which for an annual subscription guaranteed sick pay; see document in Fossier, *Paysans d'Occident*, p. 358.

7. *The Coutumes de Beauvaisis of Philippe de Beaumanoir*, trans. and ed. F. R. P. Akehurst (Philadelphia, 1992), p. 314; and *Popular Protest*, doc. no. 9.

8. *Recueil des documents rélatifs à l'histoire de l'industrie drapière en Flandre*, II, pp. 141–143. no. 289.

9. Ibid., III, 102–109, nos. 626, 686, 851; and *Popular Protest*, doc. nos. 5–6. Also see Marc Boone, "Social Conflicts in the Cloth Industry of Ypres (Late 13th–Early 14th Centuries): The *Cockerulle* Reconsidered," in *Ypres and the Medieval Cloth Industry in Flanders: Archaeological and Historical Contributions*, ed. Marc Dewilde, Anton Ervynck, and Alexis Wielemans (*Archeologie in Vlaanderen, Monografie*, 2) (Asse-Zelik, 1998), pp. 147–153. For further examples of industrial unrest in Doornik, St. Omer, Bruges, and Ghent in the late 1270s and early 1280s, see Thomas A. Boogaart II, "Reflections of the Moerlemaye: Revolt and Reform in Late Medieval Bruges," *Revue belge de philology et d'histoire* 79 (2001): 1133–1134.

10. Ibid., I, p. 63. no. 23; and pp. 98–102, no. 38. From archival sources, examples of artisan conflicts over maximum hours of work can be added for Paris in 1251, 1256, 1277, and 1324; for Provins in 1279, Troyes in 1358, and a strike of journeymen fullers at Saint-Denis in 1321; see Geremek, *Les salariat*, pp. 102–110.

11. On Bologna, Florence, and Siena, see below. Although such activity rarely occurred in preplague England, London saw separate journeymen's guilds as early as 1303, when the journeymen cordwainers rebelled unsuccessfully against a wage cut. Further, conflict erupted in 1327 between master saddlers and their dependents in other crafts, which threatened a general strike; see Whittle and Rigby, "England: Popular Politics and Social Conflict," p. 80.

12. A. Giry, *Établissements de Rouen: Études sur l'histoire des institutions municipales* (Paris, 1883), I, p. 41, cited from the *Chronico ms. ecclesiae Rotomagensi; Popular Protest*, doc. no. 7.

13. *Chronica Aegidii Li Muisis*, pp. 170 and 173–175. Also see Maurice Houtart, *Les Tournaisiens et le Roi de Bourges* (Tournai, 1908), pp. 17–18; and *Popular Protest*, doc. nos. 15–16.

14. *Chronique latine de Guillaume de Nangis*, I, p. 282; *Popular Protest*, doc. no. 10.

15. *Chronicon Girardi de Fracheto*, p. 27; *Extrait d'une chronique anonyme finissant en MCCCLXXX*, in ibid., p. 127; *Chronique anonyme finissant en MCCCLVI*, in ibid., p. 139; *Chronique anonyme finissant en M.CCC.LXXXIII*, p. 142; *Excerpta e memoriali*

Historiarum auctore Johanne Parisiensi, Sancti Victoris Parisiensis canonico regulari, in ibid., pp. 646–647; *Chronique latine de Guillaume de Nangis (first continuation)*, I, pp. 355–356; and *Les Grandes Chroniques de France*, VIII, pp. 250–252; and *La chronique parisienne anonyme*, ed. Amédée Hellot, in *Mémoire de la société de l'histoire de Paris* (1884), pp. 1–207, p. 20.

16. *Les Grandes Chroniques de France*, VIII, pp. 250–252.

17. Before the Black Death, plebes revolted at Huy in 1254–1255, 1285, 1298, 1299, 1314, and 1344; at Liège in 1200, 1253, 1254, 1275, 1302, 1303, 1310, 1312, 1327, 1329, 1331, 1343, 1345, 1346, and 1347; and at Sint-Truiden in 1242, 1255–1256, 1298–1302, 1302–1304, and 1314. For these see *La chronique de Jean de Hocsem*, ed. Godefroid Kurth, Commission Royale d'histoire: Recueil de textes pour servir à l'études de l'histoire de Belgique (Brussels, 1927); *Chronicon Cornelii Zanteliet;* Pirenne, *Histoire de Belgique*, II, pp. 31–35; *La chronique liégeoise de 1402*, ed. Eugène Bacha (Brussels, 1900); *Ly Myreur des histors, Chronique de Jean des Preis dit d'Outremeuse*, ed. Stanislas Bormas, Corps des chroniques liégeoises, 7 vols. (Brussels, 1880); Kurth, *La cité de Liège au moyen-âge*, 3 vols. (Brussels, 1909–1910), vols. I and II; and Charles, *La ville de Saint-Trond au Moyen Age*, pp. 293–317.

18. G. Villani, *Nuova Cronica*, II, pp. 88–90; *Anonymum S. Martialis Chronicon ab anno MCCVII ad ann. MCCCXX*, in *Chroniques de Saint-Martial de Limoges*, ed. H. Duplès-Agier, SHF, CLXVII (Paris, 1874), p. 141; and *Cronaca senese attribuita ad Agnolo di Tura*, p. 268.

19. Pirenne, *Histoire de Belgique*, II, p. 62.

20. See Marc Boone and Maarten Prak, "Rulers, Patricians and Burghers: The Great and the Little Traditions of Urban Revolt in the Low Countries," in *A Miracle Mirrored: The Dutch Republic in European Perspective*, ed. Karel Davids and Jan Lucassen (Cambridge, 1995), p. 104.

21. See TeBrake, *A Plague of Insurrection*, pp. 51, 93, and 98.

22. *Chronicon Comitum Flandrensium*, pp. 215–221. Conflicts between craftsmen in the cloth industry, especially between fullers and weavers, was not only common in the Low Countries; for fourteenth- and fifteenth-century Paris, See Geremek, *Les salariat*, pp. 18–20.

23. Ibid., p. 215.

24. See, W. P. Blockmans, "The Formation of a Political Union, 1300–1600," *History of the Low Countries*, ed. J. C. H. Blom and E. Lamberts, tr. J. C. Kennedy (New York, 1999), pp. 70–71; and Prevenier and Boone, "The 'City-State' Dream," pp. 87–88.

25. *Chronica Aegidii Li Muisis*, pp. 284–288.

26. The earliest revolt of *populares* against *nobiles* that I know of occurred in Milan in 909; another erupted there in 1000; see *Chronica Mediolani seu Manipulus Florum auctore Fratre Gualvaneo de la Flamma, Ordinis Praedicatorum*, Muratori, XI, cols. 620–622.

27. Salimbene de Adam, *Cronica*, II, p. 649.

28. *Pietri Cantinelli Chronicon* [*AA. 1228–1306*], ed. Francesco Torraca, RIS, XXVIII/2 (Città di Castello, 1902), p. 9.

29. *Annales Parmenses maiores, 1165–1355,* in MGH: SS, XVIII, p. 709.

30. For instance, on 25 July 1316 "the four professions" marched with their flags into the main square of Parma, charged the house of Lord Oppiçone de la Porta, and hanged him in the square. In the same year, they sacked the house of the de Sacca magnates to vindicate an offense the family had committed against a fellow ironmonger; *Chronica Parmensia a sec. XI. ad exitum sec. XIV.* ed. L. Barbieri Monumenta Historica (Parma, 1858), pp. 194 and 196.

31. *Cronaca . . . fratre Hyeronimo de Bursellis,* p. 34; and *Corpus Chronicorum Bononiensium* [Cronache A, B, Vill. Bolog.], II, pp. 241–242.

32. *Corpus Chronicorum Bononiensium* [Vill.], II, p. 271. The chronicler does not list these guilds.

33. *Frammento di Cronaca senese di anonimò (1313–1320),* in *Cronache senesi,* p. 171.

34. *Cronaca senese di Donato di Neri,* pp. 639–640; *Popular Protest,* doc. no. 83.

35. *Cronaca senese di Donato di Neri,* pp. 640–642.

36. *The Laboring Classes,* pp. 151–152. The vast majority of Florence's nonguild workers were involved in wool production, but the mixing of occupations was nonetheless revolutionary.

37. *Cronaca seconda d'anonimo,* in *Il Tumulto dei Ciompi,* pp. 110–111.

38. *Cronaca terza d'anonimo (1378–1382),* also known as "Cronichetta Strozziana," in *Il Tumulto dei Ciompi,* pp. 130–131.

39. On the votes and rights of election granted to the *popolo minuto* in its first constitutional act, 21 July 1378, see Provv. reg., no. 67, 1r–13v.

40. *Cronaca fiorentina di Marchionne di Coppo Stefani,* ed. Niccolò Rodolico, RIS, XXX/1 (Città di Castello, 1903) (hereafter, *Stefani*), p. 386.

41. *Cronaca seconda d'anonimo,* pp. 110–111; *Popular Protest,* doc. no. 122.

42. Ibid.

43. Ibid.

44. Screpanti, *L'Angelo delle liberazione,* pp. 33–34. On 26–27 October 1380 the Government of the Minor Guilds lowered still further the value of the florin against the common currency of the marketplace; *Stefani,* p. 382.

45. *Stefani,* p. 328.

46. *Diario d'anonimo fiorentino,* p. 436.

47. *Stefani,* pp. 397 (24 January 1382), 403 (15 February 1382), 407 (11 March 1382), 413–414 (April 1382), 415 (May 1382), 423 (November 1382), and 426 (July 1383). Also, see *Popular Protest,* doc. nos. 186–190.

48. *Alle bocche della piazza: Diario di anonimo fiorentino (1382–1401),* ed. Anthony Molho and Franek Sznura (Florence, 1986), p. xxiv–xxxv.

49. Ibid., pp. 25 (11 February), 33 (3 March), 34–35 (10 March), 39 (19 March), 43 (9 December), and 46 (14 June 1383).

50. ASF, Atti dell'Esecutore degli Ordinamenti di Giustizia (hereafter AEOG), no. 870, 37r–38v; no. 950, 17v–18v, 24r–27v, 29r–30v, 33r–34r, 35v–36v; Atti del Capitano del Popolo (hereafter ACP), 1198, 47v–49v; no. 1313, 26r–27r; AP, no. 3053, 102v–103v; no. 3147, 47v–48v; no. 3178, 37r, 153v–154v.

51. Rodolico, *Il Popolo Minuto,* doc. no. 14, pp. 102–104. This incident escapes the notice of Florence's principal chroniclers but is briefly described in a fragment of

an anonymous chronicle published by Domenico Maria Manni in the eighteenth century; see Rodolico, *I Ciompi: Una Pagina di storia del proletariato operaio,* 3rd ed. (Florence, 1980, first ed. 1945), pp. 46–47.

52. Ibid., docs. 26 and 27; Gene Brucker, *Florentine Politics and Society 1343–1378* (Princeton, 1962), pp. 194–195; and Screpanti, *L'Angelo della liberazione,* pp. 37–38.

53. Rodolico, *Il Popolo Minuto,* doc. 9, pp. 93–94.

54. *Stefani,* pp. 215–216. *Popular Protest,* doc. nos. 44–45.

55. *Storie Pistoresi [MCCC–MCCCXLVIII],* ed. Silvio Adrasto Barbi, RIS, XI/5 (Città di Castello, 1907), p. 196. Also see Chapter 5.

56. *Cronaca senese di Donato di Neri,* p. 577.

57. *Documenti . . . del Comune di Siena dal 1354 al 1369,* ed. Giuliano Luchaire (Lyon, 1906), no. 12, 1–9 December 1355: Statuto 31, Riforma delle Arti, pp. 43–46; and *Popular Protest,* doc. nos. 71–72.

58. *Cronaca senese di Donato di Neri,* p. 639; and *Popular Protest,* doc. no.71. I know of no contemporary sources from Perugia for this revolt. The principal chronicler of Perugia, the late-fifteenth-century Graziani *(Cronaca della città di Perugia dal 1309 al 1491 nota col nome di Diario del Graziani,* ed. A. Fabretti, in *Archivio Storico Italiano,* 16 (1850), pp. 215–216) presents this conflict as one between the *popolo* and the Raspanti, which exploded over whether the legate of Pope Gregory XI should come to Perugia. The people took up arms, cried "Long live the People," and burnt and sacked a number of houses. Maire Vigueur ("Comuni e signorie in Umbria, Marche e Lazio," pp. 543–544) argues that this was essentially a struggle between wool workers and their bosses but produces no documents to support his claim.

59. *Cronaca . . . Graziani,* p. 288.

60. *Le Croniche di Giovanni Sercambi,* I, pp. 204–205; and Archivio di Stato, Lucca, Sentenze e Bandi, no. 43, np, 1370.vii.20; see *Popular Protest,* doc. nos. 80–81.

61. *Journal de Nicolas de Baye, Greffier du Parlement de Paris 1400–1417,* ed. Alexandre Tuetey, SHF, CCXXII, 2 vols. (Paris, 1885), I, pp. 281–282.

62. *Extraits d'une chronique anonyme finissant en MCCCLXXXIII,* pp. 142–143. For six other descriptions of this revolt, see note 15.

63. *Les Grandes Chroniques de France,* VIII, pp. 250–252; *Ly Myreur des histors,* VI, pp. 104–105; and other chronicles.

64. See *Chronique latine de Guillaume de Nangis* (first continuator), I, pp. 387–388 (for 1311); and ibid., I, pp. 398–399.

65. *Richardi Scoti chronici continuatio,* pp. 107–108; and *Chronique des règnes de Jean II et de Charles V,* I, pp. 92–94.

66. *Journal d'un bourgeois de Paris de 1405 à 1449,* ed. Colette Beaune (Paris, 1990), p. 171.

67. Ibid., pp. 188–189.

68. Ibid., p. 223.

69. *Stefani,* p. 382. His figures seem mistaken. Because artisans controlled sixteen of the twenty-three guilds in the major councils, they were able to push through laws that favored them and lowered the value of the florin further (according to Stefani), from 3 lire 18 soldi (or 78 shillings) to 3 lire 12 soldi (72 shillings).

70. *Chronique de Richard Lescot*, pp. 60–61, says there were 15 rebels.

71. Ibid., pp. 60–61; and *Les Grandes Chroniques de France*, IX, pp. 237–238.

72. *Choix de pièces relatives au règne de Charles VI*, I, pp. 320–321.

73. *Journal de Nicolas de Baye*, I, p. 326.

74. I am not certain what professions these would have included in the Pisan context.

75. M. Villani, *Cronica*, II, pp. 398–399. Also see *Cronaca di Pisa di Ranieri Sardo*, p. 149.

76. *Cronaca senese di Donato di Neri*, p. 634. On such efforts in the early modern period, see Thompson, "Moral Economy"; and John Bohstedt, "The Myth of the Feminine Food Riot: Women as Proto-Citizens in English Community Politics, 1790–1810," in *Women and Politics in the Age of the Democratic Revolution*, ed. Harriet Applewhite and Darline Levy (Ann Arbor, 1990), pp. 21–60.

77. *Il Diario Romano di Antonio di Pietro dello Schiavo dal 19 ottobre 1404 al 25 settembre 1417*, ed. Francesco Isoldi, RIS, XXIV/5 (Città di Castello, 1912–1917), p. 22.

78. Ibid., p. 97.

79. *Chronique des Pays-Bas*, pp. 389–390; and Houtart, *Les Tournaisiens*, pp. 216–217 and 245–247; Houtart (pp. 294–295), also records a revolt of the guilds *(bannières)* on 2–3 June 1423. Also see Marc Boone, Hanno Brand, and Walter Prevenier, "Revendications salariales et conjuncture économique: les salaries de foulons à Gand et à Leyde au XVe siècle," in *Studia Historica Œconimica. Liber Amicorum Herman Van der Wee*, ed. Erik Aerts, Brigitte Henau, Paul Janssens, and Raymond Van Uytven (Leuven, 1993), pp. 63, 6, 68, 73–74, for strikes of fullers in Ghent from 1423 to 1427, which led to a general strike and higher wages. These revolts were also struggles for political rights.

80. Ibid., p. 391.

81. See for instance Rudé, *Paris and London in the Eighteenth Century: Studies in Popular Protest* (London, 1974), p. 23; Tilly, "How Protest Modernized in France, 1845–1855," in *The Dimension of Quantitative Research*, ed. W. Aydelotte, A. Bogue, and R. Fogel (Princeton, 1972), p. 199; Yves-Marie Bercé, *Revolt and Revolution in Early Modern Europe: An Essay on the History of Political Violence*, trans. Joseph Bergin (Manchester, 1987 [1980]), pp. 100–102; and Crone, *Pre-Industrial Societies*, p. 77: in describing the protests of townsmen, she concludes, "Bread riots in response to food shortages were by far the most common." By contrast, grain prices had fallen by time of the supposed cluster of revolts 1378–1382; for the Ciompi and grain prices, see Cohn, *The Laboring Classes*, pp. 137–139; for the English Peasants' Revolt of 1381, see Rigby, *English Society in the Later Middle Ages*, pp. 122–123. For the rarity of bread riots in England during the Middle Ages, see Buchanan Sharp, "The Food Riots of 1347 and the Medieval Moral Economy," in *Moral Economy and Popular Protest*, pp. 33–54. The earliest example thus far found in England was in 1347; others have put the date as late as 1527. Later, Tilly, in "Food Supply and Public Order in Modern Europe," *The Formation of National States in Western Europe*, ed. Tilly (Princeton, 1975), pp. 380–455, saw food riots increase in importance in Europe from 1500 to 1800.

82. Further, a document from the archives of Douai describes two women who attacked hoarders and incited a riot in 1322; for this document, see Chapter 6, note 5.

83. *Chronicon Girardi de Fracheto*, p. 25.

84. William C. Jordan, in *The Great Famine: Northern Europe in the Early Fourteenth Century* (Princeton, 1996), p. 165, claims that "grain riots did characterize urban life of the famine years," but produces little evidence for it: he cites a riot by the "mob" at Magdeburg in 1316 against the archbishop, who was determined to bring down prices and thereby to gain popular support against the merchants. Thus, the "mob," rather than being the "needy," as expected from the opening sentence of Jordan's paragraph, were the merchants. His second example, at Douai on 28 October 1322, came after the famine, when Jordan admits crops had become abundant (pp. 165–166). In a later article, "Famine and Popular Resistance: Northern Europe, 1315–1322" *Power, Violence and Mass Death in Pre-Modern and Modern Times*, ed. Joseph Canning, Hartmut Lehmann, and Jay Winter (Aldershot, 2004), p. 21, Jordan repeats that "bread riots and raids on granaries" took place during the famine of 1315–1317, but this time he mentions none of them; instead he concentrates on individual acts of "petty thievery" and piracy. According to Barbara A. Hanawalt, in *"Of Good and Ill Repute": Gender and Social Control in Medieval England* (Oxford, 1998), p. 11, criminal indictments rose steeply in England during the famine years, 1315–1317, but she does not point to any examples of collective violence or rioting.

85. *Cronaca senese attribuita ad Agnolo di Tura*, pp. 272 and 278.

86. G. Villani, *Nuova Cronica*, II, p. 221.

87. *Cronaca . . . Fratre Hyeronimo de Bursellis*, pp. 36–37.

88. G. Villani, *Nuova Cronica*, II, pp. 669–672; and *Cronaca senese di autore anomino*, pp. 139–140.

89. *Cronaca senese attribuita ad Agnolo di Tura*, p. 272.

90. G. Villani, *Nuova Cronica*, II, pp. 670–672.

91. *Cronaca senese attribuita ad Agnolo di Tura*, pp. 484–485.

92. Cohn, *Creating the Florentine State*, Chapter. 3.

93. Certainly famine conditions were behind the rage of commoners, as in a pitched battle between the *popolo* of Naples and the nobility, with commoners accusing nobles of forcing them to starve to death. But it was a struggle over constitutional rights and control of neighborhoods in Naples, not a grain riot; see below.

94. Rodolico, *Popolo Minuto:* Doc. 11, pp. 97–99.

95. Again, such use of grain for political purposes anticipates the moral economy and grain riots in England during the late eighteenth century; see Thompson, "Moral Economy;" John Bohstedt, "The Myth of the Feminine Food Riot;" and the case above from Siena in 1370.

96. *Stefani*, pp. 89–90. Also see the revolt of the *pedites* at Piacenza in 1090 described in Chapter 1.

97. Stella, *Annales Genuenses*, p. 91.

98. G. Villani, *Nuova Cronica*, III, pp. 350–353.

99. This was the price of grain in good years; in the famine of 1328–1329, it reached three times that amount. Unfortunately, the records of Domenico Lenzi's *Baidaiuolo* are missing for the 1340s and 1350s; see Richard Goldthwaite, "I prezzi del grano a Firenze dal XIV al XVI secolo," *Quaderni Storici*, 28 (1975): 15–36.

100. Rodolico, *Il Popolo Minuto*, doc. 9, pp. 93–94.
101. *Cronaca senese attribuita ad Agnolo di Tura*, p. 549.
102. M. Villani, *Cronica*, I, p. 388.
103. Ibid., I, pp. 392–393.
104. *Cronaca senese di Donato di Neri*, p. 634.
105. *Cronicon Siculum incertis authoris*, p. 27.
106. AOEG, no. 950, 7r–8v, 6.viii.1383, 11r–12r, 20.viii.1383, 15r–16v, 30.viii.1383, 17r–18v, 9.ix.1383, 25r–27v, 11.ix.1383, 29r–30v, 23.ix.1383, 33r–34v, 16.ix.1383.
107. Goldthwaite, "I prezzi del grano," p. 33 (Table B).
108. Gatari, *Cronaca carrarese*, I, p. 385.
109. Ibid., I, pp. 556–557.
110. Sanuto, *Vitæ Ducum Venetorum*, col. 815.
111. See especially Le Puy's revolt in chapter 4.
112. *Chronique des règnes de Jean II et de Charles V*, pp. 368–369, says nothing about problems of scarcity or destitution prompting this revolt, but the local chronicle, *La chronique romane*, p. 398, does. For an earlier revolt in Huy (1298), A. Joris, in *La ville de Huy au Moyen Âge: Des origines à la fin du XIVe siècle* (Paris, 1959), p. 317, maintains that food shortages were among the causes of a revolt of artisans in 1298. The revolt, however, did not voice any concerns about the price of grain; instead, it was a political revolt of artisans such as weavers, who had been excluded from the city council.
113. *Alle bocche della piazza*: "Se volete regiere e mantenere, tenete il popolo afamati di pane; e per questo l'aveano in odio" (p. 90). Other contemporaries, such as Jean Froissart, saw the source of revolutionary anger as the rising wealth of commoners and the gap between their expectations and social or political realities, rather than poverty. Also, see Rigby, *English Society in the Later Middle Ages*, pp. 111 and 124; Fryde, *The Great Revolt of 1381*, p. 32; and Hatcher, "England in the Aftermath of the Black Death," esp. pp. 32–35.
114. Kurth, *La cité de Liège*, II, pp. 241–242. Vercauteren, *Luttes sociales à Liège*, concludes much the same. Recently, Marc Boone ("Urban Space," p. 639) has returned to politics as the critical key for understanding late medieval popular revolt in the Low Countries, as stressed earlier by Pirenne's teacher, Kurth. Similar notes can be heard in other places and in other historical periods; for example, in nineteenth-century Barcelona, when "political oppression, not economic exploitation, would galvanize action among disparate groups of people living in the same place" (Temma Kaplan, *Red City, Blue Period: Social Movements in Picasso's Barcelona* [Berkeley, 1992], p. 24).

4. Varieties of Revolt

1. *Cronaca senese attribuita ad Agnolo di Tura*, p. 392; and G. Villani, *Nuova Cronica*, II, p. 342. For another vision of typologies of revolt, see Graus, *Pest-Geissler-Judenmorde*, pp. 510–528.

2. G. Villani, *Nuova Cronica*, II, p. 359.

3. *The Towns of Italy in the Later Middle Ages*, ed. Trevor Dean, Manchester Medieval Sources Series (Manchester, 2000), p. 168.

4. Rycarrdi de Sancto Germano Notarii, *Chronica*, ed. C. A. Garufi, RIS, VII/2 (Bologna, 1936–1938), pp. 193–194.

5. G. Villani, *Nuova Cronica*, II, pp. 669–670.

6. M. Villani, *Cronica*, I, pp. 365–366.

7. *Cronaca . . . Minerbetti*, pp. 334–335.

8. See the revolt of the *popolo* in 1404, immediately after the death of Pope Boniface IX, when the cardinals, "as was their custom," began grabbing everything they could; *Cronaca . . . Minerbetti*, p. 321.

9. *Cronicon Siculum incertis authoris*, p. 27.

10. These are found in *Cronaca di Niccolò di Borbona* and *Cronaca aquilana rimata di Buccio di Ranallo*.

11. *Ex Primati chronicis per Iohannem de Vignay translatis*, ed. H. Brosien, in MGH: SS, XXVI, pp. 641–642; and *Chronique de Primat, traduite par Jean du Vignay*, RGFS, XXIII, pp. 21–23.

12. *Chronique latine de Guillaume de Nangis*, I, p. 224.

13. *Anonymum S. Martialis Chronicon 1235–1377* and *Anonymum S. Martialis Chronicon 1274–1315*, in *Chroniques de Saint-Martial de Limoges*, pp. 164–165, and 172.

14. *Chronicon Girardi de Fracheto*, p. 10; *Chronique latine de Guillaume de Nangis*, pp. 278–279; *Les Grandes Chroniques de France*, VIII, pp. 146–147; and Eugène Tailliar, *Chroniques de Douai*, 3 vols. (Douai, 1875–1877), I, p. 249.

15. *Chronica monasterii Sancti Bertini auctore Iohanne Longo de Ipra*, ed. O. Holder-Egger, in MGH: SS, XXV (1880), pp. 863–864. For the extensive historiography on this revolt and a new interpretation of it, see Boogaart, "Reflections on the Moorlemaye."

16. *Chronique latine de Guillaume de Nangis* (first continuation), I, pp. 419–421.

17. These are described in *La chronique de Jean de Hocsem* and *Chronicon Cornelii Zanteliet*.

18. Guenée, *States and Rulers in Later Medieval Europe*, trans. Juliet Vale (Oxford, 1985 [Paris, 1971]), pp. 194–195. Fourquin (*The Anatomy of Popular Rebellion*, p. 23) has made similar claims.

19. *Polyhistoria Fratris Bartholomaei Ferrariensi*, col. 785.

20. Ibid., cols. 784–785. On her reputation as a whore, see Dominici de Gravina notarii, *Chronicon de rebus in Apulia gestis [AA. 1333–1350]*, ed. Albano Sorbelli, RIS, XII/3 (Città di Castello, 1903–1909), pp. 14–18. Also, on Joanna (or Giovanna) I, see Nino Valeri, *L'Italia nell'età dei principati dal 1343 al 1516*, Storia d'Italia, vol. IV, 2nd ed. (Milan, 1969), pp. 28–34 and 616–617, who relies on Émile Léonard, *Histoire de Jeanne Ire reine de Naples, comtesse de Provence (1343–1382)*, 3 vols. (Paris and Monaco, 1932–1936).

21. *Cronicon Siculum incertis authoris*, p. 11.

22. Ibid., p. 11. This charter (Reg. 1346 C, p. 353 f.295, 302t.) transcribed by de Blasiis in 1887 would have been destroyed in 1943.

23. Ibid., p. 11.

24. For 1378, ibid., p. 36; and later, *Diaria Neapolitana ab anno MCCLXVI usque ad annum MCCCCLXXVIII . . . auctore anonymo*, Muratori, XXI, cols. 1039 (1379), 1041 (1384), and 1053 (1386).

25. *La chronique romane*, p. 343; and NHGL, X, cols. 645–646.

26. *Chronicon Girardi de Fracheto*, p. 34.

27. Artonne, *Le mouvement de 1314*; and Brown, "Reform and Resistance."

28. *Richardi Scoti chronici continuatio*, pp. 107–109.

29. *Chronique des règnes de Jean II et de Charles V*, pp. 147–153; *Chronographia Regum Francorum*, II, p. 265; *Chronique normande du XIVᵉ siècle*, p. 123; *Récits d'un bourgeois de Valenciennes (XIVᵉ siècle)*, ed. M. le baron Kervyn de Lettenhove (Louvain, 1877), p. 249.

30. See for instance *Chronographia Regum Francorum*, II, p. 270.

31. *Chronique des quatre premiers Valois*, p. 77; and Adolphe Chéruel, *Histoire de Rouen pendant l'époque communale 1150–1382*, 2 vols. (Rouen, 1843–1844), I, p. 203.

32. See letters of remission in Luce, *Histoire de la Jacquerie*; Jonathan Sumption, *The Hundred Years War*, II: *Trial by Fire* (London, 1999), pp. 329–331; Secousse, ed., *Recueil de pièces*, I, pp. 97–99; Denifle, *La Guerre de Cents Ans*, II, pp. 213–214; and numerous chroniclers.

33. *Chronique des Pays-Bas*, pp. 227–229.

34. *La chronique romane*, p. 376.

35. *Chronique de Jean II et de Charles V*, II, pp. 368–369; *La chronique romane*, p. 398; Jacme Mascaro, *Le "Libre de Memorias,"* ed. Charles Barbier, in *Revue des langues romanes*, 4th ser., 34 (1890): 36–100, p. 72, and for a brief account, *Chronique des quatre premiers Valois*, pp. 281–282.

36. NHGL, X, cols. 1632–1639.

37. *Chronique de Jean II et de Charles V*, III, p. 8; for Béziers, see *Chronique des quatre premiers Valois*, p. 297. Also see Borzeix et al., *Révoltes populaires en Occitanie*, pp. 55–62.

38. *Chronique du religieux de Saint-Denys*, I, pp. 150–157; and *Popular Protest*, doc. no. 132.

39. Charles M. Radding, "The Estates of Normandy and the Revolts in the Towns at the Beginning of the Reign of Charles VI," *Speculum* 47 (1972), pp. 79–80.

40. *Chronique du religieux de Saint-Denys*, I, pp. 53–56; and *Popular Protest*, doc. no. 134.

41. Ibid., I, pp. 128–143. For a similar interpretation of anti-Semitic violence as an attack on the king during the Pastoureaux of 1320, see Nirenberg, *Communities of Violence*, Ch. 2.

42. *Chronique du religieux de Saint-Denys*, I, pp. 128–143; and *Popular Protest*, doc. no. 136.

43. *Chronique normande de Pierre Cochon notaire apostolique à Rouen*, ed. Charles de Robillard de Beaurepaire (Rouen, 1870), pp. 162–166. Also see *Chronique des quatre premiers Valois*, pp. 297–301; and *Popular Protest*, doc. nos. 144–145.

44. For the insurgents' imposed charter, which still survives, see Chéruel, *Histoire de Rouen*, II, pp. 544–546 (Archive départementale, 1ᵉʳ cart. de la Harelle); and *Popular Protest*, doc. no. 153.

45. The editor Bellaguet calls these workers *"compagnons des metiers* (journeymen)"; the Latin is "et qui publicis officinis mechanicis inserviebant artibus;" also *Popular Protest,* doc. no. 144.

46. *Chronique du religieux de Saint-Denys,* I, pp. 128–143; *Histoire de Charles VI, Roy de France par Jean Juvenal des Ursins,* in *Pathéon littéraire: Choix chroniques et mémoires sur l'histoire de France, XIV* siècle, ed. J. A. C. Buchon (Paris, 1838), pp. 332–333, repeats the same story. Some have maintained that this mocked merchant simply had the family name of le-Gras; see H. Bouteiller, *Histoire de Rouen des milices et gardes bourgeoises* (Rouen, 1858), p. 31.

47. *Chronique du religieux de Saint-Denys,* III, pp. 38–39.

48. Ibid., IV, pp. 448–449.

49. Ibid., V, pp. 295–299.

50. Ibid., V, pp. 299–301.

51. Ibid., VI, pp. 92–97; *La chronique d'Enguerran de Monstrelet (1400–1444),* ed. L. Douët-D'Arcq, 6 vols., SHF, IX (Paris, 1857–1860), III, p. 247; *Chronique de Jean le Févre, Seigneur de Saint-Remy,* ed. François Morand, 2 vols., SHF, CXLVIII (Paris, 1876–1881), pp. 293–295; *Chroniques de Perceval de Cagny,* ed. H. Moranvillé, SHF, CCCVII (Paris, 1902), pp. 107–109.

52. *La chronique d'Enguerran de Monstrelet,* III, pp. 183–185.

53. *Chroniques de Perceval de Cagny,* pp. 112–113; and *Chronique du religieux de Saint-Denys,* VI, pp. 228–234.

54. *Chronique du religieux de Saint-Denys,* VI, pp. 442–445.

55. Salimbene de Adam, *Cronica,* I, p. 75.

56. Niccola della Tuccia, *Cronache di Viterbo e di altre città,* p. 50.

57. *Storie Pistoresi,* p. 52.

58. *Annali genovesi di Caffaro e suoi continuatori,* III, p. 173.

59. Rycarrdi de Sancto Germano Notarii, *Chronica,* p. 182.

60. *Cortusiii Patavini Duo sive Gulielmi et Alberigeti Cortusiorum, Historia de Novitabtibus Paduae et Lombardiae ab an. MCCLVI usque MCCLXIV,* Muratori, XII, col. 946; *Discorso Historico con molti accidenti occorsi in Orvieto et in altre parti principando dal 1342 fino al passato 1368,* in *Ephemerides Urbevetanae,* ed. Luigi Fumi, RIS, XV/5 (Città di Castello, 1903–1920), I, p. 78; Corio, *Storia di Milano,* II, p. 195; *Cronaca senese di Donato di Neri,* p. 579.

61. *Marcha di Marco Battagli da Rimini [1212–1354],* ed. Aldo Francesco Massèra, RIS, XVI/3 (Città di Castello, 1912), pp. 32 and 46.

62. *Annales Forolivienses ab origine usque ad annum MCCCCLXXIII,* ed. Giuseppe Mazzatinti, RIS, XXII/2 (Città di Castello, 1903), p. 69.

63. *Chronicon Placentinum ab anno CCXXII usque ad annum MCCCCII auctore Johanne de Mussis Cive Placentino,* Muratori, XVI (Milan, 1730), cols. 520–521.

64. *Annales Mediolanenses Anonymi autoris,* Muratori, RIS, XVI, col. 759.

65. *Continazione del codice Marciano classe X, lat. no. 69,* ed. Antonio Bonardi, in *Rolandini Patavini Cronica in factis et circa facta Marchie Trivixane,* RIS, VIII/1 (Città di Castello, 1905–1908), p. 376.

66. *Diario d'anonimo fiorentino,* pp. 305–307.

67. *Cronaca malatestiana,* p. 38.

68. *Diario d'anonimo fiorentino,* p. 307: "E tutti quanti libertà gridaro" and "Gridando libertà, con buono ischermo." Also see Vancini, *La rivolta dei Bolognesi;* Richard Trexler, *The Spiritual Power: Republican Florence under the Interdict* (Leiden, 1974).

69. See Cohn, *Creating the Florentine State,* p. 127; and Alison Brown, "The Language of Empire," in *Florentine Tuscany: Structures and Practices of Power,* ed. William J. Connell and Andrea Zorzi (Cambridge, 2000), pp. 32–47.

70. Cohn, *Creating the Florentine State,* p. 174

71. *Corpus Chronicorum Bononiensium,* III, pp. 476–479; and *Cronaca . . . Fratre Hyeronimo de Bursellis,* p. 68.

72. On the Nine and its fall, see William Bowsky, *A Medieval Italian Commune: Siena under the Nine, 1287–1355* (Berkeley, 1981).

73. *Cronaca senese di autore anomino,* p. 151; and *Cronaca senese di Donato di Neri,* pp. 581–582 and 585.

74. *Cronaca senese attribuita ad Agnolo di Tura,* pp. 561 and 563; *Cronaca senese di Donato di Neri,* p. 570.

75. *Cronaca senese di autore anomino,* p. 160; *Cronaca senese di Donato di Neri,* p. 670.

76. Sanuto, *Vitæ Ducum Venetorum,* col. 643.

77. Ibid., col. 611; *Cronica Jadretina* cited in Andrea Danduli, *Chronica per extensium descripta,* p. x; Andreas Naugerii, patritius Veneti, *Historia Veneta ab origine urbis usque ad annum MCDXCVIII,* Muratori, XXIII, col. 1032; *Polyhistoria Fratris Bartholomaei Ferrariensi,* col. 781.

78. Sanuto, *Vitæ Ducum Venetorum,* cols. 669–671.

79. *Majus Chronicon Lemovicense a Petro Coral et aliis conscriptum,* RGFS, XXI, p. 775.

80. *Chronico ms. ecclesiae Rotomagensi,* in Giry, *Les Établissements de Rouen,* I, p. 41.

81. *Chronique des règnes de Jean II et de Charles V,* I, p. 62.

82. *E Chronico Alberici monachi Trium Fontium,* RGFS, XXI, p. 599.

83. *Extraits des chroniques de Saint-Denis,* in ibid., pp. 117–118; also *Histoire de Saint Louis par Jean sire de Joinville,* ed. N. de Wailly, SHF, CXLIV (Paris, 1868), pp. 249–252. On Boileau and his famous codification of the statutes of Parisian trades, see Geremek, *Les salariat,* pp. 27–28.

84. *Chronique de Guillaume Bardin,* in NHGL, X, pp. 26–29.

85. Tailliar, *Chroniques de Douai,* I, p. 274; Espinas, *La vie urbaine de Douai,* II, pp. 1111–1117. Perhaps because of the absence of a chronicle tradition at Douai, little notice has been taken of its "epoque révolutionnaire" between 1296 and 1311, when butchers and other workers threatened the échevins' lives and the stability of bourgeois government in 1302, 1303, 1304, 1305, 1306, and 1311; ibid., I, pp. 229–269, and IV, doc. nos. 877–881. For other revolts in Tournai in 1279–1281, Damme in 1280, Saint-Omer in 1280–1283, as well as the more famous *Moerlemaye* of Bruges in 1280–1281, see Dumolyn and Haemers, "Patterns of Urban Rebellion"; for Huy in 1299 and Liège and Fossa (in the Liégeois) in 1302, *Chronicon Cornelii Zanteliet,* cols. 140 and 145–146; for Valenciennes in 1302, *Croniques de Franche, d'Engleterre, de Flandres, de Lile et espécialment de Tournay,* p. 14; and for Damme in 1303, *Chronique latine de Guillaume de Nangis,* I, p. 317.

86. *Chronica Aegidii Li Muisis,* p. 170.

87. Ibid., pp. 173–175.

88. *Chronique latine de Guillaume de Nangis,* I, p. 282.

89. *Corpus Chronicorum Bononiensium,* II, pp. 234; Matteo Griffoni, *Memoriale Historicum de rebus Bononiensium,* ed. Lodovico Frati and Sorbelli, RIS, XVIII/2 (Città di Castello), p. 25; and *Popular Protest,* doc. no. 27.

90. M. Villani, *Cronica,* I, pp. 390–392.

91. Ibid., I, p. 388.

92. *Chronique du religieux de Saint-Denys,* VI, pp. 248–249 and 262–263.

93. For instance, the sixty heretics Fra Giovanni had burnt at the stake in Padua on 21 July 1233 were "men and women;" Gerardi Maurisii, *Cronica Dominorum Ecelini et Alberici fratrum de Romano (AA. 1183–1237),* ed. Giovanni Soranzo, RIS, VIII/4 (Città Castello, 1913–1914), p. 33; and the "more than 3,000" who followed a man in the countryside of Siena, preaching that he was an apostle of Christ in 1315, included both men and women; *Cronaca senese attribuita ad Agnolo di Tura,* p. 350.

94. *Corpus Chronicorum Bononiensium,* II, pp. 364 and 366.

95. *Excerpta e memoriali Historiarum auctore Johanne Parisiensi, Sancti Victoris Parisiensis canonico regulari,* RGFS, XXI, p. 642.

96. See Chapter 1.

97. Benedict "XIII" was the opposition pope during the papacy of Gregory XII (1406–1415).

98. *Journal de Nicolas de Baye,* I, pp. 194–196. According to Wolff *(Histoire de Toulouse,* pp. 169–170), this revolt occurred at the beginning of 1406.

99. *Journal de Nicolas de Baye,* I, pp. 110–114, is the only source that explains the origins of this attack.

100. *La chronique d'Enguerran de Monstrelet,* I, pp. 73–75; the more meticulous account of *Chronique du religieux de Saint-Denys,* III, pp. 184–196; and *Popular Protest,* doc. no. 178. On this gallery see *Paris, 1400: Les arts sous Charles VI: Paris, Musée du Louvre, 22 mars, 12 juillet 2004* (Paris, 2004), pp. 19 and 88. I wish to thank Mary Whiteley for this reference.

101. *Cronicon Siculum incertis authoris,* p. 8.

102. *Chronica Parmensia,* pp. 270–275.

103. G. Villani, *Nuova Cronica,* II, pp. 397–400.

104. *Cronaca . . . Graziani,* p. 288.

105. Leonardo Bruni, *Rerum suo tempore gestorum commentarius [AA. 1378–1440],* ed. Carmine di Pierro, RIS, XIX/3 (Città di Castello, 1914–1926), p. 445–446; and Giovanni Cavalcanti, *Istorie fiorentine* (Florence, 1838), I, pp. 66–67. Braccio dal Montone, signore of Perugia and Assisi, led the Bolognese against the pope.

106. *Chronique des Pays-Bas,* p. 209; and *Popular Protest,* doc. no. 60. For the biting satire of children's ditties against the Hussites' enemies, see Thomas A. Fudge, *The Magnificent Ride: The First Reformation in Hussite Bohemia* (Aldershot, 1998), p. 207.

107. No doubt this was an exaggeration; he also claimed that the plague of that year killed 60,000 *(Chronique de Jean le Févre,* p. 337).

108. Ibid., I, pp. 331–332.

109. *Alle bocche della piazza*, p. 18. For examples of adolescent violence that occasionally spilled into social protest against the church in late medieval France, see Jacques Rossiaud, "Fraternités de jeunesse et niveux de culture dans les villes du Sud-Est à la fin du Moyen Âge," *Cahiers d'histoire*, 21 (1976): 85–86. His examples, however, come after our period, during the second half of the fifteenth and early sixteenth centuries.

110. Bercé, *Revolt and revolution*, p. 106.

111. *Annales Gandenses*, p. 95.

112. *Cronaca senese attribuita ad Agnolo di Tura*, p. 549.

113. Cohn, *Creating the Florentine State*, pp. 142–143 and 182–183. Rigby *(English Society in the Later Middle Ages*, p. 122) sees much the same for the Peasants' Revolt of 1381: "Far from being composed of poor, rootless, marginal social elements, the revolt included many wealthier peasants, the kind of men chosen to serve as ale-tasters, rent-collectors, bailiffs and constables."

114. Andrae Danduli, *Chronicon*, p. 374; and *Venetiarum Historia vulgo Petro Iustiniano Iustiniani*, p. 176.

115. G. Villani, *Nuova Cronica*, III, pp. 350–353; also, see Rodolico, *Il Popolo Minuto*, Doc. 9, pp. 93–94.

116. NHGL, X, cols. 887–891.

117. Ibid., X, cols. 1609–1612. Also, see the above-mentioned revolt in Siena during the scarcity of 1329–1330; it was not, however, a tax revolt.

118. See note 27.

119. *Extraits des chroniques de Saint-Denis*, pp. 117–118.

120. *Chronique du religieux de Saint-Denys*, I, pp. 22–23.

121. M. Villani, *Cronica*, I, p. 702.

122. *Cronaca del Conte Francesco*, p. 240.

123. Stella, *Annales Genuenses*, pp. 184–185.

124. *Cronaca di Ser Guerriero da Gubbio*, p. 18.

125. Mirot, *Les insurrections urbaines*, pp. 112–113.

126. NHGL, X, cols. 1609–1612. Furthermore, according to Georges Lecarpentier ("La Harelle, révolte rouennaise de 1382," *Le Moyen Âge*, 2nd series, VII [1903], p. 92), Rouen "revolted not because of taxes but because they were illegal." Further, letters of remission issued to weavers and cobblers after the anti-Semitic riots in Gerona, 1391, report similar rebel demands to reduce taxes and have them assessed "according to 'the faculties' of the citizens" (Wolff, "The 1391 Pogrom in Spain: Social Crisis or Not?" *Past & Present* 50 (1971), p. 15).

127. The Cathar movement in Languedoc of the late twelfth and early thirteenth centuries appears to have cut across class lines from peasants to the highest echelons of the local aristocracy, including the counts of Toulouse. Nonetheless, they challenged the authority of the church and the crown; see Barber, *The Cathars: Dualist Heretics in Languedoc in the High Middle Ages* (Harlow, 2000), pp. 65–70.

128. NHGL, X, cols. 645–646.

129. *Chronicon Girardi de Fracheto*, p. 22.

130. *Fragmenta Libelli de ordine Praedicatorum auctore Bernardo Guidonis*, RGFS, XXI, p. 747.

131. *Chronique de Guillaume Bardin*, p. 25.

132. See for instance Gino Franceschini, "La Lotta contro il Barbarossa," in *Storia di Milano*, IV: *Dalle lotte contro il Barbarossa al primo signore (1152–1310)*, ed. Giovanni Treccani degli Alfieri (Milan, 1954), pp. 163–164.

133. *Chronique tirée d'un ancien manuscrit de l'abbaye de Berdouea, au diocèse d'Auch*, in NHGL, VIII, p. 214. This was from a population of 415. Some historians have denied that the massacre took place; see Barber, *The Cathars*, pp. 156–158. The historiography on the Cathars and Albigensians is immense; for a recent survey, see ibid., pp. 244–253.

134. At least thirteen chroniclers in my sample reported the 1251 movement, among them, *Chronique latine de Guillaume de Nangis*, I, pp. 207–208; and *Chronique anonyme des rois de France finissant en MCCLXXXVI*, RGFS, XXI, p. 83. Also, thirteen reported the 1320 crusade.

135. See for instance *Chronique latine de Guillaume de Nangis*, I, pp. 208 and 435; and II, pp. 25–28.

136. A number of chroniclers reported this heretical movement and its persecution, even ones far removed, such as the Liégeoise *Ly Myreur des histors*, VI, pp. 109–110. *Historia Fratris Dulcini Heresiarche di Anonimo Sincrono*, ed. Arnaldo Segarizzi, RIS, IX/5 (Città di Castello, 1907) was closest to the events. Also, see *Popular Protest*, doc. nos. 31–32; and Andrew P. Roach, *The Devil's World: Heresy and Society 1100–1300* (Harlow, 2005), pp. 194–198.

137. *Chronique latine de Guillaume de Nangis*, I, p. 76.

138. Maurisii, *Cronica Dominorum Ecelini*, p. 33.

139. *Annales Urbevetani: Cronica antique*, in *Ephemerides Urbevetanae*, p. 150; on heresy in Orvieto, see Carol Lansing, *Power and Purity: Cathar Heresy in Medieval Italy* (Oxford, 1998).

140. *Cronaca senese attribuita ad Agnolo di Tura*, p. 293.

141. G. Villani, *Nuova Cronica*, II, p. 354.

142. General surveys of medieval heresy, such as Gordon Leff, *Heresy in the Later Middle Ages: The Relation of Heterodoxy to Dissent, c. 1250–c.1450* (Manchester, 1967), or works on John XXII and his crusade against Ludwig of Bavaria and the Italian Ghibellines, such as Guillaume Mollat, *The Popes at Avignon 1305–1378*, trans. from 9th ed. (London, 1949), pp. 9–25 and 76–110, make no mention of the Recanati episode. Malcolm Lambert, *Medieval Heresy: Popular Movements from Bogomil to Hus*, 3rd ed. (Oxford, 2002), p. 198, alludes only to the "Ghibellines of Umbria."

143. He was the pope's military captain in the region, who would conquer various Ghibelline cities in the region over the next couple of years.

144. G. Villani, *Nuova Cronica*, II, p. 343; and *Cronaca senese attribuita ad Agnolo di Tura*, p. 392. The details of the mock funeral come from a parchment scroll of the proceedings against Federico held in the Vatican. The parchment is 10 meters long; see F. Bock, "I processi di Giovanni XXII contro i Ghebellini delle Marche,"

in *Bullettino dell'Istituto Storico per il Medio Evo,* 57 (1941): 19–70; L. Fumi, "Eretici e ribelli nell'Umbria dal 1320 al 1330," *Bollettino della R. deputazione di storia patria per l'Umbria,* III (1897): 34–95, esp. doc. 28; Antonio de Santis, *Ascoli nel Trecento,* 2 vols. (Rimini, 1984), I, pp. 28–32 and 232; and Natalucci, "Lotte di parte e manifestazioni ereticali nella Marca," pp. 125–144.

145. G. Villani, *Nuova Cronica,* II, p. 343.

146. *La chronique d'Enguerran de Monstrelet,* IV, p. 86; *Chronique de Jean de Stavelot,* ed. A. Borgnet. Commission royale d'histoire de Belgique (Brussels, 1861), p. 187.

147. On the change in strategy of church and state to combat heresy, see Paul Ormerod and Andrew Roach, "The Medieval Inquisition: Scale-free Networks and the Suppression of Heresy" *Physica A* 339 (2004): 645–652. They argue that the change from mass burning to a surgical killing of key figures took place before the fourteenth century, but as the previous examples show, such attempts to stamp out all heretics by indiscriminant mass burning persisted through the 1320s and 1330s. For the spread of Hussite beliefs in Poitou slightly later and mostly in the aristocracy, see Robert Favreau, "La Praguerie en Poitou," *Bibliothèque de l'École des chartes* 129 (1971): 277–301.

148. *La chronique d'Enguerran de Monstrelet,* IV, p. 87. The appearance of Hussites in northern France is not so far-fetched as it might appear. In 1420 Gilles Meursault traveled to Prague. He returned to his native city of Tournai in 1423, where he began converting townsmen to the Hussite cause. His arrest prompted rioting in the city, but eventually he was burned at the stake; see Houtart, *Les Tournaisiens,* p. 184; and Fudge, *The Magnificent Ride,* p. 260.

149. In addition to numerous chronicles, see Barber, "Lepers, Jews and Moslems."

150. See Chapter 9, note 68.

151. *Chronicon Neritinum,* Muratori, XXIV, col. 901.

152. Among many chronicles, see *Due cronache del Vespro in volgare siciliano del secolo XIII,* ed. Enrico Sicardi, RIS, XXXIV/1 (Bologna, 1935), pp. 19–20; and *Die Chronik des Saba Malaspina,* pp. 287–290.

153. Henri Bresc, "1282: Classes sociales et révolution nationale," in *La società mediterranea all'epoca del Vespro, XI Congresso di storia della corona d'Aragona, Palermo-Trapani-Erice 25–30 aprile 1982,* 4 vols. (Palermo, 1983), II, pp. 241–258. Also, for the broader social, economic, political, and cultural consequences of the Vespers, see Bresc, *Un monde méditerranéen: Economie et société en Sicile 1300–1450,* École française de Rome, 2 vols. (Rome, 1986), I, pp. 4–5, II, 643–648, 709–719, 758–762, 780, 799, and 917.

154. *Die Chronik des Saba Malaspina,* p. 287.

155. *Due cronache del Vespro in volgare siciliano,* pp. 19–20.

156. Capitoli del "Tesoro" di Brunetto Latini sui fatti del "Vespero," in *Due cronache del Vespro,* p. 116.

157. *Cronaca malatestiana,* pp. 42–43. By other accounts, butchers began the revolt against the Bretons.

158. Ibid., p. 43. Many other chroniclers tell much the same story. For more on this massacre, see Chapter 6.

159. In 1353 Scarlano had been the scene of an uprising against Viterbo's ruling prefect. That uprising failed and many heads rolled, including members of the church; see Niccola della Tuccia, *Cronache di Viterbo*, p. 34.

160. For various accounts, see *Le croniche di Viterbo scritte da Frate Francesco d'Andrea*, in *Archivio di R. società Romana di storia patria*, XXIV (1901), pp. 235–237; Niccola della Tuccia, *Cronache di Viterbo*, p. 35; *Cronaca senese di Donato di Neri*, p. 616; *Cronaca di Ser Guerriero da Gubbio*, p. 16; *La chronique romane*, pp. 380–381; *Chronique des règnes de Jean II et de Charles V*, II, p. 32; *Istoria della città di Viterbo di Feliciano Bussi* (Rome, 1742), pp. 204–205; and Pellini, *Dell'Historia di Perugia*, I, p. 1031.

161. *Chronique latine de Guillaume de Nangis*, I, pp. 288–289.

162. *Chronica Aegidii Li Muisis*, pp. 269–270.'

163. G. Villani, *Nuova Cronica*, II, pp. 88–90.

164. AP, no. 334, 40r–v.

165. The 1378 revolt received greater attention from chronicles than any other case of crowds pressuring cardinals during or after a papal election.

166. *Journal de Nicolas de Baye*, I, pp. 194–196.

167. *Chronique des quatre premiers Valois*, p. 311.

168. Ibid., p. 321.

169. *Annales Parmenses maiores, 1165–1355*, p. 709.

170. *Chronicon Regiense: La Cronaca di Pietro della Gazzata*, p. 216.

171. NHGL, X, cols. 1858–1861.

172. Sanuto, *Vitæ Ducum Venetorum*, col. 691.

173. I imagine nunneries as well, but no examples appear in my samples.

174. Followers of Stephen of Muret founded this order in the early twelfth century; it received papal approbation in 1189; see Lester Little, *Religious Poverty and the Profit Economy in Medieval Europe* (London, 1978), pp. 79–81.

175. *Anonymum S. Martialis Chronicon 1274–1315*, p. 183.

176. Cited in *The Black Death*, ed. Rosemary Horrox, Manchester Medieval Sources Series (Manchester, 1994), p. 128.

177. Stella, *Annales Genuenses*, pp. 128–129; and Epstein, *Genoa and the Genoese*, p. 203.

5. Leaders

1. Tilly, "How Protest Modernized in France, 1845–1855," p. 199. He later developed other categories for social conflict, such as "competitive," "reactive," and "proactive action." The third of these was similar to his earlier associational forms in that it was characterized by strike action, which came about only by the mid-nineteenth century; see "Hauptformen kollektiver Aktion in Westeuropa, 1500–1975," in *Geschichte und Gesellschaft* (1975): Heft 2: *Sozialer Protest*, ed. Richard Tilly (Göttingen, 1977): 154–163.

2. Rudé, *Paris and London in the Eighteenth Century*, p. 23. Later, Tilly, in "Food Supply and Public Order in Modern Europe," saw the food riot increase in Europe between 1500 and 1800, as "states intervened in the production and distribution of food with increasing directness and energy" (p. 443). Still, he characterized

the food riot as "old fashioned" (p. 392), a conflict that "has permeated two thousand years of European history" (p. 395). Like E. P. Thompson ("The Moral Economy of the English Crowd"), Tilly did not regard the grain riot as spontaneous or "in any simple sense responses to hunger" (p. 393) but instead as collective and conscious political action. Also see Louise A. Tilly, "The Food Riot as a Form of Political Conflict in France," *Journal of Interdisciplinary History* 2 (1971): 23–57, who saw the grain riot increasing in France after 1750 with the rise of a "laissez-faire" model of the state.

3. William Reddy, "The Textile Trades and the Language of the Crowd at Rouen, 1752–1871," *Past & Present,* 74 (1977): 62–89. In passing, Blickle ("Peasant Revolts in the German Empire," p. 237) commented that Tilly's model of "reactive revolts" for the early modern period and "proactive" for the industrial period did not consider late-fifteenth- and early-sixteenth century peasant revolts in Germany, which were also "pro-active."

4. Gordon, "Women, Work, and Collective Action: Dundee Jute Workers 1870–1906," *Journal of Social History,* 21 (1987): 27–47; Kaplan, *Red City, Blue Period;* Kaplan, "Female Consciousness and Collective Action: The Case of Barcelona, 1910–1918," *Signs,* 7 (1982): 545–566.

5. Bohstedt, "The Myth of the Feminine Food Riot." Somewhat in opposition to Bohstedt's generalizations but also to older models of "moral economy," see Pamela Beth Radcliff, "Women's Politics: Consumer Riots in Twentieth-Century Spain" in *Constructing Spanish Womanhood: Female Identity in Modern Spain,* ed. Victoria Lorée Enders and Radcliff (Albany, 1999), pp. 301–323. I wish to thank Lynn Abrams for these references.

6. *The Laboring Classes in Renaissance Florence,* pp. 129–154.

7. See for instance David Sabean, "The Communal Basis of Pre-1800 Peasant Uprisings in Western Europe," *Comparative Politics* 8 (1976): 355–364.

8. Bercé, *Revolt and Revolution in Early Modern Europe,* pp. 100–102. Also, see Crone, *Pre-Industrial Societies,* p. 75.

9. Bercé, *Revolt and Revolution in Early Modern Europe,* p. 107. Also see his *History of Peasant Revolts: The Social Origins of Rebellion in Early Modern France,* trans. Amanda Whitmore (Cambridge, 1990), pp. 174–175, where he explains the predominance of women in French early modern bread riots as "biological" in nature.

10. Bercé, *Revolt and Revolution in Early Modern Europe,* p. 64; and Crone, *Pre-Industrial Societies,* pp. 72–73. Medievalists such as Fourquin *(The Anatomy of Popular Rebellion)* have maintained the same; see Chapter 4, "The Preponderance of Elites in Rebellions." Sabean, "The Communal Basis," p. 359, has drawn the same generalization for all peasant revolts before 1800.

11. Bercé, *Revolt and Revolution,* p. 124. Similarly, in *History of Peasant Revolts,* p. 276, Bercé emphasizes that "people waited nostalgically for the return of a mythical past. They located this past in the reign of a king with a legendary reputation for justice." Also, see Fourquin, *The Anatomy of Popular Rebellion,* pp. 24 and 78; and Crone *(Pre-Industrial Societies,* p. 75), who concludes that when peasants could not flee, their frustrations might "boil over and engage in *jacqueries,* spontaneous outbursts of violence."

12. For these views of peasants in fifteenth-century Tuscany, see my "Piety and Religious Practice in the Rural Dependencies of Renaissance Florence," *English Historical Review* 114 (1999): 1–22.

13. On such claims about elites and masses, see Bertelli ("Oligarchies et gouvernement," p. 623). See also Crone *(Pre-Industrial Societies,* p. 72–73): "in keeping with the fact that politics were enacted by members of the elite, the vast majority of revolts were started by members of the elite in pursuit of by now familiar aims: autonomy or better terms vis-à-vis the monarch, be it individually or collectively."

14. *Chronique de Primat, traduite par Jean du Vignay,* pp. 21–213.

15. Naugerii, *Historia Veneta,* col. 1012; Sanuto, *Vitæ Ducum Venetorum,* col. 833. On the history of colonial revolts in Crete from Venetian control in 1211 to 1363, see Sally McKee "The Revolt of St Vito in Fourteenth-Century Venetian Crete: A Reassessment," *Mediterranean Historical Review* 9 (1994): 173–204. The revolt of 1363 began as a feudal reaction against Venetian taxes but quickly spread across social classes.

16. *Chronique des quatre premiers Valois,* pp. 77–80.

17. G. Villani, *Nuova Cronica,* II, pp. 29–31.

18. *Cronaca aquilana rimata di Buccio di Ranallo,* pp. 30–34.

19. Kurth, *La cité de Liège,* I, p. 188; Pirenne, *Les anciennes démocraties,* p. 169 ; Pirenne, *Histoire de Belgique,* I, p. 383; and Vercauteren, *Luttes sociales à Liège,* p. 49.

20. *La chronique de Jean de Hocsem,* pp. 11–15; *Chronicon Cornelii Zanteliet,* V, pp. 99–100; Kurth, *La cité de Liège,* I, pp. 179–215; and Kurth, "Henri de Dinant et la démocratie liégeoise," *Academie royale des Sciences des Lettres et de Beaux-arts de Belgique: Bulletins de la classe des lettres* (1908): 384–410.

21. Kurth, *La cité de Liège,* I, p. 199; Kurth, "Henri de Dinant," esp. 389–390; and Vercauteren, *Luttes sociales à Liège,* pp. 50–59; also see *La chronique Liégeoise de 1402,* pp. 179–183.

22. See Nicholas, *The van Arteveldes of Ghent: The Varieties of Vendetta and the Hero in History* (Ithaca, 1988), pp. 19–38; Blockmans and Prevenier, *The Promised Lands: The Low Countries under Burgundian Rule, 1369–1530,* ed. Edward Peters, trans. Elizabeth Fackelman (Philadelphia, 1999; Houten, 1988), p. 23; and Prevenier and Boone, "The 'City-State' Dream," pp. 85–87.

23. Nicholas, *The van Arteveldes,* p. 21. According to Bercé *(Revolt and Revolution in Early Modern Europe,* p. 77), a third of Ghent's city councilors were weavers before Jacob took power.

24. See for instance the struggle of 2 May 1345 in *Chronicon Comitum Flandrensium,* pp. 215–221.

25. *Chronicon Aegidii Li Muisis,* pp. 349–350.

26. Among the many sources, see *Chronique latine de Guillaume de Nangis,* I, pp. 207–208.

27. *Extraits des chroniques de Saint-Denis,* p. 115.

28. See Chapter 4, note 136.

29. Salimbene de Adam, *Cronica,* I, p. 581.

30. G. Villani, *Nuova Cronica,* II, p. 354.

31. NHGL, X, cols. 645–646. For earlier insurrections of "heretics" in Carcassonne, 1304–1305, see *Fragmenta Libelli de ordine Praedicatorum auctore Bernardo Guidonis*, p. 747; and *La chronique romane*, p. 343.

32. NHGL, X, cols. 459–460 and 461–463.

33. M. Villani, *Cronica*, II, pp. 398–399.

34. *Cronaca di Pisa di Ranieri Sardo*, p. 149.

35. Maurisii, *Cronica Dominorum Ecelini*, p. 43.

36. I cannot find Bibianello in *Annuario generale dei comuni e delle frazioni d'Italia* (Turin, 1980). Perhaps this was Bibbiano, 14 km from Reggio nell'Emilia.

37. Salimbene de Adam, *Cronica*, II, p. 920.

38. *Chronica Aegidii Li Muisis*, p. 212.

39. Schio: 24 km northwest of Vicenza.

40. *Cronaca di Antonio Godi Vicentino dall'anno MCXCIV all'anno MCCLX*, ed. Giovanni Soranzo, RIS, VIII/2 (Città di Castello, 1909), p. 10; Battista Pagliarino, *Croniche di Vicenza dal principio di questa città, sino al tempo, ch'ella si diede sotto al Serenissimo dominio Veneto 1404 . . . date in luce da Giorgio Giacomo Alcaini* (Vicenza, 1663), pp. 37–38.

41. *Monachi Patavini Chronicon*, Muratori, VIII, col. 674.

42. *La chronique de Jean de Hocsem*, pp. 185–189; and Kurth, *La cité de Liège*, II, p. 28. On Hocsem's prejudices in reporting social conflict, see Charles, *La ville de Saint-Trond*, pp. 293–294.

43. The other was an immigrant priest, who with two other immigrants organized an unsuccessful revolt in Verona. The chronicle gives no indication that this priest used his pulpit to rally his forces or invoked any religious ideology for the uprising; see Chapter 7.

44. M. Villani, *Cronica*, I, pp. 751–752.

45. Azarii, *Liber gestorum in Lombardia*, p. 122.

46. Ibid.; and M. Villani, *Cronica*, II, pp. 139–41.

47. M. Villani, *Cronica*, II, p. 141.

48. Ibid., II, p. 206; and Azarii, *Liber gestorum in Lombardia*, p. 122.

49. M. Villani, *Cronica*, II, pp. 364–366.

50. Azarii, *Liber gestorum in Lombardia*, p. 123–124.

51. *Storia di Milano*, II, p. 203; Alessandro Visconti, *Storia di Milano* (Milan, 1979), pp. 301–302; Conte Giorgio Giulini, *Memorie . . . città e campagna di Milano*, 7 vols. (Milan, 1854–1857), V, pp. 441–442; and Azarii, *Liber gestorum in Lombardia*, p. 123.

52. Azari, *Liber gestorum in Lombardia*, p. 120. The editor, Francesco Cognasso, speculates that Bussolari was influenced by Cola di Rienzo.

53. Ibid., p. 121.

54. Ibid., p. 123.

55. Boris Porchnev, *Les soulèvements populaires en France de 1623 à 1648* (Paris, 1963; Russian edition, 1951), pp. 76–115.

56. *Chronicon Parmense*, cols 870–871.

57. *Chronicon estense*, col. 511.

Notes to Pages 117–122

58. See Chapter 1, note 93; *Cronaca . . . a Fratre Hyeronimo de Bursellis*, pp. 53–55; various chronicles in *Corpus Chronicorum Bononiensium*, III: *Cronaca A*, pp. 312–313; *Cronaca B* and *Cronica Bolognetti*, pp. 306–308.

59. Today Polesella.

60. Ferrariensus, *Annalium Libris Marchionum Estensium*, pp. 15–17.

61. *Cronica . . . Minerbetti*, p. 279; Morelli, *Ricordi*, pp. 262–263. Of the principal archival sources, see AP, no. 3886 [1402], 9r–10v; ASF, Provv. reg. 92, fols. 87v–90v; for others, see Cohn, *Creating the Florentine State*, pp. 158–165; and Cohn, *Popular Protest*, pp. 362–366.

62. *Annali genovesi di Caffaro*, III, pp. 69–72. Epstein, *Genoa and the Genoese*, p. 122.

63. *Corpus Chronicorum Bononiensium*, II, pp. 432 and 435.

64. See Chapter 1.

65. *Istore et croniques de Flandres*, I, p. 553; and TeBrake, *A Plague of Insurrection*.

66. Bessen, "The Jacquerie: Class War or Co-opted Rebellion?"

67. The documents are published in Luce, *Histoire de la Jacquerie*, pp. 253–254, 260, 263–264, and 293–294. For other village leaders, see Jacques d'Avout, *Le Meutre d'Étienne Marcel* (Paris, 1960), pp. 196–197.

68. Denifle, *La Guerre de Cents Ans*, II, p. 214.

69. See for instance *La chronique des quatre premiers Valois*, pp. 69–77; *La chronique de règnes de Jean II et Charles V*, I, pp. 177–188; *Ordonnances des Roys de France de la troisième race*, ed. Denis-François Secousse, 21 vols. (Paris, 1723–1849), IV, pp. 346–347.

70. "Lettre d'Étienne Marcel aux communes de Picardie et de Flandre," in *Œuvres de Froissart*, ed. Kervyn de Lettenhove (Brussels, 1868), VI, pp. 470–471; and Luce, *Histoire de la Jacquerie*, pp. 263–264.

71. Bercé, *Revolt and Revolution in Early Modern Europe*, p. 217.

72. *Cronaca senese di autore anomino*, p. 114.

73. *Cronaca senese attribuita ad Agnolo di Tura*, pp. 371–373; *Popular Protest*, doc. no. 33.

74. *Cronaca senese attribuita ad Agnolo di Tura*, pp. 375–380; and *Frammento di cronaca senese di anonimo*, p. 172.

75. *Cronaca senese attribuita ad Agnolo di Tura*, p. 494. Exactly who the *popolo minuto* may have been in a town the size of Massa without a substantial cloth industry is difficult to know. The chronicler does not list any of the rebels by profession.

76. Ibid., p. 549.

77. The treasury of the Commune of Siena, see Bowsky, *The Finance of the Commune of Siena, 1287–1355* (Oxford, 1970).

78. *Cronaca senese di Donato di Neri*, pp. 577–579.

79. Ibid., p. 579.

80. M. Villani, *Cronica*, I, pp. 655–656.

81. Ibid., I, pp. 679–680.

82. *Documenti . . . del Comune di Siena*, no. 12, 1–9 December 1355, pp. 43–46. Yet as Bowsky (*A Medieval Italian Commune*, pp. 302–304) shows from the Biccherna archives, the revolt of 1355 did not clear Siena of the hated Nine; several continued to hold key offices in the government of the Twelve and thereafter.

83. Rodolico, *La Democrazia fiorentina nel suo tramonto (1378–1382)* (Bologna, 1905), doc. I, pp. 441–445.

84. *Corpus Chronicorum Bononiensium*, III, p. 466.

85. Niccola della Tuccia, *Cronache di Viterbo*, pp. 41–42.

86. See R. C. Famiglietti, *Royal Intrigue: Crisis at the Court of Charles VI, 1392–1420* (New York, 1986), pp. 117–119. This author also stressed that the vagaries of Charles VI's mental health influenced these political events.

87. See *L'Ordonnance Cabochienne (26–27 Mai 1413)*, ed. A. Coville (Paris, 1891); *Chronique du religieux de Saint-Denys*, V, pp. 6–13; Guillaume Cousinot I, *Geste des Nobles*, in *Chronique de la Pucelle ou chronique de Cousinot*, ed. M. Vallet de Viriville (Paris, 1859), pp. 145–146.

88. *Chronica Aegidii Li Muisis*, p. 170.

89. *Corpus Chronicorum Bononiensium*, II, pp. 232–233; and Griffoni, *Memoriale Historicum de rebus Bononiensium*, p. 25.

90. *Annales Gandenses*, p. 95.

91. *Chronica Aegidii Li Muisis*, p. 175.

92. *Corpus Chronicorum Bononiensium*, II, pp. 394, and 397–398.

93. Stella, *Annales Genuenses*, pp. 128–129. Also, see Chapter 4 and Epstein, *Genoa and the Genoese*, p. 203.

94. *Cronaca senese attribuita ad Agnolo di Tura*, p. 549.

95. Rodolico, *Il Popolo Minuto*, doc. 10, pp. 94–97.

96. *Cronaca prima d'anonimo* (called the *squintinatore*) in *Il Tumulto dei Ciompi*, p. 75.

97. Screpanti, *L'Angelo delle liberazione*, p. 104, speculates that this Simone may have been the same man as Simoncino.

98. "Neighbors and Comrades: The Revolutionaries of Florence, 1378" in Richard Trexler, *The Workers of Renaissance Florence: Power and Dependence in Renaissance Florence* (Asheville, N.C., 1998), p. 69, table 1.

99. Ibid., p. 74; and Provv. reg., no. 67, 3r.

100. Stefani, pp. 292–293.

101. *Cronaca senese conosciuta sotto il nome di Paolo di Tommaso Montauri (continuazione— anni 1381–1431)* in *Cronache senesi*, p. 691; and AP, no. 3053, 31r–32v, 1381(2).ii.12, 131r–132v, 1381(2).ii.12.

102. Trexler, "Neighbors and Comrades," pp. 61–115.

103. *Cronaca seconda d'anonimo*, pp. 110–111. This fact seems to have been lost on historians such as de Roover and Bertelli, who have claimed that the Ciompi were totally beholden to their social betters, such as Salvestro de' Medici. Screpanti (*L'Angelo della Liberazione*, p. 228) has listed all the "Cavalieri del Popolo Minuto." He identifies Guido as a carder and includes another carder, Chimento. Historians have also failed to mention that the revolt of Santa Maria Novella in August attempted to strip Salvestro and other patricians of the financial benefits granted to them on 21 July.

104. *Cronaca senese di Donato di Neri*, p. 634.

105. Ibid., pp. 639–640.

106. *Cronaca della città di Perugia. . . di Diario del Graziani*, p. 288.

107. Niccola della Tuccia, *Cronache di Viterbo*, pp. 41–42.

108. *Chronique de Jean le Févre*, I, pp. 337–342.

109. *Chronique des Pays-Bas*, pp. 389–390.

110. Ibid., pp. 391–394.

111. Houtart, *Les Tournaisiens*, p. 321.

112. Other artisan leaders can easily be added, for instance, Lello Pocadota or Bonadota, "a modest cobbler" from a "totally obscure background," who in 1362 led a revolt of the *popolo minuto* that changed the government of Rome and banished the nobility from the city; see Eugenio Duprè Theseider, *Roma dal comune di popolo alla signoria pontificia (1252–1377)*, Storia di Roma, XI (Bologna, 1952), p. 665; and *Chronicon Cornelii Zanteliet*, p. 281.

113. *Croniche fiorentine di Ser Naddo da Montecatini*, p. 37. Also Stefani, pp. 392–393.

114. G. Villani, *Nuova Cronica*, II, pp. 88–90.

115. Bertelli, "Oligarchies et gouvernement," p. 623; and Crone, *Pre-Industrial Societies*, pp. 72–73; see criticisms in Cohn, *The Laboring Classes in Renaissance Florence*, pp. 7–8; and John Najemy, "The Dialogue of Power in Florentine Politics," in *City-States in Classical Antiquity and Medieval Italy*, pp. 269–288.

116. G. Villani, *Nuova Cronica*, III, pp. 350–353.

117. *Storie Pistoresi*, pp. 195–196.

118. *Stefani*, pp. 217–218.

119. Florentine criminal records survive from 1343 with fragments from 1342.

120. A better case of clan conflict among elites sparking workers and artisans to action might be made for the *Cockerulle* in 1280. The two instigators of the revolt, Henry de la Eechout and Henri Oudewin, were members of important Ypres families and were said to have financed operations in Poperinge; see Boone, "Social Conflicts in the Cloth Industry."

6. Women, Ideology, and Repression

1. Bercé, *Revolt and Revolution in Early Modern Europe*, p. 107.

2. Rudé, *Paris and London in the Eighteenth Century*, p. 23.

3. See Chapter 3, note 81.

4. For instance, the charitable records of religious confraternities such as the brothers of San Frediano and Orsanmichele show that women, especially widows, were overwhelmingly the recipients of alms and handouts of bread; see John Henderson, "The Parish and the Poor in Florence at the Time of the Black Death: The Case of S. Frediano," *Continuity and Change* 3 (1988): 247–272; and Henderson, *Piety and Charity in Late Medieval Florence* (Oxford, 1994), Ch. 7 and 8.

5. Espinas, *La vie urbaine de Douai*, II, pp. 663–665, and IV, doc. no. 1006.

6. *Alle bocche della piazza*, p. 33.

7. *Cronica fiorentina compilata nel secolo XIII*, in *Testi fiorentini del Dugento e dei primi del Trecento*, ed. Alfredo Schiaffini (Florence, 1954), p. 126.

8. *Ly Myreur des histors*, VI, p. 262.

9. *La chronique de Jean de Hocsem*, pp. 199–200; and Kurth, *La cité de Liège*, II, p. 32.

10. Matteo Villani, *Cronica*, I, pp. 374–375. Women also were members of the Hussite standing armies and engaged in combat against the crusaders of the church and the emperor; see Fudge, *The Magnificent Ride*, pp. 170–171.

11. Corio, *Storia di Milano*, I, p. 690.

12. *Cronaca senese. . .di Paolo di Tommaso Montauri*, p. 834.

13. Rigby *(English Society in the Later Middle Ages*, pp. 280–281) also finds little evidence of women as rebels in late medieval English society and explains it by turning to "the official ideology," which "portrayed women's inequality as natural, inevitable and divinely sanctioned" (p. 280). Yet, as Rigby says elsewhere (pp. 306 and 322), the dominant ideology of medieval society stressed social harmony, but various marginals and social classes—peasants, disenfranchised workers, skilled artisans, and bourgeois—were able to overcome this "official ideology" and struggle for their own sense of freedom, liberties, and privileges.

14. *Chronicon Aegidii li Muisis*, p. 352. For women flagellants at Ghent, see *Breve Chronicon Flandriae*, in *Corpus Chronicorum Flandriae*, III, p. 23.

15. Salimbene de Adam, *Cronica*, I, p. 99. On the political aspects of the Great Alleluia as a peace movement and primarily one of the *popolo*, see Koenig, *Il "popolo" dell'Italia del Nord*, pp. 46, 203, and 209. Beyond the horizons of this study, women were active in the Hussite movement in Bohemia and, as with many other medieval heretical movements, benefited from these movements' greater sense of sexual equality. Women fought alongside men, were responsible for religious instruction, and were allowed to preach; see Fudge, *The Magnificent Ride*, pp. 93, 170–172 and 255.

16. *Annales Parmenses maiores*, p. 688.

17. Bonaccorso Pitti, *Ricordi*, in *Mercanti Scrittori*, pp. 383–385; and *Popular Protest*, doc. no. 150. According to one of the chronicles in *Istore et croniques de Flandres*, II, pp. 201–202, these new taxes burdened particularly "girl vendors [*li puelles*]."

18. For the numerous sources on this revolt, see *Popular Protest*, doc. no. 77.

19. *Diario d'anonimo fiorentino*, p. 407. In Kent the head of the poll tax commission personally examined young girls to judge whether they were virgins and thus exempt from the poll tax. The practice was one of the sparks to light the English Uprising of 1381. He was beheaded on Tower Hill on 14 June; see Nicholas Brooks, "The Organization and Achievements of the Peasants of Kent and Essex in 1381," *Studies in Medieval History Presented to R. H. C. Davis*, ed. Henry Mayr-Harting and R. I. Moore (London, 1985), pp. 254–255.

20. Niccola della Tuccia, *Cronache di Viterbo*, p. 24.

21. G. Villani, *Nuova Cronica*, II, pp. 88–90; *Popular Protest*, doc. no. 13.

22. *Chronique artésienne (1295–1304) et Chronique tournaisienne (1296–1314)*, ed. Frantz Funck-Brentano, Collection de textes pour servir a l'étude et a l'enseignement de l'histoire (Paris, 1899), p. 42.

23. See Chapter 4.

24. *Chronica Aegidii Li Muisis*, pp. 287–288.

25. See Chapter 5.

26. *La chronique d'Enguerran de Monstrelet*, IV, p. 135.

27. Archives nationales, series JJ 71, f. 65, no. 86; and 75, f. 186r–187v, no. 316.

28. *Les pays de la Loire,* no. 1077.

29. In one of the counterrevolutionary conspiracies hatched in Bologna to topple the Florentine government of minor guildsmen, a man from the Medici family is listed alongside his wife; ACP, no. 1198, 55r–59r, 1379(80).ii.15. Christopher Dyer, in "The Social and Economic Background to the Rural Revolt of 1381," in *The English Rising of 1381,* pp. 9–42, finds a case during the English Peasants' Revolt of 1381 when a man from Essex had to pay an amercement of 12 pennies because his wife "was a rebel and spoke badly of the affeerers" (p. 32). More significantly, Sylvia Federico, in "The Imaginary Society: Women in 1381," *Journal of British Studies* 40 (2001): 159–183, has found in court rolls and imaginary literature evidence of women as members of the rank and file and as leaders of the English Peasants Revolt of 1381. Most remarkably, Johanna Ferrour with her husband led the insurgents of Kent in burning the Palace of Savoy and a day later (14 July) arrested and ordered the murder of Archbishop Simon Sudbury and Treasurer Robert Hales. As with other aspects, the English Uprising appears to have differed from late medieval popular uprising in continental Europe.

30. *Stefani,* p. 377.

31. *Cartulaire historique et généologique des Artevelde,* ed. Napoléon de Pauw (Brussels, 1920), pp. 711–718.

32. Sanuto, *Vitæ Ducum Venetorum,* pp. 585–586.

33. *Chronique de Jean le Févre,* I, p. 286. Also see the counterrevolutionary conspiracy hatched in Bologna against Florence, note 29.

34. For these views see Fourquin, *The Anatomy of Popular Rebellion,* pp. 24 and 78; Bercé, *Revolt and Revolution in Early Modern Europe,* p. 276; and Graus, "From Resistance to Revolt: The Late Medieval Peasant Wars in the Context of Social Crisis," *Journal of Peasant Studies* 3 (1975), p. 5.

35. In this regard, the continental revolts contrast sharply with the English Peasants' Revolt of 1381, "when throughout the rebellion, the rebels showed loyalty to the monarchy, in the person of the fourteen-year-old boy-king, Richard II"; among other places, see Whittle and Rigby, "England: Popular Politics and Social Conflict," p. 73; Brooks, "The Organization and Achievements of the Peasants," pp. 254–255 and 265; Fryde, *The Great Revolt of 1381,* pp. 8 and 18; and Hilton, *Bond Men Made Free,* pp. 192–196. According to Dyer, in *Making a Living in the Middle Ages: The People of Britain 850–1520* (New Haven, 2002), p. 288, the English rebels of 1381 saw themselves as the king's agents and targeted his advisers as traitors and the cause of England's misrule.

36. The traditional battle cry of the king of France.

37. *Chronique des règnes de Jean II et de Charles V,* pp. 205–210; *Fragment d'une chronique latine* (I), in Secousse, ed., *Recueil de pièces,* II, p. 616; *Fragment d'une chronique françoise,* ibid., p. 638; and *Fragment d'une chronique latine* (II), ibid., p. 665.

38. See for instance *Ordonnances des Roys de France,* IV, pp. 346–347; and the letter of King John II to the inhabitants of the city of Paris declaring his intention to pardon those involved in the revolt; Secousse, *Recueil de pièces,* I, pp. 87–88.

39. The two marshals and chief advisers were Jean de Conflans and Robert of Clermont; see Sumption, *The Hundred Years War*, II, p. 312, and numerous chronicle descriptions.

40. *Chronique du religieux de Saint-Denys*, I, pp. 44–53. Further, the letters of remission are filled with acts of disobedience to the crown from individual rebels as well as from communities. The most extensive of these was the 800,000-livres fine levied in 1384 against the districts of most of Languedoc—Beaucaire, Nîmes, and Carcassonne—because of their acts of rebellion and disobedience to the crown over the past four years; Archives nationales, JJ 124, no. 236, fol. 157v. Popular insurgents of the union of six cities staged similar theaters of insult against their king in March 1348: after breaking into the royal palace, they forced Pere III (called the Ceremonious) and the queen to dance with them to satirical tunes played by a barber; see Antoni Furio, *Història del País Valencià* (València, 1995), p. 109; and Pere III of Catalonia (Pedro IV of Aragon), *Chronicle*, trans. Mary Hillgarth and ed. J. N. Hillgarth, *Medieval Sources in Translation*, 2 vols. (Toronto, 1980), I, p. 429.

41. *Diaria Neapolitana*, col. 1078.

42. *Cronicon Siculum incertis authoris*, p. 27.

43. Ibid., p. 36.

44. *I Diurnali del Duca di Monteleone*, p. 28.

45. *Cronaca aquilana rimata di Buccio di Ranallo*, p. 34.

46. Ibid., p. 207.

47. Michele da Piazza, *Chronica*, I, pp. 129, 174, and 288–289. Earlier, in a popular revolt at Messina against the local aristocracy (1342), the *popolo* mixed their cries for the *popolo* with appeals to the king of Sicily before burning and robbing the homes of aristocrats and their friends; *Anonymi Historia Sicula vulgari dialecto conscripta ab anno MCCCXXXVII ad MCCCCXII*, in *Bibliotheca Scriptorum qui Res in Sicilia Gesta sub Aragonum imperio*, ed. Rasarius Gregorio (Palermo, 1792), II, p. 280.

48. Michele da Piazza, *Chronica*, p. 298.

49. Ibid., pp. 172–174.

50. *Chronographia Regum Francorum*, I, p. 265.

51. Mario Natalucci, "Lotte di parte e manifestazioni ereticali nella Marca agli inizi del secolo XIV," *Studi Picena* 24 (1956): 125–144; and Luigi Martorelli, *Memoire historiche dell'antichissima e nobile città d'Osimo* (Venice, 1725), pp. 140–151.

52. For instance in 1303 (*Cronache senese . . . di Paolo di Tommaso Montauri*, p. 231), 1378 (*Diario d'anonimo fiorentino*, p. 377), twice in 1405 (*Cronaca . . . Minerbetti*, pp. 328 and 334–335), and in 1407 (*Cronaca di Ser Guerriero da Gubbio*, p. 35).

53. See Musto, *Apocalypse in Rome*, p. 61.

54. M. Villani, *Cronica*, I, p. 711.

55. Parma's council of the *popolo* numbered two thousand.

56. *Annales Parmenses maiores*, pp. 777–778.

57. Niccola della Tuccia, *Cronache di Viterbo*, p. 40.

58. Ordinance issued by the assembly of the three estates of Langue d'oïl abolishing all the taxes set since the reign of Philippe le Bel; *Ordonnances des roys de France*,

VI, pp. 552–554; also see *Chronographia Regum Francorum,* III, pp. 24–33; and *Popular Protest,* doc. nos. 152 and 146.

59. *Chronographia Regum Francorum,* I, p. 277.
60. *Chronique du religieux de Saint-Denys,* VI, pp. 92–97.
61. *Chronicon Cornelii Zanteliet,* pp. 344–345.
62. M. Villani, *Cronica,* I, p. 711.
63. Crone, *Pre-Industrial Societies,* pp. 75–77.
64. Naugerii, *Historia Veneta,* col. 1015.
65. Salimbene de Adam, *Cronica,* II, pp. 736–737; and *Annales Parmenses maiores,* p. 688.
66. Hilton, *Bond Men Made Free,* pp. 130–132. In other places, however, Hilton stressed the "ethos of freedom" and liberty as the defining ideology of late medieval rebels, or at least of those in the English Uprising of 1381; see *The Decline of Serfdom in Medieval England,* Studies in Economic History (London, 1969), p. 35; "Social Concepts in the English Rising of 1381," pp. 216–226; "Popular Movements in England at the End of the Fourteenth Century," p. 159; and "Inherent and Derived Ideology in the English Rising of 1381," in *Campagnes médiévales: l'homme et son espace, études offertes à Robert Fossier,* Histoire ancienne et médiévale, 31 (Paris, 1995), pp. 399–405. Did Hilton wish to distinguish the English Uprising of 1381 from other late medieval revolts, as the only one that possessed a positive sense of class consciousness?
67. Remission granted to Jean Hersent, who announced Étienne Marcel's order to assemble all the men of the region to arm themselves, in Luce, *Histoire de la Jacquerie,* pp. 263–264.
68. See remission granted to Jean Flageolet, elected leader of several villages of Perthois (ibid., pp. 293–294); remission granted to Hue of Sailleville, elected by the villagers of Angicourt as their captain (ibid., pp. 253–254); and general remission granted to the villagers of Bettancourt and Vroil, in Perthois (ibid., pp. 266–268).
69. M. Villani, *Cronica,* I, p. 388.
70. NHGL, X, cols. 1818–1820.
71. Captain for the king of France in the Agenais in March 1370.
72. There are many villages named Sauveterre, but most likely this one is just south of Toulouse.
73. *Due cronache del Vespro in volgare siciliano,* pp. 19 and 116.
74. See *Specimen historiae Sozomeni Pistoriensis,* col. 1099; *Cronaca malatestiana,* pp. 42–43; and *Chronicon estense,* col. 499.
75. On this point see Koenig, *Il "popolo" dell'Italia del Nord.*
76. *Popular Protest,* doc. nos. 121 and 129. During the revolt of 20 July, the commune's hangman Ser Nuto was the only victim singled out by the Ciompi crowds, and at the end of August the Ciompi did not target any victims or sack any palaces; see Rodolico, *I Ciompi,* pp. 118 and 166.
77. See for instance Brucker, "The Ciompi Revolution," in *Florentine Studies: Politics and Society in Renaissance Florence,* ed. Nicolai Rubinstein (Evanston, 1968),

pp. 314–356; Raymond de Roover, "Labour Conditions in Florence around 1400: Theory, Policy, and Reality," ibid., pp. 277–313; and Bertelli, "Oligarchies et gouvernement."

78. Perhaps this was the case with the guild of cobblers at Bologna, which set fire to the communal palace in 1267 because of a miscarriage of justice to one of its members; see *Pietri Cantinelli Chronicon,* p. 9.

79. *Annales Parmenses maiores,* p. 709.

80. Antonio Gramsci *(Quaderni del Carcere,* ed. Valentino Gerratana [Turin, 1975], III, p. 2287) contrasted the revolt of the Ciompi with slave revolts of the ancient world, claiming that the Ciompi was more successful because workers, unlike slaves, could make alliances with other classes. Cited in Epstein, *Speaking of Slavery: Color, Ethnicity, and Human Bondage in Italy* (Ithaca, 2001), p. 60.

81. For a definition of social class, see Pitirim A. Sorokin, "What Is a Social Class?" in *Class, Status and Power,* pp. 87–92 (first published in 1947). Given his definition of social classes as groups that are "semiclosed," "partly organized," "partly aware of their own unity and existence," and "multibonded," I would disagree with his conclusion that such groups did not play an important part in Western societies before the eighteenth century (p. 88). On the distinction between classes and orders for the late Middle Ages, see the excellent summary of Whittle and Rigby, "England: Popular Politics and Social Conflict," pp. 65–69.

82. *Extraits d'une chronique anonyme finissant en MCCCLXXXIII,* p. 142.

83. *Les Grandes Chroniques de France,* VIII, pp. 250–252.

84. *Recueil des documents relatifs à l'histoire de l'industrie drapière,* III, pp. 679–685, no. 849 (1 April 1281).

85. *Stefani,* p. 386; and Rodolico, *La Democrazia fiorentina,* doc. II., pp. 445–452. Similar to chroniclers in the north, writers such as Stefani (p. 322) listed specific occupations when describing the *gente minuta;* see Rodolico, *I Ciompi,* p. 102. In fact, chroniclers defined these lower classes with more precision than they did for the bourgeois, *popolo, popolani,* or *popolani grassi.*

86. Even the case of the English Peasants' Revolt of 1381 goes against Hilton's claim of "negative class consciousness." In contrast to the Jacquerie, "almost nobody was killed in England in 1381 merely because he was a substantial landowner, and there is no evidence of women and children being killed;" Fryde, *The Great Revolt of 1381,* p. 30. On the discipline of the crowds and the selectivity of their targets in 1381, see, among other places, Whittle and Rigby, "England: Popular Politics and Social Conflict," pp. 71–72.

87. Pitti, *Ricordi.*

88. Fourquin, *The Anatomy of Popular Rebellion,* p. 25. Genicot, in *Rural Communities,* p. 80, maintains that peasant uprisings had only two successes in the Middle Ages: forming the Swiss cantons and the Spanish *remensas* at the end of the fifteenth century.

89. *The Chronicle of Jean de Venette,* pp. 76–77.

90. *Cronaca malatestiana,* pp. 42–43. On the massacre, see Jan Robertson, "Cesena: Governo e società dal sacco dei Brettoni al dominio di Cesare Borgia," in *Storia*

di Cesena, II/2, ed. B. D. Maraldi (Rimini, 1985), pp. 5–15; and Duccio Balestracci, *Le armi, i cavalli, l'oro: Giovanni Acuto e i condottieri nell'Italia del Trecento* (Bari, 2003), pp. 133–139. The next major retaliation against an entire city population that led to a city's destruction (that I know of) was Charles the Bold's punishment of Liège in 1468, but even here it did not amount to the complete depopulation of a city; see Boone, "Urban Space," pp. 636–637.

91. *Chronique latine de Guillaume de Nangis*, I, p. 76.
92. *Excerpta e chronico Gaufridi de Collone*, p. 3.
93. *Ly Myreur des histors*, VI, pp. 109–110.
94. *Chronique tirée d'un ancien manuscrit de l'abbaye de Berdouea*, col. 214. Some have questioned whether the massacre of 200 in the fields below Montségur took place; see Roach, *The Devil's World*, p. 125.
95. See Ormerod and Roach, "The Medieval Inquisition."
96. *Cronaca . . . Minerbetti*, pp. 127–128. Minerbetti in fact overstated Florentine violence and its punishments of these rebels; see Cohn, *Creating the Florentine State*, p. 126.
97. Rutenburg, *Popolo e movimenti popolari nell'Italia del '300 e '400*, trans. Gianpiero Borghini (Bologna, 1971; Moscow, 1958), pp. 315–316 and 335–336; Rodolico *(I Ciompi: Una pagina di storia del proletariato operaio*, 3rd ed. [Florence, 1980; first published 1945], p. 209) asserts that the Florentine tribunals had condemned 8,000 rebels, most of them receiving death sentences, but he supplies no source. Certainly this figure does not come from any quantitative reckoning of the criminal records, which survive intact for these years.
98. Only one source I know claims sentences of mass exile were imposed with the fall of the Ciompi, and that a foreign one: according to *Cronaca senese di Donato di Neri*, p. 673, "over a thousand carders and combers were chased from town and exiled [*cacciaro e sbandiro*]" in September 1378. However, no Florentine chronicle or judicial record confirms this claim. Neither Rutenburg nor Rodolico cites this Sienese source. The only allusion to mass migration after the Ciompi's defeat on 1 September is *Diario del Monaldi*, in *Istorie pistolesi ovvero, Dalle cose avvenute in Toscana dall'anno MCCC al MCCCXLVIII e Diario del Monaldi* (Prato, 1835), p. 521: "A great number of the *popolo minuto* left, mainly for the *contado*, and several to Pisa and other dispersed places." Monaldi, however, lists only fourteen men who were banished by the Florentine government on 2 September. Furthermore, population statistics taken from the *Estimo* of 1379 suggest that the "grandissimo numero" who left on 2 September either were not "so great" or soon slipped back into the city: the Florentine urban population rose sharply from the famine and plague of 1374 to 1379; for these statistics, see David Herlihy and Christiane Klapisch-Zuber, *Les Toscans et leurs familles: Une étude du Catasto de 1427* (Paris, 1978), pp. 173–177; Cohn, *The Black Death Transformed: Disease and Culture in Renaissance Europe* (London, 2002), p. 200; and Cohn, *Women in the Streets: Essays on Sex and Violence in Renaissance Italy* (Baltimore, 1996), p. 22.
99. *Diario d'anonimo fiorentino*, p. 384; *Stefani*, pp. 336–337, lists only thirty-seven.
100. *Stefani*, pp. 399–401.

101. Ibid., p. 403.
102. Brucker, *The Civic World of Early Renaissance Florence* (Princeton, 1977), p. 61.
103. Sanuto, *Vitæ Ducum Venetorum*, col. 607.
104. *Cronaca senese attribuita ad Agnolo di Tura*, pp. 416–417.
105. *Chronica Aegidii Li Muisis*, p. 170.
106. Ibid., p. 175.
107. See Martines *(April Blood: Florence and the Plot against the Medici* [London, 2003], pp. 12–24) for examples of the terror, including cannibalism, that awaited conspirators such as those who assassinated Milan's head of state Galeazzo Maria Sforza on 26 December 1476.
108. For examples, see Andrew Cunningham and Ole Peter Grell, *The Four Horsemen of the Apocalypse: Religion, War, Famine and Death in Reformation Europe* (Cambridge, 2000).
109. *Chronographia Regum Francorum*, III, pp. 24–33.
110. *Chronicon Parmense*, pp. 792–793.
111. *Chronica Aegidii Li Muisis*, pp. 173–175.
112. M. Villani, *Cronica*, II, p. 88; and Wolff, *Histoire de Toulouse*, p. 153; and Wolff, *Commerces et marchands*, pp. 38–39. The revolt was called the "capage." At the same time, similar disruptions unfolded nearby at Lavaur. Moreover, the English Peasants' Revolt of 1381 did not end with savage repression, as the Jacquerie did. Only one notable, Bishop Henry le Despenser of Norwich, committed atrocities, and fewer than 200 were executed; Fryde, *The Great Revolt of 1381*, p. 30.
113. I have not considered letters of remission here because this would unduly inflate the statistics toward clemency: almost without fail these documents pardoned rebels.
114. *Chronique du religieux de Saint-Denys*, I, pp. 16–23.
115. *Ordonnances des roys de France*, VI, pp. 552–554.
116. Chéruel, *Histoire de Rouen*, II, pp. 544–546.
117. For chronicle descriptions of the *Harelle*, see *Chronique des quatre premiers Valois*, 297–301; *Chronique normande de Pierre Cochon*, pp. 162–166; and *Chronique du religieux de Saint-Denys*, I, pp. 128–143. No new archival or sustained interpretive research on the *Harelle* has appeared since Chéruel. Lecarpentier, in "La Harelle," retells the story from a comprehensive survey of the chronicles. Harry A. Miskimin ("The Last Act of Charles V: The Background of the Revolts of 1382," *Speculum* 38 (1963): 433–442) and Radding ("The Estates of Normandy") deal more with the prelude to the revolts—taxation and the character of Charles V's kingship.
118. *La Cronica di Dino Compagni delle cose occorrenti ne' tempi suoi*, ed. Isidoro del Lungo, RIS, IX/2 (Città di Castello, 1907–1916), pp. 18–19. I have also consulted the newer edition, Dino Compagni, *Cronica*, ed. Davide Cappi (Rome, 2000), pp. 9–10, but for the passages I have cited, I find no improvement over del Lungo's edition, and del Lungo's notes are more extensive and useful than those of the new edition.
119. *Chronicon Placentinum*, pp. 1–2.

120. On the constitutional importance of these revolts and their class composition, see Koenig, *Il "popolo" dell'Italia del Nord*.

121. *Corpus Chronicorum Bononiensium*, III, pp. 551–552.

122. According to the traditional historiography, the close connection between Guelfs and Ghibellines, with factions that favored either the church or the emperor, began to unravel in the early fourteenth century; the ideologies lasted in places such as Florence, however, into the fifteenth century; see Ronald Witt, "A Note on Guelfism in Late Medieval Florence," *Nuova Rivista Storica* 53 (1969): 134–145.

123. *Chronique d'Antonio Morosini, extraits rélatifs à l'histoire de France*, ed. Germain Lefèvre-Pontalis SHF, CCXC (Paris 1898–1899), II, p. 25; and see Epstein, *Genoa and the Genoese*, pp. 263–264.

124. *Extraits des chroniques de Saint-Denis*, pp. 117–118.

125. *Corpus Chronicorum Bononiensium*, II, pp. 232–233.

126. *Chronique liégeoise de 1402*, pp. 242–243; and *Fragments de la chronique de Jean le Prêtre publiés par Chapeaville*, in *Chronique liégeoise de 1402*, pp. 455–456.

127. Ibid., II, p. 272.

128. *Chronique des Pays-Bas*, pp. 143–144; M. Villani, *Cronica*, II, pp. 536–537; and the numerous chroniclers of the Ciompi's victory in July 1378.

129. M. Villani, *Cronica*, II, pp. 536–537.

130. *Chronica Mediolani seu Manipulus Florum*, cols. 677–678, 685–686, and 686–687; and Isaia Ghiron, "La Credenza di Sant'Ambrogio, o la Lotta dei nobili e del popolo in Milano, 1198–1292," *Archivio Storico Lombardo* 3 (1876): 583–609.

131. *De Romano (Annales Veronenses)*, in *Antiche cronache veronesi*, ed. Carlo Cipolla, Monumenti storici publicati dalla R. Deputazione veneta du storia patria, 3rd ser.: *Cronache e Diarii* (Venice, 1890), II, p. 410.

132. G. Villani, *Nuova Cronica*, II, pp. 397–400; and *Storie pistoresi*, pp. 196–197.

133. M. Villani, *Cronica*, II, pp. 679–680; *Cronaca senese di Donato di Neri*, pp. 577–579, 628–634, and 639–642.

134. M. Villani, *Cronica*, II, pp. 150–151.

135. Niccola della Tuccia, *Cronache di Viterbo*, pp. 32, and 40–42.

136. *Chronique des règnes de Jean II et de Charles V*, I, p. 62.

137. *Annales Estenses Jacobi de Delayto*, col. 956; and *Cronaca . . . Hyeronimo de Bursellis*, pp. 66–67.

138. *Chronique du religieux de Saint-Denys*, I, pp. 16–23, 44–53, 66–69; V, 35–37, 41–47; and VI, 229–237, 243–249; and *Chronique de Jean le Févre*, I, pp. 35–36, 330–334, 337–342.

139. *Chronique des Pays-Bas*, pp. 207–209; *La chronique d'Enguerran de Monstrelet*, VI, pp. 145, 174, 198–199.

140. *La chronique de Jean de Hocsem*, pp. 11–15, 106–108, 185–191, *Chronique latine de Jean de Stavelot*, I, p. 129; *Chronicon Cornelii Zanteliet*, pp. 99–100, 145–146, 163, 188, 239, 243, 344–345, and 402.

141. *La chronique de Jean de Hocsem*, p. 100; and *Chronicon Cornelii Zanteliet*, p. 100.

142. *Chronique latine de Jean de Stavelot*, p. 82.

143. Michele da Piazza, *Chronica*, p. 198.

144. Ibid., pp. 172–174 and 298.

145. Ibid., p. 254–259.

146. *Die Chronik des Saba Malaspina,* p. 360.

147. Ibid., p. 120; *Cronaca aquilana rimata di Buccio di Ranallo,* pp. 18, 20, 31, and 74; and *Cronaca di Niccolò di Borbona,* cols. 855–856.

148. P. S. Lewis *(Later Medieval France: The Polity* [London, 1968], pp. 266–267) sees this change taking place already by the early fifteenth century: in "the bright days of the 1350s . . . ruling groups in a number of towns thought that insurrection could be profitable. In the fifteenth century insurrection was more clearly foolish." Further, Lewis has shown that the change in France derived not solely from force but by the crown's "seduction" of oligarchs, as in Lyon in 1423; see ibid., pp. 272–275. Despite the Burgundians' violent repression of revolts in Bruges (1436–1438) and Ghent (1449–1453), such a shift away from the old coalition of various urban groups against centralized princely power may have been less marked in the Low Countries; see the sketch of revolts from 1127 to 1584 by Dumolyn and Haemers, in "Patterns of Urban Rebellion." However, the authors, along with Blockmans and others, stress that "the centralizing Burgundian dynasty" and the siding of urban elites with the dukes meant that urban revolt became far less successful after 1382. In German territories the shift may have occurred slightly later. Blickle, in "Peasant Revolts in the German Empire," has argued that regional revolts in Germany increased over the fifteenth century to the German peasants' war of 1524. With its repression, however, "the German countryside yielded to a variety of more authoritarian outcomes" (Wayne Te Brake, *Shaping History: Ordinary People in European Politics, 1500–1700* [Berkeley, 1998], p. 45).

149. On changes in military technology and "the needs of war" as the driving forces behind the development of the early modern state, see most prominently Geoffrey Parker, *The Military Revolution: Military Innovation and the Rise of the West, 1500–1800* (Cambridge, 1988). For the Hundred Years' War as the principal factor strengthening the French monarchy in the fifteenth century, see Miskimin, "L'or, l'argent, la guerre dans la France médiévale," *Annales: E. S. C.* 40 (1985): 171–184. For "the suffocating effects of monarchical warfare" in the subordination of towns across Europe in the fifteenth century, see Wim P. Blockmans, "Voracious States and Obstructing Cities: An Aspect of State Formation in Preindustrial Europe," in *Cities and the Rise of States in Europe, A.D. 1000 to 1800,* ed. Tilly and Blockmans (Boulder, 1994), pp. 218–250, esp. 237–245; as well as other essays in this volume.

150. See my arguments in *Creating the Florentine State.*

7. Communication and Alliances

1. This was my aim in "Florentine Insurrections, 1342–1385, in Comparative Perspective," in *The English Rising of 1381,* pp. 143–164, ed. R. H. Hilton and T. H. Aston (Cambridge, 1984).

2. Corio, *Storia di Milano*, I, pp. 439 and pp. 492–493; Jacobo Malvecio, *Chronicon Brixianum ab origine urbis ad annum usque MCCCXXXII*, Muratori, XIV, col. 938; Koenig, *Il "popolo" dell'Italia del Nord*, pp. 95–141. The *popolo* had its artisan component in the Credenza di Sant'Ambrogio, which allied with other groups, including a society of ousted nobility called "la Motta." On the Credenza and the Milanese *popolo minuto*, see *Chronica Mediolani seu Manipulus Florum*, cols. 677–678; Ghiron, "La Credenza di Sant'Ambrogio;" Luigi Salvatorelli, *L'Italia comunale dal secolo XI alla metà del secolo XIV*, Storia d'Italia, IV (Milan, 1940), pp. 435 and 453; and Grillo, *Milano in età comunale*, pp. 431–449.

3. Chapter 1, note 59.

4. *Cronaca senese attribuita ad Agnolo di Tura*, p. 399.

5. G. Villani, *Nuova Cronica*, II, p. 558.

6. *Croniche fiorentine di Ser Naddo da Montecatini*, pp. 77–78.

7. See Corio, *Storia di Milano*, II, pp. 466–472; also, Florentine chroniclers such as Gregorio Dati *(L'Istoria di Firenze*, pp. 83–84) gloated over the Milanese disaster and celebrated the rebellions of dependent city-states against Milanese "tyranny."

8. Corio, *Storia di Milano*, II, pp. 465–466.

9. *Cronaca . . . Minerbetti*, p. 323.

10. See Denis Romano, *Patricians and Popolani: The Social Foundations of the Venetian Renaissance State* (Baltimore, 1987).

11. Sanuto, *Vitae ducum Venetorum*, col. 564; Danduli, *Chronica per extensium descripta*, p. 314; Danduli, *Chronica brevis*, in Danduli, *Chronica per extensium descripta*, p. 369; and *Venetiarum Historia vulgo Petro Iustiniano Iustiniani*, p. 176.

12. Sanuto, *Vitae ducum Venetorum*, col. 583.

13. Ibid., cols. 691–692; and Naugerii, *Historia Veneta*, col. 1061.

14. Danduli, *Chronica brevis*, p. 321 and 371; Naugerii, *Historia Veneta*, cols. 1016–1017 and 1040; Sanuto, *Vitae ducum Venetorum*, cols. 585–586 and 634.

15. Danduli, *Chronica brevis*, p. 321.

16. Naugerii, *Historia Veneta*, col. 1040.

17. Again, an exception may have been the mid-thirteenth-century Credenza di Sant'Ambrogio, which Koenig, in *Il "popolo" dell'Italia del Nord*, p. 103, has characterized as a party of the *popolo minuto* and *Chronica mediolani seu Manipulus Florum* (col. 600), defined as comprising butchers, bakers, and leather and wool workers. It may have constituted the kernel of a revolt in 1259 that established rule of the *popolo* in Milan for a decade, but even here the leaders and beneficiaries of the revolt were the noble family of the della Torre. As Ghiron, concludes in "La Credenza di Sant'Ambrogio," p. 102, unlike revolts of the *popolo* in Florence, Bologna, Siena, Perugia, and other city-states, the "Credenza" never challenged the hegemony of the nobility. No Ordinances of Justice or other special laws or taxes were promulgated against the nobility, and no efforts were made to exclude them from office.

18. On this conflict, see Cohn, *Creating the Florentine State*, pp. 154–158; and William Connell, *La città dei crucci: fazioni e clientele in uno stato reppublicano del '400* (Florence, 2000).

19. As Pirenne *(Les anciennes démocraties,* pp. 169–175) acknowledged, cloth manufacturing was not a necessary condition for the rise of popular and "democratic" movements. No industry dominated the economy of Liège, yet, according to Pirenne, "it was the most democratic city the Low Countries ever knew" (p. 175). From chronicles alone, Liège counts 26 revolts in my samples, more than Ghent (16) or Bruges (12).

20. See Chapter 1.

21. See Appendix and NHGL, VIII, pp. 214–218. Another three fragmentary chronicles appear in this volume, but I found no popular revolts in them (other than the Albigensian movement) and have not counted them.

22. Pirenne, *Les anciennes démocraties des Pays-Bas,* p. 166. The patricians sent letters through Brabant asking cloth manufacturers not to hire these workers.

23. *Annales Gandenses,* p. 34.

24. An example of rebel recruitment across cities is found in an inquest following the defeat of the Flemish rebels at Cassel in 1328: an anonymous rebel from Bruges confessed to having had ties with rebels from the city of Geraardsbergen, who had brought him into contact with rebel weavers in Ghent; cited in Dumolyn and Haemers, "Patterns of Urban Rebellion," *Journal of Medieval History* 31 (2005), p. 383.

25. Artisan organization beyond city walls also can be seen in other avenues of social life in Flanders. Shooting guilds of archers (Saint Sebastian), crossbowmen (Saint George), and later rifle societies held competitions across various different towns. Although they would become expensive affairs of the bourgeois, they originated in the early fourteenth century as confraternities of artisan guild militia. See Stabel, *Dwarfs among Giants,* pp. 221–222; Arnade, "City, State, and Public Ritual in the Late-Medieval Burgundian Netherlands," *Comparative Studies in Society and History* 39 (1997), pp. 313–315; Arnade, *Realms of Ritual: Burgundian Ceremony and Civic Life in Late Medieval Ghent* (Ithaca, 1996), pp. 65–94; Andrew Brown, "Civic Ritual: Bruges and the Counts of Flanders in the Later Middle Ages," *The English Historical Review* 112 (1997), p. 283; Nicholas, "In the Pit of the Burgundian Theater State: Urban Traditions and Princely Ambitions in Ghent, 1360–1420," in *City and Spectacle in Medieval Europe,* ed. Barbara A. Hanawalt and Kathyrn L. Reyerson (Minneapolis, 1994), p. 277. I know of no similar supracity organizations in Italy.

26. Kurth, *La cité de Liège,* I, p. 219.

27. Ibid., I, pp. 255 and 268–269.

28. *Chronique des règnes de Jean II et de Charles V,* I, pp. 130 and 157–158.

29. "Lettre d'Etienne Marcel 'aux communes de Picardie et de Flandre,'" *Popular Protest,* doc. no. 101. He also made specific appeals to Ypres and Ghent, which inspired the weavers to revolt against the Flemish nobility in 1359 and 1360; see d'Avout, *Le Meutre d'Étienne Marcel,* pp. 175, 220–221, and 303–310; and Prevenier and Boone, "The 'City-State' Dream," p. 87.

30. Prevenier and Boone, "The 'City-State' Dream."

31. d'Avout, *Le Meutre d'Étienne Marcel,* pp. 303–310; and Blockmans and Prevenier, *The Promised Lands,* p. 10.

32. Vercauteren, *Luttes sociales à Liège*, p. 98.

33. *Chronique du religieux de Saint-Denys*, I, p. 131; and Pirenne, *Histoire de Belgique*, II, p. 214.

34. *La chronique des quatre premiers Valois*, pp. 69–77; *Popular Protest*, doc. no. 93. Also, John Ball and other rebels of the English Uprising of 1381 sent letters to rebels and villagers; see Dyer, *Making a Living in the Middle Ages*, p. 289.

35. Among the many accounts of the siege at Meaux, see *La Chronique de règnes de Jean II et Charles V*, I, pp. 177–188.

36. Today it is called Chilly-Mazarin.

37. Luce, *Histoire de la Jacquerie*, pp. 263–264; *Popular Protest*, doc. no. 110.

38. Ibid., pp. 291–292; *Popular Protest*, doc. no. 113.

39. *Chronique du religieux de Saint-Denys*, p. 131; *Popular Protest*, doc. no. 136.

40. *La chronique du bon duc Loys de Bourbon*, ed. A.-M. Chazaud, SHF, CXLV (Paris, 1876), p. 165.

41. For these chants, see Mirot, *Les insurrections urbaines*, pp. 92, 98, and 110. The same impression is given by Froissart. His description of Philippe van Artevelde and the revolt of Ghent fills two chapters and twelve pages in the latest edition, based on the Pierpont Morgan Library manuscript (*Jean Froissart Chroniques, Livres I et II*, ed. Peter F. Ainsworth and George T. Diller [Paris, 2001], pp. 849–860), while the *Maillotins* of Paris are confined to one paragraph at the end of a chapter on famine and war preparations in Ghent (pp. 853–854). Further, Froissart presents the Hammer men's uprising not as a popular revolt, but as one of "the rich and powerful" who had had their "valets armed to the nines."

42. *Chronique du religieux de Saint-Denys*, I, p. 132.

43. Also, according to Kurth, in *La cité de Liège*, I, p. lxix, "those in the workshops of Liège, Paris, and Rouen would mourn over the Flemish defeat at Rozebeke."

44. NHGL, X, cols. 1630–1632 and 1632–1639; *Chronique des quatre premiers Valois*, p. 297; *Chronique de Jean II et de Charles V*, II, pp. 368–369; and *La chronique romane*, p. 398.

45. NHGL, X, cols. 1632–1639.

46. *Chronique du religieux de Saint-Denys*, V, pp. 299–301.

47. Interregional communication between artisan rebels can also be seen in the German Empire. At Augsburg in 1368 and Cologne in 1396, artisans who wanted to topple their patrician governments formed study groups and sent their delegates to cities to learn about constitutions and electoral procedures. Those from Augsburg went to Basle, Constance, Mayence, Speyer, and Strasbourg, while those from Cologne went to Liège, Utrecht, and Deventer; Kurth, *La cité de Liège*, I, lxv.

48. For instance, Florence intervened to prosecute the rebels who tried to overthrow Siena's regime of the Nine in 1346; Rodolico, *Il Popolo Minuto*, doc. 10, pp. 94–97. During the Florentine Government of the Arti Minori, Siena harbored political exiles from Florence's old oligarchy and their exiled Ciompi comrades, who hatched numerous raids and conspiracies to bring down the Florentine artisan government between 1379 and 1382, terrorizing small towns in the countryside such as Figline Valdarno, Bucine, Montevarchi, and Laterina; see *Stefani*,

pp. 343, 349–350, and 387; AEOG, no. 870, 41r–42v, 3 December 1380; 48r–49v, 20 December 1380; 59r–60r, 11 January 1380(1), no. 885, 15r–16r, 2 March 1380(1); AP, no. 1198, 39v–44v, 12 December 1379; 47v–49v, 2 January 1379(80); ACP, no. 1313, 26r–29r, 16 February 1380(1), 127r–128r, 5 January 1380(1). In addition, Bonaccorso Pitti *(Ricordi,* pp. 370–379) shows the support he and other exiled enemies of the Governments of the Ciompi and the Minor Guilds received in Pisa, Genoa, Bologna, Arezzo, and Siena. The judicial records point to these and other cities where Florentine elite bandits could plot their return—Bologna, Parma, Padua, and Arezzo; see AEOG, no. 870, 13r–v, 1 September 1380; AP no. 1198, 55r–59r, 15 February 1379(80), 103r–106v, 24 October, 1379(80); ACP no. 1313, 20r–21v, 1 February 1380(1); 24r–25v, 16 February 1380(1); 26r–29r, 127r–128r.

49. *Cronaca . . . Minerbetti,* p. 194.

50. Rutenburg, *Popolo e movimenti popolari,* p. 149.

51. The most important popular rebel in Florence bearing a Sienese prominence, however, came before the Ciompi and the Bruco revolts. In 1343, Aldobrando di Ciecharino, called Trolquelio, who was from Siena but resided in the Florentine parish of San Lorenzo, led an armed insurrection of wool workers; AP, no. 23, fol. 87r–v; and Cohn, *The Laboring Classes,* p. 139.

52. Nicholas, *Medieval Flanders,* p. 228; and Nicholas, *The van Arteveldes,* pp. 111–112.

53. G. Villani, *Nuova Cronica,* II, pp. 686–687.

54. Ibid., III, p. 164; also see Daniel Waley, *Mediaeval Orvieto: The Political History of an Italian City-state 1157–1334* (Cambridge, 1952), pp. 130–131.

55. *Cronaca del Conte Francesco di Montemarte,* p. 248.

56. *Cronaca . . . Minerbetti,* pp. 104–105.

57. Salvatorelli, *L'Italia comunale,* p. 672. For the letter sent by Palermo to Messina to rally revolt against the French king—the "Pharaoh Prince"—see *Chronicon Siciliae auctore anonymo,* Muratori, X, cols. 830–832. Confederations of Sicilian cities—Messina, Catania, and Palermo—are found earlier in opposition to Frederick II; see Nicolai de Jamsilla, *Historia de rebus gestis Friderici II,* Muratori, VIII, col. 549.

58. Salvatorelli, *L'Italia comunale,* pp. 672–673.

59. *Cronaca malatestiana,* p. 38.

60. *Annales Mediolanenses Anonymi autoris,* col. 759. Corio *(Storia di Milano,* II, p. 273) adds that the flag was red and it was unfurled in Bologna's revolt against church rule in 1376.

61. *Annales Mediolanenses Anonymi autoris,* col. 759.

62. *Cronaca di Ser Guerriero da Gubbio,* p. 18.

63. *Diario d'anonimo fiorentino,* p. 304.

64. *Continazione del codice Marciano classe X, lat. no. 69,* p. 376.

65. Corio, *Storia di Milano,* II, pp. 272–273.

66. *Cronaca fermana di Antonio di Niccolò,* in *Cronache della città di Fermo,* ed. Gaetano de Minicis, Documenti di Storia Italiana, IV (Florence, 1870), p. 4.

67. Corio, *Storia di Milano,* p. 273.

68. Ibid., p. 273; and *Cronaca A* and *Cronaca di Pietro and Floriano da Villola*, in *Corpus Chronicorum Bononiensium*, III, pp. 304–312.

69. *Cronaca A* and *Cronaca . . . da Villola*, pp. 304–312.

70. *Die Briefwechsel des Cola di Rienzo*, ed. Konrad Burdach and Paul Piur, 5 vols. (Berlin, 1913–1929).

71. G. Villani, *Nuova Cronica*, III, p. 496.

72. Another example of an established government of the *popolo* as opposed to rebels seeking aid and guidance from a foreign city-state came in 1339, when Rome sent two of its syndics to Florence to fetch a copy of its Ordinances of Justice; see Kurth, *La cité de Liège*, I, p. lxv.

73. Anonimo romano, *Cronica*, ed. Giuseppe Porta (Milan, 1979), p. 114; Carmela Crescenti, *Cola di Rienzo: simboli e allegorie* (Parma, 2003), pp. 103–106; and Musto, *Apocalypse in Rome*, p. 134.

74. In part, these city-countryside links may have been enhanced in Flanders by the institution of "external bourgeois," or what Peter Stabel *(Dwarfs among Giants*, pp. 96–105) calls "out-burghership," in which numerous residents of the Franc or surrounding countryside possessed urban rights.

75. Pirenne, *Les anciennes démocraties des Pays-Bas*, p. 172. In Flanders this integration of city and countryside may have been aided by the large numbers of "external burghers" residing in the countryside; see Chapter 2, note 27. Further, early urban planning, especially in Bruges and Ghent, with the building of canals and "the networks of little harbors and towns" along them, extended urban space into the countryside; see Boone, "Urban Space," pp. 623–624.

76. *Recueil des documents relatifs à l'histoire de l'industrie drapière*, III, pp. 102–109; the revolt of textile workers in 1280, known as the Cockerulle, Ypres, 1281; ibid., III, p. 686; and *Prisma van de geschiedenis van Ieper: Een bundel historische opstellen verzameld door O. Mus onder leiding van prof. J. A. van Houtte* (Ypres, 1974), especially G. Doudelez, "La révolution communale de 1280 à Ypres," pp. 188–294.

77. See Sumption, *The Hundred Years War*, II, pp. 329–331.

78. Secousse, *Recueil de pièces*, I, pp. 97–99; and *La chronique normande du XIVᵉ siècle*, pp. 127–132.

79. *La chronique des quatre premiers Valois*, p. 77.

80. See Challet, "La révolte des Tuchins," pp. 104–109; and Boudet, *La Jacquerie des Tuchins*, especially letters of remission concerning Tuchin raids in the mountains around Saint-Flour.

81. NHGL, X, cols. 1689–1690.

82. Ibid., X, cols. 1632–1639.

83. *Annales Veteres Mutinensium*, p. 77.

84. *Chronicon estense*, cols. 511–512.

85. M. Villani, *Cronica*, II, pp. 653–655; *Monumenta Pisana*, cols. 1031–1032.

86. Pezzana, *Storia della città di Parma*, I, pp. 153–154.

87. Gatari, *Cronaca carrarese*, pp. 326–329.

88. Raphayni de Caresinis, *Chronica*, p. 72.

89. Stella, *Annales Genuenses*, p. 185.

90. Ibid., p. 207.
91. Ibid., p. 243–244.
92. Sanuto, *Vitae ducum Venetorum,* col. 865.
93. See Chapter 2.
94. See examples in Chapter 2 and in Cohn *(Creating the Florentine State;* and *Women in the Streets,* pp. 122–124), where the village or small town of Rocca di San Casciano in the Florentine Romagna turned to their ex-feudal lords "to liberate" them from the "tyranny" of republican Florence.
95. See Chapter 1, note 63.
96. *Cronaca di Niccolò di Borbona delle cose dell'Aquila,* cols. 855–856.
97. See Chapter 1, note 92.
98. Provv. reg., 67, 1r; and *Diario d'anonimo fiorentino,* p. 359.
99. *Cronaca seconda d'anonimo,* pp. 110–111.
100. *Diario d'anonimo fiorentino,* p. 372.
101. *Stefani,* p. 328.
102. Screpanti, *L'Angelo della liberazione,* p. 84; note 48 above; and Rodolico, *I Ciompi,* p. 227.
103. *Cronaca senese di autore anomino,* p. 151; and *Cronaca senese di Donato di Neri,* pp. 581–582.
104. For the siege of Firenzuola and the numerous raids and uprisings against the Florentine commune in 1402, see *Cronaca . . . Minerbetti,* p. 275; for other references in chronicles and archival records, see Cohn, *Creating the Florentine State,* pp. 157–171; for peasant plans to stir up rebellion in Firenzuola and their failure to achieve their goals, see AP, no. 3886, 9r–10v.
105. Sanuto, *Vitæ Ducum Venetorum,* col. 876.
106. On the coordination and cooperation between peasants and certain elements of urban populations in the Uprising of 1381 as well as other peasant uprisings in late medieval England, see Hilton, "Popular Movements in England," pp. 159–163; and "Social Concepts in the English Rising of 1381," pp. 216–218.
107. Ferrariensus, *Annalium Libris Marchionum Estensium,* pp. 15–17.
108. Corio, *Storia di Milano,* II, p. 467.
109. *Cronaca senese . . . di Paolo di Tommaso Montauri,* p. 780.
110. Stella, *Annales Genuenses,* p. 208.
111. Ibid., pp. 251–252.
112. Ibid., p. 344.
113. Ibid., pp. 222–224.
114. Ibid., p. 233.
115. Ibid., p. 244.
116. Ibid., pp. 267–268.
117. Ibid., p. 275.
118. Ibid., p. 274.
119. Ibid., p. 275.
120. Ibid., p. 328.
121. Ibid., p. 344.

122. On the unique geopolitical character of the Italian city-state, see Giorgio Chittolini, "A Geography of the 'Contadi' in Communal Italy," in *Portraits of Medieval and Renaissance Living: Essays in Honor of David Herlihy,* ed. Cohn and Steven A. Epstein (Ann Arbor, 1996), pp. 417–438. Exceptions included Turin, which hardly possessed a *contado,* at least by the end of the thirteenth century; see Giampietro Casiraghi, Enrico Artifoni, and Guido Castelnuovo, "Il secolo XIII: apogeo e crisi di un'autonomia municipale," in *Storia di Torino: I. Dalla preistoria al comune medievale,* ed. Giuseppe Sergi (Turin, 1997), pp. 657–714.

123. Herlihy and Klapisch, *Les Toscans et leurs familles,* part 3, "Population et fortunes."

124. See Epstein, "Cities, Regions and the Late Medieval Crisis: Sicily and Tuscany Compared," *Past & Present* 130 (1991): 3–50; and "Regional Fairs, Institutional Innovation and Economic Growth in Late Medieval Europe," *Economic History Review* 2nd ser. 47 (1994): 459–482.

125. John Larner, *The Lords of Romagna: Romagnol Society and the Origins of the Signorie* (New York, 1965).

126. Kurth, *La cité de Liège,* II, pp. 136–138.

127. See Cohn, *Women in the Streets;* Cohn, "Piety and Religious Practice"; and Christian Bec, "La paysan dans la nouvelle toscane (1350–1530)," in *Civiltà ed economia agricola in Toscana nei secc. XIII–XV: Problemi della vita delle campagne nel tardo medioevo (Pistoia, 21–24 aprile 1977)* (Pistoia, 1981), pp. 29–52.

8. Flags and Words

1. In three articles—"Neighbors and Comrades: The Revolutionaries of Florence, 1378," *Social Analysis* 14 (1983): 53–105; "Follow the Flag: The Ciompi Revolt Seen from the Streets," *Bibliothèque d'Humanisme et Renaissance* 46 (1984): 357–392; and "Herald of the Ciompi: The Authorship of an Anonymous Florentine Chronicle," *Quellen und Forschungen* 65 (1985): 159–191—Trexler was the first to point to the significance of flags in the Revolt of the Ciompi (although Rodolico was certainly aware of them; see *I Ciompi,* pp. 144, 168–169, 174–175, 177, 226, and 233). Trexler's discussion focused on the use of flags by radicals in San Frediano with the Eight of Santa Maria Novella at the end of August 1378.

2. See Screpanti, *L'Angelo della liberazione,* p. 77, and note 80 below.

3. On the iconography of this flag and speculations on which angel this was, see ibid., pp. 126–127.

4. When the *popolo minuto* presented their first petitions passed as laws on 21 July, the workers stood as a single body, "the *popolo minuto*" without guild divisions. They became eligible for office (two priors, three of the Twelve Good Men, and four of the sixteen gonfalonieri) as members of this new group called the *"Popolo minuto."* After 22 July, there were no new sessions of the Councils of the People and the Commune that appear until 11 September 1378, after the defeat of the Eight of Santa Maria Novella. At this point, the three new revolutionary guilds were first described, that is, at the very moment when the third guild—

that of the Ciompi, also called the guild of the carders and the *Popolo di Dio*—was disbanded; Provv. reg., no. 67, fol. 1r–13v and 15r. According to *Stefani*, p. 327, these guilds were created toward the end of July; by *Cronaca prima d'anonimo*, p. 77, it was on or after 28 August. For a description of these three flags, see ibid., p. 77.

5. *Cronaca prima d'anonimo*, p. 75; and *Popular Protest*, doc. no. 121.

6. *Stefani*, pp. 199–200.

7. *Diario d'anonimo fiorentino*, p. 370.

8. Ibid., pp. 377–378.

9. *Cronaca prima d'anonimo*, p. 82; *Popular Protest*, doc. no. 126.

10. *Stefani*, p. 397; *Popular Protest*, doc. no. 186.

11. Ibid., p. 377. With the defeat of the Otto di Santa Maria Novella, Florence passed a law condemning to death anyone who painted any flag that was not authorized by the government; see Rodolico, *I Ciompi*, p. 177.

12. Ibid., pp. 423–424. The following year (on 21 July 1383—the anniversary of the Ciompi uprising), these two city nodes, the Ponte alla Carraia and the church of Santa Maria Novella, were again central to the ex-Ciompi organization. They gathered first at this bridge with their "insegna" and cries of "Vivano le vinti quatro arti" and "Vivano le vinti quatro arti et muogano li tradeturi che ce fanno morire de fame." They then marched to Santa Maria Novella, where they were dispersed and their leader captured and condemned to death; AEOG, no. 950, 15r–16v, 1383.viii.30.

13. *Alle bocche della piazza*, p. 43.

14. See ACP, no. 1198, 39v–44v, 17 December 1379, 55r–59r, 15 February 1379(80); AEOG, no. 950, 7r–8v, 6 August 1383; 11r–12r, 20 August 1383; 15r–16v, 30 August 1383; 17r–18v, 7 September 1383; 25r–27v, 11 September 1383; 29r–30v, 23 September 1383; 33r–34v, 16 September 1383; 35r–36v, 23 September 1383.

15. ACP, no. 1198, 55r–59r.

16. In the fifth revolt of Zara against Venice (1242), the Jaderatini raised the flag of the King of Hungary in their struggle against Venetian domination; Danduli, *Chronica per extensium descripta*, p. 299.

17. For flag-waving revolts in these Sicilian cities, see Michele da Piazza, *Chronica*, pp. 129, 198, and 258.

18. Bartolomaei de Neocastro, *Historia Sicula [AA. 1250–1293]*, ed. Giuseppe Paladino, RIS, XIII/3 (Bologna, 1921–1922), p. 19.

19. *Cronaca di Niccolò di Borbona*, col. 864. Earlier in 1293, the *popolo* raised their flags in a rebellion against the Neapolitan crown; *Cronaca aquilana rimata di Buccio di Ranallo*, p. 34.

20. *Il Diario romano di Antonio di Pietro dello Schiavo*, pp. 20–21.

21. *Annales Estenses Jacobi de Delayto*, col. 1026.

22. Gatari, *Cronaca carrarese*, p. 556.

23. Sanuto, *Vitae ducum Venetorum*, col. 865.

24. *Annales Urbevetani: Cronica antique*, p. 181; also, see Waley, *Mediaeval Orvieto*, p. 101.

25. *Cronaca di Luca di Domenico Manenti (1174–1413)*, in *Ephemerides Urbevetanae*, p. 380.

26. *Le Croniche di Giovanni Sercambi,* I, pp. 204–205.

27. *Cronica di Pisa,* Muratori, XV, cols. 1051–1052bis; and *Cronaca di Pisa di Ranieri Sardo,* p. 184.

28. *Discorso Historico,* pp. 8–9.

29. *Alle bocche della piazza,* p. 139.

30. Such ritual humiliation is seen in other contexts, as in 1214, when people of Treviso held games in honor of Padua, which led to a scuffle between Paduans and Venetians. In response to Venice's unsportsmanlike conduct, the Paduans broke the flags of San Marco; *Chronicon Patavinum ab MCLXXIV usque ad MCCCXCIX auctore anonymo,* Muratori, *Antiquitates Italicae medii Aevi,* II, cols. 1127–1128.

31. *Cronaca senese di Donato di Neri,* pp. 577–579; *Popular Protest,* doc. no. 71. In another revolt in 1368, the Twelve revolted against the emperor, beginning their revolt by ritualistically desecrating the imperial insignia and flags, throwing them on the ground; *Cronaca di Pisa di Ranieri Sardo,* pp. 178–179. Furthermore, according to the *Cronaca prima d'anonimo,* p. 83, with the defeat of the Eight of Santa Maria Novella, the counterrevolutionary crowds threw the Ciompi flag of the angel from the Palazzo Signoria, tore it to shreds, and stomped their feet on what remained. Ten days later, the government celebrated their victory over the Eight, which included a ritual vilification of the Ciompi flag; also see Rodolico, *I Ciompi,* p. 174.

32. On the list and division of professions, see *Documenti . . . del Comune di Siena,* pp. 43–46; *Popular Protest,* doc. no. 72.

33. M. Villani, *Cronica,* I, pp. 645–646.

34. *Cronaca senese di Donato di Neri,* pp. 639–640.

35. *Cronaca . . . Fratre Hyeronimo de Bursellis,* pp. 53–55.

36. Ibid., pp. 57–58.

37. *Annales Estenses Jacobi de Delayto,* col. 970.

38. *Chronicon Regiense,* p. 94.

39. *Annali genovesi di Caffaro e suoi continuatori,* III, p. 109.

40. Corio, *Storia di Milano,* II, p. 273; and *Annales Mediolanenses Anonymi autoris,* col. 759.

41. *Chronica Parmensia a sec. XI. ad exitum sec. XIV,* pp. 194 and 196; *Chronicon Parmense,* pp. 147–148 and 208; and Ferrariensius, *Excerpta ex annalibus Principium Estensium ab anno MCDIX usque ad MCDLIV,* Muratori, XX, col. 447.

42. *Chronica Parmensia a sec. XI. ad exitum sec. XIV,* p. 194.

43. Ibid., pp. 270–275.

44. *Cronicon Siculum incertis authoris,* p. 8; and *Popular Protest,* doc. no. 55.

45. *Polyhistoria Fratris Bartholomaei Ferrariensi,* col. 784.

46. Ibid., col. 785.

47. *Cronicon Siculum incertis authoris,* pp. 11–12; *Chronicon suessanum ab an. MCI. ad an. MCCCXLVIII,* in *Raccolta di varie croniche, diarj, ed altri opuscoli così italiani, come latini appartenenti alla storia del Regno di Napoli,* ed. Alessio A. Pelliccia (Naples, 1780), I, p. 72.

48. *Cronicon Siculum incertis authoris,* p. 11.

49. Ibid., pp. 11–12; and *Chronicon suessanum,* p. 72.

50. *Chronicon suessanum,* p. 72.

51. *Cronicon Siculum incertis authoris,* p. 27.

52. *Diaria Neapolitana,* col. 1053.

53. Stella, *Annales Genuenses,* p. 186.

54. Sanuto, *Vitæ Ducum Venetorum,* cols. 585–586.

55. Ibid., col. 587.

56. Ibid., col. 669. Another colonial revolt against Venice, that of Crete in 1363, was in part a battle over flags and symbols. Cretan rebels refused to fly the banner of San Marco and instead raised above the bell-tower of Candia the standard of its own patron, Saint Tito, with cries of "Long live San Tito!"; see McKee, "The Revolt of St Vito," pp. 179, 204–205.

57. Cohn, *Creating the Florentine State,* p. 140.

58. *Corpus Chronicorum Bononiensium,* III, p. 479.

59. AP, no. 3856; Provv. reg., no. 40, 34r–36v; and Cohn, *Creating the Florentine State,* pp. 30–31 and 219.

60. Cohn, *Creating the Florentine State,* p. 164; and *Popular Protest,* doc. no. 198.

61. Cohn, *Women in the Streets,* pp. 123–125; and Cohn, *Creating the Florentine State,* p. 271.

62. Cohn, *Women in the Streets,* pp. 123–124 and 135.

63. *Diario d'anonimo fiorentino,* p. 435.

64. *Alle bocche della piazza,* pp. 158–159.

65. See Cohn, *Creating the Florentine State,* pp. 181–184; and Chittolini, "Civic Religion and the Countryside in Late Medieval Italy," in *City and Countryside in Late Medieval and Renaissance Italy: Essays Presented to Philip Jones,* ed. Trevor Dean and Chris Wickham (London, 1990), pp. 69–91. The document of submission and negotiations with Florence is Provv. reg., no 92, fols. 87v–90v; translated in part in *Popular Protest,* doc. no. 199.

66. Johan Huizinga, *The Waning of the Middle Ages: A Study of the Forms of Life, Thought and Art in France and the Netherlands in the Down of the Renaissance,* trans. Fritz Hopman (New York, 1924 and 1954 [Dutch ed., 1919 and 1921]). Although this translation abridged the original, it was translated in collaboration with Huizinga. The new unabridged translation, *The Autumn of the Middle Ages,* trans. Rodney J. Payton and Ultich Mammitzsch (Chicago, 1996) has been attacked for its overdependence on the German translation and stylistic flatness. For an even-handed assessment of this translation, see Edward Peters and Walter P. Simons, "The New Huizinga and the Old Middle Ages," *Speculum* 74 (1999): 587–620, esp. pp. 588–595.

67. *Chronica Aegidii Li Muisis,* pp. 173–175; *Chronique des Pays-Bas,* pp. 227–229 and 391; and *La chronique d'Enguerran de Monstrelet,* I, p. 145. Joris, *La ville de Huy au Moyen Âge,* p. 318, mentions that guild banners accompanied the bakers, millers, and weavers in their revolt against the mayor and bishop in 1299.

68. Peter Arnade, *Realms of Ritual,* pp. 105–107. *Annales Gandenses:* 13 March 1302—Ghent's commoners rallied against patricians with their battle standards firmly in hand (p. 18); on July 12, 1302 urban patricians mobilized a procession across Ghent, in which soldiers raised unspecified banners aloft. After a tax revolt in

Bruges, 1407, John the Fearless issued an ordinance limiting the use of banners by Bruges's guildsmen. According to Wim P. Blockmans ("The Formation of a Political Union," p. 61), in Ghent on 1 April 1302, "leaders of the protest summoned their followers by drums, instructing them to assemble their weapons at home and join under the banners of their respective trades." But he gives no source for this use of banners.

69. In the revolt of Ghent against the count of Flanders on 5 September 1378, the commoners grabbed the flag of the count, threw it to the ground, and ripped it apart; *Croniques de Franche, d'Engleterre, de Flandres*, pp. 218–219. According to the *Partie inédite des chroniques de Saint-Denis*, (ed. Baron J. Pichon [Paris, 1864]) p. 14, Philippe d'Artevelde's military captain had a woman sorcerer carry the Flemish banner in a battle against Charles VI in November 1382. She was killed, and the captain fled badly wounded.

70. See for instance *Istore et croniques de Flandres*, II, p. 184.

71. In Paris guild organizations reach back to the mid-twelfth century, and by 1260 over a hundred craft guilds had their own statutes; see Lewis, *Later Medieval France*, p. 251.

72. For the narrative sources on the Jacquerie, see Marie-Thérèse de Medeiros, *Jacques et chroniqueurs: Une étude comparée de récits contemporains relatant la Jacquerie de 1358* (Paris, 1979); and Luce, *Histoire de la Jacquerie;* for the *Maillotins*, see Mirot, *Les insurrections urbaines*.

73. *La chronique des quatre premiers Valois*, p. 74.

74. *Chronique des règnes de Jean II et de Charles V*, I, p. 207; and *Chronique normande du XIVᵉ siècle*, pp. 134–135.

75. *Chronique du religieux de Saint-Denys*, IV, pp. 454–458

76. *Jean Froissart Chroniques, Livres I et II*, pp. 923–924. Pitti, *Ricordi*, p. 382, who was employed as a mercenary in the troops that defeated Artevelde on that day, describes the unfurling of the *oriflambe (olifiama)* and the consequent magical lifting of the mist in almost the same words (though his were Italian). There is no evidence that either chronicler borrowed from the other. Further, *Partie inédite des chroniques de Saint-Denis* (p. 26), describes Charles VI solemnly returning the *oriflambe* to the altar of Saint-Denis after his Flemish victory. Also, the Count of Foix, the Duke of Orléans, and the Captal de Buch in their massacre of the Jacques at Meaux, charged with pennants and *oriflambes*; d'Avout, *Le Meutre d'Étienne Marcel*, p. 208.

77. *Croniques de Franche, d'Engleterre, de Flandres*, p. 203.

78. *Chronique de Guillaume de Nangis*, II, pp. 246–247.

79. *La chronique d'Enguerran de Monstrelet (1400–1444)*, II, p. 349. By contrast, the Hussite movement was also rich in banners and used pictorial devices in their street demonstrations and miltary formations. Their banners illustrated the chalice, the goose (symbolic of Jan Hus) and the Taborite war captain, Jan Žižka, mounted on a white horse; see Fudge, *The Magnificent Ride*, pp. 128, 146, 164, 227, 234, 247, and 252.

80. G. Villani, *Nuova Cronica*, III, p. 497; and Anonimo romano, *Cronica*, p. 154. On this iconography and its earlier use on coins minted by Rome's popular leader

Brancaleone degli Andalò in 1250, see Musto, *Apocalypse in Rome,* p. 177. Further, Cola's use of pictorial propaganda went beyond flags; he commissioned paintings at the Campidoglio and the churches of Sant'Angelo in Pescheria and Mary Madeline; Musto, *Apocalypse in Rome,* pp. 104, 126, and 253. Also see Duprè Theseider, *Roma dal comune di popolo,* pp. 544 and 588.

81. *Chronique de Guillaume de Nangis,* II, pp. 246–247.

82. *Chronique des règnes de Jean II et de Charles V,* p. 130.

83. *Fragment d'une chronique latine (I),* p. 611.

84. *Fragment d'une chronique françoise,* pp. 634–635.

85. *Fragment d'une chronique latine (II),* p. 664.

86. On the "White Hoods" of Ghent, a gang who in 1379 terrorized the rural population and attacked workers who were digging the New Leie to divert trade from Ghent, see Nicholas, *Medieval Flanders,* p. 228; and Prevenier and Boone, "The 'City-State' Dream," pp. 90–93.

87. *Journal d'un bourgeois de Paris,* p. 57.

88. On the late-thirteenth-century *Chaperons Blancs,* see Kurth, *La cité de Liège,* I, pp. 255 and 268–269.

89. Anonimo romano, *Cronica,* p. 154.

90. Even Crescenti, *Cola di Rienzo,* who concentrates on Cola's use of symbols, does not draw the connection.

91. See Chapter 4, note 144.

92. Maire Vigueur, "Comuni e signorie in Umbria, Marche e Lazio," pp. 449.

93. M. Villani, *Cronica,* II, pp. 536–537; *Popular Protest,* doc. no. 59.

94. Numerous accounts of the *Harelle* are found in contemporary chronicles and in letters of remission; see Chéruel, *Histoire de Rouen,* II, pp. 119–125; and Mirot, *Les insurrections urbaines; Chronique des quatre premiers Valois,* pp. 297–301; and *Chronique normande de Pierre Cochon,* pp. 162–166.

95. On this literature for northern France, Burgundy, and the Low Countries, see Peters and Simons, "The New Huizinga," pp. 605–606; and Arnade, "City, State, and Public Ritual." For the most part this literature concentrates on the fifteenth century or later. Beyond the scope of this study, the Hussites made use of mock parades in which they ceremoniously burned papal bulls; see Fudge, *The Magnificent Ride,* pp. 253–254.

96. Bercé, *Revolt and Revolution in Early Modern Europe,* p. 124: "The fleeting character of popular enthusiasm, the apparent spontaneity of their gatherings and the ease with which they dispersed showed a contempt for such happenings among political figures." Also, see Guenée, *States and Rulers,* pp. 194–195: "The revolts of the fourteenth century were born of hatred, which explains their spontaneous, inorganic and sporadic nature"; and Sabean, "The Communal Basis," p. 361. For a robust counterargument regarding the English Uprising of 1381, see Brooks ("The Organization and Achievements of the Peasants") who argues that the revolt's speed, military precision, and synchronization between actions in Essex and Kent necessitated skilled and careful planning. Also, from the standpoint of German and central European revolts in the fourteenth century, Graus *(Pest-Geissler-Judenmorde,* pp. 446–448) comments that spontaneous upris-

ings were rare and describes the prior organization and assemblies that led to the Hussite revolts.

97. AP, no. 3886, 9r–10v, and Cohn, *Creating the Florentine State*, pp. 162–164.

98. *Annales Gandenses*, p. 16.

99. *Chronique artésienne*, pp. 37–38.

100. Giambrida in Villani's Italian; Jehan Biede (Bride).

101. G. Villani, *Nuova Cronica*, II, pp. 88–90.

102. *Cronaca senese attribuita ad Agnolo di Tura*, p. 267.

103. *Cronache senese . . . di Paolo di Tommaso Montauri*, p. 230.

104. *La chronique de Jean de Hocsem*, p. 22.

105. *Chronicon Cornelii Zanteliet*, cols. 99–100.

106. *Les Grandes Chroniques de France*, VIII, pp. 250–252.

107. *Chronica Aegidii Li Muisis*, pp. 173–175.

108. Espinas, *La vie urbaine de Douai*, IV, doc. no. 1006.

109. *La chronique de Jean de Hocsem*, pp. 185–191 and 214–215; *Chronique liégeoise de 1402*, p. 309; and *Ly Myreur des histors*, VI, pp. 294–295.

110. Kurth, *La cité de Liège*, II, p. 28; and Vercauteren, *Luttes sociales à Liège*, pp. 86–87.

111. *La chronique des quatre premiers Valois*, p. 71.

112. See Arthur Layton Funk, "Robert Le Coq and Étienne Marcel," *Speculum* 19 (1944): 470–487.

113. *Histoire de la Jacquerie*, pp. 291–292.

114. Secousse, *Recueil de pièces*, I, pp. 120–121.

115. *Chronique du religieux de Saint-Denys*, I, pp. 306–307.

116. *Chronique des Pays-Bas*, pp. 207–209.

117. *Chronique du religieux de Saint-Denys*, I, pp. 16–23.

118. Ibid., I, pp. 44–53.

119. From fear of attacks by Regent Charles, Étienne Marcel employed Pierre de Villiers as captain of the Parisian city guard—in effect, chief of police—in January 1358. Already in 1358, Villiers, a Norman knight, was an experienced soldier who had served in campaigns in Brittany and Scotland; see Sumption, *The Hundred Years War*, II, pp. 305–306; and Delachenal, *Histoire de Charles V*, 5 vols. (Paris, 1909–1931), V, p. 76.

120. Jean des Marès or Jehan des Marets or Mariez was advocate general of the Parlement and one of Charles V's most able advisers; see Delachenal, *Histoire de Charles V*, II, p. 127.

121. *Chronique du religieux de Saint-Denys*, I, pp. 128–129.

122. Ibid., I, pp. 142–143 and 144–149.

123. Ibid., I, pp. 150–157.

124. Ibid., I, pp. 204–211; *Popular Protest*, pp. 285–286.

125. *Jean Froissart Chroniques*, p. 858.

126. Ibid., pp. 858–859.

127. Kurth, *La cité de Liège*, II, p. 122–126. The speech is copied in full, pp. 123–125.

128. *Chronique du religieux de Saint-Denys*, V, pp. 86–87.

129. Ibid., V, pp. 41–42.

130. Ibid., V, pp. 42–43.

131. Ibid., V, pp. 311–315.

132. Houtart, *Les tournaisiens,* pp. 216–217.

133. *Choix de pieces inédites relatives au règne de Charles VI,* I, pp. 399–400.

134. Pirenne, *Histoire de Belgique,* II, p. 92.

135. Anonimo romano, *Cronica,* p. 143. For Cola's education, see Musto, *Apocalypse in Rome,* pp. 34–44.

136. According to Musto *(Apocalypse in Rome,* p. 70), when Cola was sent as the notary and advocate of the Thirteen Good Men to Avignon in 1342 to present the commune's petitions to Pope Clement VI, he was already regarded as the best orator in Rome. In Avignon he impressed the foremost intellectual of the age, Francesco Petrarch, who in one of his "Letters without Names" probably referred to Cola's rhetorical skills: "you probed our wounds with the shafts of your eloquence to such depths that whenever I recall the sound and the meaning of your words, tears leap to my eyes, and grief again grips my soul." (Cited in Musto, *Apocalypse in Rome,* p. 76.)

137. G. Villani, *Nuova Cronica,* III, pp. 495–498.

138. See note 80.

139. *Cronaca di Antonio Godi,* p. 10; Pagliarino, *Croniche di Vicenza,* pp. 37–38.

140. *Monachi Patavini Chronicon,* col. 674.

141. Azarii, *Liber gestorum in Lombardia,* p. 123.

142. Bussolari's reputation for oratory skill had spread through northern Italy: see ibid., p. 123; M. Villani, *Cronica,* I, pp. 751–752; II, 139–141; and P. A. Williams, *Benvenuto da Imola's Commentary: A Trecento Reading of Dante* (Cambridge, 1983).

143. Kurth, *La cité de Liège,* I, p. lix; Mollat and Wolff, *The Popular Revolutions,* p. 294; Fourquin, *The Anatomy of Popular Rebellion,* p. 71; Brucker, "The Medici of the Fourteenth Century," *Speculum* 32 (1957), pp. 19–20; Philip Jacks and William Caferro, *The Spinelli of Florence: Fortunes of a Renaissance Merchant Family* (University Park, Pa., 2001), p. 24, who claim that "Salvestro was known more for his oratorical skill than political prudence . . . he fanned the flames of discontent with his inflated rhetoric." They cite the chronicler Stefani, p. 324, but he says nothing of the sort either on this page or elsewhere. More accurately, Rodolico, *I Ciompi,* p. 184, characterized him as "furbescamente prudente e silenzionso." Furthermore, according to Mattvej A. Gukowski, in "Chi fu a capo della sommossa dei Ciompi?" in *Studio in onore di Armando Sapori,* 2 vols. (Milan, 1957), I, p. 712, neither Michele de Lando nor Salvestro de' Medici was a true leader of the Ciompi; instead, the leaders were the wool workers Meo del Grasso and Luca del Melano.

144. See for instance *Diario d'anonimo fiorentino,* pp. 377; and *Cronaca prima d'anonimo,* p. 75. Similarly, in 1292, when Giano della Bella led the *popolo* and four thousand *pedoni* to rise up against the "rich and powerful" of Florence—a revolt that led to the famous Ordinance of Justice—his authority over the people rested not on any speeches or eloquence recorded by the chronicles but, instead, on creating the new flag of justice *(Gonfaloniere di giustizia),* a vermilion cross on a white field, "behind which they all followed;" *Cronica fiorentina compilata nel secolo XIII,* pp. 138–139.

145. Ser Nofri di ser Piero della Riformagioni, *Cronaca,* in *Il tumulto dei Ciompi,* p. 57.

146. *La Cronica di Dino Compagni,* pp. 16–18.

147. *Chronica Parmensia,* p. 270.

148. *Cronica di Pisa,* col. 1052 bis.

149. Bruni, *Rerum suo tempore gestorum commentarius,* pp. 445–446.

150. Pitti, *Ricordi,* pp. 383–385.

151. M. Villani, *Cronica,* II, pp. 185, 214–216, 274–275.

152. Moreover, these craft guilds had militia bands with flags and were called *bannières;* see Chevalier, "Corporations, conflits politiques et paix sociale," pp. 291–298.

153. See for instance Giles Meersseman, *Ordo Fraternitas: Confraternite e pietà dei laici nel medioevo,* 3 vols. (Rome, 1977); Catherine Vincent, *Des charités bien ordonnées: Les confréries normandes de la fin du XIIIᵉ siécle au début du XVIᵉ siècle* (Paris, 1988); Lewis, *Late Medieval France,* pp. 276–280; Kurth, *La cité de Liège,* II, p. 231; for the twelfth-century spread of Marian confraternities at Le Puy en Velai, see Mundy, *Liberty and Political Power in Toulouse,* p. 65. For confraternities of craft associations, see Petit-Dutaillis, *Les communes françaises,* pp. 170–171, and 205 (for Amiens); Vercauteren, *Luttes sociales à Liège,* pp. 36–38; Chevalier, "Corporations, conflits politiques et paix sociale," pp. 277–284; and Heers, *L'Occident aux XIVᵉ et XVᵉ siècle,* pp. 306–313. For English craft confraternities in the late fourteenth century, see Hilton, "Popular Movements in England," p. 163.

154. Wolff, *Histoire de Toulouse,* pp. 113–114. In the late fourteenth and fifteenth centuries, Toulousains distributed pious legacies to "many religious confraternities," and often the same person belonged to more than one (ibid., p. 169).

155. *Chronique de Jean de Stavelot,* ed. A. Borgnet (Brussels, 1861), p. 133. For the importance of the Holy Blood procession and other religious festivities as "civic ritual" in Flemish towns during the fourteenth century, see Brown, "Civic Ritual," 277–299, esp. pp. 280–285.

156. For evidence from mid-fifteenth-century Flanders of guild and confraternity symbols and revolt, see Boone, "Urban Space," pp. 631–632 and 634–635; and Arnade, "Crowds, Banners, and the Marketplace: Symbols of Defiance and Defeat during the Ghent War of 1452–1453," *Journal of Medieval and Renaissance Studies* 24 (1994): 471–497. Boone, in "Urban Space," p. 640, even suggests (but does not explore) that urban space became "an even sharper element of division and strife because of the increasing interference of princely power," first with Burgundian, then Habsburg rule: princely rule heightened the importance of symbols for social conflict and collective humiliation.

157. "City, State, and Public Ritual," p. 314. His conclusions are based largely on the research of Paul Trio.

158. Nicholas, "In the Pit of the Burgundian Theater State," p. 273.

169. Salimbene de Adam, *Cronica,* p. 99.

160. *Alberti milioni notarii regeni Liber de Temporibus et aetatibus et cronica imperatorum,* ed. Holder-Egger in MGH: SS, XXXI, pt. 1 (Hanover, 1901), p. 526.

161. Anonimo romano, *Cronica,* pp. 24–247. On Venturino's preaching and "peace pilgrimage," see Musto, *Apocalypse in Rome,* pp. 122–123.

162. *Historiae Romanae Fragmenta ab anno MCCCXXVII usque ad MCCCLIV,* in *Antiqui-tates Italicae Medii Aevi,* ed. Muratori, III, col. 273.

163. On Bernardino's and other Italian preachers' use of symbols, see most recently, Francesco Bruni, *La città divisa: Le parti e il bene comune da Dante a Guicciardini* (Bologna, 2003), pp. 343–403.

164. See *Chronique anonyme finissant en MCCLXXXVI,* p. 83; and Graus, *Pest-Geissler-Judenmorde,* pp. 455–456, who claims that banners and standards were common in the ranks of popular revolt. He gives few examples of them, however, and these come exclusively from fifteenth- and sixteenth-century Germany.

165. *Chronique de Jean le Bel,* I, p. 223; and *Ly Myreur des histors,* VI, p. 386, which bor-rowed heavily from le Bel.

166. See the descriptions of these groups in Chapter 9.

9. The Black Death and Change over Time

1. Mollat and Wolff's own examples from Flanders and the bread riots of Barcelona in the 1330s and Florence in the 1340s weaken their argument. Previously, Edward P. Cheyney, in *The Dawn of a New Era 1250–1453* (New York, 1936), p. 129, pointed to the years 1378–1383 as a remarkable "half decade of revolt" throughout Europe, but he listed only five revolts.

2. See Jordan, *The Great Famine,* and examples supplied earlier for Italy in the late 1320s and 1340s.

3. The economic and social literature on these broad European trends is vast; see for instance Dyer, "The Social and Economic Background to the Rural Revolt of 1381," pp. 8–9; Dyer, *Standards of Living in the Middle Ages: Social Change in En-gland, c. 1200–1520* (Cambridge, 1989); Dyer, *Making a Living in the Middle Ages;* Herlihy, *The Black Death and the Transformation of the West,* ed. Cohn (Cambridge, Mass., 1997); N. J. G. Pounds, *An Economic History of Medieval Europe* (New York, 1974); *The Brenner Debate: Agrarian Class Structure and Economic Development in Pre-industrial Europe,* ed. T. H. Aston and C. H.E. Philpin (Cambridge, 1985).

4. Legislation against strikes in Douai in 1245; *Recueil des documents relatifs à l'his-toire de l'industrie drapière,* II, p. 22; strikes and disturbances to work in Douai, 1266; ibid., p. 109; sentences against cloth workers on strike in Douai, 1280; ibid., II, pp. 141–143; the breaking of tools at Saint-Omer in 1325, ibid., I, p. 63 and pp. 98–102; strikes at Béthune in the latter half of the fourteenth century, ibid., p. 313 and pp. 328–330. Legislation against strikes for higher wages: *The Coutumes de Beauvaisis,* p. 314; commoners' revolt against changes in currency and the rise of rents in Paris, 1307; *Les Grandes Chroniques de France,* VIII, pp. 250–252, and *Chronique anonyme finissant en M.CCC.LXXXIII,* p. 142.

5. See for instance the rebellion of textile workers in Ypres and Poperinge, 3 April 1280; *Recueil de documents relatifs à l'histoire de l'industrie drapière,* III, pp. 102–109; the revolt of textile workers in 1280, known as the Cockerulle, Ypres, 1281; ibid., III, p. 686; and G. Doudelez, "La révolution communale de 1280 à Ypres," pp. 188–294; weavers' revolt in Tournai, 1281; *Chronica Aegidii Li Muisis,* II, p. 170;

revolt of fullers, Tournai, 1307; ibid., II, p. 175; revolt of Flanders, 1323–1328: *Chronicon comitum Flandrensium*, I, pp. 34–261, esp. pp. 187, 191, and 206; *Anciennes chroniques de Flandre*, pp. 418–419; TeBrake, *A Plague of Insurrection*; and Nicholas, *Medieval Flanders*, pp. 212–216. Also, from archival sources, Geremek, in *Le salariat*, pp. 102–104, finds struggles between fullers and their bosses in Paris in 1251, 1256, and 1277. These concerned maximum hours of work and efforts to constrict access to their work force by limiting the number of apprentices and prohibiting women from their craft.

6. See Pirenne, *Histoire de Belgique*, II, p. 127; Doudelez, "La révolution communale de 1280 à Ypres," and Prevenier, "Conscience et perception de la condition sociale," pp. 175–189.

7. Revolt in Flanders of the people of little wealth *(gens de petitte chavanche)*, 1297; *Chronique des Pays-Bas, de France, etc.*, pp. 121–122; revolt in Bruges and Ghent against the patricians and taxes, 1301–1302; *Annales Gandenses*, pp. 16–18; rent strike in Paris, 1306; see Chapter 3, notes 15 and 16; tax revolt in Tournai, 1307; *Chronica Aegidii Li Muisis*, pp. 173–175; two clerics accused of heresy for leading a communal revolt in Carcassonne, 1306; NHGL, X, cols. 645–646.

8. For instance, the 1306 Parisian rent strike.

9. See Chapter 3.

10. Twenty-five tax revolts appear in chronicles sampled for France and Flanders from c. 1200 to 1348.

11. See Pirenne, *Histoire de Belgique*, vols. I–II; Pirenne, *Les anciennes démocraties des Pays-Bas;* and TeBrake, *A Plague of Insurrection.*

12. The literature on the German Peasants' War of the sixteenth century is vast; for an introduction, see Peter Blickle, *The Revolution of 1525: The German Peasants' War from a New Perspective*, trans. Thomas Brady, Jr. and H. C. Erik Midelfort (Baltimore, 1981). Also, see Norman Houseley ("Historiographical Essay: Insurrection as Religious War, 1400–1536," *Journal of Medieval History* 25 [1999]: 141–154) for other large-scale revolts of the early sixteenth century, such as the Hungarian uprising of 1514, called the Dózsa revolt, the *Comunidades* of 1520–1521 in Castile, and the *Germanías* of 1519–23 in Valencia.

13. Douai is a striking example: according to Espinas *(La vie urbaine de Douai*, I, pp. 229–269), its "revolutionary epoch" ended in 1311; afterward (even to the fifteenth century), "class hatred" all but disappeared and social relations became "very pacific" (p. 270). A similar trend is seen in other places, particularly in northern France from the chronicles and Flanders in the documents on strikes, workingmen's associations, and riots published in Pirenne and Espinas, *Recueil des documents relatifs à l'histoire de l'industrie drapière en Flandre.*

14. On such models, see Chapter 2. As for grain and other riots during this famine, see Chapter 3, note 84.

15. See Artonne, *Le mouvement de 1314;* Brown, "Reform and Resistance."

16. At least this was the case for Douai in 1322–1323; see Jordan, *The Great Famine*, pp. 165–166.

17. Nicholas, *Medieval Flanders*, p. 211.

18. See TeBrake, *A Plague of Insurrection;* and Nicholas, *Medieval Flanders,* pp. 212–216.

19. According to Pirenne, in *Les anciennes démocraties des Pays-Bas,* p. 173, after the Peace of Jeneffe (1330), craftsmen at Liège ceased to exert political opposition as before; half the magistrates came from their ranks.

20. In addition, after the repression of 1328, with their city walls dismantled and artisan militias disarmed, Bruges and Ypres were less eager to risk new revolts; see Pirenne, *Histoire de Belgique,* II, p. 110.

21. Nicholas, *The van Arteveldes of Ghent,* pp. 67–68. Already, Pirenne, in *Histoire de Belgique,* II, pp. 113–114, had debunked earlier notions from Froissart that the Arteveldes were men of the people. Pirenne, in *Histoire de Belgique,* II, p. 121, characterized Ghent's struggle for hegemony within Flanders as akin to Florence's for control of Tuscan in the fifteenth century. I believe the Florence-Milan struggle is a better analogue. Later, Hans Van Werveke, "Industrial Growth in the Middle Ages: The Cloth Industry in Flanders," *Economic History Review* 6 (1954), pp. 243–234, argued that comparisons between the Ghent revolt of 1379 and the Florentine Ciompi were misleading. The Ghent revolt had nothing to do with wages or working conditions. Blockmans, in "The Formation of a Political Union," pp. 70–71, characterizes the struggles from 1337 to the Black Death as "the imperialism of the big three cities."

22. Blockmans and Prevenier, *The Promised Lands,* p. 22.

23. The literature on the rise of the *popolo* is immense; see Cristiani, *Nobiltà e popolo del comune di Pisa;* Lansing, *The Florentine Magnates;* Maire Vigueur, "Comuni e signorie in Umbria, Marche e Lazio;" Koenig, *Il popolo dell'Italia del Nord;* and Grillo, *Milano in età comunale (1183–1276).*

24. See G. Villani, *Nuova Cronica,* II, pp. 22–25 and 29–31.

25. *Corpus Chronicorum Bononiensium,* II, pp. 232–233; and Griffoni, *Memoriale Historicum de Rebus Bononiensium,* p. 25.

26. For the privileged place of butchers as the aristocracy of labor and traditional leaders of artisan revolts in late medieval Bologna, see Francesca Bocchi, "I Bentivoglio da cittadini a signori," *Atti e memorie deputazione di storia patria per le province di Romagna,* new series, XXII (1971), p. 64.

27. *Cronaca senese attribuita ad Agnolo di Tura,* pp. 371–373.

28. Bowsky, "The Anatomy of Rebellion in Fourteenth-Century Siena: from Commune to Signory?" in *Violence and Disorder in Italian Cities, 1200–1500,* ed. Martines (Berkeley, 1972), pp. 229–272; *Cronaca senese attribuita ad Agnolo di Tura,* pp. 371–373, 380, and 416–417; *Cronaca senese di autore anomino,* pp. 114–115 and 128.

29. *Cronaca senese di autore anonimo,* pp. 127–128; *Cronaca senese attribuita ad Agnolo di Tura,* pp. 416–417; *Popular Protest,* no. 36.

30. *Corpus Chronicorum Bononiensium,* II, p. 276.

31. Ibid., II, pp. 394, 397–398.

32. Salimbene de Adam, *Cronica,* II, p. 649.

33. *Annales Parmenses maiores,* p. 709.

34. *Chronicon Parmense,* pp. 147–148; *Chronica Parmensia,* pp. 194–196.

35. See Chapter 2.
36. *Annales Genuenses*, p. 133.
37. G. Villani, *Nuova Cronica*, II, pp. 784–785; *Stefani*, p. 173.
38. G. Villani, *Nuova Cronica*, III, pp. 295–300; *Stefani*, p. 206; *Popular Protest*, no. 42.
39. Rutenburg, *Popolo e movimenti popolari*, pp. 95–96; Rodolico, *Il Popolo Minuto*, pp. 24–27; Screpanti, *L'Angelo della liberazione*, p. 35; and Cesare Paoli, "Della signoria di Gualtieri duca di Atene in Firenze," *Giornale storico degli archivi toscani*, VI (1862): 81–121 and 169–286, esp. doc. no. 83.
40. Rodolico, *Il Popolo Minuto*, p. 24. Moreover, sixteenth-century transcriptions of now lost sources from the fourteenth century name an official of the guild of carders during the period of the Duke of Athens.
41. G. Villani, *Nuova Cronica*, III, pp. 295–345; *Stefani*, pp. 194–195, 202–206; *Cronaca senese di autore anomino*, p. 147; *Cronaca senese attribuita ad Agnolo di Tura*, p. 533; *Monumenta Pisana*, col. 1012.
42. Screpanti, *L'Angelo della liberazione*, p. 154.
43. G. Villani, *Nuova Cronica*, III, pp. 350–353.
44. Rodolico, *Il Popolo Minuto*, doc. 9, pp. 93–94; *Popular Protest*, nos. 45–46.
45. *Storie Pistoresi*, p. 196; see Chapter 3.
46. Rodolico, *Il Popolo Minuto*, doc. no. 14, pp. 102–104; *Popular Protest*, no. 47.
47. Rodolico, *Il Popolo Minuto.*, doc. no. 25, pp. 114–115; *Popular Protest*, no. 51. In 1344, artisans attacked the palace of the Rucellai with cries of "Long live the Guilds" and "Death to the fat cats *(li populari grassi);*" Rodolico, *Il Popolo Minuto*, doc. no. 19, pp. 108–109.
48. *Cronaca senese attribuita ad Agnolo di Tura*, p. 549; Rodolico, *Il Popolo Minuto*, doc. 10, pp. 94–97; *Popular Protest*, nos. 48–49.
49. AP, no. 334, 40r-v; *Popular Protest*, no. 68.
50. Unfortunately, the sentences for this case, which would have appeared in Podestà, no. 204, do not survive; nor have I been able to find the case in the surviving inquisitions for 1347. The inquest of 1348, however, summarizes this revolt.
51. *Corpus Chronicorum Bononiensium*, II, pp. 603 and 607; *Popular Protest*, no. 69.
52. The late-sixteenth-century historian Pellini, in *Dell'Historia di Perugia* I, pp. 909–910, mentions "un poco di tumulto" in front of the town hall, whose participants chanted "Long live the People," but he gives no source for the incident, and I find no trace of it in the published chronicles.
53. *Venetiarum Historia vulgo Petro Iustiniano Iustiniani*, p. 230; *Corpus Chronicorum Bononiensium*, II, p. 594; Raphayni de Caresinis, *Chronica*, p. 49; and Sanuto, *Vitae ducum Venetorum*, col. 616.
54. M. Villani, *Cronica*, I, pp. 49–50.
55. *Cronaca senese attribuita ad Agnolo di Tura*, p. 561.
56. Ibid., p. 563.
57. *Cronaca senese di Donato di Neri*, p. 570.
58. M. Villani, *Cronica*, I, pp. 276–278. Also, see Eugenio Duprè Theseider, *Roma dal comune di popolo*, p. 628.

59. *Cronaca aquilana rimata di Buccio di Ranallo*, p. 207.

60. *Chronique normande de Pierre Cochon*, pp. 75–76. From exhaustive research into the secondary literature, Chevalier, in "Corporations, conflits politiques et paix sociale," p. 285, finds even less evidence of popular insurrection in this period: "De 1340 à 1355, la chronique de l'agitation dans les villes françaises semble vide."

61. *Registres des Trésor des chartes*, III/3: *JJ 76 à 79b*, nos. 6888–6889. Also, archival sources reveal that crowds at Provins devastated the monastery of Saint-Ayoul in 1349; see Petit-Dutaillis, *Les communes françaises*, p. 183.

62. *Les pays de la Loire*, no. 98.

63. NHGL, X, cols. 1074–1077.

64. *Chronica Aegidii Li Muisis*, pp. 283–288; also see Nicholas, *Medieval Flanders*, pp. 225 and 308; Nicholas, *The Metamorphosis of a Medieval City: Ghent in the Age of the Arteveldes, 1302–1390* (Leiden, 1987), pp. 5 and 135–154; and Pirenne, *Histoire de Belgique*, II, p. 135.

65. M. Villani, *Cronica*, II, pp. 536–537; Pirenne, *Histoire de Belgique*, II, pp. 200–201; and *Popular Protest*, no. 59. For Ghent, see Prevenier and Boone, "The 'City-State' Dream," p. 87. Other areas of Europe show a similar social quiescence with few exceptions. In 1348 the smiths of Nuremberg revolted against the oligarchy to gain guild recognition, but plague did not reach Nuremberg until later in the fourteenth century. Besides, more recent historiography has reinterpreted this revolt: instead of one dominated by craftsmen, the hand of Nuremberg's most important families directed it for their own political and economic interests; see Alfred Haverkamp, " 'Conflitti interni' e collegamenti sovralocali nelle città tedesche durante la prima méta del XIV secolo," *Aristocrazia cittadina e ceti popolari nel tardo Medioevo in Italia e in Germania*, Annali dell'Istituto storico italo-germanico, no. 13, ed. Reinhard Elze and Gina Fasoli (Bologna, 1984), pp. 160–161. In 1348, the cities of Aragon continued their resistance to King Pere III and were brutally repressed. The union of the six principal cities of Aragon and the brief success of their revolt for independence, however, began in early 1347, well before the plague had arrived; Pere III, *Chronicle*, pp. 400–449.

66. Pirenne, *Histoire de Belgique*, II, p. 134. This is also the view of Prevenier and Boone ("The 'City-State' Dream," p. 87): "Fed up with their arrogance they [the coalition of fullers, small guilds, and burghers] expelled the weavers from the city government, after numerous weavers were killed in another bloodbath on 13th January 1349."

67. England may have been exceptional as well, since it had few Jews to attack, having expelled them in 1290; see Christopher Harper-Bill, "The English Church and English Religion after the Black Death," in *The Black Death in England*, ed. Mark Ormerod and Phillip Lindley (Stamford, 1996), p. 107. However, according to Raymond Crawfurd, in *Plague and Pestilence in Literature and Art* (Oxford, 1914), p. 125: "In England the Black Death served to revive the perennial charges brought against the Jews."

68. Cecil Roth, *The History of the Jews of Italy* (Philadelphia, 1946), p. 142. However, Shlomo Simonsohn, in *History of the Jews in the Duchy of Mantua* (Jerusalem, 1977), mentions no massacres in 1348–1349.

69. Michele da Piazza, *Chronica*, p. 92. In "The Black Death and the Burning of Jews" (in press), I argue that the persecution of Jews in Germany in 1348–1349 was neither perpetrated by the rabble nor caused by class outrage against Jews as tax collectors or moneylenders. By contrast, later outbreaks of anti-Semitic violence in Paris and Rouen in the early 1380s and in Spain in 1391 saw the lower classes attack Jews because of their role as usurers and tax collectors. Also, criminal and factional violence among feuding families may have escalated in the immediate aftermath of the plague; see Bowsky, "The Medieval Commune and Internal Violence: Police, Power and Public Safety in Siena, 1287–1355," *American Historical Review* 73 (1967), p. 16; and Smail, "Telling Tales in Angevin Courts," *French Historical Studies* 20 (1997), pp. 186–187.

70. For examples of these immediate postplague acts of violence, see *Chronique de Guillaume de Nangis*, II, pp. 213–2214 and 217–218; *Breve Chronicon Flandriae*, III, p. 23; *Annales Floreffienses*, ed. L. C. Bethmann in MGH: SS., XVIII, p. 629; *Chronicon Aegidii Li Muisis . . . alterum*, II, pp. 341–348; *The Black Death*, ed. Horrox, doc. nos. 68–75; Simonsohn, *The Apostolic See and the Jews, Documents: 492–1404* (Toronto, 1988), nos. 373–374 and 399–400; and *The Jew in the Medieval World: A Source Book, 315–1791*, ed. Jacob Rader Marcus, 2nd ed. (Cincinnati, 1999), pp. 49–55. Many more examples can be found in the German chronicles.

71. *Chronique de Jean le Bel*, p. 223.

72. Ibid., p. 225.

73. *Les Grandes Chroniques de France*, VIII, pp. 323–325.

74. *Chronicon Aegidii Li Muisis . . . alterum*, pp. 341–342. The SHF edition distinguishes the two chronicles by calling the first one "Chronique" and the second "Annales": *Chronique et Annales de Gilles le Muisit*, ed. H. Lemaître, SHF, CCCXXIII (Paris, 1906), especially pp. 221–259.

75. *Chronicon Aegidii Li Muisis . . . alterum*, pp. 345–346.

76. Ibid., p. 348.

77. Ibid., pp. 349–350.

78. Ibid., pp. 350–354. Norman Cohn, in *The Pursuit of the Millennium: Revolutionary Millenarians and Mystical Anarchists of the Middle Ages*, 2nd ed. (London, 1970 [1957]), p. 137, maintains that "the movement always consisted in the main of peasants and artisans" but supplies no evidence to back his claim. Certainly, by li Muisis's account, the most detailed one I know, it was not a popular movement but one led by noblemen and -women and backed by the town's bourgeois. Also, Richard Kieckhefer ("Radical Tendencies in the Flagellant Movement of the Fourteenth Century," *Journal of Medieval and Renaissance Studies* 4 (1974), p. 160) questions whether the flagellants had a lower-class composition generally through German-speaking areas and the Low Countries. According to the *Breve chronicon Flandriae*, even sons of dukes and princes formed their ranks. For Graus, in *Pest-Geissler-Judenmorde*, pp. 49, 53–54, it was a "mass movement" but hardly one dominated by the rabble or lower classes. He shows that farm laborers even needed the permission of their lords to join the movement.

79. See translation in *The Black Death*, ed. Horrox, pp. 150–153: "They suddenly sprang up in all parts of Germany . . . They were said, as if in confirmation of

the prophecy, to be without a head either because they literally had no head—that is to say no one to organize and lead them—or because they had no head in the sense of having no brain and no judgement" (p. 150). This source also describes the violence between the flagellants and the clergy, the Dominicans in particular. Furthermore, numerous other German chronicles describe the flagellants as "the headless sect"; see Klaus Arnold, "Pest—Geißler—Judenmorde: Das Beispiel Würzburg," in *Strukturen der Gesellschaft im Mittelalten: Interdisziplinäre Mediävistik un Würzburg*, ed. Dieter Rödel and Joachim Schneider (Wiesbaden, 1996), p. 367. Graus, in *Pest-Geissler-Judenmorde*, pp. 49–51, emphasizes the flagellants' organization, given their detailed dress and rituals but points to no elected leaders, assemblies, or social programs. Instead, he maintains the opposite: the flagellants of 1349 did not constitute a social movement; nor did they have any social or political agenda (pp. 54–55).

80. According to Kervyn de Lettenhove, *Histoire de Flandre*, 4 vols. (Brussels, 1847), III, p. 358, Tournai had three leaders: two were knights and the other a canon of Saint-Nicolas des Près.

81. *The Black Death*, ed. Horrox, p. 223.

82. M. Villani, *Cronica*, I, pp. 365–366; *Popular Protest*, no. 70.

83. Ibid., I, p. 388.

84. Niccola della Tuccia, *Cronache di Viterbo*, p. 34.

85. *Polyhistoria Fratris Bartholomaei Ferrariensi*, col. 835.

86. On the Bentivoglio's artisan origins and power within the butcher's guild, see Bocchi, "I Bentivoglio da cittadini a signori," pp. 43–64.

87. *Cronaca . . . Fratre Hyeronimo de Bursellis*, p. 45.

88. M. Villani, *Cronica*, I, pp. 485–487; *Corpus Chronicorum Bononiensium*, III, pp. 32–33.

89. *Cronaca senese di Donato di Neri*, pp. 577–579 and 581; and M. Villani, *Cronica*, II, pp. 645–646 and 655–656.

90. *Cronaca senese di Donato di Neri*, p. 579; Cortusii, *Historia de Novitabtibus Paduae*, col. 946; *Monumenta Pisana*, cols. 1029–1031.

91. M. Villani, *Cronica*, I, pp. 653–655; *Monumenta Pisana*, cols. 1031–1032. For a brief overview, see Valeri, *L'Italia nell'età dei principati*, pp. 134–137.

92. M. Villani, *Cronica*, I, p. 711.

93. Near Alessandria.

94. M. Villani, *Cronica*, I, pp. 716–717.

95. Sanuto, *Vitæ Ducum Venetorum*, col. 634.

96. Naugerii, *Historia Veneta*, cols. 1040–1041: "ho usato carnalmente con tua moglie, sorella, ovvero figliuola."

97. M. Villani, *Cronica*, I, pp. 624–626; and *Venetiarum Historia vulgo Petro Iustiniano Iustiniani*, pp. 243–244.

98. M. Villani, *Cronica*, I, p. 702.

99. *Cronaca malatestiana del secolo XIV*, p. 19.

100. M. Villani, *Cronica*, I, p. 681.

101. *Cronaca malatestiana del secolo XIV*, p. 20.

102. *Cronaca senese di Donato di Neri*, p. 586.

103. *Venetiarum Historia vulgo Petro Iustiniano Iustiniani,* p. 248.

104. Azarii, *Liber gestorum in Lombardia,* p. 77; Stella, *Annales Genuenses,* pp. 154–156; Epstein, *Genoa and the Genoese,* p. 221.

105. M. Villani, *Cronica,* I, pp. 751–752.

106. *Cronaca senese di Donato di Neri,* p. 584.

107. Ibid., p. 585.

108. *Venetiarum Historia vulgo Petro Iustiniano Iustiniani,* pp. 250–252.

109. Sanuto, *Vitae ducum Venetorum,* col. 643.

110. M. Villani, *Cronica,* II, p. 77.

111. Ibid., II, pp. 94–95, and 107–109.

112. Ibid., II, pp. 150–151.

113. Ibid., II, p. 181.

114. Ibid., II, pp. 139–140, 140–141, 141, and 206.

115. *Cronaca senese di Donato di Neri,* p. 592.

116. M. Villani, *Cronica,* II, pp. 387–388.

117. Ibid., II, pp. 301–303.

118. Ibid., II, pp. 364–366.

119. *Richardi Scoti chronici continuatio,* p. 118. The chronicler maintains that Taussac, not Marcel, was provost of the merchants in 1357.

120. Ibid., p. 120, and numerous other chronicles; also see Sumption, *The Hundred Years War,* II, pp. 312–313.

121. Sumption, *The Hundred Years War,* II, pp. 316 and 323.

122. Chéruel, *Histoire de Rouen,* I, p. 203.

123. One exception is Caen; Luce, *Histoire de la Jacquerie,* pp. 291–292.

124. See for instance *The Chronicle of Jean de Venette,* pp. 76–77; and *Richardi Scoti chronici continuatio,* pp. 126–127.

125. Chéruel, *Histoire de Rouen,* II, p. 170.

126. *Richardi Scoti chronici continuatio,* p. 98; and *Chroniques de J. Froissart,* IV, pp. 174–175.

127. Sumption, *The Hundred Years War,* II, p. 284; and Fournial, *Les villes et l'économie d'échange en Forez,* pp. 374–375.

128. M. Villani, *Cronica,* II, p. 88.

129. See Pirenne, *Histoire de Belgique,* II, p. 200; Nicholas, *Medieval Flanders,* p. 266; and M. Villani, *Cronica,* II, pp. 338–340 and 536–537.

130. M. Villani, *Cronica,* II, pp. 536–537. The same united front arose again against the count in 1368; see *Chronique des Pays-Bas,* p. 246.

131. The most thorough survey of revolts in Western Europe, Mollat and Wolff's, *The Popular Revolutions,* gives the impression of a generational absence of serious revolts after the Jacquerie, not only for northern France, but throughout Europe: "As always on the morrow of great ordeals, there first came a period not of equilibrium or of quiet, but of a sense of respite and expectation" (p. 131). Further, they do not mention a single revolt in France during this generation, attributing the quiet to "the marked languor produced by the epidemic of 1361–1362."

132. *Chronique de Guillaume de Nangis,* II, pp. 288–289; *Chronique normande du XIVe siè*cle, pp. 146–147; and *Richardi Scoti chronici continuatio,* p. 127.

133. *Chronique de Guillaume de Nangis,* II, pp. 306–307.

134. *Chronique de Guillaume de Nangis,* II, pp. 304–305.

135. For references to poverty and desperation as supposed causes of late medieval revolts and especially those after the Black Death, see my comments in Chapter 1. For the English Peasants' Revolt of 1381, historians such as Hilton, in *Bond Men Made Free,* pp. 144–164 and "Popular Movements in England," pp. 158–159; and Rigby *(English Society in the Later Middle Ages,* p. 111) emphasize rising expectations and a subjective sense of injustice. The same can be found in the chronicles such as those of Froissart and Michel Pintoin.

136. *Chronique de Guillaume de Nangis,* II, pp. 322–328.

137. Ibid., II, pp. 325–328.

138. Douglas Aiton is now studying this question.

139. Arch. nat. JJ 93, f. 66r, no. 164.

140. Arch. nat. JJ 93, f. 115v, no. 277.

141. Arch. nat. JJ 93, f. 79r, no. 194.

142. *Croniques de Franche, d'Engleterre, de Flandres,* pp. 122–123.

143. Ibid., p. 123, transcribed by Hoquet. This letter was kept in the municipal archives of Tournai, which were completely destroyed by a German firebomb in 1940.

144. *Chronique de Guillaume de Nangis,* II, pp. 349–350, and 355–356; *Chronique des Pays-Bas,* pp. 207–209.

145. *Croniques de Franche, d'Engleterre, de Flandres,* pp. 131–138.

146. *Chronique des Pays-Bas,* pp. 227–229.

147. Ibid., pp. 246 and 248–249.

148. *Recueil des documents relatifs à l'histoire de l'industrie drapière,* II, pp. 503, 512, and 535.

149. *Chronicon Comitum Flandrensium,* p. 232, and see Pirenne, *Histoire de Belgique,* II, pp. 200–201.

150. *Chronique des quatre premiers Valois,* p. 202.

151. Boudet, *La Jacquerie des Tuchins.* Similar bands, however, continued to pillage and organize cattle raids in the Massif Central and other parts of Languedoc well into the fifteenth century.

152. See NHGL, X, cols. 1688–1690, nos. 675–676.

153. NHGL, X, cols. 1180–1182.

154. Ibid., X, cols. 1351–1352.

155. Arch. nat. JJ 91, f. 266v.

156. Arch. nat. JJ 91, f. 155r, no. 302.

157. NHGL, X, cols. 1351–1355.

158. Ibid., col. 1329–1331, no. 511; *Popular Protest,* no. 67.

159. Ibid., cols. 1818–1820, no. 732; *Popular Protest,* no. 66.

160. Ibid., cols. 1332–1335.

161. Ibid., cols. 1349–1350.

162. Ibid., cols. 1412–1413.

163. *Chroniques de J. Froissart,* pp. lxxxix, 210–211, and 398; and *Chronique des quatre premiers Valois,* p. 195 (who dates it 1368).

164. *Cronaca senese di Donato di Neri,* pp. 618–625.

165. Ibid., pp. 639–640.
166. Among other places for these "années révolutionaires," 1378–1382, see Challet, "La révolte des Tuchins," p. 108.
167. In contrast, our statistics show that popular revolts hardly declined in the last decade of the fourteenth or early fifteenth centuries. Scholars such as Boone, in "Echecs des réseaux" in *Le prince et le peuple: Images de la société du temps des ducs de Bourgogne 1384–1530,* ed. Prevenier (Antwerp, 1998), pp. 344–355, have shown that the rich tradition of revolts in the Low Countries continued apace through the fifteenth century.
168. M. Villani, *Cronica,* II, pp. 94–95 and 107–108.
169. See Chapter 3, note 60.
170. *Cronaca senese di Donato di Neri,* p. 639.
171. Ibid., p. 640.
172. See Chapter 1.
173. See note 163 above.
174. *Cronaca senese di Donato di Neri,* p. 639.
175. *Cronaca . . . Fratre Hyeronimo de Bursellis,* pp. 57–58.
176. *Cronaca di Ser Guerriero da Gubbio,* p. 16.
177. *Chronicon Placentinum . . . Johanne de Mussis,* col. 521. By contrast, Mollat and Wolff, in *The Popular Revolutions,* pp. 139–141, find only 42 across Europe, and some of these, such as the wars led by Philippe van Artevelde, I would not classify as popular revolts.
178. *Cronaca malatestiana,* p. 38.
179. Brucker, *Florentine Politics and Society,* pp. 294–295.
180. Screpanti, *L'Angelo della liberazione,* p. 64.
181. *Diario d'anonimo fiorentino,* p. 329. Even where the initiative may have come from aristocrats, as in Bologna, the revolt resulted in sweeping popular reforms, a return to guild-based government and the creation of a legislative council of 500, where the *popolo minuto* began to raise their voices; see Oreste Vancini, *La rivolta dei Bolognesi,* pp. 29, 45–47, and 53.
182. *Chronica abbreviata, Fr. Johannis de Cornazano O.P* in *Chronica Parmensia a sec. XI. ad exitum sec. XIV,* p. 397.
183. Ser Andrea de Redusiis de Quero, Cancellario Communis Tarvisii, *Chronicon Tarvisinum, a. 1368–1428,* Muratori, XIX, col. 789. Also, in the German-speaking towns, postplague revolts that appear before the cluster may have predominated over those during the years 1378–1382; for instance, Rhiman A. Rotz, in "Urban Uprisings in Germany: Revolutionary or Reformist? The Case of Brunswick, 1374," *Viator* 4 (1973): 207–223, mentions collective demonstrations and revolts at Augsburg (1368), Brunswick (1374), Nordhausen (1375), and Hamburg (1376) but none during the years 1378–1382. Of the most important revolts of the later fourteenth century listed by Graus, *Pest-Geissler-Judenmorde,* p. 432 (Wetzlar, 1372; Nordhausen, 1375; Lübeck, 1376; München, 1385; Dortmund, 1386; Augsburg, 1387, and Iglau in 1391), only one (Rottweill in 1387), appears within the cluster.
184. Kurth, *La cité de Liège,* II, pp. 122–126.

185. On Charles VI's mental health and its political consequences, see Famiglietti, *Royal Intrigue.*

186. See Rudolph Binion, "Europe's Culture of Death," in *The Psychology of Death in Fantasy and History,* ed. Jerry S. Piven (Westport, Conn., 2004), pp. 119–120. Jones, in *The Italian City-State,* p. 690, sees a similar blurring of differences across the north and south of Italy during "the Renaissance age," which he attributes to "common or shared experiences" in economic structures and state systems. He does not, however, pinpoint the chronology of this age.

10. A New Appetite for Liberty

1. Although the numbers are lower, the fourteenth century also registered an increase in popular rebellion in Germany, especially between 1361 and 1380; see Haverkamp, " 'Conflitti interni,' " pp. 123–125. He relies largely on statistics gathered by Erich Maschke.

2. The spark of the English Peasants' Revolt of 1381 was taxation, first the third poll tax of 1380 and second, the subsidy owed by villages and towns, fixed in 1334, which now had to be shared by greatly reduced populations; among other sources, see Dyer, *Making a Living in the Middle Ages,* p. 282; Fryde, *The Great Revolt of 1381,* pp. 10–12; and Fryde, "Peasant Rebellion and Discontents," pp. 768–772. Other places, such as France and Siena, confronted their fiscal problems with more flexibility, shifting the tax burden to indirect (or sales) taxes or forced loans; see John B. Henneman, Jr., "The Black Death and Royal Taxation in France, 1347–1351," *Speculum* 43 (1968), p. 416; and Bowsky, "The Impact of the Black Death upon Sienese Government and Society," *Speculum* 39 (1964), pp. 21–22. But such shifts still meant increased taxation, and as regressive forms of taxation they struck commoners as even more unfair, as evinced in the *Harelle, Maillotins,* and tax revolts that swept through southern France in 1379–1381. At Le Puy, the city's oligarchy converted direct taxes into indirect ones "to off-load a greater burden of taxation upon the poor;" Lewis, *Late Medieval France,* p. 262.

3. This is the hypothesis of many, including Rodolico, *La Democrazia fiorentina,* pp. 35–36, but I know of no statistics until the tax surveys *(estimi)* of 1371, which recorded the migration of peasants in the *contado* of Florence. On migration in the *contado* of Florence during the second half of the fourteenth century, see Cohn, *Creating the Florentine State,* pp. 36–39 and 67–70. Hilton, in "Popular Movements in England," p. 158, makes a similar argument for England: by 1377, cities such as London had regained much of their plague losses through rural migration.

4. Hilton, "Popular Movements in England," p. 158. E. B. Fryde, in *Peasants and Landlords in Later Medieval England c. 1380–1525* (London, 1996), pp. 32–33, argues that this labor scarcity prompted greater risk taking, mobility, and disobedience among the English peasantry.

5. Cohn, *Creating the Florentine State,* pp. 229–231.

6. See Dobson, *The Peasants' Revolt of 1381,* pp. 63–69; Bertha Putnam, *The Enforcement of the Statutes of Labourers, 1349–1359* (New York, 1908). This was not necessarily the case with labor legislation elsewhere; see Robert Braid, " 'Et non ultra': Politiques royals du travail en Europe occidentale au XIVe siècle," *Bibliothèque d'École des chartes,* 161 (2003): 437–491. Outside of England, Petit-Dutaillis, in *Les communes françaises,* p. 200, is the only historian I know to consider this confrontation between the postplague advantage of laborers and labor legislation as a reason for the increasing numbers of revolts.

7. Cited by Fryde, *The Great Revolt of 1381,* p. 26; and Fryde, "Peasant Rebellion and Discontents," p. 760, from Putnam, ed. *Proceedings before the Justices of the Peace in the Fourteenth and Fifteenth Centuries, Edward III to Richard III* (London, 1938), p. cxxiii. For succinct descriptions of various causes of the English Peasants' Revolt of 1381, which trace its long-term causes back to the Black Death and the Statute of Labourers, see Fryde, *The Great Revolt of 1381,* pp. 25–30; Fryde, "Peasant Rebellion and Discontents," pp. 759–760; and Whittle and Rigby, "England: Popular Politics and Social Conflict," pp. 73–74.

8. Cohn, *Creating the Florentine State,* Ch. 3.

9. Cohn, *Women in the Streets,* pp. 122–123.

10. Brucker, "The Ciompi Revolution," p. 328.

11. Franco Franceschi, *Oltre il "Tumulto": I lavoratori fiorentini dell'Arte della lana tra Tre e Quattrocento* (Florence, 1993), p. 11.

12. From 1360 to 1371, dyers pressured the wool guild for special privileges, rioted, and went on strike; see Rodolico, *Il Popolo Minuto,* pp. 72–77 and 116–118.

13. Franceschi, *Oltre il "Tumulto,"* p. 13.

14. According to the *Estimo* of 1379, Florence's urban population stood at 13,779 households, not including clerics. With a cautious coefficient of four per household, which is less than in 1427 (when it can be measured), Florence would have had an urban population or around 55,116. This is almost 40 percent more than were counted in the city at the time of the 1352 estimo, when the population stood at around 40,000. However, as Rodolico, in *La Democrazia fiorentina,* p. 39, has argued, because of a rush of rural laborers into Florence in the intervening four years, the true population of Florence immediately after the Black Death must have been considerably smaller. He estimates it as low as 25,000. According to Charles-M. de la Roncière, in *Prix et salaires à Florence au XIVe siècle (1280–1380)* (Rome, 1982), p. 676, Florence's population was around 70,000 on the eve of the plague of 1363. That plague reduced the population by around one-third. On these statistics and their sources, see Cohn, *Women in the Streets,* p. 22; and *The Black Death Transformed,* pp. 199–200.

15. See Screpanti, *L'Angelo della liberazione,* pp. 119–120. On the leaders who previously had been crossbowmen or leaders of crossbowmen divisions, see Brucker, "The Ciompi Revolution," p. 329; and Trexler, "Neighbours and Comrades," pp. 64, 67, 97–100.

16. In August, the new Ciompi government "passed ordinances that all the wool bosses must produce [at least] 2,000 wool cloths [*panni*] a month, whether

they wanted to or not, or suffer great penalties"; *Cronaca terza d'anonimo*, pp. 130–131.

17. Wolff, "The 1391 Pogrom in Spain," p. 16.

18. *Chronicon Cornelii Zanteliet*, p. 325.

19. Kurth, *La cité de Liège*, II, p. 123; and *Chronique Liégeoise de 1402*, pp. 399–404.

20. Kurth, *La cité de Liège*, II, p. 125.

21. This formulation is most prominently stated in Skocpol, *States and Social Revolutions*. She is quick to caution, however, that no "general theory of revolution" can be extended beyond her study of the French, Russian, and Chinese revolutions (p. 288).

22. On centralization of power and the rise of territorial states, see Marvin Becker, "The Florentine Territorial State and Civic Humanism in the Early Renaissance," in *Florentine Studies*, pp. 109–139; and Chittolini, *La formazione dello stato regionale e le istituzioni del contado: secoli XIV e XV* (Turin, 1978).

23. For this history and its popes, see among many other places, Mollat, *The Popes at Avignon*.

24. Pirenne, *Histoire de Belgique*, II, p. 92.

25. Pirenne, *Le soulèvement de la Flandre Maritime de 1323–1328: Documents inédits* (Bruxelles, 1900); and Jacques Heers, *L'Occident aux XIVe et XVe siècle: Aspects économiques et sociaux*, "Nouvelle Clio," no. 23 (Paris, 1963), p. 100.

26. Blockmans, "The Formation of a Political Union," p. 70.

27. *La chronique d'Enguerran de Monstrelet*, IV, p. 87. Also see Chapter 4, note 148, on the Hussite rioting in Tournai in 1423. I do not, however, have any chronicle description of that riot.

28. Fudge, *The Magnificent Ride*, p. 211.

29. Houseley, "Historiographical Essay: Insurrection as Religious War," pp. 153–154.

30. Cazelles, *Société politique, noblesse et couronne sous Jean le Bon et Charles V* (Geneva, 1982), p. 323; and Bessen, "The Jacquerie," follows Cazelles' lead.

31. Luce, *Histoire de la Jacquerie*, pp. 228–229; and *Popular Protest*, no. 106.

32. Luce, *Histoire de la Jacquerie*, pp. 270–272; and *Popular Protest*, no. 112. The English Peasants' Revolt of 1381 is again exceptional; Hilton, in *Bond Men Made Free*, p. 207–210, has identified around twenty clerics as local leaders; the most prominent were John Ball and John Wrawe. Furthermore, in other essays such as "Popular Movements in England," pp. 159 and 164; "Ideology and Social Order in Late Medieval England," p. 248; and "Social Concepts in the English Rising of 1381," pp. 222–226, Hilton emphasizes the importance of popular preaching and ideas that anticipated the Lollards in forming a socioreligious ideology of peasant rebels in 1381. Finally, Walsingham and other chroniclers in the late fourteenth and fifteenth centuries tried to tarnish followers of Wycliffe by retrospectively accusing John Ball of preaching "the perverse doctrines of the perfidious John Wycliffe"; see M. E. Aston, "Lollardy and Sedition, 1381–1431," *Past & Present* 17 (1960): 4.

33. Crone, *Pre-Industrial Societies*, p. 75.

34. M. Villani, *Cronica*, II, pp. 398–399.

35. Rodolico, *La Democrazia Fiorentina*, pp. 82–86; Rodolico, *I Ciompi*, pp. 57–58; Becker, "Florentine Politics and the Diffusion of Heresy in the Trecento: A Socio-Economic Inquiry," *Speculum* 34 (1959): 60–75; Becker, "Heresy in Medieval and Renaissance Florence: A Comment," *Past & Present* 62 (1974): 153–161; Screpanti, *L'Angelo della liberazione*, Ch. 5: pp. 156–206; Donald Weinstein, "The Myth of Florence," in *Florentine Studies*, pp. 30–31. On the other side of the argument, see John Stephens, "Heresy in Medieval and Renaissance Florence," *Past & Present* 54 (1972): 25–60; Stephens, "Rejoinder," *Past & Present* 62 (1974): 162–166; and Brucker, *Florentine Politics and Society*, p. 390. In regard to Becker's and Rodolico's thesis "that the Fraticelli doctrines were a potent factor in stimulating proletarian unrest [of the Ciompi]," I concur with Brucker's judgment: "I do not believe that this thesis is proved by the very scanty and fragmentary evidence which is extant." And as Stephens, in "Heresy in Medieval and Renaissance Florence," p. 38, comments: "despite some pleas to the contrary [Rodolico's and Becker's argument], it would not seem that it [the Fraticelli] acted as an ideology of the *popolo minuto*, or of the *Ciompi*, since the poorer sort in the city wanted economic equality, and not apostolic poverty."

36. Screpanti, *L'Angelo della liberazione*, p. 200; and *Cronaca prima d'anonimo*, pp. 92–93.

37. Screpanti, *L'Angelo della liberazione*, p. 201; Gukowski, "Chi fu a capo della sommossa dei Ciompi?" p. 713.

38. For instance, on 18 July the Ciompi insurgents discussed their plans in the Hospital of the Priests and other places in Belletri; on 31 August 1378 the *popolo minuto* assembled in Santa Maria Novella, San Frediano, and Sant'Ambrogio to organize an uprising; see *Diario d'anonimo*, p. 377. After the fall of the Government of the Minor Guilds, those wishing to revive the three revolutionary guilds met at Sant'Ambrogio on 11 March 1382 to plan a revolt; see *Alle bocche della piazza*, p. 35.

39. *Alle bocche della piazza*, p. 36.

40. "Die Pestschriften des Johann von Burgund und Johann von Bordeaux," in *Archiv für Geschichte der Medizin* 5 (1911), p. 67.

41. "Das Pestwerken des Raymundus Chalin de Vivario" in *Archiv für Geschichte der Medizin* 17 (1925), pp. 38–39.

42. "Ein Paduaner Pestkonsilium von Dr. Stephanus de Doctoribus," in *Archiv für Geschichte der Medizin* 6 (1913), p. 356. For a further discussion of this change in sentiment, see Cohn, *The Black Death Transformed*, Ch. 9.

43. On these trends, see Cohn, *The Black Death Transformed*, Ch. 8.

44. Villani also condemned it in other cases, as in 1354 when "in the name of liberty" the people of Rome rose up and "tyrannously" killed their tribune, "the valiant and wise" Pandolfo de'Pandolfucci; *Cronaca*, I, pp. 509–511.

45. See for instance *Annales Mediolanenses Anonymi Autoris*, col. 759; *Cronaca malatestiana del secolo XIV*, p. 38 and pp. 42–43; *Estratti delle "Historie" di Cipriano Manenti (supplemento alla Cronica di Luca di Domenico Manetti, 1325–1376)*, p. 470; and *Diario d'anonimo fiorentino*, pp. 303–306 and 319.

46. According to Anonimo romano, in *Cronica*, p. 143, Cola's father was a tavern keeper and his mother lived by washing clothes and carrying water, but by the time he became tribune, his supporters were merchants and even the lower nobility; see Ch. 7. On Cola's triad of liberty-peace-justice that filled his letters and speeches, see Eugenio Duprè Theseider, *Roma dal comune di popolo*, p. 546.

47. On this distinction between noble franchises and rights, on the one hand, and those of the community or territorial immunity, on the other, see Alan Harding, "Political Liberty in the Middle Ages," *Speculum* 55 (1980): 423–442. Harding saw a shift from "the licence of the magnates" to "the liberties of the whole community" occurring with the antimagnate legislation of Florence in the 1290s (p. 442). He did not, however, consider the transition studied here and revealed by the sources on popular revolt—one for community rights defined by elites as opposed to those initiated by commoners and the disenfranchised on behalf of the community as a whole.

48. For documents that define liberty as privilege, see the "libertates et consuedines" Philip Augustus granted to citizens of Carcassonne around 1204; the 1216 "Charter of Liberties and Customs" granted by Henry III, king of England, "to his subjects," but which pertained only to the feudal elites, lay and ecclesiastic; or the royal "privilegiorum et libertatum" granted to the bourgeois *(burgensibus)* of Poitou in 1222; *Layettes du Trésor des chartes*, ed. Alexandre Teulet, 5 vols. (Paris, 1863–1909), I, pp. 273–281, 434–437, and 552–553. For notions of liberty and freedom in late-twelfth and early-thirteenth-century Toulouse, which centered on the urban patriciate's struggle with their count, see Mundy, *Liberty and Political Power in Toulouse.*

49. Rycarrdi de Sancto Germano, *Chronica*, p. 182.

50. *La chronique de Jean de Hocsem*, pp. 11–15.

51. *La Cronica di Dino Compagni*, pp. 16–18.

52. Naugerii, *Historia Veneta*, col. 1012.

53. *Chronique de Guillaume Bardin*, cols. 26–28.

54. *Corpus Chronicorum Bononiensium*, II, pp. 341–342.

55. Naugerii, *Historia Veneta*, col. 1028.

56. *Stefani*, pp. 204–205; *Cronaca senese di autore anomino*, p. 147; *Cronaca senese attribuita ad Agnolo di Tura*, pp. 535–536; G. Villani, *Nuova Cronica*, III, pp. 331–342; and *Popular Protest*, no. 43. On liberties as the urban privileges of the bourgeoisie in late medieval France, see Lewis, *Later Medieval France*, pp. 238–240.

57. See Screpanti, *L'Angelo della liberazione*: "the hounding out of the Duke of Athens, instead of a triumph of liberty and democracy, was a victory for the reactionary bourgeoisie," p. 154.

58. On these thinkers and preachers and notions of liberty, equality, and liberty, see Screpanti, *L'Angelo della liberazione*, Ch. 5; and la Roncière, "Pauvres et pauvreté à Florence au XIVe siècle," in Michel Mollat, *Études sur l'histoire de la pauvreté (Moyen Age-XVIe siècle)*, 2 vols. (Paris, 1974), II, pp. 661–745.

59. See Chapter 5.

60. M. Villani, *Cronica*, I, pp. 653–655.

61. *Corpus Chronicorum Bononiensium,* III, p. 476.

62. M. Villani, *Cronica,* I, pp. 679–680.

63. *Alle bocche della piazza,* p. 164.

64. *Chronique du religieux de Saint-Denys,* I, pp. 128–143.

65. *Chronique normande de Pierre Cochon,* pp. 162–166.

66. *Chronique du religieux de Saint-Denys,* I, pp. 44–153.

67. *Chronographia Regum Francorum,* III, 24–33.

68. Ibid.; Guillaume Cousinot I, *Geste de Nobles,* pp. 106–107; *Ordonnances des roys de France,* VI, 552–554.

69. *Chronique du religieux de Saint-Denys,* I, pp. 16–23.

70. Also see Hilton, "Inherent and Derived Ideology in the English Rising of 1381," p. 402: "It is worth emphasising strongly that the demand for freedom was perhaps the most powerful element of inherent ideology in 1381;" and Hilton, "Popular Movements in England," p. 159: "the demands of popular preachers and of the rebel leaders in 1381 show freedom became a central feature of peasant class consciousness." In addition, see *Chronicon Angliae:* "The peasants . . . coveting greater things . . . came together in a great multitude and began to make great tumult, demanding their liberty . . . They intended in future to be bound to pay service to no man," cited in Leonard W. Cowie, *The Black Death and Peasants' Revolt* (London, 1972), p. 87.

71. Such impulses and ideology continued to propel popular revolts beyond the chronological borders of this study. The revolts in Ghent from 1447 to 1453 were battles to preserve rights of citizenship as workers and guildsmen pushed their elites and moderate aldermen to extend these revolts against their more conservative desires to placate the duke; see Arnade, *Realms of Ritual,* Ch. 4.

Sources

Archival Sources

Archives nationales de France (Paris): JJ series
Archivio di Stato, Bologna: Curia del Podestà: Guidici ad Maleficia
Archivio di Stato, Firenze:
  Atti del Capitano del Popolo (ACP)
  Atti dell'Esecutore degli Ordinamenti di Giustizia (AEOG)
  Atti del Podestà (AP)
  Provvisioni registri (Provv. reg.)
Archivio di Stato, Lucca: Sentenze e Bandi

Histories, Chronicles, Diaries, Journals, and Lives

Collections

Antiquitates Italicae medii aevi. Ed. Ludovico Antonio Muratori. 6 vols. Milan,
1738–1742:
  vol. III:
    Historiae Romanae Fragmenta ab anno MCCCXXVII usque ad MCCCLIV, cols. 247–398.
  vol. IV:
    Excerpta ex chronico Jordani ad anno DCCCCL usque ad MCCCXX, cols. 949–1034.
    Chronicon Patavinum ab MCLXXIV usque ad MCCCXCIX auctore anonymo, cols.
      1115–1168.
  vol. V:
    Aliprandina, sive Chronicon Mantuanum . . . ab origine . . . usque 1415, cols.
      1061–1242.
  vol. VI:
    Cronaca di Niccolò di Borbona delle cose dell'Aquila, dall'anno 1363 all'anno 1424,
      cols. 853–876.

Bibliotheca Scriptorum qui res in Sicilia Gesta sub Aragonum imperio. Ed. Rasarius
Gregorio. 2 vols. Palermo, 1791–1792:
  vol. I:
    Bartholomei de Neocastro, *Historia conspirationis Johannis Prochytae,* pp. 249–274.

Nicolai Specialis, *Historia Sicula ab anno MCCLXXXII ad MCCCXXXVII*, pp. 283–508.
vol. II:
Anonymi Historia Sicula vulgari dialecto conscripta ab anno MCCCXXXVII ad MCCC-CXII, pp. 273–301.
Simonis Leontinensis Chronicon ab anonymo inde continuatum ad annum usque MCCC-CXXXIV, pp. 303–423

Collections de chroniques belges, Commission royale d'histoire:
Corpus Chronicorum Flandriae. Ed. J.-J. de Smet. 4 vols. Brussels, 1837–1865.
vol. I:
Chronicon Comitum Flandrensium.
Chronicon Flandriae inde a Liderico I° usque ad mortem Joannis.
Annales Sancti Bavonis Gandensis.
vol. II:
Chronica Aegidii Li Muisis, abbatis XVII Sancti-Martini Tornacensis.
Chronicon Aegidii Li Muisis, abbatis Sancti-Martini Tornacensis alterum.
vol. III:
Breve Chronicon Jacobi Muevin, XVIII abbatis Sancti-Martini Tornacensis.
Chronique des Pays-Bas, de France, d'Angleterre et de Tournai.

Documenti di Storia Italiano:
vol. IV:
Cronaca fermana di Antonio di Niccolò. In *Cronache della città di Fermo.* Ed. Gaetano de Minicis. Florence, 1870.
vol. V:
Niccola della Tuccia, *Cronache di Viterbo e di altre città*, in *Cronache e statuti della città di Viterbo.* Ed. Ignazio Ciampi. Florence, 1872.
vol. VI:
Cronache dei secoli XIII e XIV. Florence, 1876.
Ptolemaei Lucensis Annales. Ed. Carlo Minuto.
Diario di Ser Giovanni di Lemmo da Comugnori dal 1299 al 1320.
Diario d'anonimo fiorentino dall'anno 1358 al 1389. Ed. A. Gherardi.
Chronicon Tolosani canonici. Ed. G. B. Borsieri.

Fonti per la Storia d'Italia dall'Istituto Storico Italiano: Studi e Testi:
n. 5: Diario della città di Roma di Stefano Infessura scribasenato. Ed. Oreste Tommasini. Roma, 1890.
nn. 19–21: *Le Croniche di Giovanni Sercambi Lucchese.* Ed. Salvatore Bongi, 3 vols. Rome, 1892.
n. 41: *Cronaca aquilana rimata di Buccio di Ranallo.* Ed. Vincenzo de Bartholomaeis. Rome, 1907.
n. 99: *Cronaca di Pisa di Ranieri Sardo.* Ed. Ottavio Banti. Roma, 1963.

Monumenta Germaniae Historica: Scriptores (MGH:SS)
vol. XVI:
Annales Floreffienses, a. 1–1482. Ed. L. C. Bethmann.

vol. XVIII:

Annales Placentini Guelfi.

Annales Placentini Gibellini auctore Mutio de Modoetia.

Annales Parmenses maiores a 1165–1355.

vol. XIX:

Annales Veronenses, pp. 1–18.

Annali Siculi, pp. 494–500.

vol. XXV:

Chronica monasterii Sancti Bertini auctore Iohanne Longo de Ipra. Ed. O. Holder-Egger, pp. 736–872.

vol. XXX:

Martin de Troppau, Martinus Polonus, Chronicon pontificum: Continuations. Ed. O. Holder-Egger, pp. 708–719.

vol. XXXI/1:

Annales Cremonenses. Ed. O. Holder-Egger, pp. 1–21.

Alberti milioni notarii regeni Liber de Temporibus et aetatibus et cronica imperatorum, pp. 336–461 and 504–668.

vol. XXXV:

Die Chronik des Saba Malaspina. Ed. Walter Koller and August Nitschke.

Scriptores Rerum Germanicarum in usum scholarum ex Monumentis Germaniae Historicus separatim editi:

Iohannis Codagnelli Annales Placentini. Ed. O. Holder-Egger. Hannover, 1901.

Rerum Gallicarum et Francicarum Scriptores, Recueil des Historiens des Gaules et de la France Paris, 1855) (RGFS):

vol. XX:

Vie de Saint Louis par Guillaume de Nangis.

vol. XXI:

Chronicon Girardi de Fracheto et anonyma ejusdem operis continuatio.

Selecta e speculo historiali Vincenti Bellovacensis.

Chronique anonyme des rois de France finissant en MCCLXXXVI.

Extraits des chroniques de Saint-Denis.

Extrait d'une chronique anonyme finissant en MCCCLXXX.

Extraits d'une chronique anomyme française, finissant en MCCCVIII.

Chronique anonyme finissant en MCCCLVI.

Extraits d'une chronique anonyme finissant en MCCLXXX.

Extraits d'une chronique anonyme finissant en MCCCLXXXIII.

Fragment d'une chronique anonyme finissant en MCCCXXVIII, et continuée jusqu'e . . . MCCCLXXXIII.

Extraits de la chronique attribuée a Baudoin D'Avesnes, fils de la comtesse Marguerite de Flandre.

Extraits de la chronique attribuée a Jean Desnouelles, abbé de Saint-Vincent de Laon.

Pars ultima chronici anno MCCCXVII a Guillelmo Scoto, Sancti Dionysii monacho.

E Chronico Alberici monachi Trium Fontium.

Excerpta e memoriali Historiarum auctore Johanne Parisiensi, Sancti Victoris Parisiensis canonico regulari.

E floribus chronicorum seu catalogo Romanorum Pontificum necnon e chronico regum Francorum auctore Bernardo Guidonis, episcopo Lodovensi.

Fragmenta Libelli de ordine Praedicatorum auctore Bernardo Guidonis.

Majus Chronicon Lemovicense a Petro Coral et aliis conscriptum.

Majoris chronici Lemovicensis quartum Supplementum sive chronicon abbatiae Sancti Martini Lemovicensis auctore Petro Corali, ejusdem monasterii abate.

Anonymum S. Martialis chronicon ad annum MCCCXV continuatum.

vol. XXII:

Excerpta e chronico Gaufridi de Collone.

Ex Histoira satirica regum, regnorum et summorum pontificum ab anonymo auctore ante annum MCCCXXVIII scripta.

Ex anonymo regum Franciae chronico circa annum MCCCXLII scripto.

Extraits d'une chronique anonyme intitulée Anciennes chroniques de Flandre.

vol. XXIII:

Chronique de Primat, traduite par Jean du Vignay.

E Mari historiarum auctore Johanne de Columna ord. praedicatorum.

Ex Brevi chronoico ecclesiae S. Dionysii.

Extrait des chroniques de Pierre Cochon.

E Chronici Rotomagensis continatione.

E Chronico Sancti Laudi Rotomagensis.

E Chronico Sanctae Catharinae de Monte Rotomagi.

Rerum Italicarum Scriptores. Ed. Godovico Muratori, 28 vols. Milan, 1723–1751 (Muratori):

vol. VIII:

Antonio Godi, *Chronica ab anno MXCIV usque ad MCCLX*, cols. 66–93.

Nicolai de Jamsilla, *Historia de rebus gestis Friderici II, ab anno MCCX usque ad MCCLVIII*, cols. 491–615.

Monachi Patavini Chronicon, 1207–1270, cols. 661–734.

vol. IX:

Chronicon fratris Francisci Pipini Bononiensis ordinis praedicatorum ab 1176 ad 1314, cols. 581–752.

Chronicon Parmense 1008–1309 anonymo synchrono, cols. 755–880.

Ferreti Vicentini Historia: Rerum in Italia Gestarum 1250–1318, cols., 935–1182.

vol. X:

Albertino Mussato, *De Gestis Henrici VII. Caesaris*, cols. 27–527.

Albertino Mussato, *De gestis Italicorum post mortem Henrici VII*, cols. 569–784.

Chronicon Siciliae auctore anonymo, DCCCXX usque MCCCXXVIII, cols. 801–904.

Nicolai Specialis, *Historia Sicula in VIII libros . . . ad MCCLXXII usque MCCCXXXVII*, cols. 918–1092.

vol. XI:

Annales Veteres Mutinensium ab anno MCXXXI usque ad MCCCXXXVI . . . cum additamentis Auctore Anonymo, col. 48–86.

Chronicon Mutinenese ab anno MCCCVI ad MCCCXLII auctore Bonifacio de Morano, cols. 89–130.

Secundino Ventura, MCCCCXIX usque MCCCLVII, cols. 140–281.

Memoriale Guilielmi Venturae civis astensis, De Gestis Civium.

Astemsium et plurium illorum, cols. 153–268.

Chronica Mediolani seu Manipulus Florum auctore Fratre Gualvaneo de la Flamma, Ordinis Praedicatorum, cols. 537–740.

Ptolomaei Lucensis ordinis praedicatorum, Historia ecclesiastica a Nativiate Christi usque ad annum circiter MCCCXII, cols. 757–1242.

Ptolomaei Lucensis, *Breves Annales,* cols. 1250–1306.

vol. XII:

Andrae Danduli, *Chronicon,* (to 1339 RIS to 1280 only) cols. 1–398.

Raphaynus Caresini, Cancellarius Veneti, *Chronicon: continuation Andreae Danduli,* cols. 399–524.

Cortusii Patavini Duo sive Guilielmi et Alberigeti Cortusiorum, Historia de Novitatibus Paduae et Lombardiae ab anno MCCLVI usque MCCLXIV, cols. 757–954.

Historia Parmensis Fragmenta ab anno MCCCI usque . . . MCCLV, col. 725–750.

Istoria di Parma: Additamenta recentioris scriptoris ad hanc historiam, cols. 751–754.

Additamenta duo ad Chronicon Cortusiorum: unum ab 1359–1365; Alterum, 1354–1391 Patavina dialecto, cols. 955–988.

vol. XIII:

Conforti Pulicis Vicentini, *Annalium Patriae Fragmenta ab anno MCCCLXXI usque ad annum MCCCLXXXVII,* cols. 1238–1270.

vol. XIV:

Jacobo Malvecio, *Chronicon Brixianum ab origine urbis ad annum usque MCCCXXXII [MCCCXII],* cols. 777–1004.

Annales Caesenates ab anno MCLXII ad MCCCLXII, also called *Chronico antique civitatis Caesenae et aliarum Civitatum Romandiolae & extra dictam Provinciam,* cols. 1089–1186.

vol. XV:

Chronicon estense gesta Marchionum estensium, cols. 299–548.

Continuatio Annalium Arimensium per alterum Auctorem Anonymum, cols. 927–68.

Monumenta Pisana, 1089–1389 auctore anonymo, Cronica di Pisa, cols. 975–1086.

vol. XVI:

Johannis de Mussis, *Chronicon Placentinum ab anno CCXXII usque ad annum MCCCCII,* cols. 441–560.

Annales Mediolanenses Anonymi autoris, cols. 642–844.

Specimen historiae Sozomeni Pistoriensis, cols. 1063–1198.

vol. XVIII:

Annales Estenses Jacobi de Delayto cancellarii D. Nicolai Estensis . . . ab MCCCXCIII usque MCCCCIX, cols. 899–1098.

vol. XIX:

Andreas Billius, *Rerum Mediolanensium Historiae 1402–1431,* cols. 9–76.

Annali Sanesi, 1385–1422, cols. 387–428.

Ser Andrea de Redusiis de Quero, Cancellario Communis Tarvisii, *Chronicon Tarvisinum, a. 1368–1428*, cols. 741–866.

vol. XX:

Johannes Bandini de Bartholomaeis, *Historia senensis ab anno MCCCCII usque ad annum MCCCCXXII*, cols. 5–22.

Johannes Ferrariensi, Ordinis Minorum, *Excerpta ex annalibus Principium Estensium ab anno MCDIX usque ad MCDLIV*, cols. 437–474.

Bartholomaeus Sacchus, Cremonensus, called *Platina, Historia Urbis Mantuae ab ejus origine usque ad annum MCDLXIV*, cols. 611–862.

Antonius de Ripalta et Albertus ejus filius, *Annales Placentini, a. 1401–1484*, cols. 869–978.

vol. XXI:

Laurentius Bonincontri Miniatensis, *Annales ab anno MCCLX usque MCCCCLVIII*, cols. 9–162.

Diaria Neapolitana ab anno MCCLXVI usque ad annum MCCCCLXXVIII . . . auctore anonymo, cols. 1031–1137.

vol. XXII:

Marino Sanuto, *Vitæ Ducum Venetorum italice scriptæ ab origine urbis, sive ab CCCXXI usque MCCCCXCIII*, cols. 599–1252.

vol. XXIII:

Annales de Raimo sive Brevis Historia rerum in Regno Neapolitano gestarum ab anno MCXCVII ad MCCCCLXXXVI, cols. 221–240.

Andreas Naugerii, patritius Veneti, *Historia Veneta ab origine urbis usque ad Annum MCDXCVIII, Storia Veneziana*, cols. 923–1426.

Annales Bononienses F. Hieronymi de Bursellis bononiensis ordinis praedicatorum ab anno MCDXVIII usque ad MCDLXXXVII, cols. 863–916.

vol. XXIV:

Fragmenta Historiae Pisanae Pisana dialecto conscripta ab anno MCXCI usque ad MCCCXXXVII, cols. 643–694.

Polyhistoria Fratris Bartholomaei Ferrariensi Ord. Praed. MCCLXXXVIII usque ad annum MCCCLXVII, cols. 699–848.

Chronicon Neritinum, 1090–1368: cols. 859–922.

Rerum Italicarum Scriptores. Nuova edizione riveduta . . . con la direzione di Giosue Carducci, Vittorio Fiorini, Pietro Fedele. Bologna and Città di Castello, 1900–(RIS):

VI/2: *Gli Annales Pisani di Bernardo Maragone*. Ed. M. Lupo Gentile. 1930–1936.

VII/2: Rycarrdi de Sancto Germano Notarii, *Chronica*. Ed. C. A. Garufi. Bologna, 1936–1938.

VIII/1: *Rolandini Patavini Cronica in factis et circa facta Marchie Trivixane (1200 cc. 1262)*. Città di Castello, 1905–1908.

Annales Patavini. Ed. Antonio Bonardi.

Continazione del codice Marciano classe X, lat. n. 69.

VIII/2: *Cronaca di Antonio Godi Vicentino dall'anno MCXCIV all'anno MCCLX.* Ed.
Giovanni Soranzo. Città di Castello, 1909.

VIII/3: *Chronicon Marchiae Tarvisinae et Lombardiae [AA. 1207–1270].* Ed. L. A.
Bottehi. Città di Castello, 1914–1916.

VIII/4: Gerardi Maurisii, *Cronica Dominorum Ecelini et Alberici fratrum de Romano
(AA. 1183–1237).* Ed. Giovanni Soranzo. Città di Castello, 1913–1914.

VIII/5: Nicolai Smeregli Vincentini, *Annales Civitatis Vincentaie [AA. 1200–1312].* Ed.
Giovanni Soranzo. Bologna, 1921.

XI/2: *La Cronica di Dino Compagni delle cose occorrenti ne' tempi suoi.* Ed. Isidoro del
Lungo. Città di Castello, 1907–1916.

IX/5: *Historia Fratris Dulcini Heresiarche di Anonimo Sincrono.* Ed. Arnaldo Segarizzi.
Città di Castello, 1907.

XI/5: *Storie Pistoresi [MCCC–MCCCXLVIII].* Ed. Silvio Adrasto Barbi. Città di
Castello, 1907.

XI/9: *Chronicon Parmense ab anno MXXXVIII usque ad annum MCCCXXXVIII.* Ed.
Giuliano Bonazzi. Città di Castello, 1903.

XII/1: Andrea Danduli, Ducis Venetiarum, *Chronica per extensium descripta, aa.
46–1280.* Ed. Ester Pastorello. Bologna, 1938–1958.
A. Danduli, *Chronica brevis.*

XII/2: Raphayni de Caresinis, cancellarii Venetiarum, *Chronica aa. 1343–1388.* Ed.
Ester Pastorello. Bologna, 1922.

XII/3: Dominici de Gravina notarii, *Chronicon de rebus in Apulia gestis [AA.
1333–1350].* Ed. Albano Sorbelli. Città di Castello, 1903–1909.

XII/5: Guillelmi de Cortusis, *Chronica de Novitatibus Padue et Lombardie.* Ed. Beni-
amino Pagnin. Bologna, 1941.

XIII/1: Conforto da Costoza, *Frammenti di Storia vicentina [AA. 1371–1387].* Ed.
Carlo Steiner. Città di Castello, 1915.

XIII/3: Bartolomaei de Neocastro, *Historia Sicula [AA. 1250–1293].* Ed. Giuseppe
Paladino. Bologna, 1921–1922.

XIV/1: Antonii Astesani, *De eius vita et fortuna varietate Carmen (AA. 380–1341).* Ed.
A. Tallone. Città di Castello, 1908–1912.

XV/1: *Cronica dei fatti di Arezzo di Ser Bartolomeo di Ser Gorello.* Ed. A. Bini and G.
Grazzini. Bologna, 1917–1933.

XV/2: *Cronaca malatestiana del secolo XIV (AA. 1295–1385).* Ed. Aldo Francesco
Massèra. Bologna, 1922–1924.
Cronaca Malatestiana del secolo XV (AA. 1416–1452).

XV/3: *Chronicon estense cum additamentis usque ad annum 1478.* Ed. Giulio Bertoni
and Emilio Paolo Vicini. Città di Castello, 1908–1929 (only up to 1354).

XV/4: *Chronicon Mutinense Iohannis de Bazano [AA. 1188–1363].* Ed. Tommaso
Casini Bologna, 1917–1919. (incomplete).

XV/5: *Ephemerides Urbevetanae.* Ed. Luigi Fumi. Città di Castello, 1903–1920, vol. I:
*Discorso Historico con molti accidenti occorsi in Orvieto et in altre parti principando dal
1342 fino al passato 1368.*
Annales Urbevetani: Cronica antique (1161–1313).

Cronaca del Conte Francesco di Montemarte e Corbara (1330–1400).

Cronaca di Luca di Domenico Manenti (1174–1413).

Estratti delle 'Historie' di Cipriano Manenti (supplemento alla Cronica di Luca di Domenico Manetti (1325–1376).

XV/6.1: *Cronache Senesi.* Ed. A. Lisini and F. Iacometti. Bologna, 1939:

Cronaca senese di autore anomino della metà del secolo XIV dall'anno 1202 al 1362, con aggiunte . . . fino al 1391.

Frammento di cronaca senese di anonimo (1313–1320).

Cronache senese conosciuta sotto il nome di Paolo di Tommaso Montauri.

Cronaca senese attribuita ad Agnolo di Tura del Grasso detta la cronaca maggiore.

Cronaca senese di Donato di Neri e di suo figlio Neri.

Cronaca senese conosciuta sotto il nome di Paolo di Tommaso Montauri (Continuazione—Anni 1381–1431).

XVI/1: *Sozomeni Pistoriensis Presbyteri, Chronicon Universale [AA.1411–1455].* Ed. Guido Zaccagnini. Città di Castello, 1907–1908.

XVI/2: *Chronicon Bergomense Guelpho-Ghibellinum ab anno 1378 usque ad annum 1407.* Ed. Carlo Capasso. Bologna, 1926–1940.

XVI/3: *Marcha di Marco Battagli da Rimini [1212–1354].* Ed. Aldo Francesco Massèra. Città di Castello, 1912.

XVI/4: Petrus Azarii, *Liber gestorum in Lombardia.* Ed. Francesco Cognasso. Bologna, 1925–1939.

XVII/1: Galeazzo and Bartolomeo Gatari, *Cronaca carrarese confrontata con la redazione di Andrea Gatari (1318–1407).* Ed. Antonio Medin and Guido Tolomei. Città di Castello, 1942–1948.

XVII/2: Georgius and Iohannes Stella, *Annales Genuenses.* Ed. Giovanna Petti Balbi. Bologna, 1975.

XVII/3: *Chronicon Parvum Ripaltae seu Chronica pedemontana minora.* Ed. Ferdinando Gabotto. Città di Castello, 1911–1912.

XVIII/1: *Corpus Chronicorum Bononiensium.* Ed. Albano Sorbelli, 3 vols. Città di Castello, 1910–1938:

Cronaca A.

Cronaca B (called *Varignana*).

Cronica Bolognetti

Cronaca di Pietro and Floriano da Villola.

XVIII/2: Matteo Griffoni, *Memoriale Historicum de rebus Bononiensium.* Ed. Lodovico Frati and Sorbelli. Città di Castello, 1902.

XVIII/3: *Il Tumulto dei Ciompi: Cronache e Memorie.* Ed. Gino Scaramella. Bologna, 1917–1934:

Cronaca di Alamanno Acciaioli.

Cronaca seconda d'anonimo.

Cronaca terza d'anonimo (1378–1382), also known as "Cronichetta Strozziana."

Ser Nofri di ser Piero della Riformagioni, *Cronaca.*

Cronaca prima d'anonimo (called the *Squintinatore*).

XIX/3: Leonardo Bruni Aretino, *Historiarum Florentini populi.* Ed. Emilio Santini and Carmine di Pierro. Città di Castello, 1914–1926.

Leonardo Bruni, *Rerum suo tempore gestorum commentarius* [*AA. 1378–1440*]. Ed. Carmine di Pierro.

XIX/5: *Chronicon Fratris Hieronymi de Forlivio ab anno MCCCXCVII usque ad annum MCCCCXXXIII*. Ed. Adam Pasini. Bologna, 1931.

XX/2: Fr. Johannes Ferrariensus, *Annalium Libris Marchionum Estensium Excerpta* [*AA. 00–1454*]. Ed. Luigi Simeoni. Bologna, 1920–1936.

XXI/4: *Cronaca di Ser Guerriero da Gubbio dall'anno MCCCL all'anno MCCCCLXXII*. Ed. Giuseppe Mazzatinti. Città di Castello, 1902.

XXI/5: *I Diurnali del Duca di Monteleone*. Ed. Michele Manfredi. Bologna, 1958. (see Muratori, *Diaria Neapolitana*).

XXII/2: *Annales Forolivienses ab origine usque an annum MCCCCLXXIII*. Ed. Giuseppe Mazzatinti. Città di Castello, 1903.

XXIII/2: *Cronaca gestorum ac factorum memorabilium civitatis Bononie a fratre Hyeronimo de Bursellis* [*ab urbe condita ad a. 1497*]. Ed. Albano Sorbelli. Città di Castello, 1911–1929.

Annales Arretinorum Minores, 1200–1336.

XXIV/5: *Il Diario Romano di Antonio di Pietro dello Schiavo dal 19 Ottobre 1404 al 25 settembre 1417*. Ed. Francesco Isoldi. Città di Castello, 1912–1917.

XXIV/6: *Chronicon Sublacense (AA. 593–1369)*. Ed. Raffaello Morghen. Bologna, 1927.

XXIV/7: *Diario ferrarese all'anno 1409 sino al 1502 di auctori incerti*. Ed. Giuseppe Pardi. Bologna, 1928–1937.

XXIV/13: *Breve Chronicon Monasterii mantuani sancti Andree ord. Bened. di Antonio Nerli (AA. 800–1431)*. Ed. Orsini Begani. Città di Castello, 1908–1910.

XXIV/14: *Juliani Canonici Civitatensis Chronica* [*AA. 1252–1364*]. Ed. Giovanni Tambara. Città di Castello, 1906.

XXVI/1: *Matthei Palmerii Liber de Temporibus* [*AA. 1–1448*]. Ed. Gino Scaramella. Città di Castello, 1906–1915.

XXVI/2: *Fragmenta Fulginatis Historiae*. Ed. Michele Faloci-Pulignani. Bologna, 1932–1933.

XXVII/2: *Cronaca volgare di Anonimo fiorentino dall'anno 1385 al 1409 già attribuita a Piero di Giovanni Minerbetti*. Ed. Elina Bellondi. Città di Castello, 1915–1918.

XXVIII/2: *Pietri Cantinelli Chronicon* [*AA. 1228–1306*]. Ed. Francesco Torraca. Città di Castello, 1902.

XXX/1: *Cronaca fiorentina di Marchionne di Coppo Stefani*. Ed. Niccolò Rodolico. Città di Castello, 1903.

XXXIII/1: *Due cronache del Vespro in volgare siciliano del secolo XIII*. Ed. Enrico Sicardi. Bologna, 1935.

Capitoli del "Tesoro" di Brunetto Latini sui fatti del "Vespero."

Société de l'histoire de France (Paris, 1835–), 366 vols. (SHF)

    vol. VIII. *Mémoires de Pierre de Fenin, comprenant le récit des événements qui se sont passés en France et en Bourgogne sous les règnes de Charles VI et Charles VII (1407–1427.)* Ed. Mlle. DuPont, Paris, 1837.

    vol. IX. *La chronique d'Enguerran de Monstrelet (1400–1444)*. Ed. L. Douët-D'Arcq, 6 vols. Paris, 1857–1860.

vols. XXXIII and XXXV. *Chronique latine de Guillaume de Nangis de 1113 à 1300 avec les continuations de cette chronique de 1300 à 1368.* Ed. H. Géraud, 2 vols. Paris, 1843.

vol. LXXXI. *Histoire des règnes de Charles VII et de Louis XI par Thomas Basin,* 3 vols. Paris, 1855.

vol. CIX. *Chronique des quatre premiers Valois (1327–1393).* Ed. Siméon Luce. Paris, 1862.

vol. CXLIV. *Histoire de Saint Louis par Jean sire de Joinville.* Ed. N. de Wailly. Paris, 1868.

vol. CXLV. *La chronique du bon duc Loys de Bourbon.* Ed. A.-M. Chazaud. Paris, 1876.

vol. CXLVII and CDLVI. *Chroniques de J. Froissart.* Ed. Siméon Luce, Léon Mirot, and Albert Mirot. 15 vols. Paris, 1869–1975.

vol. CXLVII. *Chroniques des églises d'Anjou.* Ed. Paul Marchegay and Émile Mabille. Paris, 1869:

Chronicon Vindocinense seu de Aquaria.

Historia Sancti Florentii Salurensis.

vol. CXLVIII. *Chronique de Jean le Févre, Seigneur de Saint-Remy.* Ed. François Morand. 2 vols. Paris, 1876–1881.

vol. CLXVII. *Chroniques de Saint-Martial de Limoges.* Ed. H. Duplès-Agier. Paris, 1874:

Anonymum S. Martialis Chronicon ab anno MCCVII ad annum MCCCXX.

Fragments d'une petite chronique limousine de l'an 804 a l'an 1370.

Anonymum S. Martialis Chronicon 1235–1377.

Varia Chronicorum fragmenta ab anno 848 ad annum 1658.

vol. CCV. *Chronique normande du XIVe siècle.* Ed. Auguste and Émile Molinier. Paris, 1882.

vol. CCXXII. *Journal de Nicolas de Baye, Greffier du Parlement de Paris 1400–1417.* Ed. Alexandre Tuetey. 2 vols. Paris, 1885.

vol. CCLII. *Chronographia Regum Francorum.* Ed. H. Moranvillé. 3 vols. Paris, 1891–1892.

vol. CCLXXVIII. *Chronique de Richard Lescot, religieux de Saint-Denis (1328–1344) suivie de la continuation de cette chronique (1344–1364).* Ed. Jean Lemoine. Paris, 1896.

vol. CCXC. *Chronique d'Antonio Morosini, extraits rélatifs à l'histoire de France.* Ed. Germain Lefèvre-Pontalis. 3 vols. Paris, 1898–1899.

vol. CCCVII. *Chroniques de Perceval de Cagny.* Ed. H. Moranvillé. Paris, 1902.

vol. CCCXVII. *Chronique de Jean le Bel.* Ed. Jules Viard et Eugène Déprez. Paris, 1904–1905.

vol. CCCXXIII. *Chronique et Annales de Gilles le Muisit.* Ed. H. Lemaître. Paris, 1906.

vol. CCCXLVIII. *Chronique des règnes de Jean II et de Charles V.* Ed. R. Delachenal. 4 vols. Paris, 1910–1920.

vol. CDXXIII. *Les Grandes Chroniques de France.* Ed. Jules Viard. 10 vols. Paris, 1920–1937.

vol. CDXC. *Les chroniques du roi Charles VII par Gilles le Bouvier dit Hérault Berry.* Ed. Henri Courteault and Léonce Celier. Paris, 1979.

Chronicles Outside Collections or in Smaller Numbers from Collections

Alle bocche della piazza: Diario di anonimo fiorentino (1382–1401). Ed. Anthony Molho and Franek Sznura. Florence, 1986.

Annales Florentini 1288–1431. In *Fontes Rerum Germanicarum.* Ed. Joh. F. Boehmer. Stuttgart, 1868, IV, pp. 672–686.

Annales Gandenses. Ed. and tr. Hilda Johnstone. London, 1951.

Annali genovesi di Caffaro e de' suoi continuatori dal MCLXXIV al MCCXXIV. Ed. Luigi Tommaso Belgrano and Cesare Imperiale di Sant'Angelo. 5 vols. Genoa, 1890–1929:

  Marchisii scribae Annales 1220–1224.

  Annales Ianvenses ann . . . MCCXXV–MCCL.

  Annales Ianvenses ann. MCCLI–MCCLXIV.

  Iacobi Aurie Annales ann. MCCLXXX–MCCLXXXXIII.

The Anonimalle Chronicle. Ed. V. H. Galbraith. Manchester, 1927.

Anonimo romano, *Cronica.* Ed. Giuseppe Porta. Milan, 1979.

Antiche Cronache Veronesi. Ed. Carlo Cipolla. In Monumenti storici publicati dalla R. Deputazione veneta du storia patria, 3rd ser.: *Cronache e Diarii.* vol. 2 Venice, 1890:

  Syllabus Potestatum Veron. 1194–1306.

  De Romano (Annales Veronenses).

Cavalcanti, Giovanni. *Istorie fiorentine.* 2 vols. Florence, 1838–1839.

Corio, Bernardino. *Storia di Milano.* Ed. Angelo Butti and Luigi Ferrario. 3 vols. Milan, 1855–1856.

Cronaca di Bindino da Travale (1315–1416). Ed. Vittorio Lusini. Siena, 1900.

Le Cronache di Todi (secoli XIII–XVI). Ed. G. Italiani, C. Leonardi, F. Mancini, E. Menestò, C. Santini, G. Scentoni. Florence, 1979.

Chronica Parmensia a sec. XI. ad exitum sec. XIV. Ed. L. Barbier, Monumenta Historica. Parma, 1858.

  Chronica abreviata, Fr. Johannis de Cornazano O. P., pp. 355–399.

Croniche fiorentine di Ser Naddo da Montecatini in *Delizie degli eruditi toscani.* Ed. Fr. Idelfonso di San Luigi. 24 vols. Florence, 1770–1789. vol. XVIII.

The Chronicle of Jean de Venette. Trans. Jean Birdsall. Ed. Richard Newhall. New York, 1953.

Chronico ms. ecclesiae Rotomagensi, in *Etablissements de Rouen: Etudes sur l'histoire des institutions municipales.* Ed. A. Giry. Paris, 1883. I, p. 41.

Chronicon Cornelii Zanteliet S. Jacobi Leodiensis monachi, in *Veterum Scriptorum et Monumentorum Historicorum, Dogmaticorum, Moralium amplissima Collectio.* Ed. Emund Martène. Paris, 1729. V, cols. 67–506.

Chronicon Laurentanum MCLXXXVII–MCCLXXI, (Bibliotheca Nazionale di Napoli IX, C. 24), in Vincenzo Bindi, *Monumenti storici e artistici degli Abruzzi,* 4 vols. Naples, 1889. II, pp. 587–589.

Chronicon Placentinum ab anno MXII ad annum MCCXXXV, in *Chronica Tria Placentina a Johanne Codagnello, ab anonymo, et a Guerino.* Ed. B. Pallastrelli, Monumenta historica, vol III. Parma, 1859.

  Chronicon Placentium ab MCLIV ad annum MCCLXXXIV.

Chronicon Regiense: La Cronaca di Pietro della Gazzata nella tradizione del codice Crispi. Ed. Laura Artioli, Corrado Corradini, Clementina Santi. Reggio Emilia, 2000.

Cronicon Siculum incertis authoris ab a. 340 ad a. 1396. Ed. Joseph de Blasiis Monumenti storici, ser 1a: Cronache Naples, 1887.

Chronicon suessanum ab anno MCI. ad annum MCCCXLVIII. In *Raccolta di varie croniche, diarj, ed altri opuscoli così italiani, come latini appartenenti alla storia del Regno di Napoli.* Ed. Alessio A. Pelliccia, 4 vols. Naples, 1780. I, pp. 51–81.

Chronique artésienne (1295–1304) et Chronique tournaisienne (1296–1314). Ed. Frantz Funck-Brentano. Collection de textes pour servir a l'étude et a l'enseignement de l'histoire. Paris, 1899.

Chronique de Guillaume Bardin, in *Histoire générale de Languedoc,* X, cols. 4–78.

La chronique de Jean de Hocsem. Ed. Godefroid Kurth. Commission Royale d'histoire: Recueil de textes pour servir à l'études de l'histoire de Belgique. Brussels, 1927.

Chronique de Jean de Stavelot. Commission royale d'histoire de Belgique. Ed. A. Borgnet. Brussels, 1861.

Chronique du religieux de Saint-Denys. Ed. M. L. Bellaguet. Collection de Documents inédits sur l'histoire de France, 6 vols. Paris, 1839–1842.

Chronique liégeoise de 1402. Ed. Eugène Bacha. Brussels, 1900.

Chronique normande de Pierre Cochon notaire apostolique a Rouen. Ed. Ch. de Robillard de Beaurepaire. Rouen, 1870.

La chronique parisienne anonyme. Ed. Amédée Hellot, in *Mémoire de la société de l'histoire de Paris* (1884), pp. 1–207.

La chronique romane. Ed. Pegat Ferdinand, Eugène Thomas, and Desmazes. In *Thalamus Parvus: Le Petit Thalamus de Montpellier.* Société archéologique de Montpellier. Montpellier, 1840.

Chronique rouennaise, 1371–1434. In *Chronique normande de Pierre Cochon,* pp. 316–356.

Chronique tirée d'un ancien manuscrit de l'abbaye de Berdouea, au diocèse d'Auch. In NHGL, VIII, pp. 214–216.

Chroniques liégeoises : textes latins. Ed. Slyvain Balau. Brussels, 1913:
    Chronique latine de Jean de Stavelot.
    Chronique du règne de Jean de Bavière.

Cousinot I, Guillaume. *Geste des Nobles,* in *Chronique de la Pucelle ou chronique de cousinot.* Ed. M. Vallet de Viriville. Paris, 1859.

Cronaca della città di Perugia dal 1309 al 1491 nota col nome di Diario del Graziani. Ed. A. Fabretti, in *Archivio Storico Italiano,* 16 (1850).

Cronaca del Tocco di Cefalonia di Anonimo. Ed. Giuseppe Schirò. Rome, 1975.

Cronaca di Cremona. Frammento dall'anno 1399 al 1442. Ed. Fr. Robolotti. In *Bibliotheca Historica Italica cura et studio Societatis Longobardicae.* Milan, 1886. vol. I.

Cronaca di Partenope. Ed. Antonio Altamura. Studi e testi di letteratura italiana, II. Naples, 1974.

Cronache siciliane inedite della fine del medioevo. Ed. Francesco Giunta. Documenti per servire alla storia di Sicilia. Palermo, 1955:
    Brevis cronica de factis insule sicilie (1257–1396).
    Cronica brevis (827–1396).
    Nicolò da Marsala, *Cronica.*

Cronica di Paolino Piero Fiorentino delle cose d'Italia dall'anno 1080 fino all'anno 1305. Ed. Anton Filippo Adami. Rome, 1755.

Cronica fiorentina compilata nel secolo XIII. In *Testi fiorentini del Dugento e dei primi del Trecento.* Ed. Alfredo Schiaffini. Florence, 1954, pp. 82–150.

Le croniche di Viterbo scritte da Frate Francesco d'Andrea. Ed. P. Egidi. In *Archivio di R. società romana di storia patria,* XXIV (1901), pp. 197–252 and 299–71.

Croniques de Franche, d'Engleterre, de Flandres, de Lile et espécialment de Tournay. Ed. Adolphe Hoquet. Mons, 1938.

Fragments de la chronique de Jean le Prêtre publiés par Chapeaville. In *Chronique liégeoise de 1402,* pp. 447–478.

Fragments de la chronique du Conte Rouge (ame VII Conte de Savoye) par Perrinet du-Pin. In *Monumenta Historiae Patriae,* III: Scriptorum, I (1840), cols. 390–592.

Istoria della città di Viterbo di Feliciano Bussi. Rome, 1742.

L'Istoria di Firenze di Gregorio Dati dal 1380 al 1405. Ed. Luigi Pratesi. Norcia, 1902.

Istorie Pistolesi ovvero, Delle cose avvenute in Toscana dall'anno MCCC. al MCCCXLVIII e Diario del Monaldi. Prato, 1835.

Istore et croniques de Flandres, d'après les textes de divers manuscrits. Ed. Joseph Kervyn de Lettenhove. 2 vols. Brussels, 1879–1880.

Jean Froissart Chroniques, Livres I et II. Ed. Peter F. Ainsworth and George T. Diller Paris, 2001.

Journal d'un bourgeois de Paris de 1405 à 1449. Ed. Colette Beaune. Paris, 1990.

Ly Myreur des histors, chronique de Jean des Preis dit d'Outremeuse. Ed. Stanislas Bormas. Corps des Chroniques Liégeoises. 7 vols. Brussels, 1864–1887.

Mascaro, Jacme. *Le "Libre de Memorias."* Ed. Charles Barbier. In *Revue des langues romanes,* 4th ser., 34 (1890): 36–100.

Michele da Piazza, *Chronica.* Ed. Antonino Giuffrida. Palermo, 1980.

Morelli, Giovanni di Pagolo. *Ricordi.* In *Mercanti Scrittori: Ricordi nella Firenze tra Medioevo e Rinascimento.* Ed. Vittore Branca. Milan, 1985.

Pagliarino, Battista. *Croniche di Vicenza dal principio di questa città, sino al tempo, ch'ella si diede sotto al Serenissimo dominio Veneto 1404 . . . date in luce da Giorgio Giacomo Alcaini.* Vicenza, 1663.

Partie inédite des chroniques de Saint-Denis. Ed. Baron J. Pichon. Paris, 1864.

Pathéon littéraire: Choix chroniques et mémoires sur l'histoire de France, XIVe siècle. Ed. J. A. C. Buchon. Paris, 1838:

Histoire de Charles VI roy de France par Jean Juvenal des Ursins.

Chronique dels comtes de Foix et senhors de Bearn feyt l'an de l'incarnacion de N.-S. 1445, per Miguel del Verms.

Pellini, Pompeo. *Dell'Historia di Perugia.* 2 vols. Venice, 1664.

Pere III of Catalonia (Pedro IV of Aragon). *Chronicle,* Tr. Mary Hillgarth and ed. J. N. Hillgarth, Medieval Sources in Translation. 2 vols. Toronto, 1980.

Pitti, Bonaccorso. *Ricordi,* in *Mercanti Scrittori,* pp. 341–503.

Récits d'un bourgeois de Valenciennes (XIVe siècle). Ed. Kervyn de Lettenhove. Louvain, 1877.

Recueil de pièces. Ed. Secousse, vol. II:

Fragment d'une chronique latine (I), 1350 à 1368, pp. 599–630.

Fragment d'une chronique Françoise, pp. 631–655.

Fragment d'une chronique Latine (II), 1350 à 1380, pp. 656–678.

Salimbene de Adam, *Cronica.* Ed. Giuseppe Scalia. 2 vols. Scrittori d'Italia. Nn. 232–233. Bari, 1966.

Venetiarum Historia vulgo Petro Iustiniano Iustiniani filio adiudicata. Ed. Roberto Cessi and Fanny Bennato. Monumenti Storici: Deputazione di Storia Patria per le Venezie, XVII. Venice, 1964.

Villani, Giovanni. *Nuova Cronica.* Ed. Giuseppe Porta. 3 vols. Parma, 1990.

Villani, Matteo. *Cronica con la continuazione di Filippo Villani.* Ed. Porta. 2 vols. Parma, 1995.

More chronicles were consulted but were not listed if no popular revolts were found in them.

Other Printed Sources

The Apostolic See and the Jews. Documents: 492–1404. Ed. Shlomo Simonsohn. Toronto, 1988.

The Black Death. Tr. and ed. Rosemary Horrox. Manchester Medieval Sources Series. Manchester, 1994.

Boudet, Marcellin. *La Jacquerie des Tuchins, 1363–1384:* Appendice. Riom, 1895.

Die Briefwechsel des Cola di Rienzo. Ed. Konrad Burdach and Paul Piur. 5 vols. Berlin, 1913–1929.

Cartulaire historique et généologique des Artevelde. Ed. Napoléon de Pauw. Brussels, 1920.

Choix de pièces inédites relatives au règne de Charles VI. Ed. L. Douët D'arcq. 2 vols. SHF, CXIX. Paris, 1864.

The Coutumes de Beauvaisis of Philippe de Beaumanoir. Trans. and ed. F. R. P. Akehurst. Philadephia, 1992.

Documenti . . . del Comune di Siena dal 1354 al 1369. Ed. Giuliano Luchaire. Lyon, 1906.

Établissements de Rouen: Études sur l'histoire des institutions municipales. Ed. A. Giry. Paris, 1883.

La Gascogne dans les registres du Trésor des chartes. Ed. Charles Samaran. Paris, 1966.

Histoire générale de Languedoc, Ed. Cl. Devic & J. Vaissete, et al. New ed., 16 vols. Toulouse, 1872–1904.

The Jew in the Medieval World: A Source Book, 315–1791. Ed. Jacob Rader Marcus, 2nd ed. Cincinnati, 1999.

Le Languedoc et le Rouerge dans le Trésor des chartes. Ed. Yves Dossat, Anne-Marie Lemasson, and Philippe Wolff. Paris, 1983.

Layettes du Trésor des chartes. Ed. Alexandre Teulet. 5 vols. Paris, 1863–1909.

"Lettre d'Étienne Marcel aux communes de Picardie et de Flandre," in *Œuvres de Froissart.* Ed. Kervyn de Lettenhove (Brussels, 1868), VI, pp. 470–471.

Luce, Siméon. *Histoire de la Jacquerie d'après des documents inédits,* 2nd ed. Paris, 1894. Appendix of royal letters of remission.

L'Ordonnance Cabochienne (26–27 Mai 1413). Ed. A. Coville. Paris, 1891.

Ordonnances des Roys de France de la troisième race. Ed. Denis-François Secousse. 21 vols. Paris, 1723–1849.

Les pays de la Loire Moyenne dans le Trésor des chartes: Berry, Blésois, Chartrain, Orléanais, Touraine, 1350–1502 (Archives nationales, JJ 80–235). Ed. Bernard Chevalier. Paris, 1993.

Recueil de pièces servant de preuves aux mémoires sur les troubles excités en France par Charles II dit le Mauvais, Roi de Navarre et comte d'Evreux. Ed. Denis-François Secousse. 2 vols. Paris, 1755.

Recueil des documents concernant le Poitou contenus dans les registres de la Chancellerie de France. Ed. Paul Guérin. In *Archives Historiques du Poitou,* XI–XXVI (1881–1896).

Recueil des documents relatifs à l'histoire de l'industrie drapière en Flandre. Ed. Georges Espinas, Pirenne, and Henri-E. de Sagher. 4 vols. Brussels, 1906–1924.

Registres du Trésor des chartes, I: Règne de Philippe le Bel: Inventaire Analytique. Ed. Robert Fawtier. Paris, 1958.

Registres du Trésor des chartes, II: Règnes des fils de Philippe le Bel. Ed. Jean Guerout and Fawtier. Paris, 1966.

Registres du Trésor des chartes, III/1 (JJ 65A à 69) and *III/2 (JJ 70 à 75).* Ed. J. Viard and Aline Vallée. Paris, 1978–1979.

I Registri della Cancelleria angioina ricostruiti da Riccardo Filangieri, II: (1265–1281). Naples, 1951.

Rodolico, Niccolò. *La Democrazia fiorentina nel suo tramonto (1378–1382).* Bologna, 1905. Documenti.

———. *Il Popolo Minuto: Note di storia fiorentina (1343–1378).* Florence, 1899; new ed., 1968. Documenti.

"The testimony of Bascot de Mauléon in 1388." In *Chroniques de J. Froissart.* SHF, CXLVII. Ed. Léon Mirot. Paris, 1931. XII, p. 97.

Secondary Sources

Annuario generale dei comuni e delle frazioni d'Italia. Turin, 1980.

Arnade, Peter. "City, State, and Public Ritual in the Late-Medieval Burgundian Netherlands." *Comparative Studies in Society and History* 39 (1997): 300–318.

———. "Crowds, Banners, and the Marketplace: Symbols of Defiance and Defeat during the Ghent War of 1452–1453." *Journal of Medieval and Renaissance Studies* 24 (1994): 471–497.

———. *Realms of Ritual: Burgundian Ceremony and Civic Life in Late Medieval Ghent.* Ithaca, 1996.

Arnold, Klaus. "Pest—Geißler—Judenmorde: Das Beispiel Würzburg." In *Strukturen der Gesellschaft im Mittelalten: Interdisziplinäre Mediävistik un Würzburg,* pp. 358–369. Ed. Dieter Rödel and Joachim Schneider. Wiesbaden, 1996.

Artonne, André. *Le mouvement de 1314 et les chartes provinciales de 1315, Bibliothèque de la faculté des lettres de l'université de Paris,* XXIX. Paris, 1912.

Balestracci, Duccio. *Le armi, i cavalli, l'oro: Giovanni Acuto e i condottieri nell'Italia del Trecento.* Bari, 2003.

Barber, Malcolm. *The Cathars: Dualist Heretics in Languedoc in the High Middle Ages.* Harlow, 2000.

———. "Lepers, Jews and Moslems: The Plot to Overthrow Christendom in 1321." *History* 66 (1981): 1–17.

Baron, Hans. *The Crisis of the Early Renaissance,* 2 vols. Princeton, 1955; rev. ed., 1966.

Bates, David. *Normandy before 1066.* London, 1982.

Bec, Christian. "La paysan dans la nouvelle toscane (1350–1530)." In *Civiltà ed economia agricola in Toscana nei secc. XIII–XV: Problemi della vita delle campagne nel tardo medioevo (Pistoia, 21–24 aprile 1977),* pp. 29–52. Pistoia, 1981.

Becker, Marvin. "Florentine Politics and the Diffusion of Heresy in the Trecento: A Socio-Economic Inquiry," *Speculum* 34 (1959): 60–75.

———. "The Florentine Territorial State and Civic Humanism in the Early Renaissance." In *Florentine Studies: Politics and Society in Renaissance Florence,* pp. 109–139. Ed. Nicolai Rubinstein. Evanston, Ill., 1968.

———. "Heresy in Medieval and Renaissance Florence: A Comment," *Past & Present* 62 (1974): 153–161.

Bercé, Yves-Marie. *History of Peasant Revolts: The Social Origins of Rebellion in Early Modern France.* Trans. Amanda Whitmore. Cambridge, 1990.

———. *Revolt and Revolution in Early Modern Europe: An Essay on the History of political violence.* Trans. Joseph Bergin. Manchester, 1987 [1980].

Bertelli, Sergio. "Oligarchies et gouvernement dans la ville de la Renaissance." *Social Science: Information sur les sciences sociales* 15 (1976): 601–623.

Bessen, David M. "The Jacquerie: Class War or Co-opted Rebellion?" *Journal of Medieval History* 11 (1985): 43–59.

Bettelheim, Charles. *Les luttes de classes en URSS: Première pèriode, 1917–1923.* Paris, 1974.

Binion, Rudolph. "Europe's Culture of Death." In *The Psychology of Death in Fantasy and History,* pp. 119–135. Ed. Jerry S. Piven. Westport, Conn., 2004.

Blickle, Peter. *The Revolution of 1525: The German Peasants' War from a New Perspective.* Trans. Thomas Brady, Jr., and H. C. Erik Midelfort. Baltimore, 1981.

———. "Peasant Revolts in the German Empire in the Late Middle Ages." *Social History* 4 (1979): 223–239.

Bloch, Marc. "Blanche de Castille et les serfs du chapitre de Paris." *Mémoire de la Société de l'histoire de Paris et de l'Île-de-France,* XXXVIII (1911): 224–272. Reprinted in *Mélanges historiques,* I, pp. 462–490. Ed. Charles-Edmond Perrin. Paris, 1963.

———. *French Rural History: An Essay on Its Basic Characteristics.* London, 1966. [Antwerp, 1931].

Blockmans, Wim P. "The Formation of a Political Union, 1300–1600." In *History of the Low Countries,* pp. 55–140. Ed. J. C. H. Blom and E. Lamberts, trans. J. C. Kennedy. New York, 1999.

———. "Voracious States and Obstructing Cities: An Aspect of State Formation in Preindustrial Europe." In *Cities and the Rise of States in Europe, A.D. 1000 to 1800,* pp. 218–250. Ed. Charles Tilly and Wim P. Blockmans. Boulder, 1994.

Blockmans, Wim P., and Walter Prevenier. *The Promised Lands: The Low Countries under Burgundian Rule, 1369–1530.* Ed. Edward Peters, trans. Elizabeth Fackelman. Philadelphia, 1999; Houten, 1988.

Bocchi, Francesca. "I Bentivoglio da cittadini a signori." *Atti e memorie deputazione di storia patria per le province di Romagna,* new series, 22 (1971): 43–64.

Bock, F. "I processi di Giovanni XXII contro i Ghebellini delle Marche." *Bullettino dell'Istituto Storico per il Medio Evo,* 57 (1941): 19–70.

Bohstedt, John. "The Myth of the Feminine Food Riot: Women as Proto-Citizens in English Community Politics, 1790–1810." In *Women and Politics in the Age of the Democratic Revolution,* pp. 21–60. Ed. Harriet Applewhite and Darline Levy. Ann Arbor, 1990.

Boogaart II, Thomas A. "Reflections on the Moerlemaye: Revolt and Reform in Late Medieval Bruges." *Revue belge de philologie et d'histoire* 79 (2001): 1133–1157.

Boone, Marc. "Echecs des réseaux." In *Le prince et le peuple: Images de la société du temps des ducs de Bourgogne 1384–1530,* pp. 344–355. Ed. Walter Prevenier. Antwerp, 1998.

———. "Social conflicts in the cloth industry of Ypres (late 13th–early 14th centuries): The *Cockerulle* reconsidered." In *Ypres and the Medieval Cloth Industry in Flanders: Archaeological and Historical Contributions,* pp. 147–153. Ed. Marc Dewilde, Anton Ervynck and Alexis Wielemans. *(Archeologie in Vlaanderen, Monografie, 2.)* Asse-Zelik, 1998.

———. "Urban Space and Political Conflict in Late Medieval Flanders." *Journal of Interdisciplinary History* 32 (2002): 621–640.

Boone, Marc, Hanno Brand, and Walter Prevenier, "Revendications salariales et conjuncture économique: Les salaries de foulons à Gand et à Leyde au XVᵉ siècle." In *Studia Historica Œconomica. Liber Amicorum Herman Ver de Wee,* pp. 59–74. Ed. Erik Aerts, Brigitte Henau, Paul Janssens, and Raymond Van Uytven. Leuven, 1993.

Boone, Marc, and Maarten Prak. "Rulers, Patricians and Burghers: The Great and the Little Traditions of Urban Revolt in the Low Countries." In *A Miracle Mirrored: The Dutch Republic in European Perspective,* pp. 99–134. Ed. Karel Davids and Jan Lucassen. Cambridge, 1995.

Borzeix, Daniel, René Pautal, and Jacques Serbat. *Révoltes populaires en Occitanie: Moyen Âge et Ancien Régime.* Treignac, 1982.

Bouteiller, H. *Histoire de Rouen des milices et gardes bourgeoises.* Rouen, 1858.

Boutruche, Robert. *La crise d'une société: Seigneurs et paysans du Bordelais pendant la Guerre de Cent Ans.* Paris, 1963.

Bowsky, William. "The Anatomy of Rebellion in Fourteenth-Century Siena: From Commune to Signory?" In *Violence and Disorder in Italian Cities, 1200–1500,* pp. 229–272, Ed. Lauro Martines. Berkeley, 1972.

———. *The Finance of the Commune of Siena, 1287–1355.* Oxford, 1970.

———. "The Impact of the Black Death upon Sienese Government and Society." *Speculum* 39 (1964): 1–34.

———. "The Medieval Commune and Internal Violence: Police, Power, and Public Safety in Siena, 1287–1355." *American Historical Review* 73 (1967): 1–17.

———. *A Medieval Italian Commune: Siena under the Nine, 1287–1355.* Berkeley, 1981.

Braid, Robert. "'Et non ultra': Politiques royales du travail en Europe occidentale au XIVᵉ siècle." *Bibliothèque d'École des chartes* 161 (2003): 437–491.

The Brenner Debate: Agrarian Class Structure and Economic Development in Pre-industrial Europe. Ed. T. H. Aston and C. H. E. Philpin. Cambridge, 1985.

Bresc, Henri. "1282: classes sociales et révolution nationale." In *La società mediterranea all'epoca del Vespro, XI Congresso di storia della corona d'Aragona, Palermo-Trapani-Erice 25–30 aprile 1982,* 4 vols., II, pp. 241–258. Palermo, 1983.

————. *Un monde méditerranéen: Économie et société en Sicile 1300–1450*. École française de Rome, 2 vols. Rome, 1986.

Brooks, Nicholas. "The Organization and Achievements of the Peasants of Kent and Essex in 1381." *Studies in Medieval History Presented to R. H. C. Davis*, pp. 247–270. Ed. Henry Mayr-Harting and R. I. Moore. London, 1985.

Brown, Alison. "The Language of Empire." In *Florentine Tuscany: Structures and Practices of Power*, pp. 32–47. Ed. William J. Connell and Andrea Zorzi. Cambridge, 2000.

Brown, Andrew. "Civic Ritual: Bruges and the Counts of Flanders in the Later Middle Ages." *The English Historical Review* 112 (1997): 277–299.

Brown, Elizabeth R. "Reform and Resistance to Royal Authority in Fourteenth-Century France: The Leagues of 1314–1315." In *Parliaments, Estates and Representation*, 1, pp. 109–137. London, 1981.

Brucker, Gene. "The Ciompi Revolution." In *Florentine Studies*, pp. 314–356.

————. *The Civic World of Early Renaissance Florence*. Princeton, 1977.

————. *Florentine Politics and Society 1343–1378*. Princeton, 1962.

————. "The Medici of the Fourteenth Century." *Speculum* 32 (1957): 1–26.

Bruni, Francesco. *La città divisa: Le parti e il bene comune da Dante a Guicciardini*. Bologna, 2003.

Caffero, William. *Mercenary Companies and the Decline of Siena*. Baltimore, 1998.

Caggese, Romolo. *Roberto d'Angiò ed i suoi tempi*, 2 vols. Florence, 1922–1930.

Carile, A. *La cronachistica veneziana (s. XIII–XVI)*. Florence, 1969.

Casiraghi, Giampietro, Enrico Artifoni, and Guido Castelnuovo. "Il secolo XIII: apogeo e crisi di un'autonomia municipale." In *Storia di Torino: I. Dalla preistoria al comune medievale*, pp. 657–714. Ed. Giuseppe Sergi. Turin, 1997.

Cazelles, Raymond. "The Jacquerie." In *The English Rising of 1381*, pp. 74–84. Ed. R. H. Hilton and T. H. Aston. Cambridge, 1984.

————. *Société politique, noblesse et couronne sous Jean le Bon et Charles V*. Geneva, 1982.

Cessi, Roberto. *Il tumulto di Treviso (1388)*. Padova, 1908.

Challet, Vincent. "La révolt des Tuchins: Banditisme social ou sociabilité villageoise?" *Médiévales* 34 (1998): 101–112.

Charles, J. L. *La ville de Saint-Trond au Moyen Âge: Des origines à la fin du XIVᵉ siècle*. Paris, 1965.

Chéruel, Alfonse. *Histoire de Rouen pendant l'époque communale 1150–1382*. 2 vols. Rouen, 1843–1844.

Chevalier, Bernard. "Corporations, conflits politiques et paix sociale en France aux XIVᵉ et XVᵉ siècles." In *Les bonnes villes, l'état et la société dans la France du XVᵉ siècle*, pp. 271–298. Ed. Chevalier. Orléans, 1995.

Cheyney, Edward P. *The Dawn of a New Era, 1250–1453*. New York, 1936.

Chittolini, Giorgio. "Civic Religion and the Countryside in Late Medieval Italy." In *City and Countryside in Late Medieval and Renaissance Italy: Essays presented to Philip Jones*, pp. 69–91. Ed. Trevor Dean and Chris Wickham. London, 1990.

————. *La formazione dello stato regionale e le istituzioni del contado: secoli XIV e XV*. Turin, 1978.

————. "A Geography of the "Contadi" in Communal Italy." In *Portraits of Medieval and Renaissance Living: Essays in Honor of David Herlihy,* pp. 417–438. Ed. Cohn and Steven A. Epstein. Ann Arbor, 1996.

Cohn, Norman. *The Pursuit of the Millennium: Revolutionary Millennarians and Mystical Anarchists of the Middle Ages.* 2nd ed. London, 1970 [1957].

Cohn, Samuel K., Jr. "The Black Death and the Burning of Jews." (In press).

————. *The Black Death Transformed: Disease and Culture in Renaissance Europe.* London, 2002.

————. *Creating the Florentine State: Peasants and Rebellion, 1348–1432.* Cambridge, 1999.

————. "Florentine Insurrections, 1342–1385, in Comparative Perspective." In *The English Rising of 1381,* pp. 143–164. Ed. R. H. Hilton and T. H. Aston. Cambridge, 1984.

————. *The Laboring Classes in Renaissance Florence.* New York, 1980.

————. "Piety and Religious Practice in the Rural Dependencies of Renaissance Florence." *English Historical Review* 114 (1999): 1–22.

————. *Women in the Streets: Essays on Sex and Violence in Renaissance Italy.* Baltimore, 1996.

Comba, Rinaldo. "Rivolte e ribellioni fra tre e quattrocento." In *La storia: I grandi problemi,* vol. II, part 2, pp. 673–691. Ed. Nicola Tranfaglia and Massimo Firpo. Turin, 1988.

Connell, William. *La città dei crucci: fazioni e clientele in uno stato reppublicano del '400.* Florence, 2000.

Cowie, Leonard W. *The Black Death and Peasants' Revolt.* London, 1972.

Crawfurd, Raymond. *Plague and Pestilence in Literature and Art.* Oxford, 1914.

Crescenti, Carmela. *Cola di Rienzo: simboli e allegorie.* Parma, 2003.

Cristiani, Emilio. *Nobiltà e popolo nel comune di Pisa dalle origini del podestariato alla signoria dei Donoratico.* Naples, 1962.

Crone, Patricia. *Pre-Industrial Societies.* Oxford, 1989.

Cunningham, Andrew, and Ole Peter Grell. *The Four Horsemen of the Apocalypse: Religion, War, Famine and Death in Reformation Europe.* Cambridge, 2000.

Daris, Joseph. *Histoire du diocèse et de la principauté de Liège.* Liège, 1890.

"Das Pestwerken des Raymundus Chalin de Vivario." In *Archiv für Geschichte der Medizin* 17 (1925): 35–39.

Davies, R. R. *The Age of Conquest: Wales, 1063–1415.* Oxford, 1987.

————. *The Revolt of Owain Glyn Dwr.* Oxford, 1995.

d'Avout, Jacques. *Le Meutre d'Etienne Marcel.* Paris, 1960.

Delachenal, Roland. *Histoire de Charles V.* 5 vols. Paris, 1909–1931.

de Medeiros, Marie-Thérèse. *Jacques et chroniqueurs: Une étude comparée de récits contemporains relatant la Jacquerie de 1358.* Paris, 1979.

Denifle, Henri. *La Guerre de Cent Ans et la désolation des églises, monastères & hôpitaux en France,* 2 vols. Paris 1897–1879.

de Roover, Raymond. "Labour Conditions in Florence around 1400: Theory, Policy, and Reality." In *Florentine Studies: Politics and Society in Renaissance Florence,* pp. 277–313. Ed. Nicolai Rubinstein. Evanston, Ill., 1968.

de Santis, Antonio. *Ascoli nel Trecento,* 2 vols. Rimini, 1984.

Dictionnaire des lettres françaises: Le Moyen Âge. Ed. Geneviève Haenohr and Michel Zink. Paris, 1992.

"Die Pestschriften des Johann von Burgund und Johann von Bordeaux." *Archiv für Geschichte der Medizin* 5 (1911): 58–75.

Dobson, R. B. *The Peasants' Revolt of 1381,* 2nd ed. London, 1983.

Doudelez, G. "La révolution communale de 1280 à Ypres." In *Prisma van de geschiedenis van Ieper: Een bundel historische opstellen verzameld door O. Mus onder leiding van prof. J. A. van Houtte,* pp. 188–294. Ypres, 1974.

Dumolyn, Jan, and Jelle Haemers. "Patterns of Urban Rebellion in Medieval Flanders." *Journal of Medieval History* 31 (2005): 369–393.

Duprè Theseider, Eugenio. *Roma dal comune di popolo alla signoria pontificia (1252–1377).* Storia di Roma, 11. Bologna, 1952.

Dyer, Christopher. *Making a Living in the Middle Ages: The People of Britain, 850–1520.* New Haven, 2002.

———. "The Social and Economic Background to the Rural Revolt of 1381." In *The English Rising of 1381,* pp. 9–42. Ed. R. H. Hilton and T. H. Aston. Cambridge, 1984.

———. *Standards of Living in the Middle Ages: Social Change in England, c. 1200–1520.* Cambridge, 1989.

"Ein Paduaner Pestkonsilium von Dr. Stephanus de Doctoribus." *Archiv für Geschichte der Medizin* 6 (1913): 355–361.

Epstein, Stephan. "Cities, Regions and the Late Medieval Crisis: Sicily and Tuscany Compared." *Past & Present* 130 (1991): 3–50.

———. "Regional Fairs, Institutional Innovation and Economic Growth in Late Medieval Europe." *Economic History Review* 2nd ser. 47 (1994): 459–482.

Epstein, Steven A. *Genoa and the Genoese, 958–1528.* Chapel Hill, N.C., 1996.

———. *Speaking of Slavery: Color, Ethnicity, and Human Bondage in Italy.* Ithaca, 2001.

Espinas, Georges. *La vie urbaine de Douai au Moyen Âge.* 4 vols. Paris, 1913.

Evan-Pritchard, Sir Edward. *Kinship and Marriage among the Nuer.* Oxford, 1951.

Faith, Rosamond. "The 'Great Rumour' of 1377 and Peasant Ideology." In *The English Rising,* pp. 43–83. Ed. R. H. Hilton and T. H. Aston. Cambridge, 1984.

Famiglietti, R. C. *Royal Intrigue: Crisis at the Court of Charles VI, 1392–1420.* New York, 1986.

Favreau, Robert. "La Praguerie en Poitou," *Bibliotèque de l'École des chartes* 129 (1971): 277–301.

———. *La ville de Poitiers à la fin du Moyen Âge: une capitale régionale.* 2 vols. Poitiers, 1978.

Federico, Sylvia. "The Imaginary Society: Women in 1381." *Journal of British Studies* 40 (2001): 159–183.

Figueira, Thomas J. "A Typology of Social Conflict in Greek Poleis" In *City-States in Classical Antiquity and Medieval Italy: Athens and Rome, Florence and Venice.* pp. 289–329. Ed. Anthony Molho, Kurt Raaflaub, and Julia Emlen. Stuttgart, 1991.

Flammeront, Jean. "La Jacquerie en Beauvaisis." *Revue Historique* 4 (1879): 123–143.

Fossier, Robert. *Paysans d'Occident (XIᵉ–XIVᵉ siècle).* Paris, 1984.

Fournial, Étienne. *Les villes et l'économie d'échange en Forez aux XIIIe et XIVe siècles.* Paris, 1967.

Fourquin, Guy. *Les campagnes de la région parisienne à la fin du Moyen Age.* Paris, 1964.

———. *Les soulèvements populaires au Moyen Age* (Paris, 1972), translated as *The Anatomy of Popular Rebellion in the Middle Ages.* Trans. A. Chesters. Amsterdam, 1978.

Fowler, Kenneth. "'A World of Visual Images': Froissart's Legacy to Burgundy." In *The Burgundian Hero: Proceedings of the Annual Conference of the Centre Européen d'études Bourguignonnes (XIVe–XVIe siècles),* pp. 15–25. Ed. Andrew Brown, Jean-Marie Cauchies, and Graeme Small. Neuchâtel, 2001.

Franceschi, Franco. *Oltre il "Tumulto": I lavoratori fiorentini dell'Arte della lana tra Tre e Quattrocento.* Florence, 1993.

Franceschini, Gino. "La Lotta contro il Barbarossa." In *Storia di Milano,* IV: *Dalle lotte contro il Barbarossa al primo signore (1152–1310).* Ed. Giovanni Treccani degli Alfieri. Milan, 1954.

François, Michel. "Note sur les lettres de rémission transcrits dans les registres du Trésor des chartes." *Bibliothèque de l'École des chartes* 103 (1942): 317–324.

Freedman, Paul. "Peasant Anger." In *Anger's Past: The Social Uses of an Emotion in the Middle Ages,* pp. 171–188. Ed. Barbara H. Rosenwein. Ithaca, 1998.

Fryde, E. B. "The Financial Policies of the Royal Governments and Popular Resistance to Them in France and England, c. 1270–c.1420." *Revue belge de philologie et d'histoire* 57 (1979): 824–860.

———. *The Great Revolt of 1381.* Historical Association, n. 100. London, 1981.

———. "Peasant Rebellion and Peasant Discontents." In *The Agrarian History of England and Wales* III: *1348–1500,* pp. 744–819. Ed. Edward Miller. Cambridge, 1991.

———. *Peasants and Landlords in Later Medieval England c. 1380–c. 1525.* London, 1996.

Fudge, Thomas A. *The Magnificent Ride: The First Reformation in Hussite Bohemia.* Aldershot, 1998.

Fumi, Luigi. "Eretici e ribelli nell'Umbria dal 1320 al 1330." *Bollettino della R. deputazione di Storia patria per l'Umbria* 3 (1897): 34–95.

Furio, Antoni. *Història del País Valencià.* València, 1995.

Gauvard, Claude. *"De Grace especial": crime, état et société en France à la fin du Moyen Age.* 2 vols. Paris, 1991.

———. "Le petit peuple au Moyen Âge." In *Le petit peuple dans l'Occident médiéval: Terminologies, perceptions, réalités,* pp. 707–722. Ed. Pierre Boglioni, Robert Delort, and Gauvard. Paris, 2002.

Genicot, Léopold. *Rural Communities in the Medieval West.* Baltimore, 1990.

Geremek, Bronisław. *Le Salariat dans l'artisanat parisien aux XIIIe et XVe siècles: Étude sur le marché de la main-d'œuvre au Moyen Âge.* Trans. Anna Posner and Christiane Klapisch-Zuber. Paris, 1968.

Ghiron, Isaia. "La Credenza di Sant'Ambrogio, o la Lotta dei nobili e del popolo in Milano, 1198–1292." *Archivio Storico Lombardo* 3 (1876): 583–609.

Giulini, Conte Giorgio. *Memorie . . . città e campagna di Milano.* 7 vols. Milan, 1854–1857.

Goldthwaite, Richard. "I prezzi del grano a Firenze dal XIV al XVI secolo." *Quaderni Storici* 28 (1975): 15–36.

Gordon, Eleanor. "Women, Work, and Collective Action: Dundee Jute Workers 1870–1906." *Journal of Social History* 21 (1987): 27–47.

Gramsci, Antonio. *Quaderni del Carcere*. Ed. Valentino Gerratana, 4 vols. Turin, 1975.

Graus, František. "Au bas Moyen Âge: Pauvres des villes et pauvres des campagnes." *Annales: E. S. C.* 16 (1961): 1053–1065.

———. "The Crisis of the Middle Ages and the Hussites." In *The Reformation in Medieval Perspective*, pp. 76–103. Ed. Steven E. Ozment. Chicago, 1971.

———. "From Resistance to Revolt: The Late Medieval Peasant Wars in the Context of Social Crisis." *The Journal of Peasant Studies* 3 (1975): 1–9.

———. *Pest-Geissler-Judenmorde. Das 14. Jahrhundert als Krisenzeit.* Göttingen, 1987.

Grillo, Paolo. *Milano in età comunale (1183–1276): Istituzioni, società, economia.* Spoleto, 2001.

Guenée, Bernard. *States and Rulers in Later Medieval Europe.* Trans. Juliet Vale. Oxford, 1985 [Paris, 1971].

Gukowski, Mattvej. "Chi fu a capo della sommossa dei Ciompi?" In *Studi in onore di Armando Sapori.* 2 vols., I, pp. 707–713. Milan, 1957.

Hanawalt, Barbara A. *"Of Good and Ill Repute": Gender and Social Control in Medieval England.* Oxford, 1998.

Hansen, Harriet Merete. "The Peasants' Revolt of 1381 and the Chronicles." *Journal of Medieval History* 6 (1980): 393–415.

Harding, Alan. "Political Liberty in the Middle Ages." *Speculum* 55 (1980): 423–442.

Harper-Bill, Christopher. "The English Church and English Religion after the Black Death." In *The Black Death in England*, pp. 79–124. Ed. Mark Ormerod and Phillip Lindley. Stamford, 1996.

Hatcher, John. "England in the Aftermath of the Black Death." *Past & Present* 144 (1994): 3–35.

Haverkamp, Alfred. "'Conflitti interni' e collegamenti sovralocali nelle città tedesche durante la prima méta del XIV secolo." *Aristocrazia cittadina e ceti popolari nel tardo Medioevo in Italia e in Germania*, pp. 123–176. Annali dell'Istituto storico italo-germanico, no. 13. Ed. Reinhard Elze and Gina Fasoli. Bologna, 1984.

Heers, Jacques. *Family Clans in the Middle Ages: A Study of Political and Social Structures in Urban Areas.* Amsterdam, 1977 [Paris, 1974].

———. *L'Occident aux XIVᵉ et XVᵉ siècle: Aspects économiques et sociaux.* "Nouvelle Clio," 23. Paris, 1963.

Henderson, "The Parish and the Poor in Florence at the Time of the Black Death: The Case of S. Frediano." *Continuity and Change* 3 (1988): 247–272.

———. *Piety and Charity in Late Medieval Florence.* Oxford, 1994.

Henneman, John B., Jr. "The Black Death and Royal Taxation in France, 1347–1351," *Speculum* 43 (1968): 405–428.

Herlihy, David. *The Black Death and the Transformation of the West.* Ed. Samuel K. Cohn, Jr. Cambridge, Mass., 1997.

Herlihy, David, and Christiane Klapish-Zuber. *Les Toscans et leurs familles: Une étude du Catasto de 1427.* Paris, 1978.

Hilton, R. H. *Bond Men Made Free: Medieval Peasant Movements and the English Rising of 1381.* London, 1973.

————. *The Decline of Serfdom in Medieval England*. Studies in Economic History. London, 1969.

————. "Ideology and Social Order in Late Medieval England." In *Class Conflict and the Crisis of Feudalism: Essays in Medieval Social History*, pp. 246–252 and 332–333. London, 1985. (First published as "Idéologie et ordre social," in *George Duby. L'Arc* 72 (1978): 32–37.)

————. "Inherent and Derived Ideology in the English Rising of 1381." In *Campagnes médiévales: l'homme et son espace, études offertes à Robert Fossier*, pp. 399–405. Histoire ancienne et médiévale, 31. Paris, 1995.

————. "Peasant Movements in England before 1381." In *Class Conflict and the Crisis of Feudalism*, pp. 122–138 and 315–318. London, 1985. (First appeared in *Journal of Peasant Studies* 1 [1974]: 207–219.)

————. "Popular Movements in England at the End of the Fourteenth Century." In *Class Conflict and the Crisis of Feudalism*, pp. 152–164 and 322–323. London, 1985. (First appeared in *Il Tumulto dei Ciompi*, pp. 223–240 [Florence, 1981].)

————. "Social Concepts in the English Rising of 1381." in *Class Conflict and the Crisis of Feudalism*, pp. 216–226 and 330–331. London, 1985. (First published as "Soziale Programme in Englische Aufstand von 1381." In *Revolte und Revolution in Europa*. Ed. P. Blickle. In *Historische Zeitschrift* 4 [1975]: 31–46.)

Histoire de Nîmes. Ed. Raymond Huard. Aix-en-Provence, 1982.

Hobsbawm, Eric J. *The Age of Revolution, 1789–1848*. New York, 1962.

————. *Primitive Rebels: Studies in Archaic Forms of Social Movement in the 19th and 20th Centuries*. New York, 1966.

Houseley, Norman. "Historiographical Essay: Insurrection as Religious War, 1400–1536." *Journal of Medieval History* 25 (1999): 141–154.

Houtart, Maurice. *Les Tournaisiens et le Roi de Bourges*. Tournai, 1908.

Huizinga, Johan. *The Waning of the Middle Ages: A Study of the Forms of Life, Thought and Art in France and the Netherlands in the Dawn of the Renaissance*. Trans. J. Hoppman. New York, 1945 [Dutch ed., 1924].

Jacks, Philip, and William Caferro. *The Spinelli of Florence: Fortunes of a Renaissance Merchant Family*. University Park, Pa., 2001.

Jones, Philip J. *The Italian City-State: From Commune to Signoria*. Oxford, 1997.

Jordan, William C. "Famine and Popular Resistance: Northern Europe, 1315–22." In *Power, Violence and Mass Death in Pre-Modern and Modern Times*, pp. 13–24. Ed. Joseph Canning, Hartmut Lehmann, and Jay Winter. Aldershot, 2004.

————. *The Great Famine: Northern Europe in the Early Fourteenth Century*. Princeton, 1996.

Joris, A. *La ville de Huy au Moyen Âge: Des origines à la fin du XIVe siècle*. Paris, 1959.

Justice, Steven. *Writing and Rebellion: England in 1381*. Berkeley, 1994.

Kaplan, Temma. "Female Consciousness and Collective Action: The Case of Barcelona, 1910–1918." *Signs* 7 (1982): 545–566.

————. *Red City, Blue Period: Social Movements in Picasso's Barcelona*. Berkeley, 1992.

Kervyn de Lettenhove, Joseph. *Histoire de Flandre*. 4 vols. Brussels, 1847.

Kieckhefer, Richard. "Radical Tendencies in the Flagellant Movement of the Fourteenth Century." *Journal of Medieval and Renaissance Studies* 4 (1974): 157–176.

Klassen, John. "The Disadvantaged and the Hussite Revolution." *International Review of Social History* 35 (1990): 249–272.

Koenig, John. *Il "popolo" dell'Italia del Nord nel XIII secolo.* Bologna, 1986.

Kurth, Godefroid. *La cité de Liège au moyen-âge.* 3 vols. Brussels, 1909–1910.

———. "Henri de Dinant et la démocratie liégeoise." *Academie royale des Sciences des Lettres et de Beaux-arts de Belgique: Bulletins de la classe des lettres* (1908): 384–410.

Lambert, Malcolm. *Medieval Heresy: Popular Movements from Bogomil to Hus,* 3rd ed. Oxford, 2002.

Lansing, Carol. *The Florentine Magnates: Lineage and Faction in a Medieval Commune.* Princeton, 1991.

———. *Power and Purity: Cathar Heresy in Medieval Italy.* Oxford, 1998.

Lanza, Antonio. *Firenze contro Milano: Gli intellettuali fiorentini nelle guerre con i Visconti (1390–1440).* Rome, 1991.

Larner, John. *The Lords of Romagna: Romagnol Society and the Origins of the Signorie.* New York, 1965.

la Roncière, Charles-Marie. "Pauvres et pauvreté à Florence au XIVe siècle." In Michel Mollat, *Études sur l'histoire de la pauvreté (Moyen Age–XVIe siècle).* 2 vols., II, pp. 661–745. Paris, 1974

———. *Prix et salaires à Florence au XIVe siècle (1280–1380).* Rome, 1982.

Layton Funk, Arthur. "Robert Le Coq and Étienne Marcel." *Speculum* 19 (1944): 470–487.

Lecarpentier, Georges. "La Harelle, révolte rouennaise de 1382," *Le Moyen Âge.* 2nd series, 7 (1903): 12–100.

Leff, Gordon. *Heresy in the Later Middle Ages: The Relation of Heterodoxy to Dissent, c. 1250–c.1450.* Manchester, 1967.

Le Goff, Jacques. *La civilisation de l'Occident médiéval.* Paris, 1964.

Leguai, André. "Les révoltes rurales dans le royaume de France du milieu du XIVe siècle à la fin du XVe." *Le Moyen Âge* 88 (1982): 49–76.

———. "Les troubles urbains dans le Nord de la France à la fin du XIIIe et au début du XIVe siècle." *Revue d'histoire économique et sociale* 54 (1976): 281–303.

Léonard, Émile. *Histoire de Jeanne Ire reine de Naples, comtesse de Provence (1343–1382).* 3 vols. Paris and Monaco, 1932–1936.

Lewis, P. S. *Later Medieval France: The Polity.* London, 1968.

Little, Lester. *Religious Poverty and the Profit Economy in Medieval Europe.* London, 1978.

Luce, Siméon. "Notice sur Guillaume l'Aloue." *Annuaire-Bulletin de la Sociéte d'Histoire de France* (1875): 149–156.

McKee, Sally. "The Revolt of St Vito in Fourteenth-Century Venetian Crete: A Reassessment." *Mediterranean Historical Review* 9 (1994): 173–204.

Maire Vigueur, Jean-Claude. "Comuni e signorie in Umbria, Marche e Lazio." In *Storia d'Italia.* Ed. G. Galasso, VII/2. Turin, 1987.

Mallet, Michael. "Dal Verme, Iacopo." In *Dizionario biografico degli Italiani,* vol. 32. pp. 262–267. Rome, 1986.

Marshall, T. H. "The Nature of Class Conflict." In *Class, Status and Power.* pp. 81–87. Ed. R. Bendix and S. M. Lipset. London, 1954. First published in 1938.

Martines, Lauro. *April Blood: Florence and the Plot against the Medici.* London, 2003.

———. *Power and Imagination: City-States in Renaissance Italy.* New York, 1979.

Martorelli, Luigi. *Memoire Historiche dell'antichissima e nobile città d'Osimo.* Venice, 1725.

Meek, Catherine. *Lucca, 1369–1400: Politics and Society in an Early Renaissance City-State.* Oxford, 1978.

Meersseman, Giles. *Ordo Fraternitas: Confraternite e pietà dei laici nel medioevo.* 3 vols. Rome, 1977.

Miliband, Ralph. *Class Power and State Power.* London, 1983.

Mirot, Léon. *Les insurrections urbaines au début du règne de Charles VI (1380–1383): Leurs causes, leurs conséquences.* Paris, 1905.

Miskimin, Harry A. "The Last Act of Charles V: The Background of the Revolts of 1382." *Speculum* 38 (1963): 433–442.

———. "L'or, l'argent, la guerre dans la France médiévale." *Annales: E. S. C.* 40 (1985): 171–184.

Mollat, Guillaume. *The Popes at Avignon, 1305–1378.* Trans. from 9th ed. London, 1949.

Mollat, Michel, and Philippe Wolff. *Ongles bleus, Jacques et Ciompi: Les révolutions populaires en Europe aux XIVe et XVe siècles.* Paris, 1970. Trans. as *The Popular Revolutions of the Late Middle Ages* by A. L. Lytton-Sells. London, 1973.

Moore, Barrington. *Social Origins of Dictatorship and Democracy.* Boston, 1966.

Moral Economy and Popular Protest. Ed. Adrian Randall and Andrew Charlesworth. Houndmills, 2000.

Muir, Edward. *Mad Blood Stirring: Vendetta and Factions in Friuli during the Renaissance.* Baltimore, 1993.

Mundy, John H. *Liberty and Political Power in Toulouse, 1050–1230.* New York, 1954.

Munro, John H. "Medieval woolens: Textiles, Textile Technology and Industrial Organization, c. 800–1500." In *The Cambridge History of Western Textiles,* I, pp. 181–277. Ed. David Jenkins. Cambridge, 2003.

Musto, Ronald G. *Apocalypse in Rome: Cola di Rienzo and the Politics of the New Age.* Berkeley, 2003.

Najemy, John. "The Dialogue of Power in Florentine Politics." In *City-States in Classical Antiquity and Medieval Italy,* pp. 269–288. Ed. Anthony Molho, Kurt Raaflaub, and Julia Emlen. Ann Arbor, 1991.

Natalucci, Mario. "Lotte di parte e manifestazioni ereticali nella Marca agli inizi del secolo XIV." *Studi Picena* 24 (1956): 125–144.

Nicholas, David. "In the Pit of the Burgundian Theater State: Urban Traditions and Princely Ambitions in Ghent, 1360–1420." In *City and Spectacle in Medieval Europe,* pp. 271–295. Ed. Barbara A. Hanawalt and Kathyrn L. Reyerson. Minneapolis, 1994.

———. *Medieval Flanders.* London, 1992.

———. *The Metamorphosis of a Medieval City: Ghent in the Age of the Arteveldes, 1302–1390.* Leiden, 1987.

———. *The van Arteveldes of Ghent: The Varieties of Vendetta and the Hero in History.* Ithaca, 1988.

Nirenberg, David. *Communities of Violence: Persecution of Minorities in the Middle Ages.* Princeton, 1996.

Ormerod, Paul, and Andrew Roach. "The Medieval Inquisition: Scale-Free Networks and the Suppression of Heresy." *Physica A* 339 (2004): 645–652.

Ottokar, Nicola. *Il Comune di Firenze alla fine del Dugento,* 2nd ed. Turin, 1962; first published in 1926.

Paoli, Cesare. "Della signoria di Gualtieri duca di Atene in Firenze." *Giornale storico degli archivi toscani* 6 (1862): 81–121, 169–286.

Paris, 1400: Les arts sous Charles VI: Paris, Musée du Louvre, 22 mars, 12 juillet 2004. Paris, 2004.

Parker, Geoffrey. *The Military Revolution: Military Innovation and the Rise of the West, 1500–1800.* Cambridge, 1988.

Peters, Edward, and Walter P. Simons. "The New Huizinga and the Old Middle Ages." *Speculum* 74 (1999): 587–620.

Petit-Dutaillis, Charles. *Les communes françaises: Caractères et évolution des origins au XVIIIe siècle.* Paris, 1947.

Pezzana, Angelo. *Storia della città di Parma,* I: 1346–1400. Parma, 1837.

Pirenne, Henri. *Les anciennes démocraties des Pays-Bas.* Paris, 1910.

———. *Histoire de Belgique: Des origines à nos jours,* 3rd ed. 7 vols. Brussels, 1922–1932; first edition, 1900.

———. *Le soulèvement de la Flandre Maritime de 1323–1328: Documents inédits.* Bruxelles, 1900.

Polanyi, Karl. *The Great Transformation.* Boston, 1957; first published 1944.

Popular Protest in Late Medieval Europe. Ed. and trans. Samuel K. Cohn, Jr. Manchester Medieval Sources Series. Manchester, 2004.

Porchnev, Boris. *Les soulèvements populaires en France de 1623 à 1648.* Paris, 1963; Russian edition, 1951.

Pounds, N. J. G. *An Economic History of Medieval Europe.* New York, 1974.

Prescott, Andrew. "Writing about Rebellion: Using the Records of the Peasants' Revolt of 1381." *History Workshop Journal* 45 (1998): 1–27.

Prevenier, Walter. "Conscience et perception de la condition sociale chez les gens du commun dans les anciens Pays-Bas des XIIIe et XIVe siècles." In *Le petit peuple dans l'Occident médiéval,* pp. 175–189. Ed. Pierre Boglioni, Robert Delort, and Gauvard. Paris, 2002.

Prevenier, Walter, and Marc Boone. "The 'City-State' Dream." In *Ghent: In Defence of a Rebellious City,* pp. 81–87. Ed. Johan Decavele, Antwerp, 1989.

Protesta e rivolta contadina nell'Italia medievale. Ed. Giovanni Cherubini. In *Annali dell'Istituto "Alcide Cervi"* 16 (1994).

Putnam, Bertha. *The Enforcement of the Statutes of Labourers, 1349–1359.* New York, 1908.

Radcliff, Pamela Beth. "Women's Politics: Consumer Riots in Twentieth-Century Spain." In *Constructing Spanish Womanhood: Female Identity in Modern Spain,* pp. 301–323. Ed. Victoria Lorée Enders and Radcliff. Albany, 1999.

Radding, Charles M. "The Estates of Normandy and the Revolts in the Towns at the Beginning of the Reign of Charles VI." *Speculum* 47 (1972): 72–90.

Reddy, William. "The Textile Trades and the Language of the Crowd at Rouen, 1752–1871." *Past & Present* 74 (1977): 62–89.

Régis de Chauveron, *Des Maillotins aux Marmousets: Audouin Chauveron, Prévôt de Paris sous Charles VI*. Paris, 1992.

Repertorium fontium historiae medii aevi. Istituto storico italiano per il Medio Evo. Rome, 1962–.

Rigby, S. H. *English Society in the Later Middle Ages: Class, Status and Gender*. Basingstoke, U.K., 1995.

Roach, Andrew P. *The Devil's World: Heresy and Society, 1100–1300*. Harlow, 2005.

Robertson, Jan. "Cesena: Governo e società dal sacco dei Brettoni al dominio di Cesare Borgia." In *Storia di Cesena*, II/2, pp. 5–15. Ed. B. D. Maraldi. Rimini, 1985.

Rodolico, Niccolò. *I Ciompi: Una pagina di storia del proletariato operaio*, 3rd ed. Florence, 1980; first published 1945.

Rogozinski, Jan. *Power, Caste, and Law: Social Conflict in Fourteenth-Century Montpellier*. Cambridge, Mass., 1982.

Romano, Denis. *Patricians and Popolani: The Social Foundations of the Venetian Renaissance State*. Baltimore, 1987.

Rossiaud, Jacques. "Fraternités de jeunesse et niveux de culture dans les villes du Sud-Est à la fin du Moyen Âge." *Cahiers d'histoire* 21 (1976): 67–102.

Roth, Cecil. *The History of the Jews of Italy*. Philadelphia, 1946.

Rotz, Rhiman A. "Urban uprisings in Germany: Revolutionary or Reformist? The Case of Brunswick, 1374." *Viator* 4 (1973): 207–223

Rudé, George. *The Crowd in History, 1730–1848*. New York, 1964.

———. *Paris and London in the Eighteenth Century: Studies in Popular Protest*. London, 1974.

Rutenburg, Victor. *Popolo e movimenti popolari nell'Italia del '300 e '400*. Trans. Gianpiero Borghini. Bologna, 1971; Moscow, 1958.

Sabean, David. "The Communal Basis of Pre-1800 Peasant Uprisings in Western Europe." *Comparative Politics* 8 (1976): 355–364.

Salvatorelli, Luigi. *L'Italia comunale dal secolo XI alla metà del secolo XIV*. Storia d'Italia, IV. Milan, 1940.

Salvemini, Gaetano. *Magnati e popolani in Firenze dal 1280 al 1295*. Florence, 1899.

Sambin, Paolo. "Di un'ignota fonte dei Diarii di Marin Sanudo," *Atti Istituto Veneto* 104 (1944–1945): 21–53.

Scott, James C. *Domination and the Art of Resistance: Hidden Transcripts*. New Haven, 1990.

———. *Weapons of the Weak: Everyday Forms of Peasant Resistance*. New Haven, 1985.

Screpanti, Ernesto. "L'Angelo delle liberazione e il Tumulto dei Ciompi, Firenze, giugno-agosto 1378." Unpublished MS., January 2005.

Sharp, Buchanan. "The Food Riots of 1347 and the Medieval Moral Economy." In *Moral Economy and Popular Protest*, pp. 33–54. Ed. Adrian Randall and Andrew Charlesworth. Houndmills, 2000.

Simonsohn, Shlomo. *History of the Jews in the Duchy of Mantua*. Jerusalem, 1977.

Skocpol, Theda. *States and Social Revolution: A Comparative Analysis of France, Russia, and China*. Cambridge, 1979.

Smail, Daniel Lord. "Telling Tales in Angevin Courts." *French Historical Studies* 20 (1997): 183–215.

Sorokin, Pitirim A. "What Is a Social Class?" In *Class, Status and Power*, pp. 87–92. Ed. R. Bendix and S. M. Lipset. London, 1954. First published 1947.

Spiegel, Gabrielle M. "History, Historicism, and the Social Logic of the Text in the Middle Ages." *Speculum* 65 (1990): 59–86.

Stabel, Peter. *Dwarfs among Giants: The Flemish Urban Network in the Late Middle Ages.* Leuven, 1997.

Stephens, John. "Heresy in Medieval and Renaissance Florence." *Past & Present* 54 (1972): 25–60.

———. "Rejoinder." *Past & Present* 62 (1974): 162–166.

Sumption, Jonathan. *The Hundred Years War.* Vol. 2: *Trial by Fire.* London, 1999.

Swetz, Frank J. "*Figura Mercantesco*: Merchants and the Evolution of a Number Concept in the Latter Middle Ages." In *Word, Image, Number: Communication in the Middle Ages,* pp. 391–412. Ed. John J. Contreni and Santa Casciani. Florence, 2002.

Tailliar, Eugène. *Chroniques de Douai.* 3 vols. Douai, 1875–1877.

Tamba, G. "Giovanni d'Andrea." In *Dizionario Biografico degli Italiani,* vol. 55, pp. 667–672. Rome, 2000.

TeBrake, William H. *A Plague of Insurrection: Popular Politics and Peasant Revolt in Flanders, 1323–1328.* Philadelphia, 1993.

Thompson, E. P. "The Moral Economy of the English Crowd in the Eighteenth Century." *Past & Present* 50 (1971): 76–136.

Tilly, Charles. "Food Supply and Public Order in Modern Europe." In *The Formation of National States in Western Europe,* pp. 380–455. Ed. Tilly. Princeton, 1975.

———. "Hauptformen kollektiver Aktion in Westeuropa, 1500–1975." In *Geschichte und Gesellschaft* (1975): Heft 2: *Sozialer Protest,* pp. 154–163. Ed. Richard Tilly. Göttingen, 1977.

———. "How Protest Modernized in France, 1845–1855." In *The Dimension of Quantitative Research,* pp. 192–256. Ed. W. Aydelotte, A. Bogue, and R. Fogel. Princeton, 1972.

Tilly, Louise A. "The Food Riot as a Form of Political Conflict in France." *Journal of Interdisciplinary History* 2 (1971): 23–57.

The Towns of Italy in the Later Middle Ages. Ed. Trevor Dean. Manchester Medieval Sources Series. Manchester, 2000.

Trexler, Richard. "Follow the Flag: The Ciompi Revolt Seen from the Streets." *Bibliothèque d'Humanisme et Renaissance* 46 (1984): 357–392.

———. "Herald of the Ciompi: The Authorship of an Anonymous Florentine Chronicle." *Quellen und Forschungen* 65 (1985): 159–191.

———. "Neighbors and Comrades: The Revolutionaries of Florence, 1378." *Social Analysis* 14 (1983): 53–105.

———. *The Spiritual Power: Republican Florence under the Interdict.* Leiden, 1974.

———. *The Workers of Renaissance Florence: Power and Dependence in Renaissance Florence.* Asheville, N.C., 1998.

Valeri, Nino. *L'Italia nell'età dei principati dal 1343 al 1516.* Storia d'Italia, vol. IV. 2nd ed. Milan, 1969.

Vancini, Oreste. *La rivolta dei Bolognesi al Governo dei Vicari della Chiesa (1376–1377): L'origine dei tribuni della plebe.* Bologna, 1906.

Vanderkindere, Léon. *Le siècle des Artevelde: Études sur la civilisation morale et politique de la Flandre et du Brabant.* 2nd ed. Brussels, 1909.

Vercauteren, Fernand. *Luttes sociales à Liège (XIIIme et XIVme siècles).* 2nd ed. Brussels, 1946.

Vincent, Catherine. *Des charités bien ordonnées: Les confréries normandes de la fin du XIIIe siècle au début du XVIe siècle.* Paris, 1988.

Visconti, Alessandro. *Storia di Milano.* Milan, 1979.

Waley, Daniel. *Mediaeval Orvieto: The Political History of an Italian City-state, 1157–1334.* Cambridge, 1952.

Wardi, Emmanuel P. *Le Strategie familiari di un doge di Genova: Antoniotto Adorno (1378–1398).* Turin, 1996.

Weinstein, Donald. "The Myth of Florence." In *Florentine Studies: Politics and Society in Renaissance Florence,* pp. 15–44. Ed. Nicolai Rubinstein. Evanston, Ill. 1968.

Werveke, Hans Van. "Industrial Growth in the Middle Ages: The Cloth Industry in Flanders." *Economic History Review* 6 (1954): 237–245.

Whittle, Jane, and S. H. Rigby. "England: Popular Politics and Social Conflict." In *A Companion to Britain in the Later Middle Ages,* pp. 65–86. Ed. Rigby. Oxford, 2003.

Wickham, Christopher. *Framing the Early Middle Ages: Europe and the Mediterranean, 400–800.* Oxford, 2005.

Williams, P. A. *Benvenuto da Imola's commentary: A Trecento Reading of Dante.* Cambridge, 1983.

Witt, Ronald. "A Note on Guelfism in Late Medieval Florence." *Nuova Rivista Storica* 53 (1969): 134–145.

Wolff, Philippe. "The 1391 Pogrom in Spain: Social Crisis or Not?" *Past & Present* 50 (1971): 4–18.

———. *Commerces et marchands de Toulouse (vers 1350–vers 1450).* Paris, 1954.

———. *Histoire de Toulouse.* Toulouse, 1958.

Index

Note: Readers are advised to check under both names of persons, as second names are not necessarily last names.